Baedeker

G000275669

Mexico

www.baedeker.com

Verlag Karl Baedeker

TOP SIGHTS ★ ★

Mexico has everything you need for a holiday of tremendous variety: deserts and waterfalls, white Caribbean beaches, jungle and cactus landscapes, pre-Hispanic archaeological sites, lonely villages, modern metropolises and magnificent colonial cities. Experience at first hand the culture of the country with its numerous festivals, colourful markets and delicious culinary specialities!

Monarch butterfly
Every year, thousands spend the winter in Mexico.

2 ★ ★ Teotihuacán
No single city, state or people has had a greater influence on the rest of Central America. ▶ page 551

3 ★ ★ Guanajuato
A jewel of colonial architecture, whose historic centre and mines are world heritage sites. Page 318 ▶ page 318

4 ★ ★ San Miguel de Allende
Once a mission, today a favourite meeting place for artists and art students from all over the world ▶ page 533

1 ★ ★ Barranca del Cobre
The sheer scale of the Copper Canyon – four times the size of the Grand Canyon – makes it one of Mexico's most spectacular sights. ▶ page 216

5 ★ ★ Mexico City
A true Moloch, but at the same time a

©Baedeker

1 Barranca del Cobre

14 Chic Itzá

3 Guanajuato   2 Teotihuacán   13 Uxmal

4 San Miguel de Allende

5 Mexico City   6 Jalapa
7 Popocatépetl
Iztaccíhuatl   12 Palenque

8 Taxco

9 Acapulco   10 Oaxaca
11 Monte Albán

Uxmal
Pyramid of the Magician

Mexico City
Aztec dancers perform outside the cathedral

BAEDEKER'S BEST TIPS

Of all the Baedeker tips in this guidebook here are the most interesting ones. Experience and enjoy the most beautiful side of Mexico!

🔳 Construction in progress
Luis Barragán's houses were always composed of light, colour and generous space. In the meantime, his own house in Mexico City has been opened to the public. ▶ **page 88**

🔳 See more of the sea
Those who want to do more than just swim and sunbathe in Cancún can observe sea-dwellers up close in the first inter-active aquarium in Latin America.
▶ **page 237**

🔳 Olas Verdes
Visitors to the Costa Alegre in spring can witness a unique natural spectacle: the up to 8m/26ft-high waves glow green due to the presence of fluorescent micro-organisms. ▶ **page 278**

🔳 Riding the Tequila Express
Every Saturday and Sunday at 11am, the Tequila Express leaves Guadalajara station for a train ride through the central highlands. Mariachi musicians – and high-proof tequila – ensure a party atmosphere on board. ▶ **page 304**

🔳 Songs of Mérida
The art of the troubadours, the »trova«, is a typical aspect of the culture of Mérida. Every Thursday, singers and musicians show off their abilities at the Serenata de Santa Lucía. ▶ **page 344**

🔳 A nighttime temple visit
See the archaeological zone in Mexico City at the periphery of the Zócalo in a new light – by taking part in a special guided tour after nightfall. ▶ **page 378**

🔳 Help us St Anthony!
Every Morelia local knows the restaurant San Miguelito and likes to show strangers its special atmosphere. Here, in a special ritual, and either just for fun or rather more seriously, the single women of Morelia ask St Anthony for a husband. Some women making the plea to the saint have already had success – though only those who entered their email address.
▶ **page 436**

At Pátzcuaro Lake
the fishermen try their luck for a morning catch with the help of butterfly nets.

🔲 Baile de Viejitos

On 8 December the Dance of the Old Men takes place in Pátzcuaro, in which the dancers at first make a very frail impression…   ▶ **page 474**

🔲 Raisin glasses

Opposite the Plazuela de los Sapos, on which a flea-market takes place on Sundays, stands the La Pasita bar where the popular raisin liquor of the same name is served; it normally comes with a raisin in the glass.   ▶ **page 486**

🔲 Pelota game

In Yucatán's Xcaret leisure park it is not only ecology that is writ large – Maya history is also presented, and in a lively way at that. Every afternoon, the show programme includes the demonstration of a Pelota game in appropriate historical costume on an authentic replica of a Pelota court.   ▶ **page 516**

🔲 How did the Maya heal?

Predominantly with herbs, natural remedies and magic rituals. In the Casa de Curación in the museum of Maya medicine, visitors can experience how illnesses were diagnosed and treated at first hand…   ▶ **page 520**

🔲 Wellness the Mexican way

Fancy being spoilt for a couple of days? If so, the health resort in Ixtapán de la Sal is just the place for you.   ▶ **page 576**

The descendents of the Maya
are closely bound to the old traditions, whether in medicine, agriculture or architecture.

Tequila
along with a little salt and a hearty bite into the lime…

Dancers with Mariachi musicians
► page 89

BACKGROUND

PRACTICALITIES

Price categories

Hotels
Luxury: over 1,300 Mex$
Mid-range: 650 – 1,300 Mex$
Budget: under 650 Mex$
(double room per night)
Restaurants
Expensive: over 290 Mex$
Moderate: 87 – 290 Mex$
Inexpensive: under 87 Mex$
(one meal without drinks)

The colours of paradise, south of Isla Mujeres
► page 328

► Content

The best place for hammocks is Mérida.
► **page 346**

*Hierve el Agua:
petrified waterfalls near Mitla* →

Background

»MÉXICO ES UN OTRO MUNDO« – MEXICO REALLY IS A DIFFERENT, FASCINATING WORLD WITH A RICH CULTURAL HISTORY, A VARIETY OF UNIQUE LAND-SCAPES AND ANCIENT TRADITIONS. ABOVE ALL, MEXICANS THEMSELVES ARE A SPECIAL DELIGHT.

¡VIVA MÉXICO!

Mexico – hear the name and start dreaming. Dream of magical beaches, fascinating archaeological sites, colourful folklore, huge cacti, tropical forests, and the pure joy of life. Visit Mexico and experience the dream. Discover the country's fascinating history and its nature, enter into distant Indian cultures and then step back into the realities of modern Mexico!

The Spanish conquerors were the first Europeans to travel to Mexico. In search of a new world and riches, they found highly developed cultures which they did not begin to understand. Their desire for money and power prevailed: within a short time, they had destroyed what generation after generation had built over centuries. While this remains a heavy historic burden to this day, Mexico is also conscious of the value of its treasures from the past. Today's many visitors often come to trace the unparalleled legacy of the Maya and the Aztec.

Perfect beaches
With 10,000 km (6,000 mi) of coast on the Pacific, the Gulf of Mexico and the Caribbean, every visitor finds the perfect beach.

Palms and Pyramids

The wonderful thing about Mexico is that it is possible to experience its ancient cultures in a direct way. There are pyramids to climb and excavation sites to visit. The visitor sees how one layer of history after another is unearthed. In their villages, Mesoamerican natives still practice their ancient crafts to create genuine traditional art; it is still also possible to taste the delicious traditional foods. Culture and recreation lie side-by-side in the southern part of Mexico: a paradise for swimmers and divers stretches along the coastlines; the evening enchants with dinner under the palm trees while the morning's awe of the pyramids still lingers.

Cacti and Sombreros

The approximately 4,000 different types of Mexican cacti have little in common with that small, green, domestic succulent on the window sill. Some of northern Mexico's cacti stand like giant monuments, and there are entire cactus forests. Interesting experiences await everywhere: visitors can observe the most artful survivors in

Relics of significant high cultures
Chichén Itzá is the largest and best known Maya site in Yucatán and was once a monumental centre of power.

Mariachi
The hallmark of Mexican music are the Mariachis, popular ensembles with guitars, trumpets and violins.

Cacti
thrive above all on Baja California.

Margaritas
That holiday feeling: let the day come to a relaxed close with a drink like this.

Día de los Muertos
This is how the Mexicans celebrate the dead – as part of life.

Tacos
Many people don't know the difference between taco and tortillas, burritos or fajitas. In fact, tortillas are always used: it's just the fillings, preparation and presentation that vary.

the animal and plant kingdoms, admire the beauty of a desert in bloom or enjoy delicious fresh prickly pears. The sombrero is often thought of as Mexico's typical form of practical sun protection. It was however a mere Hollywood fancy that made the sombrero synonymous with Mexico. Smaller hats have long since replaced the sombrero in everyday life: a sombrero really isn't all that practical.

Home to Millions

Passengers often fall silent as their plane approaches Mexico City for landing. The view from the plane onto the vast, seemingly limitless capital is for many the first impression of Mexico. The capital is as fascinating as the country. Having pushed past the 25 million mark a while ago, the population is growing steadily. Visitors find everything imaginable in this metropolis: Mexico City is the capital, the centre for economy and trade, and the seat of government agencies. It also serves as a transportation hub and is home to the most important educational and cultural institutions. Exclusive residential areas and slums, theatres and street performances, luxury restaurants and fast food stands, museums and archaeological sites – the list is endless. There is something for everyone in Mexico City, just waiting to be discovered.

Colourful and Spicy

Not only is tequila a cult drink enjoyed internationally, but also Mexican cuisine has won over the world's taste buds. It is especially

Sunsets
Spectacular and breathtaking

known for its variety and creativity, not surprising given the plentiful supply of a wide range of fresh fruit and vegetables in the country. Clearly, without corn, beans and every kind of chili, a meal is just not complete. It is impossible to get bored with the countless variety of delicious tortillas alone. The use of spices such as cinnamon and coriander makes Mexican cuisine special, as do dishes in the Mayan and Aztec tradition. Mexico's popular culture is as colourful as its fruit and vegetable markets. Whether silverwork, ceramics, fine metalwork or embroidery, arts and crafts are created in all regions, mostly of the highest quality. The colours, patterns, forms and symbols of these artefacts mirror many of the old traditions. The enticing colours lure and tempt shoppers. Don't fight it – souvenirs always go down well with the folks back home.

Facts

Mexico overwhelms the visitor with its unique mixture of culture, natural beauty, traditions and modernity. History, magic rituals and modern living merge more naturally here than anywhere else in the Americas.

Nature

In the Cretaceous period, i.e. more than 65 million years ago, the ocean covered large parts of what is now Mexico. According to modern geophysical research, a very large meteorite hit the region during the transition from the Cretaceous to the Tertiary period. This meteorite penetrated the earth's crust in the area now known as the Yucatán peninsula, leaving behind the Chicxulub crater with a diameter of 200km/124mi.

Geology

The major Mexican mountain ranges, the Western and Eastern Sierra Madre, can be understood as a continuation of the North American Rocky Mountains and the mountains of the Basin and Range Province. Accompanied by severe earthquakes and **volcanic activity**, they were formed in the Tertiary period. The Isthmus of Tehuantepec, which connects North and South America, was formed only between 2 and 5 million years ago.

The earth under Mexico is still restless: individual tectonic plates continue to move. The eastern Pacific Cocos plate, for example, is moving under the American and the Caribbean plates, frequently causing severe earth tremors or volcanic activity at the plate edges. The Mexico City region experienced its last devastating **earthquake** in 1985. The quake took the lives of about 10,000 people and the damage to buildings and infrastructure was immense. The Puebla region registered the most recent severe earthquake in the summer of 1999: 23 people perished. The volcanoes of the Cordillera Neovolcánica create upheaval time and time again. The volcanic mountains are part of the circum-Pacific seismic belt, better known as the Pacific Ring of Fire. As recently as 1943 Paricutin, Mexico's youngest volcano, came to life. Several times in recent years, Popocatépetl has made its presence felt to the more than 30 million people living in its shadow.

◄ Restless earth

The highlands are Mexico's principal region. They span the northern and central part of Mexico and add to the country's extraordinary geographic and geological contrasts. From north to south, the elevation increases from 900m/2,953ft to 2,400m/7,874ft and up to 3,000m/9,843ft. The highlands are framed by the Sierra Madre Occidental and the Sierra Madre Oriental. Very little precipitation reaches the central part of the country over these immense mountain ranges. Mountain ridges and deep canyons stretch across the seven large basins that make up the highlands.

The Mexican highlands
◄ (Altiplanos)

The lower northern highlands feature mostly wide valleys, the so-called **bolsones**. The largest of these broad hollows – which are without drainage to the ocean – are the bolsones of Mapimí and San Luis Potosí. The right tributaries of the Río Bravo del Norte (Río Grande)

◄ The northern highlands

← *A little girl from Chiapas*

take care of the drainage into the Gulf of Mexico. The northern part of the wide valley base (elevation 900m/2,953ft–1,200m/3,937ft) is in some places covered with lakes, sand dunes, salt plains and, on the mountain slopes, alluvial deposits. On average, the mountain peaks tower 800m/2,625ft–900m/2,953ft above the desert basin. Several deposits of gold, silver, lead, zinc, mercury, oil shale, coal and iron ore have been discovered in the mountains.

Southern highlands ▸ Wide basins make up the principle part of the central southern highlands, such as the valleys of Bajío, Toluca, México and Puebla among others. The valley floors consist of volcanic material. The different valleys are separated from each other and from southern Mexico by uplands distinguished by softly sloping knolls as well as steep, rugged volcanic peaks. Lakes, swamps and thermal springs have formed on the valley floors at an elevation of between 1,500m/4,921ft and 2,600m/8,530ft where the drainage has been blocked by lava. Best known among these are lakes Chapala, Cuitzeo and Pátzcuaro. Three of Mexico's most important river systems originate in this area and run to the ocean: the Mezcala-Balsas system in Puebla; the Río Lerma/Río Grande de Santiago system in the area west of the Basin of Mexico; and the Río Montezuma/Río Pánuco system which drains the Basin of Mexico. This large area was already densely populated in the pre-Hispanic era. One of Mexico's most fertile grain producing

Mexico Landforms

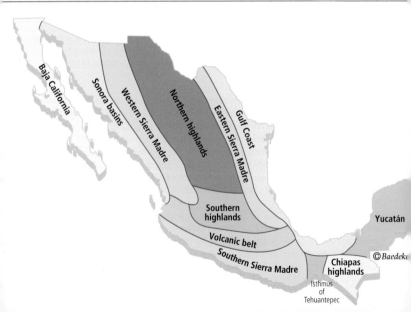

Because Popocatépetl frequently casts out ashes, it is often closed to climbers.

areas is the Bajío, i.e. the region stretching along the Río Lemma. The largest portions of this grain area belong to the federal states Michoacán and Guanajuato.

A volcanic belt crosses the southern central highlands. It extends approximately from San Blás on the Pacific to Veracruz on the Gulf of Mexico. This volcanic mountain range separates northern and central Mexico from the southern part of the country. This is where Mexico's highest **volcanoes** are found, such as Citlaltépetl (Pico de Orizaba, 5,747m/18,855ft above sea level), Popocatépetl (5,465m/17,930ft), Iztaccíhuatl (5,286m/17,343ft), Nevado de Toluca (Cinantecátl, 4,575m/15,010ft) and La Malinche (Matlalcuéyetl, 4,461m/14,636ft). The southern slopes of the volcanic belt are very rugged and the Río Mezcala tributaries have eroded the volcanic rock. The Sierra Mixteca features a similar landscape. This mountain range connects the highlands with the Southern Sierra Madre.

◄ Volcanic belt (Sistema Volcánico Transversal)

The western Sierra Madre spans about 1,100km/684mi from northwestern to south-eastern Mexico. The mountain range is about 160km/100mi wide, and its peaks average more than 1,800m/5,906ft, with the highest peaks 3,000m/9,843 feet high. The course of the mountain chains and grand ravines (barrancos) mostly reflect the folding of the earth in the Mesozoic era and earlier periods in the earth's history. With a depth of more than 1,500 m/4,921ft, the **barrancos** (gorges) in the west are so magnificent that they rival in every

◄ Western Sierra Madre (Sierra Madre Occidental)

way the world renowned Grand Canyon in the US state of Arizona. Waters from the Sierra Madre Occidental irrigate the »oases« of the highlands and the lowlands bordering the Gulf of California. The rivers Carmen, Conchos, Nazas and Aguanaval feed water to the highlands; the rivers Yaqui, Mayo, Fuerte, Sinaloa and Culiacán flow westward.

Eastern Sierra Madre (Sierra Madre Oriental) ► A chain of relatively low mountains stretches in a south-easterly direction from the great river bend of the Río Bravo del Norte (also known as Río Grande). South of Monterrey, these low mountains are taller and turn into a **magnificent mountain range**, the Eastern Sierra Madre. The peaks average about 2,100m/6,890ft but some exceed 3,000m/9,843ft. Several rivers break through the eastern edge of the highlands and rush toward the Gulf of Mexico, among them the Pánuco.

The northern Pacific region The northern Pacific region consists of the parallel mountain chains and wide valleys of the federal state of Sonora, the flat coastal corridor of the Baja California (Lower California) peninsula and the Gulf of California (Mar de Cortés, Sea of Cortés).

Sonora basins ► Detrital rock sediments flank the Sonora basins. Toward the northeast, these rock sediments gradually take the form of several mountain ranges. Aside from the mostly straight, flat and sandy coastal regions, there are also deep bays and lagoons surrounded by protective rocks. None of the rivers actually run all the way to the ocean between the Río Sonora and the Colorado River. However, there are »**oases**« in the southern region where cotton, wheat, sugar cane, fruits and vegetables can grow. Rich copper deposits are mined in the north-easternmost region.

Baja California ► The Baja California peninsula stretches 1,250km/777mi along the southern continuation of the infamous San Andreas Fault. The peninsula is only 90km/56mi wide. More than 20 million years ago, the peninsula broke off from the continent along this deep crack in the earth's crust and has been moving north-west ever since – causing severe earthquakes and volcanic activity. In a geological time frame, this **volcanism** is only a recent phenomenon.

In the north, near the border to the United States of America, the waters of the Laguna des los Volcanoes churn with activity. The peninsula landscape consists mostly of high mountains and desert. The land is dry, and few people live there. Crystalline mountains – most of them more than 1,500m/4,921ft high – run the length of the Baja California peninsula; some of them reach 3,000m/9,843ft. On both sides of the Sierra de Santa Clara are not only uplands but also fairly wide strips of flat desert land. Natural bays form excellent natural harbours on both coasts, and there are long, for the most part still pristine beaches. The Colorado River forms its delta at the end of the Gulf of California.

Islands ► Most of the numerous islands in Baja California's coastal waters are uninhabited. Only a few sea lions, goats and other animals live there.

The south-western parts of the coastal lowlands around the Gulf of **The Gulf Coast**
Mexico gradually give way to the Eastern Sierra Madre. The northern
and central basement was formed in the Cretaceous period. The typical regional landscape consists of low sediment hills which are
rarely higher than 200m/656ft; this is especially true for the vast
»Huasteca« south of Tampico. The coastal plain is known for its
long beaches, sand dunes, swamps and lagoons. The northern Gulf
Coast lacks good natural harbours.

The foothills of the Eastern Sierra Madre encroach upon the coastal
plain in the middle part of the state of Veracruz. The rocky coast and
the hills around San Andrés Tuxtla enliven the otherwise flat landscape. Two mighty rivers, the Río Bravo del Norte (Río Grande) and
the Río Pánuco traverse the northern coastal plain, and the Río
Grande marks the border to the USA. South and east of the state capital and harbour Veracruz, the rivers Papaloapán, Coatzacoalcos,
Grijalva and Usumacinta fan out to form large swamps and wetlands
before they reach the ocean.

The Yucatán peninsula is the widest part of the lowlands. Geological- ◀ Yucatán
ly, it is the youngest part of Mexico. Not until the last few million peninsula
years did the flat layers of limestone on the crystalline rock bed fold
up over the Gulf of Mexico. The highest elevations in the peninsula
are found in the centre (some of them in neighbouring Guatemala);
however, the elevations rarely exceed 150m/492ft. Precipitation

A perfect holiday setting on the Bahía de Zihuatanejo

quickly seeps through the porous, soluble limestone so that there are practically no surface rivers or streams. Instead, the richest of karst formations are seen here: sinkholes (collapsed underground channels called »dzonots« by the Maya, »cenotes« to Spanish ears), grottoes, caves with dripstone formations, sandbanks and lagoons are present all along the northern and western coasts of Yucatán. There are coral reefs on the eastern coast, and mangrove swamps exist around the peninsula.

Islands ▶ The barrier islands off the coast of the Yucatán peninsula offer marvellous beaches and diving areas. The islands are built of coral reef carbonate. Cancún, Isla Mujeres and Cozumel have become popular holiday destinations in the last three decades.

Southern Mexico Southern Mexico has a mountainous terrain. South of the volcanic belt, the elevation of the central plateau increases toward the Sierra Madre del Sur. This area includes the Southern Sierra Madre, the Isthmus of Tehuantepec and the Chiapas highlands.

The Southern Sierra Madre (Sierra Madre del Sur) ▶ A labyrinth of narrow ridges and deep valleys characterize the Southern Sierra Madre. The bedrock of the very rugged mountains consists of Cretaceous deposits; the volcanic rock cover from the Mesozoic era is heavily eroded. The peaks average more than 2,000m/6,562ft, some even exceed 3,000m/9,843ft. In the east, the mountainous terrain ends rather abruptly and the land leads into the Isthmus of Tehuantepec. A narrow, discontinuous coastal plain in the southwest and the lowlands around the Balsas-Mezcala river system in the north frame the principle part of the Sierra Madre del Sur.

Sierra Mixteca ▶ The Sierra Mixteca extends east of these lowlands and forms a highland bridge between the volcanic belt and the Sierra Madre del Sur. The mountains are relatively rich in natural resources, especially iron ore, lead, silver and gold. In this part of the country, the Pacific coastline parallels the mountain range of the Sierra Madre. In some spots, a rocky coast plunges down to the ocean; in other places, as is the case around Acapulco and Manzanillo, bays form excellent natural harbours. Only a few roads run across the mountains to the ocean, and access to the Sierra is very difficult, which has helped the native Indians maintain their own culture and way of life to a large degree.

Isthmus of Tehuantepec (Istmo de Tehuantepec) ▶ Topographically, the soft hills of the Isthmus of Tehuantepec resemble the hills of the coastal plains on the Gulf of Mexico. However, the regional geology has more in common with that of the neighbouring regions, the Southern Sierra Madre to the west and the Chiapas highlands to the east. The hills formed only in the most recent geological past. They connect two important mountain ranges. The isthmus has been a natural connecting corridor throughout the ages and nowadays roads, rail lines and oil pipelines cross it. Plans have existed for several hundred years to build a channel between the Pacific and Atlantic across this, the **narrowest part of Mexico** (225km/140m). The plan has, however, never been executed.

Typical highland vegetation: shrubs and cacti

Only 40 km/25mi inland, the Chiapas highlands reach heights of more than 1,500m/4,921ft above sea level. A few peaks even exceed 3,000m/9,843ft, among them the Tacaná volcano. The central plateau (Meseta Centra) has formed only recently, i.e. in the last few million years. It consists mostly of limestone and sandstone. The Sierra Madre de Chiapas continues to form and change, as it has for more than 500 million years. Longer phases of surface ablation and sedimentation interrupt this process. The most recent mountain formation started in the Tertiary era and has not yet ended. Several rivers start their short journey to the coast in the mountains and carry water to the many lagoons on the coastal plain. Wide lowlands at an elevation of between 300m/984ft and 600m/1,969ft stretch between the two mountain ranges. The Río Grijalva and its tributaries run through these lowlands. The Chiapas region is predominantly characterized by farmland, forests and meadows. Coffee is cultivated on some mountain slopes. Not until the early 1980s did »civilization« end the isolation of this part of the country through rail connections and new roads.

◄ Chiapas highlands

Climate

Mexico is located at the northern edge of the tropics; in addition, the differences in elevation are pronounced. Consequently, the entire range of subtropical and tropical climates is seen here. In some areas it is extremely dry and hot as is especially the case in the northern Sonora desert. In other places, the climate is often very hot and humid all year round, such as in the subtropical Lacandon jungle in the

From dry heat to tropical humidity

Chiapas region. The lower southern regions are tropical (hot and humid), while in the northern regions the climate becomes increasingly arid as the land approaches the horse latitudes with their steppes and desert belts. All year, the trade winds blow against the eastern Atlantic coastal regions and the ocean-side flanks of the Sierra Madre Oriental: tropical forests thrive where these winds create hot and humid conditions. In contrast, the Pacific coast is much drier. Precipitation decreases with distance from the oceans and is rare on the lee-side of the mountains.

Highland zones The climate is cooler at higher elevations, leading to typical changes in the natural vegetation and farming opportunities. The Spanish conquerors gave these climate zones names that are still used to this day. The lowest zone, the **Tierra Caliente** (hot zone), extends up to elevations of 800m/2,625ft, which corresponds to the border for growing cocoa. Given sufficient precipitation, tropical rain forests prevail in the southern regions of Mexico. The region at elevations between 800m/2600ft and 1,700m/5,577ft is called the **Tierra Templada**. This is the temperate, warm zone, which extends to the upper altitude limit for the cultivation of coffee, cotton and sugar cane. The zone above 1,700m/5,577ft is the **Tierra Fría**, the cool zone. Snow covers the highest peaks of the volcanoes all year.

Climate zones Humid summers with moderate temperatures characterize the southern central highlands. In the northern central highlands, a steppe climate with humid summers prevails, which further north turns into a subtropical semi-desert and desert climate. The southern Gulf Coast region with the Yucatán peninsula displays the entire range of climates, from the constantly humid tropical forest climate in the south to a seasonally more or less humid savannah climate. Humid summers and an otherwise subtropical steppe climate characterize the northern Gulf Coast region. The southern Pacific coast on the other hand is dominated by a tropical savannah climate with changing humidity, while the coastal regions around the Gulf of California show a subtropical semi-desert and desert climate. Mexico's extreme

Mexico *West-east cross section*

Western Sierra Madre

Ciudad de Mexico (2240m/7,280ft ASL)

Tierra Fria

1700 m ©Baedeker

Tierra Templada

800 m

Manzanillo

Tierra Caliente

north-west already extends into a climate zone whose distinguishing feature is winter rainfall.

Southern central highlands (Mexico City climate station)

Almost half of all Mexican territory lies at an altitude above 1,500m/ 4,921ft. The altitude of the capital, Mexico City (Ciudad de México) is 2,240m/7,349ft. Like the major part of the Mexican highlands, the capital is located in the cool climate zone, the Tierra Fría. The altitude accounts for the fact that, despite its location in the tropics, Mexico City has neither high temperatures nor high precipitation. When visiting Mexico in mid-October for example, travellers from Central Europe will be quite familiar with the nightly low temperatures. Most of the precipitation occurs in violent downpours between June and September. For the rest of the year, there is much less precipitation than in Central Europe. Frequent dust storms occur in the dry season. The high altitude brings with it some other climatic characteristics. The barometric pressure is considerably lower, and on occasion, the thinner air may cause breathing and circulatory problems. At this altitude, the rays of the sun are considerably more intense than in the lowlands. It feels warm, even at air temperatures between 10 and 15°C (50 and 59°F). With the sun high in the sky, protection against ultraviolet rays is absolutely necessary.

Northern central highlands (City of Juárez climate station)

The Juárez city climate station at the border to the USA registers considerable temperature differences between summer and winter. The median night temperatures in January are as low as –8°C/17.6°F, while the daily summer highs are just under 40°C/104°F. Daily temperature fluctuations have increased to almost 30°C/86°F, meaning that in winter in the middle of the day the temperature is as high as in Mexico City, but the nights are bitterly cold. Here as elsewhere in Mexico, most rain falls in the summer. The north sees far less rain than the more southern regions.

Yucatán (Mérida climate station)

This area has a hot and humid tropical climate. North of here, dry spells in the winter become more prevalent. Quite often, cold northern air masses cause temperatures to drop considerably between

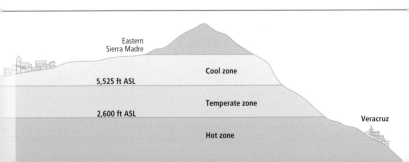

October and March. On the uphill slopes west of Veracruz, the trade winds from the ocean blow inland and lead to orographic rainfall. From the lowlands up to 2,000m/6,562ft, the amount of precipitation also increases with increasing altitude from 1,500mm/59in to 4,000mm/158in. All mountain zones are present, from tropical rainforest to permafrost on the high volcanoes. The Mérida climate sta-

Mexico   *Five region-typical climate stations*

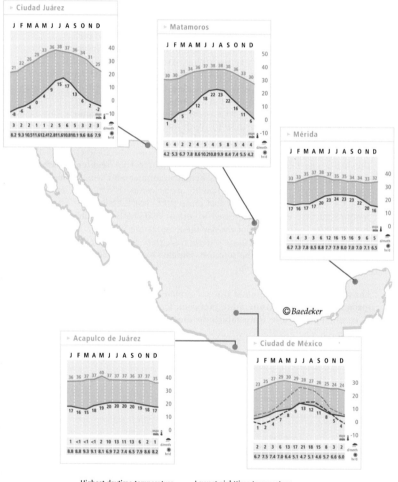

—— Highest daytime temperature   —— Lowest nighttime temperature

Days of rain   Hours of sun/day   Water temperature in °C

tion is situated in the drier north-west part of the Yucatán peninsula. Most rain falls between May and October. While summer temperatures with daily highs of 34°C/93.2°F are 3°C/5.4°F lower than the temperatures in May, high humidity makes the summer harder to endure. All year, about 10m/32.8ft to 30m/98ft above the ground or dense forest, a light breeze freshens the air.

Between July and October, tropical storms and hurricanes may occasionally also make their way from the Gulf of Mexico or the Caribbean to southern Mexico. The island Cozumel on the east coast of Yucatán shows the same temperature patterns as the ones recorded in the Mérida climate station. However, Cozumel gets more rain, as do the eastern parts of Yucatán which are exposed to the trade winds.

The Northern Gulf Coast (Matamoros climate station)

The climate changes in many ways in the north and around the Río Grande. Daily temperature highs are still relatively high (28°C/82.4°F in January, 36°C/96.8°F in July and August), but in January the nightly lows go down to −1°C/30.2 °F. Moving north, less and less rain falls, but winter rains add to the precipitation. As a result, the climate is always humid, mild in winter and hot in summer.

The Southern Pacific Coast (Acapulco climate station)

Mexico's entire southern Pacific coast features all-year-round high temperatures with maximal precipitation in the summer months. The weather remains sunny for the rest of the year when there is practically no rain. Sea breezes refresh the air. A comparison with the climate in Mexico City, a region that lies 2,500m/8,200ft higher, clearly shows that the temperatures are higher throughout, namely by 10°C/18°F for the nightly lows, and by up to 7°C/13.6°F for the daily highs in the afternoon. The daily temperature fluctuations in the coastal regions are far less pronounced than those inland in the more central regions.

Tolerable air temperatures, warm waters and plenty of sunshine attract tourists from cold northern climates, especially in winter, to the beaches of Acapulco and Mazatlán among others. The temperatures in Acapulco hardly vary through the year and are even higher than in Mazatlán. The median daily temperatures are around 35°C/95°F, the nightly lows are around 17°C/62.6°F. With 1,377 mm/54.2in, Acapulco has more rain than Mazatlán; it falls almost exclusively between June and October.

Around the Gulf of California

The climate in this region is that of subtropical semi-desert or desert. In summer, the Colorado delta with the city of Mexicali and the Sonora Desert are among the hottest places on earth. On average, the sun shines here 10.5 hours per day.

North-west region

It rains in winter in the northernmost part of Mexico, a pattern also typical for California over the border to the north with its Mediterranean climate.

Flora and Fauna

Flora

Rich variety The flora of Mexico is richly diverse, and a whole slew of today's useful and edible plants trace their origins to the country, such as corn (maize), potatoes, tomatoes, tobacco, cocoa, coffee and vanilla, as well as many different fruits and nuts.

The flora in Mexico's **deserts and semi-deserts**, i.e. mostly in the north-eastern parts of the country, but also in Lower California (Baja California peninsula) consists of drought-resistant plants, such as succulents, which can retain and store large amounts of water in their tissue. Prickly pear (opuntia) species are abundant. Slightly more vegetation grows in the **grass and bush steppe** in the southern central Mexican highlands: after a good rain, this steppe can temporarily turn into lush grassland. Many forms of cactus exist here as well, as do mesquite bushes, yucca palm trees and the thorny bushes of the Chaparrales (shrubland), agaves and the intoxicating mescaline cactus named Peyotl by the Indians. The Western, Eastern and Southern Sierra Madre and the volcanic belt which frame the central highlands are rich in **deciduous and coniferous woodlands**: evergreens, defoliating oak tree varieties, arbour vitae, juniper and pine trees and other conifers grow in these forests. Nest grasses and cushion plants cover the ground. **Tropical evergreen forests** grow mostly close to the south-western coastline on the Gulf of Mexico. Swamp plants, bamboo and mangroves thrive in the coastal wetlands and swamps. Climbing plants and epiphytic ferns cover the trees. There are also orchids, swamp cypresses and a tree called the Montezuma cypress or Ahuehuetl (ahuehuete in Spanish). **Wide scrublands** characterize the Pacific coastline of Central and South Mexico and the Northern Yucatán peninsula. Low scrub is found amongst the grassland. **Tropical rainforest** abounds in the southern Yucatán peninsula, in Chiapas, Tabasco and in the state of Veracruz. Among other trees, there are mahogany and kapok (java cotton) trees, logwood, and the chicle tree, which provides the raw material for chewing gum. Trees and bushes are often covered with clinging, climbing or epiphytic plants.

Fauna

Mammals Mexico's fauna, too, shows great diversity. North and South American animals have made their habitats in Mexico since the Pliocene. Wolf, coyote, black bear and beaver moved south and found a new habitat in Mexico's highlands. The lowlands attracted jaguars, pumas, monkeys and other species from South America. Mexico's animals also include the ocelot, lynx, badger, otter, armadillo, desert bighorn sheep, sloth, racoon, squirrel, tapir and anteater. There are also several species of wild boar, deer and small rodent. Although bats make themselves useful keeping insects at bay, farmers fear and combat them as carriers of livestock disease.

Reptiles and amphibians

Among the small and large reptiles and amphibians are large saurians, sometimes called earth monsters (iguanas), small saurians, alligators, tortoises and many frog and toad varieties. The Gila monster, a poisonous lizard, lives in the north-west. The neotenic newt Axolotl (Ambystoma mexicana) is the most wondrous of the amphibians; it lives in underground water pools and reaches sexual maturity in the larval stage. Mexico has the most **snakes** of any country in the world: there are 705 different snake species. Among the venomous snakes are several kinds of rattlesnake, the coral snake, the bushmaster snake (also called surucucu) and the fer-de-lance. The non-venomous boa constrictor can reach several metres in length.

Birds

The Indian native population was in awe of the birds' ability to fly. Birds therefore played an important role in mythology, and the Indians made festive garments for their rulers using the feathers of the **quetzal**. The quetzal has become very rare as has the eagle, Mexico's heraldic animal. The **hummingbird** and the **parrot** also play a part in mythology. Other Mexican birds include turkeys, vultures, buz-

Humming birds feed predominantly on richly nourishing nectar, making possible their energy-demanding style of flight.

Sea lions on the Baja California peninsula

zards, cormorants, pelicans, toucans, egrets (herons) and flamingos. Woodpeckers, wild geese, mallard ducks, wild pigeons, quails, sea-gulls, swallows (martins) and partridges migrate to Mexico from the north.

Insects Insects and arachnids can become a nuisance in Mexico. Various kinds of mosquitoes, flies, ticks and mites are prevalent. Scorpions live in almost all dry regions. Their bite is painful and may be dangerous. Some spiders are also venomous, such as the tarantula (bird-eating spider) and the black widow. The bites of red ants are also unpleasant.

Butterflies The colourful multitude of butterflies should not be overlooked, with species such as the red admiral, the **monarch butterfly**, the copper-headed sooty wing, the malachite and the iridescent blue morpho butterfly, as well as saturniid moths and the cracker butterfly, also known as the calico butterfly.

Maritime fauna The maritime fauna has a rich with a variety of species. From the coast of the northern Pacific visitors can observe **sea lions**, and at certain times of year also **grey whales**. Shrimp (an important export item), crustaceans (crayfish, crabs) and plaice are harvested from shallow coastal waters. Among the ocean fish are the goliath grouper (sea perch), mackerel, mullet, sardine, bonito (tuna, albacore), barracuda, swordfish, moray eel and various kinds of shark and ray. Now and then, dolphins can be observed near the more secluded beaches of the Pacific coast. Freshwater fish include trout, perch, carp and catfish.

Facts and Figures Mexico

Location
► The southern part of North America
► between 32° 43' and 14° 14' northern latitude and 88° 48' and 117° 07' western longitude
► Neighbouring countries: USA, Guatemala and Belize

Area
► 1,972,550 sq km/710,280 sq mi (England: 130,000 sq km/50,000 sq mi)

Population
► approx. 105 million
► Average age: 24.6 years (in UK: 38.8 years)
► Birth rate: 2.1%

The state
► Federal republic consisting of 31 states (estados) and one federal district (Distrito Federal, D.F. for short) with the capital Mexico City and its surroundings
► Head of state is the president, who is elected for six years and also serves as the head of government.
► Each individual federal Mexican state commands regional autonomy and is run by a governor.

Economy
► Largest national economy and most significant export nation in Latin America

► Gross national product: US$ 626.1 billion (2004)
► Inflation: approx. 4%
► Trading partners: USA (77% of import goods and 85% of export goods), Canada, Japan, Spain and Germany
► Natural resources: crude oil, natural gas, zinc, salt, silver, copper, marble, manganese, phosphate and uranium
► Industry: oil production and refining, automotive industry, chemistry, food, tobacco and alcohol preparation, as well as mining of iron ore
► Agriculture: corn (maize), sugar cane, fruit, vegetable, coffee, cotton, grain, beans
► Tourism: uptrending, in 2004 almost 20.5 million visitors

Language and religion
► Official language: Spanish; various indigenous tongues
► Predominantly Roman Catholic (about 89%) with other Christian, Jewish and Baha'i faith groups; elements and rites from ancient Indian faiths

Name, flag and emblems
► The Aztec called themselves the »México« and so coined the name for the country. Furthermore, the Spanish built a city on the ruins of Teotihuacán and called it »Méjico«.
► Emblazoned in the Mexican emblem is the story of the legendary founding of the Aztec capital Tenochtitlán. Following a divine oracle, the Aztec built their city in the place where they found an eagle perched on a cactus with its wings spread and a snake in its beak.
► The flag takes its symbolism from the French tricolour. Green stands for freedom, white for purity of religion and red for national unity.

Population · Politics · Economy

Racial melting pot
Mexico is the only country on the American continent in which the predominant part of the population has a mixed ancestry of all the different races. At the time of the conquistadores, the ancestors of today's approximately **105 million** Mexicans (2004) were 6 to 7 million Indian natives, around 200,000 Spanish immigrants and about an equal number of slaves who were brought into the country from Africa during colonial times.

Precise population data are not always available. According to estimates, about 80% of Mexicans are mestizos with mostly Indian-Spa-

Mexico *Indian population*

Indigenous groups of Mexico
Source: Instituto Nacional Indigenista

1 Kumiai	15 Mazateco	29 Pima Bajo	43 Tzeltal
2 Cucapá	16 Popoloca	30 Tepehuano	44 Tzotzil
3 Paipai (akwa'ala)	17 Ixcateco	31 Yaqui	45 Tojolabal
4 Cochimí	18 Chocho-Popoloca	32 Mayo	46 Chuj
5 Kiliwa	19 Mixteco	33 Tarahumara	47 Jacalteco
6 Seri	20 Cuicateco	34 Guarijio	48 Mame
7 Tequistlateco/Chontal de Oaxaca	21 Trique	35 Cora	49 Motozintle
8 Tlapaneco	22 Amuzgo	36 Huichol	50 Mixe
9 Pame	23 Chatino	37 Nahua	51 Popoluca
10 Chichimeco Jonaz	24 Zapoteco	38 Huasteco	52 Zoque
11 Otomi	25 Chinanteco	39 Maya Peninsular	53 Totonaco
12 Mazahua	26 Huave	40 Lacandón	54 Tepehua
13 Matlatzinca	27 Pápago	41 Chontal (de Tabasco)	55 Purépecha
14 Ocuilteco	28 Pima Alto	42 Chol	56 Kikapú

nish, but also African and Asian ancestry. Another 8 to 10% are Indians, slightly more than 10% are Caucasian, mostly from old Spanish ancestry (Criollos). Whites make up only a small percentage of the population. Yet, they still play a dominant role in politics, industry and trade.

Even as late as 1870, the population was mostly Indian. But this changed quickly. By 1921, only 30 to 35 percent of the population was Indian. The majority of the natives is grouped in the central highlands (México, Hidalgo, Puebla), in the south (Guerrero, Oaxaca, Chiapas), on the Gulf Coast (Veracruz) and in the east (Yucatán peninsula). Today, probably about one quarter of the 10 to 15 million Indians **do not speak Spanish**, i.e. about 8% of the total population. The more than 130 languages of the natives could not survive. Among the few Indian languages still in use are more than 20 different Mayan and 6 Náhuatl (Aztec) language variants.

Indian natives (Indigenas)

Today, Mexico recognizes 52 individual groups of Indians. Unofficial estimates however set the number of such groups at 115. Among the largest and best known Indian tribes that in part still live according to their unique cultural traditions are the Náhua, Otomí, Purepechan (Tarascan), Huichol, Cora, Tarahumara, Mayo, Yaqui, Totonac, Huastec, Matlatzínca, Mazatec, Mazahua, Amuzgo, Triqui, Míxtec, Zapotec, Chinantec, Tzeltal, Tzotzil, Tojolobal, Chol and Maya (Yucatán). Two dozen or more Indian tribes have been able to a large extent to claim their right to local self-government. The Mexican Government displays with pride the rich historic legacy of the original Indian inhabitants of the country. Nevertheless, social and economic conditions leave their immediate descendents **out of the mainstream**. The integration efforts of the National Indigenous Institute (Instituto Nacional Indígenista) are also plagued with contradictions, the natural result of striving for economic progress for the rural Indian population while at the same time working to preserve their cultural inheritance. Lately, individual tribes have shown growing confidence: on 1 January 1994, the Tzotzil and Tzeltal in Chiapas actively protested against economic and other conditions.

Lacandon Maya children wear their hair long.

Mexico States

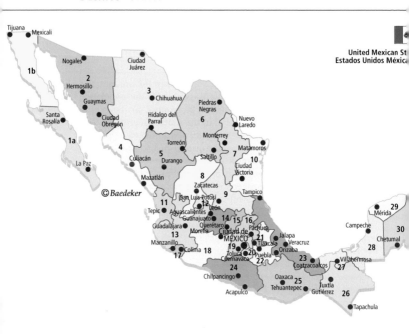

United Mexican St
Estados Unidos Méxic

©*Baedeker*

1a Baja California
Sur (B.C.S.)
1b Baja California
Norte (B.C.)
2 Sonora (Son.)
3 Chihuahua (Chih.)
4 Sinaloa (Sin.)
5 Durango (Dgo.)
6 Coahuila (Coah.)
7 Nuevo León (N.L.)
8 Zacatecas (Zac.)

9 San Luis Potosí (S.L.P.)
10 Tamaulipas (Tamps.)
11 Nayarit (Nay.)
12 Aguascalientes (Ags.)
13 Jalisco (Jal.)
14 Guanajuato (Gto.)
15 Querétaro (Qro.)
16 Hidalgo (Hgo.)
17 Colima (Col.)
18 Michoacán (Mich.)
19 México (Mex.)

20 Morelos (Mor.)
21 Tlaxcala (Tlax.)
22 Puebla (Pue.)
23 Veracruz (Ver.)
24 Guerrero (Gro.)
25 Oaxaca (Oax.)
26 Chiapas (Chis.)
27 Tabasco (Tab.)
28 Campeche (Cam
29 Yucatán (Yuc.)
30 Quintana Roo (Q

Population structure In contrast to a number of other Latin American countries, Mexico has a relatively broad middle class. However, the crises of the 1980s and the 1990s put severe stress on this social group. A wide gap exists between the small, enormously rich upper class and the often extremely poor rural and urban immigrant populations.

Worldwide, Mexico is still one of the countries with the **least equitable distribution of wealth**. While the upper 10% of the population with the highest incomes control 41% of the wealth, half of the population must subsist on 16% of the national income. Large cities are magnets for young people who want to leave rural poverty behind. This situation is partially alleviated by the stream of legal and illegal emigrants to the United States of America.

With the battle cry »Tierra y Libertad« (land and freedom) Mexican revolutionists called for the return of the large, fertile farms (haciendas) to the rural populations.

The rural population

However, land reform did not take place until the 1930s. The farmers were given land either for collective cultivation (ejidos colectivos) or for private use (ejidos individuales).

The government remained the owner of the land. At the end of 1991, the Ejido system was radically liberalized. Only every fourth farmer owns a plough, and owning a tractor is still rare. The hoe is the most common tool.

Most of the harvest is used to sustain the farmers and villagers themselves. Only a small portion is sold on the market to obtain funds for the purchase of consumer goods. Small farmers must also compete with large farm corporations. Many family farmers give up their piece of land and hire themselves out as field hands or move to urban areas.

Only about 20% of the urbanites can afford to live in relative comfort. Two out of three however live very close to the poverty line, or below it. When work is scarce people take on temporary jobs. Many women subsidize their budgets with jobs as maids, and some earn their entire living in this way. Children also contribute to the family income: some peddle gum and sweets, some earn money washing windscreens or even entertaining as fire-eaters. One of the most striking manifestations of urban poverty are the slums on the outskirts of the cities, the »ciudades perdidas« (lost cities). Faced with a housing emergency, the authorities tolerate the illegal living quarters.

The urban population

Mexicans now spend almost 6% of the gross national product on education (OECD average: 5.6%). This amounts to almost one quarter (24%) of all public spending (OECD countries: 12.7%). Compulsory education since the 1920s (6 years of primary and 3 years of secondary school) and literacy campaigns have reduced the illiteracy rate to 5.6%. Nonetheless, many children still leave school without qualifications, a particular problem in poorer rural regions.

Educational system

The number of Mexican colleges has all but exploded in recent decades. While there were only 39 colleges in 1950, today their number has reached about 1,300 (515 public, 736 private colleges). More than 2 million students attend one of Mexico's universities. The number of universities has grown to 70.

Politics

From its inception in 1929 until 2000 the Partido Revolucionario Institucional, the **PRI**, was by far the strongest Mexican party. Throughout this period, the PRI appointed all presidents. Political opponents were intimidated and sometimes murdered. Elections were rigged. However, on 2 July 2000, the election of **Vicente Fox** as

Political parties

Mexican president ended long years in opposition for the conservative catholic party, the Partido Acción Nacional (PAN).

Moreover, since the 2006 elections, Mexico's congress has been roughly split three ways between the PRI, president Felipe Calderon's PAN and Lopez Obrador's left-leaning PRD (Partido de Revolución Democrática). The other party of significance is the green ecology party, the PVEM.

Presidential elections 2006

The PRD politician **Andrés Manuel López Obrador** and the PAN party's **Felipe Calderón Hinojosa** were seen as the frontrunners in the presidential elections of 2006. In polls, Obrador had for many months come out ahead of both PAN and PRI candidates (Fox was not allowed to run again after six years as president). Obrador had made a name for himself as the mayor of Mexico City where he gained popularity because of his comprehensive social policies in favour of the poor. The administration under President Fox and his PAN party therefore left no stone unturned to stop their PRD competitor. A huge political conflict ensued in October 2004 when the federal government attempted to interfere with financial decisions in the capital.

The objective was clear enough: the Fox administration wanted to cut López Obrador's social programmes to harm his popularity. In April 2005, the ruling conservative parties in parliament revoked Obrador's immunity and cleared the way for a lawsuit against him. The district attorney accused him of approving road construction in spite of a legal injunction. If convicted, Obrador would no longer have been eligible to run for office in the presidential elections. This brought several hundred thousand citizens to Mexico City and triggered the largest demonstration in the history of the country ever.

Campaigning for the 2006 elections began in an atmosphere of fierce competition. When the voting began, it became clear that the difference between the two frontrunners was very small, smaller than the margin of error of the official quick count by the Federal Electoral Institute (IFE). Nevertheless, both Obrador and Calderón claimed victory based on their own exit polls.

President Calderón

The election was held on 2 July 2006; on 6 July the IFE announced the victory of Felipe Calderón Hinojosa, by a narrow margin of 0.58 percentage points. Obrador challenged the result, and the PRD made allegations of election irregularities. The protest that followed was largely peaceful; it included a demonstration on Mexico City's Zócalo in support of Obrador and what he referred to as the »defence of the popular vote«.

However, although many observers found examples of fraud and demanded a full recount, election monitors from the European Union stated on 8 July that they had found no evidence of irregularities which could have affected the results. On 5 September 2006 the Federal Electoral Court declared Calderón the definitive winner.

Over the border at Tijuana the United States beckons.

Mexico's economic dependency on its »big brother« in the north has scarcely diminished. The influx of illegal Mexican migrant workers to the USA weighs heavy on the relations between the two countries. While the farming industry and small business needs the cheap Mexican labour force, the American labour movements resent the competition. For Mexico, the illegal workers represent a welcome relief for the labour market, but the lack of legal rights of migrant workers in the USA is cause for concern.

Mexico and the USA

After lengthy debates in the US political arena, a new immigration law (the Simpson Rodino Act) came into force in November 1986. Among other provisions, this law provides for an amnesty program for illegal immigrants who have been in the USA since 1982, and fines for employers who hire illegal workers. Most illegal immigrants are however wary of going to the authorities.

Economy

In recent years, Mexico's economy has experienced remarkable changes. The declared objective of these changes is to break with socialism and the protectionism of the past. The hallmarks of these new economic policies are privatization of government-owned companies, economic liberalization and opening up to the world markets as well as lifting regulatory restrictions for both Mexican and foreign investors. Although it is becoming more and more apparent that planned reform projects, such as the opening of the energy sectors to foreign investors, the creation of a more flexible labour market and

Breaking with protectionism and socialization

the removal of structural problems in the public financing sector will take time to complete, the improved economic climate points to an **uptrend**.

Problems include the unfair distribution of wealth with high poverty rates, a banking system in dire need of reform, high debt loads for private households and enterprise and the resulting strong dependency on foreign corporations (foreign companies produce about two thirds of the Mexican export goods). What is more, the Mexican labour market is coming under increasing pressure from competitors in Asia.

Labour market   Mexico's workforce numbers about 43.3 million people, of a total population of 105 million. Officially, the unemployment rate is currently around 3.3%, though the rate is much higher in rural areas. The daily minimum wage is US$4.43 (2007). Surveys by the Mexican Social Security Institute (IMSS) show that almost one million people are paid this minimum daily wage; more than 20 million wage earners receive less.

Industry   Industrial goods, in particular cars and car parts, are the most important source of foreign currency bringing in more than 50% of all export revenue. They account for more than one quarter of the gross national product. The largest industries are automotive assembly (Ford, among others), steel, textiles, brewing, and processing and refining of foods. In recent years, manufacturers of electronics and computers have experienced a real boom. Despite attempts to decentralize, most industries are concentrated in and around Mexico City, Puebla, Guadalajara, Monterrey, Mérida and Mexicali. The finishing industries contribute much to Mexican exports. In 2004, these industries grew by about 15%.

The »**maquiladoras**« are also very important. Maquiladoras are foreign companies which use the relatively low wages in Mexico to their advantage. The companies produce or process semi-finished products, such as textiles, automotive components, and electrical and electronic devices. Today, there are about 3,500 of such companies (called industry parks) with about 1.5 million employees. Originally, these companies were mostly located near the US border, but in the mean time they are also settling in other parts of the country. The new enterprise brought some life to the Mexican labour market – despite miserable work contracts (up to 12-hour days, no unions) and low wages.

Agriculture   Advancing industrialization notwithstanding, Mexico is still a predominantly agrarian country. Agriculture contributes approximately 4% to the gross national product (GNP). The productivity is relatively low, as in spite of increasing irrigation only one sixth of the country can be cultivated; about 40% is pasture. Agricultural areas are the southern highlands and the abutting boundary ranges of the mountains as well as the Pacific coastal regions and the lands on the Gulf of Mexico. The most important agricultural goods are coffee, fruit and vegetables, especially tomatoes. Agricultural exports have more than doubled since Mexico joined NAFTA; most of the agricultural export goods are however produced on a very small number of industry-sized farms on vast areas of privately owned land.

Small farmers (**campesinos**) make up the large part of the Mexican farm population. They cultivate their pieces of land and use the harvest mostly for personal consumption. The campesinos still widely use the traditional Indian Milpa system with corn (maize), beans and some fruit. Haciendas and the modern agricultural industry on the other hand dominate the delivery of agricultural goods to the markets. Based on the reform law of 1917, land reforms were undertaken in the 1930s, which concluded with a second phase in the 1970s. These reforms covered almost 60% of the cultivated land, representing about three quarters of the agrarian business. Three forms of property rights to agricultural land exist today in Mexico: the

A short break after a long, hard working day: approx. 70% of workers at so-called maquiladoras are women. Their daily wage, 3 to 4 US dollars, is even less than their male colleagues.

Today, Mexico is the fifth largest exporter of oil in the world. After nationalization in 1938 it was possible to build up a sizeable oil industry.

farm property (more than 5ha/12.4ac) and the »**ejido**«. Ejidos are a form of community property management. The government owns the real estate but it is either let to individual members of the community for agricultural use, or used and maintained collectively. As long as the land is used and maintained properly the government does not exercise its ownership rights. In 1991, the system was changed radically. The ejidatario now has the right to sell or lease his lands, either to Mexicans or to foreigners.

Forestry Forests cover almost 30% of Mexico. Although forestry shows a lack of productivity, more than 5,000 sq km/1,931 sq mi are deforested for wood every year with no ecological considerations. Exhaustive deforestation is mainly seen in the tropical rainforests of southern Mexico, especially in the problem region of Chiapas. The American consumer appreciates such Mexican forestry exports as valuable tropical woods, oak timber and soft coniferous woods, as well as natural resin, tanning agents and chicle for the production of chewing gum.

Fishery Mexico has more than 9,000km/5,593mi of coastline and its fishing industry has the potential to be one of the most productive in the world. The waters around Baja California in particular are rich in fish. In recent years, the fishing fleet has been modernized and the existing bureaucratic stumbling blocks reduced. Important Mexican fishery exports are shrimp, crayfish, lobster, mackerel, bonito (tuna), anchovy, sardine and squid (octopus).

Mexico is rich in mineral resources. The country's crude oil deposits are substantial and their sale brings important foreign currency into the country. Recently, the income from crude oil exports has increased by 33.5%, due in no small degree to higher oil prices. 31% of Mexico's export revenue is based on the sale of petroleum products. Mining of silver, bismuth, arsenic and antimony plays a considerable role; nevertheless, mining generates only 4% of the gross national product (GNP). **Energy and mining**

Tourism plays an ever more important role and is today already the **second most important source of foreign currency income**. According to the WTO, about 20.5 million tourists visited Mexico in 2004, the large majority of them from the USA. American visitors contributed US$ 16.6 million to the Mexican economy, 12.3% more than in 2003. Today, more than 6 million Mexicans already make a living either directly or indirectly from tourism. **Tourism**

The wonderful beaches on the Riviera Maya will help boost the tourist industry.

History

How did the great ancient American civilizations originate, and how were architecture and the arts and sciences able to soar to such heights? Why did the Spanish conquistadores destroy this civilization so swiftly and so completely? Why did it take so many insurrections and revolutionaries to turn Mexico into a modern state?

Origins

Pre-Colonial Era	Significant high cultures: Olmec in Southern Mexico (1st millennium BC) Teotihuacán (key period AD 600) Maya (key period AD 600) Aztec (since AD 1300)
1325	Foundation of Tenochtitlán (today's Mexico City) by the Aztec

Aborigines from Asia (50,000 to 5000 BC)

The first settlers came around 50,000 BC via the Bering land bridge from Asia to South and Central America. These Paleo-Indians lived as hunter-gatherers, wandering throughout the entire subcontinent. Between 10,000 and 5000 BC, this nomadic existence gave way to settling and farming. The cultivation of corn (maize) and beans has been the mainstay of nutrition in Central and South America ever since. Small villages grew into larger settlements, which in due course blossomed into the pre-Columbian high cultures.

The Olmec (1200 to 500 BC)

The first high culture in the region of Tabasco between 1200 and 500 BC is attributed to the Olmec. Their legendary worship of the jaguar god and colossal head monuments are as mysterious as the culture's sudden disappearance.

The Maya and other high cultures (2000 BC to AD 900)

The first Maya settlements in the region of Belize date back to times as early as 2000 BC. However, the Maya reached the high point of their civilization only around the beginning of the Common Era (the year 0) in the Yucatán region. The cities of the Maya started to deteriorate around AD 900, but remnants of their culture and traditions are still alive, mostly in remote rural communities. The Zapotec and Mixtec developed comparable **cultural centres** in today's Oaxaca region. Who is responsible for creating the grandiose city of Teotihuacán in central Mexico is a mystery to this very day.

The Toltec (AD 900 to 1200)

The Toltec were a warrior society. They came to central and southern Mexico from the north. In his guise as a feathered serpent, the legendary **Quetzalcóatl** was both king and god to his people. His city of Tula was a masterful new creation. The great days of the Toltec only lasted from AD 900 to 1200.

Aztec (1400–1519)

In the 15th century, the Aztec superseded the mighty civilizations of the Toltec and Tepanec. The centre of Aztec power and splendour was the city of Tenochtitlán, which was built in what was originally the swamp-like Texcoco lake region, a system of five lakes in the Val-

← *Montezuma II, Hernán Cortés's adversary (1623)*

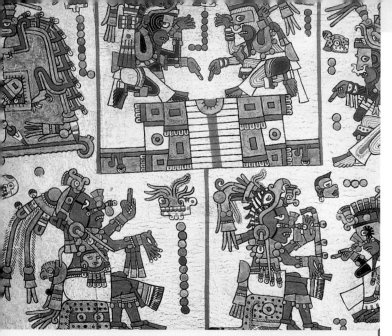

Mixtec Codex (around 1400)

ley of Mexico. According to oral tradition, an eagle was seen here, sitting on a cactus devouring a snake. This was the sign to the Aztec that this was the place to build their city. Today, the scene is depicted on the **national flag of Mexico**. Mexico City is nowadays expanding much faster than the Aztec capital ever did.

Aztec society Until their empire fell apart, the Aztec ruled a region of enormous size for their time. They subjugated many of the indigenous populations. The king was elected from Aztec nobility and ruled **a strictly hierarchical society**. The ruling classes of the Aztec included priests, administrative scribes and famous warriors. Traders not only supplied the capital city with the required goods but were also the only people to travel the entire empire. The real centre of power however was in the highland valley of Anahuac.

In the circle of the sun and the calendar The Mexican aborigines created comprehensive history books, in which they described the Aztec origins in mythical terms and laid the foundations for their power in religion. A **complex sun myth** bound history, tradition and life tightly together and was expressed in the architecture of the city, in religious ball games and human sacrifice, as well as other aspects of living. So holy was the circle as a symbol of the sun that even the use of the wheel was taboo. The cycles of day and year also had their mythical foundation. The amazing side effects of these myths are **precise calendars** (see pp.64/65). The length of each calendar round was 52 years or about one human lifetime. Apocalypse loomed at the end of each calendar round and had to be averted with many religious rites.

The Aztec were enmeshed in legends and myths. This not only gave rise to remarkable cultural achievements in architecture, literature and the arts, but also contributed to the fall of the civilization. When confronted with the vehemence of the Spanish conquerors, the Aztec lost their power, which was based on suppression and conquest. They also lost because the Aztec not only feared the strength of the foreign warriors but also believed that they might be new gods.

Fall of the empire

The Spanish Conquest

1492	Columbus »discovers« America.
1519 to 1521	Subjugation of the Aztec by the conquistadores (Hernán Cortés)

From 1492, when Columbus discovered Haiti and Cuba, the conquistadores stood at the gates of Mexico. The first contact between Spaniards and the Maya came about in 1512 on the Yucatán peninsula. Following this contact, Hernández de Córdoba explored the Gulf Coast region. The Spanish priest Juan de Aguilar was captured and became the first European to learn Indian languages.

First contact

In 1519, Cortés left Cuba without permission of his superiors with eleven ships and about 600 men. His immediate destination was Yucatán where he was able to liberate the priest Aguilar. He then went to the Tabasco coast, but was driven out by Maya warriors. On his departure, he took with him his Indian lover Malinche who was to bear him several children. In **the priest Aguilar and Malinche**, Cortés now had two assistants whose knowledge of the language and culture later became invaluable to him.

Hernán Cortés

The first place where the Spaniards were able to settle was Veracruz. It became both base and fallback point for the ensuing conquests. Here, Cortés found the Indian tribes eager to shake off Aztec suppression and recruited them. The Aztec prince **Montezuma II** sent magnificent welcoming gifts to Cortés a few days after his arrival. The Indians marvelled at the Spaniards, their ships, horses and destructive weapons. Few if any suspected the Spaniards to be potential enemies, which proved to be fatal.

The beginning of the end

Gifts and the dead

For Cortés, these gifts confirmed the presence of untold treasures in the country. The power of the Aztec had existed for less than 200 years and was based on suppression and myths. On this basis, Cortés doubted its stability and moved toward the capital Tenochtitlán. During his campaign, he demonstratively destroyed the important cities Tlaxcala and Cholula and killed about 15,000 people who had greeted him peacefully. This destructive form of war took the Aztec completely by surprise: Aztec wars were about taking as many prisoners as possible for later sacrifice to the gods, and also annexing intact cities to their empire. Although his 60,000 Aztec warriors outnumbered the 450 Spaniards, Montezuma II received Cortés in Tenochtitlán **without resistance** on 8 November 1519. In this way, Montezuma II presumably hoped to appease the Spaniards and convince them to leave. This however turned out to be a fateful error.

Resistance (1519–1520)

To legitimize his rather arbitrary expedition, Cortés sent a ship-load of precious gifts to Spain, just in time for the coronation of Emperor Karl V. Having first lived as a guest in Tenochtitlán, Cortés then fortified his own residence as a stronghold and put weapons in place. At the end of 1519, he placed Montezuma II under the supervision of Pedro de Alvarado and made him prisoner in his own palace. He himself hurried back to Veracruz in 1520 to defeat Spanish troops on a mission to end Cortés' wilful behaviour. Meanwhile, on the occasion of a religious celebration, Alvarado killed several Aztec noblemen. This finally triggered resistance against the uninvited guests.

Returning to the Aztec capital in June of 1520, Cortés had no choice but to barricade himself in with his treasure. The situation escalated when Montezuma II refused to appease the population and had to pay for this with his life. The Spaniards took their chance to escape during »the sad night«(»**la noche triste**«) from 30 June to 1 July 1520. 800 of the fleeing Spaniards paid with their lives, many of them presumed drowned in the channel system of Tenochtitlán because they were so heavily loaded down with loot.

Bloodthirsty conquest (1521)

Even after this defeat Cortés was able to rebuild his army. Four Spanish ships were sent against him, yet they merely supplied him with the needed weapons, horses and soldiers. He promised great wealth to the ship crews and they joined him. Cortés also recruited troops from neighbouring Indian tribes. In order to take the swamp-logged Aztec capital, he commissioned boats and transported them over the mountains. In 1521, Cortés once again approached the gates of the city. The population was badly weakened by a **smallpox epidemic**, a disease brought in by the Spaniards. It nevertheless took the Spanish troops three months to take Tenochtitlán. The conquest cost at least 10,000 Aztec lives. On 13 August 1521, the Spaniards occupied the completely destroyed city. The Aztec Empire was totally defeated, its culture destroyed and the population close to annihilation. In light of this, many other Indian tribes bowed to Spanish power.

The Colonial New Spain

1521 to 1810	Colonial New Spain: Christianization, enslavement of the Indians, exploitation of natural resources
1531	Worship of the Virgin of Guadalupe
1600	Economic fall

After conquering the Aztec, the Spaniards built their colonial empire swiftly and consistently. They established cities and governed the conquered regions with an administrative system in the Spanish

The connection between religion and cult: the Virgin of Guadalupe is a national symbol. She appeared at the place where, up until that point, the Aztec goddess Tonantzin had been worshipped.

style. The **Christian faith** was declared the official state religion, and the Indians were converted by force. Indian culture was eradicated. Throughout the country places of worship were demolished; scriptures, works of art and objects of cultural value were destroyed. Religious and political leaders were persecuted. National treasures were plundered and found their way into European collections.

While the new capital Mexico City grew out of the ruins of Tenochtitlán, some of the more remote regions remained relatively untouched. This preserved the lifestyle of some smaller Maya communities over hundreds of years.

Help from Our Lady of Guadalupe

The population was brought under Christian hierarchy as soon as the military conquest was concluded. Within a few years, a large number of churches and convents rose up, which also usually involved the taking of vast stretches of land.

As of 1531, the veneration of the Virgin of Guadalupe became more and more popular with the Indians, for whom the appearance of the Virgin Mary as a dark skinned figure **easily fitted into the realm between Indian identity and the new religion**. To this day, elements of Christianity and Indian spirituality and myth flow into her worship. Churches and religious orders stabilized the expanding colonial structures.

Since 1535: goldmine New Spain

By declaring Antonio de Mendoza viceroy, Karl V officially gave New Spain the status of **colony**. Starting in 1547, Indians were moved from their small rural communities into larger settlements. New cities emerged, and the systematic exploitation of country and people began. In a few years, the rich Mexican silver deposits made Spain the largest silver merchant in the world.

Bartolomé de las Casas

The Indian population shrank drastically in the space of only a few years due to indiscriminate murder, slave labour and newly introduced epidemics. Bartolomé de las Casas, the archbishop of Chiapas, attempted to stem the genocide in the »New World« – but to no avail. To protect the Mexican aborigines he argued for the use of African slaves, in doing so starting a course of long-lasting human misery in many countries of the Americas.

A social powder keg

Only a few upper crust Spaniards actually lived in Mexico. Whites who were born in the colony, **the Creoles**, had to make a living as craftsmen or lower ranking officials. Following the deliberate decimation of the Indian population, the **Mestizos** made up the majority of the population. The keeping of concubines was tolerated, and many Spaniards had many offspring without ever acknowledging them. Although the traditional village communities tolerated these Mestizos, they did not fully integrate them. This gave rise to tension and identity problems which colour the fabric of Mexican society to this day.

The path to independence

| 1810–1821 | The War of Independence costs 650,000 human lives |
| 1821 | Mexico gains independence. The initial revolutionary movement for social change is however quashed by the Spanish upper class, which is not inclined to make way for reforms. |

The ideas of the French Revolution not only influenced the North American Declaration of Independence. The first demands for sovereignty were also being heard in Mexico.

»Death to bad government!«

These ideas gained momentum after Napoleon's victory in Spain in 1808 and after his brother, Joseph Bonaparte, became King of Spain. Mexicans rejected the imposed ruler.

The Creoles in particular believed that the time for independence had come, and found their radical leader in the priest **Miguel Hidalgo y Costilla**. In 1810, he called on his flock from the pulpit to fight for land reform and better social conditions.

Hidalgo was captured and executed promptly, in 1811. However, he set in motion the avalanche of protest that ended in Mexico's independence in 1821.

In 1811, the priest **José Maria Morelos** stepped into Hidalgo's shoes. He successfully formulated the objectives of the uprising, i.e. the abolition of slavery, torture, government monopolies and the class system. He demanded constitutional sovereignty and the right of each citizen to vote. In 1815, he too was captured and executed. European developments undermined Spanish power in Mexico. Still the bloody conflict dragged on.

The price of independence in blood (1811–1821)

In 1821, the Spanish king Ferdinand VII saw no other solution but to sign a constitution which officially gave Mexico its independence. About 650,000 Mexicans gave their lives in the fight. Still, even the proclamation of a constitutional monarchy did not end the grave social conflicts.

The Century of Revolutions

| 1823 | Mexico officially becomes a republic. |
| 1846 to 1848 | War with the USA. Mexico loses half its territory (Texas, New Mexico, Arizona, California, Utah, Nevada and parts of Colorado). |

1861 to 1872	The presidency of Benito Juárez, who proclaims a liberal constitution. Napoleon III appoints the Austrian Archduke Maximilian emperor of Mexico. Juárez, now supported by the USA, wins against Maximilian who is shot in 1867.
1876 to 1911	Porfirio Díaz comes to power through a coup and establishes his dictatorship, the so-called »Porfiriato«.
1910 and beyond	The civil war was won by farmers (Emiliano Zapata, Pancho Villa), workers and the progressive middle class who carried the revolution on their shoulders.
1917	Adoption of the constitution, which is still in force today.

War against the USA

The first 30 years of independence were characterized by dictators and revolutionists. Armed conflicts plunged the country into chaos. There were fights to take the last Spanish strongholds, battles with Indian tribes and skirmishes over land ownership with farmers. In 1848, Mexico lost half its territory in the war against the USA. California, Arizona, New Mexico and Texas became states of the United States of America.

Benito Juárez

Benito Juárez was the first president of Indian descent. In 1858, he created a new liberal constitution, which curtailed the privileges of the upper classes and the clerics. However, the constitution could be put into force only after three years of civil war. Reforms, and then interference by Mexican and foreign powers followed. Finally, the French armed intervention under the pretext of exacting foreign debt interrupted the Juárez presidency.

Puppet monarch Maximilian I (1863–1867)

England, Spain and especially France were set on further exploitation of riches from the colonies. They therefore used Mexican foreign debt as a pretext for military intervention. In 1863, Napoleon III put the Austrian Maximilian I on the Mexican throne. Maximilian had the reputation of being a weakling. Influential groups believed to have found in him the kind of puppet monarch who would serve their interests. Initially, Maximilian endeared himself to the upper classes through lavish celebrations. However, the rich Mexicans turned away from Maximilian when he did not rescind the liberal reforms of Juárez. Maximilian's unfortunate regency ended when troops under the command of Porfirio Díaz shot him dead in 1867.

Modernization

A coup put General Díaz in power in 1876, and so began his **30 years of dictatorship**, the so-called »Porfiriato«. Mexico underwent an industrial revolution during this time. Modernization blossomed, but at the expense of social structure. Farmers and industrial workers rapidly sank into poverty. Large-scale landed property ownership increasingly prevailed. The winners of the economic boom were mostly foreign investors who could always count on General Díaz to quash any protests with military force.

The Mexican revolution was caused by social conditions which were no longer acceptable to the people. The trigger occurred in 1910 when gross election fraud was attempted in order to preserve the Díaz dictatorship. The real winner of the election, Francisco Madero, announced his fight against Díaz from exile in the USA on 20 November 1910. Aided by the armed militia of Francisco (Pancho) Villa in the north of Mexico and **Emiliano Zapata** in the south, Madero became Mexican President in 1911. This alone, however, did not satisfy Zapata's farmer troops with their typical white shirts (► Baedeker Special pp.52–54).

Zapata and the consequences

The farmers demanded land as a basis to earn a livelihood through their own work. At long last, traditional community ownership and a new distribution of land were expected to break the vicious cycle of wage dependency and encumbrance by large-scale landed property owners. In the south of Mexico, the revolution gained strong momentum under Zapata's charismatic leadership.

The battle cry of the revolution was »**Tierra y Libertad!**« (land and freedom). However, government troops had their work cut out in other parts of the country as well. A coup put the new dictator Victoriano Huerta in power in 1913. He became the main enemy of the revolutionists. United, **Pancho Villa**, the »Robin Hood of the North«, Álvaro Obregón, the leader of the western farmers, and the southern

Leaflet with a portrait of Zapata

leader Emiliano Zapata took the capital in 1914. However, their stay in the Mexico City was short-lived: the hearts of the revolutionary fighters belonged in their home regions, to which they soon returned. Their thoughts were not of political power, but of freeing the land.

In 1917, the upper middle-class liberal **Venustiano Carranza** became president of the revolutionary Mexico. He put in place a modern

Victory for the revolution

Zapatist columns, led by Sub-comandante Marcos (r) and Major Moises (l)

¡VIVA ZAPATA!

A man with a determined gaze, a large moustache, wearing a large sombrero and holding a long rifle – this is the image of Emiliano Zapata that will be remembered. Always a legend, he is just as much a part of Mexico as tequila and sun. Why did this man have such an impact? And what makes the mighty shake in their boots at the mention of his name even today?

Roots

Around 1877, **Emiliano Zapata** was born the eighth child of a poor farming family in the Morelos region. His earliest years gave him intimate knowledge of the vicious cycle of poverty and the life that awaits the landless farmer. Poverty, hard labour, hunger and the death of several siblings put their stamp on Zapata and gave him an early awareness of social realities.

Zapata learnt to break in horses and travelled the country. He observed the same grievances wherever he went. At the age of 30, his village voted him their delegate, an official office that inspired his ambitions. Determined to

re-establish the traditional community property with the old community rights for the landless farmers who worked like slaves for their masters, the »patrones«, he commenced on a fight that was finally to cost him his life, but one that was to give him **immortality**.

»Land and Freedom«

Zapata's battle cry rallied many followers among the southern farmers who had set their hearts on land and water rights. In their tens of thousands they took up weapons against the large landholders, their mission an equitable distribution of land.

Eventually, the land reform activist Francisco Madero proclaimed the revolution. This was also the signal for the Zapata and his »**white shirts**« (the white shirt of the farm worker had become the »uniform« of Zapata and his followers). It was crunch time, and the movement succeeded bril-liantly in the south of Mexico. Together with the other revolutionists, they defeated the old regime.

Character and Charisma

Soon after Mexico City had fallen to the revolutionaries, Zapata returned from the centre of power to the south. His goal was the redistribution of the land. Zapata preferred to see his »white shirts« till the lands and take care of their families than meddle in political affairs in the capital with rifle and ammunition belt.

However, Mexico's revolution destroyed its own. Venustiano Carranza, the first president in the revolutionary Mexico, may have been Zapata's ally, but he was unwilling to support Zapata's **land reform**; instead, he used troops to bring the south into line with his politics. Zapata on the other hand had no intention of betraying his cause and his compatriots: his character was too steadfast for that.

The continuing loyalty of the population rested upon his charisma and integrity.

A long and bloody guerrilla war appearing unavoidable, Carranza chose the route of intrigue and murder instead of political change. On 10 April 1919, he had a trap set for Zapata in Chinameca. Zapata walked into it and died in a hail of bullets. A few months later, the leaders of Zapata's movement agreed to support Alvaro Obregón in his fight for political power against Carranza. Zapata's grave is in Cuautla.

Chiapas: Zapata Lives On

Zapata had become a **legend and national hero** long before he died. Social and economic conditions of the poor farming population show to this day how right his demands were and still are.

There is a discrepancy between Mexico's impoverished south and the northern regions which participate in the economic wealth of the neighbouring USA. This discrepancy became more pronounced towards the end of the 20th century in the 1990s. When Mexico joined NAFTA and celebrated this event on 1 January 1994, guerrillas fired a clear warning shot. Still using Zapata as their role model and with his demands for reform on their lips, the Indian guerrillas occupied several cities in Chiapas. Today's demands are the same as before: land reform. The official uprising has ended, but the **Zapata National Liberation Army** is still active behind the scenes and represents the interests of a large percentage of the population. Emiliano Zapata's spirit will remain alive as long as Mexico does not resolve this old conflict. Zapata is not just glorified as a heroic revolutionist; his spirit is a real presence, fighting for change for as long as it must.

constitution that, with its many social and political reforms, is still the life blood of Mexico. The radical nature of the land reforms however became a bone of contention between Carranza and Zapata. Soon, as early as 1918, Carranza set government troops against the southern farmers.

The government arranged for Emiliano Zapata to be lured into a trap and **murdered** in 1919; to this day, Zapata is enormously popular in his home state of Morelos and in the neighbouring states. Four years later, the second leader of the revolution, Pancho Villa, suffered the same fate.

The Institutionalized Revolution

The 1920s	The revolution is »institutionalized«; the national party (PRI) is established.
1942	Mexico joins the allies in the Second World War.
1994	North American Free Trade Agreement with the USA and Canada (NAFTA) while protests rise up in southern Chiapas.
2000	After 70 years the PRI loses its position as the ruling party when Vicente Fox Quesada is elected Mexico's president.
2006	Amid protests and allegations of fraud, Felipe Calderón Hinojosa of the PAN party narrowly defeats Andrés Manuel López Obrador of the PRD in the presidential elections.

The party of institutionalized revolution, the constitutional 6-year term limit for the presidency, the unions and corruption held Mexico together in the 20th century. It may sound absurd, but these factors prevented coups, long-term dictatorships and civil wars.

Álvaro Obregón became Carranza's successor (1921–1924). He carried out important reforms. He saw to it that schools and unions were established, the land redistributed and the power of the clerics curtailed. President Calles ran the country only from 1924 to 1928, but he maintained a strong influence on his successors until 1933. The nationalization of foreign-owned commercial assets was expected to bring economic independence. Targets for nationalization were in particular US and British-held oil assets.

Stabilization

The party of institutionalized revolution, the Partido Revolucionario Institucional, (**PRI**) has existed since 1929 under various names. The members of the PRI held all important political offices in the country until the year 2000.

Rebound   While the Second World War raged, Mexico enjoyed a phase of relative tranquility. The left-wing oriented country offered asylum to **exiles**, among them Leon Trotsky, the author Anna Seghers and the journalist Egon Erwin Kisch. In 1942, Mexico declared war against Germany and Japan but did not actively participate in the fight until 1945 when it engaged in air strikes in the Pacific. Further significant population growth in the 1950s and 1960s was accompanied by an economic upturn, which counteracted unemployment and pauperization. On the contrary, the infrastructure, social security and the educational system improved.

Corruption, inflation, rebellion   Only a small, elite group profited from the economic boom, the rest of the population having no part in it. This created new social unrest. Corruption and inflation added more fuel to the fire. Bribery of political officials and cronyism were business as usual in Mexico. Protests against political fraud grew louder by the end of the 1960s.

The man who put an end to more than 70 years of PRI rule: Vicente Fox

The criticism came mostly from the intellectuals. Sadly, President Gustavo Díaz Ordaz made himself a name through his cruel actions against student protests in 1968. After hundreds had been killed in the Tlatelolco massacre, he presented Mexico as a peaceful country to international guests at the 1968 Olympic Games and the Soccer World Cup in 1970.

Oil boom (1976–1981)

The difficulties only got worse in the early 1970s when Mexico was swept up in a global economic crisis and the boom ended. The country experienced a vigorous but short-lived oil bonanza under the presidency of José López Portillos (1976–1982). Inflated investment and increasing foreign debt followed. Mexico still suffers from the consequences of this mismanagement.

A path to a better future

Politicians have been seeking a way out of this crisis ever since with debt conversion and debt relief agreements with foreign banks and internal political change as their main issues. The first successes became visible in the 1980s. It was a political surprise when a candidate from the opposition party won the presidential election for the first time in 1988. Fearful of a power vacuum and chaos, the PRI resorted to election fraud.

Pre-millennial unrest

The **Chiapas uprising** started in 1994. Zapatist activists from the neighbouring regions joined in. This revival of revolutionary demands clearly showed that years of institutionalized revolution had not solved the social and ethnic problems in the south. Although the situation calmed down after 1996, the Zapatist guerrilla movement still exists.

Presidential elections in 2000 and 2006

The opposition party (PAN) candidate, **Vicente Fox**, won the presidential elections on 2 July 2000, thus ending the 71-year unbroken run of the PRI. In 2006, the elections caused PRD supporters to take to the streets when their candidate, **Andrés Manuel López Obrador**, was narrowly defeated by the PAN party's **Felipe Calderón Hinojosa** amid allegations of election fraud. Today, power in Mexico's congress is shared by the conservative catholic PAN, the reformed PRI and the left-leaning PRD.

Pre-Columbian Cultures

High cultures have existed in Central America for almost 2000 years. They were responsible for the step pyramids, and the development of writing. Tenochtitlán, the capital of the mighty Aztec Empire, was larger and richer than any European city of the 15th century. Nevertheless, the Spaniards completely destroyed this impressive culture around 1520.

Lacking reliable sources for this period, the origins of the ancient Indian cultures in Mesoamerica are still not fully known. The Indians' history of their origins mixes historical fact with myths and legends. Aside from a few epi-Olmec letter symbols, only the Maya had a fully developed script in the pre-Spanish period, which has not yet been fully deciphered. This makes it more difficult to fill in the gaps in the story of Indian origins in Mesoamerica.

So far, about 13,000 archaeological sites have been registered in Mexico, but only a few of these sites have been excavated and explored. Recent excavations have revealed finds with **ever earlier dating**. Clearly, the historical account of the origins of the »New World« is still far from complete.

Investigative problems

The term »pre-Columbian« should not bring up the notion of a culture which abruptly ended when Columbus landed on the shores of North America in 1492. The high cultures however did meet an abrupt end when the Spanish conquistadores invaded. We have since learnt to date the cultural origins to the transitional period between the archaic (8000–1000 BC) and formative eras (about 1500 BC).

Timeline and geography

The Aztec empire was the last pre-Columbian Mesoamerican high culture. It was destroyed in 1521, not quite 30 years after Columbus first set foot on the American continent. The Mesoamerican high cultures thrived predominantly in four large regions: the coastal regions on the Gulf of Mexico (Tabasco, Veracruz); the central highlands (Federal District, México, Puebla, Hidalgo); the southern regions (Oaxaca, Chiapas and also in Guatemala, El Salvador and Honduras); and the eastern region (Campeche, Yucatán, Quintana Roo and also in Belize, the former British Honduras).

The Olmec (High Culture 1400–400 BC)

Not much is known about the Olmec or the La Venta Culture (in Náhuatl language, the people from ÕlmAn, the land of olli [rubber]). The Olmec formed the first important Mesoamerican city states on the Gulf Coast such as La Venta, Tres Zapotes and San Lorenzo Tenochtitlán. They used some kind of hieroglyphic script and numeric system. The find of the stela of La Mojarra near Veracruz in 1986 was sensational: it displayed 400 recognizable hieroglyphs in a so-called epi-Olmec script. This proves the existence of an advanced script 100 to 150 years before the Maya scripts.

The Olmec influence spread to places a great distance from their metropolis. Quite often, these places were not Olmec settlements but rather trading posts with religious affiliations to the Olmec centre of power on the Gulf Coast. Tlatilco, Gualupita, Tlapacoya, Chalcatzingo, Xochipala, Juxtlahuaca, Oxtotitlán, Izapa, Monte Alto (Guatema-

Olmec influence on other cultures

← *The »plumed serpent« Quetzalcóatl (Codex Telleriano-Remensis)*

Olmec altar with seated figure of a priest and jaguar mask

la) and Las Victorias (El Salvador) were probably such outposts. The Olmec ventured far and wide to trade luxury items, such as the cherished jade. They went to the Pacific coast and via Chiapas, Guatemala and San Salvador all the way to Costa Rica. Many of the ancient artefacts found in these areas bear the stamp of Olmec artists or show Olmec influence. Among these finds are ceramic, stone and jade artefacts as well as reliefs and murals on rock faces and in caves. Symbolic images showing man as part human and part sacred jaguar have been found both in the Olmec Culture and the Chavin Culture in Peru. Both cultures existed at about the same time, and some researchers see a stylistic relatedness between them.

The influence of the Olmec lived on in later Mesoamerican high cultures, such as the cultures of the Maya, Monte Albán I, Dainzú and El Tajín. In particular, reliefs, numbers and glyphs show Olmec influence. Olmec gods continued to rule over later cultures as well, among them the gods Xipe Tótec, Quetzalcóatl and Huehuetéotl. The Olmec ball game also became a tradition in later cultures.

Olmec art

The people of the Gulf Coast were masters at working with hard stone. Their legacy includes the famous colossal heads, made from basalt and measuring up to 3.40m/11ft. They presumably represent religious leaders. Also among the Olmec artefacts are monumental altars and intricate jade figurines. The unique figure of the jaguar with more or less-expressed human features is ubiquitous. It is obviously the image of the rain god. The Olmec depicted the typical human face with fleshy lips and a wide fleshy nose, inspiring some to speculate about a negro descent. The oldest precisely dated artefact is stela C of Tres Zapotes (3 September 32 BC).

The finds from the Olmec Period are now in museums in Villahermosa, Santiago Tuxtla, Tres Zapotes and Jalapa as well as the National Museum of Anthropology in Mexico City.

Teotihuacán (~200 BC– AD 750)

Mesoamerican metropolis

Teotihuacán was the religious and urban centre in the classical era. Its religious, political and economic might made it the most important Mesoamerican metropolis of its time. The city builders probably came from the north and later integrated immigrants from Cuicuilco, Copilco and the Huasteca region.

Pre-Columbian high cultures *Overview*

Period	Olmec Gulf Coast	Central highlands	Maya	Oaxaca valley Zapotec Míxtec	El Tajín Huastec Totonac Gulf Coast	Aztec (México)
Pre-classical (formative)						
1500	S. Lorenzo → Tlatilco	Tlatilco		Tierras Largas		
1400						
1200	El Manatí El Azuzul La Venta →	Tlapacoya Teopante-cuanitlán		S. José Mogote		
1000		Chalcatzingo Juxtlahuaca Oxtotitlán				
800	Tres Zapotes	Cuicuilco		(transition) Huijazoo Dainzú Monte Albán I		
600						
400			(transition) Lol-tún Izapa			
Proto-classical						
200		Teotihuacán I	Chiapa de Corzo	Monte Albán II		
BC/BCE AD/CE	La Mojarra					
		II	Dzibilchaltún Yaxuná			
200				Monte Albán III A		
Early classical					El Pital	
400		III	Chichén Itzá (foundation) Oxkintok			
600		IV	Palenque Yaxchilán Calakmul	Monte Albán III B	Remojadas El Tajín	
800		Xochicalco Tula Chico	Uxmal	Monte Albán IV	El Tamuín	
Post-classical						
1000		Tollán (Tula)	Chichén Itzá (Renaissance under Toltec influence)	Yagul Mitla	El Tajín Chico	
1200			Mayapán Tulum	Monte Albán V		
1400				Zaachila		
Conquista from 1519			Maní	Giengola	Zempoala	Tenochtitlán

©Baedeker

History Teotihuacán developed in several eras. The first lasted to the common era (the year 0 CE) and the second ended about AD 350. The city reached its height in the third era (until about AD 650). A cultural exchange existed between the city and Monte Albán, Pánuco, El Tajín and the Maya region. This exchange was not just about trade but also involved flourishing artist colonies. The general opinion today is that Teotihuacán controlled settlements as far away as Kaminaljuyú in Guatemala (1,100km/684mi as the crow flies) as well as Maya settlements in the lowlands. The central city also exerted its influence on the religious centres of Xochicalco, Cholula, early El Tajín and several places in today's federal state Guerrero. The metropolis met its in-part violent demise in AD 750.

Culture Teotihuacán's exemplary architecture is expressed in its pyramids, ceremonial buildings, palaces and dwellings for workers and farmers. One of the main architectural principles is the design called Talud-Tablero. The name for the design alludes to the use of a platform structure (tablero, table) on top of a sloped wall (talud). This architectural design, with the help of horizontal cornices, created optically divided units and stabilized the buildings. Other civilizations imitated and modified this design principle. Sculptures pale somewhat against the grandiose architectural scale of the city. With the exception of snake head sculptures and stone reliefs, artistic expression was focussed on magnificent masks and stone figures. The masks often showed intricate inlay work. The large number of murals shows an astounding range of motives, such as gods, animals and religious scenes. The maize god played a dominant role in myths as did the rain god and the god of fire. Animal forms often characterized the gods.

Maya (500 BC– AD 1450)

Origins The origins of the Maya are also mysterious. Until recently, the first appearance of the Maya was dated at around 500 BC when they were traced to the temperate highlands of Chiapas and Guatemala as well as to the lowlands of El Petén. Recent data however has proved that a larger Maya centre already existed around 2000 BC in Cuello (Belize). One Maya tribe, which later became known as the Huastec, seems to have split off and settled on the northern Gulf Coast as early as 1500 to 2000 BC.

The classical Maya region The Maya land of origin was densely populated as early as around 1500 BC. However, a definite connection between the development of the Maya civilization and the sites at Chiapa de Corzo, Izapa, Ocós and El Baúl is not clearly established. At this juncture, self-contained, still unknown civilizations mixed with the Olmec culture and the newly emerging Maya culture. Not including the early sites in Guatemala (Nakbé, El Mirador) and Belize, the first larger settle-

Maya stone relief (National Anthropological Museum, Mexico City)

ments of the Maya formed in Dzibilchaltún and Yaxuná in the northern parts of Yucatán. The Maya influence already reached as far as Oaxaca (Monte Albán II) in the early period and later, in the classical period, their influence even reached Teotihuacán, Cacaxtla and Xochicalco. Of course, the Olmec city-state Teotihuacán in turn also put its stamp on the Maya cities between 400 and 600.

The Maya achieved their most significant feats in the classical period (AD 200–900), in particular in their central region. They accomplished much without metal tools, draught or pack animals and even without the wheel, which the Maya used only for children's toys. The Maya flourished in locations and city-states like Palenque, Bonampak, Toniná, Yaxchilán and Chinkultic in the federal state of Chiapas and also in Guatemala, Belize and Honduras. In Tikal (Guatemala),

Cultural achievements

Maya calendar Plan

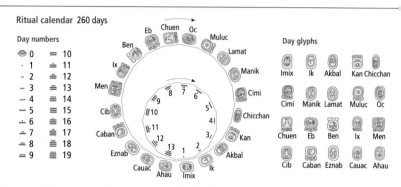

Ritual calendar 260 days

Day numbers

0	= 10
1	≐ 11
2	≟ 12
3	≡ 13
4	≣ 14
5	≣ 15
6	≣ 16
7	≣ 17
8	≣ 18
9	≣ 19

Day glyphs

Imix, Ik, Akbal, Kan Chicchan

Cimi, Manik, Lamat, Muluc, Oc

Chuen, Eb, Ben, Ix, Men

Cib, Caban, Eznab, Cauac, Ahau

the Maya built their highest pyramid (65m/213ft). Builders and artists created palaces, courts for ball games, altars and stelae and aligned them with specific dates of the calendar. The stelae designs show magnificent artistry. In bas-relief or sometimes in detached statuary, they show hieroglyphs, portraits of rulers and historical scenes. The Maya calendar was the most accurate of its time and astronomy and mathematics were also highly developed.

The Maya calendar The Maya used two different calendar systems. With minor modifications, similar calendars have been found in other Mesoamerican high cultures.

The most important calendar in the system was the common Mesoamerican ritual calendar known among the Maya as the Tzolkin (count of days). It covered a complete cycle of 260 days. Each day was characterized by a combination of a number and a day glyph. The numbers ran from 1 to 13 and the day glyphs from 1 to 20. The number and glyph series ran independent of each other so that e.g. day 1 of the second trecena (13) cycle would combine with the 14th day glyph of the veintena (20) cycle.

In contrast, the solar calendar covered 18 periods of 20 days each. In this Haab calendar, 5 days were not counted to adjust for the real length of the solar year. The Maya went in fear of calamity in these »empty« (undefined) 5 days (uayeb). The word »kin« means day, the »unial« consists of 20 days and the »tun« of 360 days, the »katun« is 7,200 days long (20 years), the »baktun« is a span of 20 katun or 144,000 days (400 years) and 13 baktun are an epoch. A cycle of 52 Haabs (solar years) made up one calendar round in the Maya calendar. A calendar round consisted of 18,980 days and ended when the last day of the ritual calendar and the last day of the solar calendar fell on the same date. Dates were expressed in script with numeral signs (dot and bar system) or face glyphs (mostly on monuments). Glyphs for days and months pinpointed each day of a calendar cycle.

Solar calendar

365 days - 18 months, each with 20 days, 5 »empty« days

©Baedeker

Month glyphs

Pop Uo Zip Zotz Tzec Xul Yaxkin Mol Chen Yax Zac Ceh Mac Kankin Muan Pax Kayab Cumhu Uayeb

The designation for each solar year was determined using the date from the ritual calendar for the beginning of the 365-day solar year. The calendar played a pivotal role in Maya religion and myth. The Maya lived by astronomy and astrology. They associated the passing of days and cycles with their deities and, as in a horoscope, the dates of their calendars served to predict human fortunes. People consulted the calendar shaman before embarking on an important task because even the gods and their workings were subject to the constellations of the heavenly time keepers. The complex mathematics of time-keeping enabled the Maya to think in very long time spans. Their time keepers (shamans) handled events several million years in the past.

Downfall

In the 9th century, the Maya abandoned their shining cities, which were soon swallowed by vegetation. The reasons for this exodus are still unknown. The latest research has shed light on the decline of the Maya culture: Feeding such a large population had long since strained the land to the extreme. Three large droughts can be proven for the 9th century. Today it is assumed that they started the process of decline.

Other Maya sites

Maya culture outside the central area was also at its height in the classical period. There were Maya north of the central area in Kohunlich and in the southern Campeche regions (Hormiguero, Calakmul, Xpuhil, Becán, Chicaná), who are known for their art in the Río-Bec style. In the late classical period, when sculpted stelae became rare, other styles flourished such as the Chenes style (Hochob, Dzibilnocac) and the Puuc style (Uxmal, Kabah, Sayil, Labná) in northern Yucatán. Buildings in this style feature elaborate ornamentation with complex patterns that are put together from hundreds of elements. The predominant motif is the image of the rain god Chac. These centres were deserted in the 11th and 12th centuries.

The integration of other cultures Cultural activities once again flourished when the Toltec and other Central American cultures settled in Northern Yucatán. Toltec and Maya styles merged, particularly in Chichén Itzá as seen in the large stone sculptures of the **Chac Mool** and the **Atlantean columns or kouroi** (male figures as part of columns). The dominant motif is the feathered serpent.

Chichén Itzá's zenith ended around 1200 when it became second to the city of Mayapán. This last grandiose Mayan metropolis went under around 1450 and with it the 2000-year-old Maya high culture came to an end. Some smaller principalities survived, but they were without cultural significance. It took the Spaniards 20 years of fierce warfare to subjugate the Yucatán Maya in 1542.

The Zapotec and Mixtec (500 BC– AD 1521)

History Five phases (Monte Albán I, II, III, IV and V) define the history of the great ceremonial centre in the valley of Oaxaca in southern Mexico. Stone reliefs, burial places and ceramic finds from pre-Christian times show influences first of the Olmec and then the Maya. Only at the beginning of the Common Era did the Zapotec make their presence known and, in the classical period, put their stamp on the culture with their sacred places like Dauya-quch (later named Monte Albán). There are signs of **a lively cultural exchange with Teotihua-**

View of the Monte Albán site

cán between the years 300 and 600. Decline followed stagnation in the years between 800 and 1000. By all accounts, the Zapotec abandoned Monte Albán and the Mixtec used it solely as a burial ground. Close to the end of the 15th century, the Aztec took over the region around Oaxaca. South-east of Oaxaca, the city Mitla was alternately under the influence of the Zapotec, the Mixtec, and another still unknown culture.

In pre-Christian times, artists created large, impressive clay sculptures of upright human forms and jaguars, as well as figures in bas-relief on large stone slabs known as »**Los Danzantes**« (the dancers). The first pre-Spanish (hieroglyphic) writing system was presumably used between 400 and 300 BC. So far, the vertical script columns have not been deciphered.

Aside from following the influence of Teotihuacán and erecting monumental buildings, in the classical period artists also made vessels in the shape of figurines. Most of the figurine vessels depicted priest-deities and were found in tombs. The veneration of the ancestors in a **cult of death** plays an important role. The tombs had a cruciform design, they were decorated with frescoes and reliefs and the dead were provided with rich burial objects. The Mixtec created exquisite jewellery and polychrome ceramics. The logographic pictorial writing has provided us with important historical insights. The most important gods in the lives of the people of Oaxaca Valley were the rain god Cocijo, the maize god Pitao Cozobi, the wind god Quetzalcóatl, and Xipe Tótec, the god of renewal and of the jewellers.

Culture

El Tajín (600–1200)

The ceremonial centre El Tajín is situated between Tampico and Veracruz close to the Gulf of Mexico. It was a long-held belief that the Totonac built the site. However, the Totonac moved into the already abandoned city only in the 13th century. Today, it is not clear who actually built El Tajín. Artefacts show cultural influences of the late Olmec and of Teotihuacán.

History

In all probability, El Tajín was at its height between 700 and 900. The city builders used a unique style, which did not spread far to other areas. The most significant testimonial to their art is the six-storey Pyramid of the Niches. Typical finds in El Tajín are the often elaborate ornamented stone sculptures. According to their shape, the ornamental shapes are named the yugo (yoke), hacha (a thin axe head) and palma (a regional palm). The forms are presumably inspired by the protective regalia worn by the players of the **ritual ball game**, which occupied an important place in the belief system of the people. 13 ball courts have been found in El Tajín alone. It remains unclear whether it was the winner or the loser who was offered as a sacrifice to the gods.

Culture

The Toltec (950–1200)

Origins The creation of the Toltec metropolis Tollán (**Tula**) marks the beginning of the post-classical period of the pre-Columbian cultures. Two groups likely merged to form the tribe called the Toltec. One group consisted of the Náhuatl-speaking Chichimec who came from Western areas while the other group, the Nonoalca, came from Tabasco.

History According to a legend, the Toltec founded their city Tollán only in the year 968. Their ruler at the time was Ce'Acatl Topiltzín who later assumed the name of the god-king Quetzalcóatl (feathered serpent). About 20 years later, after a conflict, the ruler probably left Tollán with a small group of people and moved via Cholula to the Yucatán Gulf Coast. Around AD 1000, the cultures of the Toltec and the Maya began to mix in a striking fashion. The Toltec also influenced the cultures, by means of trade and military might, in the northern part of the Mexican highlands (with Teotenango and Malinalco) and the regions around the northern cities La Quemada, Chalchihuites and probably also Casas Grandes.

Downfall The zenith of the Toltec culture was relatively short and ended in 1175 with the fall of Tula. The reason for this demise is attributed to internal strife and the pressure of a new wave of immigrant Chichimec people. Some of the fleeing Toltec settled in the Mexican highlands (Culhuacán and Cholula), others moved to the region that is now Nicaragua.

Culture Architecture and sculpture show a coarser style in the Toltec period than in the classical period. The Toltec legacy includes large porticos, up to 4.60m/15ft-high giant Atlantean statues, the unique prone figures of the **Chac Mool** (red jaguar), the snake wall (coatepantli) and the wall of skulls (**tzompantli**). Warriors and their orders of the eagle and the jaguar represented an important aspect of the civilization: reliefs showing skulls and scenes of battle and sacrifice tell of proud warriors. The most impressive examples of Toltec art can be seen in **Chichén Itzá** in Yucatán. The basic concept of this art is obviously Toltec while the decorations were executed by Maya artists. In the Tollán era, people started to work with metal in the way they had seen it done in Guerrero. They also used the wharve (a pulley or flywheel on a spinning device) for the first time. **Quetzalcóatl** reigned

Tzompantli (wall of skulls)

in the divine hierarchy, and his symbolic expressions and various appearances had all-encompassing significance. His brother Tezcatlipoca, who reigned over the night sky and was in charge of magic and punitive justice was Quetzalcóatl's counterpart. In general, the heavenly deities and warrior gods began to displace the earth and agricultural gods of the classical period. This shift gave more importance to the warriors at the expense of the formerly all-powerful priest caste.

The Aztec (1300–1521)

History

In the 12th century, the Aztec (the people from Aztlán) migrated from the north-west to the Mexican central highlands, and in the 14th century they built their capital on an island in the Texcoco Lake. Today, Mexico City is situated where the Aztec metropolis **Tenochtitlán** once was. The Aztec referred to their tribe as the »Méxica«, and so this name became familiar in their new region. In the following 150 years, the Aztec expanded the reach of their power: in the north and east, they reached the area of the Huastec in the coastal regions on the Gulf of Mexico; in the south-west and south, they expanded to Colima via Oaxaca up to the border of today's Guatemala. However, these regions did not form a uniformly ruled empire but rather a federation of 40 provinces in addition to the core region; these provinces had to pay tribute to the Aztec. The invasion by Spaniards and their Indian allies between 1519 and 1521 put a violent end to this last Mesoamerican high culture.

Culture

In comparison with the other pre-Columbian high cultures, Aztec art had less cultural significance. Aztec prowess was mostly expressed in technical and economic successes. Religious life was well organized. Often, the Aztec embraced the skills of their predecessors and neighbours and honed them to higher perfection. They considered themselves the **descendants of the Toltec**; this is apparent in their architecture and sculpture. There was a flow of techniques from subjugated peoples into the Aztec culture, which was also enriched by artefacts and artisans imported from occupied regions. In the core region of the Aztec, many artefacts have been found which have their origin in the cultures of the Mixtec Puebla, the Huastec and the Purépecha (Tarasca). Most of the great Aztec ceremonial sites were destroyed by the Spaniards and the materials recycled for their own buildings. For this reason, few accomplished Aztec works have been preserved.

In recent years, parts of the temple complexes of Tenochtitlán and Tlatelolco have been excavated in the area around Mexico City. The main temple (figure 3D, p.376) was discovered in Mexico City. The most significant artefacts left to us from the Aztec culture are the colossal stone sculptures, such as the Stone of the Fifth Sun (see p.394) or the stone of the moon goddess Coyolxauhqui.

Life in the Aztec Empire

Tenochtitlán

The Spanish conquistadores were awestruck when they first saw Tenochtitlán, the giant metropolis of the Aztec Empire. They were overwhelmed by its size and splendour and admired the well-organized city plan. They were impressed by the markets in particular. Hernán Cortés himself later wrote to Emperor Karl V about **the market of Tlatelolco**: »Among us were soldiers who had visited places in the world such as Constantinople, Italy, even Rome. They said that they had never seen such a large, organized market so crammed with goods and people«. According to the chronicler Bernal Díaz del Castillo, 25,000 people visited this market daily, and every fifth day a special market attracted 40,000 to 50,000 people.

When the Spaniards arrived, Tenochtitlán (place of the cactus fruit) and Tlatelolco (which had been captured by the Aztec in 1473) were divided into four large districts, which were left in place long after the Spanish conquest. The traditional lower level administrative units were however the smaller calpulli (Aztec for »clans«), neighbourhoods which owned land in common, each one electing its own leader. Three large dams connected the centre of the city on the lake with the shore. The northern overpass originated in Tlatelolco and from there reached the shore at Tepeyacac close to today's place of pilgrimage known as Guadalupe. The western dam connected Tenochtitlán with Tlacopan. The southern dam split into two passageways, one going south-west to Coyoacán and the other running east to Iztapalapa. There were also two aqueducts, one passing from Chapultepec to the centre of the city and the other carrying drinking water from Coyoacán alongside the street of Iztapalapa.

Social Order

Dignitaries   Aztec society was hierarchical but allowed people to rise through the ranks. The senior nobles of the military, government and the courts had to be addressed as tecuhtlí (chief, lord). The ruler himself had this title. The general title of the ruler was tlatoaní (speaker, i.e. leader of men in the highest council [tlatocan]) and tlacatecuhtlí (warrior chieftain). In Tenochtitlán, the ruler was elected by a special assembly of senior noblemen. As of the reign of Montezuma I, the highest ruler was assisted by Cihuacóatl or the »serpent woman«. The name alludes to the serpent goddess and her role was that of a prime minister. Four high noblemen and advisers were the immediate subordinates to the ruler and Cihuacóatl, followed in rank by the members of the Tlatocan, the high council.

Tlatelolco Market (Diego Rivera, 1929 – 1935) →

Priests Priests were considered the equals of warriors and noblemen. Future priests were prepared for their role in schools, called Calmecac. At the age of 22, the apprentice had the choice of assuming the exulted title of Tlamacazqui (priest) and remaining celibate. The leaders of the priesthood were two high priests. One of them was the Quetzal-cóatl Tótec Tlamacazqui (priest of the feathered serpent god of the universe) who served the sun and warrior god Huitzilopochtli. The other high priest, the Quetzalcóatl Tláloc Tlamacazqui (priest of the feathered serpent god of the Tláloc), served the rain god. Priestesses served the female gods.

Warriors Office and rank in the Aztec empire were assigned for life. On principle, nobility was not inherited: the son of a tecuhtli was a pilli (child, son) and had no claim to a title. Instead, rank had to be earned, especially through prowess as a warrior. Only access to higher education at the calmecac (temple school) was made easier for the son of a nobleman. The nobility was usually supplemented by members of the plebeian macehualtin (singular: macehualli, in Nahuatl: vassal, townsman). These commoners, but not merchants, were able to attain the rank of Iyac by taking their first enemy prisoner. Higher ranks were named after northern warrior tribes: Quauhchichimecatl (Chichimec Eagle) or Otomitl (Otomí warrior).

Merchants The merchants inherited their trade membership. They were called pochteca after the famous Pocthlan trading quarter in the city of Tlatelolco. While they were not admitted to the warrior class, they were valued as spies because their trade involved adventurous journeys to the most remote regions. The merchants often accumulated great riches as a result of a monopoly on trade with communities outside the empire.

Artists and craftsmen Artists and craftsmen were important. Among the Aztec they were known as the tolteca. Their artistic skills and prowess were perceived as toltecayotl (Toltec business), since Toltec was synonymous with culture to the Aztec. The craft guilds deemed most important were those of the feather weavers (amanteca) and goldsmiths (teocuitlahuaque). The scribe or »painter of books« (tlacuilo) commanded special respect.

Slaves The Aztec had slaves called tlatlacotin (singular: tlacotli). The living conditions for these slaves were however much less inhumane than in Europe. Aztec slaves could own property; they could save money and buy their freedom, and marriage between free people and slaves was permitted. Slaves were prisoners of war who had not been sacrificed, or individuals doing penance for committing a crime. However most slaves seem to have volunteered of their own free will: these future slaves then lived free until the money that they had received in trade for their freedom was used up, usually about a year later.

Quetzalcóatl sculpture (Teotihuacán)

Mythology

Just as in the cosmology of other Mesoamerican civilizations, so too the Aztec believed that other worlds had preceded this, the fifth world. Cosmic catastrophe had destroyed these four prior worlds. According to Aztec belief, they lived in the fifth world, hence the name of the famous calendar stone is the **stone of the fifth sun** (see p.394). The fourth world destroyed, the gods had assembled in Teotihuacán, where a humble god assented to turn into the new sun. However, the new sun did not move through the skies. The other gods then sacrificed themselves and gave their power to set the sun in motion. Since the universe had taken shape only through **sacrifice**, only continued sacrifice could keep it safe. This sacrifice had to be something most precious, namely human blood, which is called chalchiuatl (precious water) in Nahuatl.

Human sacrifice was especially important for the México at the close of each calendar round of 52 years. A calendar round related to the sacred calendar system, which was also used to construct horoscopes. As in other Mesoamerican cultures, the calendar days were assigned 20 day glyphs and 13 numerals. The beginning of the year could only fall on four of the glyphs. These four glyphs, multiplied by the series of 13 day numerals, yield 52 cycles or one calendar round. The first days of each calendar round have the same combination of day glyph and day numeral: this calendar and the solar calendar were resynchronized on this day.

The Aztec lived in particular fear of a cosmic catastrophe on this day. Throughout the land, fires were extinguished and the colourful stucco on the walls of pyramids and temples broken. In the dark of night, the high priests ascended to the summit of the mountain Ui-xachtecatl close to their capital, from where they observed the heavens. If the cosmos defied their expectations and continued moving they lit a flame in the chest of a human sacrifice using a piece of hardwood. Emissaries then relit all fires from this flame. The sacred objects then received their new coverings.

Gods **Huitzilopochtli** (hummingbird of the south) was the focus of Aztec religious belief. He was the war god and the symbol of the sun. Like the sun, he died every evening and was reborn every morning.

Other gods were mostly adopted from subjugated tribes. Among those are **Tláloc** (rain god and god of growth, tlalli = earth), Tezcatlipoca (god of the smoking mirror, god of the night sky, of destruction, magic and of punitive justice), Xipe Tótec (our god the flayed one, god of suffering and diseases, god of fertility and renewal in the spring, also patron god of the jewellers), **Quetzalcóatl** (feathered serpent, deity of the morning star, the wind and technical progress), **Coatlícue** (she with the skirt of the serpent, earth goddess and mother of Huitzilopochtlis) and her daughter **Coyolxauhqui** (the one who paints her face with golden bells, goddess of the moon and the night).

Warfare

The history of the earlier Aztec military conquests tells of a war strategy very unlike the one used by Europeans. This explains the bafflement of the Aztec when attacked by the Spaniards. The Aztec did not engage in surprise attacks. Before war was declared, they would always send emissaries to conduct long negotiations, in which they repeatedly offered the enemy a choice of voluntary submission or war. The war strategy was not to kill but to capture enemy warriors.

The successful conquest of the main temple of the enemy city was immediately taken as a verdict of the gods: Huitzilopochtli, the Aztec war god, had proven his superiority. Immediately, the hostilities ended and negotiations began over the size of the tribute, which was set in a way that left the economy of the losing party intact. The losers were also allowed to keep their lifestyles and habits.

Flower wars When the Spanish conquistadores first set foot on Aztec territory, the Aztec had already ceased adding more regions to their empire and new conquests were rare. For this reason, prisoners of war were no longer available for sacrifices, and the ruling city-states Tenochtitlán, Texcoco and Tlacopan therefore came to an agreement with the fiefdoms Tlaxcala, Huejotzingo and Cholula **to conduct ritual combat at regular intervals** with the sole purpose of taking captives.

This mock combat was called xochíyáoyotl (flower war). The Tlaxcala republic in particular paid heavily in blood. Rancour naturally grew, and as a result the Tlaxcaltec became allies of the Spaniards against the Aztec. Without these allies, the Spaniards would very likely have failed to conquer Tenochtitlán.

Codices

Our knowledge about Aztec life is based on written sources, the codices. There are also reports from the conquistadores and the first monks sent to the New World. The most important codices are the Codex Mendoza, the Codex Magliabecchiano, the Codex Ríos and, as a parallel volume, the Codex Telleriano. Some priests had a command of the indigenous language and provided transcriptions of the hieroglyphs in Latin along with Spanish commentaries.

The commentaries were necessary because the original sources exist as an ideographic script. Picture a book painter at work. He wants to record that, for example, the emperor Montezuma is making preparations for war. To express this he draws the sitting figure of the ruler, puts the appropriate name glyph alongside the figure and then draws weapons around him to make his point. But such a writing system is not sufficient to convey the intricacies of Náhuatl literature with its excellent contributions in the areas of rhetoric, lyrics and epics. Therefore, the students of a priest school had to memorize text of considerable length with the pictorial signs serving as a mnemonic for recitals. Fortunately, Christian monks who took over the education of the Indians could still locate a sufficient number of young noblemen from Indian society who had mastered the pictorial script. With their help the monks wrote down the Náhuatl texts in Latin, or taught the young scholars the western phonetic writing system.

Body of traditions

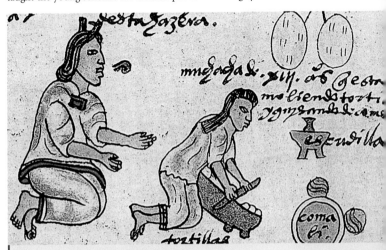

Education of an Aztec girl (Codex Mendoza)

The Arts and Culture

Most people know of the impressive monumental pre-Hispanic buildings and the sometimes light-hearted, sometimes disturbing pictures of Frida Kahlo. On the following pages much more is shown, such as the influence of the colonial period (especially on the architecture), genuine Mexican muralism, and traditions like the charreada or Jai alai. Curious?

Painting

Before the Spanish conquistadores invaded, until about 1520, the art of the pre-Columbian murals dominated in Mexico. Excellent examples of this art are the frescoes of the Maya temple in Bonampak or the paintings in Teotihuacán, Tepantitla, Atetelco, Cacaxtla and Cholula near Puebla City. Regrettably, only a few of these **ancient Indian artefacts** still attest to their great artistry. The red and orange hues, the gold and the famous blue of the Bonampak frescoes give an impression of the high standard of painting techniques in classical Maya culture. In addition to the frescoes, skilfully painted ceramics have been found, and pictorial writings with drawings of figures and hieroglyphs have also been attributed to this era.

Soon after the Spanish victory, Franciscan monks established a school in Mexico City and European artists started to teach there. Like most European painters of their time, they were influenced by the Dutch style of painting. The Flemish painter **Simon Pereyns** (1566–1603) who settled in Mexico was the only significant painter among his European peers.

At the beginning of the 17th century, an independent colonial art emerged as documented by **Baltazar de Echave Orío** (1548–1620), **Baltazar de Echave Ibía** (1585–1645) and **Luis Juárez** (1600–1635). Artists who later continued this style were **José Juárez** (1615–1667), **Baltazar de Echave Rioja** (1632–1682) and **Pedro Ramírez** (1650–1678). These latter artists found their own characteristic style which combined elements of such diverse painters as Murillo and Rubens.

Significant artists to define the first phase of the Mexican Baroque (end of the 17th century/beginning of the 18th century) are **Cristóbal de Villalpando** (1652–1714), **Juan Correa** (1674–1739) and **Juan Rodríguez Juárez** (1675–1728). Their pictures clearly show a European influence.

The Correa students **José María de Ibarra** (1688–1756) and **Miguel Cabrera** (1695–1768) defined Mexican painting in the 18th century. In contrast to Mexican architecture and the Mestizo schools in Cuzco and Potosi in South America, Mexican painting remained almost completely free of Indian influences.

Among the important artists in the middle and second half of the 19th century are the portraitist and representative of naïve art **José María Estrada** (1830–1862), and the landscape painter **José María Velasco** (1840–1912), who would later become the teacher of Diego

← Colonial art: painting of the nun Sor Juana de la Cruz
(anonymous, 17th century, see also p.96)

Rivera. At this time, a popular, expressive style of painting developed in the province; the best examples of this style can be seen in many village chapels. Towards the end of the 19th century and at the beginning of the 20th century, the influence of French Impressionism became more pronounced. This is evident in the landscape paintings of **Joaquín Claussel** (1866–1935) and **Mateos Saldaña**.

Murals The next era of Mexican painting began in the 20th century at the time of the revolution (1910–1920), when muralismo became an autonomous art form. The new trend started at a secessionist exhibition in 1910 at which the central figure was Gerardo Murillo (1875–1964), who called himself **Dr. Atl** (Náhuatl: water). The metal engraver and political caricaturist José Guadalupe Posada (1851–1913) is considered the forerunner of this school.

To this day, the three leading artists of the new style are called »Los Tres Grandes«, (the three greats). They were **Diego Rivera** (1886–1957), **José Clemente Orozco** (1883–1949) and **David Álfaro Siquieros** (1896–1974). Inspired by love for their country and the Mexican people, they enthusiastically painted murals on public buildings telling of Indian origins, the country's changing fortunes in history and life in health and prosperity.

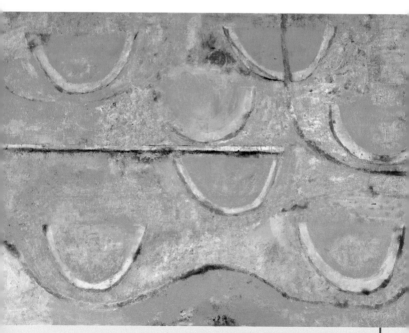

Rufino Tamayo: »Watermelons« (1968)

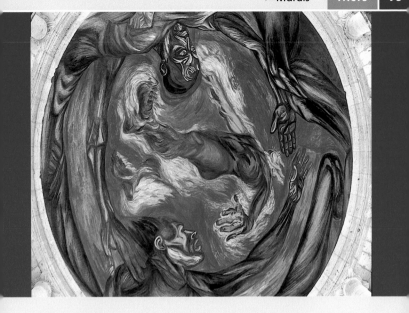

THE THREE GREATS OF MURAL PAINTING

In essence, the history of Mexican muralismo parallels the history of »Los Tres Grandes«, the three greats: Diego Rivera, José Orozco and David Álfaro Siqueiros. This is not to say that there were not many other artists involved from the beginning. Muralismo was the new Mexican folk art with strong ties to the Mexican identity. Very importantly, everybody had easy access to the large scale murals.

Although **José Orozco** (1883–1949) and **David Álfaro Siqueiros** (1896–1974) had collaborated on plans for an artistic and social revolution as early as 1914, the desire to artistically express the unity and identity of Mexico **(Mexicanidad)** took shape only after the upheaval of the revolution 7 years later. Mexico's then minister of education, José Vasconcelos, provided the basis for the beginning and the rise of the new art form in the 1920s, furnishing the artists with the walls of schools and other

public buildings for use as giant canvases. In 1921, after returning from a stay in Paris, **Diego Rivera** (1886–1957) joined the team of artists who wanted to develop a freely accessible Mexican form of large-scale modern art.

Tradition and Vision

The old folk art was still alive in the population, and the painters turned to it. They embraced its forms, colours and subjects from pre-Columbian times. Their murals showed themes

See p. 79: »Man of Fire« by Josés Clemente Orozco in Guadalajara (originated 1938/39)

Portrait of Pater Hidalgo by Orozco in the Governor's Palace in Guadalajara

from **Mexican history** and also expressed their vision of a **better future for the masses,** which was to come about through mechanization, modern agriculture and medicine. Artists' studios, museums and galleries were not the venues for exhibiting this work; instead, public places were chosen so that people from all walks of life could access the art. The artists did feel obliged to depict a certain ideology as far as their faith in progress and the education of illiterate people was concerned, but were never constrained by any kind of doctrinaire socialistic realism.

Ideological Conflicts

Good intentions notwithstanding, there was no future for the movement of the muralists, as they were now called. Ideological conflicts in particular soon broke the group apart. An argument over the (communistic) content of some murals ensued and

led to a long **artistic and ideological discourse between Siqueiros and Rivera.** The height of the debate took place on 28 August 1935 when Rivera – pistol in hand – gatecrashed a presentation by Siqueiros in the Palacio Bellas Artes (hall of fine arts) and forced a discussion about the nature of Mexican muralismo. The ensuing exchange lasted several days, the participants finally agreeing to disagree. Despite all these obstacles, the mural painters brought forth a great wealth of extraordinary works of art over many years, which are dynamic and full of dramatic lights effects. Now and then, Siqueiros spent time in prison or exile, so the three greats shrank to the two greats. Rivera worked mostly in Mexico City and Orozco in Guadalajara. In the end, Siqueiros outlived them both. He remained a proponent of the muralismo idea and the revolution throughout his life.

The Most Significant Works

Scepticism, weariness and compassion for the human fate often weave through the strict composition of Orozcos's paintings. His main works of art are the giant murals in the Instituto Cultural Cabañas in Guadalajara, (1938/1939), among them his famous painting *Man of Fire* inside the dome of the chapel. Orozcos also painted the frescoes in the stairway of the Governor's Palace in Guadalajara. In Mexico City, he created magnificent murals for the EPN (Educator/Practitioner Network) and for the Palacio Nacional de Bellas Artes (National Fine Arts Institute). Diego Rivera's large frescoes usually depict scenes from Mexico's political or social life. Particularly noteworthy amongst his numerous works are the murals in the Palacio Nacional (see fig. p.71) and in the Escuela Nacional de la Agricultura (National School of Agriculture) in Chapingo. His famous painting *Dream of a Sunday Afternoon in the Central Alameda Park* can be seen in Mexico City near the Plaza de la Solidaridad. More of his frescoes are on display in the Ministry of Education building, in the Museum of Fine Arts (Palacio de Bellas Artes), on the premises of the Ministry of Health (all in Mexico City) and in the Cortés Palace in Cuernavaca.

The especially striking characteristic in the works of Siqueiros is his rendition of motion, machines and technology. He created large, extremely moving frescoes for public buildings as commissioned by various governments. His works can be seen mostly in Mexico City, e.g. in the Hospital de la Raza, the National Palace (Palacio Nacional), the Museum of Fine Arts (Palacio de Bellas Artes) and at the **rectorate of the university** (see fig. p.408). He was also responsible for the concept and the artistic design of the Polyforum.

Modern art **Frida Kahlo** (1907–1854) was a celebrity painter (Baedeker Special p. 82). She was married twice to Diego Rivera: their marriages were turbulent. Her art was easel painting. After a serious accident in her youth, she had to cope with severe disabilities for the rest of her life, and her fears and pain became part of her painting. Frida Kahlo developed a surrealistic style which made a strong impression even on André Breton, the French master of surrealism.

A follower of Zapotec's ideology, **Rufino Tamayo** (1899–1991) is considered the seasoned master of Mexican modern painting. He meshed elements of Mexican folk-art with elements of modern painting, cubism in particular. Like Rivera, he fought for an Indian renaissance. Rufino Tamayo became the originator of modern Mexican painting and painted in daylight only in order to have control over the entire range of shades and colours (see fig. on p. 78).

Life in remote villages, the ritualized way of life and the bonds with ancestors, plants and animals are the main subjects in modern painting. This subjective folk art has a dream-like quality. It can be seen particularly in the works of **Rufino Tamayo**, **Rodolfo Morales** (1925–2001) and **Francisco Toledo** (born in 1940). A unique form of expression emerged in the small region of Oaxaca: while Tamayo creates perceptive images from the animal kingdom, Toledo's art is inspired by poetic childhood dreams and Morales deals with the mystery of women.

The magic-realistic Oaxaca style is now well accepted in the art world. The style lives on through artists like **Sergio Hernández**, **Luis Zárate**, **Fernando Andracci** and **José Villalobos**.

Sculpture

The Maya, Aztec and other ancient American tribes used sculpture mostly as **decoration of ceremonial buildings**. Cult and worship were at the centre of their artistic work; the materials for the sculptures were stone, stucco or clay. Figures are displayed on the temples, e.g. the famous danzantes (dancers) of Monte Albán, and there are also geometrical wall reliefs whose designs are reminiscent of patterns used in textile weaving. Artists produced sculpted items for daily use, some of them simple and some very elaborate. These smaller sculpted objects have mostly been found as burial objects. Small female figurines, which some archaeologists interpret as fertility goddesses, are particularly abundant.

The Olmec The incomparable art of the Olmec gave us **colossal stone sculptures** with particularly outstanding examples in the Olmec city of La Venta. Especially impressive are the colossal heads with their flat wide noses and fleshy lips. They can be up to 3.40m/11ft in height and weigh up to 50 tons. Olmec artistry not only expresses its excellence in the form of colossal statuary but also through smaller scaled sculpture. The Olmec jade sculptures often show a very minimal design. A few simple lines aptly express the essence of a living object.

The Maya

In their classical period, the Maya created **artworks of the highest calibre from stone or stucco**, such as the stucco reliefs on the buildings of Palenque. The Maya produced stucco by adding natural rubber to the plaster/water mixture. The rubber additive gave the stucco a particularly hard, polishable surface. The Maya also created artful smaller sculptures like the figurines seen in the many burial objects from the island Jaina, a necropolis for the nobility. The paintings on the terracotta figurines clearly show what the priests and warriors looked like and how the nobility dressed. Aside from artistic works in stone and clay, the Maya also created masks or jewellery and feather mosaics. The feathers were dyed and woven into a pattern together with textiles.

Colonial times

The Spanish conquest marks a drastic change for the Mesoamerican sculptors as well as for the painters and architects. Decorative sculptures on public buildings and churches notwithstanding, Mexican sculptures of colonial times lacked individual expression. At the beginning of the 18th century, the painter **Jerónimo Balbás** settled in Mexico and achieved fame, creating among other works the magnificent *Altar of Kings* in Mexico City's cathedral. His works greatly influenced other Mexican artists.

At the end of the 18th and the beginning of the 19th centuries, Mexican sculptures showed less and less refinement and three-dimensional depth. In Puebla during the mid-19th century the sculptors José Villegas de Cora, his nephew Zacarías de Cora and his adopted son José Villegas, as well as the Querétaro artists Mariano Perusquía, Mariano Arce and Mariano Montenegro, set out to give their art new impulses. Their sculptures are on display mainly in museums in Puebla and Querétaro.

Artists created many village altars and sacred figurines, which show the development of a simple but uniquely Mexican style of sculpture.

20th century

After the revolution (1910–1920), Mexican sculptors preferred to work on monumental sculpture often commissioned by politicians. Only in the second half of the 20th century did a generation of sculptors as well as architects emerge who expressed themselves in unique, imaginative ways. **Juan F. Olaguíbel** (1889–1971), an artist of this new generation, designed the fountain with the *Diana Cazadora* cast in bronze in Mexico City. **Germán Cueto** (1893–1975) gave us the copper sheet statue of a native from the isthmus of Tehuantepec, *La Tehuana*, in the Palacio Nacional de Bellas Artes also in Mexico City. **Ignacio Asúnsulo** (1890–1965) created the Obregón memorial in the San Ángel district of the capital. The *Yucatecas en el Parque* (Yucateca women in the park) by **Francisco Zúñigas**

(1913–1998) can be seen in the Galeria Tasende in Acapulco. **Sebastián** (in fact: Enrique Carbajal, born in 1947) created *Las Puertas de Monterrey* and *La Puerta de Chihuahua* in the cities of the same names.

Architecture

Colonial architecture

After the Spaniards had conquered the Aztec empire, they destroyed much of the magnificent Indian architecture. Many a European architectural style came to the »New World« as a European, mostly Spanish import. Quite often, these European styles developed local variants. The natural abundance of building materials explains why so many examples of colonial architecture were built in a relatively short architectural period, another reason for the colonial building boom being the ready army of cheap labourers. The porous volcanic red scoria known as tezontle or blood stone was, and still is, quarried mostly in the central highlands. It has many uses; the Aztec used the rose-coloured to dark-brown stone, and modern builders use it in most palaces in Mexico City. There are also many attractive shades of limestone (cantera) which can easily be put to use in construction.

Early religious architecture

The first generation of buildings after the Spanish conquest arose in the style of fortified medieval monasteries. The Franciscan monks built their churches and convents where the ancient Indian pyramids or temples had stood before, often simply using the plentiful supply of materials from the flattened Indian ceremonial buildings. These buildings featured strong walls and massive supporting columns so they could also serve as strongholds. The design featured only a few windows, which were spaced widely and placed high up in the building. The interior had ribbed or vaulted ceilings. A uniquely Mexican design element of these 16th-century monasteries was the walled atrium with a chapel in each corner. These chapels were called **capillas posas** because the Christ figure was put there during processions. A further typically Mexican element was the Indian chapel or capillas abiertas (open chapel), a vaulted room on one side of the main nave of the church with one open side, a design which accommodated the Indian dislike of closed ceremonial buildings. The Franciscan architectural style with atrium and posas is exquisitely represented in Izamal (Yucatán) and in the church of San Francisco in Tlaxcala (eastern Central Mexico). Visit the very interesting Indian chapels in Teposcolula (state of Tlaxcala) and the cathedral in Cuernavaca (40mi/66km south of Mexico City).

Mudéjar style

The Spanish Mudéjar style is named after the Arab (Moorish) artists who were allowed to remain in Spain after the Reconquista. The style

The colourful murals in the interior of the Tlacochahuya church were done by Indians.

is a symbiosis of **Moorish and Gothic style elements**. The »alfiz«, a small rectangular frieze that frames the Moorish arch (horseshoe arch), is a special characteristic of this style. On some 16th-century buildings, the reproduction of the cord girding the Franciscan frock is part of the frieze, as seen in the posas of Huejotzingo. Other characteristics of the Mexican Mudéjar style appeared only later, such as the use of azulejos (floor and wall tiles), the design of the Moorish horseshoe arches and ceilings as well as the style of wood working (alfarje and artesonado).

The early Plateresque style (an elaborate style, the Spanish »platero« means silversmith) dates back to the 16th century. The stonemason's filigree work, in the main showing elements of heraldry or tendrilled patterns and decorating the portals, was borrowed from the works of Spanish silversmiths. Variations of this style developed in New Spain. These can be classified as follows: **Plateresque style**
– **the pure Renaissance style** with Italian characteristics as seen in the church of San Francisco in Morelio;
– **the Spanish Plateresque style** with Renaissance elements as seen e. g. on the Montejo House in Mérida;
– **the colonial Plateresque style**, which combines Spanish Renaissance elements and local traditional elements. An example is the side portal of the cathedral in Cuernavaca;

– **Indian Plateresque style**, which combines the skills of local crafts-men with those of the pre-Columbian period. This is the style seen on the façade and the northern portal of the parish church in Xochi-milco (Mexico City).

Baroque

In the 17th century the Baroque style slowly gained ground. It was first seen in a relatively prosaic form as for example in La Soledad in Oaxaca. During this period the major construction work on the great cathedrals, such as those in Mexico City, Puebla, Morelia, Guadalaja-ra, San Luis Potosí and Oaxaca, was carried out; at the same time convents and parish churches were built. These buildings expressed the growing power of the church, which directly answered to the Spanish crown, while the independent religious orders lost influence. The increasingly exuberant nature of the Mexican Baroque in its ma-ny different expressions also reflects the growing influence of the Mexico-born Spaniards (criollos) as against that of the Spaniards from Spain (gachupines).

Ultra-Baroque

Ultra-Baroque marks the height of the Mexican late Baroque of the 18th century. The style is also known as Churriguerism, named after the architect (1665–1723) who worked in Spain. It was mostly defi-ned by the estipites, upward flaring pedestals which often decorate façades and retables. Among the many examples of the **Ultra-Baro-que** in New Spain are the following: the façades of the Sagrario Met-ropolitano, the La Santísima church and the Casa de los Mascarones as well as the Altar of Kings in the cathedral (all in Mexico City); the San Francisco Xavier church (Tepotzotlán); the basilica of Ocotlán (Tlaxcala); the San Sebastián y Santa Prisca church (Taxco); the pa-rish church in Dolores Hidalgo; the La Valenciana church (Guana-juato); the chapel of Aránzazu (San Luis Potosí); and the cathedral of Zacatecas.

Puebla or Andean Baroque

The Puebla Baroque is a particularly original variation on the Mexi-can Baroque. The style is named after Puebla City and is characte-rized by the regional architecture **between Tlaxcala and Puebla**. The imaginative stucco ornamentation was often influenced by Indian art and also integrated colourful tiles and red bricks. The chapel of San Antonio in Puebla City and the House of Tiles (Casa de los Azulejos) in Mexico City are excellent examples of this style.

Neo-classicism

European neo-classicism reached Mexico in the late 18th century. The movement often destroyed irreplaceable cultural treasures in its fervour to part with everything old. For example, the architect and sculptor **Manuel Tolsá** (1757–1816) who had immigrated from Spain tried to strip Mexican churches of their rich style to bring their ap-

An example of the excessively rich decorative style typical of Mexican Baroque: Santo Domingo in San Cristóbal de las Casas (Chiapas) →

! *Baedeker* TIP

Construction in progress

In the 20th and 21st centuries, architects in Mexico have embraced the traditions of the Maya and pursue their skilful art in creative and modern ways. Luis Barragán (1902–1988) is considered the forerunner of new Mexican architecture: his houses are hailed as a symphony of light, colour and generous space. In celebration of Barragán's 100th birthday memorial, his house in the suburb of Tacubaya (in Mexico City, Francisco Ramiréz 14, tel. 55 15 49 08) was opened as a museum.

pearance more in line with classicist ideas of architecture. However, he also created the grand statue of Emperor Karl IV on a horse (»el Caballito«) and worked out plans for the school of engineering in Mexico City.

The foremost personality to foster this new trend in the arts was the universally talented Mexican artist **Francisco Eduardo Tresguerras** (1759–1833) who made a name for himself as a poet, musician, painter, sculptor, copperplate engraver and architect. Two of his most beautiful buildings are reconstructions of the church of Santa Clara in Querétaro and the city domicile of Earl Rul in Guanajuato. The main altar of the Sagrario Metropolitano in Mexico City is an important neo-classical work by **Pedro Patino Ixtilinque** (1774–1835) who was an Indian apprentice of Manuel Tolsá. Its style definitely has its roots in the Baroque. **José Damián Ortiz de Castro** (1750–1793) also played an important role. He created the bell towers and made the last adjustments to the façade of the cathedral in Mexico City.

Neo-Gothic works, Art Nouveau

In the hundred years between Mexico's independence and the revolution (1910–1920) there were no significant architectural developments with the exception of extensions to existing buildings and works under emperor Maximilian, such as the original, mostly neo-Gothic works of Ceferino Gutiérrez who died in 1896. There are also a few exceptional buildings in the Art Nouveau style.

Modern architecture

The Bauhaus style influenced Mexican architects after the revolutionary wars, exposing them to the new forms of modern **functionalism**. The artistic value of the colossal constructions of this era is still controversial. It wasn't until the 1950s and 1960s that Mexican architects achieved success with impressive buildings. **Enrique del Moral** (1906–1987) did most of the design work for the university in Mexico City. **Mathias Goeritz** (1915–1990) designed for example the *Functionless Towers* in the suburb Ciudad Satélite (also Mexico City). Together with these designers, **Luis Barragán** (1902–1988) created an architectural style that strives for mastery in colour composition and spatial arrangement and integrates the natural environment as much as possible (Pritzker Award 1980). Not to be overlooked among these architects is **Pedro Ramírez Vázquez** (born 1919) who designed the world-renowned building for the National Anthropology Museum in Mexico City.

Folklore

Many of the current Mexican folk dances go back to pre-Columbian times, others have their origins in Europe and are traditions of the newer immigrants. While the conquistadores tried to abolish the non-Christian dances, the proselytizing Franciscan and Dominican monks wanted to make the Indian songs and dances part of catholicism by way of interpretation. For example, the **dance of the Aztec** which symbolized the fight between light and darkness, good and evil, was interpreted by the friars as a symbol for the fight of the church against the machinations of the devil. Similarly, the ceremonial dances honouring the Aztec earth mother Tonantzin are danced almost in their original form in reverence to the Virgin Mary, Our Lady of Guadalupe. The dances are an essential part of many celebrations.

Folk dances

Dancers with Mariachi band

On the occasion of the **Quetzal dance** in the federal states of Vera-cruz and Puebla, the dancers wear colourful costumes and a giant round headdress. The dance of the little old men, the **viejito dance**, has its origin in the Spanish conquest of the Tarasca: the Tarascan ruler came before the conquistadores in the symbolic garb of an old man to offer his surrender, and accordingly the dancers wear masks and imitate the tired movements of old men, though in time they emerge as young dancers again. The **penachos dance** (dance of the headdresses) is still a tradition in Oaxaca: the dancers wear towering feather headdresses adorned with mirrors. Rattles are the essential props of the **sonajero dancers** who also use bows and arrows as well as wearing an elaborate headdress. Their dance venerates the symbol of the cross and acknowledges the power of nature.

Ballroom dancing

Popular ballroom dances consist mostly of Spanish melodies and steps. Examples of these dances are the jarabe tapatio from Guadala-jara, the zandunga from Tehuantepec, the huapango from Veracruz and the jarana from Yucatán.

Corrida (bullfight)

The Spanish bullfight (corrida de toros) has also become a tradition in Mexico. Mexico City is home to the world's largest bullfight arena (40,000 seats), and there are arenas (plazas de toros) in all major cities. The best bullfighters present themselves during the main bull-fighting season (from November to March, during the summer months in northern Mexico), while newcomers to the art will fight the bull during the rest of the year. Usually, the **corridas** take place on Sundays or a holiday afternoon at 4pm on the dot. The best seats offer some shadow (sombra) while the cheap seats are exposed to the sun. Fighting bulls are raised on specialized farms; they are carefully selected according to strict principles and enter the arena at the age of four or five.

Cockfight

The cockfight (pelea de gallos) is still popular in rural areas despite protests from animal rights groups worldwide. The owners affix sharp steel blades to the feet of their animals, which naturally cause severe injury to the animals in a fight. Spectators bet large sums of money on the outcome of cruel and bloody fights.

Charreadas (Mexican rodeo)

The charreadas are Mexican-style rodeos. Most of the horsemen (charros) belong to clubs, which provide the arenas. The rodeos are held in the tradition of the cattle drovers on horseback who used to work on the large farms (haciendas). The participants make their entrance in picturesque costumes and then show their skills riding horses, handling the lasso and roping in wild bulls and mustangs. The intermissions are filled with folk dances and mariachi music.

Jai alai

Jai alai (happy festival) is called pelota in Mexico (pelota vasca in Spain). It originated in Spain's Basque region and came to Mexico

Women, too, present daring feats of horsemanship at the Charreadas.

with the Spaniards along with many other games. Pelota is quite likely the **fastest and most dangerous of all ball games**. The game takes place in a rectangular, three-walled court, which usually has a roof. Teams of 2 (in most cases) play by catapulting an about 8cm/3in hard rubber ball against the front wall. The players catch and throw the ball with a cesta, a long, curved wicker scoop strapped to one arm.

Only one generation ago, men in many Mexican regions still donned the **charro suit**, a dress code originating with the festive attire of the cattle drovers and ranchers. The attire consists of a fine leather jacket and trousers with rows of silver buttons. A shirt with ruffles and a large sombrero complements the outfit. The large hat is made of felt and embroidered with gold and silver threads. Today, this outfit is worn only in charro clubs and by mariachi ensembles. The **china poblana dress** of Mexican women consisted of a red and green embroidered skirt over several petticoats, a white blouse and a woollen or linen scarf (rebozo) to cover head and shoulders. A Chinese immigrant woman is credited with having brought the scarf fashion from the Philippines to Puebla. Today, the china poblana dress is normally only seen at folk dances or fancy-dress balls.

Traditional garb

Traditional Indian
outfits ▶

In contrast, traditional Indian outfits are still common in many villages. The ancient methods of spinning and weaving are unchanged to this day; only the plant dyes used in times past have now given way to synthetic dyes. A variety of old traditional wear is still common in the federal states of Oaxaca, Veracruz, Yucatán and Chiapas. It is mostly women who wear the traditional outfits, while most men prefer modern clothing, such as a plain white shirt and trousers with a woollen or linen waistband.

Heavy woollen cloaks (**sarapes**) adorned with geometric patterns protect from the cold and rain. Wide pleated shirts with many pockets (**guayaberas**) are the usual fashion in the warmer gulf regions of Yucatán. The women wear the **huipil**, a rectangular piece of embroidered cotton fabric with openings for head and arms. The **Quechquémetl** is customary in North and Central Mexico and has a similar design but uses two panels of fabric. The Spaniards took on the customary Mexican straw hat, the **sombrero**. Only the Indian tribes of the Tarahumara, Huicholes, Amuzgo, Tzotzil and Tzeltzal still wear the pre-Hispanic traditional garb.

For many the classic Mexican accessory par excellence – but in fact the sombrero was imported from Spain.

Textiles from Zinacantán

The quality and variety of Mexican arts and crafts can easily compete **Arts and Crafts** with the best in the world. Certainly, there has been a recent trend to mass-produce industrial goods of lower quality, but the offerings of solid and imaginative handcrafted art is still plentiful. Like so much in today's Mexico, folk art shows a delightful combination of Mexican and Spanish elements; in many regions, people have developed their own style. The rural parts of Mexico therefore offer a particularly rich range of art and craft objects. (►Practicalities, Shopping).

Famous People

Why did Montezuma II hand over his power to Hernán Cortés? How did an Austrian get to be emperor of Mexico in 1863? Is it true that Leon Trotsky lived and died in Mexico? Has there ever been a Mexican winner of the Nobel prize for literature? Did you know that celebrities like Carlos Santana and Salma Hayek were born in Mexico?

Baedeker Specials have discussed in detail the lives and works of the following notable persons: Frederick Catherwood and John Lloyd Stevens (p.471), Frida Kahlo (p.405), José Orozco, Diego Rivera and David Siquieros (p.79) and Emiliano Zapata (p.52)

Lázaro Cárdenas (1895–1970)

Lázaro Cárdenas was born in Jiquilpan in Michoacán. He joined the revolutionary army of General Guillermo Garcia in 1913 and in 1920 became a member of the constitutionalists. From 1928 to 1932, he was Governor of Michoacán. After accepting several more government positions, Cárdenas was elected Mexican President in 1934. His name is connected with the largest **land reform** in Mexico's history, in which 18 million ha/45 million ac of land were returned to farming families and the »ejidos« (communal properties). He earned much public acclaim when he nationalized the foreign oil companies and bolstered the union movements.

General and politician

Hernán Cortés (1485–1547)

Hernán Cortés was the son of an aristocratic Spanish captain from Medellín in Spain. When Diego de Velásquez, governor of Cuba, gave him command of an expedition to explore the Central American continent, Cortés saw his great opportunity. He set sail on 18 February 1519 commanding a fleet of eleven ships, a crew of about 100 men and 500 soldiers.

On the Gulf Coast, Cortés established a city by the name of Villa Rica de la Vera Cruz (close to today's Veracruz). The ruler of the Aztec, Montezuma II, sent delegates carrying lavish gifts to greet him. At this point, most men in his crew were ready to turn around and leave; Cortés responded by burning all the ships but one and heading inland. He entered **Tenochtitlán** on 3 November 1519, and mistaking the Spaniard for the returning god Quetzalcóatl, Montezuma II submitted to him.

In May of 1520, Cortés was forced to temporarily leave Tenochtitlán to face troops under the command of Panfilo de Narváez, sent by the Cuban governor because of Cortés's insubordination. Cortés prevailed and returned to the Aztec capital Tenochtitlán only to find the city in uproar: delegates he had left behind had massacred Aztec noblemen, which had finally sparked anger in the population. Again, the Spaniards were forced to flee from Tenochtitlán. More than a year later, on 13 August 1521, Cortés's soldiers and their Indian allies again conquered the Aztec capital. This time they razed Tenochtitlán to the ground. Emperor Karl V appointed Cortés governor of the new colony, New Spain, in 1522. In the subsequent period, his troops subjugated almost all Indian regions.

Conquistadore of the Aztec empire

← *Inventor of Latin rock: Carlos Santana*

1519: Montezuma II receives Cortés and Malinche (contemporary miniature from the Lienzo de Tlascala)

From 1528 to 1530, Cortés resided in Spain. He was honoured upon his return but lost his post as governor because of the hostility of his opponents. Still, he kept the rank of supreme commander of the armed forces and was given the title of Marqués del Valle de Oaxaca (marquess of the valley of Oaxaca). Cortés returned to Mexico and embarked on several expeditions, but with little success. His attempts at conquest brought him, for example, to Honduras and the California Peninsula. Having returned to Spain once more, he participated in the military action against Algiers. He died a bitter man in Castilleja de la Cuesta near Seville (Spain).

Juana Inés de la Cruz (1651–1695)

Nun and poet (fig. p.76)   Juana Inés de la Cruz, was one of Mexico's foremost Spanish-speaking poets of the 17th century. Born on the hacienda San Miguel Nepantla in Amecameca in today's state of México, her talents became obvious early in her life. After studying Latin in Mexico City, she was accepted at the court of the viceroy, and even there her thirst for knowledge shone brightly. When, on the request of the viceroy, 40 scholars examined her, she passed with flying colours. She entered a convent two years later; according to her own statements, only there did she hope to find deliverance. In the **convent of San Jerónimo**, she worked as a housekeeper and registrar while devoting herself to her studies and literature. Among her literary works are three religious plays, two comedies (*Los empeños de una casa* (pawns of a house) and *Amor es más laberinto* (love, the greater labyrinth)) and many love poems which eloquently tell of the inner conflicts of a nun.

Cuauhtémoc (1496–1525)

Cuauhtémoc, the last of the free Aztec emperors, succeeded Cuitlá-huac who had ruled a mere three months. Cuauhtémoc (the name means descending eagle or, by extension, setting sun) enjoyed the excellent education and cultured upbringing given to the sons of Aztec noblemen. The emperor defended his people against the conquistadores with great valour and prudence. When the Spaniards took him captive on 13 August 1521, Cuauhtémoc responded by asking Cortés for the mercy of his death. Instead, Cortés forced the former Aztec ruler to accompany him on his journey to Honduras. In 1525, Cortés hanged Cuauhtémoc for alleged treason in a city known as Izancanac (now Yaxchilan in the state of Chiapas). **The last free Aztec ruler**

Porfirio Díaz (1830–1915)

General Porfirio Diaz was born in Oaxaca. For more than 30 years, he was the dominant figure in Mexican politics. While he fostered the modernization of Mexico, that very process also deepened the abyss between rich and poor which still exists today. **General and politician**

Díaz started out fighting the conservatives and then the French, side by side with Benito Juárez, making him a folk hero and the most powerful general in the country's history. In 1871, he surprised everyone by running for the office of president against his former companion Juárez, a race Díaz lost. Afterwards, he openly rebelled but was defeated and disappeared from public life as a result. After the death of Juárez, Díaz usurped power with a military coup in 1876; from then on, he ruled ruthlessly and suppressed all opposition with the help of the army. Díaz opened Mexico to foreign investment and thereby **bound Mexico's politics and economy to its relationship with the USA**. However, few Mexicans profited from this modernization, and large-scale land ownership in the hands of a very few finally led to the farmer revolt under Emiliano Zapata. Díaz blatantly rigged his re-election and arrested the opposition candidate Francisco Madero, acts which led to the revolution in November 1910. Eventually, in May 1911, Díaz resigned and lived until his death in exile in Paris.

Salma Hayek (born 1966)

The daughter of a Lebanese oil manager and a Mexican opera singer, actress Salma Hayek was born in Coatzacoalcos (Veracruz). The dream role of **Frida** in the opulent movie about the Mexican painter Frida Kahlo brought her international recognition, although she had **Actress**

Salma Hayek in her best known acting role so far, as Frida Kahlo

been a celebrity before this based on her appearance as »Teresa« in one of Mexico's most successful TV shows. She landed this role very soon after completing her studies in international relations and drama.

Hollywood initially relegated her to smaller roles. However, her part in Robert Rodriguez's **Desperado**, with Antonio Banderas as her partner, gave her Hollywood success. Salma Hayek has now starred in almost three dozen movies. Among them are *Fools Rush In*, *Studio 54*, *Dogma* and *Wild Wild West*.

After her dream project *Frida* (the Mexican fashion czar **Armando Mafud** provided the costumes), Hayek worked again under the direction of Rodriguez on *Sometime in Mexico*, a sequel to *Desperado*, and played a reformed jewel thief in *After the Sunset*. Among her most recent movies are the drama *Ask the Dust*, the Western *Bandidas* and a satire about the New York art scene entitled *Paint*.

Miguel Hidalgo y Costilla (1753–1811)

Freedom fighter This year as every year, on 15 September at one hour to midnight, a cheer will disturb the quiet of the night all over Mexico. Hidalgo's **Cry of Dolores** (grito de Dolores) runs as follows: »Mexicans! Viva Mexico! Viva Our Lady of Guadalupe! Viva Ferdinand!« (These days of course, Mexicans omit the last sentence, »Death to the gachupines!«, a battle cry directed against the Spanish-born privileged class.) The priest Miguel Hidalgo y Costilla delivered his cry from the village church in Dolores, north-west of Querétaro. His actions made him a folk hero that night. Along with the mayor of Querétaro, Miguel Domínguez, his wife and captain Ignacio Allende, the priest participated in a plot to attain Mexico's independence from Spain. In danger of being discovered, Hidalgo forged ahead, and within a short time had activated an army of tens of thousands. Hidalgo and his army conquered Guanajuato, Morelia and Guadalajara, a fight characterized by equal brutality and terror on both sides. Close to Puerto Calderón however, he and his army had to face General Calleja and his troops. Hidalgo's side lost, and he and his officers unsuccessfully tried to escape to the USA. They were shot in Chihuahua.

Agustín de Iturbide (1783–1824)

Agustín de Iturbide, the first emperor of Mexico, was born in Valladolid (now Morelia). Initially, he made a name for himself as a loyal officer of the Spanish viceroy and successfully fought the rebels who demanded independence. In 1820, after a liberal Spanish constitution had given new life to the Mexican independence movement, Iturbide joined a conservative group which also wanted to separate from Spain but planned on establishing a Mexican monarchy. As the commander of the conservative troops he moved against the rebel army of Vicente Guerrero. In pursuit of his own goals, Iturbide negotiated with Guerrero, and they agreed on the Plan of Iguala, i.e. on an independent Mexico as a constitutional catholic monarchy. He convinced the new Spanish viceroy Juan O'Donojú to agree to this plan. Contrary to these agreements, Iturbide dissolved the constituent assembly in May 1822 and proclaimed himself **Emperor Agustín I.** His days of glory were however numbered. The pressure of a new rebellion ended his reign as the Mexican emperor after only eleven months and the rebel leader became President Santa Ana. The emperor fled to Italy with the congress accusing him of treason. In 1824, when he attempted to sneak back into Mexico incognito, he was recognized and shot.

First emperor of Mexico

Benito Juárez (1806–1872)

Benito Juárez was born to Zapatist parents in San Pablo Guelatao in Oaxaca. At the age of 13 he learnt to read and write and then studied to become a lawyer. He was elected governor of Oaxaca in 1848. From the very beginning until the end of his period in office in 1852, Juárez worked towards reforms.

Mexican president

He fled abroad ahead of Santa Ana's persecution of liberals, where he had contact with like-minded people. Following Santa Ana's final departure, he designed a liberal constitution while working as the lord chancellor for the Comonfort government. However, the ideas of Juárez and those of the government were not compatible. In 1858, Juárez himself became president.

In his first years in office Juárez was occupied with military skirmishes. This seriously hampered his **reform plans** to abolish church privileges, introduce legal marriages and public schools, nationalize church property and advance the industrialization. But first, he and his government had to flee the conservatives and go to Guadalajara and Veracruz. Then, in 1861, there were conflicts with the French because he had ceased repaying foreign debt. To protect their investments England, Spain and France invaded in 1862 After the Habsburg episode – when Austrian archduke Maximilian was appointed Mexican emperor by the French – Juárez again became president in 1867 and continued his reforms. Despite a stroke in 1870 he ran again for election in 1871. He died in 1872 of natural causes.

Bartolomé de Las Casas (1474–1566)

Missionary The father of the Dominican monk Bartolomé de Las Casas, Don Francisco, was a passenger on Columbus's *Santa María*. In 1502, after completing his studies of theology and law in Salamanca (Spain), Bartolomé journeyed to his country's colonial properties in Central America. He visited Cuba in 1512.

He soon became aware of the unjust and cruel treatment of the Indians at the hands of the Spaniards. From 1514, he vehemently fought for the rights of the Indians against countless intrigues and hostilities, amongst other things embarking on 14 voyages by ship for this purpose. The great inquisitor gave him the title »Defensor universal de los Indios« (general defender of the Indians). When Ferdinand IV granted him an audience he presented his ideas about improving the Indians' living conditions, but seeing that his efforts were in vain he spent ten years (1523–1533) in the Dominican monastery on Hispaniola (Cuba). There he worked on his *Apológetica Historia de las Indias* (Apologetic History of the Indies) and the *Historia General de las Indias* (**General History of the Indies**). In 1539, he provoked Spanish soldiers in Nicaragua to desert, and was forced to go back to Spain to stand trial.

In his four years in Spain, he created his arguably most famous book, entitled *Brevísima relación de la destrucción de las Indias occidentales* (Short Account of the Destruction of the Indies). This work prompted Emperor Karl V in 1542 to proclaim his »new laws«, aimed at giving far-reaching protection to the Indians. Unfortunately, they were revised in 1545. De Las Casas was appointed bishop of Chiapas in Mexico; again he aggravated the colonialists and again he was summoned to Spain. He left Mexico in 1547. In his famous disputation of Valladolid in the year 1550 he expounded his views one last time. De Las Casas died in 1566 in Madrid; the location of his grave is not known.

Maximilian I (1832–1867)

Emperor of Mexico Maximilian of Habsburg, one of the younger brothers of Emperor Franz Joseph I, was born in the castle of Schönbrunn in Vienna, Austria. He embarked on a military career and was appointed governor-general of Lombardo-Veneto in 1857. Following the loss of this Italian province, Maximilian I retreated to Miramare Castle near Trieste.

Here, a conservative, clerical Mexican group asked him to become emperor of Mexico. The proposal came from Emperor Napoleon III of France who had ordered his army to march against the republican government under Benito Juárez. Maximilian I accepted the offer and took his first steps on Mexican soil in Veracruz on 28 May 1864. To the horror of his conservative clerical proponents, he continued Juárez's **reforms**. Among other things, he established the freedom of

»The Execution of Emperor Maximilian of Mexico«
Painting by Eduard Manet (1868/69)

the press and enforced the nationalization of church property. When the French left Mexico, Maximilian I was still surrounded by a raging civil war against republican forces, without any support. He fled to Querétaro, and there fell into the hands of troops under General Corona and General Escobedo on 15 March 1867. He was brought before a military tribunal and was shot, as were his generals Mejia and Miramón. His remains were shipped to Vienna and buried in December 1867.

Montezuma

At least two significant Aztec rulers bore the name Montezuma (or Moctezuma, sometimes also Motecuhzoma). The name means »he who is angry in a noble manner« or »he who frowns like a lord« in the Náhuatl language. It is also a reference to the cloud-covered sun. **Significant Aztec rulers**

The name **Montezuma Ilhuicamina** means »solitary one who shoots an arrow into the sky«. This elder Montezuma built the political empire Tenochtitlán and made it the superior power in Central Mexico by expanding trade relations far beyond the Valley of Anahuac and by exacting taxes and tributes from defeated regions. He also established the alliance between Tenochtitlán, Texcoco and Tlacopan. He initiated the construction of many buildings in the city of Tenochtitlán and started building an aqueduct to supply the city with drinking water.

Montezuma II Xocoyotzin (the younger) is arguably one of the most tragic figures in the history of Mexico. He reigned from 1502 to 1520. His fatal error was to mistake Hernán Cortés for the returning god-king Quetzalcoátl, an error the Aztec ruler recognized too late. Some Mexican researchers describe Montezuma II as tough, tyranni- **Fig. p.42**

cal and deeply religious. Under his reign, he expanded the power of Tenochtitlán to the Isthmus of Panama and the city itself reached the high-point of its civilization. Even the Spaniards were in awe of its splendour. According to Spanish sources, Montezuma II died when he was trying to calm a crowd that had gathered at Cortés's house on 27 June 1520: a stone was thrown by a member of the crowd and killed him. Indian sources however say that the Spaniards murdered him.

Tina Modotti (1896–1942)

Photographer

Tina Modotti was born in Udine (Italy) where she spent her childhood. In 1913, she settled with her family in San Francisco. There

Tina Modotti: »Woman from Tehuantepec« (1929)

she initially earned a living as a textile worker. Together with her husband, the painter and poet Roubaix Richey, she moved to Los Angeles in 1918. She played several parts in Hollywood silent movies and started an affair with the photographer **Edward Weston**, who followed when she and her husband moved to Mexico in 1922. Once in Mexico, she met **Diego Rivera** and his circle. After Richey's death, Modotti and Weston settled together in Mexico City, and Weston taught her the art of photography. Soon, she had graduated from the role of assistant and become an artist in her own right. Her first subjects of interest were plant still lifes, which she photographed in a surreal, symbolic manner, but as her involvement in revolutionary Mexican politics expanded so her artistic interest in human portraits increased. Her companion Weston

set scenes for photographs of Tina's body and also photographed famous Mexican artists and revolutionaries. In contrast, Modotti's photography was soon dominated by urban street scenes and **social studies of the rural population**. Egon Erwin Kisch wrote about Tina Modotti that »her camera creates perfect paintings«, and saw the secret of her artistry in the fact that »she portrayed the essence of her world with the eye of kindness«. After the newly-elected Mexican president was assassinated Modotti, the self-confessed communist, had to leave the country. She went to Cuba where she started an affair with the Cuban revolutionary Julio Mella. When her lover was murdered she travelled to Europe and to Moscow. There, she actively involved herself with the Red Aid organization. Numerous myths around Modotti's life still exist today. The stories go that she was involved both in the assassination of the president and in the death of Mellas, that she spied for Stalin and was finally poisoned. Tina Modotti died in Mexico City while taking a taxi home from a dinner party.

Octavio Paz (1914–1998)

As early as the 19th century, the members of the Indian-Spanish Paz family were among the foremost figures in Mexico. Octavio Paz's grandfather Ireneo was considered one of the outstanding personalities in Mexican liberalism. He was a minister and a biographer of Porfirio Díaz. Octavio's father worked for the social revolutionary Zapata. Octavio himself was born in Mixcoac, Mexico City. At the young age of 17, he had already become a co-founder of a literary journal and a published author. After studying philosophy and the law, he worked as a teacher and got involved in politics. In 1937, he travelled to Spain and a year later founded the periodical for poetry and reviews *Taller*. From 1946 to 1952, Octavio Paz lived and worked in Paris where he participated in the surrealist movement led by André Breton. In this period of his life, he also made his first journeys to India and Japan. In 1962, Paz was named ambassador to India, a post he resigned as a protest against the massacre of demonstrating students in Mexico City in 1968. Afterwards, he taught as a visiting

Lyricist and essayist

King Carl Gustaf presents Octavio Paz with the Nobel Prize for Literature in 1990.

professor in the USA until his return to Mexico in 1971. It was then his main domicile though he occasionally taught at North American universities. He continued to live and write in Mexico until his death. Along with many other awards, he received the **Nobel Prize for Literature** in 1990 for his work as lyricist and essayist, the highpoint of his stellar career as an author. His best known book is entitled ***The Labyrinth of Solitude*** and analyzes the various and very complex cultures in Latin America. The volume was published in 1950 and is still considered the key to Mexico's soul today.

Carlos Santana (born 1947)

Rock musician
(fig. p.94)

When Carlos Santana was five, his father arranged violin lessons for him. But that was before the young Santana got a taste of rock and roll, and in 1955 he switched to the guitar. In the same year, his family moved from his birthplace Autlán (in the Mexican Federal State of Jalisco) to Tijuana, where the young musician honed his playing in clubs. His family moved to San Francisco in 1960 and Carlos followed a year later. There, he met like-minded people, and in 1966 he formed the Santana Blues Band together with Gregg Rolie, Gus Rodriguez, Michael Carabello and Danny Haro. They created their own unmistakable sound, a mixture of rock'n'roll, blues and Latin American rhythms. The music soon became popular in and around San Francisco. Music historians refer to their style as **Latin Rock**. Their first record, *Santana*, came out in 1969 and was an overnight success. This secured the band an appearance at the legendary Woodstock festival. Their second album, entitled *Abraxas* contains the classics ***Samba Pa Ti*** and ***Black Magic Woman***. Carlos Santana released his first solo-album in 1972. As time went on, the success of the band waned as did Santana's ambitions to be a solo artist. Still, he remained a cherished guest of the music greats of the time. In 1999, Santana and his band staged one of the greatest comebacks in pop-music history. The album ***Supernatural*** became an international success and with nine prizes set a record at the Grammy awards in 2000. Once again, Santana is the talk of the town.

Leon Trotsky (1879–1940)

Russian
revolutionary

From 1902, Trotsky was the alias for the Russian revolutionary Lev Davidovich Bronstein, born in Janowska. He became the organizer of the armed revolution in Russia, and he also established the Red Army. In his ideology he envisioned the population and the government engaged in a »**permanent revolution**«. In his estimation, socialism in the Soviet Union would only be secure after a successful revolution in capitalist countries as well. Stalin's views on this issue were opposed to Trotsky's; he propagated »socialism in one country«. The ensuing rivalry became more extreme when Trotsky expressed his opinion that the Stalin dictatorship was not in line with the ideas of Lenin, and Trotsky was exiled from the Soviet Union in 1929. He arrived in Mexico City in 1937, where he lived with his wife and stepson in a fortress-like house in Coyoacán until he was murdered in 1940.

Francisco »Pancho« Villa (1878 – 1923)

Mexican
revolutionist

Francisco »Pancho« Villa – his real name was Doroteo Arango – was a multifaceted and unique figure in the Mexican revolution. In 1910, he participated in the armed fight against the dictator Díaz. He es-

Together with Zapata, »Pancho« Villa marched into Mexico City in 1914. The famous photograph of him on the Mexican president's chair is from the same time.

tablished his famous-infamous cavalry troops, the **División del Norte** in September 1913. These troops were invaluable in fights against government troops; unfortunately, they also did not shy away from looting. Pancho Villa celebrated his biggest triumph when he marched into Mexico City in December 1914, side by side with **Emiliano Zapata**. Just like Zapata, he was inefficient as a politician. Upon returning to northern Mexico, his power was used up in many skirmishes. When US troops moved against him, his division even attacked the US city Columbus in New Mexico. Under President Álvaro Obregón, Pancho Villa was granted amnesty and received a hacienda (large farm) near Hidalgo de Parral in the Federal State of Chihuahua. His past eventually caught up with him however. Together with his companion from the revolutionary days Miguel Trillo, he was shot dead in 1923.

Practicalities

WHICH MEXICAN CULINARY SPECIALITIES
SHOULD ON NO ACCOUNT BE MISSED?
WHAT SHOULD TRAVELLERS TO MEXICO
KEEP IN MIND, AND WHICH ITEMS
SHOULD DEFINITELY BE BROUGHT
ALONG? FIND OUT HERE –
PREFERABLY BEFORE THE TRIP!

Accommodation

Camping and caravanning

»Trailer parks« for motor homes or campers (campos para remolques) are quite common; they are firmly in the hands of US operators. Campsites (campamentos) are less common. The Mexican Ministry for Tourism will provide a list of economical places to stay. This includes a list of campsites (directorio de albuerges, cabañas, campamentos, campos para remolques) (►Information). When travelling to Mexico via the USA information can be obtained from the US motoring organization the AAA (Triple A, American Automobile Association) or from one of the Mexican insurance companies at the border. Even though it is not against the law, it is not advisable to pitch a tent just anywhere, no matter how much the beautiful beaches and landscapes may invite such an idea.

Hotels

First class hotels in large cities and vacation spots comply with Central European quality standards, but they usually cater to the demands of US travellers (practical comfort but little atmosphere). Some Mexican-owned hotels have a more individual character. Hotels may not be quite as comfortable in places with less tourism.

Prices   Hotel price controls were dropped in 1993 and prices fluctuate with supply and demand. Prices quoted here are therefore no more than rough ball park figures. Regional situations and the season are factors, too. In some cases it is possible to haggle over the price.

Value added tax of 15% must be added and – at this point in time only in Mexico City and some beach resorts – an additional **hotel tax** of 2%.

Hacienda hotels   Haciendas are very large farm properties or manors which were given as rewards to the Spanish conquerors for their actions on behalf of Spain. Some of these haciendas have been turned into colonial-style luxury hotels. This guide lists the locations of the best-known hacienda hotels.

Many historic city palaces have been turned into first rate lodgings (e.g. around Morelia or Oaxaca). At the same time, bold modern hotel buildings are rising up with no more than a handful of rooms, maybe up to two dozen at the most. These solitary architectural novelties are located in large cities or tourist centres (e.g. Mexico City, Playa del Carmen, Isla Mujeres or Cancún).

A stay in simple but pleasant surroundings comes at a very reasonable price in one of many casas de huéspedes (inns, motels) or one of the posadas familiares (family-run hotels).

Motels, inns and family-run hotels

Youth Hostels / Backpackers' Lodges

Accommodation in youth hostels (albergues de la juventud) is available in the following places: Aguascalientes, Campeche, Cancún, Chetumal, Durango, Guadalajara (2x), La Paz, Monterrey, Morelia, Playa del Carmen, Puerto Vallarta, Querétaro, Tuxtla Gutiérrez and Zacatecas. No age limit applies. Reservations must be made before 8pm and guests can stay up to 15 days in a single hostel.

▶ YOUTH HOSTLES

▶ **Instituto Mexicano de la Juventud**
Serapio Rendón 76
Col. San Rafael
06470 México, D. F.
Tel. (018 00) 228 00 92
www.imjuventud.gob.mx

▶ **Other reasonably-priced accommodation**
www.hostels.com
www.lugaresdemexico.com
www.hostellingmexico.com

Arrivals · Before the Journey

Holidays are usually not long enough to consider reaching your destination by anything but aeroplane. It takes about 12–14 hours to fly from any of the important European airports to Mexico City.

By aeroplane

There are **direct flights** to Mexico City from London Heathrow, but using another UK airport or flying to another Mexican city usually involves changing planes either in Europe or in the USA.

Aeromexico, Mexicana and several US airlines offer flights from US cities to Mexico. These flights are convenient for those travelling to the USA and planning a side trip to Mexico.

The airlines Mexicana de Aviación and Aeromexico offer competitively priced tickets for domestic flights to and from more than 30 cities. Travellers must purchase package flights such as Mexico Airpass, Mexi-Pass, Mexi-Plan and Maya-Pass when booking tickets for the transatlantic flight. They will not be available after arrival in Mexico.

⏺ AIRLINES

AIRLINES

▶ **Aeromexico**
Tel. +44 (0)20 7801 6234
Shakespeare House, 168
Lavender Hill,
London, SW11 5TG, England
www.aeromexico.com

▶ **Mexicana**
Tel. +44 (0)870 8900040
75, St. Margarets Avenue,
London, N20 9LD, England
www.mexicana.com.mx

▶ **United Airlines**
Tel. 1 800 538 2929 (USA and
Canada) or
+44 (0)845 8 444 777 (UK)
www.united.com

▶ **KLM**
Tel. +44 (0)20 8750 9200
Plesman House, Cains Lane, Feltham, Middlesex TW14 9RL,
England
www.klm.com

▶ **Air Canada**
Tel. (00 800) 8712 7786
www.aircanada.com.de

▶ **British Airways**
Tel. +44 (0)870 850 9 850
Fax +44 (0)20 8759 4314
www.britishairways.com or
www.ba.com

TRAVELLING ABOARD
FREIGHTERS

▶ **Cruise & Freighter Travel Club International**
2700 Rufus Rockhead 313
Montreal, QC H3J 2Z7, Canada
www.freightercruises.com
Tel. 1 203 222 1500 Fax 1 203 222 9191

▶ **Cruise & Freighter Travel Association**

P.O. Box 580188, Flushing, New
York 11358, USA
Tel. 800 872 8584 (toll-free in USA
and Canada)
www.travltips.com

Overland · Most travellers who enter Mexico overland cross the border from the USA. The usual border crossings are San Diego (California)/Tijuana (BCN), Calexico (California)/Mexicali (BCN), Nogales (Arizona)/Nogales (Sonora), El Paso (Texas)/Ciudad Juárez (Chih.), Presidio (Texas)/Ojinaga (Chih.), Del Río (Texas)/Ciudad Acuña (Coah.), Eagle Pass (Texas)/Piedras Negras (Coah.), Laredo (Texas)/Nuevo Laredo (N.L.), McAllen (Texas)/Reynosa (Tamaulipas, Mexico) and Brownsville (Texas)/Matamoros (Tamps.)

By car ▶ Buying a car is an economical option only for a longer stay. It is best to buy the car in the USA. The vehicle is registered on the tourist card and in the passport, and it must be properly exported.
The import licence is granted for up to 180 days. Apply for an extension well in advance because those in possession of an expired licence may be subject to considerable fines.

US car insurance does not extend to Mexico. While third party motor vehicle liability insurance is not mandatory in Mexico, purchasing insurance for a car is a good idea. The Sanborn insurance company, with offices in all major border cities, has a reliable record.

US bus companies offer services to the major border crossings. Once at the border, much less costly Mexican buses bring passengers to Mexico City and many other destinations in Mexico. It is possible to get bus tickets for direct routes from the border cities to Mexico City or elsewhere. ◀ By bus

Transfers from the US to the Mexican rail systems are possible from the US-Mexican border cities Calexico (California, travelling by bus from Phoenix or San Diego), Nogales (Arizona, travelling by bus from Tucson), El Paso (Texas), Presidio (Texas, travelling by bus), Del Río (Texas), Eagle Pass (Texas), McAllen (Texas, travelling by bus) and Nuevo Laredo (Texas). Transfer to the rail stations on the Mexican side of the border. Please note that rail travel is by far the slowest means of transportation in Mexico. ◀ By train

Travellers with plenty of time (about 2-3 weeks) can also board a ship to Mexico. It is possible to buy passage aboard regular freighters (liner traffic) with passenger cabins. Round-trip tickets are also available, for example around the east coast of the US or the Gulf of Mexico. Ocean liners regularly depart from European ports in Liverpool, Hamburg, Bremen, Kiel, Rotterdam, Antwerp and Geneva to Tampico or Veracruz. Shipping companies based at US ports will also carry passengers to Mexico. By ship

Travel Documents

Citizens of the UK, US, Canada, Australia, New Zealand and many Western European countries need only a tourist card and a passport for a trip to Mexico lasting less than 180 days. The passport must be valid for at least 6 months, and the tourist card is issued in the respective home country by Mexican embassies, consulates, tourist offices and tour operators, or in flight by airline staff. The documents are issued in duplicate, and the original is presented on entry into Mexico. The copy is required on leaving Mexico and should therefore be kept in a safe place. An entry fee is payable if travelling overland; it is usually included in the price of an air ticket. A tourist card can be extended for longer stays. While in Mexico, this can be done only at the immigration office in Mexico City (Secretaría de Gobernación, Ave. Chapultepec 284), which also replaces lost cards. Proof of financial means for the extended stay is required. Be prepared for long waits when processing the papers at this office; for this reason, it is better to obtain approval for a longer stay before the trip. Further information can be obtained from the Embassy of Mexico to the United Kingdom on 020 7235 6393 or at www.mexicanconsulate.org.uk (▶ Information). It is also possible to travel into one of Tourist card

Loaded to the hilt!

the neighbouring countries (carrying the necessary visa) and return to Mexico a day later with a fresh new tourist card.

Driving licence A national driving licence suffices to drive in Mexico. Taking along an international driving licence is however recommended.

Animals Animals require an anti-rabies inoculation record not more than six months old, certified by the Mexican consulate.

Customs Regulations

Entry Tourists may bring in items and equipment for daily use duty free. This includes 400 (a carton of) cigarettes, 50 cigars or 250g/8.8oz of tobacco, 2/3 of a gallon or 3 litres of alcoholic beverages (persons over 18 years of age only), one camera/video camera with 12 rolls of film or cassettes, gifts valued at up to US$ 300 and three items of in-use sports equipment. In addition, each traveller is permitted to import a portable TV, a radio, a cassette player/recorder, a CD player/recorder, a typewriter and a computer. It is prohibited to import harpoons, spears or lances for underwater hunting, weapons, plants, fruits and pornography of any kind.

Exit The export of gold, antiques and archaeological items is prohibited. Under no circumstances should drugs be taken out of the country, not even the smallest amount.

Re-entry into EU Countries All articles of daily use that were taken on the outward journey to Mexico are duty free (see above), as well as 200 cigarettes or 100 small cigars, 50 cigars or 250g/8.8oz of tobacco, 1 litre/1.8pt of alcoholic beverages with over 22% alcohol by volume or 2 litres/3.5pt of alcoholic beverages with less than 22% alcohol by volume or 2 litres/ 3.5pt of sparkling wine. Duty free items also include 2 litres/3.5pt of wine, 500g/17.6oz of coffee or 200g/7oz instant coffee, 100g/3.5oz of tea or 40g/1.4oz tea extract, 50g/1.7oz of perfume or 0.25litres/0.5pt of eau de toilette. Tobacco products and alcoholic beverages are allowed only for persons aged 17 or older; coffee is allowed only for persons over the age of 15. Other goods and gifts are duty free up to a value of €175. Goods obtained in duty-free shops may not exceed a value of €85. The limits for duty free goods are more generous when re-entering the UK from another EU country.

Every traveller can show cooperation and support for the Washington convention on biodiversity by avoiding the purchase of souvenirs that require materials from rare or endangered species or importing and exporting live animals or plants living in the wild. Among others, the following species or items are protected in Mexico: cacti, tortoise shell, black coral, saurian skins, crocodiles (live or cured as a trophy), parakeets, turtles and tarantulas. Visitors should not capture animals or dig up plants. Any violation of one of the species protection acts will be noticed at the latest by European customs officials; such violations are punishable by fines up to €50,000 or up to five years' imprisonment.

Washington convention on biodiversity

Beach Holidays

Mexico has a coastline of almost 10,000km/6,200mi. The **beaches** (playas) on the Pacific and the Gulf of Mexico offer a wide range of interesting recreational activities.

The oceans are usually calm. That is true not only of the Atlantic side, i.e. the Gulf Coast, but also of the Gulf of California on the Pacific with the Baja Peninsula shielding it from the open ocean. In contrast, coastal areas that are directly exposed to the Pacific have to weather stronger waves and tides at times. The variety of settings allows every holidaymaker to make their very personal choice of beach, whether it features the lively entertainment of one of the large tourist centres like Acapulco, Cancún or Puerto Vallarta, or the peace and quiet of a remote paradisical bay.

i The best beaches

- Acapulco: classic holiday destination; watch the famous cliff divers.
- Cancún: tourist centre and a good base when planning trips to Maya sites.
- Cozumel: this island in the Caribbean Sea off the eastern Yucatán shore beckons divers and snorkellers.
- Huatulco: aquatic sports and remote bays
- Los Cabos: more than 33km/21mi of desert and coastal scenery
- Playa del Carmen: rambling beaches, relaxing atmosphere and aquatic sports
- Puerto Escondido: a surfer's paradise, calm waters and ecology parks

A wonderful evening atmosphere on the beach in Acapulco

The best place for scuba diving is on the Pacific or the Caribbean coast. There is, for example, the island of Cozumel, which features the world's second largest live coral reef.

The Mexican Pacific coast offers the best environment for windsurfing.

Water quality The water quality is not good near large port cities, such as Tampico, Veracruz, Coatzacoalcos and Lázaro Cárdenas. The oil boom and the petrochemical industry has taken its toll especially on the Gulf Coast; the coast around Coatzocoalcos is a glaring and appalling example of this.

The water quality may vary in large beach holiday centres, such as Acapulco, Puerto Vallarta and Mazatlán, while it is good to excellent at all other beach resorts.

Most of the Mexican **thermal springs** are found in the southern part of the Western Sierra Madre and in the southern central highlands. Only the most frequented and largest cities with healing springs are well organized as health resorts with all the usual trappings. Among the structured health resorts are Aguascalientes, Ixtapán de la Sal, Río Caliente, Comanjilla and Tehuacán, where the best known Mexican mineral water is bottled (Agua Tehuacán). In other places, the health spa amenities may be quite simple. Mineral springs often surface naturally and only serve the needs of the local population.

Children in Mexico

Mexicans are very kind to children. The little ones are welcome everywhere, and complaints about noisy offspring will usually meet with anything from surprise to disapproval. Children's needs on the trip can usually be met locally; it is not necessary to carry a lot of extra provisions.

▷ CHILDREN

▶ **Aktun Chen Natural Park**
www.aktunchen.com
4km/2.4mi south of Akumal
(2km/1.2mi west of the MEX 307)
www.aktunchen.com
Children can have an adventure in this small nature park with dripstone caves and animals including a snake enclosure.

▶ **Hípico La Golondrina**
Bordo del Río Atoyac 800
San Jacinto Amilpas
Tel. / Fax (01951) 512 75 70
www.mexonline.com/hipico.htm
Special riding programme for children (day trips, also dressage and jumping) with ponies and small horses, approximately 10km/6mi north of Oaxaca

▶ **Papalote Museo del Niño**
Mexico City, Chapultepec Park

Segunda Sección,
(opp. Museo Tecnológico)
Here, children can actively experience the worlds of science, technology and art, learning for example how the human body functions or about life deep in the oceans

▶ **Tortugranja**
Carretera a Garrafón
A turtle station situated on the west coast of Isla Mujeres with various pools and a clinic for sick and injured animals

▶ **Wet'n'Wild water park**
Cancún, Paseo Kukulkán Km 25
(at the southern end of the hotel zone)
This part of the huge leisure park Parque Nizuc features water slides, pools and more.

It can't get any better than this: sun, sea and sand!

But do remember the heat. The little travellers should be sure to drink enough water and wear sunscreen and hats. Of course, children especially love to be on the beach, where they can happily play in the sand and water and build sand castles. Many hotels offer children's programmes and excursions.

Electricity

In general, the Mexican mains supply is 110 Volts AC, sometimes also 126 Volts or 220 Volts AC. Most plugs are similar to those in the USA (flat connexion). An adapter is required for European electrical devices.

Emergency Numbers

▶ **Tourist hotline**
of the Mexican Tourism Ministry
SECTUR:
Tel. 01 800 90 39 28
(nationwide free service, available
around the clock, English and
Spanish)

▶ **Emergency services**
Tel. 080

▶ **Police**
Tel. 060

▶ **Traffic police**
Tel. (5) 250 01 23 (Mexico City)
Tel. (998) 884 07 10 (Cancún)

▶ **FCO (Foreign and Commonwealth Office)**
Tel. +44 (0) 845 850 28 29

Etiquette and Customs

Mexico fascinates most visitors with its mixture of tradition, history and vibrant modern life. The colourful street scene, strolling couples and chaotic traffic of Mexico City, for example, contrasts with the magnificent ruins of a long dead civilization just a few miles from the city, where the traveller sees how pre-Columbian sites are excavated. History has put its stamp on Mexico. The Spanish conquistadores destroyed the ancient civilizations and then built their colonial empire, forcing the proud builders of a high culture into submission. The colonial exploitation of the former Aztec empire lasted for centuries, and much blood was shed before Mexico finally became a free nation. Indian roots are therefore part of the Mexican identity, as are the Spanish influences and today's social and economic conditions. But historic burdens and current problems notwithstanding, Mexicans have one character trait in common: they are **proud to be Mexican!**

Promises and burdens from the past

Before taking a photo, please ask:
this Indigena woman in San Juan Chamula has no objections

Mariachi musicians sing of unfulfilled love and unshakable macho pride.

Indigenous population After the 1910 revolution, Mexicans made the ancient Mesoamerican history an integral part of their national identity. Mexicans love to tell of the historic accomplishments of the Indians, and eat meals prepared according to ancient Indian traditions; the memory of brutal colonial practices will raise their ire. In contrast, the contributions made by the living heirs of the old civilizations do not quite find such heartfelt appreciation. Today, the natives or aborigines (indígenas) make up a considerable 14% of the population. Most of the natives live in remote areas and over the centuries they have retained an **amazing degree of cultural integrity**. Indian lives revolve around the small family farm and village community with communal tasks and activities. Land reform and thoughtless social reforms have often destroyed these structures and caused huge problems. It is small wonder that outside influences and outsiders, including visitors from abroad, are viewed with scepticism. Many natives do not appreciate being photographed without their consent. The negative Mexican view of the natives is based on their **perceived lack of progress**. It is true that many uprooted natives fail in modern society. Stubborn prejudices and discrimination hamper their integration, as does the threat posed by economic developments in Mexico's modern consumer society. Establishing a sustainable role for the native Indians in modern Mexico remains a challenge.

Virility is imperative – for Mexican men that is. To most tourists, it seems more like typical machismo posturing. Mexicans however don't mind the show: in fact, society tolerates a lot of the resulting contradictions in daily life. Mexicans adore their mothers; wives on the other hand are not so highly honoured. Virginity before marriage is still an important male requirement of women, and loss of virginity means less or no value as a future wife. Once married, women can only hope to acquire further exalted status as mothers of children. Jealously guarded by their husbands, women are at the centre of domestic life and shoulder the main responsibilities for daily necessities. Most men separate their domestic lives from their social lives without much problem. Having a lover outside the marriage is often regarded as a sign of manhood, and society doesn't frown upon men who visit prostitutes. It is hardly surprising that there is a lack of respect and understanding for homosexuals or emancipated women. Unaccompanied women, short skirts, or provocative shorts and tops can be perceived as a sexual challenge by Mexican men. A consistent but friendly distance and unobtrusive attire go a long way when a female traveller in Mexico wishes to avoid obnoxious teasing or aggressive come-ons. Meanwhile, change is taking place: urban women quite often display their abilities in both the family and the workforce, and many women make considerable contributions to the family income. Some Mexicans are accepting of females who acquire an education, a profession and independence. It would appear that the traditional gender stereotypes are on their way out.

Machismo

It is hard to know who ranks higher in Mexican esteem: mothers or Our Lade of Guadalupe. The national saint is a pervasive presence in Mexican life, and every day masses of people stream to her altar in the cathedral. Foreigners often marvel at expressions of Mexican religiosity: soccer players make the sign of the cross before a penalty kick and send quick prayers to the heavens; small home altars are given pride of place in the living room and small glossy pictures of saints protect cars; a Mexican may make a quick visit to a church during a lunch break. Seen globally, Mexico is a country with one of the highest percentages (90%) of Catholics, and – another Mexican contradiction – pre-Columbian traditions easily mesh with Catholic rites. In many communities, the missionaries seamlessly turned local Indian gods into Catholic saints. This worked well for the acceptance of the new religion – not to mention the new political powers. Tolerance for certain Indian traditions and holy places also helped the transition. Today, this mixture of Indian and Catholic traditions is played out at fiestas. Mexicans will even return home from foreign countries to participate for several days in lavish festivals in honour of the patron saint of their home town. Aside from Masses and pro-

Religion

cessions, there is music, dance and fireworks as well as competitions or trials of courage. A special Mexican tradition involves the yearly days of veneration of the dead on 1 and 2 November. A festive, happy mood characterizes the celebrations. The house altar is decorated with pictures or mementos of the dead and the party then proceeds to the burial place, bringing along the dead person's favourite foods. The whole family then gathers for an extended picnic at the grave site. Children and friends receive gifts of skulls, skeletons and bones made of sugar or sweet pastry. Several customs from Indian death cults have found their way into this informal and happy commemoration (Baedeker Special pp.128/129) .

Rich and poor While Mexico has gone from being a third world country to a newly industrializing country in recent decades, the country still suffers severely from the continuing discrepancy between rich and poor. Travellers to Mexico cannot help but see the drastic social conditions.

Patience: tomorrow is another day!

Mexico City is not the only city surrounded by slums of giant proportions. Hawkers harass cars waiting at red lights, while street children and beggars do their best to make a living. One of the main reasons for widespread, serious poverty is the unfair distribution of land, which in parts goes back to colonial times. Another reason is the habit of the country's wealthy elite to share the wealth only among each other: not quite 20% of the population gets more than half of all revenue. Cronyism, corruption and frozen political structures keep the system in place. People from rural areas try to flee from poverty into the cities in hope of work and a better life. The unemployment rate is high and many seek better conditions in the USA, often working there as illegal immigrants. The current average wage in Mexico is about one tenth of that in the UK or North America. Whatever is left after inflation must often sustain an entire family, something visitors may like to remember when leaving tips or bringing hostess gifts.

Mexicans face many social and economic problems in their country. This and the economic discrepancy between the USA and Mexico may often cause rather restrained reactions toward American tourists, who like to use the lower prices over the border to indulge in uninhibited drinking excursions into Mexico. When granted due respect, Mexicans will be gracious hosts. A few words of Spanish, friendly manners and respect for the country's magnificent culture will open many doors.

Time is relative in Mexico, and patience is a national virtue. Good intentions to be punctual often vanish when confronted with life's realities: there is a traffic jam in the city, the signature of the employee who just happens to be away is required, this or that little detail is missing ... In Mexico, there are many reasons for doing something mañana (tomorrow). In these situations, tips and even bribes will not help – only patience will do. While most departure times are reliable, arrivals may be delayed due to life's many imponderables, and arriving late is therefore not a sign of bad manners. As a dinner guest it is even impolite to appear at the appointed time: it will only embarrass the host. Besides, there is plenty of time for dinner among friends in Mexico.

Mañana!

Festivals, Holidays and Events

Every Mexican village or city has its own traditions of fiestas to honour patron saints. These fiestas are a mixture of ancient Indian rites, Christian traditions and people simply expressing the joy of life. To list them all would exceed the boundaries of this book, so here is a selection:

⏵ EVENTS CALENDAR

i The most beautiful fiestas and celebrations

- Carnival: lively celebrations with colourful parades or processions in Veracruz, Mérida and Mazatlán.
- Equinoccio (Equinox): watch the snake god slither down the Great Pyramid in an architectural play of light and shadow in Chichén Itzá, illumination in Dzibilchaltún.
- Feast of Corpus Christi: »Dance of the old men« (baile de los viejitos) in Pátzcuaro (Michoacàn) and the treasured ritual »voladores de Papantla« (the theme is a symbolic ceremonial dialogue between the forces of nature and humans).
- Guelaguetza (»offerings« in Zapotec): large scale dance celebration with pre-Columbian traditions in Oaxaca on the last two Mondays in July. (The offerings are to propitiate the gods who bring the necessary rain and a good harvest.)

HOLIDAYS

1 January: New Year's Day
6 January: Día de los Reyes (day of the three kings; Epiphany, Catholics celebrate the baptism of Christ)
5 February: Día de la constitución (constitution day)
21 March: birthday of the national hero and Mexican president Benito Juárez
Semana Santa (Christian holy week)
Jueves de Corpus (feast of Corpus Christi)
1 May: Día del Trabajo (Mexican Labour Day)
5 May (Cinco de Mayo): commemorates the Battle of Puebla in 1862
1 September: Day of the Nation
16 September: Día de la Independencia (independence day)

12th of October: Día de la Raza (day of the human races)
1 and 2 November: Todos los Santos, Día de los Muertos (All Saints' day, All Souls' day)
20 November: Día de la Revolución (day of the revolution)
12 December: Día de la Virgen de Guadalupe (day of Our Lady of Guadalupe)
25 December: Navidad (Christmas)

FIESTAS

⏵ New Year's Celebration
The New Year is greeted all over Mexico with festive meals, parades and processions, music and dance.

⏵ Día de los Reyes
On 6 January, the day of the magi, Mexican children put their plates out in front of the door expecting to find them filled with sweets.

⏵ Fiesta Grande
A city-wide celebration to honour various saints takes place in Chiapa de Corzo between 9 and 23 January.

⏵ San Antonio Abad
On 17 January, Mexicans all over the country bring their pets to church for a blessing and to deck them out with flowers. The ceremony is particularly beautiful in Taxco, Tlalpan and in Mexico City where great ceremonies take place in Coyoacán in the church of San Juan Bautista, in the Plaza de las Tres Culturas, in the church Santiago and in Mexico City's playground, the Floating Xochimilco Gardens

► Día de la Inmaculada Concepción (31 January)

On the day of the immaculate conception, Morelia citizens decorate their city with flowers and lights.

► Día de la Candelaria

Candlemas is celebrated everywhere in Mexico. The celebrations are particularly colourful in Cholula, Taxco and Tlacotalpan (Veracruz).

► Día de la Constitución

The Mexican constitution is celebrated all over Mexico on 5 February. Equestrian parades and bullfights are part of the festivities.

► Second half of February

Of course, carnival is celebrated everywhere in Mexico, but the carnival in the city of Veracruz is special. The carnivals in Mazatlán (►Baedeker Tip p.342), Villahermosa and Mérida are not far behind with their lavish celebrations.

► Ash Wednesday

Pilgrimage to the Señor de Sacromonte in Amecameca de Juárez (State of Mexico)

► Holy Week/Easter

Processions and pilgrimages take place in all of Mexico. Well worth seeing: the recreations of Christ's Way to the Cross in Mexico City in the suburb of Ixtapalapa on Good Friday, and all through Holy Week the passion plays near the church of Santa Prisca in Taxco.

► April

Familiar occasions are the celebration on 3 April in Izamal

Parachico dancers at the January festivals in Chiapa de Corzo

(Yucatán), the celebration of the patron saint Ildefonso two days later Ticul (Yucatán), the tobacco celebration, the corn and honey fiesta in Hopelchén (Campeche) in mid-April as well as the flower fiesta in Fortín de las Flores (Veracruz), which may sometimes be scheduled as late as mid-May.

▶ **Fería de San Marcos**
The religious celebration to honour the patron saint of the city of Aguascalientes has taken place since 1604 on 25 April. It is one of the most lively and beautiful celebrations in Mexico. With the religious celebrations over, lavish celebrations follow with bullfights, cockfights, singing, dancing and much more. The festivities begin a week ahead of the official starting date and last for three full weeks!

▶ **Día de la Santa Cruz**
On the day of the holy cross on 3 May, Mexican construction workers decorate their work sites as is the custom in Mexico. There are also celebrations with fireworks and dancing. The celebrations in Tepotzlán and Valle de Bravo are particularly beautiful.

▶ **Feria de San Isidro**
San Isidro is the patron saint of farm workers. In his honour, Mexicans all over the country decorate their working animals and bless the fields on 15 May. The celebrations in Huistan (Chiapas) offer a special attraction: the Tzotzil Indians perform dances on very long stilts.

▶ **Feast of Corpus Christi**
All over the country, Mexicans celebrate the Feast of Corpus

Christi. The children wear farmer's garb, and sing, dance and display toy donkeys made of maize husks. For eight days, the »flying men« (Voladores de Papantla) perform in Papantla (Veracruz) (▶Baedeker Special p.302).

▶ **Día de San Juan Bautista**
Mexicans celebrate the day of St John the Baptist on 24 June with entertainment, fairs and baptisms in rivers. The Maya living in the southern highlands stage a widely recognized festive flag procession in San Juan Chamula (Chiapas).

▶ **Día de Nuestra Señora del Carmen**
The day of the Holy Virgin of Mt. Carmel, also called »Virgin Carmen Day«, on 16 July is a nationwide holiday. One of the celebrations in Mexico City's district San Ángel involves a fair and a flower show.

▶ **The dance exhibition of Cuetzalán**
Another very interesting celebration is the dance exhibition of Cuetzalán from 15 to 18 July where many folklore groups from surrounding areas perform their traditional dances.

▶ **Guelaguetza**
In Oaxaca, the last two Mondays of July are reserved for harvest celebrations in honour of the maize goddess. The Guelaguetza features a combination of pre-Hispanic and Christian traditions. Indian dancers wear traditional costume.

▶ **13 August**
Two important celebrations make

Guelaguetza festival in Oaxaca

13 August extra special. A 4-day dance celebration takes place in Juchitán (Oaxaca), and in Mexico City Indians perform their traditional dances in the Square of the Three Cultures (Plaza de las Tres Culturas) to commemorate the Battle of Tenochtitlán.

▶ Assumption Day

Artistic mosaics (xocipecate) made from flowers cover the ground on 15 August in Huamantla (Tlaxcala). All over Mexico, people go on pilgrimages or celebrate with dances and fairs.

▶ San Agustín

On 20 August, the city of Tapachula (Chiapas) starts the 10 days of celebration in honour of their patron saint, Augustin

▶ Feast of the Patron Saint San Luis Potosí

Five days later, the feast days celebrating the patron saint San Luis Potosí start with the dances of the Matachines and sometimes also of the Malinches (with reference to Malinche, or by her Indian name Malintzin, a Christian convert and Cortés's mistress).

▶ Día de la Santa Rosa

The day of the Holy Rosa in San Juan Chamula is 30 August.

▶ Vela Pineda

Regional candle festivals from 3 to 5 September in Juchitán (Oaxaca)

▶ Tepozteco

Indian dance presentation inside the ruins of Tepozteco (Morelia) from 7 to 8 September

▶ Presentations of myths and legends

The dance presentation takes place on the market in Tepotztlán (Morelia) on 8 September.

For the Day of the Dead, skulls and skeletons are made of papier maché, clay, metal, wood or sugar and put on display.

FROM BEYOND THE GRAVE

For visitors, the noisy fiesta that takes place on the Day of the Dead (Día de los Muertos) may seem alien and puzzling. Decorated skulls made of icing grin at you, people wear miniature coffins as tie pins and bakers serve loaves in the shape of bones. Why then do the Mexicans treat death so utterly differently to Europeans or Americans?

The Day of the Dead (Día de los Muertos), held on 1 and 2 November each year, appears to be the climax of all the annual festivals that take place in Mexico. It coincides with the Catholic festival of All Souls but, rather than being a time for gentle contemplation of the deceased, here it sparks a huge, and occasionally rather strident, celebration. The reason for this is that in Mexico death is seen as part of life itself. Octavio Paz described the difference between Europeans or Americans and Mexicans in the following way: »To the inhabitant of New York, Paris, or London death is a word that is never uttered because it burns the lips. The Mexican, on the other hand, frequents it, mocks it, caresses it, sleeps with it, entertains it, it is one of his favourite playthings and his most enduring love.« This

attitude dates back to the days before Columbus. Back then it was believed that death is only the end of life on earth but the existence of the soul continues. The Aztecs even saw death as vital for the creation of new life. They would wage war on their allies simply to have prisoners that they could sacrifice to their gods, who would then allow the sun to remain in the sky and reward the people with a good harvest.

The end of life not of being

Nowadays death is something to be feared, but nevertheless also something to be challenged. We make our challenge and laugh in the face of death. In this way it is possible for a quite remarkable way of thinking about death to arise. For there is no need for those remaining on earth to

be saddened, instead they can look forward to being reacquainted with deceased friends and relatives.

Encounters with the dead

In the weeks before the major event, people give their imagination full rein to decorate the surroundings. At the end of October there are already icing skeletons and marzipan coffins and the traditional death loaves to be seen in the windows of bakers and confectioners. Many private homes are also decorated with skulls in the windows or with a grinning skeleton leaning in the doorway.

In the market places especially in and around Mexico City, food and other original items like decorated candles, smoke boxes, flowers and clay skulls are on sale at the markets. People clean and decorate their homes brightly then prepare splendid meals like mole, tamales desserts and, of course, calaveras or skulls. All these things are laid on an altar to the dead along with white flowers and sometimes cigarettes or a glass of tequila. The Mexicans do not actually believe that any of these things will really be drunk or eaten but they are nevertheless sure that sweet aromas and pretty colours are things that make the souls of the dead happy. To make sure that any visitors from the other side end up at the right altar, pictures of the deceased are placed on them as well.

Picnics at the graveyard

On 1 November families go to the graves of their forebears to decorate them with colourful flowers. Since those who have only died within the last year do not yet know the way to their graves a trail of petals is specially laid for them. In the evening there is then a big party. Whole families come to the cemetery to laugh, drink and enjoy a picnic. They sing songs and even talk to the deceased. It is a lively scene amongst the dead.

Día de la Independencia
On 16 September Mexicans celebrate their independence. Military parades in Mexico City with patriotic displays attract big crowds.

Día de San Miguel Arcángel
Large scale city-wide celebrations in San Miguel de Allende (Guanajuato) to honour the city's patron saint and archangel Michael on the 29th of September.

Beginning of October
Coffee celebration (2 October) and feast of San Francisco (4 October) in Cuetzalán (Puebla)

Virgen de Zapopán
The great celebration on 12 October to honour Our Lady of Zapopán in Guadalajara (Jalisco) is particularly popular. There are processions and dances as well as bullfights and cockfights. In an impressive procession, the picture of the virgin is carried from the cathedral to its place in the church of Zapopán.

Todos los Santos y Día de los Muertos
All Saints and All Souls (1 and 2 November) are among the very important Mexican holidays. Relatives and friends visit their dead at their burial places and bring gifts, food and drink. Alternatively, they may arrange a table with gifts, provisions and sometimes also with personal belongings of the dead.

People offer each other sugar skulls and the bread of the dead (pan de muertos), which is often decorated with bones made of sugar or pastry dough. The occasion is especially celebratory on the island Janitzio at Pátzcuaro Lake (► Baedeker Special pp.126/127).

Feast of the Mariachis
This feast takes place on 22 November in Zapotitlán (Jalisco)

Día de San Andrés
The day of St Andrew is celebrated with a holy cross procession on the first Sunday in December in Coyutla (Veracruz).

Día de Nuestra Señora de la Salud
On 8 December, people in Pátzcuaro (Michoacan) have a fair in honour of the Day of Our Lady of Redemption.

Día de la Virgen de Guadalupe
Mexico's highest religious holiday on 12 December is in honour of the national saint, Our Lady of Guadalupe. People come out in force for the celebrations. Many representations of folkloristic or religious nature take place in front of the Basilica of the Holy Virgin of Guadalupe in Mexico City amid a large festive crowd.

Pre-Christmas days
Mexican villages and cities arrange »posadas« from 16 to 24 December. These are processions and plays which symbolize the journey of Mary and Joseph and their search for a place to stay in Bethlehem.

Día de los Niños Inocentes
8 December is the day of the innocent children, much like the similar celebration on 1 April.

Food and Drink

Mexico offers many culinary treats, from top class restaurants with international chefs to fast food restaurants. Even street vendors offer simple foods, though for reasons of hygiene some prudence is advised before purchasing food on the street, on the beach or in buses.

True Mexican cuisine is good and inexpensive, especially at the tiled food counters (fondas) in the markets. Meals in **restaurants** usually come in generous portions and consist of several courses. The choice almost always includes a lunch menu and an often lower-priced special of the day (comida corrida).

Mexico's **meal-times** are a little later than in Western Europe: lunch is between 2pm and 4pm and dinner is generally served after 8pm.

Price categories

■ In the section »Sights from A to Z«, this travel guide recommends meal services in restaurants in the following classes (menu without beverages):

Expensive: over 290 Mex$
Moderate: 87 – 290 Mex$
Inexpensive: under 87 Mex$

Mexican Cuisine

Mexico has its own culinary traditions. Over time, Indian traditions have merged with culinary arts from various immigrant nations. Different regions have their own **local specialities**. The mainstays of the delicious recipes are usually maize (corn) and beans (► Baedeker Special p.120). However, Mexican cuisine wouldn't be Mexican cuisine without the famous **chili peppers** to supply the right kind of zest. Of course, the type, amount and preparation are of the essence, and not all chili peppers will bite back so viciously that they are inedible. Chili peppers come in all **colours, shapes and degrees of spiciness**. They may be light yellow, orange, bright red, green or brown. The »chile de árbol« (from the group of chili peppers that also includes cayenne and Tabasco peppers) is quite small and hot, while the reddish brown »chile poblano« (Pueblo pepper, the same cultivar of Capsicum annuum as bell peppers and jalapeño) is mild and quite suitable for enriching soups, stews and sauces. From Yucatán comes the »chile habanero« (Capsicum chinense), which is extremely hot, not to put too fine a point on it. Fresh and dried chili peppers may have very different attributes as far as taste, colour and shape are concerned.

Less adventurous eaters may still have difficulty finding the right meals. The larger hotels and restaurants therefore offer international cuisine.

Traditional foods, hot and not so hot

Chili peppers are available at the markets in a variety of shapes, sizes and colours, as well as dried. They can be very hot – beware!

Typical Beverages

Beer

It is the Germans that have to answer for the beer in Mexico. German immigrants to Mexico who often worked as miners in the 1900s brought the art of brewing beer with them. Today, Mexican beer is in style all over the world. The brands **Corona**, **Negra Modelo** and **Dos Equis** have in the meantime conquered the European taste buds and supermarkets. In Mexico, beer is sometimes served with a slice of lemon or lime – only to be used to cleanse the mouth of the bottle.

Tequila, mezcal and pulque

That definitely does not apply to tequila, the **ultimate Mexican speciality among alcoholic beverages**. The customary way to drink ordinary tequila is as follows: first put some salt on the back of the hand and lick it, then down all the high-proof alcohol in the glass in one swallow (if you can). Afterwards, bite into a piece of lemon or lime with conviction. Genuine tequila is made in and around a little city which goes by the telling name of Tequila (Santiago de Tequila, Jalisco) near Guadalajara where it is made from a special kind of blue agave (►Baedeker Special pp.314–317). Tequila is often the main ingredient in a cocktail.

A real temptation: a well-mixed Margarita, made from tequila, lemon juice and Cointreau or Triple Sec

Mezcal is made from one of five kinds of agave in the region of Oaxcaca. A **worm in the bottle** is considered proof of its high alcohol content. The Maya produced (the once sacred) pulque from yet another kind of agave even in ancient times. The alcohol content in pulque is low and it is still widely available.

While Mexican viniculture has a long tradition, wine is mostly exported. Wine cellars with bars (bodegas) with a good reputation exist in the north of Mexico in particular, but the wines do not reach the quality of their Californian neighbours. Mexicans are not especially keen wine drinkers. Given the opportunity though, taking a wine tasting side trip is fun and the wines go well with the spicy food.

Wine

When ordering a cup of coffee the foreign visitor usually gets a »café americano« (regular filtered coffee). What is internationally known as espresso goes by the name »café solo«, »café tinto« or »café negro« in Mexico. »Chocolate caliente« (hot chocolate) is a Mexican speciality. The old Mexican recipes for it include spices, added according to individual preference and ranging from cinnamon and vanilla to pepper and chili.

Coffee and chocolate

*A real treat: tacos and
tortillas with various fillings*

HOT, SPICY AND TASTY

In Mexico, practically every dish seems to include maize and beans. These two
ingredients can form the basis for delicacies featuring fish or meat, all served
with helpings of fruit and vegetables and topped with sauces that can range
from gently piquant to ferociously spicy. For that extra something special, try
out the traditional Mexican cuisine and its surprising combinations of spices.

Anyone who has come to know and love their local Mexican restaurant may be in for a surprise when they visit Mexico itself. What the world regards as typically Mexican is highly coloured by the American experience and particularly by the local Tex-Mex cuisine there, which differs from the Mexican original in a variety of respects. »Chili con carne«, for example, is unheard of in Mexico. There are very few such casserole dishes at all, instead the recipes tend to feature fillings, coverings and plenty of grilled food. It is the fresh ingredients and spices that give what are, after all, primarily common staples their in-comparable taste. Restaurants that offer the authentic cuisine might seem rather plain at first sight, but nevertheless serve food of the highest quality. For true Mexicans, what really matters is not only the food on the plate but also the time spent together enjoying it.

Typically Mexican

Maize is the staple foodstuff in Mexico, although it is seldom served in whole cobs or as grain. The yellow maize goes through a complex process in which it is cured, dried and finally milled into maize flour. This forms the basis for tortillas, enchiladas, tacos

and many other recipes. One special form of white maize is used to make a stew speciality by the name of pozole. Alongside maize, there is also a second key ingredient to Mexican food – beans. Commonly, black beans are used. They can be boiled, baked, grilled or fried. They are the primary providers of protein in the Mexican diet and are included in countless recipes.

No Mexican would let a day go by without eating tortillas. They are best eaten when freshly baked and can be bought as such at markets, from special bakeries or in a few top restaurants. Nevertheless, even packaged from a supermarket, these extra-thin pancakes taste fabulous. For a succulent breakfast, try some huevos rancheros, tortillas with fried egg and tomato sauce. At any other time of the day they may also be served as an appetizer in various forms, in which case they are called antojitos. Rolled

tortillas are called enchiladas and when folded they are tacos. Depending on the preparation and type of filling they may be sold as quesilladas with cheese or enfrijoladas with beans and may be accompanied by all manner of sauces and side dishes. Even dried tortillas can be magically transformed into delicious titbits. Broken into pieces and fried, they become totopos, served as a side dish to guacamole (avocado purée) or salsa, one of the many exquisite spicy sauces. Tortillas can equally well be served as an appetizer, a side dish or even as the main course. Freshly made tortilla specialities can be obtained well into the evening. Give yourself the chance to try out as many as possible.

Meat and fish

Mexican cuisine uses both pork and beef as well as plenty of poultry and lamb. The meat is often spread with

In Marisquerías, fish and seafood are on offer, mostly fresh from the sea.

spicy patés or skilfully marinated then fried or grilled. The ancient Indian methods of preparation include roasting the meat in a cooking trench dug out of the ground where it rests on stones heated in a fire and wrapped in banana or maize leaves. This gives the food a smoky aroma. At family gatherings or fiestas, you may get the chance to taste cochinita pibil (pig roasted on a spit). Many tasty tortilla fillings consist of meat minced with various vegetables. What makes many of these meat dishes so succulent is the spices that are added, such as chili, cumin, coriander, cinnamon or even dark chocolate. It is only the classic mole sauce made of nuts, chili, dark chocolate and various spices that gives the turkey in the national dish mole poblano its incomparable taste. Whenever the sea is close by Mexico has outstanding fish and seafood to offer. They are usually prepared quite simply, using a pan, oven or grill but

they are turned into something truly special by the gorgeous marinades or sauces made of vegetables, exotic fruit and spices. Mussels, shrimps and, in particular, the red snapper are properly served as pescado a la Veracruzana in tomato sauce or rustically prepared and wrapped in a covering of onions and bacon.

Fruit and vegetables

You will fall in love with Mexican markets. Amid the irresistible colours of exotic fruit and vegetables, many unknown to European cuisine, amid mountains of limes, all kinds of avocados, paprika or chili in unexpected shapes and colours, amid the pumpkins, melons, tomatoes of red, yellow and green, green bananas, papayas, quince and guava, you will simply swoon. Few, if any though, are produced or marketed directly by small farmers. Mexican agriculture is dominated by large-scale export-

oriented plantation farming, primarily supplying the American market. The Mexican may enjoy meat, but without vegetables there is no meal. They may appear in salads, side dishes, as ingredients in fillings or as the basis of sauces. There is no recipe in which they do not feature. The most popular vegetables are beans, chili, tomatoes and onions but avocados, pumpkins, potatoes and green bananas are all staples, too. Creative and traditional combinations of nuts, spices and various fruits give rise to the most luscious dishes, such as chiles en nogada, green peppers filled with minced meat and served with walnut sauce and crab apples. The chicken recipe pollo verde almendra is distinguished by a sauce made of tomatillo berries, similar to ground cherries and flavoured with almonds. Nopal or fresh cactus figs are another Mexican speciality, as is huitlacoche (Mexican corn truffle), a dark fungus that only grows on wheat. Another popular dish is ate, a fruit jelly made of quince or guava for example, cut into slices and served with cheese.

Sweets

While many Mexicans enjoy a rich and tasty meal in the form of a second breakfast at around 10am, the first meal of the day usually consists simply of coffee and sweet foods. Cuernos (croissants) or orejas (puff pastry in the shape of an ear, known as palm leaves in English) are popular, as are various biscuits as small cakes. There is also one breakfast speciality, perhaps best avoided by those counting the calories, that consists of hot chocolate into which are dipped fried churros. This has also gained popularity in Spain. Desserts include such internationally popular recipes as flans, but also various crème dishes based on chocolate, quark, fruit or eggs and often enhanced with spices.

Health

Immunizations Travellers must present a yellow fever inoculation certificate if entering Mexico from a region where this disease is prevalent. No other immunizations are required. However, immunizations against typhus (typhoid fever), tetanus, polio and precautionary treatment against hepatitis with immunoglobulins are prudent. A malaria prophylaxis for those travelling to the tropical lowlands is also a wise precaution.

Climate The Mexican climate may be stressful unless certain precautionary measures are taken. Central Europeans may not be accustomed to the elevation and suffer circulatory problems as a result. This problem is more prevalent with travellers who pack a lot of activities into the first days of their trip, eat a lot of fatty foods or drink alcohol. This is also true, incidentally, for the hot and humid lowlands. Allow a few relaxed days to acclimatize and get over the jet lag. The intense rays of the sun necessitate UV protection. Choose clothes made of light fabrics, wear a hat or cap and use sunscreen. An insect repellent is also recommended. In the tropical climate, food spoils much faster and pathogens grow quickly. This increases the **risk of stomach and intestinal ailments** (known as »Montezuma's revenge«).

Precautions Don't drink tap water under any circumstances. Most restaurants and hotels provide »agua purificado« (filtered and bottled water). The extra careful traveller may prefer to drink only mineral water (»agua mineral«) directly from its bottle. To be absolutely sure, don't brush your teeth with tap water either. Beverages with ice cubes are also a risk, and vegetables and salads should be washed with filtered water; fruit should be washed and peeled. In any case, every traveller should make up their own mind before eating fast food and the food on offer in the ubiquitous markets. It is always a good idea to have a close look at the conditions of hygiene.

Assistance If, despite all precautions, Montezuma's revenge strikes, the most important response is to lie down and drink a lot of water to compensate for the loss of liquid. A tried and tested remedy for such an ailment is the over-the-counter medicine Imodium. If the intestinal infection is accompanied by a serious fever, consult a doctor; in most

 HEALTH

▶ **Hospital Inglés (American-British Cowdray)**
Calle Sur 136, Col. Américas
01120 México 18, D.F.
Tel. (55) 52 30 80 00

▶ **Hospital México-Americano**
Colomos 2110
44100 Guadalajara (Jal.)
Tel. (33) 36 41 31 41

hotels someone will be able to refer you to one. Otherwise, contact the local tourist office or the consulate of your home country (▶diplomatic and consular representations), both of which can recommend English-speaking doctors. Always take a dictionary when visiting the doctor. The invoice for medical treatment must be paid immediately; remember to ask for a receipt.

There are hospitals with English-speaking staff in Mexico City and Guadalajara, among other places.

Hospitals (hospitales)

Aside from medicine, other items are found in pharmacies (chemist's, drugstores). Visitors may be surprised at how many drugs are available without prescription. First rate pharmacies are run by doctors.

Pharmacies (farmacias)

Information

▶ USEFUL ADDRESSES

TOURISM BOARD IN MEXICO

▶ **Hotline**
Tel. 01 800 90 39 28
(Information or help in English and Spanish)

▶ **Ministry of Tourism SECTUR**
Secretaría de Turismo
Av. Presidente Masaryk 172
11587 México, D.F.
Tel. (55) 30 02 63 00

Hotline (span./engl.)
Tel. (55) 250 01 23, 250 05 89
www.sectur.gob.mx

IN CANADA

▶ **Mexican Tourism Board Montreal**
1 Place Ville Marie, Suite 1931
Montreal, Quebec H3B 2C3
Tel. (514) 871 1103
Fax. (514) 871 3825
www.visitmexico.com

IN THE UNITED KINGDOM

▶ **Mexican Tourism Board London**
1 Trinity Square, Wakefield House
London EC3N 4DJ
Tel. (020) 7488 9392
Fax (020) 7265 0704
www.visitmexico.com

IN THE USA

▶ **Mexican Tourism Board New York**
400 Madison Avenue, Suite 11C
New York, NY 10017
Tel. (212) 308 21 10 ext. 103
Fax. (212) 308 90 60
www.visitmexico.com

EMBASSIES IN MEXICO

▶ **Australian Embassy**
Ruben Dario 55, Col. Polanco
Mexico D.F.
Tel. 1101 2200
Fax. 1101 2201
www.mexico.embassy.gov.au

▶ **Embassy of Canada**
Schiller 529, Col. Polanco
11560 México City
Tel. (55) 57 24 79 00
Fax. (55) 5724-7980
www.canada.org.mx

▶ **Embassy of the Republic
of Ireland**
Cda. Boulevard Avila Camacho
76-3, Col. Lomas de Chapultepec
C.P. 11000, México, D.F.
Tel. (55) 5520 5803
Fax. (55) 5520 5892
Email: embajada@irlanda.org.mx

▶ **British Embassy**
Río Lerma 71, Col Cuauhtémoc
06500 México DF
Tel. (55) 52 42 85 00
Fax. (55) 5242 8517
www.britishembassy.gov.uk/
mexico

▶ **US Embassy**
Paseo de la Reforma 305
Col. Cuauhtemoc
06500 Mexico, D.F
Tel. (55) 50 80 20 00
www.mexico.usembassy.com

MEXICAN EMBASSIES

▶ **Australia**
14 Perth Ave
Yarralulma, ACT 2600
Tel. (02) 62 73 39 63
www.mexico.org.au

▶ **Canada**
45 O'Connor Suite 1000
Ottawa, Ontario K1P 1A4
Tel. (613) 233 89 88
www.embamexcan.com

▶ **Republic of Ireland**
43 Ailesbury Rd, Ballsbridge
Dublin 4

Very popular in Mexico: in the cities, new internet cafés open every day.

Tel. 01 260 0699
www.sre.gob.mx/irlanda

► **United Kingdom**
42 Hertford Street, Mayfair
London W1Y 7TF
Tel. (020) 74 99 85 86
www.embamex.co.uk

► **USA**
1911 Pennsylvania Av.
Washington DC 20006
Tel. (202) 72 81 60
Fax. (202) 728 1698
www.sre.gob.mx/eua

INTERNET

► **www.mexconnect.com**
In-depth information on Mexico;
features, articles and forums

► **www.mexicotravel.net**
Extensive information on all
regions of Mexico – from accommodation, sports, and traditional
fiestas, to Spanish courses and
honeymoon arrangements.

► **www.arts-history.mx**
Background information on cultural themes, museums (Spanish)

► **www.mayadiscovery.com**
Website of the magazine Mundo
Maya (English and Spanish)

► **www.visitmexico.com**
Website of the Mexican Tourism
Board with information on sporting activities, ecotourism, arts and
crafts, architecture and much
more

Language

SPANISH LANGUAGE GUIDE

At a glance

Yes./No.	Sí./No.
Maybe./Probably.	Quizás./Tal vez.
Sure!/OK	¡De acuerdo!/¡Está bien!
Please./Thank you.	Por favor./Gracias.
Thank you very much.	Muchas gracias.
You're welcome.	No hay de qué./De nada.
Excuse me, please!	¡Perdón!
Can you please repeat that?	¿Cómo dice/dices?
I don't understand.	No le/la/te entiendo.
I only speak a little…	Hablo sólo un poco de…
Could you please help me?	¿Puede usted ayudarme, por favor?
I'd like…	Quiero ?/Quisiera ?
I (don't) like it.	(No) me gusta.

Do you have…?	¿Tiene usted ??
How much is this?	¿Cuánto cuesta?
What time is it?	¿Qué hora es?

Social interaction/Greetings

Good morning!	¡Buenos días!
Good day!	¡Buenos días!/¡Buenos tardes!
Good evening!	¡Buenos tardes!/¡Buenos noches!
Hello! Hi!	¡Hola!
My name is…	Me llamo…
What's your name, please?	¿Cómo se llama usted, por favor?
How are you?	¿Qué tal está usted?/¿Qué tal?
I'm fine, thanks. How are you?	Bien, gracias. ¿Y usted/tú?
Good bye!	¡Hasta la vista!/¡Adiós!
See you!/Take care!	¡Adiós!/¡Hasta luego!
See you soon!	¡Hasta pronto!
See you tomorrow!	¡Hasta mañana!

En Route

left/right	a la izquierda/a la derecha
straight ahead	todo seguido/derecho
near/far	cerca/lejos
How far is it?	¿A qué distancia está?
I'd like to rent…	Quisiera alquilar…
a car	un coche.
a boat	una barca/un bote/un barco.
Excuse me, where do I find…?	Perdón, dónde está…?
the railway station?	la estación (de trenes)?
the bus stop?	la estación de autobuses/ la terminal?
the airport?	el aeropuerto?

Car breakdown

My car's broken down.	Tengo una avería.
Would you please send me a tow truck?	¿Pueden ustedes enviarme un cochegrúa, por favor?
Where is the next garage, please?	¿Hay algún taller por aquí cerca?
Where is the next petrol station, please?	¿Dónde está la estación de servicio/a gasolinera más cercana, por favor?
I'd like … litres of ?	Quisiera ? litros de ?
regular petrol	gasolina normal.

... super./ diesel.	... súper./ diesel.
... unleaded./ ?leaded.	... sin plomo./ con plomo.
Fill her up, please.	Lleno, por favor.

Accident

Help!	¡Ayuda!, ¡Socorro!
Look out!	¡Atención!
Careful!	¡Cuidado!
Please call.... quickly! ?	Llame enseguida ?
... an ambulance.	... una ambulancia.
... the police.	... a la policía.
... the fire brigade (fire department).	... a los bomberos.
Do you have a first aid kit?	¿Tiene usted botiquín de urgencia?
It was my fault.	Ha sido por mi (su) culpa.
Would you please let me have your name and your address?	¿Puede usted darme su nombre y dirección?

Food

Please, where can I find?	¿Dónde hay por aquí cerca ?
... a good restaurant?	... un buen restaurante?
... an inexpensive restaurant?	... un restaurante no demasiado caro?
I'd like to make a reservation for a table tonight for 4 people.	¿Puede reservarnos para esta noche una mesa para cuatro personas
To your health!/Cheers!	¡Salud!
The bill please!	¡La cuenta, por favor!
Did you enjoy your meal?	¿Le/Les ha gustado la comida?
Excellent, thank you very much!	La comida estaba écelente.

Shopping

Please, where can I find ...	Por favor, dónde hay ?
... a market?	... un mercado?
... a pharmacy/drugstore/chemist's?	... una farmacia?
... a shopping centre?	... un centro comercial?

Accommodation

Excuse me. Can you please recommend…?	Perdón, señor/señora/señorita. Podría usted recomendarme ?

¿Cuánto cuestan las flores? How much are the flowers?

... a hotel	... un hotel?
... a small bed and breakfast?	... una pensión?
I have a reservation for a room.	He reservado una habitación.
Do you still have a vacancy for ?	¿Tienen ustedes ?
... a single room?	... una habitación individual?
... a room with two beds?	... una habitación doble?
... with a shower/bath?	... con ducha/baño?
... for one night?	... para una noche?
... for one week?	... para una semana?
How much is the room with ?	¿Cuánto cuesta la habitación con
... breakfast?	... desayuno?
... half-board?	... media pensión?

Doctor

Can you recommend a good doctor?	¿Puede usted indicarme un buen médico?

I have ? . . . . Tengo ?
   ... diarrhoea. . . . . diarrea.
   ... a fever. . . . . fiebre.
   ... a headache. . . . . dolor de cabeza.

Bank

Please, where can I find ? . . . . Por favor, dónde hay por aquí ?
   ... a bank? . . . . un banco?
   ... a bureau de change? . . . . una oficina/casa de cambio?
I would like to exchange British pounds   Quisiera cambiar ?
     into pesos. . . . . libra esterlina en pesos.

Post office

How much is a stamp ? . . . . ¿Cuánto cuesta ?
   ... for a letter ? . . . . una carta ?
   ... for a post card ? . . . . una postal ?

How many balloons are there?

to England?	para Inglaterra?
postage stamps	sellos
prepaid phone cards	tarjetas para el teléfono

Numbers

0	cero	11	once
1	un, uno, una	12	doce
2	dos	13	trece
3	tres	14	catorce
4	cuatro	15	quince
5	cinco	16	dieciséis
6	seis	17	diecisiete
7	siete	18	dieciocho
8	ocho	19	diecinueve
9	nueve	20	veinte
10	diez	21	veintiuno(a)
22	veintidós	100	cien, ciento
30	treinta	200	doscientos, -as
40	cuarenta	1000	mil
50	cincuenta	2000	dos mil
60	sesenta	10 000	diez mil
70	setenta	1/2	medio
80	ochenta	1/4	un cuatro
90	noventa		

Restaurante/Restaurant

desayuno	breakfast
almuerzo, comida	lunch
cena	dinner
camarero	waiter
cubierto	plates, cutlery (silverware, flatware)
cuchara	spoon
cucharita	teaspoon
cuchillo	knife
lista de comida	menu
plato	plate
sacacorchos	corkscrew
tenedor	fork
taza	cup
vaso	glass

Desayuno/Breakfast

café américano	white coffee/coffee and cream
café con leche	latte/white coffee
café negro	black coffee
café descafeinado	decaffeinated coffee
té con leche/limón	tea with milk/lemon
chocolate	chocolate
jugo de fruta	fruit juice
huevo tibio	soft-boiled egg
huevos rancheros	fried eggs on a burrito with Mexican sauce
huevos revueltos	scrambled eggs
pan/bolillo/pan tostado	bread/bread roll/toast
bizcocho/pan de dulce	sweet pastry
churros	fritters/fried pastry
mantequilla	butter
queso	cheese
carnes frías	cold cuts
paté/jamón	ham
miel	honey
mermelada	jam/fruit spread

Entradas, Sopas / Appetizers, Soups

botana mexicana	pickled vegetables with chili
caldo de camarón	shrimp broth
camarones al ajillo	shrimp with garlic sauce
ceviche	fish/seafood cocktail
consomé de pollo/res	chicken/beef broth
crema de elote	creamed corn
crema del día	soup of the day
ensalada de nopales	salad made from prickly pear pads
sopa de ajo	garlic soup
sopa de fideos	noodle soup
sopa de pescado	fish soup/chowder
sopa de tortilla	burrito and tortilla chips soup
sopa de verduras/sopa juliana	vegetable soup
tortilla	burritos

Pescados y Mariscos/Seafood and Fish

atún	tuna/bonito
bacalao	codfish, stockfish (dried cod)
camarones	shrimp
dorado	ocean perch
huachinango	redfish
langostinos	crayfish

A hearty breakfast: huevos rancheros

lenguado	sole
ostras	oysters
pulpo	octopus
róbalo	sea perch, sea bass
salmón	salmon
trucha	trout

Carne y Aves/Meat and Poultry

asado	roast
bistec	thin breaded cutlet (Viennese schnitzel)
cabrito	kid (goatling)
carne molida	minced (ground) meat (hamburger)
cerdo/puerco	pork
chuleta	cutlet
cocido/puchero	stew (meat and vegetables)
conejo	rabbit
cordero	lamb, mutton
guisado	goulash, ragout
hamburguesa	hamburger
hígado	liver
lechón	suckling-pig
lengua	tongue
lomo/filete	sirloin, tenderloin
milanesa	breaded cutlet
parrillada	grill platter (meat, BBQ)
pato	duck

pavo/guajolote	turkey
pollo/gallina	chicken
res	beef
ternera	veal

Ensalada y Verduras/Salad and Vegetables

aguacate	avocado
berenjenas	aubergine (eggplant)
calabacitas	zucchini
camote	sweet potato (yam)
cebollas	onions
chícharos	peas
chile verde	fresh green pepper
cilantro	fresh coriander/cilantro
colecitas de Bruselas	Brussels sprouts
coliflor	cauliflower
ejotes/fríjoles	green beans or string beans/pinto beans
elote	corn on the cob
espárragos	asparagus
hongos/champiñones	mushrooms/champignons
jítomate	(red) tomatoes
lechuga	lettuce
maíz	maize/corn
papas	potatoes
patatas fritas	French fries/chips
pepinos	cucumbers
perejil	parsley
pimiento morrón	fresh paprika
plátano macho	plantain
tomates	green tomatoes

Postres, Helados, Pasteles/Desserts, Ice Cream, Pastry

arroz con leche	rice pudding
ate con queso	quince jelly with Manchego cheese
buñuelos	thin doughnuts with syrup
café helado/copa de helado	coffee ice/sundae
crema	heavy cream
donas	crullers/doughnuts
dulces	sweets/desserts
flan	crème caramel
frutas en almíbar	stewed fruit
galletas	biscuits (cookies/crackers)
gelatina	jelly/jello
helados	ice cream

nieve .... sorbet
panqué .... pound cake
pastel/pay de frutas .... cake/fruit flan/tart

Antojitos Mexicanos/Snacks

barbacoa .... mutton (wrapped in agave leaves and cooked in an earth oven)
burritas .... wheat burritos with ham and cheese
chalupas .... small tortillas with a very spicy sauce
chilaquiles .... tortilla chips with a zesty sauce, cheese and heavy cream
enchiladas .... enchiladas filled with different sauces or cheeses
guacamole .... guacamole (creamed avocado)
menude .... savoury tripe stew (tripe: stomach lining from ruminants, an acquired taste!)

Making tortillas

mole poblano	thick brown sauce with more than 20 ingredients
panuchos	fried corn tortillas with pinto beans and sauce
pozole	maize (corn) stew with pork, chili and onions
quesadillas	fried filled corn tortillas
tacos	tacos (filled tortilla rolls)
tamales	tamales (spicy mixture of chopped meat and crushed peppers wrapped in corn husks and spread with masa)
tostadas	tostadas (fried tortillas, spread with creamed beans, beef or chicken, cheese and salad)
tortas	Mexican sandwich, i.e. a crusty sandwich (bolillo or telera), generously filled with meat, cheeses and vegetables according to taste (hot or cold)
tortillas	maize (corn) tortillas

Bebidas/Beverages

botella	bottle
cerveza clara/obscura	light/dark beer
copa	glass/shot glass/small glass
margarita	margarita (lime juice, ice cubes and tequila)
mezcal/tequila	mezcal/tequila (double or triple distilled high proof alcohol from different types of agave)
pulque	traditional agave drink with low alcohol content
sidra	cider/apple cider
vaso	glass
vino	wine
blanco/tinto	white/red
rosado	rosé
seco/dulce	dry/sweet
agua mineral	mineral water
con/sin gas	carbonated/still
cerveza	beer
café de olla	strong coffee with cinnamon
horchata	rice milk
leche	milk
refresco	refreshing beverage
limonada	fresh lemonade
jugo de zanahória	carrot juice
jugo de naranja	orange juice
licuado de agua	mixed fruit and water

Literature · Movies

Michael Coe: *Reading the Maya Glyphs* and *Breaking the Maya Code* (Thames & 2 Rev Ed edition, 1996). This is a very good description of the Book of the Council, the Mayan creation story, the legends and the theology of the Quiché Maya.

Nigel Davies: *The Aztecs, a history* (Univ of Oklahoma Pr; New Ed edition, 1980) A lively Aztec political history, one of Davies's many books on Aztec and Toltec cultures)

Linda Schele/David Friedel: *A Forest of Kings: The Untold Story of the Ancient Maya* (William Morrow; Reprint edition, 1993). The well-known archaeologists and hieroglyph researchers have revolutionized and popularized the way we read about the Maya.

Hernán Cortés: *The Dispatches of Hernando Cortes Addressed to the Emperor Charles V During the Conquest* (Kessinger Publishing, 2005). A report of the conquest of Tenochtitlán and the life of the Aztec as seen by the conquistador Hernán Cortés. Edited and translated by George Folsom.

Pre-Columbian cultures and mythology

The conquest of Mexico

Viva Zapata: Chihuahua-born Anthony Quinn received his first Oscar in 1953 for his portrayal of Zapata's brother. Marlon Brando was honoured in Cannes as best leading actor.

i Recommended films

- *Amores Perros* (2002): three interrelated stories of everyday life from the moloch that is Mexico City.
- *Like Water for Chocolate*: a tragic love story interspersed with culinary treats. The backdrop to the story is the Mexican revolution.
- *Frida* (2003): the painter Frida Kahlo (played by Salma Hayek) and the famous fresco painter and communist intellectual Diego Rivera were quite a colourful pair. Actually, they may have been the most unique couple in the history of art.
- *Once Upon a Time in Mexico* (2003): actor Antonio Banderas as El Mariachi once again shoots his way through chaotic events. This is the third, and most elaborate part of the Mexico trilogy (*El Mariachi*, *Desperado*) by Robert Rodriguez.
- *Los Olvidados* (1950): Luis Buñuels's masterpiece about a gang of stray youngsters roaming the slums of Mexico City.
- *The Mexican* (2001): a mixture of road movie, love story and action comedy starring Julia Roberts and Brad Pitt.
- *Viva Zapata* (1951): a fictionalized version of the peasant Emiliano Zapata's rise to become a national hero – starring Marlon Brando in the title role.

Bernal Díaz del Castillo: *The Conquest of New Spain* (Penguin Books Ltd; New Impression edition, 1969) This is a very interesting and lively account of the conquest written by a simple soldier and companion in arms of Hernán Cortés.

William Prescott: *History of the Conquest of Mexico* (Cooper Square Press, 2000). This is still the most profound history of the conquest.

Bernardino de Sahagún: *Florentine Codex: General History of the Things of New Spain. Introductions and Indices* (Monographs of the School of American Research, University of Utah Press, 1982).
Authoritative writings of the famous monk about the Aztec after the conquest.

Recent history and the present: Tony Cohan: *On Mexican Time: A New Life in San Miguel* (New York: Broadway Books, 2000). The famous writer perceptively and with humour describes his everyday experiences during his move from California to a small Mexican town.

Andrés Oppenheimer: *Bordering on Chaos: Mexico's Roller-Coaster Journey Toward Peace* (Little, Brown, 1998). The best informed account of Mexican national politics (1993–1996) by the former correspondent of the Miami Herald.

Alan Riding: *Distant Neighbors: A Portrait of the Mexicans* (Vintage Books USA; Reissue edition, 1989). A study of Mexico's politics, society, economy and culture, and an attempt to find out what makes Mexicans tick.

Novels **Laura Esquivel:** *Like Water for Chocolate* (Black Swan, 1993). A funny and sensitive story woven around the magical effects of Mexican cuisine with traditional recipes after every chapter.
The book was made into a movie; both book and movie were a huge success.

Carlos Fuentes: *The Old Gringo* (HarperPerennial). The Mexican writer Carlos Fuentes is also known outside his native country's borders. The basis for this book is the mysterious disappearance and ensuing fate of the US author Ambrose Bierce during the Mexican revolution.

Graham Greene: *The Power and the Glory* (Vintage; New Ed edition, 2001). This is the tragic story of a priest during the time of religious persecution in Mexico.

Juan Rulfo: *Pedro Páramo* (Serpent's Tail; New Ed edition, 2000). The author of the so-called »new« novel uses his mighty linguistic skills to write about the times of revolution. In January of 2000, the author received the award for the best novel in the Spanish language of the century.

Frida Kahlo: *Frida Kahlo: An Intimate Self-Portrait* (Harry N. Abrams, Inc., 2006). The book includes a remarkable introduction by the world-renowned Mexican writer Carlos Fuentes.

Art and culture

Elizabeth Wilder Weismann: *Art and Time in Mexico* (New York: Harper & Row, 1985). Interesting texts and excellent photographs of religious, public and private Mexican architecture.

Money

The Mexican currency is the **peso** with the short symbol $ – not to be mistaken for the US dollar with the same symbol.
Denominations for bank notes are 20, 50, 100, 200 or 500 pesos. Coins come in 5, 10, 20 or 50 centavos and 1, 2 or 5 pesos.
It is practical to always have a small amount of cash in small denominations at hand for tips and small purchases. Bus and taxi drivers or vendors often do not have enough change to break a larger bank note.

The **currency exchange rate** is based on the US dollar and fluctuates on the free market against the euro and other European currencies. Tourist currencies are accepted at a US$-oriented exchange rate.

According to the **currency regulations** in Mexico, the import and export of more than US$ 10,000 in foreign or Mexican currency must be registered.

It is possible to **change currency** at banks and in some hotels. However, money can be exchanged more straightforwardly in one of the

▶ **British pounds**
1 mx peso =
0.05 British pounds
1 British pound =
21.7 mx pesos

▶ **US-Dollar**
1 mx peso = 0.09 US $
1 US-$ = 10.98 mx pesos

▶ **Euro**
1 mx peso = 0.07 euros
1 euro = 14.7 mx pesos

many casas de cambio (small bureaux de change). It is best to take along some traveller's cheques in US dollars and a few US dollars in cash. European currencies are more difficult to exchange.

Banks The most important Mexican banks are the Banco Nacional de México (BANAMEX), Bancomer, Banco Bital, Banco del Atlántico and Serfin. In general, banks are open Monday to Friday from 9am to 1:30pm. The offices of some larger banks are open to 5pm and maybe even on Saturdays from 9am to 12 noon.

Credit cards and cash cards Hotels, restaurants, car rental agencies, larger or high-end stores and large chain stores accept major credit cards. Away from major tourist centres, credit card payments are not possible. Fortunately, there is an increasing number of **automatic cash dispensers** in Mexico which enable visitors to withdraw money via credit card or cash card.

Lost or stolen cards In the case of a card being lost or stolen, call the international emergency service number on the back of your credit card without delay. The Visa Global Card Assistance Service will arrange for lost visa cards to be cancelled: in Mexico, call 001-800-847-2911 for this free and multi-lingual service.

Newspapers

Newspapers, magazines The newspaper industry in Mexico is quite active, both on a regional and international level. There are also two English-language daily newspapers, the *Mexico City Times* and the *Mexico City - The News*. These newspapers are available everywhere in Mexico and report on home and international topics; they also include an events calendar for Mexico City. A few of the many daily newspapers are *El Universal* and *Excelsior* (news and commentary), *El Financiero* (financial news) and *La Jornada* (an independent newspaper, critical of the government). European and US newspapers are available in Mexico City and sometimes (irregularly) also in major vacation spots, though they may be a few days old and fairly expensive.

Post and Communications

Different postage stamps are required for **postcards** (tarjeta postal) and **letters** (carta) via airmail (correo aéreo, por avión) to Europe. Mail delivery to Europe will take about two to three weeks. The cost of stamps may change several times a year, and it is therefore not very helpful to publish the rates in this travel guide. The current rates are displayed in post offices. For safe delivery it is best to post the properly stamped mail into a postbox (buzón) at the post office rather than using a postbox in the street. Sending a **package** (paquete) to Europe by ship from Mexico may take three to five months, though sending packages by airmail is quite expensive. **Mail sent poste restante** to Mexico must be marked »lista de correos« and addressed to a specific post office; it must be claimed within ten days. Post offices are usually open Monday to Friday from 9am to 6pm and on Saturdays from 9am to 1pm.

Post

Prepaid Ladatel phone cards, for both local and long distance phone calls, are available from telephone offices and stores near public telephones or next to railway stations or airports. Coin-operated telephones have become very rare. **Long distance calls** (larga distancia) can be made using public telephones bearing the label »Ladatel«. Alternatively, use one of the »oficina de larga distancia« (long distance offices) which operate almost everywhere. In these offices, calls are put through manually, including calls to foreign countries. After giving the desired phone number to the clerk, the caller waits until the connection is established, at which point the clerk will notify the caller and assign them a telephone booth. Some stores and pharmacies have »casetas de larga distancia«, i.e. blue telephones especially for long distance calls; they also work for inland long distance calls. Phone calls to foreign countries are very expensive: charges apply for every new 3-minute unit whether you use the entire 3-minute interval or not, and value added tax (VAT) of 15 % is added. Hotels apply an additional hefty charge. It is possible to ask the operator what the estimated costs for a telephone call will be. European **mobile phones** are incompatible with the standard Mexican mobile network. There

Telephone

► INTERNATIONAL DIALLING CODES

► **from Mexico**
   to UK: Tel. 00 44
   to the USA: Tel. 00 1
   to Australia: Tel. 00 61
   to Canada: Tel. 00 1
   to Republic of Ireland: Tel. 00 353

► **calling Mexico**
   Tel. 00 52, then area code
   without the 0

There are public telephones in abundance in Mexico.

are rare exceptions (triband), but often these connections do not cover a sufficient network area to be useful. Telcel (www.telcel.com) provides the usual AMPS net (advanced mobile phone services, provider IUSACELL, www.iusacell.com.mx) and the digital GSM net (GSM 1900, global system for mobile communications). Travellers can rent a local mobile phone for the duration of their stay.

Email and internet
Internet cafés are springing up in all tourist destinations. Tourist offices or hotel clerks will provide you with the addresses.

Telegram services and fax
Telegram services (telegrama) are not part of the postal services. Telegrams are handled by offices for this specific purpose (oficinas de telégrafos). Larger hotels provide fax connections.

Prices

▶ PRICES

Double room
665 – 1330 mx peso

3-course meal
from 120 mx peso

Simple meal
27 – 40 mx peso

Drink
20 – 27 mx peso

Petrol (1 l)
9 mx peso

**Trip by bus
(100 km/60 mi)**
from 133 mx Peso

Safety

Travellers to Mexico are in no more danger than in many other countries. Nevertheless – Mexico is by no means completely safe. The usual precautions also apply when travelling in Mexico: be sure to leave cash and valuables in the hotel safe, and don't carry more cash than necessary; keep wallets and documents in a place that is not easily accessible; and don't have an expensive camera or handbag hanging loosely around your neck. If more cash is required, use traveller's cheques or credit cards, which can be used all over the country. Conveniently, most credit card companies will issue a replacement card within 24 hours. Leave your travel documents (ID, passport and tourist card) in the hotel safe if possible and carry legible copies instead. Use cash dispensers only when accompanied and not after sunset.

Take the usual safety precautions!

In Mexico City, only use cabs from official taxi companies (sitios); important indicators for a reputable taxi service are a functional meter and a certificate with the name of the taxi driver. Interurban travel – particularly when using roads through remote areas – can be dangerous due to increased incidents of robbery by armed gangs. The southern states Guerrero, Oaxaca and Chiapas are sadly infamous for such crimes. Use buses if possible only during daylight hours and do not consider hitchhiking. This is not common practice in Mexico and therefore particularly dangerous.

Most drugs sold in the USA either come from Mexico (marihuana and heroin) or come through Mexico (cocaine). Opium poppy, the raw material for heroin production, is cultivated especially in those Mexican federal states that border the USA, such as Baja California, Sonora or Chihuahua, amongst others. Mexican law prohibits the use of drugs. Yielding to pressure from the USA, the police vigorously enforce the laws against cultivation, smuggling and possession of even the smallest amounts. Travellers, and in particular younger single travellers, must be prepared to be searched and have their luggage searched when crossing the Mexican border but also while in the country. The best advice is not to carry drugs at any time, not even small amounts for personal use.

Drugs

Shopping

Mexican retail stores don't have generally applicable business hours (horarios). Stores are often open late at night and sometimes even on Sundays. In hot regions, the time between 2pm and 5pm is reserved for an afternoon break.

Business hours

People like to bring home various arts and crafts objects as memen-tos. It is best to buy these items where they are made or at markets. It is not prudent to buy silver and gold items from street vendors. Again, the manufacturers of such items or reputable stores are good sources (especially in Taxco). Genuine silver displays a stamp (»Ster-ling« or »925«).

Souvenirs

The export of antique items is against the law, so buying them is in any case ill advised. However, the National Museum of Anthropology in Mexico City sells excellent replicas. At archaeological sites visitors may be offered what the seller calls a »major archaeological find«. All these so-called finds are fakes, often hastily buried shortly before-hand. Because the art of making ceramic items has been kept alive to this day, even experts have a hard time distinguishing the fakes from the real antiques.

Antiques

The quality and creativity of Mexi-can **arts and crafts** is second to no-ne. While there has been a trend toward the industrial manufacture of goods of lesser quality, opportu-nities to buy high-class, creative artwork are still plentiful. Like most means of human expression in Mexico, the arts and crafts also display the delightful merging of Mexican and Spanish elements. Many regions have developed artis-tic styles of their own. There is a range of creative art objects to be discovered in the countryside to suit every taste and wallet.

> **? DID YOU KNOW ...?**
>
> ■ ... that Talavera originated in Spain? The invading Spaniards brought with them their Iberian arts, among them the art of making coloured clay pottery called Talavera. Home of the Talavera art was a city near Toledo of the name Talavera de la Reina. No sooner was the technique imported, than the clay items had become common articles in Mexican everyday life. Among the early centres of Talavera manufacture are Dolores Hidalgo and Puebla, and to this day many manufacturing plants produce these traditional ceramics, not only tiles but also vases, washbasins and more. Located just outside Puebla, the company Manufaktur Uriarte (Ave. 4 Poniente No. 911) has been making Talavera ceramics since 1827, and offers visitors the chance to watch the manufacturing process. Guided tours take place from Monday to Friday at 11am and 1pm (telephone: 222/232 15 98).

Ceramics (cerámica) come in many different forms. The pottery from the federal state of Michoacán is very beautiful, as are the green ceramics of the Tarasca. The off-white/white/black patterns used in Tzintzuntzán may appeal to some, while in the Puebla region the azulejos, i.e. yellow-and-blue wall tiles in arabesque patterns, Talave-ra pottery and the tree of life sculptures (see p.571) are to be found. In Oaxaca, black vases are produced with an almost metallic sheen. The best known of all are the ceramics from the pottery village Tona-lá, where people diligently paint the ceramics with bright colours. In

← *A rich and colourful variety of textiles and other souvenirs from Mexico*

Chiapas, small clay animal figures (animalitos) are manufactured and children sell them in the streets.

Weaving and embroidery The elaborately woven textiles are bound to make a strong impression. Indian women make the traditional wide blouses (huipiles), scarves, skirts, dresses, napkins and tablecloths. It pays to obtain these treasures directly from the diligent hands of the women rather than buying them at much higher prices in stores. The prices vary by a wide margin, often explained by differences in material, pattern and the complexity of the embroidery.

Silver Silver was already being worked in Mexico in pre-Hispanic times. The city of Taxco, south of Mexico City, is famous as the silver city. Here, silversmiths create beautiful pieces of jewellery from the precious metal. Silver rings, earrings, chains and belt buckles are often studded with coral and turquoises.

Always an eye-catcher: whether as sun-protection, decoration or as an unusual gift

The artisans of Santa Clara del Cobre famously work with copper. The Tarasca manufacture very beautiful vessels, pans and plates from the metal. Religious images (milagros) are often formed from tin-plate. Because it is easy to work with this material, it is used to produce tree-of-life sculptures with symbolic birds or fruit motifs, mirror frames and candle holders.

Items made from onyx are mostly made for tourists or exported. The precious stone is often used to make chess sets, bookends and figurines.

Metals and precious stones

The market (mercado) is one of the central elements in the daily lives of Mexicans. When the Spanish conquistadores first saw the Aztec markets even they were impressed by their size, scope, the variety of traded goods and in particular their perfect organization. To this day, markets in Mexico proceed much more calmly than elsewhere in South America. Haggling about the price of goods is common practice; it is even expected. There is an impressive abundance of goods, including handcrafted items, folk art, flowers, fruit and vegetables. Indian travelling markets are called »tianguis«.

Markets

Beautiful wood carvings and lacquered wood items make reasonably priced souvenirs. Such goods are a regional speciality around Uruapán where traders offer lacquered and painted wood items, ranging from small boxes to chests and bowls, as well as small painted wooden animal figures from Oaxaca. A hammock (hamacas, see p.346) is another typical present to bring home from Mexico, its very look conjuring up images of holidays and relaxation.

Souvenirs

Sports

Mexico offers not only beaches and ancient ruins but also many opportunities to be active. Surfing and diving naturally come at the top of this list of activities, but there is also golf (mostly in Baja California and Acapulco), biking, mountain climbing and white-water rafting. The national parks (Chipinque, Cumbresde, el Salto) around Monterrey are the Eldorado of mountain bikers. Mountain climbers can challenge themselves on the steep sides of the Canyon de la Huasteco, south-west of Monterrey, a favourite location for climbers in Mexico. Rafters discover spectacular opportunities to navigate the Río Filobobos around the El Canbot Waterfall in Veracruz.

More than beaches and ancient ruins

The inland reservoirs offer opportunities for practically all aquatic sports (deportes acuáticos), such as boating, sailing, windsurfing, water skiing etc. On the Pacific coast (west coast of Lower California and the continental coast south of Mazatlán) the strong swell from

Aquatic sports

the open ocean provides good conditions for surfing. There are very good opportunities to go diving (buceo). Snorkellers and divers find excellent waters particularly in Acapulco, Akumal, Cancún, Cozumel, at the Chinchorro Banks Reef in Quintana Roo, in Huatulco, Los Cabos, Paamul, Playa del Carmen, Puerto Escondido, Puerto Vallarta and Zihuatanejo. The flora and fauna of the coral reefs in these places provide magnificent images for underwater photography.

Extreme sports have rapidly grown into favoured tourist attractions. An example is the sport of **rafting** in Veracruz, San Luis Potosí, Chiapas and other Mexican states. The very popular centre for this sport is Jacomulco on the banks of the Río Pescados; for more than five years now, tour guides have been taking travellers down the in parts raging river. However, the less adventurous can opt for less difficult rides. Pescados river rides come in five degrees of difficulty (from I–V on the international scale), covering the range from a contemplative trip along the river to very challenging rides down wild rapids (mostly after the rainy season). It is possible to book day trips or expeditions spending a few nights in a tent on the river banks.

Fish are abundant in the Mexican coastal waters and the continental Fishing shelf zones, a fact much appreciated by offshore anglers. Angling for large fish by boat is very popular. Harpoons and spears are not permitted. Freshwater fishing is not very common because few Mexican rivers carry water all year.
Some reservoirs and lakes are however quite suitable for fishing. The sport of fishing is regulated in Mexico. Please enquire about the rules with the appropriate tourist office.

Tourism has made tennis much more popular in Mexico. It is no Tennis longer the sport of the privileged lounging in private clubs. Many of the larger hotels feature well-maintained tennis courts. Local tennis clubs may welcome visitors as a guest player.

Golf courses are mostly run by local clubs or hotels. Most of them Golf are located near larger cities and in tourist centres, such as Acapulco,

i **Recommendations**

- Surfing: popular waters on the long Pacific shores and offshore Yucatán
- Diving and snorkelling: rich underwater world, aficionados are drawn to the eastern Yucatán coast
- White-water rafting: numerous wild rivers in the Mexican highlands
- Mountain climbing and hiking: climbing the Pico de Orizaba and hiking tours of several days across the Copper Canyon (Barranca del Cobre) are very special experiences.
- Nature tours: learn about the Mexican environment and particularly the flora and fauna in new ways.

← *The best surfing areas lie on the Oaxaca coast and in Baja California, but the Caribbean is not to be overlooked.*

▶ SPORTS, FUN AND ACTIVITIES

MOUNTAIN CLIMBING

▶ **Club Alpino Chomolumna**
C. Lago Superior 188
Colonia Torre Blanca
11280 México, D. F.
Tel. (55) 5 27 14 71

▶ **Desafio**
Avenida Poniente 3 No. 586
Orizaba
Tel. (01 272) 725 06 96
www.desafio.cjb.net

ECOTOURISM

▶ **Grupo Ecológico Sierra Gorda**
Avenida Benito Juárez 9
Jalpan de Serra
Tel. (01 441) 296 08 18

*Fascinating underwater worlds
with coral, fish and crustaceans*

▶ **Ecoturismo Yucatán**
Calle 3 No. 235
Mérida
Colonia Pensiones
Tel. (01 999) 925 21 87
Fax (01 999) 925 90 47
www.ecoyuc.com

BIKING

▶ **Bici Tours »Los Pingüinos«**
Ave. 5 de Mayo No. 10 B
29240 San Cristóbal d. l. Casas
Tel. (967) 802 02
Fax (967) 866 38

▶ **Bike Mex**
Calle Guerrero 361
Puerto Vallarta, Jal.
Tel. (322) 318 34
Fax (322 31680

RAFTING

▶ **Aventura y Rafting B. Martínez**
Ave. Revolución 1546-6
Col. Guadalupe Inn
0100 México, D. F.
Tel. (55) 207 88 55, 208 71 67

▶ **Adventures Selvazul**
Avenida 41 Poniente 2120
Puebla
Tel. / Fax (01 222) 240 64 55
www.mexicorivers.com

AQUATIC SPORTS

▶ **Coral Scuba Dive Center**
Ave. Matamoros 13a
Ila Mujeres
Tel. (01 998) 877 07 63
www.coralscubadivecenter.com

▶ **Aqua World**
Paseo Kukulkán Km 15,3
Cancún
Tel. (01 998) 848 83 27
www.aquaworld.com.mx

Cancún, Chalapa, Cuernavaca, Guadalajara, Huatulco, Ixtapa de la Sal, Los Cabos, Manzanillo, Mazatlán, Mexico City, Mérida, Monterrey, Morelia, Puebla, Puerto Vallarta, Querétaro, San Carlos, San Miguel de Allende, Taxco, Valle de Bravo and Veracruz.

The Mexicans love their horses. Quite a few hotels offer horse-riding (equitación). An outing on horseback can usually be arranged when visiting a hacienda.   **Riding**

Ecotourism is another new trend all over Mexico. Eco-groups, travel agencies and travel operators put together interesting tours, which show the traveller the environment and natural beauty of Mexico.   **Ecotourism**

Chances for extreme mountain climbing (alpinismo) are limited in Mexico. However, the large mountain ranges, the Sierra Madre Oriental, Occidental and del Sur provide good conditions for hiking tours in the mountains. The timberline is at about 4,000m/13,000ft. Therefore, the mountains don't have the same kind of alpine character as the Rocky Mountains in the USA or the European high mountain ranges. Since very little accommodation exists in the Mexican mountain regions, plan on making day trips only. Vegetation often obscures the view of the landscape and there are numerous obstacles to negotiate. Hikers may suddenly find themselves standing at the rim of a gorge that had escaped their notice, and have to find a different route. Mountains with high alpine character are the volcanic mountains Popocatépetl (5,452m/17,800ft), Iztaccíhuatl (5,286m/17,200ft) and Citlaltépetl (Pico de Orizaba; 5,700m/18,700ft). Suitable terrain for mountain climbing is usually located at elevations of about 4,000m/13,000ft. At higher elevations, hikers find extended fields of volcanic ash and penitent snow (conical, tilted snow formations; formed through alternate melting and freezing in wind and sun).   **Mountain climbing and hiking**

Hiking tours across the Copper Canyon (Western Sierra Madre) lasting several days enjoy increasing popularity, and almost every hotel along the railway line offers such tours. Many hikers start out in Creel where there is a particularly wide range of tours on offer.

Increasingly, guided tours for mountain bikers are offered. The terrain is ideal for biking in the federal state of Chiapas, in the southeast of Mexico and on the peninsula Baja California.   **Biking tours**

Mexicans love to watch bullfights, although some will hardly consider this a sport.   **Spectator sports**

Charreadas, the Mexican version of a rodeo, are less bloody than bullfights. The stars are the charros (riders) who show their professional skills. (▶Art and Culture, Folklore)   ◀ **Charreadas – Mexican rodeo**

Jai alai attracts much attention. The players throw a small ball against a wall and catch it using a cesta (a long, curved wicker scoop that is   ◀ **Jai alai (Frontón)** strapped to one arm). In Mexico City, Jai alai games take place every evening except Mondays and Fridays. The court is located at the Frontón México at the Plaza de la Revolución.

Time

Time zones Mexico has three time zones that are each one hour apart:
hora oficial del Centro (CET minus 7 hrs), in the East and the highlands
hora oficial de las Montañas (CET minus 8 hrs) in Nayarit, Sinaloa, Sonora and Chihuahua
hora oficial del Pacífico (CET minus 9 hrs) in Baja California Norte

Summer daylight saving time (hora de verano) In 1996, Mexico adopted summer daylight saving time for the entire country and almost all states comply. This means that almost everywhere in Mexico the time is the US EST (Eastern Standard Time) minus one hour.

Transports

Road Traffic

Roads Mexico has a road network of about 370,000km/230,000mi, of which 45,000km/28,000mi are motorways or similar highways. The network varies according to demand: not many roads cross the inner regions of Baja California, for example; only the very important north-south connections are very well executed. There is better coverage in the central and southern parts of the country like the connection Mazatlán – Monterrey – Matamoros to the borders of Guatemala or Honduras.

Motorways (autopistas) exist mostly near large cities or traffic hubs, such as Mexico City, Guadalajara, Monterrey, Saltillo, Coatzacoalcos, Villahermosa, Veracruz, Hermosillo, Mazatlán, Tijuana, Chihuahua, Puebla, Querétaro or Colima. Most motorways are toll roads as are many bridges. The national highways (rutas federales) are the backbone of the Mexican road network. These routes are assigned numbers following the letters MEX, such as MEX 180. The road systems of the individual federal states are identified by letters for the individual state and numbers, such as GTO 49. Narrow, not very well-constructed side roads often make the connection to smaller villages and remote areas.

Caution! Small side roads and byways often become impassable for regular vehicles during the rainy season. Even all-terrain vehicles have trouble negotiating these roads after heavy rains. The Ministry for Tourism issues monthly reports on the road conditions (►Information).

Mexicans drive on the right side of the road. At crossings and junctions, the vehicle approaching from the right has the right of way. Roundabout traffic also has the right of way. The traffic signs generally conform to international standards. The speed limits are 25mph/40km/h in cities and villages, 50mph/80km/h for highways and 68mph/110km/h on motorways. Speed bumps (»topes«) ahead of city limits or villages are effective in slowing down the traffic.

Traffic rules

Traffic rules are more or less theoretical. Experience will soon teach the driver not to count too heavily on fellow road users following the rules. The prudent driver is therefore defensive. Diving into the chaotic traffic of Mexico City is an exercise in patience, control and stoicism; the practice will definitely increase your reaction times. Incidentally, the Mexican capital has a good mass transit system.

Tip

Please note: do not park in a no-parking zone. The Mexican traffic police have adopted a very practical enforcement method – they remove the licence plates from the car. The police will give it back to

There's always time for a little small-talk at the road-side

you in return for your signature on a ticket or a (sometimes considerable) »fee«.

In contrast to international traffic rules, a Mexican driver may use his/her left signal lights to indicate to the following cars that he/she will let you pass. In preparation for a left-turn, go to the right hand side of the road, turn on your left signal, wait there and observe the traffic in both directions until you can safely turn left. Mexican drivers will flash their headlights to warn other drivers about obstacles like cows or mules. On one-lane bridges or other narrow passages, the car that first flashes its headlights always goes first.

Car breakdowns: Ángeles Verdes

The Mexican Ministry of Tourism maintains a fleet of emergency repair vehicles. The operators patrol the streets, make repairs, deliver first aid and provide information: they are known as Ángeles Verdes (green angels). The car owner only pays for parts and petrol. The Mexican motoring association (Automobile Association) and its yellow fleet also runs an emergency repair service.

The Ángeles Verdes don't have a unique nationwide phone number. Drivers may therefore be left with no other choice but to sit and wait by the road-side and let the car's open bonnet indicate their predicament. Travellers stranded in a remote area must take matters into their own hands, though at petrol stations, service stations or in villages it is often possible to find a person who can repair a car without too much difficulty. When going on longer trips or travelling to remote areas it is a good idea to take along some important replacement parts.

Petrol stations

Nationalized PEMEX petrol stations may not always be within close reach, so always keep the tank filled up well ahead of time. The PEMEX street guide indicates where petrol stations are located. Most of these stations can supply you with lead-free petrol (»magna sin« and »premium«).

Hire Cars

Hire cars (rental cars, coches de alquiler) cost dearly in Mexico. Car hire companies are located in all larger cities and tourist centres. International hire companies will in general provide a car in proper condition; it may pay to give cars from smaller local companies a closer look.

A national driver's licence should suffice to rent a car, but an international driver's licence is recommended. In general, you must be at least 25 years old to rent a car. A car hire company expects payment by credit card; if they accept cash they will usually demand a rather high security deposit. Value added tax of 10% (less in some places) is applicable and the car must be returned in Mexico. An additional return fee applies should the car be picked up in one place and returned in another.

TRAVEL INFORMATION

MOTORING ORGANIZATION

► **Asociación Mexicana Automovilista (AMA)**
Orizaba 7, Colonia Roma
06700 México, D. F.
Tel. (55) 2 08 83 29
The AMA's offices are found in all large Mexican cities.

HIRE CARS

► **Alamo**
Uxmal 21
Cancún
Tel. (998) 886 01 68

► **AVIS**
Reforma 308, Col. Juárez
06600 México, D. F.
Tel. (55) 762 36 88

Cancún
Tel. (998) 883 00 44
or (998) 886 02 21
(airport)

► **Budget**
Atenas no. 40
06600 México, D. F.
Tel. (55) 566 88 15

Cancún
Av. Tulum sm 20
Tel. (998) 884 07 30 or 886 00 26
(airport)

► **Europcar**
Av. Cuauhtémoc 1025,
Col. Narvarte
03020 México, D. F.
Tel. (55) 575 16 44

► **Hertz**
Versailles No. 6, Col. Juárez
06600 México, D. F.
Tel. (55) 592 70 82

FERRIES

► **Grupo Sematur de California**
Calle Arizona 58,
03810 México, D. F.
Tel. (55) 56 87 78 39
www.ferrysematur.com.mx

RAIL (see also p. 183)

► **Ferrocarriles Nacionales de México**
Estación Buenavista
(main station in Mexico City)
Departamento de Tráfico de Pasajeros
Av. Insurgentes Norte 140
Colonia Buena Vista,
06358 México, D. F.
Tel. (55) 37 09 36

► **Ferrocarril de Chihuahua al Pacífico, S.A. de C.V.**
Apartado Postal 46
Chihuahua, Chih.
Tel. (614) 15 77 56
Tickets are available in advance at
www.nativetrails.com
www.nativetrails.com

BUS SERVICES FROM MEXICO CITY

► **Terminal Indios Verdes**
Metro station: Indios Verdes
(line 3)
Buses to Teotihuacán and the northern suburbs

► **Terminal del Norte (T. A. N.)**
Av. de los Cien Metros 4907
Col. Magdalena
Tel. (015) 587 15 52
Metro station: Terminal del Norte
(line 5)
Buses to Tula, Querétaro, Guanajuato, San Luis Potosí, north Mexico and the USA

▶ **Terminal del Oriente (T. A. P. O.)**
Calz. Ignacio Zaragoza 200
Col. 1er de Mayo
Tel. (015) 762 59 77
Metro station: San Lázaro
(line 1)
Buses to Puebla, Oaxaca, Mérida
and Yucatán

▶ **Terminal del Sur (T. A. S.)**
Av. Taxqueña 1320
Col. Campestre Churubusco
Tel. (015) 689 97 45
Metro station: Taxqueña
(line 2)
Buses to Cuernavaca, Taxco,
Acapulco and the south

▶ **Terminal del Poniente (T. A. P.)**
Av. Sur 122, Esq. Río Tacubaya,
Col. Real del Monte
Tel. (015) 271 04 81
Metro station: Observatorio
(line 1)
Buses to Toluca, Morelia and the
west coast

AIR TRAVEL

▶ **Aeroméxico**
Paseo de la Reforma 445
Col. Cuauhtémoc
06500 México, D. F.
Tel. (55) 327 40 00

▶ **Mexicana**
Paseo de la Reforma 302
06600 México, D. F.
Tel. (55) 514 53 86

▶ **Aero California**
Paseo de la Reforma 33
206500 México, D. F.
Tel. (55) 207 53 11

Hangar 7 Zona E
Col. Federal
15620 México, D. F.
Tel. (55) 627 02 05

▶ **British Airways**
Paseo de la Reforma 10-14
México, D.F.
Tel. (55) 628 05 00

▶ **American Airlines**
Paseo de la Reforma 314
México, D.F.
Tel. (55) 209 14 00

▶ **Canadian Airlines Intl.**
Paseo de la Reforma 389
México, D.F.
Tel. (55) 208 18 83 /
207 66 11

Rail Travel

Routes   The Mexican railway system (ferrocarriles or FFCC for short) has a total length of about 31,000km/20,000mi but leaves many areas underserved. The exception is the region between Mananillo at the Pacific and Veracruz at the Gulf of Mexico where rail services are quite good. There is no railway in the federal states of Baja California Sur (Lower California) and Quintana Roo.

Most rail services are run by the state-owned railway company Ferrocarriles Nacionales de México. Private companies, such as Ferrocarril del Pacífico, Ferrocarril de Chihuahua al Pacífico and Ferrocar-

Stunning scenery: a trip by train through the Copper Canyons

ril Sonora to Baja California cover additional routes. The tickets are valid for all routes, regardless of where they have been issued.

Special characteristics

Travelling by train is by far the least expensive way of getting around in Mexico. Compared with European rail services, the lower price also means little comfort, unreliable timetables and extremely long travel times.

Until further notice, the Mexican rail companies no longer offer 1st class accommodation or sleeper cabins. Only the tourist rail connection offers 1st class. Often, the trains have been in service since the 1940s or 1950s and may not be in the best state of repair. In general, but especially for overnight travel (risk of theft), buy a 1st class ticket if available.

The inconveniences notwithstanding, and with enough time on hand, a trip by rail can be an interesting experience. Trains may go through regions and towns not regularly seen by tourists; travelling by train, you are part of the regular Mexican lifestyle. Enterprising people in the countryside offer refreshments and food at stations.

Ferries

Pacific coast   The shipping company Grupo Sematur de California operates car ferries between the Mexican continent and the Baja California peninsula. This solution is ideal for travellers who want to save the time and effort of a drive around the Gulf of California. Make reservations well in advance in the company offices in Mexico City or in the individual ports.

Routes and travel times: Guaymas – Santa Rosalía: 8 hours
Topolobampo – La Paz (Pichilingue): 10 hours
Mazatlán – La Paz (Pichilingue): 18 hours

Caribbean   Ferries go from continental Mexico to the island of Cozumel and Isla Mujeres. The shipping companies Cruceros Marítimos del Caribe and Naviera Turística de Quintana Roo provide ferry services several times daily.

Tickets are on sale at the pier. Reservations are not required.
Routes and travel times:
Playa del Carmen – Cozumel: ten daily trips from Cruceros to the island (7:30am – 9pm) and back (6:30am – 8pm), six daily trips from Naviera to the island (6:30am – 8pm) and back (7:30am – 9pm), travel time is about 1 hour.
Puerto Aventuras – Cozumel: daily to the island at 9:30am and 5:30pm, and back at 8:30am and 4:30pm, travel time is about 2 hours (Naviera)
Puerto Morelos – Cozumel: regular connection (car ferry) between Puerto Morelos and Cozumel
Cancún – Isla Mujeres: four trips daily to the island (9am – 7pm) and back (10am – 8pm), travel time: 1/2 hour (Cruceros).
Puerto Juárez – Isla Mujeres: regular connection by car ferry between Puerto Juárez (Punta Sam) and Isla Mujeres.

Travelling by Bus

The bus (camión, autobús) is the most popular way for Mexicans to travel. Almost every little place can be reached by bus with one of the various bus service providers. Buses serving the most important inland cities and border or coastal towns leave several times a day, some even every hour. Aside from local buses, there are also first and second class buses.

First class   Travellers may consider taking a first or luxury class bus (primero, de lujo, ejecutivo) for long rides through the countryside. The tickets cost about 10 to 20% more than second class but there is a chance that the air conditioning may be working and the seats are sure to be more comfortable. Reserve seats well in advance, maybe as much as a day ahead of time. Once a bus is full, companies will simply promise a seat on the next bus.

Without doubt, one of the most original Mexican experiences is a ride on a bus.

With a second class ticket the bus may be somewhat older and slower; it will make frequent stops to pick up more (or too many) passengers and give vendors a chance to offer their food or goods. It is an ideal way to mix with Mexicans.

Second class

It is always a good idea to enquire well in advance about departure times, tickets, connecting travel and reservations. This is particularly true for the school holidays, Easter holidays, in August and around Christmas and the New Year, when bus services are in demand. During these holiday periods it may be better to use other modes of transportation; if not, make reservations weeks ahead of time.

Tips

Information and tickets are available at the bus terminals (camionera), usually located on the outskirts of a city or town.
Some places have different bus terminals for individual bus operators and/or service classes.

Information

There are five large bus terminals in the peripheral districts of Mexico City. Buses depart from there to the different parts of Mexico (see p.170).

Bus terminals in the federal district of Mexico

Travelling by Air

There are 59 national and international airports in Mexico.
The country's most important hub is the Aeropuerto Internacional Benito Juárez in Mexico City with US, South American and European airline services among others.

Airports

British Airways offers direct flights from London Heathrow to Mexico City, but at the time of writing only on Mondays, Wednesdays, Fridays and Sundays; on other days it is necessary to change in airports like Chicago O'Hare or New York JFK. The direct flight from Heathrow takes a little over 10 hours.

Airlines   The privately-owned airline Aeromexico is part of Aervías de México, which also has the controlling interest at Mexicana Airlines. These airlines together cover about 85% of the Mexican air traffic market. Aeromexico flies domestic routes and also offers daily flights to New York, Miami, Houston, Los Angeles, Tucson, San Diego and New Orleans. The airline's international routes include daily flights to Madrid, Paris, Rome and Frankfurt.

Mexicana serves mostly domestic routes as well as offering flights to the USA and Central American countries.

Several regional airlines fill the gaps in airline services.

Flight passes   Aeromexico and Mexicana offer bargain packages for European and US air travellers (Mexi Pass). These passes include connecting flights inside Mexico. (►Getting There).

Travellers with Disabilities

Most airports and good hotels or restaurants in larger cities have proper ramps and toilets for persons with disabilities. In rural areas on the other hand, the situation could be more difficult. Please contact the following sources for more information:

► **RADAR (UK)**
12 City Forum
250 City Road
London EC1V 8AF
Tel. 020 7250 3222
Fax: 020 7250 0212
www.radar.org.uk

► **Mobility International USA**
132 E. Broadway, Suite 343
Eugene, Oregon USA 97401
Tel. Tel: (541) 343-1284
Fax: (541) 343-6812
www.miusa.org

► **MossRehab ResourceNet**
MossRehab Hospital
1200 West Tabor Road
Philadelphia, PA USA
Tel. 215 456 9900
www.mossresourcenet.org

► **Accessible Travel (UK)**
Avionics House
Naas Lane
Quedgeley
Gloucester GL2 2SN
Tel. 01452 729 739
Fax 01452 729853
www.accessibletravel.co.uk

When to Go

Best holiday times

While it is quite possible to travel in Mexico all year round, it is also true that the summer months can be very hot and humid. In addition, there might be summer rains. June to October is the season for hurricanes and tropical storms with deluges of rain and wind hitting parts of the country.

With these considerations in mind, it may be best to plan your trip to discover Mexico from **mid-September to mid-May,** when the weather is unlikely to be too hot or too rainy. In the Mexican highlands, including the region around Mexico City, winter nights and early mornings can be quite cool. The higher levels of humidity in the coastal regions and the Yucatán peninsula should be taken into consideration; humidity may reach 100% in these regions and in other Mexican jungle areas, where the temperatures rarely sink below 27°C/80°F. Popular beaches and tourist destinations, such as Acapulco, Cancún, Cuernavaca and San Miguel de Allende are fairly crowded around Christmas and Easter, and also on Mexican holidays. For more detailed information about climates in Mexico please see p.23ff.

If you are in Mexico on 1 November you will experience the impressive and unusual All Saints Day festival, where sweets including ones shaped like skulls are sold.

Tours

ENTER INTO THE WORLD OF THE MAYA, WALK
HISTORIC TRAILS TO DISCOVER THE OLD COLONIAL
CITIES AROUND THE
CAPITAL, TAKE A TRIP TO
ACAPULCO AND THE OCEAN
OR VISIT AN INDIAN VILLAGE.

*Colourful façades
in the streets
of San Miguel de Allende*

TOURS THROUGH MEXICO

In all its rich variety, there are many different aspects to Mexico.
The following routes reveal some of them.

TOUR 1 **On the Trail of the Ancient Maya**
The majority of the most beautiful Maya sites are located
on the Yucatán peninsula. Chichén Itzá and Uxmal are a
must, and the tour leads on via the colonial cities Mérida
and Campeche to Palenque, hidden deep in the rainforest.   ▶ **page 184**

TOUR 2 **Heading South**
The journey from Mexico City to the famous resort of
Acapulco passes through wonderful mountain scenery, and
invites side trips to fascinating caves as well as a visit to
the silver mining town of Taxco.   ▶ **page 186**

TOUR 3 **Silver and Freedom**
The next stops after Mexico City are the colonial towns of
Querétaro, San Miguel de Allende, Dolores Hidalgo,
Guanajuato and then the listed old town of Morelia, at the
gates of which lies the Pátzcuaro Lake.   ▶ **page 188**

TOUR 4 **Across the Centre**
Mole poblano, the famous hot chili-chocolate sauce, was
invented in Puebla. From here, the route leads to the
magnificent colonial city of Oaxaca with the impressive pre-
Hispanic temples of Monte Albán. After a visit to the Gulf
from Tehuantepec the tour continues into the highlands –
to the Indio-regions in Chiapas centred around San
Cristóbal.   ▶ **page 190**

Find from Palenque: Maya head

Beautiful view from the fort at Campeche

The emblem of Chichén Itzá: Chac-mool

TOUR 3

Dolores Hidalgo
San Miguel de Allende
Guanajuato
Querétaro
Morelia
Mexico City
Pátzcuaro Lake
Puebla
Taxco
Cuernavaca
TOUR 4
Chilpancingo
Oaxaca
TOUR 2
Mitla
Acapulco
Monte Albán
Cañon de Sumidero
Tuxtla Gutiérrez

Chichén Itzá
Izamal
Cancún
Cobá
Mérida
Riviera Maya
Uxmal
Tulum
Campeche
Puuc Route
Edzná
TOUR 1
Palenque
San Cristóbal de las Casas

Daring cliff-divers demonstrate their art to an amazed public in Acapulco.

A wonderful combination of rich history and unique landscape: Tulum on the Caribbean coast

Travelling Mexico

Organized round trips

Many travellers choose an all-inclusive package tour when visiting Mexico for the first time. After all, Mexico is a very large country with many different aspects. Travel agents offer such packages in particular for the Yucatán peninsula with its many Maya sites. In the meantime, organizers have added more tours to their programmes. Some trips go south from Mexico City to places like Puebla or Oaxaca; others turn north from the capital to visit the old northern colonial cities.

Mexico Your Way

... by aeroplane

Exploring Mexico on your own is fairly easy – especially with some planning. If time is short it is worth considering covering large distances by plane. The Mexican domestic air traffic system is quite good: half a dozen airlines offer daily flights to and from more than two dozen cities. The largest of these airlines are Aerocaribe, Mexicana and Aero California. Tickets are available in advance through ma-

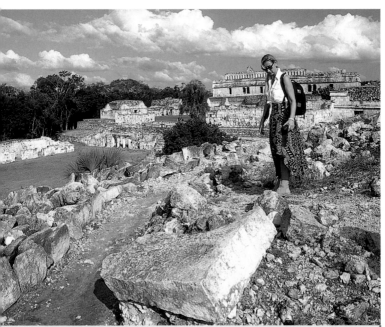

Exploring extensive archaeological sites in the hot sun can be tiring.

ny travel agencies or online (either direct from the airlines, e.g. www.ba.com, or through tour organizers). Also worthy of consideration are the economically priced flight passes, such as the Mexi Pass and the Maya Pass, or good value round-trip fares. Flights are normally on time, and the airlines do take connecting flights into account.

A hired car offers the most flexibility on your Mexican tour of discovery. However, this kind of transportation is not exactly cheap, and long car rides can be boring or drain your energy. For instance, travelling the route between Cancún and Mérida necessitates negotiating 400km/250mi of straight highway through nothing but jungle. Some will recommend hiring a car from an international rental car agency well in advance while still at home. However, there are quite a few local car rental companies offering fair deals. It is possible to keep your options open and negotiate with managers who like to keep all their cars on the road, though speaking at least a few words of Spanish may improve the chances of getting a fair deal.

... by hire car

> ### Baedeker TIP
>
> **Protection from heat and thirst**
> When visiting archaeological sites it is always a good idea to take along some head protection (a hat or scarf) as well as sufficient water. Many sites cover such a large area that a visit will take several hours, often during the midday heat.

Be that as it may, here are the basics: to rent a car, drivers must be at least around 25 years of age and have a credit card. An international driving licence is recommended by some authorities, but normally not required. It is best to choose a car with working air conditioning if driving in hot weather (even small cars usually have this feature). When planning a trip, remember that dropping off a rented car in a location other than the pick-up point can be very expensive in Mexico. Of course, it is possible to rent a car in location A and drop it off in location B – but for a fee that may come as a shock. Rental agencies explain this fee by claiming that they have to hire a driver to bring the car back to its original location.

The main interurban roads are almost all in good condition, and there are petrol stations in all cities. To reach remote villages and lesser known Maya sites or national parks, less well-maintained byways must be used; in these more remote areas, petrol stations may be few and far between. The way of joining and leaving highways is not the same as the European model but rather works like a zip. A »tope« (speed bump) may be strategically placed on entering a township; this convincing and potentially damaging reminder to heed the speed limits may be hidden in the shadow of trees or in other poorly visible spots.

Authorities warn that travellers on solitary roads or in remote areas face the risk of falling prey to gangs of armed robbers, especially in the southern states of Guerrero, Oaxaca and Chiapas. The FCO (Foreign and Commonwealth Office, **www.fco.gov.uk**) advises special caution in Oaxaca City where recent protests have led to violence. Though most visits to Mexico are trouble-free, travellers should be particularly alert in tourist areas and when withdrawing money from cash points or exchanging money at bureaux de change.

... by bus or shared taxi service

The »authentic« way to travel in Mexico is by bus. Mexico has an excellent bus system, which covers about 360,000km/223,000mi of road. The buses and bus terminals are often highly modern, and bus companies all over Mexico offer local and country-wide services.

It's definitely easier to explore Mexico City by taxi or Metro.

These bus services come in several classes. First class (primera) and express buses (rápido, express) feature air conditioning, TV and toilet facilities. A snack may be part of the service.

Tickets for first class buses may cost up to 50% more than those for second (economy) class buses (segunda clase, clase económica); in the latter, passengers should be prepared for open windows and well-worn plastic seats. The reward for travelling economy class, though, is the company of Mexicans. In general, buses arrive and depart very punctually; the destination is either clearly displayed or somebody will call it out before departure. Tickets are available in the bus terminals, a few days in advance if desired. Bulky luggage is stowed in the luggage compartment, and the bus driver provides a receipt for the stored luggage.

Shared taxis (peseros, colectivos) are a good solution for travelling shorter distances. The price depends on the distance travelled and is paid on arrival; if you are unsure about the price, watch what local people pay for the same service, usually amounting to only a few coins counted into the hands of the driver. The destination is sometimes displayed on the vehicle and at some bus stops; in all other cases, ask for information, in Spanish if possible. Shared taxis are usually Volkswagen buses but can also be regular cars – be prepared for somewhat cramped conditions.

At a stop on the Chihuahua al Pacífico railway line (Chepe)

Mexican taxis are rather inexpensive compared to the USA or Europe. Especially in Cancún and Mexico City, beware of cab drivers who try to charge you many times the regular price. A taxi hailed right in front of a hotel or at the airport is usually more expensive than a taxi hailed in the street. The FCO advises the use of only authorized pre-paid taxi services at airports. In Mexico City, they say, travellers should use the better regulated »sitio« taxis from authorized cab ranks. Passengers have been robbed and/or assaulted by unlicensed taxi drivers, particularly in the capital (March 2007).

More and more Mexican rail routes are being abandoned. In all of Yucatán, there is no rail system for personal travel; only goods are transported by rail. Everywhere else in Mexico, rail travel is not particularly efficient and not very comfortable. In very beautiful tourist regions however, the »Ferrocariles de México« are now bucking the trend and creating rail services such as the route across the Copper Canyon in the Western Sierra Madre (p.216): tickets are available at **www.nativetrails.com**. Rail companies also bank on the success of tourist trains such as the Tequila Express (see p.304). The luxury train the Maya Express (Espreso Maya) is privately run. Tickets are available in Mérida (Tel. +999 944-93-93), and booking information can be obtained from the USA/Canada at 1-800-717-0108/503-292-5055); the company's website is **www.expresomaya.com**. The only ferry service between the Mexican continent and the peninsula Baja California, i.e. from Topolobamp/Los Mochis to La Paz is also in private hands. Tickets are also available at www.nativetrails.com.

... by train

Tour 1 On the Trail of the Maya

Start and destination: from Cancún to Palenque
Length of trip: 6 to 7 days

Distance: about 2,000 km/1,250 mi

On this tour, a must for all who want more than a lazy beach holiday, travellers get to know the different Maya civilizations. With the exception of Tulum, all the splendid temples and pyramids are located in the heart of Yucatán peninsula. Combine this with a trip to study the colonial influences on Mérida and Campeche.

The round trip starts in ❶ ✳ **Cancún.** This is where European charter planes land. There are similar charter flights to Playa del Carmen south of Cancún, which has become an alternative (and competitive destination) to Cancún on the ❷ ✳ **Mayan Riviera**. After driving along the coast for 60km/37mi or 130km/81mi respectively, a unique experience awaits. Right at the edge of the ocean, on a walled rock plateau stands the Maya city of ❸ ✳ **Tulum,** formerly also known as Zama (city of dawn), with its towering majestic temple. The jungle north-west of Tulum surrounds the ruins of the Maya city❹ ✳ **Cobá** with the highest pyramid in the region. Cobá is located equidistant between Tulum and the small, very laid-back colonial township Valladolid, a natural choice for a stopover on the way to ❺ ✳ ✳ **Chichén Itzá.** This is the largest, most famous and most visited pyramid complex in Yucatán. Half a day is not nearly enough to even get a glimpse of this magnificent civilization. Highpoints are visits to the Kukulkán pyramid, the Temple of the Warriors, the ball court, the Venus Temple and the observatory, nicknamed »el Caracol« or »the snail« after its architecture.

Turning north-west, you will reach the »Yellow City« (most houses are painted yellow), called ❻ ✳ **Izamal**. An important Maya centre once existed where the city now prospers. The enclosed church square in the city centre has existed since the 16th century and is the largest in Mexico. The church was constructed on top of the Popol Chac Pyramid and built with stones from it. The next destination is ❼ ✳ **Mérida**, in the western part of the peninsula. The city is nicknamed the »White City«, a reference to the colour of most of the houses and the city's cleanliness. To this day, the façades of the houses in Paseo Montejo reveal the wealth of the sisal-barons. Colonial architecture and the hustle and bustle of everyday life characterize

✓ DON'T MISS

- Tulum: fortified temple on the ocean
- Chichén Itzá: most visited archaeological site in Yucatán
- Mérida: capital of Yucatán, cultural centre
- Uxmal: ruins of Maya buildings in the classical Puuc style
- Palenque: magnificent Maya pyramids in the middle of the jungle

the streets around the city square (Zócalo). Many of the sisal haciendas have now been turned into luxury lodges or museums.

Another archaeological gem from the Maya civilization awaits about 90km/56mi south of Mérida. The name of the site is ❽ ✶ ✶ **Uxmal** and its main attractions are the Adivino Pyramid, also called the Pyramid of the Magician, and the Governor's Palace (nicknamed »Nunnery Quadrangle« by the Spaniards). The isolated archaeological site is located between the villages Muna and Ticul. Recently, a few smaller hotels have been built around the Uxmal excavation site, which is considered the highlight of the ❾ ✶ **Puuc Route**. Other ancient Maya sites in a related style are located south of Uxmal (Kabah, Labna, Sayil) near the country road 261 to Hopelchen. A convenient side trip runs from Uxmal to the ancient Maya city of ❿ ✶ **Edzná** with the Small Acropolis and the Grand Acropolis as well as the Temple of the Five Floors. Enjoy the views.

The port city of ⓫ **Campeche** is now only 65km/40mi away. Originally, Campeche was a Maya city but the Spaniards destroyed it, replacing it with a city in the colonial style. The historic centre of the city has been restored. Today it is a UNESCO World Heritage Site.

A side trip from Campeche to ⓬ ✶ ✶ **Palenque is well worth the effort. The long trip may be exhausting**, but the sight of the abandoned ancient ruins is ample reward. Palenque is surrounded by rainforest where howler monkeys live in the trees.

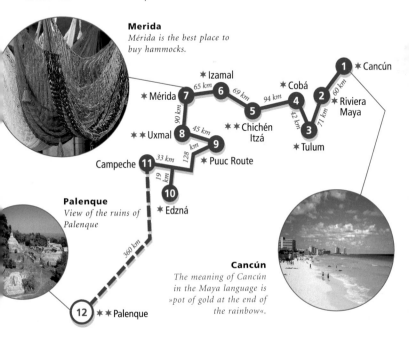

Merida
Mérida is the best place to buy hammocks.

✶ Izamal
✶ Cancún
65 km
✶ Cobá
60 km
✶ Mérida **7**
6 69 km 94 km **4**
2 ✶ Riviera Maya
5
90 km
45 km
✶ ✶ Chichén Itzá
71 km
42 km
✶ ✶ Uxmal **8**
3
128 km
9
✶ Tulum
✶ Puuc Route
Campeche **11** 33 km
19 km
10
✶ Edzná

Palenque
View of the ruins of Palenque

360 km

Cancún
The meaning of Cancún in the Maya language is »pot of gold at the end of the rainbow«.

12 ✶ ✶ Palenque

Tour 2 Heading South

Start and destination: from Mexico City to Acapulco
Length of the trip: 1 to 2 days

Distance: about 400 km/250 mi

Impressive mountains, ancient caves with glorious murals and impressive stalagmites and stalactites, the legendary silver town Taxco and the famous beach resort Acapulco are the highpoints of this trip south of Mexico City.

From ❶ ✷ ✷ **Mexico City,** take the avenue Insurgentes Sur (south), passing the Aztec Stadium and catching a glimpse of the floating Xochimilco Gardens in the distance, and negotiate about 80km/50mi of bends up and downhill on the MEX 95 freeway to reach ❷ ○ **Cuernavaca.** The town with its old colonial centre is charming. In ancient times, Aztec rulers chose to build their palaces in this beautiful place; Emperor Maximilian followed suit. The revolutionary leader Emiliano Zapata sent out his battle cry »Tierra y libertad!« (land and freedom) from this »city of eternal spring«. It was here that Malcom Lowry wrote his famous novel »Under the Volcano« which was made into a movie. Cuernavaca marks the end of your freeway ride; the next destination is Taxco via an old country road. A short side trip to ❸ ✷ **Xochicalco** is worthwhile for the magnificent sight of a pre-Columbian ceremonial centre high on an artificially levelled mountain top. The large dripstone grotto system of the ❹ **Grutas de Cacahuamilpa** is situated further along the route to Taxco.

Soon, the Silver City ❺ ✷ ✷ **Taxco** comes into view, nestled in the foothills of two mountain ranges. The narrow streets ascend at very steep angles, lined with small villas, small one-storey houses and countless platerias (silversmith shops). Above the houses at a small town square (Zocaló) rises the majestic, lavishly decorated cathedral San Sebastián y Santa Prisca. José Borda from the French Basque region donated the monumental church to the community in the mid-18th century. He had become very rich almost overnight after a gigantic silver vein had been discovered near Taxco in the el Atache Mountains. Taxco, a protected historic site, is the image of a self-contained colonial town. It is one of the most beautiful places to visit in Mexico: when darkness falls and the lights from the many houses sparkle in the night the city shines like a jewel.

Before moving south on the MEX 95 or, alternatively, on the parallel country road, the city of Iguala is worth a visit. Here, as in Taxco, vi-

 DON'T MISS

- Tulum: impressive fortress on the seaside
- Chichén Itzá: most frequently visited Maya site in Yucatán
- Merida: cultural centre
- Uxmal: classical Puuc-style ruins

sitors marvel at the art of the silversmiths and goldsmiths. In the last week of February, a grand flag festival entertains Iguala citizens and visitors with parades, cockfights and great arts and crafts fairs. A side trip to the lagoon of Tuxpan is worth considering on the way south. A ride of about 100km/62mi leads to the Sierra Madre valley with the city of ⑥ **Chilpancingo**, where the historic city hall has been turned into a museum. Other sights are the Casa Los Bravos, the arts and crafts centre and the parish church. 9km/6mi south of Chilpancingo a small country road branches off leading to Colotilipa, and a further 7 km/4 mi north of Colotilipa are the dripstone caves of ⑦ **Juxtlahuaca** with 3,000 year old wall paintings.

Leaving the foothills of the Sierra Madre del Sur behind, travel another 130km/81mi on from Chilpancingo to reach the legendary, lively beach resort of ⑧ ＊ ＊ **Acapulco**.

Mexico City
Unforgettable: a view over an ocean of houses in Mexico City

＊＊ Mexico City ①

76 km

＊ Xochicalco ② ＊ Cuernavaca
27 km
30 km ③

Grutas de ④
Cacahuamilpa

＊＊ Taxco ⑤

147 km

Chilpancingo ⑥
42 km
⑦ Grutas de
Juxtlahuaca

133 km

⑧ ＊＊ Acapulco

Tepotzlán
East of Cuernavaca: the unique Dominican monastery of Tepotzlán

Xochicalco
The Pyramid of the Feathered Serpent in Xochicalco

Acapulco
Definitely not vertigo sufferers: the »clavadistas« in Acapulco

Tour 3 Silver and Freedom

Start and destination: : from Querétaro to Lake Pátzcuaro
Distance: about 400 km/250 mi

Length of trip: 4 to 5 days

The Spaniards obviously appreciated the highlands. They liked the blue mountains, the red rocks, the narrow canyons and wide valleys, the vast flatlands and large lakes. For this reason they built their most beautiful and important colonial cities here.

In 1996, UNESCO gave the historical centre of ❶ ✳ **Querétaro** the rank of World Heritage Site. The well-kept city with its colonial architecture is about 2 hours away from Mexico's capital by car. Querétaro has witnessed many important events in Mexican history, such as the first stirrings of the Mexican War of Independence. The current Mexican constitution was signed here in 1824. Continuing on the same route leads on to ❷ ✳ ✳ **San Miguel de Allende**, the capital of the federal state of Querétaro. This metropolis is quite tranquil despite its industrial belt. The charming Eldorado for artists with its internationally renowned academy is nestled against a hill. The grandiose style of the old colonial mansions and palaces still shows the wealth of their original owners who exploited nearby mines. Today, the city enjoys protection as a historic monument. The freedom fighter Ignacio de Allende was born here and the peo-

Guanajuatos
View of the historic centre

San Miguel de Allende
Balloon sellers at the Zócalo

Pátzcuaro
Morning fishing on the lake

54 km
❸ Dolores Hidalgo
74 km
✳ ✳ Guanajuato ❹
✳ ✳ San Miguel de Allende
❷
28 km
❶ ✳ Querétaro
177 km
❺ Morelia
45 km
❻ ✳ Pátzcuaro Lake

Morelia
The winter habitat of the Monarc butterfly is Angangueo near More.

ple honoured his memory by naming their city after him. In the early years of the 19th century, Ignacio de Allende and the cleric Pater Miguel Hidalgo y Costilla initiated the Mexican War of Independence from Spain (1810-1821). Hildalgo operated from a now quiet town north-west of San Miguel Allende, known for its colourful ceramics, by the name of ❸ **Dolores Hidalgo**. The politically engaged priest was standing in front of his parish church portal in 1810 when he yelled his fateful »grito de Dolores« (cry of Dolores) and initiated the revolt against the Spanish-born privileged class (criollos). The small Independence Museum (Museo de la Independencia) in the former Dolores prison is a reminder of Hidalgo's initiatives. His statue is located in the Plaza Principal amid tropical greenery. Leaving Dolores Hidalgo, the jour-

✔ DON'T MISS

- San Miguel de Allende: city of the arts and artists
- Guanajuato: One of the most beautiful colonial cities in Mexico
- Lago de Pátzcuaro: a wonderful location amid wooded hills

ney continues through forest-green hills. A 50km/31mi car ride south-west leads to the city of ❹ ✳ ✳ **Guanajuato**. The colonial city with its maize-yellow, ochre-red or light-blue painted houses is surrounded by silver and gold mines. Mountain slopes limit the city's expansion in the narrow valley. Guanajuato, too, has its place in the annals of Mexican history: a few days after Pater Hidalgo's cry of Dolores, the first battle between the revolutionists and the royalists' army took place here. The Spanish royalists barricaded themselves in a disused granary (alhóndiga); today, this building is a historical museum, and the city a World Heritage Site. Nowadays, however, any disturbance in town is likely to be caused by the numerous students, or the band of international artists and tourists attending the annual Cervantes Festival. During the festival, the street restaurants in the small, pie-shaped park Jardín de la Unión are constantly overflowing with guests. With its ancient fig trees, this park is the heart of the city. By the way, Guanajuato is also the birth place of the painter Diego Rivera (the building where he was born still stands, and now houses an oddity: a mummy museum). The tour continues further south, via Irapuato and Salamanca, leading after about 180km/112mi to ❺ **Morelia** in the centre of a wide valley. The historic colonial part of town is also a UNESCO Heritage Site and subject to historic monument protection. The city has the oldest conservatory in America and an impressive library in its former Jesuit church. It was named after its famous son and freedom fighter José María Morelos.

Less than 60km/37mi away from Morelia lies the ❻ ✳ **Lago de Pátzcuaro**, arguably Mexico's most beautiful lake. The lake shores stretch almost 20km/12.4mi between wooded hills and dormant volcanoes. Along the shoreline, there are picture-perfect Indian villages; a boat brings visitors to the islands in the lake. The ride back to Mexico City from Pátzcuaro is about 350km/220mi.

Tour 4   Across the Centre

Start and destination: from Mexico City to San Cristóbal de las Casas
Distance: about 1000 km/ 620 mi

Length of the trip: 4 days (without extended trip to Palenque)

Experience the fascinating landscapes, impressive archaeological sites and the pomp of colonial cities. Make contact with the descendants of the people who built the pre-Columbian civilizations, giving Mexico its cultural riches. Come to know Mexico on this tour from the present-day capital to the Indian capital.

Travellers heading south-east from ❶ ✳ ✳ **Mexico City** towards Puebla are greeted at the halfway point by the majestic ❷ ✳ ✳ **Popocatépetl** on the right hand side. ❸ ✳ **Puebla** was originally named Ciudad de los Ángeles (city of angels). Legend has it that angels convinced the Franciscan friars from Spain to settle there. Today, Puebla is an industrial town (Volkswagen) with a charming historic centre. The city has also made the list of UNESCO Heritage Sites. Shiny Talavera wall tiles embellish the façades, and countless church domes point toward the heavens. The former convent of Santa Rosa now houses an impressive museum with records of cultural history as well as the arts, crafts and skills of ancient artists. The museum also tells of regional culinary specialities.

A short side trip runs from Puebla to the Indian ceremonial site ❹ ✳ **Cholula**. The Great Pyramid of Cholula is the tallest building of its kind in Mexico and by volume the largest man-made structure in the world, larger even than the Cheops pyramid in Cairo.

✓ DON'T MISS

- Oaxaca: contemplative peace and quiet in the historic centre
- Monte Albán: pyramid complex
- San Cristóbal de las Casas: colonial city with Indian style elements
- Palenque: Maya archaeological site

The journey continues from Cholula through the Sierra Mixteca with its lonely ridges, colourful eroded rocks and giant candelabra cacti on to ❺ ✳ ✳ **Oaxaca**. The region is one of Mexico's treasures. The capital, also named Oaxaca, has a beautiful Spanish colonial centre, a picturesque market and impressive museums. The cathedral is located next to important archaeological sites. The most significant of these sites, towering like a giant over the valley of Oaxaca, is the old Zapotec settlement of ❻ ✳ ✳ **Monte Albán,** another UNESCO Heritage Site.

Travelling further south, take a look at the Tule tree (according to Aztec legend the Tree of Life, which is said to be 2,000 years old now). Next stop are the excavations in ❼ ✳ **Mitla.** Mighty cactus fences guard the magnificent pre-Hispanic buildings and their artistically worked stones.

Mexico City
Highlight: the National Museum of Anthropology

Palenque
Maya head

Puebla
The unique Casa del Alfeñique (Almond Cake House)

The next leg of the tour runs through the narrowest part of Mexico, the Isthmus of Tehuantepec. Then, again up in the mountains, comes ❽**Tuxtla Gutièrrez**, which is also reachable by plane from Oaxaca. Don't miss the breathtaking view into the ❾**Cañon del Sumidero** about 15km/9mi west of Chiapa de Corzo. The Río Grijalva flows through the almost 1,000m/3,280ft-deep canyon.

❿ ✳ **San Cristóbal de las Casas**, the »Indian Capital« of Mexico, is now about 50km/31mi away. The city consists mostly of brightly painted one-storey buildings; it made a name for itself as the centre of the Zapatist movement.

The majority of the indigenous Indian population of Mexico lives in the region around San Cristóbal; 125 Maya communities and ten different tribal languages are officially registered in the mountain regions of Chiapas. In the colonial centre of San Cristóbal and especially at the traditional arts and crafts market in front of the Santo Domingo church, the native Tzotzil dominate the street scene in their colourful garb. Most Indian villages are hidden in deep gorges or cling to the edge of a mountain ledge at the end of a path somewhere. Of those villages in the very nearly 3,000m/10,000ft high, intensely wooded mountains, the one called Chamula is the easiest to reach. In particular, the market in front of the white church with its turquoise-blue ornaments works its magic on all visitors.

For those with another day to spare, about 200km/124mi from San Cristóbal in the tropical part of Chiapas the sunken Maya city of ⓫ ✳ ✳ **Palenque** awaits.

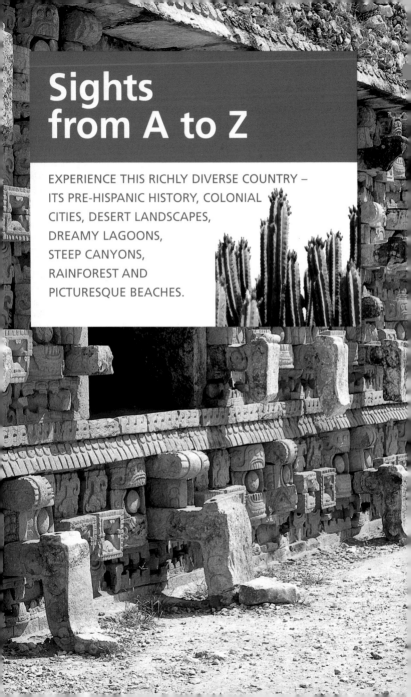

Sights
from A to Z

EXPERIENCE THIS RICHLY DIVERSE COUNTRY –
ITS PRE-HISPANIC HISTORY, COLONIAL
CITIES, DESERT LANDSCAPES,
DREAMY LAGOONS,
STEEP CANYONS,
RAINFOREST AND
PICTURESQUE BEACHES.

★ ★ Acapulco

S 19

Federal state: Guerrero (Gro.)
Population: 700,000

Altitude: 2 m/6.6 ft
Distance: 420 km/261 mi south of Mexico City

Is there anybody who has never heard of the world-renowned beach resort Acapulco? The name stands for glamour, luxury, sand and sun. Acapulco has it all: blue ocean, white beaches and cliffs. Furthermore, this paradise by the sea is also an excellent natural harbour on Mexico's Pacific coast.

Although Acapulco attracts many – maybe too many – visitors, the resort is still worth seeing. Besides, good alternative locations are within easy reach. The best-known tourist feature is without doubt **La Quebrada**, a 42m/138ft high cliff, from which daring divers (clavadistas) jump into the rough surf below. Their target is only 5m/16ft wide and not very deep.

History   People have probably lived in and around Acapulco for a very long time, but it was first explicitly mentioned after the conquest of the Aztec Empire at the end of the 15th century. In 1521, the Spanish conquistador **Gil Gonzales Ávila** became the first European to set eyes on the bay. In the years that followed the Spanish conquest, Acapulco became the harbour for ships bringing supplies for expeditions to South America and sailing north along the Pacific coast, and by the end of the 16th century Acapulco had developed into the port of registry for ships going to the Philippines, China, India and South America. Its decline as a harbour began at the end of the 18th century, with the opening of a new trade route from the Philippines to Spain through the Indian Ocean and around the Cape of Good Hope. Acapulco lost its significance with Mexican independence; the city experienced a revival only after the completion of the highway to Mexico City in 1927. Its stellar rise began after the Second World War as a result of it being frequented by **celebrities** like Elizabeth Taylor and Frank Sinatra and by tourists from the USA. Recently, visitors to Mexico have learnt to avoid Acapulco because of the high number of tourists and increasing water contamination.

What to See in Acapulco

City panorama   Aside from its beautiful landscapes and hotel palaces, Acapulco offers few remarkable sights. Life for tourists revolves around the Avenida Costera Miguel Alemán which has the majority of the large hotels, restaurants, bars and shops. But old Acapulco also has shops which sell leather goods and crafts. In spring the city is invaded by students from the USA and Canada during the spring vacation

At lunchtime around 1 pm, and in the evening between 7 pm and 10 pm (the times vary), the famous cliff-divers (clavadistas) show off their diving skills, descending head-first into the rough surf from the **42m/137ft-high Quebrada cliff**. Before they jump, the daring divers say a prayer in front of a Madonna statue, as portrayed in the well-known Elvis Presley movie Fun in Acapulco. Floodlights illuminate the cliff-diving spectacle in the evenings when some of the divers jump carrying torches. Located next to the Quebrada cliff is the hotel plaza Las Glorias El Mirador with the restaurant La Perla, opened in 1949 by Swiss swing musician Teddy Stauffer (1909–1991) after he moved to Mexico. Through this business venture, Acapulco became well-known in Europe.

Clavadistas

The Mágico Mundo Marino aquarium is located on a small tongue of land between Caleta and Caletilla beach. Visitors can see a show with sea lions and the feeding of sharks and piranhas or use the swimming pool and water slides. There is also a small marine science museum.

Mágico Mundo Marino

Daring clavadistas dive from the famous Quebrada cliffs.

▶ VISITING ACAPULCO

INFORMATION

Tourist information
La Costera 4455 (in front of the
Centro Convenciones, Playa Icacos)
Tel. (744) 484 44 16
Information is also available at
www.acapulco.org.mx or
www.acapulco.com.

GETTING AROUND

by plane
Flights to Acapulco depart from Mexico City (hourly) as well as from other Mexican and US airports.

by car
By car, the journey takes about 3.5
hours on the Autopista del Sol (sunshine highway, MEX 95).

by bus
When travelling by bus (about 4.5
hours), make return travel arrangements immediately upon arrival.

WHERE TO EAT

▶ **Expensive**
① *Coyuca 22*
Avenida Coyuca 22,
Fracc. Las Playas
Tel. (744) 483 50 30 or 482 34 68
www.hamacas.com.mx/coyuca/
The Coyuca 22 is arguably the most
famous restaurant in Acapulco. Film
directors use its romantic ambience to
set scenes in movies. Try the grill
specialities, especially the meat and
fish; be sure to make a reservation.

▶ **Moderate**
② *Madeiras*
Carretera Escénica 33
Tel. (744) 446 56 36
www.madeiras.com.mx
The restaurant is very popular because

of its international cuisine and spectacular view. Tables are therefore
rarely available without a reservation.

WHERE TO STAY

▶ **Luxury**
① *The Fairmont Acapulco Princess*
Playa Revolcadero s/n Col. Granjas del
Marqués
Tel. (744) 469 10 00, Fax 469 10 16
aca.reservations@fairmont.com
The Princess, with its 1019 rooms, is
the largest hotel in Acapulco. Among
its features are a park, small lakes and
waterfalls.
Choose from seven restaurants, seven
bars, five swimming pools, an 18-hole
golf course, seven tennis courts and a
basketball court.

③ *El Mirador Acapulco*
Plazoleta La Quebrada 74
Tel. (744) 483 11 55
Fax (744) 485 55 43
www.hotelelmiradoracapulco.com.mx
The view over the town from the old
Hotel El Mirador Acapulco (130
rooms) is magnificent. Next to this
hotel, the famous cliff-divers, also
known as Quebrada divers (clavadistas), entertain the public with their
dives from a 40m/130ft rocky cliff into
the surf below.

▶ **Mid-range**
② *Hotel Misión*
Calle Felipe Valle 12
Tel. (744) 482 36 43
Fax (744) 482 20 76
The Hotel Misión (20 rooms) is a
colonial building. Many years ago, it
housed the American embassy. Centrally located, the hotel is only about
two minutes away from the main city
square (Zócalo).

Acapulco *Plan*

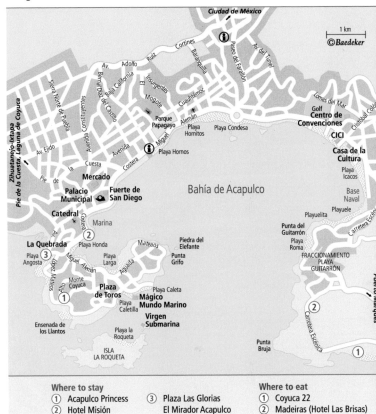

Ciudad de México

1 km
©Baedeker

Where to stay
1. Acapulco Princess
2. Hotel Misión
3. Plaza Las Glorias
   El Mirador Acapulco

Where to eat
1. Coyuca 22
2. Madeiras (Hotel Las Brisas)

The cathedral in the Moorish-Byzantine style is situated at the town square (Zócalo). It was built in the 1930s.

Cathedral

Fort San Diego was originally built between 1615 and 1617. The fortress was reconstructed after an earthquake in 1776 as a stronghold against pirates. Today, it houses a history museum (**Museo Histórico de Acapulco**), whith exhibits on the Spanish conquest, the history of the fortress and trade relations with Asia. The museum also gives an account of piracy in the Pacific.

★ Fort San Diego

This large amusement park is located near the Hornitos Plaza. It is filled with fragrant tropical plants and offers a roller skating rink, a lake perfect for boating and a marvellous view from a hill that can be reached by cable railway.

Papagayo Park

The CICI (Centro Internacional de Convivencia Infantil) is situated   CICI
east of Acapulco on the coastal road. This family park for aquatic
sports offers many highlights, such as dolphin and sea lion shows, a
20m/66ft slide and a swimming pool with simulated tides.

The convention centre (Centro de Convenciones) is situated on the   **Convention**
coastal road (Costera M. Alemán 4455). The centre features confer-   **centre**
ence rooms, a theatre, a folk art exhibition and a small archaeological museum, and puts on regular folkloristic shows.

Nearby, in the Casa de la Cultura (along the La Costera 4834), an ar-   **Casa de la**
chaeological museum, an art gallery and an arts and crafts shop at-   **Cultura**
tract visitors. There are also occasional theatre performances and
concerts.

Beaches around Acapulco

There are more than 20 beaches in and around Acapulco. The most
popular are named Hornos, Hornitos, Condesa and Icacos.

Mostly before noon, Mexicans visit the beaches Caleta and Caletilla.   **Caleta and**
These small, wind-protected beaches are to be found south of the   **Caletilla**
Península de Playas. They offer calm, clear water and beautiful
underwater fauna, which can be admired from the glass-bottom
boats.

The boats go from Playa Caletilla to La Roqueta island, which has a   ✳
beach of the same name. The island has been turned into a magnifi-   **Isla**
cent national park, where visitors can take a walk, dive, snorkel or   **La Roqueta**
visit a zoo. North-east, off the coast of La Roqueta, a bronze statue
of the Virgin of Guadalupe (Virgen Submarina) is submerged in
about 2m/6ft of water.

Playa La Angosta, a small, wind-protected beach, is situated on the   **La Angosta**
western side of the peninsula.

Acapulco offers all kinds of aquatic activities, such as water skiing,   **Aquatic sports**
jet skiing, banana boat rides and para-sailing. It is possible to rent
sailing boats, pedal boats, canoes, snorkel and other equipment along
the smaller beaches. Tour operators offer night and daytime cruises.

Coastal Drive from Acapulco toward Zihuatanejo

The north-west motorway (expressway) Carretera 200 connects Acapulco and Zihuatanejo. In the main, small villages and farms are to
be seen to the right and left of the motorway.

← *Playa Condesa – with the small island Farallón – is said to be Acapulco's
most beautiful beach.*

✳
Pie de la Cuesta Pie de la Cuesta (12 km/7.5 mi north-west of Acapulco) is built on a sand dune. The sandbar separates the Coyuca lagoon from the ocean. The panorama is particularly beautiful at sunset, and at night there is a great view of the glittering lights of Acapulco. Pie de la Cuesta is much calmer, cleaner and more peaceful than its famous neighbour. However, the undertow and the often wild surf can make swimming dangerous.

Laguna de Coyuca Take a boat trip from here to the freshwater lagoon Laguna de Coyuca. This is a natural paradise with freshwater fish and exotic birds living amongst the very dense tropical vegetation. It is possible to find overnight accommodation at the beaches of El Carrizol and Playas de San Jerónimo; you can reach them from Coyuca de Benítez.

Papanoa About 50 km/31 mi from Acapulco, before reaching Zihuatanejo, the almost 15 km/9.3 mi-long beautiful beach of Papanoa beckons beach-goers and swimmers. Arrangements for food and lodging can be made in the hotel Club Papanoa.

Coastal Drive from Acapulco to Puerto Escondido

The MEX 200 runs south-east from Acapulco to the coastal region named Costa Chica. On starting out from Acapulco, travellers immediately marvel at the breathtaking view onto Acapulco Bay from the Carretera Escénica.

Puerto Marqués The next destination is the bay and port of Puerto Marqués (13km/8mi east of Acapulco). The picturesque lagoon Tres Palos is another beautiful choice for your itinerary. The ocean around the fishing village Puerto Marqués is on the quiet side and ideal for sailing and water skiing. Just 1km/0.6mi further on is the **Playa Revolcadero**, a long beach directly on the Pacific with a strong surf and undertow, where annual surfing competitions take place. There are great opportunities to go horse-riding here.

From San Marcos to the Pacific The next towns include San Marcos (about 80 km/50 mi), Cruz Grande (about 120 km/75 mi), San Luis Acatlán (junction after about 27 km/16.8 mi), Ometepec (junction after about 16km/10mi), Cuajinicuilapa (about 234 km/145 mi), Montecillos (junction after 17 km/10 mi) and Punta Maldonado (junction after about 14 km/8.7 mi); they are located at the indicated distances between the Sierra Madre del Sur and the Pacific.

Idyllic region Do make a trip to this region. There are rich rewards in the forms of lush tropical vegetation, small rivers, idyllic lagoons and bizarre rock formations. Some of the locations are home to the descendants of escaped former slaves who have made a life here, founded families and had children with their Indian neighbours.

Venturing Out from Acapulco

Chilpancingo (population 120,000) is the capital of the federal Mexican state of Guerrero. Located 80km/50mi north of Acapulco, the city nestles in a valley at the foot of a mountainside of the Sierra Madre del Sur. While not offering too many tourist attractions, the city may serve as a strategic stop en route to Cuernavaca. This is a convenient place from which to venture out into remote mountain regions near and far. The region around Chilpancingo was settled by Indians from ancient times; the earliest to leave signs of their culture in this area were the Olmec. In colonial times, the city played a role as an intermediate stopover for transports from the Pacific coast to the Highlands. Chilpancingo experienced its most important moment in recent history when the **first Mexican National Congress** assembled here in 1813. The congressional leader was José María Morelos. Today, the city is the centre for the surrounding agricultural and forestry business.

Chilpancingo

Among the few tourist attractions are the Government Palace (Palacio de Gobierno) with historic frescoes, the parish church and the zoo. The regional museum, with its archaeological finds from the federal state of Guerrero, is the most worthwhile place to visit.

Near Chilpancingos, in Oxtotitlán and Juxtlahuaca, cave paintings are witness to Olmec artistry. Travelling south from Chilpancingo on the MEX 95 and turning left after about 9km/5.6mi at Petaquillas, it is another 38km/24mi to Colotlipa; the caves of Juxtlahuaca, which have been known since the 1930s, but which were mapped only in 1966, are approximately 7km/4.3mi north-east of Colotlipa. Taking a guided tour is the only way to visit the dripstone caves: among the finds inside are 3,000-year-old skeletal fragments, ceramics and cave paintings. The artistic motifs of the paintings in black, red, yellow and green hues represent Olmec rulers, jaguars and snakes. The **Oxtotitlán caves** are equally interesting but they are harder to reach: 7km/4.3mi north of Chilapa is the village Acatlán, and from there a 45-minute hike up the mountains leads to the caves.

★ **Caves of Juxtlahuaca**

Chilapa (population 21,000) is located about 55km/34mi east of Chilpancingo. The city used to be the capital of the state of Guerrero and features a modern cathedral

> ! *Baedeker* TIP
>
> ### Feast of the jaguar
> Chilapa puts on a large celebration on Assumption Day (Día de la Virgen de la Asunción) on 15 August. The highpoint is the feast of the jaguar »La Tigrada« with processions involving allegorically decorated carriages. Men and boys run noisily through the streets masquerading as jaguars and frightening young girls and children in the process. Historically, the celebrations were once a request to the gods for a good harvest.

and a 16th-century Augustinian monastery. A celebration on 3/4 June and a Sunday market (Aztec market) on the wider city square explains the popularity of Chilapa. There are bargains to be found among the beautiful lacquered boxes from Olinalá, wood carvings, textiles and leather items.

Aguascalientes

Federal state: Aguascalientes (Ags.)
Population: 640,000

Altitude: 1,889 m/6,200 ft
Distance: about 500 km/311 mi north-west of Mexico City, 131 km/81 mi from Zacatecas

Aguascalientes, a Spanish-style city in the heart of Mexico, is known for its ceramics and woven or embroidered textiles. The city is also famous for its lively spring festivals. The »Feria de San Marcos« has been the topic of many folk songs.

The friendly colonial town is surrounded by fruit orchards and vineyards and has a comfortable climate. There are also haciendas where the owners raise fighting bulls. The area is mostly famous for the **healing hot thermal springs** (aguas calientes) in and around the city.

History   The Spaniards fought hard against the natives before taking the city in 1575. They gave it the elaborate name Nuestra Señora de la Asunción de las Aguas Calientes. For a long period, the Spaniards used the place only as an outpost to fight their Indian enemies. Aguasca-

▶ VISITING AGUASCALIENTES

INFORMATION

Dirección General de Turismo
Avenida Universidad 1001
Edificio Torreplaza Bosques, 8°piso,
Tel. (449) 12 35 11

GETTING AROUND

By car, take the MEX 57 from Mexico City to Querétaro and then the MEX 45 via Salamanca and Léon to Aguascalientes. The travel time by bus is a little more than 6 hours.

WHERE TO EAT

▶ **Moderate**
Mitla Restaurante
Calle Madero 222

This popular traditional Mexican restaurant offers tasty meals and snacks. The lunch menu and the buffet on Sundays are both particularly impressive.

WHERE TO STAY

▶ **Budget**
Hotel Señorial
Calle Colón 104
(on the Plaza Principal)
Tel. (915) 16 30 or
Tel. (915) 14 73
Central location and simple, clean rooms. Some rooms have a view of the plaza.

lientes became the capital after the state of Aguascalientes was created in 1957.

An important railway junction, the city became the target and stronghold of different sides in the battles during the revolution. Today, more than half the citizens of the state of Aguascalientes live in the state capital, where agriculture along with the orchards and vineyards provide most employment.

What to See in Aguascalientes

Directly in the city square (Plaza de la Patria) is the town hall (Palacio Municipal) and the Governor's Palace (Palacio del Gobierno, built in the 17th and 18th centuries), which used to be the Palais des Marqués de Guadalupe (palace of the Marques of Guadalupe). Rivera-student Osvaldo Barra Cunningham's murals decorate the inner courtyard of the grand Baroque building. The murals depict agricultural life and industry in Aguascalientes.

★
Palacio de Gobierno

On the opposite side of the Plaza de la Patria is the 18th-century church of Nuestra Señora de Asunción (Our Lady at her Ascension), which contains works by Miguel Cabreras.

Cathedral

Next to it stands the Teatro Morelos: this building was executed in the Porfiriato style. In 1914, the Aguascalientes Convention was signed here, which unified the leaders of the revolution. The collaborative spirit however dissolved quickly.

Teatro Morelos

Half a block from the city square on the Carranza is the Casa de la Cultura (cultural centre). The centre was built in the 17th century as a monastery. After serving as a mansion for a while, the building is now the venue for many cultural events. The little café on the patio offers some peace and quiet.

Casa de la Cultura

The Museo Regional de Aguascalientes (regional museum) is not far away from the Carranza on the opposite side of the street. The museum's subject is the history of the region, and features pictures by Santurnino Herrán (1887–1918).

Museo Regional

The Posada Museum is located in the Encino Gardens (Jardín del Encino) next to the church of the same name. The museum shows prints and drawings by the artist Juan Guadalupe Posada (1852–1913) who was born in Aguascalientes. He was known for his **socio-critical caricatures**. In his drawings he dealt satirically with death. (Open: Tue–Sun 11 am–6 pm).

★
Museo Posada

🕓

About 1 km/0.6 mi west of the city square (Plaza de la Patria) stands the Expo Plaza, which is a modern shopping and entertainment centre. A broad pedestrian passage leads directly to the new bullfight

Around the Expo Plaza

arena in the Plaza de Toros Monumental. There are a few restaurants in the Calle Paní and Paseo de la Feria. The street also leads to the San Marcos church and the Jardín de San Marcos, a park with welcome shade. Also located in Calle Pani is the Casino de la Feria. Among other attractions, it contains an arena for cockfights.

Los Arquitos

Recently, one of the former thermal springs took on new life as a cultural centre. The 19th-century bathhouse in the Avenida Alameda now features Moorish galleries, lush greenery, and small chambers with mineral bathing, as well as open basins and some public laundries. The water comes from a small underground viaduct. Today, part of the complex is a museum. Other buildings house a stage, seating and a cafeteria. There are also rooms for students of music and the theatre, aspiring artists and writers.

Museo Ferrocarrilero

The city council applied the same concept to the now dormant railway station. Inaugurated in 1884, its central location soon made it the most important railway hub in Mexico. Its facilities stretched over 90 ha/222 ac and the machine repair park was the largest in all of Mexico. In the meantime, the freight and station hall have been turned into an interesting exhibition hall for travel and crafts-related topics. To complete the picture, there are historic rail cars, computer animations and a garden with musical fountains that operate in rhythm with well-known Mexican songs.

Festival of San Marcos

The annual Feria de San Marcos in April and May is the strongest draw for visitors. Since 1604, these celebrations have been held in honour of the city's patron saint. Bull and cockfights are part of the festivities, as are charreadas (Mexican style rodeos), nightly music and fireworks.

Around Aguascalientes

León

The road south from Aguascalientes runs via Lagos de Moreno to León (population 970,000), 60 km/37 mi away. León is a vital **industrial town**, well-known for its leather goods (shoes, saddles etc).

It has developed from a city of craftsmen into a mostly modern industrial centre. There are quite a few beautiful colonial buildings here, and the city square is remarkable for its arcades; the Baroque 18th-century cathedral is also here. The town hall's elaborate façade invites attention. The 20th century new-Gothic Church of Atonement has more than 20 altars; its many crypts were used as hiding places during the Cristero War between peasants and priests and the Marxist government (1926–1929). Also located near the centre is a museum of local history and an archaeological museum with interesting finds from the Chupícuaro and Chichimec cultures. In addition, a well-visited market and the sport city (ciudad deportiva) are well-known attractions.

Baja California

B – M 1 – 9

Federal states: Baja California Norte
(B.C.N.) and / Baja California Sur (B.C.S.)

Area: 144,000 sq km/55,600 sq mi

Baja California is the long peninsula stretching like an arm into the Pacific off the shore of mainland Mexico. The Gulf of Mexico separates Baja California from continental Mexico. The peninsula is 1,250 km/777 mi long and on average 90km/56mi wide. Two federal states make up this Mexican territory, Baja California Norte and Baja California Sur. The border between the two states runs exactly along the 28th degree of latitude, which is also the border between time zones.

Baja California peninsula is hot and dry. It has mountain ranges and an interesting coastline with many different features. The main mountain ridge is the Sierra de San Pedro Mártir with Cerro de la Encantada (3,080 m/10,105 ft) as its highest peak. The Río Colorado marks the border of the state of Sonora. The river's mouth opens into the northern tip of the Gulf of California. The northern neighbour, the USA, makes its presence known; tourism and other influences have widely **Americanized** cities and villages. The desert flora

Native cave paintings are hidden in the canyons of Sierra San Francisco.

▶ VISITING BAJA CALIFORNIA

INFORMATION

Baja California Norte
Secretario Estatal de Turismo
Paseo de los Héroes No. 10289
Edificio Nacional Financiera, 4° piso
Tijuana, B.C.N. 22320
Tel. (666) 34 63 30, 34 65 74
Fax (666) 34 71 57

Baja California Sur
Coordinator Estatatal de Turismo
Carretera al Norte Km 5.5
Fraccionamiento Fidepaz
La Paz, B.C.S. 23090
Tel. (612) 401 00, 401 03
Fax (612) 407 22

GETTING AROUND

Flights go from Mexico City and other Mexican airports to Tijuana, La Paz, Mexicali and San José del Cabo. A bus ride to Baja California takes about 32 hours. From the USA, travel by aeroplane, bus or car.

WHERE TO EAT

▶ Moderate

① *El Bismark II*
Santos Degollados y
Avenida Altamirano
La Paz
Tel. (612) 122 48 54
This is a good Mexican family restaurant. Seafood is on the menu.

② *La Embotelladora Vieja*
Avenida Miramar 666
Ensenada
Tel. (646) 178 16 60
This is the most elegant restaurant in Ensenada. The building used to be a wine cellar of the Santo Tomás vineyards. The French-Californian cuisine is excellent.

WHERE TO STAY

▶ Luxury

② *Las Rosas Hotel Spa*
Carretera Tijuana – Ensenada
Km 105.5, Tel. (866) 337 67 27
www.lasrosas.com
This classy hotel (48 rooms) north of Tijuana only offers suites with a view of the ocean or the swimming pool. The hotel has restaurants, bars, a thermal spring and other amenities.

▶ Mid-range

① *La Concha Beach Resort*
Carretera a Pichilingue Km 5
La Paz
Tel. (612) 121 63 44, Fax 121 62 29
www.laconcha.com
This is a modern hotel (116 rooms) at La Concha beach. In the summer months (June–November), the hotel offers opportunities to take part in aquatic sports.
In winter, it arranges whale watching tours for travellers.

with its cactuses and the stark mountain ranges silhouetted against the sky are most impressive, and the coastline seems to stretch endlessly and features sandy beaches, cliffs and lagoons. With the exception of a few touristy places, Baja California offers the experience of a harsher, more solitary landscape. Barely 1,000 native Indians are left on the peninsula; their tribes include the Cucapá, Kiliwa, Pai-pai, Cochimí and Ki-nai.

Baja California Map

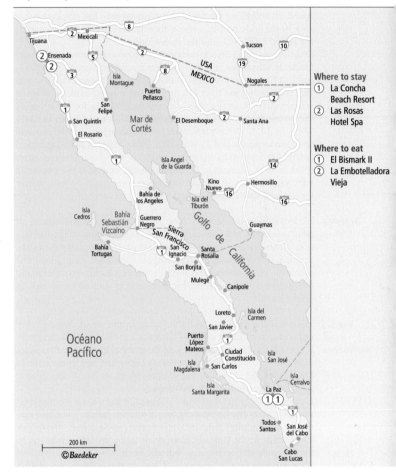

Where to stay
1. La Concha Beach Resort
2. Las Rosas Hotel Spa

Where to eat
1. El Bismark II
2. La Embotelladora Vieja

Many different animal species live in Baja California, such as mountain lions, coyotes, foxes, red deer, hares, wild geese and ducks as well as many different sea birds. The ocean is home to grey whales, sea lions, seals, dolphins, barracudas, swordfish (broadbills) and the fast-swimming bonitos (tunas).

Fauna

There are traces of human existence on the peninsula from as early as 7500 BC, but there are no indications of a high culture and nearly nothing is known about the early Indian settlers. In search of a legendary black queen named Calafia and her Amazon paradise, **Her-**

History

nán Cortés landed here in 1535 in the area of La Paz. However, the Spaniards following Cortés could not overcome the effective resistance of the Indians. Bitter about their failures, the Spaniards named the region California after the elusive queen.

Only the invading Jesuit missionaries Francisco Eusebio Kino, Juan María de Salvatierra and Juan de Ugarte could manage to colonialize parts of the country; in 1767 however, the Jesuits were expelled and first Franciscans and then Dominicans colonized the land. California was separated from Lower California in 1804; US troops occupied the peninsula during the war between the USA and Mexico in 1847/1848. In 1931, the peninsula was subdivided into a northern and southern territory, and 21 years later Baja California Norte became a federal Mexican state. Baja California Sur was given Mexican statehood in 1974. More than **50 million people now visit the peninsula each year** for duty-free shopping, whale watching or to take part in the various aquatic sports on offer here.

Economy Alongside tourism, the cultivation of cotton, corn (maize), wheat, alfalfa, vegetables and fruit play a role in regions with artificial irrigation. Cross-border industries (maquiladoras), particularly the establishment of US business activities across the border, have gained importance. The economy also profits from processing agricultural and fish products and from mining gold, copper and silver, as well as preparing salt.

Popular travel destinations Tijuana is the most visited border town in the world. Another very important destination in Baja California is the El Vizcaíno Biosphere Reserve Baja where whales, among them the **grey whales**, find sanctuary; they calve in the lagoons Ojo de Liebre and San Ignacio. While here, climb the plateau of the volcanic Sierra de San Francisco and marvel at the **pre-Hispanic paintings**.

Loreto, the first capital of Baja California, is known for its own mission as well as the one nearby, San Francisco Javier. The city's surroundings also offer welcome opportunities to be active: visitors can go kayaking in the Gulf of California or take a mountain bike out to the Sierra de la Gigante. Last but not least, every traveller can find their paradise on the beaches and bays at the southern tip of Baja California, ▶Los Cabos. There are comfortable resorts like Cabo San Lucas, neat and unpretentious places like San José del Cabo, artist colonies like Todos Santos and, a magnet for most hikers and campers, the Sierra de la Laguna with its magnificent natural marvels.

The Carretera Transpeninsular (MEX 1)

The north-south highway across Baja California, the MEX 1 (Carretera Transpeninsular) spans 1,700 km/1,100 mi from the largest city in the north at the US border ▶Tijuana, all the way down to Cabo San Lucas in the south.

SURVIVORS

A pitiless, burning sun and forests of cactus. It sounds like a film set but this scene is actually real. Mexico is the land of the cactus. More than 4,000 of the world's 6,000 species grow there and a cactus even appears on the national coat of arms. On California's Baja peninsula and in the state of Sonora, cacti can be experienced in all their glory.

Succulents is the name of the genus to which cacti belong. They are plants that store water, consisting of between 70 to 95% of water alone. It is this that makes them capable of maintaining their existence even in the most arid conditions. They can survive long periods of drought and extreme heat with ease. They even produce brightly coloured blooms. Another succulent, the agave, only produces blooms when it is about to die. In Mexico, however, it is not the flowers of the plant that are of most interest but its stalks, from which tequila and pulque are distilled

20m/65ft and can live for as many as 250 years. When the cacti are just ten years old, though, they are usually only 10cm tall. After a hundred years they can grow to 12m/39ft and start to put forth the characteristic side branches. Only then does a cactus begin producing seeds, more than 250,000 of them. Yet even with all that number, perhaps only one will germinate and grow into another cactus. A cactus can have up to 50 branches, offering plenty of food and nesting possibilities for numerous birds and bats. They are also used by people for the purposes of building.

Columnar cacti

Columnar cacti, also known as organ pipe cacti, are mightily impressive plants that can reach a height of up to

Old man cactus

This cactus certainly lives up to its name with its wrinkled skin. Its thorns even form an extra coating of fine white hair that almost completely covers the trunk. This covering provides the cactus itself with shade and reduces evaporation. Living to the biblical **age of 200 years**, the old man cactus can reach a diameter of 45cm/17in and a height of about 12m/39ft. White blooms appear only when the cactus is at an advanced age and is more than 6m/19ft tall.

Prickly pears

The prickly pear with its wide variety of sub-species is probably the best known type of cactus. It is widespread, particularly in north and central Mexico, and people have found plenty of uses for it. Its tasty and **refreshing fruits** can make the searing heat more bearable and they form the basis for the chocolate-like »queso de tuna«, which is particularly popular with children. The young shoots can also be prepared as a vegetable.

Crown of thorns cactus

The crown of thorns cactus is also popular in Europe. It doesn't grow in the desert but in tropical regions. It is one of the succulents called **wolf's milk plants** and has dozens of red or yellow flowers all along its branches.

Devil's pin cushion and other rarities

The **devil's pin cushion cactus**, like many other forms of ferocactus, forms balls up to 40cm/15in thick and has thorns of 4 to 5cm/1.5 to 2in all over it. As if this were not enough to live up to its name, the longest thorns also have extra barbs at their tips. Despite its spiky name the **sea urchin cactus** has no thorns at all. Only its shape, a grey green ball with white patches, is reminiscent of the creature for which it has been christened. Its fragrant orange blooms are intoxicating. The **prism cactus** is a real rarity. Only when the weather is damp does it unfold its 10cm/4in-long green leaves, that are actually part of the trunk with soft, fibrous thorns on the ends. It is at its best when sporting its 8cm/3in flowers in fragrant yellow.

An impressive columnar cactus →

Ensenada

The town Rosarito is situated 30km/19mi south of Tijuana, the next larger town after 80km/50mi being Ensenada (population 195,000). Stretching along the beautiful bay of Todos los Santos, this fishing port is now a **popular tourist spot for aquatic sports and offshore fishing**. The Portuguese captain Rodríguez Cabrillo was the first European to set foot here in 1542. From 1888 to 1910 Ensenada, also known as the Cinderella of the Pacific, was the capital of the northern part of Baja California before this distinction fell to today's capital Mexicali; around this time, Baja California separated into a northern and southern district. Incomes in Ensenada are mostly based on fishing and on having the region's only deep-sea port. Bodegas Santo Tomás, one of Mexico's largest and best wineries and the oldest winery in Baja California, is surrounded by Enseneda's extensive vineyards and has operated there since 1888. As the first architectural complex in Baja California, its fourteen 20th-century industrial buildings have recently been declared a national monument. The Museum of Anthropology and History (Museo de Antropología y Historia) is also remarkable.

! **Baedeker TIP**

La Bufadora

At Maneadera, 16km/10mi south of Ensenada, a road branches off north-west towards the Punta Banda headland (22km/13mi). Here, visitors can observe La Bufadora, a common natural spectacle on the Pacific coast: with terrific power, sea water is forced through a narrow opening in the rock and with a tremendous roar surf is hurled 20m/65ft into the air.

San Quintín

Back on the MEX 1, it is possible to visit several old missions on the 175 km/110 mi trip to San Quintín, for example Santo Tomás, San Vicente and Vicente Guerrero. En route, stop off at the villages La Huerta and San Miguel, which are home to Cochimi Indians. The farming and fishing village San Quintin is situated in a fertile valley near a bay (also named San Quintin) with beautiful, white beaches.

Driving on, the road south of El Rosario no longer runs parallel to the coastline; instead, it now cuts through the inner part of the peninsula. Along the highway, take the opportunity to visit more missions such as San Fernando, San Agustín and the very impressive cliff dwellings of the mission Cataviña.

Bahía de los Ángeles

Driving past the lagoon Chapala on the MEX 1, there is a junction after 50 km/31 mi. Take this branching road to the left and drive another 70 km/44 mi to reach the beautiful Bahía de los Ángeles at the Gulf of California, primarily a place to go fishing.

Border

Returning to the MEX 1, you will first reach Rosarito. Shortly before Guerrero Negro, a 40 m/130 ft-high steel eagle (Monumento Águila) marks the 28th degree of latitude and the border between the federal Mexican states Baja California (Baja California Norte) and Baja California Sur. This is also **the border between time zones** Hora del

Pacífico/Pacific Standard Time (PST) and Hora de las Montañas/ Mountain Standard Time (MST = PST + 1hr.)
The salt deposits in the immediate vicinity of Guerrero Negro, formed from salt lakes through evaporation, are among the largest in the world.

Enjoy watching the whales surface from the calm waters of the lagoons (Laguna Scammon and Laguna Ojo de Liebre) in the Bay of Sebastián Vizcaíno or in the more accessible lagoon Ignacio (located quite some distance away: take the junction on the MEX 1 at San Ignacio to the coast). Watching the grey whales return to the bay is an impressive event each year between the end of December and March. This whale sanctuary offers magnificent sights: the whales come to the surface and, usually about 2 weeks after their return, they mate or calve. Part of this bay has been a **UNESCO Natural Heritage Site** since 1993. In and around Guerrero Negro, there are several suitable whale watching spots. About 3km/2mi south of the city, a road is marked with grey whale symbols. This road leads after 27km/17mi to a National Park (Parque Natural de la Ballena Gris: »ballena gris« is the local name for grey whales). Whale watchers are obliged to follow strict rules. The trip by boat out into the bay should not last longer than 1 hour, and the number of boat trips per day is limited. Every autumn the grey whales, which can be 10–15m (30–50ft) long and weigh up to 25 tons, start their long migration from the Arctic Bering Sea to Baja California. In the first decades of the 20th century, grey whales were hunted close to extinction. However, they were placed under protection in 1947, and it was possible to remove grey whales from the list of endangered species in 1992.

Bahía Sebastián Vizcaíno

◄ Grey whales

Setting out to see grey whales up close...

San Ignacio Travel 126 km/78 mi north from Guerrero Negro into the central part of the peninsula to reach the pretty village of San Ignacio. The central point of the village is the Jesuit church, which is the best kept colonial church in Baja California. Construction began in 1728 and Juan Crisóstomo Gómez completed it in 1786. The local museum (Museo Rupestre) may also be of interest.

✳
Cave at Cuesta del Palmerito For those interested in ancient **cave paintings**, the three to four-hour trip to view the paintings of the Sierra de San Francisco, e.g. in the cave at Cuesta del Palmerito, is to be recommended. The cave paintings (100 BC to AD 1300), showing large animals and people of largely unknown origin, are a UNESCO **Human World Heritage Site**.

Baja-Indian relic

There are more caves around Santa Martha. On the way back to the coast the active volcano Las Tres Vírgenes comes into view.

The small port city of **Santa Rosalía** (population 10,000) lies 74 km/46 mi south of San Ignacio. Santa Rosalía's short history only began in the mid-1800s. Its church was built by French immigrants and former owners of the regional copper mines. Other sights of interest are the museum of anthropology in the Casa de Cultura and, at the town's northern edge, a mining museum with an old rail wagon, used to transport the ore. A ferry brings travellers from San Ignacio across the Gulf of California to Guaymas in the federal state of Sonora on the Mexican mainland.

San Borjita Caves Continuing the journey from Santa Rosalia on the peninsula, a drive of about 40 km/25 mi leads to a turn toward the Hacienda Baltasar. Proceed for about 22 km/12.7 mi on this country lane to reach the caves of San Borjita in the Sierra de la Guadalupe. There, marvellous cave paintings show hunting and war scenes. It is best to drive an all-terrain vehicle to the caves. Other caves with ancient paintings are La Trinidad, San José de los Arces, El Coyote, La Esperanza, El Rancho Guajodomi, Santa Teresa and San Baltasar del Carmen.

Mulegé Next stop is the township of Mulegé (population 5,000) on the Gulf of Mexico, with the Jesuit mission Santa Rosalía de Mulegé (1705) and the recreation of the famous Canannea jail without bars or locked doors. The jailhouse is often mentioned in folk songs and street ballads. Enjoy a nice walk through date palm groves by the river bank. The town also has several beaches and the fishing is good.

Especially lovely coastal scenery awaits you about 10km/6mi outside Mulegé at the Bahía Concepción, with beautiful beaches such as Punta Arena, Santiapac, El Coyote, El Requesón and Los Muertos.

✶
Bahía Concepción

Another picturesque township is Loreto (population 10,000). It is located an approximately 135 km/84 mi drive from Bahía Concepción. Jesuits built the town's now restored mission church in 1697, thus creating the oldest Jesuit settlement on the peninsula. The main annual festival is on 8 September, the day of Our Lady of Loreto (Día de Nuestra Señora de Loreto).

Loreto

Loreto was the place **where the European exploration and Christianization of Lower California began**, and this is documented in the mission museum. From 1776 to 1830, the town was the capital of Baja California (Spanish for lower California). Located on the Gulf of California, Loreto offers the traveller opportunities for excursions to the offshore islands, fishing on the high seas and diving.

A 40km/25mi excursion, mostly on miserable roads, leads to San Javier, where the well-maintained 18th century **mission church** honours San Francisco Javier. The beautiful Baroque façade and the gilded main altar are certain to catch the eye.

On the roadside between Loreto and San Javier, about 8km/5mi from El Pilón, there are more caves with ancient paintings and drawings.

About 40 km/25 mi south of Loreto, the MEX 1 once again turns inland. A ride of 80 km/50 mi ends in the village Villa Insurgentes. A side road leads to the wide Bahía de Magdalena (Magdalena Bay) on the Pacific coast and the port **Puerto Adolfo López Mateos**. Many whales migrate here and to the bay of Sebastián Vizcaíno for the winter months, where they mate or calve.

Whale watching excursion

There is a similarly excellent look-out point for whales south of the bay: the little port of **San Carlos**, best reached via the MEX 22 from Ciudad Constitución. The bay island Santa Margarita is home to many sea lions.

To continue the north-south route, take the Transpeninsular Highway near Ciudad Constitución and then drive about 210 km/131 mi to reach La Paz. On the MEX 1 travel the 104 km/64 mi from La Paz to the fishing village and beach resort Los Barriles. En route, you will pass San Pedro (note the junction after about 26 km/16 mi to Todos Santos and Cabo San Lucas) and the former mining city El Triunfo. A short drive of 6 km/3.7 mi further on is Buenavista, a favourite spot for those who like to fish and sail.

Travel on to San José del Cabo, about 75 km/47 mi from Buenavista, via the village of Miraflores, a former settlement of the Pericúe Indians now known for skilful leather craftsmanship. Cabo San Lucas (► Los Cabos) is at the southern end-point of the Transpeninsular Highway after another 35 km/22 mi. It is a popular port of call for cruise ships, and a great site for whale watching.

Los Cabos

✱ ✱ Barranca del Cobre

Federal state: Chihuahua (Chih.)　　**Area:** about 60,000 sq km/23,200 sq mi

**The Copper Canyon (Barranca del Cobre) actually consists of six se-
parate canyons in the Sierra Madre Occidental in Mexico's north-
west. By area, the Copper Canyons are four times as large as the
Grand Canyon in Arizona.**

The Sierra Madre Occidental with its jagged mountains is also called
the Sierra Tarahumara after the regional Indian tribe. In pre-Columbian times, Indians lived here but did not settle in one or the other
particular place. These Indians are thought to be related to today's
Tarahumara. Archaeologists have discovered ancient remnants of
buildings with storage vessels dating back to the year 1000. At the beginning of the 17th century, Jesuits conducted a search for copper,
and coming to the canyon they named it Copper Canyon or, in
Spanish, Barranca del Cobre. The Tarahumara only settled in the
often inaccessible regions around Copper Canyon when the new
holders of large properties drove them from the plateau. The Spaniards mined silver, gold, opals and other ores in the canyons. Plans
for a railroad to connect the USA (Texas) and northern Mexico with
the Pacific were first discussed in 1903. However, it took a long time
until these bold plans were finally executed between 1953 and 1961.

Excursions　The beauty of the Tarahumara Canyons (Copper Canyon) is overwhelming. Excursions can be made into the area by car, with a mule
or on horseback, or on foot. Suitable starting points are the towns
Creel, Divisadero and other stations on the railway line through the
canyons. **The 14-hour train ride** by »Ferrocarril de Chihuahua al
Pacífico« from Los Mochis to Chihuahua and back is an unforgettable experience. The train journey can be interrupted for stopovers of
various lengths or to take trips.

✱ ✱ Train Ride from Los Mochis to Chihuahua and Back

The Ferrocarril　The recently privatized Ferrocarril al Pacífico company now provides
rail services between Los Mochis and Chihuahua. The company of-
fers tourist class (first class, primero) and second class trains in both
directions. The train, called CHEPE for short, departs daily from
Chihuahua and Los Mochis at 6am (first class) and 7am (second
class). The ride takes 14 or 18 hours respectively. Tickets are sold at
all railway stations. Make reservations well in advance for rides in Ju-

*The Copper Canyons (Barranca del Cobre) are
four times the size of the Grand Canyon.* →

Barranca del Cobre Map

©Baedeker

ly, August or October and around Christmas or Easter, especially for first class trains. Also make sure to ask about schedule changes. **Information and reservations**: Tel. 01 (614) 439 72 12, www.chepe. com.mx.

Tip Travellers who start their trip to the Mexican west coast or to Baja California are likely to choose the route from Chihuahua to Los Mochis. Topolobampo on the Pacific coast is located 25 km/15.5 mi from Los Mochis; take a ferry from there to La Paz. Due to delays, night may fall before reaching the most interesting landscapes between Creel and Los Mochis. It is worth considering starting the trip in Los Mochis – then, the light of the day will reveal the beauty of the land. The train negotiates a change in altitude of **almost 2,500 m/ 8,200 ft** and goes through **86 tunnels** and over **39 bridges** in a very interesting landscape. There are highlands with cactuses, pine forests, hills and mountains, bizarre rock formations and canyons, lush mountain slopes and subtropical plantations, as well as palm and bamboo groves. The magnificent canyons, up to 1,200 m/4,000 ft

▶ VISITING BARRANCA DEL COBRE

INFORMATION
www.coppercanyonguide.com or
www.coppercanyon-mexico.com

GETTING AROUND
When travelling by car take the road
from Chihuahua to Cuauhtémoc
(104km/65mi) and then the asphalt
road via La Junta (152km/95mi) to
Creel. The train goes from Los
Mochis to Chihuahua (653km/
406mi). Small planes also fly to the
airport in Chihuahua.

WHERE TO EAT
▶ Moderate to inexpensive
El Taquito
Calle Leyva (between Hidalgo and
Independencia)
Los Mochis
Tel. (668) 812 81 19
This simple Mexican restaurant in a
central location is open around the
clock.

Tío Molcas
Avenida López Mateos 35
Creel

Tel. (635) 456 00 33
The restaurant offers good Mexican
cuisine in a rustic atmosphere.

WHERE TO STAY
▶ Mid-range
Best Western Lodge at Creel
Avenida López Mateos 61
Creel
Tel. (635) 456 00 71
Fax (635) 456 00 82
 www.thelodgeatcreel.com
The lodge has 27 rooms and consists
of several rustic cabins with four
rooms each, decorated with Tarahu-
mara folk art.

Santa Anita
Calle Leyva e Hidalgo
Los Mochis
Tel. (668) 818 70 46
Fax (668) 812 00 46
 www.santaanitahotel.com
This hotel, built in 1959, is in a
central location and has 133 rooms. It
provides travellers with an ideal base
for excursions by train into the
magnificent Copper Canyons.

deep and 1,500 m/4,900 ft wide, are located between Creel and Los
Mochis. The Copper Canyons are **in every way as impressive as the
Grand Canyon** in Arizona. Some mountain peaks are bald, some permit pine trees to grow, and all are snow-covered in winter. This is a
huge contrast to the lush tropical vegetation down on the canyon
floor, which includes citrus fruit trees and banana plants. The most
remarkable canyons are the Batopilas, Sinforosa, Tararécura, Chini-
pas, Candameña and the Río San Miguel Canyon.

The inhabitants of Creel (2338 m/7,670 ft) live from the timber in-   **Creel**
dustry. Creel is a good starting point for hikes and rides into the surrounding areas. Cusarare is located about 20 km/12.4 mi south of
Creel; you can visit an 18th-century Jesuit church there, which Indians have adorned with paintings. In the near vicinity there are also

Indian cave paintings and drawings, as well as a beautiful waterfall. The fall can be reached on foot or by all-terrain vehicle. Take an excursion to Basíhuare, Humira (52 km/32 mi), to the mining town La Bufa, to Batopilas or to the mission San Ignacio. Other Tarahumara settlements in this region are for example Rocheáchic, Norogáchic and Guachóchic.

※
Basaseáchic Falls

The beautiful Basaseáchic Falls (312 m/1,023 ft) are in easy reach from Creel (see p.266). Travel from Creel to San Juanito (31 km/ 19 mi) and from there take the road to the Cascades Nature Park (Parque Natural Cascadas). This trip is about 130km/81mi on a non-asphalted road.

Divisadero

The train usually makes a 15-minute stop for photos at Divisadero (elevation 2,250 m/7,400 ft). This is the location of the watershed between the Atlantic and Pacific oceans. The panorama is particularly beautiful here. Enjoy the great view of the Copper Canyons, Urique and Tararécura.

※ ※
Panorama ▶

Cerocahui

The village of Cerocahui is located 12km/7.5mi from the railway station Bahuichivo. The village children still attend the Jesuit mission school that has existed here since the end of the 17th century. More waterfalls cascade over rocks around the village. Upon leaving Bahuichivo, the descent down winding roads to the Pacific coast begins.

Tarahumara women at the Divisadero Barrancas railway station

Barranca del Cobre (area 60,000 sq km/23,200 sq mi) is almost ex-   **Tarahumara**
clusively part of the federal state of Chihuahua. The region is home   **Indians**
to about 50,000 Tarahumara Indians. Little is known about the origins of the Tarahumara, who refer to themselves as Rarámuri (runners). However, there is no doubt that the Rarámuri had settled throughout Chihuahua by the time of the Spanish conquest. The Indians fought the Spaniards with vigour and their fight against Caucasians and Mestizos lasted well into the 20th century. Eventually, the Indians were pushed back into the inaccessible parts of the Sierra Madre Occidental. They have managed to retain their independence to some degree.

The Tarahumara live not only in the above-mentioned regions but also in the villages of Bocoyna, Carichic, Guazápares and Guanacevi. Some of the Indians spend their winters in **cave dwellings** in the lower parts of the canyons. An elected body of 30 elders makes up the local government. The men have long hair and wear either a white or red headband, a simple tunic and a type of loincloth, while women wear a sack-like tunic and gather their wide woollen skirts with a belt. The Indians hunt, plant a few crops and raise animals. The arts and crafts of the tribe include making clay vessels to smoke meat, wicker baskets, wooden masks to symbolize other persons or animals, colourful hand-woven belts and woollen blankets.

On the surface, the Tarahumara appear to be Christians; however, many rather adhere to their own **ancient Indian religion**. The main gods represent the sun and the moon. Like the Huicholes, the Tarahumara hold the Peyotl cactus sacred. The various running contests are important Indian events, and they also mark the passing of the year. The contests last several days, during which the runners cover distances of sometimes more than 200km/124mi while kicking a wooden ball along the trail.

Bonampak · Yaxchilán

S 27/28

Federal state: Chiapas (Chis.)   **Altitude:** 360 m/1,180 ft
Distance: 130 km/81 mi south-east of
Palenque

While the trip to Bonampak may be somewhat cumbersome, it is well worth the effort. The amazing frescoes of Bonampak provide insights into the lives of the Maya and their culture. The same can be said about visiting the ruins of the ancient Maya city Yaxchilán, also located close to the Guatemalan border. A trip from Palenque taking in both Maya sites usually takes at least two days.

When Bonampak (city of murals) became known to Europeans in   **Beautiful murals**
1946, it initially did not seem to be very significant. As soon as visi-

BONAMPAK

GETTING AROUND

Trips are available from Palenque by bus or boat to Bonampak and Yaxchilán. A tour usually takes two days (camping), since the relatively long distances are covered on roads that may not be in the best of condition. Chartering a small air taxi is a good alternative, also available from Tuxtla Gutiérrez, San Cristóbal de las Casas or Ocosingo and Comitán in the federal state of Chiapas as well as from Villahermosa and Tenosique in the state of Tabasco. Drivers take the national highway (Carretera Federal) 199 toward Chancalá until they reach the Crucero de Bonampak intersection after about 200km/124mi. From there, it is only a 14km/9mi drive to the archaeological sites.

Travellers who only want to see Yaxchilán can go to the border town Frontera Corozal and from there travel 45 minutes by boat, or take a plane from San Cristóbal.

tors set their eyes on the beautiful murals from the 8th century in one of the buildings however, the archaeological site became a world sensation. Like no other find, the murals depict **Mayan life and mythology**. So far, only a small part of the ancient ruins have been excavated but the temple and city presumably did not reach the same level of religious and political importance in ancient times as the other larger Maya sites in the region, such as Palenque and Yaxchilán in Chiapas or Piedras Negras in Guatemala.

Why the temple walls in Bonampak, a now seemingly rather unimportant place, are adorned with the largest and artistically most precious Mesoamerican murals may never be explained. Most of the murals have been restored and small groups of visitors can view them. The Anthropology Museum in Mexico City and the museum in Villahermosa display very good replicas of the murals.

As far as the **site design** is concerned, the ancient Maya architects grouped the important buildings in an array with a rectangular area in the centre. Only the buildings on the southern side are still relatively intact. The main point of interest is certainly the Temple of the Murals (Templo de las Pinturas) or »Structure 1«. The murals are a window on Mayan life, their ceremonies and rites.

Opening times: daily 8am–4pm

Templo de las Pinturas

The top part of the Temple of the Murals was originally adorned with a stucco relief. However, most of this detail has been lost. All three rooms on top of the pyramid are of the same size. Their walls are covered with the famous murals (created from AD 790–792). The Maya used the **classical fresco technique** for the murals. They favoured a deep blue background colour, ochre-red for the figures, along with black, yellow, green and pink. Most of the pictures show life in the palace, celebrations, fights, as well as religious ceremonies and receptions, all in great detail.

Room 1 ► On the left, nobles attend a ceremony. They wear special tunics and shells as symbols of the earth and the underworld. Flanked by two

In the Templo de las Pinturas of Bonampak

women, the ruler of the city state sits on his platform. To the side, an underling carries the ruler's child in his arms. Three lower-ranking chiefs are depicted in a group surrounded by many underlings. In the lower centre stand three chiefs with tall Quetzal feather headdresses, in front and to the left of which are musicians with instruments as well as two people with parasols. Masked gods move amongst the musicians; on the right are spectators, also carrying parasols.

The scenes of decorated warriors with lances attacking naked men ◀ Room 2 without weapons are dated 2 August 792. The scene seems to show a surprise attack by Bonampak warriors with the objective of capturing people for sacrifices. Another picture shows the presentation of the captives. The ruler stands on a platform wearing a jaguar vest and gaiters as well as sacred jade symbols and Quetzal feathers. He is surrounded by chiefs and nobles. They look at a group of prone or seated captives at their feet.

This picture shows preparations for a feast or ceremony. A chief ◀ Room 3 honours his gods with a blood sacrifice by lancing his tongue. Also part of the scene are ten noblemen and nine seated persons. Toward the top of the picture, twelve men carry a small grotesque looking figure (earth god) on a small stretcher-like platform. The main part of the mural is the final scene with the human sacrifice and the dancers.

Lacandon-Maya Surviving families of the Lacondon-Maya live around the archaeological sites on the Río Lacan-há. Until recently, these families were considered the only **Mayan descendents untouched by modern Western lifestyles**. Their origins are not known to us because the tribe never came into contact with the Spaniards. The Lacandon call themselves the Karib and their villages are therefore called »caribal«. They keep their hair long and wear long white frocks. Until recently, these isolated Indians still used bows and arrows for their hunts and worshipped in their traditional ways in the ruins of their ancient temples. In recent years, the tribal people have lost their independence to a large degree after being targeted by missionaries, ethnologists and tourists.

Yaxchilán

Important Maya site
🕐 **Opening times: daily 8am–4pm**

Yaxchilán is an important Maya archaeological site. It is situated 40 km/25 mi north of Bonampak in the eastern part of the federal state of Chiapas. A long loop of a 200m-wide river, the Río Usumacinta, borders the area. The river is also the border of Guatemala. The town stretches about 1.5km/1mi along the river bank and extends from there on terraces far into the high surrounding hills. The excavation site is hidden by lush rain forest and therefore barely visible from the river banks. It is one of the most captivating archaeological sites in Mexico.

From 300 to 900, during the Maya classical period, **Yaxchilán was one of the large religious and political centres** in the central Mayan lowlands. The ancient city ranked equal with Palenque, Piedras Negras (located 60 km/37 mi downriver), Tikal and Quiriguá (all in Guatemala), Caracol (Belize) and also Copán (Honduras). At the height of its civilization in the 8th century, Yaxchilán seems to have ruled several of its surrounding cities, such as Bonampak. Like other Maya cities in the central region, the Maya abandoned it in the 9th century for reasons unknown to us. A German engineer was the first European to discover the ruins in 1881. The Austrian Teobert Maler was then given the chance to research the site more closely (1897–1900). He gave the site the name »Place of the Green Stones«.

Site design There are almost 100 ancient buildings along the Río Usumacinta and in the surrounding hills. Only a few buildings have been excavated and restored. The forest vegetation tends to claim back the ruins very fast, faster than people can remove the vegetation from the old stones. The buildings show no special architectural features. Long since worn down, stucco or stone figures once adorned the top ridges and higher parts of the facades. As also seen in the great Maya site of Palenque, the buildings had high sloped mansard roofs. Of particular significance in Yaxchilán are the singularly fine, yet very impressive reliefs cut into the stones of stelae, altars, door lintels and steps. The reliefs often show the transfer of power between two figures.

The most significant building is Structure 33 or the Palace of the King (Edificio 33, Palacio del Rey) on the south-west side of the square. The Hieroglyphic Stairway has 13 tablets reporting »Bird-Jaguar's« ascension to the throne in 752. His name glyph looks like a small jungle cat with feathers on its back and a bird on its head; the adornments on the three entrance lintels show the ruler and his life. Eleven of the tablets show scenes from the ball court. Niches on top of the lintels once provided the space for stone figures. The frieze still shows the remnants of original motifs. The particularly beautiful double-ridged roof has rectangular recesses in eight horizontal rows. Originally, the 2.5 m/8 ft statue of the ruler with resplendent headdress dominated the centre, but the torso of a figure from the inner palace is now placed in front of it; the head of this statue lies a small distance away from the torso. The figure has been named »the King« (el Rey).

◄ Palacio del Rey (Structure 33)

The Great Acropolis in Yaxchilán:
the temples exhibit wonderful stucco ornaments.

Structure 41 ▶ Don't miss climbing up Structure 41. It is the highest structure in Yaxchilán and a little distance away from the other buildings. The view of the entire site and the jungle around it is stunning. The hike to this structure is somewhat hard-going, and guides therefore often omit mentioning it.

Campeche

P 28

Federal state:: Campeche (Camp.)
Population: about 200,000

Altitude:: 16 m/20 ft
Distance: about 200 km/124 mi south-west of Mérida

The port city Campeche on the west coast of Yucatán on the Gulf of Mexico combines relics from the country's early history with the attributes of a modern city. The oil boom has strongly influenced the image of the town and its surroundings. In 1995, it was demolished by a hurricane. Afterwards, the historic town centre was restored and declared a UNESCO World Heritage Site.

History The Spanish conquistador Hernández de Córdoba was the first European to land here, in 1517. However, the city came into being as the town of Campeche only on 4 October 1540 through the efforts of Francisco de Montejo, the Younger (El Mozo). The name derives from the Maya settlement Ah-kin-pech. During the 16th century, the city developed into the most important **port** on the Yucatán peninsula. The harbour was repeatedly beleaguered by pirates. Many underground escape routes still exist in Campeche today; they once served as hiding places from marauding intruders. Between 1686 and 1704, the people of Campeche built a 2.5 km/1.6 mi-long, 2.5 m/8 ft-thick and up to 8 m/26 ft-high defensive wall around their city. The wall and its eight bastions secured Campeche against the pirates. In 1777, King Carlos III of Spain gave Campeche the rank of a city. A hurricane destroyed most of the city's buildings in 1807. Since 1867, Campeche has been the capital of the state of the same name. A light-and-sound spectacle at the Puerta de Tierra, one of the city's two land gates, illustrates events from Campeche's history. Until 1960, the waves of the Gulf of Mexico lapped at the other land gate, the Puerta del Mar.

What to See in Campeche

City design Even-numbered streets run parallel with the ocean and, curiously, they begin directly inside the city wall with Calle 8. Streets with odd numbers run inland and perpendicular to the even-numbered streets. Seven of the original eight bastions have been preserved. Take a stroll along the Avenida Circuito Baluartes to have a look at them.

► VISITING CAMPECHE

INFORMATION
Centro Cultural Casa No. 6
(south-west corner of the main park)
Tel. (981) 816 17 82

GETTING AROUND
By plane, Campeche is 1.5 hours away
from Mexico City.
A bus ride takes 17 hours.

WHERE TO EAT
► Expensive
La Pigua
Avenida Miguel Alemán 197 A
Tel. (529) 811 33 65
This restaurant is particularly popular
with Mexicans. It is open only from
11am to 5pm and has mostly fish on
the menu. The caviar Campechano

with spicy chili sauce is especially
tasty. The coconut shrimp (shrimp
covered with shredded coconut and
fried, served with apple sauce in a
coconut shell) are also delicious.

WHERE TO STAY
► Mid-range to budget
Colonial
Calle 14 No. 122
(between Calles 55 and 57)
Tel. (981) 816 22 22
This 31-room hotel used to be the
villa of a lieutenant. Built in 1812, it
was converted into a hotel in 1940.
Every room is furnished in a different
way. Not all rooms are air conditioned: some have fans instead.

The bastion Baluarte de la Soledad is located close to the Plaza Principal (main square). Today, the bastion houses the Maya museum,
the Museo de Estelas Mayas, with interesting stone sculptures. | **Baluarte de la Soledad**

Yucatán's first church is located opposite the museum. Construction
of the La Concepción cathedral was started in 1540 but the work was
finished only in 1705. The cathedral is flanked by beautiful old colo-
nial buildings. | **Cathedral**

A formidable arts and crafts sales exhibition is housed in the grand
villa, the Carvajal Mansion in Calle 10, No. 584. | **The Carvajal Mansion**

Enter Calle 8 and turn right to pass by the land gate Puerta del Mar
to reach the modern Governor's Palace (Palacio del Gobierno or Edificio de Poderes) and the Cámara de Diputados, the parliament of
the federal state of Campeche. | **Governor's Palace**

Calle 8 ends at the Baluarte San Carlos, which is one of the oldest
and best maintained fortifications of Campeche. An arts and crafts
centre next door has a large selection of Panama hats. | **Baluarte San Carlos**

Inside this bastion, the display in the small botanical garden Xmuch'-
haltun features palms, agaves and other local plants. | **Baluarte Santiago**

Casa del Teniente del Rey
The new regional museum has been established in the Casa del Teniente del Rey, Calle 59, No. 40 (near the Puerta de Tierra). It displays archaeological finds from the Campeche region, such as burial objects from Calakmul, including a precious mosaic mask.

Church of San Francisco
The 16th-century San Francisco church is located at the intersection of Calle 59 and Calle 18. The church contains five wood-carved altars with vermillion-red and white-painted ornamentation. The first Mass on Mexican soil is supposed to have been said in 1517 in the monastery San Francisco, which is located north of the church at the wharf Miguel Alemán (Malecón). Jerónimo, the grandson of Hernán Cortés, was likely baptized here in 1562. The baptismal font is still in use.

The market
Visiting the market is particularly enjoyable during festivities. Visitors buy mementos here, such as jipis (a type of Panama hat) and objects made from tortoise shells, sea shells or hardwoods.

Fuerte San Miguel
At the southern periphery of the city, turn off onto the coastal road to reach the fortress Fuerte San Miguel in a beautiful lofty location.

A splendid view from the San Miguel fortress

Pass the drawbridge to see the stronghold with its cannons. There is also a small but very interesting archaeological museum (Museo de Arqueología) displaying finds from Maya culture. The **Jaina terracotta figures** are especially noteworthy, as are the well-designed diagrams showing an overview of all Pre-Columbian cultures.

◄ Museum of Archaeology

For those interested in maritime finds the Museo de Marinería y Armas (maritime and weapons museum) displays interesting items, including models of ships from colonial times and the pirate era. There is a beautiful view of the town from the fortress.

Fuerte San José

A Coastal Trip to Villahermosa

The 65 km/40 mi trip south on the MEX 180 to Champotón (population 41,000) takes in the ports and fishing villages Lerma (8 km/5 mi) and Seybaplaya (33 km/21 mi).

In pre-Hispanic times, the port of Champotón was the centre of a larger Indian region and served as a hub for the cultural exchange between Guatemala, Yucatán and Central Mexico. Two cultures very likely merged here, the dominant Toltec and the Maya. After the 10th century many of these Maya migrated east and merged with other Maya tribes there. Today, Champotón is mostly a fishing harbour and port for **offshore fishing**. It is convenient to plan excursions into the state of Campeche from here. The only surface river on the Yucatán peninsula is the approximately 40km/25mi-long Río Champotón with its mouth in Champotón. From here, tourists can explore the first two thirds of the river by boat.

Champotón

The village Isla Aguada is located some 100km/62mi past Campotón. From there, the 3.4km/2.1mi-long ocean bridge Puente de Unidad leads onto the island Isla del Carmen. The bay of Campeche lies off the northern island shore; the southern shore closes off the lagoon called Laguna de Términos. This fresh-water lagoon is supplied by several rivers. Isla del Carmen, formerly known as Isla de Tris, looks like a giant sandbank off the coast. From 1558 to 1717, it was a hiding place and base for pirates, from which they menaced the Spanish ports on the Gulf of Mexico.
Situated at the south-west end of the 40km/25mi-long island is **Ciudad del Carmen** (population 100,000). Alfonso Felipe de Andrade named the city in honour of the Virgin of Mount Carmel. He made a name for himself fending off pirates. The citizens annually commemorate the victory over the pirates in 1717 with celebrations that last from 15 to 31 July. Today, the port is a centre for shrimp fishing as well as the most important trans-shipment centre for Gulf of Mexico oil. The colourful glass windows in La Virgen del Carmen cathedral are remarkable. A small archaeological museum, housed in the Liceo Carmelita (convent), displays Maya ceramics.

Isla del Carmen

Xicalango	Using a recently finished bridge, you can go back to the fishing village El Zacatal on the mainland. Only a few miles down the road stands the lighthouse of Xicalango. In pre-Columbian times, this marked a very important trading post between Mesoamerica and Yucatán. Cortés once made a stop here on his way to Veracruz. It was here that he met the Indian woman **La Malinche**, who became his lover, interpreter and guide on his Mexican conquest.
The way to Villahermosa	After about 30 km/19 mi a bridge spans the Río San Pedro y Pablo, and after a further 24 km/15 mi a second bridge crosses the Río Grijalva near Frontera. ▶Villahermosa is another 75 km/47 mi away.

From Campeche to Mérida (MEX 180)

The shorter route	The MEX 180 is the shortest route from Campeche to Mérida. However, the longer route on the MEX 261 is the better choice if the itinerary includes visits to Edzná, Kabah or Uxmal.
Hecelchakán	The next 56/35 mi leg of the route runs via Tenabo to the village of Hecelchakán with its Franciscan church from the year 1620 and an archaeological museum, the Museo Arqueológico del Camino Real. The museum displays a beautiful collection of the well-known **clay figures from the island of Jaina**. At the height of its civilization (AD 600–900), Jaina (House of Water) was an important Maya centre and ceremonial gathering site. About 1,000 pre-Hispanic burial sites have been found in Jaina. In its patio, the Jaina Museum displays stelae and door lintels from the surrounding excavation sites. Several archaeological sites exist around Hecelchakán, for example Kocha and Xcalumkin (Holactún).

> **! Baedeker TIP**
>
> **Hats with history**
>
> The village Becal, between Campeche and Mérida, is widely known for its lightweight hats that are tailor-made for hot climates. The hats or »jipijapas« are soft and pliable. They are made of palm fronds. Becal citizens have been weaving these hats since the 19th century in karst caves where the climate is perfect for keeping the fronds from breaking in the process of forming the hats.

From Campeche to Mérida (MEX 261)

✳ Edzná ⏲ Opening times: daily 8am–5pm	Some 65 km/40 mi south-east of Campeche and off the main route on the MEX 261 is the excavation site Edzná (House of Masks). The site is located on the periphery of a region with many archaeological sites. According to the often-used suffix in the names of settlements, the region was given the name Chenes (wells). The so-called Chenes style (see below) is attributed to art from this region. Edzná however does not quite fit this classification because finds also show signs of other styles, such as the Río Bec, Puuc and classical Maya architectural styles. Once, Edzná was a Maya post on the main trading route

between the highlands and the coast. Today, the buildings are ruins in a wide valley with tropical forest and agricultural lands. Low hills border on the northern and eastern parts of the valley. People had already settled in Edzná by around 400 BC, but its time of prosperity was between AD 600 and 900: according to estimates, about 60,000 people lived in Edzná around the year 650. The archaeological sites around Edzná cover about 6 sq km/2.3 sq mi. Many ancient buildings have not yet been excavated or have been reclaimed by vegetation after initial archaeological efforts. The Maya often built new constructions on top of existing ones, and dating the finds can therefore be difficult. The buildings around the central courtyard are especially remarkable; a square altar platform is located in the centre of this courtyard. On its western side, the altar has a small upright section known as La Picota.

The most interesting accessible monument in Edzná stands on the eastern side of the courtyard. This is the famous Temple of Five Storeys, also known as »the Palace« (Edificio de los Cinco Pisos, Structure of Five Storeys). Its base is almost a square measuring 60 x 58m (197 x 190ft). On the outside of the structure, pyramid steps reach up to the fourth storey. Each storey is 4.60m/15ft high. Atop the fourth storey rests the temple with its 6m/20ft-high mansard roof. The small rooms of the first four storeys were presumably places for the priests while the temple with the altar platform served as the most sacred point. The columns at the base are built from several stones in a style reminiscent of the Río-Bec style. In the fourth storey however, the columns are monolithic and have quadrangular capitals as were common in the Puuc region. In the first storey and underneath the steps is a passage with an arched cantilever roof. This passage is also the point of access to the inner room. This very impressive construction is a good example of the predominant **prosaic architectural style** in Edzná with simple ledges and plain facades; the style is clearly distinct from the architecture of regions where ceremonial buildings were constructed in the classical Chenes or Puuc style.

◄ Edificio de los Cinco Pisos

The House of the Moon (Casa de la Luna) is located at the west side of the courtyard. The building rests on a base plate and sits in the shade of a higher temple. The wide outside steps are framed by a double row of six terraces. In one corner of the courtyard stands the Temple of the South-west. This temple consists of a rectangular platform, which forms the base for tilted walls. Steps lead to the upper terrace with remnants of temple walls. The Temple of the North-west (Templo del Noroeste) occupies the other corner on the same side. A side building of the temple presumably served as a sweat bath (temazcalli).

◄ Main courtyard

Another ancient building complex is worth mentioning. The buildings are grouped around the ceremonial plaza (Grupo del Centro Ceremonial). The Great Acropolis (La Gran Acrópolis) occupies the eastern part of this plaza and the Great House takes up the western

◄ Great Ceremonial Plaza

The at least 30m/100ft-high Temple of Five Storeys (Edificio de los Cinco Pisos) towers above the whole site and is visible from a distance.

side (Casa Grande or Nohol'ná). At the northern corner is the Platform of the Knives (Plataforma de los Cuchillos), and in the southern part of the plaza stands the Temple of the South (El Templo del Sur). The Edzná building complex is in a region below sea level. Therefore, the Maya designed an ingenious drainage system for the site. The system, consisting of underground channels and retention basins, is located south of the Great Acropolis.

Chenes culture From Hopelchén (about 50 km/31 mi north-east of Edzná) those interested in archaeology will most likely want to make a trip south to the region of the Chenes culture (AD 550–830). Three Maya architectural styles dominated in the late classical period on the Yucatán peninsula: the Puuc style (►Uxmal) in the north-west; the Río Bec style (►Chetumal) in the south; and the Chenes style in the north. The styles have much in common. In contrast to the Puuc style, in Chenes-style buildings the façades are completely covered with trimmed stone or stucco. The entrances are shaped like wide open snake mouths and the long-nosed masks of gods adorn the corners of the buildings. See examples of this style at the excavation sites Dzehkabtún, El Tabasqueño and Dzibalchén (San Pedro), 20km/12.4mi south-east of Hopelchén.

Hochob The Maya site Hochobis located about 13km/8mi south-west of Dzibalchén via Chenkoh on a country road, which is passable only in the dry season. This site was built in the classical Chenes style. The Maya placed the buildings around a central square. A temple with three chambers on the north side is particularly remarkable: it is well preserved and the remnants of a roof ridge tower over the central chamber. The doorways are shaped like the wide open mouths of masks. The rest of the façade is covered with stylized snake motifs.

Another trip on almost 20km/12.4mi of country roads goes from Dzibalchén to Iturbide and the excavation site Dzibilnocac in the near vicinity. This is one of the largest excavations in the Chenes region. The main temple façade here is similar to the one in Hochob.

Dzibilnocac

Bolonchén de Rejón is 33 km/21 mi north of Hopelchén on the MEX 261. A road leads from there to the nearby Grutas Xtacumbil-xunan, where there is a giant system of dripstone caves and large sinkholes (cenotes). Only a minute portion of the system has been explored and made accessible. At the present time, it is hard even to estimate the entire size of the cave system.

Grutas Xtacumbil-xunan

Not far from Bolonchén are the temple ruins of Kichmool and Itzimté. The architecture of these archaeological sites combines elements of the Chenes and Puuc styles.

Kichmool and Itzimté

The MEX 261 leads to ►Uxmal in the state of Yucatán. A side road brings you to the ruins on the ►Puuc Route.

In the vicinity

✶ Cancún

Federal state: Quintana Roo (Q.R.)
Population: 430,000

Altitude: sea level
Distance: 320 km/320 mi east of Mérida

Cancún was designed in the 1970s on the drawing board from the following components: white, sandy beaches, the wonderful turquoise-blue waters of the Caribbean Sea, a huge lagoon and a temperate tropical climate. The plan worked and Cancún very soon became a popular beach destination.

The 22 km/13.7 mi-long and about 400 m/440 yd-wide island features about 100 hotels with a total of more than 20,000 beds. A dam separates the beachfront from the modern city of Cancún on the mainland. The city has grown with the influx of tourists: there is a futuristic looking bus terminal and a new yacht harbour, and new land developments are planned north of Punta Sam.

Originally, Cancún was a Maya village. In 1843, Stephens and Catherwood described the village and called it Can-cune (pot at the end of the rainbow). No more than 100 Maya lived in Cancún when the development project started in earnest; they lived by fishing and collecting the sap of the chicle (sapotil) tree. The Mexican government

History

Cancún Plan

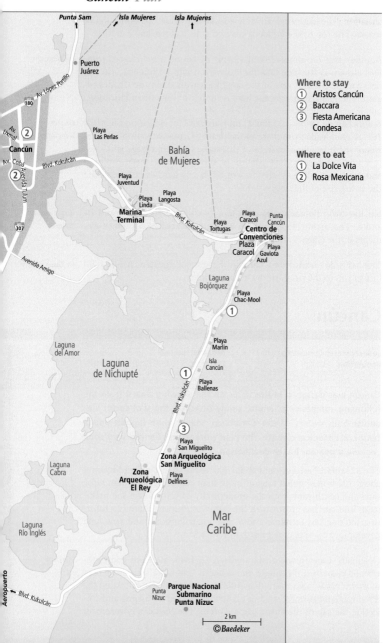

Where to stay
1. Aristos Cancún
2. Baccara
3. Fiesta Americana Condesa

Where to eat
1. La Dolce Vita
2. Rosa Mexicana

Punta Sam Isla Mujeres Isla Mujeres

Puerto Juárez

Av. López Portillo

180

Av. Uxmal

Cancún

Av. Coba

Avenida Tulum

Blvd. Kukulcán

307

Avenida Amigo

Playa Las Perlas

Bahía de Mujeres

Playa Juventud

Playa Linda

Playa Langosta

Marina Terminal

Blvd. Kukulcán

Playa Tortugas

Playa Caracol

Punta Cancún

Centro de Convenciones

Plaza Caracol

Playa Gaviota Azul

Laguna Bojórquez

Playa Chac-Mool

Laguna del Amor

Laguna de Nichupté

Playa Marlin

Isla Cancún

Playa Ballenas

Blvd. Kukulcán

Playa San Miguelito

Zona Arqueológica San Miguelito

Laguna Cabra

Zona Arqueológica El Rey

Playa Delfines

Laguna Río Inglés

Mar Caribe

Aeropuerto

Blvd. Kukulcán

Punta Nizuc

Parque Nacional Submarino Punta Nizuc

2 km

©Baedeker

and private enterprise selected the village as the best choice for an international holiday centre. The tourist spot was constructed according to a master plan.

Tourist Attractions

Cancún is a city divided. The core of the city is the commercial zone with mostly public buildings, shops and family homes, a few small hotels, a bullfight arena and the large market.

Commercial zone

The zona hotelera (hotel zone) is the tourist domain on the island connected to the mainland by bridges. Large hotels are lined up in a row along the naturally beautiful coastal strip. Holidaymakers enjoy many activities here, such as diving, off-shore fishing, para-sailing and golf.

Hotel zone

In the convention centre (**Centro de Convenciones**), the museum for anthropology and history (Museo de Antropología y Historia) displays objects from the Maya culture and presents exhibitions on the history of the federal state of Quintana Roo. Close to the convention centre, there are two of many shopping centres on the Paseo Kukulkán.

Museum of anthropology and history

From the top of the new Cancún tower (La Torre Cancún) visitors have the most **spectacular view**. The tower is located at the El Embarcadero centre next to the convention centre. A rotating panorama

La Torre Cancún

A refreshing dip – one of the perfect beaches on the Caribbean coast

► VISITING CANCÚN

INFORMATION

Avenida Tulúm 5
Tel. (998) 887 43 29
and in the Avenida Tulúm 26
Tel. (998) 88 46 53 29 or at
www.allaboutcancun.com

GETTING AROUND

The flight time from Mexico City is
about 2 hours. There are flights from
Mérida or Monterrey, from US airports and from the European airports
Zurich, London and Paris. From
London, for example, American Airlines, Air Canada and Lufthansa all
offer flights to Cancún. Travelling by
bus from Mexico City takes about 24
hours.

SHOPPING

The very modern shopping centre at
the Plaza Caracol at the Paseo Kukulkán around the major hotels can
satisfy almost any demand. Aside from
designer clothing, shops also offer the
products of local arts and crafts. There
are also well-stocked book stores. In
the Costa-Blanca-shopping centre next
to the Plaza Caracol, shoppers can find
a large selection of modern and
traditional Mexican clothing.
Smaller shops line the Avenida Tulúm.

WHERE TO EAT

► Expensive

① *La Dolce Vita*
Paseo Kukulkán Km 14.6
(across the street from the Marriott
Hotel)
Tel. (990) 885 01 61, 885 01 50
www.cancunitalianrestaurant.com
This restaurant has a romantic European atmosphere. Italian food is
served while diners enjoy the view of
the Nichupté lagoon. A reservation is
strongly recommended.

► Moderate

② *Rosa Mexicana*
Calle Claveles 4
Tel. (998) 884 63 13
The waiters in this Mexican colonial-
style restaurant wear the garb of the
charros (horsemen). Guests can eat by
candlelight on the patio.

WHERE TO STAY

► Luxury

② *Baccara Boutique Resort*
Blvd. Kukulkán Km 11.5 (opposite
Planet Hollywood)
Tel. (998) 813 90 00
The small hotel with 27 rooms has
been renovated under its new man-
agement. It is furnished with Mexican
antiques. Each room has a kitchenette.
There is a choice of three restaurants
and three bars.

③ *Fiesta Americana Condesa Cancún*
Blvd. Kukulkán Km 16.5 Lote 44
Zona Hotelera
Tel. (998) 881 42 00
Fax (998) 881 42 59
www.fiestaamericana.com
This is one of the three Fiesta Hotels in
Cancún with 602 suites. It features
three seven-storey towers around a
patio. Visitors may choose from five
restaurants, two bars, three tennis
courts and a fitness centre.

► Mid-range and budget

① *Aristos Cancún Plaza Hotel*
Blvd. Kukulkán Km 20.5
Zona Hotelera
Tel (98) 85 33 33
Fax (98) 85 02 36
www.aristoshotels.com/cancun.html
One of the prime hotels in Cancún. Its
150 rooms each have a small balcony
with a view of either the Paseo or the
lagoon.

capsule brings visitors 80 m/262 ft up to the top of the tower.

The **beaches** de las Perlas, Juventud, Linda, Langosta, Tortugas, Caracol and Chac-mool, of which the latter three are the most popular, stretch from the city limits along the Paseo Cancún and the Paseo Kukulkán.

The 18-hole public **golf course** Pok-ta-Pok is situated at the street marker Km 7.5 on the Paseo Kukulkán.

! **Baedeker** TIP

See more of the sea

Those who want to do more than just swim and sunbathe in Cancún can observe sea-dwellers up close without getting unduly wet in the first interactive aquarium in Latin America (in the Isla shopping centre, Blvd. Kukulkán, Km 12.5). The same applies to Aquaworld's submarine trip (www.aquaworld.com.mx). Fans of more genuine ocean experiences will enjoy sailing to Isla Contoy on board an exact replica of Columbus's caravel or a pirate cutter (information and bookings: tel. 01 80 07 15 33 75).

A hydrofoil brings people to the **islands** ► Cozumel and ► Isla Mujeres, departing from the convention centre. Boats go to the uninhabited Isla Contoy, the most important nesting site for sea birds in the Mexican Caribbean. Only 200 visitors with a permit are allowed on the island per day.

Several interesting Maya ruins have been found between Punta Cancún and Punta Nizuc. The buildings are mostly executed in the Puuc style. Collectively, they are known as the **El Rey** ruins. Occasionally, they are also called Pinturas, San Miguel, Yamilum, Pok-ta-poc or El Conchero. The ruins consist of pyramid stumps with temples built on top of them, sometimes with rounded corners. More than 50 graves have also been found here.   **Maya sites**

For quite a few years now, tourism has sparked the economy on the 150km/93mi-long beach strip called the ►Riviera Maya, which is the coastline between Cancún and ►Tulum. Tourists come here to enjoy the beautiful beaches.   **Riviera Maya**

★ # Catemaco Lake (Laguna de Catemaco)

Federal state: Veracruz (Ver.)   **Altitude:** 370 m/1,200 ft
Distance: 565 km/351 mi east of Mexico City

The beautiful Catemaco Lake is surrounded by several volcanic peaks; tropical vegetation adds special charm to the region. The people who live here are known for practicing witchcraft. Mexican tourists like to come here especially at weekends and during holidays; foreign travellers also visit to participate in spiritual ceremonies or to see the location of the Sean Connery movie »Medicine Man« (1992).

Catemaco Lake and its islands Ténapi and Agaltepec are only 35km/ 22mi away from the the Gulf of Mexico. Catemaco is one of Mexico's most beautiful inland lakes. The lake is 16 km/10 mi long and its surface area measures about 130 sq km/50 sq mi. The dormant volcano San Martin (1,850 m/6,070 ft) is the highest mountain in the area. The regional abundance of water is unusual for a Mexican landscape, but here plenty of water feeds the Río Cuetzalapa and the romantic, 41 m/135 ft-high Eyipantla falls 8km/5mi east of San Andrés Tuxtla. Indians live in villages on the slopes of the San Martin volcano east of Acayucan. They are Popoluca Indians, like the Mecayapan and Soteapan, who do not belong the Nahua language group.

Catemaco The most important town on the lake is Catemaco (population 30,000) on the north-western shore. The citizens live mostly from fishing and tourism. The faithful bring votive gifts to the church of the Virgen del Carmen at the plaza and choose this church as their **pilgrimage destination**. Annual celebrations honour the Virgin del Carmen on 16 July. Catemaco is also home to many **curanderos** (healers) and **brujos** (witch doctors), a strong attraction for some. From all over Mexico, the sick come here to seek help and others to receive advice on all of life's questions. The tropical forests around Catemaco provide a great variety of medicinal plants.

▶ VISITING CATEMACO LAKE

INFORMATION
in the Municipalidad Catemaco
at the Zócalo
Tel. (294) 943 00 16

GETTING AROUND
Take the bus from Veracruz to be in Catemaco in about three hours. It is necessary to change to another bus in San Andrés Tuxtla. By car, drive 155km/96mi south on the MEX 180 from Veracruz to Catemaco. After reaching Minatitlán, go another 120km/75mi north on the MEX 180.

WHERE TO EAT
▶ **Inexpensive**
Many restaurants around the city square and on the lake offer fish and seafood. Be sure to try the local specialities, such as mojarra (sea fish) or carne de chango (smoked pork with chili).

WHERE TO STAY
▶ **Mid-range to budget**
Hotel La Finca
Carretera 180 Costera del Golfo
Km 147
Tel. (294) 947 97 10
www.lafinca.com.mx
The beautiful lakefront hotel is located in a 7,000 sq m/8,370 sq yd park. Enjoy the splendid view of the lake from all 57 rooms.

Every treatment by a brujo starts with a cleansing, in which aromatic herbs are burned, prayers recited and the patient rubbed with branches.

Tanaxpilo island and Changos island (monkey island) are favourite places for excursions. Cared for by the University of Veracruz, a number of stump tail macaques (imported from Thailand) live on the island.

Isla Tanaxpilo

The ecology park (Parque Ecológico) at the northern lake shore preserves a small area of rainforest. On the guided tours visitors learn about the ecology, drink the regional mineral water and observe the toucans, turtles and monkeys.

Ecology park

Take the 40 km/25 mi trip north from Catemaco to the fishing village Montepío and see the steep mountains with lush vegetation, picturesque lagoons and attractive beaches along the way. The beaches Jicacal and Escondida are perhaps most worth a visit.

Montepío

From Catemaco to Veracruz

San Andrés Tuxtla (population 60,000) is a 15km/9mi drive west on the MEX 180. The former colonial city is situated in a caldera and surrounded by hills. In pre-Hispanic times, the town's name was Zacoalcos. The two churches, San José and Santa Rosa, are noteworthy.

San Andrés Tuxtla

In 1902, in the vicinity of the town, a 20 cm/7.9 in Olmec jade statue was found. It depicts a priest and has the date 162 inscribed upon it. Today, the so-called Tuxtla Statue is displayed in Washington. San Andrés is a centre for cigar making, and you may like to visit the cigar maker Te amo.

Laguna Encantada

The legendary crater lake Laguna Encantada (enchanted lake) is situated just 5km/3mi away, down a rough country road. Paradoxically, the water level in the lake falls during the rainy season and rises in the dry season. At times, the volcano heats the water in its caldera so much that all the fish die. As soon as the water cools down, fish return to the lake.

Santiago Tuxtla

Santiago Tuxtla (population 51,000) is another 10 km/6 mi west on the MEX 180. The Río Tuxtla flows through the town on the edge of the tropical forest. One of the typical Olmec colossal heads rests in the central town plaza, and the small Tuxteco Museum displays more Olmec finds, mostly stone sculptures from the Olmec cultural centre Tres Zapotes and from Nestepe. Two patron saints are honoured with celebrations, San Juan on 24 June and Santiago Apóstol from 23 to 25 July. The feasts involve processions and the performance of the Indian dance Liseres, in which the participants wear jaguar costumes.

Picked fresh: This stand in Santiago Tuxtla sells fresh pineapples.

In Tres Zapotes, archaeologists have excavated two of the colossal heads sculpted from basalt, as well as the stele C which bears the second oldest written date (32 BC) so far found in the Americas. The finds have been distributed over several museums. However a pleasant, small museum has been established in recent years in Tres Zapotes itself. The museum is 24km/15mi from Santiago Tuxtla via Villa Isla.

Tres Zapotes

Some 70 km/44 mi north-west of Santiago Tuxtla is Alvarado (population 50,000) on the Gulf Coast. The town is located on a spit that separates the Alvarado lagoon from the Gulf of Mexico. ►Veracruz is 70 km/44 mi from Alvarado.

Alvarado

From Catemaco to Villahermosa

The important traffic hub Acayucan (population 37,000) is located a further 80 km/50 mi south-east on the MEX 180. Take the junction to the MEX 185 to go via the Isthmus of Tehuantepec to Juchitán (195 km/121 mi), ► Tehuantepec (220 km/137 mi) and Salina Cruz (235 km/146 mi) on the Gulf of Tehuantepec.

The city of Minatitlán (population 180,000) is located 40 km/25 mi north-east of Acayucan off the MEX 180. Due to the oil boom and sulphur mining, the city has developed into an industrial centre.

Minatitlán

The hard-to-reach excavation site San Lorenzo Tenochtitlán (1200–900 BC) is situated on the banks of the Río Chiquito about 45km/28mi south-west of Minatitlán. Aside from statues, nine colossal heads have been found here. Among the finds were also many ritualistically mutilated stone statues: the destruction may relate to the death of the depicted ruler. The stone relics were obviously buried when the city perished. A recently discovered colossal head has now found a new home next to the museum.

San Lorenzo Tenochtitlán

25 km/15.5 mi of freeway in north-eastern direction lead from Minatitlán via a bridge over the Río Coatzocoalcos to the important port and industrial city Coatzacoalcos (population 400,000). The city is now a petrochemical centre and expanded fast in the years of the oil boom. The development however has come at a very high price in terms of the horrendous contamination of air, soil and water.

Coatzacoalcos

The Río Tonalá forms the border of the state of Tabasco about 40 km/25 mi south-east of Coatzacoalcos. A turning after 4.5 km/2.8 mi leads to a swampy oil field and the village of La Venta another 5km/3mi north-west.
At the periphery of the small town is the excavation site La Venta, which was once the most important **political and religious Olmec centre**. The Olmec era is therefore often also called the »La Venta

La Venta

culture«. The influence of this first Mesoamerican high culture was enormous. It stretched from the Gulf Coast through central Mexico all the way to the west coast and to El Salvador in the south. The La Venta culture also affected the early phases of the Monte Alban and the Maya civilizations. The Olmec were at the zenith of their influence between 900 and 600 BC. The once magnificent, more than 32m/105ft-high temple pyramid made from clay is now overgrown. Among the finds next to the pyramid were four of the familiar colossal heads (cut from basalt), stone altars and stelae, as well as ceramics and jade figurines. Some artefacts are on display in the local museum, and other evidence of the mysterious La Venta culture is displayed in the La Venta open-air museum of ►Villahermosa.

Chetumal

Q 30

Federal state: Quintana Roo (Q.R.)
Population: 210,000

Altitude: sea level
Distance: about 450km/280mi southeast of Mérida and about 380km/236mi south of Cancún

Before the city fell to the Spaniards, Chetumal was an important port for the Maya who traded gold, feathers and copper here and brought them to the north of Yucatán. From then until 1898, the place was only sparsely populated. Today Chetumal, situated at the mouth of the Río Hondo at the southernmost point of the Yucatán east coast, is the capital of Quintana Roo. (The Río Hondo marks the border of Belize, the former British Honduras.)

The port city developed quickly as soon as traffic connections and the free-port had been established. Beautiful lagoons and reefs around the city have made Chetumal attractive for tourists. It is also a good base for excursions to the many archaeological sites nearby. At weekends, the markets overflow with customers from neighbouring Belize.

History   Chetumal has a long and multifaceted history. The city's original name was Chactemal, i.e. in the Maya language »place where brazilwood grows«. For many centuries, it was a sea port and centre for boat building. In 1512, the first Spaniards to come here, Gerónimo de Aguilar and Gonzalo Guerrero, were shipwrecked and the Maya enslaved them. Aguilar was later freed by Cortés and then served him with his invaluable skills as an interpreter. In contrast, Guerrero married a Maya princess and for a long time successfully fought on the side of the Maya against the Spanish intruders. Chetumal's history under the Spaniards starts only in 1898. This was the year when

● VISITING CHETUMAL

INFORMATION

Secretría de Turismo
Calle Calzada del Centenario 622
Tel. (982) 835 08 60
Fax (982) 835 08 80
An additional information booth offers its services at the corner of Avenida Héroes and Aguilar.

GETTING AROUND

A bus trip from Mexico City to Chetumal takes roughly 22 hours. The travel time from Mérida is 8 hours, and from Cancún 6 hours. There are daily flights from and to Cancún, Mérida and Mexico City.

WHERE TO EAT

▶ Moderate

La Mansión Colonial
Calle Bahía 8
Tel. (983) 832 26 54
This restaurant specializes in Tampico cuisine.

WHERE TO STAY

▶ Luxury

Chicaná Ecovillage Resort
Carretera Escárcega-Chetumal
Km 150, Xpuhil
Tel. (981) 622 33
Fax (981) 116 18
This small, comfortable hotel with 32 rooms is located next to the archaeological zone of Chicaná. It is furnished in the Maya style.

▶ Mid-range

Holiday Inn Chetumal-Puerta Maya
Avenida Héroes 171, Col. Centro
Tel. (983) 83 50 400
Fax (983) 83 50 429
 www.ichotelsgroup.com
The former Hotel Continental has 85 rooms and is located across from the market and two blocks from the Maya museum (Museo de la Cultura Maya). It is one of the few air-conditioned hotels.

Captain Othón Blanco established the city, under the name of Payo Obispo. This name was later dropped. During the Caste War of Yucatán, the city served mostly as a frontier post with the objective of preventing the flow of weapons and munitions to the insurgent Indians. At this time, the city was built without a particular plan and consisted of wooden houses, and its citizens eeked out a meagre existence based on agriculture and fishing. In 1954, a hurricane almost levelled the town. The Mexican central government then built the city anew, and Chetumal is now an important trade centre for the eastern Yucatán peninsula.

Aside from a few very old log houses, modern Chetumal offers few sights for tourists. The Museum of Maya Culture (Museo de la Cultura Maya at the Avenida Niños Héroes) is worth visiting, providing a overview of the arts, architecture, religion and the daily lives of the Maya. Several models show significant Maya buildings the way they may have looked when they were new and the style was at its zenith. Using touch-screen computers, visitors can learn about the Maya cal-

✱
**Museum of
Maya Culture**

endar and their glyphs. The museum also displays replicas of stelae and murals.

North of Chetumal

Laguna Bacalar

A 35 km/22 mi trip north-west on the MEX 307 ends at the Laguna Bacalar. The 56 km/35 mi-long fresh-water lake is calm and not very deep. It attracts those keen on aquatic sports, which are offered in wide variety, and angling. Maya ruins and the remnants of Spanish settlements are located on the shores of the lagoon. An 18th-century Spanish fortress in Bacalar, the Fort San Felipe, at the south-west end of the lagoon is now a history museum. The fortress is also the location for the annual celebrations from 13 to 16 August in honour of St Joaquin.

The more than 70 m/230 ft-deep **Cenote Azul** is located about 3 km/2 mi outside the city. Visitors can rest and eat at its shore.

Chetumal Bay

Chetumal bay offers good fishing opportunities. A tongue of land separates Chetumal bay from the ocean; the fishing village Xcalak is located on the southern Caribbean side of it. The village can be reached via Majahual, continuing on a rough road from there. It is a good base for offshore fishing and scuba diving. In front of the tongue of land lies the Chinchorro reef, which is part of a giant coral reef.

Felipe Carrillo Puerto

A drive of about 150 km/93 mi north on the MEX 307 from Chetumal brings you to the traffic hub Felipe Carrillo Puerto (population 20,000). It was known by the name Chan Santa Cruz (small holy cross) when it was the centre of the **Cult of the Talking Cross**, which caused the Caste War of Yucatán (1847–1901). At this time, Chan Santa Cruz was the interim capital of the independent Maya state of Yucatán. Remnants of the original Temple of the Talking Cross still exist on the north-west corner of Calles 60 and 69. The Santuario de la Cruz Parlante museum shows documents and photographs concerning the Caste War of Yucatán and the history of the city. The church involved in the talking cross cult was built in 1858. At the main city plaza, visitors can enter the church in which the insurgent Indians listened to the »apparition of the talking cross« and decided to change their fate. However, they very likely heard the voice of a hidden human speaker or a ventriloquist.

South of Chetumal

Kohunlich
🕐 Opening times: daily 8am–5pm

The excavated ruins of Kohunlich are surrounded by tropical forest. Despite their remote location, the ruins are among the best-maintained excavation sites in Mexico. To reach them from Chetumal take the MEX 186 west; after 58 km/36 mi turn left at Francisco Villa and drive another 9km/5.6mi to the excavation site. The real name of the site is Aserradero (saw mill). Kohunlich is a corrupted version of »Cohoon Ridge«. Kohunlich was first registered in 1912 when archaeological research in the neighbouring South Campeche brought attention to its existence. People however discovered the place in earnest only after 1958, when thieves were caught in the act of taking the **large god masks** from the Temple of the Masks. The work on excavation and restoration has been exemplary ever since.

The great masks of Kohunlich are unique, both in form and in the method of their creation.

So far, archaeologists have investigated an area of 2 sq km/0.8 sq mi in Kohunlich. Former residents levelled about half of the entire site and poured cement over part of it; they also turned natural trenches into collection basins to store drinking water for the dry season.

The Pyramid of the Masks (Pirámide de los Mascarones) is a unique structure and the most interesting building of its kind in Maya territory. The pyramid was built in the 5th century. Robbers once found eight great stucco masks flanking the pyramid steps, of which five are still present. The masks seem to show the sun god (Kinich Ahau). A mythological being with spiral-shaped eyes is recognizable in the large headdress. Several eyes in the masks show the glyph Chuen: the glyph is the sign for Tzolkin, i.e. the religious Maya year of 260 days. As was the custom for Maya nobles, the noses are adorned with rings. The mouths look like those of predatory cats and wear the twirled beards of the rain god. Interestingly, these latter features show Olmec characteristics. All masks wear earrings with posts, the sides of which represent snakes, which most likely symbolize the rain. ◄ Pyramid of the Masks

The great Plaza of the Stelae (Plaza de las Estelas) was named after the four monolithic stelae in the east building (Edificio Oriente). These stelae are now embedded at the edge of the steps. The Maya prepared a base plate for the plaza using a mixture of lime and honey. Remnants of this hardened ground are still visible. ◄ Plaza of the Stelae

On to Villahermosa via Francisco Escárcega

The MEX 186 traverses the only very sparsely populated southern part of Yucatán. Tropical forests and wide savannahs cover most of this region. The Ramada Chicaná Ecovillage Resort is located at the kilometre-marker 145. About 58 km/36 mi west of Chetumal, take the turning towards the Maya site Kohunlich 9 km/5.6 mi away.

Xpuhil

🕐
Opening times:
daily 8am–5pm

The archaeological site Xpuhil (Xpujil) is located about 60km/37mi west of Francisco Villa in the federal state of Campeche. The site is to the right and within walking distance of Xpuhil junction. Although the Maya had settled in and around Xpuhil earlier, the excavated buildings are considered to be from the late Maya classical period (AD 800–900).

The main structure is a palace with one tower on each side and a middle tower placed slightly behind the others. These towers are pure decoration, mimicking the familiar front of temple pyramids in Petén (Guatemala). Once, the façades over the doors were adorned with giant masks, probably stylized cat masks. This style, a combination of purely decorative towers and façade decorations, is called the Río Bec style. It is reminiscent of the Chenes style.

It is the excavation site **Río Bec**, situated 10 km/6 mi east of Xpuhil, which gave the style its name. At the time of writing, the site is closed. Please enquire at the tourist office in Xpuhil.

Hormiguero

Those interested in archaeology may like to visit the large Maya site Hormiguero, 15 km/9.4 mi distant.

Chicaná: house of the priest

Becán is located only 4km/2.5mi further along on the right side of the road. The structures here are also in the Río Bec style. Visitors see for example the palaces with the two false towers, a pyramid with a temple, altars and a ball court. The structures I to IV stand around the first plaza; these buildings were mostly erected in the last construction phase (550–830). The most interesting structure at the site is Structure IV with its monumental outside steps. Its upper part shows still intact relief sculptures on the southern façade. The northern façade consists of several terraces and entrances, which are framed by ornamental stones. On the southern side of the Central Plaza, Structure VIII with its two towers has an entrance leading to several rooms. Structure IX on the north side is not yet fully excavated. At more than 32 m/105 ft it is the highest building in Becán.

Becán
🕐
Opening times:
daily 8am–5pm

Drive 2 km/1.2 mi along the main road and turn left: the excavation site is another 5 minutes away. Some of the decorated façades are in good condition or well restored, making it easy to study the Río Bec style here. Structure II was built between 750 and 770 and is located on the eastern side of the main plaza. The major feature of the façade is a giant mask, whose open mouth leads into the structure. Again, there is the typical covering of the entire middle façade and its decoration with stylized motifs. Other structures are flanked by towers. The outer temple corners are also remarkable: they are formed from vertically stacked masks of the rain god Chac with a trunk-shaped nose.

Chicaná
🕐
open:
daily 8am–5pm

About 20 more Maya locations exist between these three sites and the border of Guatemala in the south. Most of them can only be reached on rough roads and only in the dry season. The most important city, and arguably the largest Maya City anywhere, is Calakmul with more than 6,000 structures. Among recent new discoveries are seven causeways (sacbeob) and richly endowed grave sites, including the grave of an important Calakmul ruler. Presumably, the Maya metropolis was already playing a dominant role in the pre-classical period, together with Nakbé and El Mirador (both in Guatemala). So far, the finds include about 120 stelae that are dated between 434 and 810. The local biosphere reserve covering an area of 7,500 sq km/2,900 sq mi is named after Calakmul.

Calakmul, Balamkú and other Maya sites
🕐
open:
daily 8am–5pm

Balamkú (Temple of the Jaguar) is located about 60 km/37 mi west of Xpuhil at the Conhuas junction. Surprisingly, this well-preserved magnificent site does not conform to either the Río Bec style of nearby sites or the northern Chenes style. The most intriguing structure is La Casa de los Cuatro Reyes (House of the Four Kings) with a unique figure frieze on the upper façade. The frieze is 17 m/56 ft long and 1.5 m/4.9 ft wide and includes scenes with four kings, as well as jaguars with grotesque masks with vipers in their fangs.

The re-discovered ruins at **Nadzcaan** are located about 15km/9.3mi north-east of Balamkú. The site consists of three groups of structures. Among the at least 40 structures are two pyramids, a temple, a ball court and 13 stelae. In the early classical period (300–600) Nadzcaan, together with Balamkú, held an important cultural, commercial and social position between Edzná and Petén (Guatemala). **Dzibanché and Kinichná** are other important Maya sites in the region.

Connection to Palenque and Villahermosa
273 km/170 mi separate Chetumal and the traffic hub Francisco Escárcega. At this hub, the MEX 261 from Campeche and Champotón merges with the MEX 186. Cross the Río Usumacinta after 150km/93mi, and after another 182 km/113 mi take the Catazaja junction to ► Palenque. From here, drive a further 116 km/72 mi to ► Villahermosa, crossing the Río Grijalva shortly before entering the city.

✷ ✷ Chichén Itzá

O 30

Federal state:: Yucatán (Yuc.)   **Altitude::** 10m/33ft
Distance:: 120km/75mi east of Mérida

Workers had to clear five square kilometres (almost two square miles) of tropical forest to expose only part of the Maya ruins at Chichén Itzá. Not counting short interruptions, Chichén Itzá was a sacred Maya site for 700 years. In the 11th and 12th centuries, the city became a political and religious centre during a Maya renaissance under huge Toltec influence. Chichén Itzá is one of the largest and best-restored archaeological sites in Mexico. It is one of the UNESCO Heritage Sites.

History
Maya tribes from the south presumably established Chichén Itzá around the year 450. Experts currently assume that the site was not abandoned at the end of the classical period (around 900), as were far more important southern and central cities in the Maya region. New research even supports the belief that as early as the 7th and 8th centuries tribes from the Mexican Central Highlands migrated to this region and merged with the Maya. Some tribes may have migrated back in the 9th and 10th centuries, thus explaining the elements of Maya culture in Tula. Until recently, it was thought that around the year 1000, the Toltec migrated 1200 km/745 mi from Tollán (Tula) and settled in the city, which was then probably still called Uucil-abnal. According to old Náhua chronicles, the peaceful nature of the legendary ruler Ce Ácatl Topiltzín led to him being ousted from this region. He then became the Maya emigrant leader. Like other Toltec rulers, Ce Ácatl Topiltzín called himself Quetzalcóatl or Kukulkán (feathered serpent).
The **fusion of the Toltec and Maya high cultures** initiated a 200-year renaissance of Maya architecture immediately following the classical

period. The Náhua chronicles and Maya accounts contradict each other in many aspects. For example, the Maya reports in the books of Chilam Balam tell us about a triple alliance between Chichén Itzá, Uxmal and Mayapán, the so-called League of Mayapán, between 1007 and 1194. Modern researchers have their doubts about this because by the 11th century Uxmal was already abandoned and Mayapán was probably established only in the early 13th century.

Toltec style elements dominated when Chichén Itzá was at the height of its power. Despite many Maya characteristics, structures from this time therefore show an amazing similarity with structures in the ancient Toltec city Tollán. The chronicles describing the end of Chichén Itzá are also quite contradictory. The Maya probably abandoned Chichén Itzá around 1250. The proposed reason for this abandonment is a second wave of immigration of Maya who had been influenced by the highland culture; these immigrants gave Chichén Itzá its current name. Soon, the Itzá split into factions. Part of the tribe estab-

The Chac-mool are Toltec stone statues lying on their backs that were used as sacrificial altars. One of these figures can be admired in Chichén Itzá in the Temple of the Warriors.

Chichén Itzá *Plan*

Cenote de los Sacrificios (Sacrificial well)

Causeway

Mérida

Entrance

P

Temple Norte

Juego de Pelota (Ball court)

Edificio Sur

Tumba del Chac-mool (Tomb of Chac-mool)

NORTH

6

7

8

5

Castillo (Kukulkán Pyramid)

Templo de los Guerreros (Temple of the Warriors)

GROUP

Grupo de las Mil Columnas (Group of the Thousand Columns)

4

Tumba del Gran Sacerdote (High Priest's Tomb)

Mercado (Market)

3

2

9

1

10

11

SOUTH

South entrance

Cenote de Xtoloc (Well)

GROUP

Caracol (Observatory)

Mayaland

Edificio de las Monjas (Nunnery Complex)

13

14

12

Hacienda Chichén

Villas Arqueológicas

100 m

©Baedeker

Puerto Juarez, Cancún

1 Juego de Pelota (Ball court)
2 Temazcalli (Steam bath)
3 Juego de Pelota (Ball court)
4 Columnata del Noreste (North-east colonnade)
5 Templo de las Mesas (Temple of the Tables)
6 Tzompantli (Wall of skulls)
7 Casa de las Águilas (House of Eagles)
8 Templo de los Tigres (Temple of the Jaguars)
9 Casa de los Metates (Temple of the Grinding Stones)
10 Templo del Venado (Temple of the Deer)
11 Casa Colorada (Red House) or Chichanchob
12 Iglesia (so-called Church)
13 Templo de los Tableros (Temple of the Wall Panels)
14 Akab-D'zib (House of Unknown Scripts)

lished the city of Mayapán under the rule of the Cocom house. The Mayapán city government then ruled northern Yucatán until 1450. Obviously, Chichén Itzá no longer played a prominent role by that time because construction had all but ceased and most of the city lay deserted.

At the time of the Spanish conquest in 1533, Chichén Itzá was only sparsely populated, although it had remained a popular place of religious ceremony. Bishop Diego de Landa visited Chichén Itzá and in 1566 described some of the buildings. John Stephens researched the

► VISITING CHICHÉN ITZÁ

GETTING AROUND

On the MEX 180, the travel time by bus or car is about 1.5 to 2.5 hours from Mérida and 1 hour from Valladolid. An air taxi service from Cancún is also available.

EVENTS

The steps of the great pyramid of Kukulkán are flanked by the stone bodies of two snakes with their heads at the bottom of the pyramid. Twice a year at the important equinoxes on 21 March and 22/23 September, the play of light and shadow creates the illusion of the snake bodies slithering down to earth. This phenomenon conveys an extraordinary and powerful impression which attracts thousands of onlookers.

WHERE TO EAT

In general, the hotel restaurants are good, in particular the Dolores Alba Chichén mentioned below.

WHERE TO STAY

► **Mid-range**

Dolores Alba Chichén
Carretera Mérida-Valladolid
Km 122
Tel. (985) 858 15 55
www.doloresalba.com
40 bungalows offer clean accommodation about 3km/2mi from the ruins. The ride to the excavation sites is free.

Hacienda Chichén
Carretera Mérida–Puerto Juárez
Km 120.5
Tel. (999) 924 21 50
Fax (999) 924 50 11
www.haciendachichen.com
A beautiful 16th-century hacienda was converted into this small, quiet, 21-room hotel. Some of the rooms are in bungalows with patios.

site in 1841/42, and in 1876 the French amateur archaeologist Le Plongeon worked in Chichén Itzá. Edward Thompson, the US consul in Mérida, bought the entire site in 1885. Sylvanus Morley from the United States deserves particular credit for his work excavating and restoring Chichén Itzá in the 1920s. Since the 1960s, the US National Geographic Society and Mexican Institute for Anthropology and History (I.N.A.H.) have been especially active in striving for new insights into Chichén Itzá.

The archaeological zone stretches over 8 sq km/3 sq mi. As with all pre-Columbian sites in Mexico, only a part of Chichén Itzá's structures have been excavated. The often misleading identifications either originate from early Spanish accounts or earlier archaeologists. Almost all historical names have been forgotten. A large visitor centre offers helpful services at the main entrance. It features an interesting museum, an auditorium, a restaurant and a bookshop. A swim in one of the several cenotes is a great way to relax after the sightseeing.

The site

⏱

Opening times: daily 8am–5pm

Chichén Nuevo (North Group)

The north group shows mainly elements characteristic of the Toltec style. The figure of the **Chac-mool** (red jaguar) is an inappropriately named reclining stone figure with its face turned sideways holding a ceremonial tray on its flat stomach. The flat surface sustains the interpretation that it is a small altar meant to hold sacrificial or ceremonial items. Typical Toltec elements are the so-called **Atlantean columns**, stone figures of upright, standing warriors that served as columnar support for stone slabs or temple roofs. The ubiquitous symbol of the plumed serpent replaced the renditions of the Maya rain god Chac, and scenes of fighting and sacrifice also became much more abundant than in classical Maya art.

El Castillo (3-D image p.254) The dominant structure is El Castillo, the **Kukulkán Pyramid**. As was customary in pre-Columbian times for ceremonial structures, the design strictly followed the parameters of astronomy and astrology. The classical simplicity of the pyramid is very impressive. The 24m/79ft-high pyramid has been exquisitely restored. It has four flights of stairs on four sides and nine terraces, symbolizing the four cardinal points (the four corners of the world) and the nine heavens. Each of the four pyramid stairways has 91 steps, making 364 steps in all. Adding the top platform as another step makes 365 steps one for each day of the solar year. A large snake head rests at the base of each side of the four stairways. The stairs rise at a 45° angle and lead up to a platform where the Temple of Kukulkán stands.

There is a **fantastic view** from the top of the pyramid over the entire site. The main temple entrance is flanked by two snake columns, which are typical for the Toltec style. As discovered during excavations, the Maya built the Kukulkán Pyramid upon another, older pyramid. This older temple pyramid underneath the Castillo was built completely in the Maya style. A stone Chac-mool was found at the entrance as well as a throne in the shape of a red-coloured stone jaguar whose skin was inlaid with jade pieces. A passage to the inner pyramid provides access to these rooms.

✳ Kukulkán descending At the two equinoxes (21 March and 21/22 September), the Kukulkán pyramid becomes part of a spectacular, albeit very short, event. An axis through the north-west and south-west corners of the pyramid points to the rising point of the sun at the vernal equinox and the setting point at the autumnal equinox. As the sun passes over, the sides of the terraces throw shadows onto the sides of the northern stairway in such a way that it creates a serrated line of seven moving interlocking triangles. Looking up at the northern steps, light and shadow create the illusion of a long tail slithering down the sides of the stairway toward the snake heads at the base – imagery representing Kukulkán returning to earth when it is time to plant new seeds or when the rainy season comes to an end.

The Temple of the Warriors (Templo de los Guerreros) is located east of the Castillo. This is a grand building on top of a stepped platform and surrounded by wide porticos. Undoubtedly, it is a larger imitation of the temple of the Morning Star in Tula. Several rows of quadrangular columns lead to a staircase with a Chac-mool at its end. Two large snake columns form the portal to the main temple, and the stone altar behind the columns is supported by four Atlantean columns. Inside the pyramid, archaeologists have found remnants of an earlier, smaller warrior temple.

Temple of the Warriors

The Group of the Thousand Columns (Grupo de las Mil Columnas) is located below the Temple of the Warriors. The original purpose of this structure is unknown. It may have been a market or a meeting place. Next to it is a small ball court (juego de pelota), a market (mercado) and a steam bath (temazcalli). The anteroom of the bath, the bath itself and the heater room are still recognizable.

Group of the Thousand Columns

The Chac-mool tomb (tumba del Chac-mool, also called the Venus Platform) is located north of the Pyramid of the Warriors. 130 years ago, Augustus le Plongeon found a stone figure here. He called it Chac-mool. The reliefs on the platform are interesting, combining Kukulkán and Venus symbolism.

Tomb of Chac-mool (Venus Platform)

The great sacred well (Cenote Sagrado) is situated 300 m/330 yd further north at the end of a 6 m/6.5 yd-wide path. Its existence may

Cenote Sagrado

A symbol of the 365 days of the year, hewn from stone: the Kukulkán Pyramid, seen from the Venus Platform

KUKULKÁN PYRAMID

✱ ✱ The 24m/78ft-high Kukulkán Pyramid is without doubt the most famous building of Chichén Itza. Twice a year at the two equinoxes (21 March and 21 September) it becomes an attraction for crowds of people, all intent on seeing how the shadow of the serpent seems to slither down the stairway.

⏲ Open:
daily 8am–5pm

① Northern steps

The pyramid represents a calendar of a full solar year. The four stairways each with 91 steps add up to 364, the final platform making a total of 365 steps, one for each day of the year.

② Panels

On the four sides of the pyramid, there are 52 panels representing the 52-year cycle of the sacred Maya calendar.

③ Nine terraces

on each side of the pyramid are divided in half by the stairways making a total of 18, standing for the 18 months of the Maya calendar.

④ Temple of Kukulkán

The inner sanctum of Kukulkán, the Quetzalcóatl (feathered serpent) of the Maya, is not open to the public.

⑤ Entrance to inner pyramid

On the right hand side of the northern steps it is possible to enter the interior of the pyramid and climb to the top via a narrow flight of stairs. Because of a lack of ventilation, many visitors find that the stairs are quite slippery and the air very sticky.

⑥ Temple of the inner pyramid

Visitors find a locked chamber at the top of the stairs, which is illuminated and contains two statues. One is a Chac-mool in the typical half-prone position with a sacrificial altar on its belly, the other a bright red jaguar throne with jade inlay.

View of the pyramid from between the columns of the Temple of the Warriors

The cenote is thought to have once been a sacrificial site.

stairway provides access to the upper level, which opens towards the west and looks on to the ball court. Snake columns flank the entrance as also seen in the Temple of the Warriors. Friezes on the façade show mostly jaguars. Murals inside the temple apparently depict a battle between the Maya and Toltec.

Chichén Itzá (South Group)

Crossing the former route from Mérida to Pto. Juárez, visitors reach the south group ruins of Chichén Itzá. The site for these outer ruins is called Chichén Viejo, i.e. old Chichén Itzá.

The High Priest's Tomb (Tumba del Gran Sacerdote) is on the right. This a 10m/33 ft-high damaged pyramid atop a natural limestone cave with seven skeletons and valuable offerings.

High Priest's Tomb

»The snail« (caracol) is the nickname for one of the most interesting structures in Chichén Itzá. The round building standing on a two-step platform is located next to the High Priest's (Shaman's) Tomb; in all probability, it served as an observatory. A gently inclined spiral passage winds through the inner round building. Very narrow openings permit the sunlight to fall into the centre of the building only for seconds twice a year: a simple but reliable method which enabled the Maya priests in Chichén Itzá to determine the time. The observatory displays style elements of the central highlands and classical Maya buildings.

Caracol (Observatory)

The Nunnery Complex	Located south of the observatory are structures in the classical Chenes style of the Maya. Inaccurately, the Spaniards called the elaborately decorated building complex »the Nunnery« (Edificio de las Monjas, house of nuns). Stone decorations cover almost the entire façade with symbolized depictions of the Maya god Chac. Just east of the Nunnery is a building nicknamed »La Iglesia« (the church) in the Puuc style. Built in this earlier style, the façades show classical Chac masks as well as geometrical ornamentation and animal images. Between the Chac masks there are images of the animals which, according to Maya mythology, support the heavens: a crab and an armadillo as well as a snail and a turtle.
Other structures	Other structures are also worth mentioning in connection with this part of Chichén Itzá. There is the Temple of the Wall Panels (Templo de los Tableros) with its reliefs depicting Toltec warriors and jaguars, and the House of Unknown Scripts (Akab D'zib), so named because glyphs over the door of the second room are still not deciphered. In addition, the Temple of the Sculptured Lintels (Templo de los Dinteles) and the Red House (Casa Colorada or Chichan-chob) are mostly in the Puuc style. Also noteworthy are the Date Group (Grupo de las Fechas) with the House of the Phallus (mostly in the Toltec style), another ball court, and the Cenote Xtoloc, a sinkhole which served as a water reservoir.
Light and sound show	An interesting light and sound show (Luz y Sonido) takes place every night at 8pm. The narrative is in Spanish but headsets to listen in other languages are available for a small fee.
Yaxuná	The Maya site Yaxuná from the early period is located south-west of Chichén Itzá. The site is known as the terminal of the important 100 km/62 mi-long Cobá causeway (sacbe). In the beginning of the 1990s, a find in this area caused surprise: two graves, which were dated AD 300 to 315, showed the influence of Teotihuacán. Influences of the then-allied Calakmul were also recognized. It is thought that the fall of Yaxuná began in the 7th century.

Around Chichén Itzá

✳ **The Caves of Balankanche**	The Balankanche (Throne of the Jaguar Priest) caves are a mere 5km/3mi drive from Chichén Itzá, east on the MEX 180 toward Valladolid and Puerto Juárez. These dripstone caves were discovered by accident in 1959. Until then, quarry stones had blocked access to this **underground cult and burial site**, which had been left untouched by humans for many centuries. The Balankanche caves are probably part of a wide, elaborate, not yet explored labyrinth of caves and aquifers. In the illuminated caves, visitors see many clay trays and bowls, metates (grindstones for maize), copal smoking paraphernalia and

Throwing the ball was not allowed. It had to be propelled through the stone hoop using elbows, knees, buttocks or hips.

A DEADLY GAME

Almost all the cultures of Mexico before the voyages of Columbus played the Mesoamerican ball game or »juego de pelota«. It was not simply played, though, but rather celebrated. It was less of a sport than a ritual event. There were variations from region to region and the rite itself was modified over the centuries but some of the rules remained constant

It is thought nowadays that the Mesoamerican ball game or **juego de pelota** was invented by the Olmecs on the Gulf Coast around 1300 BC. It then spread to neighbouring peoples so that the typical I-shaped court has been found in archaeological sites all over Mexico.

The ball represents the course of the sun

The game was played between two teams of three to five players. The object was to propel a hard rubber ball through a stone ring using only the elbows, knees buttocks and hips. Rigid gloves were worn to protect the hands while the players supported themselves on the ground. Mayan and Zapotec finds have had sloping walls whereas Toltecs and Aztecs built the walls vertical. The ball represented the sun and was not allowed to touch the ground since that would ruin the symbolism of the solar journey.

Sacrifices of winners or losers?

It is not known whether the game's winners or losers were then sacrificed to the gods. It is easy to believe that the losers should have to pay for allowing the sun to fall from the sky and were compelled to atone for it with their blood.

However, there is also a theory that the gods would only have been satisfied with the best and as such the death of the winners would represent **an honourable reward**. What seems clear is that the sacrificial rite was intended to strengthen the sun and secure its path through the firmament.

many other items and offerings once placed here by priests. Many of the cult items are adorned with the likeness of the Toltec/Aztec rain god Tláloc, which is taken as evidence that the caves were purely Toltec burial grounds. The centre of the cave system is an altar room with a dripstone formation in the shape of a Ceiba tree, the holy tree of the Maya. A narrow passage leads into a lower stalactite cave. At the end of the chamber, very clear waters surround an altar in honour of the rain god Tláloc.

Valladolid Valladolid (population 60,000), the second largest city in Yucatán, is located about 40 km/25 mi east of Chichén Itzá. Few colonial buildings in the city survived the civil war or the second half of the 19th century. Among those that did are the Cathedral of San Servacio at the main plaza (built in 1706) and the restored convent San Bernardino in the city district of Sisal. San Bernardino was established by Franciscans in 1552. The church contains interesting religious art from the time of its foundation. The two sinkholes in Valladolid, cenotes Cis-ha and Zac-hi, are worth mentioning. At the cenote Zac-hi, young men follow in the footsteps of the famous cliff-divers (clavadistas) of Acapulco. For a few pesos they will jump head-first into the water 80 m/260 ft below. 5 km/3 mi before reaching Valladolid, visit the cenote Dzitnup: it is about 20 m/66 ft deep and its cobalt-blue waters are a very beautiful sight. Only a few hundred yards away, take a look down into the cenote Samula.

There is plenty to discover on a stroll through Valladolid.

Take the national road 295 to Tizimin and then turn off to Hunuku and head right to Santa Rita to reach the village Ekbalam (black jaguar) and the archaeological site of the same name (a total of 27km/17mi from Valladolid). This Maya site has 16 restored structures from the late classical period (AD 600–900). Among these is a structure named Las Gemelas (the twins), consisting of a large platform with two identical structures built on top of it. The Acropolis, or Structure 1, is located on the northern side of the plaza. At a height of 30m/98ft, it is by far the highest building at the Ekbalam site.

Tizimín is 52 km/32 mi north on the MEX 295. From 30 December to 6 January, extended festivities in honour of the three Magi take place here.

The famous flamingos, who nest by the Río Lagartos after returning from Celestún in spring.

The next stop after a 52 km/32 mi drive north is a pretty coastal town named **Río Lagartos** (Nefertiti) in a very beautiful natural setting. Of note are the breeding colonies, with countless flamingos and other protected bird species, situated around Las Coloradas (16km/10mi) and the mouth of the Río Lagartos. The 36 ha/89 ac lagoon area is also home to spider monkeys, alligators and tortoises. Plenty of opportunities for boating excursions satisfy the curiosity of visitors.

◄ Flamingo breeding colonies

Chihuahua

F 12

Federal state: Chihuahua (Chih.)
Population: 670,000

Altitude: 1,330m/4,360ft
Distance: about 1,500 km/ 930 mi north-west of Mexico City

Chihuahua is a modern, in some ways rather dilapidated city based on industry and trade, with close ties to the revolutionary movement. Pancho Villa pursued his cause here. In 1913 he occupied the city by sending his men to the Chihuahua market wearing the garb of farmhands and visitors as a disguise. Sometimes, merchants on

this market also sell the tiny hairless dogs called perritos Chihua-huenses. Chihuahua is also the start or the end of the line for the CHEPE train, which traverses the famous Copper Canyon.

Chihuahua is the capital of the federal Mexican state of the same name. The city is built in a beautiful valley, which opens to the north and is surrounded on all other sides by low mountain chains of the Sierra Madre Occidental. The citizens used to work mainly in the mining industry. This changed however in the days of the large haciendas, and since then people have been making a living raising livestock, a fact easily recognized by the way men dress in cowboy boots and hats.

History Apache (Arizona) and Comanche (Texas) from the north moved through the region in pre-Columbian times and later. In the 16th

 VISITING CHIHUAHUA

INFORMATION

Tourist information
(in the Government Bldg.)
Palacio del Gobierno
at the corner of Calle Carranza
and Aldama
Tel. (614) 410 10 77

GETTING AROUND

Travelling from Mexico City to Chihuahua, a flight takes about 2 to 3 hours and a bus about 21 hours.

WHERE TO EAT

► **Moderate**
① *Club de los Parados*
Avenida Juárez 3901
Tel. (614) 410 53 35
Historic house with numerous photos of important Chihuahua celebrities, such as Anthony Quinn. Steaks are a speciality.

► **Moderate to inexpensive**
② *Casa de los Milagros*
Calle Victoria 812
(opposite the Hotel Reforma)

The atmosphere in the restaurant and bar is relaxed. Have a pleasant time on the beautiful patio of the colonial building.

WHERE TO STAY

► **Luxury**
① *Holiday Inn Hotel & Suites Chihuahua*
Calle J. Escudero 702
San Felipe
Tel. (614) 439 00 00
Fax (614) 414 33 13
www.ichotelsgroup.com
This modern hotel is located only 10 minutes away from the city centre. All 74 rooms are suites with a kitchen.

► **Mid-range**
② *Hotel San Francisco*
Calle Victoria 409
Tel. (614) 439 90 00
Fax (614) 415 35 38
www.hotelsanfrancisco.com.mx
This modern 5-storey hotel with 132 rooms is popular with business travellers. It is located next to the main city square and the cathedral.

century, the first attempts of the Spaniards at settling and establishing missions in the region failed. Antonio de Deza y Ulloa established a settlement here in 1709 and named it San Francisco de Cuéllar. Nine years later, the city's name was changed to San Felipe El Real de Chihuahua after the Tarahumara expression for »dry place«. The discovery of large deposits of silver made Chihuahua rich, but constant attacks by Indians interfered with its development.

Pater Miguel Hidalgo y Costilla,, the father of Mexican independence, was taken prisoner in Chihuahua by troops of the Spanish crown in 1811. He and his companions were shot according to martial law. US troops temporarily occupied the city during the war between the USA and Mexico (1846–1848) and the US intervention (1862–1866). For a while, Benito Juárez resided in Chihuahua. At the end of 1910, a revolt started here, which forced President Porfirio Díaz to resign and initiated the Revolutionary War. The main acti-

Chihuahua Plan

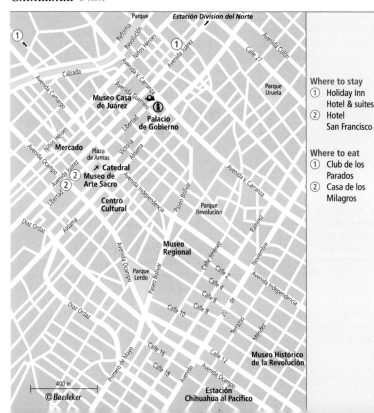

Where to stay
① Holiday Inn
   Hotel & suites
② Hotel
   San Francisco

Where to eat
① Club de los
   Parados
② Casa de los
   Milagros

400 m
© Baedeker

vists in the north were Abraham Gonzales and the group leader Pancho Villa who occupied the city in 1913 with his División del Norte and made it his headquarters.

What to See in Chihuahua

Cathedral The cathedral in the Plaza de la Constitución was built from 1717 to 1826 and was dedicated to St Francis of Assisi. Statues of the twelve disciples grace the Baroque façade. The church is the most impressive church building in North Mexico. At the back, in a small vault, catholic art is displayed in the museum of religious arts, the **Museo de Arte Sancto**.

✴ Governor's Palace (Palacio de Gobierno) The Governor's Palace (Palacio del Gobierno), a Jesuit seminary rebuilt in the 19th century, is located not far from the cathedral in the Plaza Hidalgo. This is the place where, in 1811, Pater Hidalgo and his officers were held captive and then shot dead. Their impaled heads were later displayed in Guanajuato. The Federal Government Building (Palacio Federal) is also in the Plaza Hidalgo. Miguel Hidalgo was imprisoned here during his trial. The **Church of San Francisco** is situated in Calle Libertad. It was built between 1721 and 1741. Hidalgo's remains rested here until they were transferred to Mexico City in 1823.

Regional museum ✴ Quinta Gomeros ► The regional museum of the federal state of Chihuahua (Museo Regional del Estado) is located in the Paseo Bolívar 401 (corner of Calle 4 a) in the former Palace of Justice, known as Quinta Gomeros. The palace, built between 1907 and 1910, is one of the best examples of Art Nouveau in Mexico. Inside the building are, for example, rooms with furniture in the Art Nouveau style, archaeological art mostly from the Casas Grandes (Paquimé), as well as photographs and documents about the history of Chihuahua.

✴ Pancho Villa Museum (Museo Histórico de la Revolución) Pancho Villa once lived in the Palais Quinta Lus in the Calle 10 Norte No. 3014. Once managed by his family, the history museum now goes by the name Museo Histórico de la Revolución (history museum of the revolution) and is run by the Mexican Army; it is also known as the **Pancho Villa Museum**. Aside from his death mask, the museum contains many mementos from the life of the famous-infamous bandit and hero of the revolution. Also on display is the car in which Pancho Villa was shot to death.

Benito Juárez Museum (Museo Casa de Juárez) The Benito Juárez Museum (Museo Casa de Juárez, Avenida Juárez 321) displays documents, photographs and newspapers concerning Benito Juárez's stay in the city and the constitution of 1857, as well as showing furniture from this time. The house also served as the National Palace for two years when Juárez fled during the French invasion.

The Cultural Centre of Chihuahua (Centro Cultural de Chihuahua) is housed in a beautiful 19th-century building at Aldama 430. The centre exhibits ceramics from the Casas Grandes culture.

Cultural Centre of Chihuahua

Around Chihuahua: the Near Vicinity

In the immediate vicinity of the city there are a number of reservoirs (Presa Francisco Madero, Las Vírgenes, Chuviscar) where it is possible to swim and go fishing. In addition, some of the old silver mines (Santa Eulalia or Aquiles Serdán) are well worth a visit.

The city of Cuauhtémoc (population 42,000, altitude 211 m/692 ft) is situated about 100km/62mi west of Chihuahua. The city and surrounding area is home to about 50,000 Mennonites who live on agriculture and raising livestock. Most of them still speak the old northern German dialect of their forefathers.

Cuauhtémoc

From Cuauhtémoc, drive 47 km/29 mi west on the MEX 16 to arrive in La Junta. From there travel by train, or by car on now very good roads, to ►Barranca del Cobre (Copper Canyon).

La Junta

Driving west in the direction of Yepáchic via Ocampo leads to the nearby Basaseachic Falls. These, the highest waterfalls in Mexico, are

✳
Basaseachic Falls

Revolutionary past: Chihuahua was once a stronghold of the insurgents.

located in a beautiful forested mountain region; the water cascades 250m/820ft down a gorge into the river Basaseáchic. A trip of 132km/82mi on a serviceable sand road brings you from La Junta via San Juanito to the town of Creel. This town is a convenient starting point for excursions into the ▶Barranca del Cobre.

Ciudad Camargo

A drive from Chihuahua south-east on the MEX 45 leads to the small town of Ciudad Camargo. Nearby are the well-known healing thermal springs and spas Ojo de Jabalí, Ojo Caliente and Ojo Salado, as well as the Boquilla reservoir.

Hidalgo del Parral

The mining city Hidalgo del Parral (population 85,000) is another 150km/93mi south of Ciudad Camargo on the same road. Buildings of interest are the parish church (1710) with its ultra-Baroque altar, the El Rayo church (18th century), a popular pilgrimage destination for Indians with its richly decorated retables, and also the church La Fátima (20th century) built from locally mined metal. In 1923, **Pancho Villa** was shot dead in his car in Parral. A small museum and a commemorative plaque are intended to keep his memory alive.

Around Chihuahua: Further Afield

✱
Casas Grandes

Approximately 8km/5mi south of the modern agricultural city Nuevo Casas Grandes (about 335 km/210 mi north-west of Chihuahua), lie **North Mexico's most important pre-Hispanic ruins** on the edge of the old town Casas Grandes. The archaeological site – now a UNESCO World Heritage Site – is also named Casas Grandes or Paquimé after the Náhuatl expression for »great city«. The site represents one of the oasis cultures, the most important of which are Casa Grande (Arizona), Mesa Verde (Colorado) and Pueblo Bonito (New Mexico). Casas Grandes had its first period of prosperity around the year 1000. Recent findings suggest that Casas Grandes was subject to cultural influences from the central highlands in the 13th and 14th centuries.

In all likelihood, **Paquimé** was an important centre for crafts and trade. Remnants of the tools for making ceramics and items from turquoise and sea shells provide evidence for this assumption. Finds from the early period at the archaeological site include pit houses, the first ceramics and underground cult chambers (kivas); from the middle period, remnants of multi-storey adobe houses, staircases and irrigation channels have been discovered. Aside from Anasazi ceramics, finds from the late period include structures in the Toltec-Mexican style, such as ball courts, platforms, pyramid ruins and different renditions of the Quetzalcóatl motif. Recently, the very worthwhile Museo de las Culturas del Norte was established at the Paquimé excavation site. In three large rooms, this museum offers information about the regional history, displays of archaeological and ethnological finds and other interesting items and information.

Casas Grandes is the most significant pre-Hispanic archaeological site in northern Mexico. The erstwhile settlement was built from simple adobe bricks.

Travellers who are especially interested in archaeology may like to take a trip to Nuevo Casas Grandes and visit a site named Las Cuarenta Casas (Forty Houses) in the Mesa del Huracán. These interesting cave dwellings were most likely built in the 12th or 13th century AD as a garrison of Paquimé. To reach the site, take Carretera 10 to Buenaventura and then continue on Carretera 28 via Las Varas to Gómez Farías.

Las Cuarenta Casas

Ciudad Juárez (population 100,000) on the southern banks of the Río Grande is located more than 330 km/205 mi north-west of Nuevo Casas Grandes at the border with the USA. Formerly, the city's name was Paso del Norte, but it was renamed in 1888 to honour Benito Juárez, who made his headquarters here during the Intervention War (1865/66). During the Mexican Revolution (1910–1921) **Pancho Villa**, the revolutionary hero and leader of outlaws, set up his permanent quarters here. Today, Ciudad Juárez has significance as a trans-shipment centre and border city, and is also a centre for the finishing industry (maquiladoras, US/Mexican border industry). The most important festivities in Ciudad Juárez are on 4 December (Día de Santa Bárbara), the founder's days from 5 to 12 December, and the feasts on the occasion of the cotton fair from 10 to 20 August.

Ciudad Juárez

The 17th-century mission church in Guadalupe and the new culture centre with its museum of archaeology and history are well worth seeing. The museum contains ceramics from Casas Grandes as well as pieces which commemorate the Mexican Revolution, and presents exhibitions of folk art.

✴ Cholula

P 20

Federal state: Puebla (Pue.)
Population: 150,000

Altitude: 2,150m/7,054ft
Distance: 12 km/7.5 mi west of Puebla

When Cortés first arrived at what is now called Cholula (12km/ 7.5mi north-east of Puebla) he found a Mesoamerican religious centre with 100,000 inhabitants and 400 shrines erected around the Great Pyramid of Quetzalcóatl.

All that remains of that glorious past today is a giant mound, under-neath which the world's largest pyramid by area is hidden. On top of the pyramid now stands a church, and from there the view is of the spires of churches built by the Spaniards on top of pyramids and temples after the conquest.

History   The origins of the early inhabitants and builders of Cholula are un-known to us. It is however certain that a settlement already existed here between 400 and 300 BC. Around the beginning of the com-mon era (the year 0 CE), the great classical culture of Teotihuacán started to exert its long-lasting influence on Cholula. This influence found expression in the structure of the buildings, consisting of

▶ VISITING CHOLULA

INFORMATION
opposite the pyramid or
in Calle 4 Pte 103
(between Calles 3 and 5 Nte,
north of the main city square)
Tel. (222) 247 31 16

GETTING AROUND
From Mexico City drive the 126km/ 78mi on the highway to Puebla; from there it is another 12km/7.5mi to Cholula. The bus to Puebla leaves Mexico City from the Terminal del Oriente (east terminal) and takes 1.5 hours. In Puebla, transfer to another bus for the ride to Cholula.

WHERE TO EAT
▶ **Moderate to inexpensive**
Café Enamorada
Zócalo No. 1

Popular café for a coffee break or a relaxed dinner. Now and then, music groups entertain guests.

WHERE TO STAY
▶ **Mid-range to budget**
Hotel Suites San Juan
5 Sur 103
Tel. (222) 247 02 78
Fax (222) 247 45 44
Large modern rooms with tiled floors and TV.

Hotel Reforma
Corner Morelos / 4 Sur
Tel. (222) 247 01 49
Plain rooms of various sizes with or without bath.

sloped pyramid-shaped platforms and vertical entablatures (ta-bleros). After the fall of Tula (1175), the Toltec and Chichimec in-vaded the Cholula region, finally forcing the inhabitants of Cholula to flee to the coastal region on the Gulf of Mexico. Even before the invasion, a Mixtec influence had pervaded the arts, but now this be-came more striking. The **Mixtec Puebla culture** developed, and the artists of this era produced extraordinary glazed ceramic items. Although Cholula was at times occupied by neighbouring powers, it remained relatively self-contained as a religious centre throughout its long pre-Columbian period. When the Spanish conquerors under Cortés and their Tlaxcaltec allies invaded Cholula in 1519 they esti-mated the city's population to be around 100,000. Under the pretext of avoiding a trap, the Spaniards instigated a bloodbath among the people of Chulola – during which between 3,000 and 6,000 people are thought to have been massacred – and destroyed the Great Pyra-mid. The great plague epidemic from 1544 to 1546 then killed al-most all Indians, sealing the fate of the once great Cholula civiliza-tion.

What to See in Cholula

The temple pyramid was dedicated to the god Quetzalcóatl – the light-skinned, bearded god of the wind, the morning and evening stars and the civilization technologies – who is credited with having taught the Mesoamerican people the arts, sciences and agriculture. The pyramid, still almost completely covered with earth and vegeta-tion, is considered the largest structure of its kind in the world. In the course of roughly 1,500 years, a new pyramid was built on top of the old one seven times. At its base, each side of the last pyramid measured 425 m/1,394 ft. It was once 62 m/203 ft high and covered an area of 17 ha/43 ac.

★
Great Pyramid
⏲
Opening times:
daily 9am–6pm

Only the pyramid's west side has been partially restored; an almost 9km/5.6mi-long tunnel has been built to aid current research pro-jects. So far, the finds include remnants of platforms, living spaces, temple walls and patios, as well as an unusual outside spiral staircase and interesting frescoes. Excavators have found renditions of butter-flies and locusts in the style of Teotihuacán as well as a magnificent 50m/164ft-long coloured mural (AD 200) which shows life-sized fig-ures drinking or using drugs (about AD 200); this mural is on dis-play. A small museum opposite the pyramid entrance shows the scale of the ancient site using a model.

It has been known only since 1997 that on the days of the vernal equinox (21/22 March) and the winter solstice (22/23 December) a gliding shadow appears in the mornings and evenings on the Great Temple Pyramid, which creates the illusion of **a sliding snake**, simi-lar to observations in Chichén Itzá. In contrast to Chichén Itzá, the illusions at the Cholula pyramid include the downward and upward motions of the snake.

In Cholula the Spaniards built churches over many ancient sacred sites. The Templo de Nuestra Señora de los Remedios stands on top of the former Great Pyramid.

Church of Our Lady of Perpetual Help

The Indian populations continued to adhere to their belief system involving Quetzalcóatl and other gods after the Spanish conquest. This prompted the Spaniards to build churches either on top of destroyed Indian ceremonial buildings or in place of them. In line with this strategy, they destroyed the top of the Great Pyramid and built over it the church of Nuestra Señora de los Remedios (Our Lady of Perpetual Help). The church collapsed in 1666, and the following reconstruction lasted into the 18th century. After an earthquake almost completely demolished the church in 1884, it was rebuilt in the neoclassical style. A statue of the Madonna is displayed in a glass-panelled case over the altar. Cortés supposedly gave this statue to the Franciscan friars as a gift. Visitors have a marvellous view over Cholula from the church.

Convent San Gabriel

In 1549, the Franciscans built the immense monastery San Gabriel in the town square on top of the remnants of an ancient ceremonial site. The features of the monastery include a large atrium, a Plateresque entrance, massive doors and impressive Gothic arches. The **Royal Chapel (Capilla Real)** was built in the mid-16th century and modelled on the great mosque in Córdoba (Spain). The chapel, renovated 100 years after its creation, is a huge structure consisting of seven naves with 49 small domes, which open into a generous inner courtyard with lovely decorated procession chapels.

Around Cholula

San Francisco de Acatepec

✳ There are beautiful churches in the small villages of this region as well, as the Spaniards made use of the artistic skills and craftsmanship of the Indians. This is exemplified in the church San Francisco de Acatepec, which is located only a few miles south of Cholula and 16 km/10 mi west of Puebla. The church is one of the best examples of the **regional Baroque style** in Mexico.

An impressive archway in the neo-Mudéjar style (a Moorish style unique to Spain) leads towards the church, whose entire façade is covered with glazed tiles and clay facing-tiles. The structural organization consists of three elements. The portal is framed by an irregular arch and flanked by three Corinthian columns on each side. A sculpture stands in each recess between columns. In the centre, pilasters in the shape of upturned pyramid stumps replace the columns; such pilasters (rectangular columns very close to a wall) are a major element of the ultra-Baroque style (a Spanish and Latin-American Baroque style with opulent decorations). The large window bears the symbol of St Francis. In the top part, the pilasters in the outer central section extend in a spiral pattern to hint at a gable. The sculpture of the saint is displayed in the star-shaped recess; above this, an artistic rendition of the Trinity completes the picture.

Inside the church, there are many painted and gilded stucco and wooden sculptures in the typical Pueblo style of the 18th century. An altar upright from an earlier time is interesting, with its gilded and then painted sculptures almost disappearing amid golden Solomonic columns (twisted, corkscrew-shaped columns also known as barley-sugar columns) and other ornaments. The particularly complex and opulent treatment of the entrance door to the baptistry is also worthy of note.

If the façade of the church of San Francisco de Acatepec marks the **highpoint of the Pueblo style**, the inside of the church of Santa María de Tonantzintla (1 km/0.6 mi west of Acatepec) is an interior design masterpiece of this Baroque style. On view here is the total decoration of a room with the mystic predilection for fruits, flowers and birds, so highly developed in pre-Columbian times, mixed with Christian motifs.

✳
Santa María de Tonantzintla

Other motifs are an orchestra with Indian musicians for the choir and stucco frames with reliefs depicting Jesus, the Virgin Mary and St Christopher. A group of angelic heads amid an ocean of leaves seems to descend from the dome as if spawned from a flower. The lectern arch shows remarkable stucco works, with crowned devils spitting fruit forming part of the decorated Atlantides.

Return to Acatepec and from there take the MEX 190 toward Puebla. The small town of Tlaxcalancingo (population 6,000) is situated about 4 km/2.5 mi away.

San Bernardino de Tlaxcalan- cingo

San Bernardino church (18th century), another good example of the Pueblo style Baroque, is on the right hand side. The beautiful façade with its curved gable is completely covered with glazed tiles and red facing-tiles. The left-hand side consists of an elegant tower with a tile dome and pinnacle.

Beautiful blooms by the side of the road

✳ San Francisco de Huejotzingo

The village of Huejotzingo is located at the foot of the 5,286 m/ 17,344 ft-high, snow-covered volcano Iztaccíhuatl and surrounded by fruit orchards. The village is a mere 14 km/8.7 mi north-west of Cholula, and 26km/16m from Puebla. While the city is known for its apple cider and ponchos, most visitors come to see the monastery San Francisco de Huejotzingo, one of the oldest and most beautiful monasteries in New Spain.

The monastery is entered through the atrium, reached via wide stairs and through a doorway made up of three Plateresque arches. A cut stone cross stands in the centre of the inner courtyard. **Procession chapels** (posas) are placed in all four corners of the yard; these chapels are among the most beautiful chapels of their kind in Mexico. The façade of the typical chapel-fort is decorated with columns and symbols of the order. The frame around the north portal, which is now walled shut, is an excellent example for the **colonial Plateresque style**. An architectural element frames the archway and the order's crests decorate the façade in a harmonic and imaginative way. The pyramidal merlons with openings are found only in Huejotzingo. In the generously dimensioned church nave, with its magnificent ribbed Gothic vaulting, stands a large four-part altar upright (1586), decorated with 14 statues in the Plateresque tradition. The Flemish artist and immigrant to New Spain (1566) Simon Pereyns painted the seven preserved oil paintings in the church. Once, frescoes covered the walls, but only remnants of them are left now. Enter the monastery through a gate to the right of the church portal. The Trinity chapel and the attached cloister are in the vestibule.

★ Cobá

O 31

Federal state: Quintana Roo (Q.R.)   **Altitude:** 8 m/26 ft
Distance: 43 km/27 mi north-west
of Tulum

In Cobá, in the dense rainforest of Quintana Roo between several small lakes, visitors can discover as yet unrestored ancient arte-facts in one of Mexico's largest Maya archaeological sites.

Blessed with a unusually rich water supply for Yucatán, this region was populated from the early classical period into the late 15th century. Today, the religious centre and settlement is still almost completely covered with vegetation. According to current research, Cobá's civilization appears to have experienced its height during the Maya classical period (600–900), though some of the structures here appear to be from the post-classical period (900–1450). Cobá was still populated when the Spanish conquistadores arrived but escaped discovery.

Visiting the Ruins

The archaeological site is quite large (about 80 sq km/31 sq mi) and the landscape is very beautiful. These are but two reasons to set aside plenty of time for a visit. Signposts help in locating the main attractions. Be prepared for heat, humidity and insects and always carry sufficient drinking water.

Tip

▶ VISITING COBÁ

GETTING AROUND

Drive 43km/27mi north-west from Tulum through dense rainforest to reach the Maya ruins of Cobá. Another route starts from Nuevo X-Can in the north (42km/26mi); alternatively, negotiate a dirt track from Chemax (31km/19mi). Regular bus rides to Cobá are available from Cancún, Playa del Carmen and Valladolid.

WHERE TO EAT

▶ **Inexpensive**
La Pirámide
This restaurant is located on the edge of the village, beside a lake in very idyllic surroundings. It serves local Yucatán specialities as well as delicious cuisine from other parts of Mexico.

WHERE TO STAY

▶ **Mid-range to budget**
Villa Arqueológica Cobá Club Med
Zona Arqueológica
Tel. (985) 858 15 27
This hotel (40 rooms) is situated right next to the Cobá excavation site. It has a well-stocked library and presents interesting exhibitions on the Maya.

Site design
🕐
Opening times:
daily 7am–6pm

The huge site has so far 45 local and regional roads as well as more than 6,000 structures. So far, 40 stelae from the Maya classical period have been discovered, most of them with reliefs. The oldest time designation (613) is the one on stele 6. However, the architecture of some of the buildings, which resembles that seen in Petén (Guatemala), suggests that they were built in the early classical period (300–600). The large number of causeways (sacbeob, »white ways«) in the area underpins the significance of Cobá as a metropolis. The causeways formed an extended network of raised trample paths with a hard limestone mortar surface, connecting the centre with distant trading centres. Unusually, they are sometimes as wide as 10 m/33 ft here, and the one leading to Yaxuna, at that time a religious centre south-west of Chichén Itzá, is almost 100 km/62 mi long.

Cobá Group

On the right hand side when entering the archaeological zone are the buildings of the Cobá Group (Grupo de Cobá) or Group B. The 24 m/79 ft-high pyramid is nicknamed »the Church« (La Iglesia) and is partially restored. Its base measures 40 x 50m (131 x 164ft) and, after the seventh terrace, the highest platform rests on top of a wall

All roads from Cobá lead to the Nohoch Mul pyramid.

and forms the base for a small temple. From here, visitors have a terrific view over the Cobá region with several pyramids, temples and lakes. Close to »the Church« is the ball court (juego de pelota).

About 500 m/545 yd behind the ball court, a path to the right leads to the **Macanxoc Group** (Group A). From the eight stelae found here so far, stelae 1, 4 and 6 are relatively intact. They are up to 3m/10ft high and 1.5 m/5 ft wide stone columns, and their reliefs show rulers and inscriptions in the form of Maya glyphs.

About 100 m/328 ft behind this group, a marker directs visitors left to the **Group of Pictures** (Grupo de las Pinturas or Group D). The most significant structure is a pyramid (Structure 1) that is crowned

Cobá Map

by a small temple with door openings to the east and west and a main portal on the north side. The main portal is divided by a column. The door lintel over the portal and the three horizontal stone cornices above it still clearly show the remnants of the original paintings. Through the east door visitors can enjoy a beautiful view of the pyramid known as »the Castle« (El Castillo).

A path opposite the pyramid steps leads to different stelae, on two of which human sacrifices are depicted. Walk past the stelae to the Nohoch Mul path and turn right.

The great pyramid of Nohoch Mul (big mound) is another 800m/ **Nohoch Mul**
0.5mi further on. Before the trail turns left, a path leads to a group of weathered stelae, the remnants of structure X, a platform with rounded corners and the magnificent stele 20. A relief on the stele shows a richly clad ruler with his feet on the backs of two slaves on all fours. The ruler carries a ceremonial staff in a slanted position, typical of the Cobá style. Glyphs cover the upper part and sides of the stele.

The main pyramid (**El Castillo**) is, at 42 m/138 ft, the highest accessible ancient Indian building on Yucatán peninsula. The 120 steps of the outer staircase lead via six terraces to the last platform. Shell motifs are carved in some of the steps. Two small staircases finally lead to the temple on top of the pyramid. The pyramid was built in the classical Maya style, while the temple standing on it shows similarities with the Tulum temples built much later, probably in the 14th or 15th century. A small altar stands in front of the temple. In the upper frieze of the temple are three rectangular niches. They originally contained sculptures of the descending god, and two of these are still in place. The only access door leads to a room with a cantilever dome; from here, again, the view is magnificent.

Costa Alegre

O/P 13/14

Federal states: Jalisco (Jal.) and Colima (Col.)

Length: 250km/155mi between Puerto Vallarta and Manzanillo

Recently, the 250 km/155 mi coastal region between ▶ Puerto Vallarta and Manzanillo was given the name Costa Alegre. With the new name, a new and exclusive holiday destination on Mexico's west coast was launched.

Most Costa Alegre beaches are only accessible by hotel guests, or from the ocean.

⏵ VISITING COSTA ALEGRE

INFORMATION
Tourist information:
Jalisco 67, Barra de Navidad
Tel. (315) 355 51 00

GETTING AROUND
Regular bus service from Puerto Vallarta

WHERE TO EAT
▶ Inexpensive
Yacatecuhtli
Avenida México 249
Manzanillo, Tel. (314) 332 56 70
Delicious vegetarian meals, great fruit salads, creative fruit cocktails and soy burgers.

WHERE TO STAY
▶ Luxury
Las Hadas Resort Hotel
Avenida de los Riscos y
Vista Hermosa
Península de Santiago
Manzanillo
Tel. (314) 331 01 01, Fax 331 01 25
www.brisas.com.mx
The most exclusive and best-known hotel (233 rooms) in this area offers accommodation in five categories depending on size, view and amenities. The hotel offers restaurants, bars, two swimming pools, an 18-hole golf course and a discotheque.

▶ Mid-range to budget
Cabo Blanco
Calle Armada y Bahía de la Navidad
Barra de Navidad
Tel. (315) 355 51 70, Fax 355 51 36
The 83 rooms are clean and bright with air conditioning. There are also two swimming pools and tennis courts in each location.

The coastal MEX 200 traverses palm groves, plantations with fruit trees and bushes and passes large vacation clubs and small hotels in idyllic surroundings. Resorts with beautiful gentle beaches alternate with jagged cliffs. In another century pirates often made their unwelcome appearance here, but nowadays sailing and fishing along the coast are safe, and pleasant, activities.

Careyes

It is mostly members of the international jet set who, for years now, have spent time in the mansions and luxury resorts on Bahía de Careyes (Careyes Bay) about 100km/62mi south of Puerto Vallarta. The particular beauty of the coastal area around Jalisco is breathtaking. Palm groves extend almost all the way to the ocean and small bays invite the traveller to relax.

✱
Chamela

Visitors find a 11 km/6.8 mi-long, almost completely unspoiled beach in the coastal town Chamela (160 km/100 mi south-east of Puerto Vallarta). The Mexican government have declared the coastal region between Chamela and Barra de Navidad an ecological tourist zone and in this way have secured a habitat for snapping turtles and other animals.

San Patricio Melaque San Patricio Melaque (population 8,000), often referred to simply as Melaque, is situated on the beautiful Bahía de la Navidad (60 km/ 37 mi south-east of Chamela) with a view of the neighbouring village Barra de Navidad. Families come here especially during school holidays and many yacht owners spend the winter months in this bay. The festivals in San Patricio Melaque on St Patrick's Day (Fiesta de San Patricio) in March attract visitors from far and near.

Barra de Navidad The popular ocean resort Barra de Navidad (population 3,000) was once a fishing village. In 1564, Captain Miguel López de Legazpi set out from here to cross the Pacific for the Philippines, where he established the first Spanish settlement marking the beginning of the Spanish colonialization of Asia.

Like Melaque, Barra de Navidad is situated on a sand dune between a lagoon and the ocean. The particularly beautiful beach is flanked by a promenade. The waves are higher here than in the neighbouring village, especially on the western beaches, which attracts many surfers from Melaque during the winter months.

Manzanillo Manzanillo (population 100,000) is located about 60 km/37 mi south of Barra de Navidad on a peninsula at the southern end of two curved bays (Bahía de Santiago and Bahía de Manzanillo). This important port city on the Mexican Pacific coast is surrounded by lush jungle as well as banana and coconut plantations. Manzanillo has vast beaches and offers excellent opportunities for angling and offshore fishing which has made it a popular travel destination in recent years.

Among the best known **beaches** facing the open ocean are Playa de Campos and Playa de Ventanas in the south. Some caution is required though, as the currents are strong and the waves high. Manzanillo bay offers the beaches Rompeolas, San Pedrito, Las Brisas, Playa Azul, Salagua and Las Hadas, which features a holiday colony with particularly interesting architecture. The string of beaches in Santiago Bay are La Audiencia, Santiago Olas Altas, Playa de Miramar and La Boquita; Playa de Oro beach is located beyond the Juluapán peninsula. Although Manzanillo boasts **some colonial buildings**, there are no real tourist attractions in the city. The Laguna de Cuyutlán stretches south-east into a beautiful landscape. From this lagoon it is a 24 km/15 mi drive via Armeria to reach the beach resort of Cuyutlán. This sleepy town lives from tourists who are only interested in peace and quiet.

> ! **Baedeker TIP**
>
> **Olas Verdes**
>
> The coastal region between Cuyutlán and Boca de Pascuales, 8km/5mi south-west of Tecoman, is well-known for the up to 8m/26ft-high Olas Verdes (green waves). This natural spectacle, when the ocean appears to glow green due to the presence of fluorescent micro-organisms, occurs mostly during the months of April and May.

Side trip to Colima

The city of Colima (not quite 60 km/37 mi away from the Pacific coast) seems exposed to the vagaries of nature. In the last four centuries alone, the Colima volcano (Volcán de Colima) 30 km/19 mi north of the city has erupted nine times on a large scale. The city also suffered a series of fairly major earthquakes. The quakes are the reason that only a few colonial buildings still exist in Colima (population 120,000), capital of the state of the same name. Colima was one of the first cities to be established in West Mexico. The city extends through a fertile valley along two rivers and up the slopes of surrounding mountains. In recent decades, Colima has developed into a trade and processing centre for regional ranch and hacienda-related business in the livestock, forestry and agricultural industries.

✳
Colima

The cathedral on the main city square has been rebuilt since it was first erected in 1527. Close to it, the Government Palace (built 1884–1904) displays murals by the local artist Jorge Chávez Carrillo. The national hero Miguel Hidalgo once served as a preacher in Colima; in commemoration of Hidalgo's 200th birthday, scenes from Mexican historic events were included in the murals.

Around the City Square (Zócalo)

The Colima Museum of History (**Museo de la Historia de Colima**) is located on the south side of the city square. It displays mostly pre-Hispanic ceramics and clay figurines from local excavations, along with masks, traditional costumes and items made from shells. The Teatro Hidalgo (1871–1883) is one block south of the city square. The theatre was destroyed in earthquakes in the 1930s and 40s and reconstructed in 1942.

The city's main attraction, the Museum of Western Cultures (Museo de las Culturas de Occidente) is located 1km/0.6mi from the city centre at the intersection of the streets Calzada Galván and Ejército Nacional. The museum exhibits mostly archaeological finds from tombs or burial grounds to provide a picture of **Colima culture**. The depictions of people and dogs are very impressive.

✳
◄ Museum of Western Cultures

The museum of popular culture, the **Museo Universitario de Culturas Populares** (Calle 27. Septiembre/Manuel Gallardo Zamora) displays many regional traditional costumes, Mexican musical instruments as well as a completely furnished bakery for the typical sweet pastry (pan dulce). Dances with masks are often performed in and around Colima; ask about these shows here.

Comalá is located about 10 km/6 mi north of Colima. It is the centre of the regional arts and crafts industry, which produces furniture, forged objects and other items.

Comalá

About 6 km/3.7 mi outside Comalá, you can experience a volcano-related anomaly in the magnetic field: take a taxi a certain spot on the country road; the driver will turn off the engine and the car will be pulled uphill as if by magic forces.

Nevado de Colima ✷ About 40 km/25 mi north of Colima in the federal state of Jalisco, the peaks of the Nevado de Colima (4,339 m/14,240 ft) and the Volcán de Colima (3,838 m/12,590 ft) tower majestically. The former, also known as Zapotépetl (Mountain of the Zapote Trees), is Mexico's seventh-highest mountain. **Volcán de Colima** ► ✷ The Volcán de Colima, also known as the Fiery Volcano (Volcán de Fuego) was active between 1957 and 1975 and has caused much damage having erupted several times since 1994. By government decree, a prohibited area with a radius of 8.5 km/5.3 mi has been established around the volcano. It is a 27 km/ 17 mi drive to the Parque Nacional Volcán de Colima (Volcano National Park), after taking a left turn onto a very rough road shortly before entering the village of Atenquique. To reach the Nevado de Colima National Park (Parque Nacional de Nevado de Colima), take another left turn onto a rough country or sand road when leaving Atenquique. Follow this road for 37 km/23 mi. Access to this park is also possible by taking a road 2 km/1.2 mi before reaching Ciudad Guzmán. This road leads to Albergue La Joya and the radio station Canal 13.

Suchitlán The village Suchitlán (8km/5mi north-east of Colima) has earned fame for its carved animal masks, worn by dancers during the Semana Santa (the holy week before Easter Sunday). It is possible to buy a mask on Sundays at the Indian market.

The **Tampuchamay** hotel runs an open-air museum with many sculptures. To reach it, follow the junction toward Los Los Azmoles (12 km/75 mi south of Colima) and continue the 5km/3mi to Los Ortices. Now and then, bones and ceramic pieces are to be found in burial grounds here. Various bat species and other cave-dwelling animals live in the caves at Tampuchamay (Gruta de Tampuchamay).

✷ Cozumel (Cozumel Island)

O 31/32

Federal state: Quintana Roo (Q.R.)	**Area:** about 500 sq km/193 sq mi
Population: 70,000	**Distance:** 20 km/12.4 mi off the north-eastern shore of Yucatán

Cozumel, a flat island 20km/12.4mi off the north-eastern shore of Yucatán, is covered mostly with dense green jungle vegetation. At 45 km/28 mi long and up to 18km/11mi wide it is one of Mexico's largest islands.

The beautiful white beaches are a lively contrast to the blue-green shades of the ocean. The ocean floor is covered with very fine white coral sand and the water is therefore crystal clear. Cozumel was first developed as a diving paradise for tourists in the middle of the 20th century.

In the post-classical period, particularly between 1000 and 1200, Co- **History**
zumel appears to have played an important role. Being the eastern-
most of all Maya cities, Cozumel was the **sacred place of the rising
sun**. Old chronicles suggest that some Maya tribes migrated from
Cozumel to the mainland. In any case, it was an important pilgrimage destination in honour of Ix-chel, the goddess of fertility and
birth, who was also the moon goddess and wife of Itzamná, the
dominant ruler and sun god. This gave Ix-chel a prominent position
in the Yucatán Maya mythology and sacred places were dedicated to
her. Maya women in particular paid tribute to Ix-chel.

Juan de Grijalva was the first Spaniard to discover Cozumel in 1518.
Hernán Cortés followed in 1519 and in 1527 Francisco de Montejo
came here to attempt his conquest of Yucatán. The island probably
had a population of about 40,000 when Cortés saw it. From the 17th
to the 19th centuries Cozumel mainly served as a hiding place for pirates and smugglers. Many fugitives from the mainland came here
during the Caste War of Yucatán. During the Second World War, the
old town of San Miguel was levelled to establish a US air base in its
place. Hurricane Gilbert made landfall in Cozumel in September
1988 with wind speeds of up to 330 kmh/205 mph. The effects were
devastating. Despite vocal protests from environmental protection
groups, in the late nineties the construction of a large pier close to
the Paradise Reef was started, as part of the Puerta Maya Project.

*Ideal for snorkelling: the sea in the vicinity of Laguna Chankanab
on Isla Cozumel*

Isla Cozumel *Map*

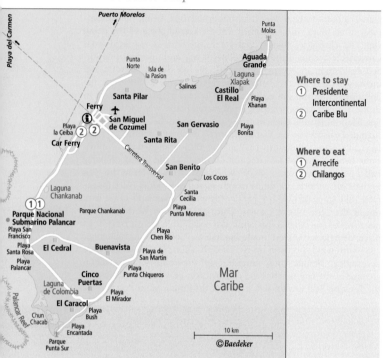

Puerto Morelos
Punta Molas
Playa del Carmen
Punta Norte
Isla de la Pasion
Salinas
Aguada Grande
Laguna Xlapak
Santa Pilar
Castillo El Real
Playa Xhanan
Ferry
San Miguel de Cozumel
San Gervasio
Playa la Ceiba
Playa Bonita
Car Ferry
Santa Rita
Carretera Transversal
San Benito
Los Cocos
Laguna Chankanab
Santa Cecilia
Parque Chankanab
Playa Punta Morena
Parque Nacional Submarino Palancar
Playa San Francisco
Playa Chen Rio
Playa Santa Rosa
El Cedral
Buenavista
Playa de San Martin
Playa Palancar
Cinco Puertas
Playa Punta Chiqueros
Mar Caribe
Laguna de Colombia
Playa El Mirador
El Caracol
Playa Bush
Palancar Reef
Chun Chacab
Playa Encantada
Parque Punta Sur
10 km
©Baedeker

Where to stay
① Presidente Intercontinental
② Caribe Blu

Where to eat
① Arrecife
② Chilangos

What to See on Cozumel Island

San Miguel de Cozumel San Miguel de Cozumel in the north-west part of the island offers its visitors an aquarium with dolphins and an island museum (Museo de la Isla, Avenida Rafael E. Melgar/Calle 4/6 Norte) with exhibitions on the island's geography, history and fascinating underwater world. Slightly outside the town, the archaeology park (Parque Arqueológico) is on the Avenida 65 with numerous replicas of artefacts from different Mesoamerican cultures. Maya in traditional costume show how tortillas or hammocks are made.

✳ Beaches A few of the most popular and beautiful beaches on Cozumel are San Juan and Pilar in the north-west and San Francisco, Santa Rosa and Palancar in the south-west. On the east coast the beaches at Encantada, Hanan, Bonita, Punta Morena, Chen Río and Chiqueros face onto the open sea.

Laguna Chankanab The Laguna Chankanab (»little sea« lagoon) is a popular vacation spot. It is a small freshwater lake 7 km/4.3 mi south of San Miguel de

▶ VISITING COZUMEL

INFORMATION

Tourist information:
Plaza del Sol at the Zócalo
(1st level)
Tel. (987) 872 09 72 or
www.islacozumel.com.mx

GETTING AROUND

A flight to Cozumel takes about 2.5 hours from Mexico City, about 40 minutes from Mérida or 15 minutes from Cancún. Of course, there are also flights to Cozumel from many other Mexican and US airports.
The passenger ferry from Playa del Carmen takes about 1 hour, the car ferry from Puerto Aventuras or from Puerto Morelos about 2 hours. Crossing by hovercraft from Cancún may also be appealing.

WHERE TO EAT

▶ **Moderate**
① *Arrecife*
About 6km/3.7mi south of San Miguel (in the hotel El Presidente Intercontinental, see below).
Tasty fish dishes and an amazing view at sunset.

② *Chilangos*
Avenida Coldwell 30

(between Calle 3 Sur and Calle Morelos)
The speciality of the house are the huaraches (»sandals«), consisting of open fried masa (tortilla with dough made of lime-water-treated maize) stuffed with beans and other goodies. There is a choice of fillings.

WHERE TO STAY

▶ **Luxury**
① *Presidente Intercontinental*
Carretera a Chankanaab
Km 6.5
Tel. (987) 872 95 00
Fax (987) 872 95 28
www.ichotelsgroup.com.mx
The hotel is located on one of the longest beaches on Cozumel. Many of the 240 rooms have their own patio to the beach or garden.

▶ **Mid-range**
② *Caribe Blu*
Costera Sur Km 2.2
Tel. (987) 872 01 88
Fax (872) 16 31
www.caribeblu.net
All rooms in this pretty hotel have a view of the ocean and separate balconies. There is also an excellent diving shop.

Cozumel. Natural underground channels connect the lake with the ocean. In its crystal clear waters live tortoises and colourful fish in large numbers. The lagoon has been closed to swimmers and snorkellers for several years now. The small museum of natural history is worth a visit.

Uncontrolled hunting with harpoons has badly decimated the populations of aquatic creatures in the waters around Cozumel. Despite this fact, the underwater world around Cozumel is still an exciting marine location for snorkellers and divers. Palancar Reef is one of

Diving

✷

◄ Palancar reef

the most beautiful diving areas. The reef on the south-west tip of Cozumel almost reaches the ocean surface from a depth of 80 m/262 ft. A statue of Christ has been placed at a depth of 17 m/56 ft. Other destinations for divers are the reefs San Francisco, Paraíso, Columbia and Maracaíbo as well as the Santa Rosa Wall.

Punta Sur Park

Opening times:
daily 9am–5pm
www.cozumel-
parks.com.mx

The Nature Reserve Punta Sur is located at the southern tip of Cozumel. Many species live here, crocodiles, flamingos and herons among them. Cars are not permitted, but there are public bus services and bicycles. Climb to the top of the look-out towers to watch the fauna in the Laguna Colombia and Laguna Chunchacaab. The park services offer a special evening programme for visitors who like to watch the tortoises. The lighthouse Faro de Celarain is also on the park premises, which now houses a maritime museum. Kayak and diving gear rentals are available. It is not permitted to carry food or beverages into the park but there is a restaurant.

Maya sites

30 small Maya sites have been discovered on the island. However, only a few sites have been investigated, let alone restored. Access to the sites is difficult and the architecture of little interest. However, the hidden archaeological sites are located in pretty places in the jungle. To visit the temple of the goddess Ix-chel go by bus, taxi or car the 16 km/10 mi from San Miguel de Cozumel to **San Gervasio**. The site is the religious centre and pilgrimage destination of the island. The ruins of Santa Rita are near this site. Other sites are **Santa Pilar** in the north and, in the north-east, the Castillo Real with the largest Maya structure on the island. The Maya left traces of their lives in Buenavista (south-east) and in El Caracol (south) near the lighthouse (in Punta Sur Park).

✶ Cuernavaca

Q 19

Federal state: Morelos (Mor.)
Population: 800,000

Altitude: 1,540 m/5,053 ft
Distance: about 80km/50mi south-west of Mexico City

The mild subtropical climate, the splendour of the flowers and the old-colonial charm of the city centre have made the capital of the federal state of Morelos a very attractive place to visit. Cuernavaca has also become a city in which to enjoy retirement.

Progressive industrialization and the rising stream of visitors have taken their toll on the once intimate atmosphere of the city. However, the lively activities in the city square still show off the ambience here. A visit to the Cortés Palace (Palacio de Cortés), the nearby ruin sites and the spas should be on the itinerary.

Cuernavaca possesses a long Indian history that most likely goes back to the Olmec. Since about 1200, Cuernavaca was the central city for the Tlahuica who fell under Aztec rule under Itzcóatl in the 15th century. Until the Spanish conquest, Aztec tribes constructed beautiful summer residences in Cuauhnáhuac (among groves), today's Cuernavaca. The Spaniards, under Hernán Cortés, invaded and destroyed Cuauhnáhuac in 1521. Having been stripped of his power by Emperor Karl V, Cortés spent some time in the city as the Count of Cuernavaca. In 1540, he finally returned to Spain. In colonial times, the Spanish upper crust liked to stay in Cuernavaca. Emperor Maximilian and his wife Charlotte resided in Cuernavaca several times during their short reign in Mexico (1864–1867). During the Mexican Revolution (1910–1920) the revolting farmers destroyed many ha-

History

Cuernavaca *Plan*

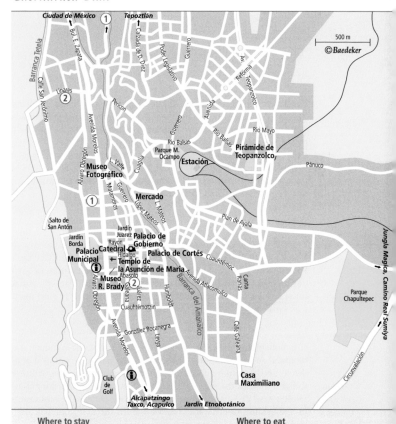

Where to stay
① Hacienda de Cortés ② Posada María Cristina

Where to eat
① La India Bonita ② Las Mañanitas

Today, the Palacio Cortés contains a large collection relating to regional archaeology, colonial history and revolution, above all concerning Emiliano Zapata.

ciendas around Cuernavaca. The leader of the revolt was Emiliano Zapata (Baedeker Special pp.52–54). Shouting »Tierra y Libertad« (land and freedom), the revolutionaries demanded that the land held by the large hacienda owners be redistributed.

Cuernavaca has also been mentioned in literature. The English writer Malcolm Lowry (1909–1957) lived in the city from 1936 to 1938 at Calle Humboldt No. 15 and made Cuernavaca the backdrop to his novel *Under the Volcano* (published in 1947).

What to See in Cuernavaca

Plaza de Armas The Cuernavaca city square is the lively Plaza de Armas. On its east side stands the Palacio de Cortés and on its west side the Governor's Palace (Palacio del Gobierno). On the south side restaurants of various kinds invite visitors to linger. North-west of the Plaza de Armas is the smaller plaza **Jardín Juárez** whose look-out point is a wrought-iron kiosk designed by Gustave Eiffel.

Palacio Cortés Close to the city square (Plaza Morelos) is the Cortés Palace. Construction of the palace started around 1530, but the building was modified several times after this. Once, the palace served as a residence and government office building; nowadays, amongst other things, it houses the regional Cuauhnáhuac museum of history (Museo Regional de Cuauhnáhuac), which shows evidence of past events in and around Cuernavaca. The view from the first floor balconies

✱

Regional Cuauhnáhuac Museum ▶

onto the city and its surroundings is magnificent. Of note are the **frescoes** by Diego Rivera that were commissioned by the US ambassador Dwight Morrow (the father-in-law of the cross-Atlantic pilot Charles Lindbergh). The frescoes, painted between 1929 and 1930, bring to life scenes from the Spanish conquest, the history of Cuernavacas, the War of Independence and the Mexican Revolution. In one of the scenes Emiliano Zapata leads the white horse on which Hernán Cortés sits – a metaphor for the people taking back their country.

★
Cathedral

In 1529, a Franciscan monastery was rebuilt into today's cathedral on the corner of Hidalgo Street and Morelos. The fortress-like structure with which the building was begun in 1533 goes back to Hernán Cortés. The side portal of the church has a colonial Plateresque façade. Over the gable, the symbols crown, cross, skull and crossbones are framed by an insignia-like architectural element. The interior of the cathedral was restored in the 1950s and in the process earlier murals came to light. They show 24 Mexican monks from the Franciscan order setting sail for a mission to Japan and then their crucifixion in 1597. In the back of the monastery is a chapel of the Third Order with the typical Mexican Baroque façade. The wood-carved altar (1735) shows a definite Indian influence. The same is true for the façade with a small figure that is meant to depict Hernán Cortés. Attached to the cathedral is the **open chapel** (capilla abierta) with a dome resting on three arches. Two bracing columns strengthen the centre columns. The cloister of the monastery contains murals depicting the origins of the Franciscan order. Every Sunday at 11am, a popular Mass with Mariachi music takes place. The Mariachis also give a performance in the cathedral on Sunday evenings.

Jardín Borda

The Borda Garden (Jardín Borda) is situated diagonally opposite the cathedral. The silver mogul of the mining town Taxco, José de la Borda, designed the garden in the second half of the 18th century. The park was restored in 1987 and now features terraced gardens, ponds, fountains and an open-air theatre. The gardens used to be the summer residence of Emperor Maximilian and wife Charlotte who gave huge glittering parties during their reign (1864–1867). Even today, the place still attracts the curious, who enter the gardens via the Calle Morelos to see how the Spanish aristocracy lived in Mexico. In a wing of the colonial building, the **Museo de Sitio** shows details of the everyday life of the time. Original documents from Maximilian, Juárez and Morelos are part of the display in the museum. Several paintings depict romantic scenes, the best known of which shows Maximilian with his lover La India Bonita.

★
Robert Brady Museum

The American artist and collector Robert Brady (1928–1986) spent 24 years of his life in Cuernavaca. His private residence at Calle Netzahualcóyotl 4 was once part of the monastery complex of the cathe-

▶ VISITING CUERNAVACA

INFORMATION

Turismo
Calle Morelos Sur 187
Tel. (777) 314 38 72, 314 39 20
or at the information kiosk on the
south side of the Jardín de los Héroes
(garden of the heroes).
Information also at
www.cuernavaca.gob.mx

GETTING AROUND

A drive of 80km/50mi on the MEX 95
from Mexico City, or a 1.5-hour bus
ride.

WHERE TO EAT

▶ **Expensive**

② *Las Mañanitas*
Calle Ricardo Linares 107
Tel. (777) 314 14 66
www.lasmananitas.com.mx
Choose your table on a shady terrace
in this exclusive restaurant and enjoy
the view of the park with its peacocks.
The Mexican-international menu is
presented on a large chalkboard. Be
sure to make a reservation.

▶ **Moderate**

① *La India Bonita*
Calle Dwight Morrow 15
Tel. (777) 318 69 67, 312 50 21

La India Bonita is located between
Matamoros Street and Morelos in the
patios of the restored former residence
of the US ambassador Dwight Morrow. The cuisine is Mexican and
Indian.

WHERE TO STAY

▶ **Luxury**

① *Hacienda de Cortés*
Plaza Kennedy 90
Col. Atlacomulco, Mor.
Tel. (777) 322 72 35
Tel. (777) 315 88 44
Fax (777) 315 00 35
www.hotelhaciendadecortes.com
This 16th- century hacienda (22
rooms) once belonged to conquistador
Hernán Cortés. The rooms are fur-
nished with exclusive Mexican furni-
ture and have patios and romantic
gardens.

▶ **Mid-range**

② *Posada María Cristina*
Calle Francisco Leyva 200
Tel. (777) 318 57 67
www.maria-cristina.com
The former Posada de Xochiquetzal
(Xochiquetzal Lodge) with 18 rooms
has a garden with a well. The rooms
are furnished in colonial style.

---

dral. It contains about 1,300 pieces of art, among them pre-Columbian and colonial art, paintings by Diego Rivera, Frida Kahlo and
Rufino Tamayo as well as arts and crafts from the Americas, Africa
and Asia. All descriptions are in English (open Tue–Sun
10am–6pm).

Municipal Palace   The city's history is the theme of the paintings on display in the Municipal Palace (Palacio Municipal) south of the Borda Gardens
(Jardín Borda) in the Avenida Morelos. The inner courtyard often
contains touring exhibitions.

About 1km/0.6mi from the city centre in the west part of Cuernava-ca, waters cascade down the 40 m/131 ft San Antón Falls (Salto de San Antón). On a path through a picturesque landscape visitors can stop right behind the falls. People living in the small village above the falls create beautiful ceramics.

San Antón Falls

It is worthwhile to take a trip to the city district and formerly inde-pendent village Acapatzingo about 1.5 km/1 mi south of the city centre. There, at Calle Matamoros 19, visit the Casa Maximiliano or Casa del Olvido (the House of Forgetfulness). Maximilian built this hideaway in a pastoral setting as a refuge for himself and his Indian lover. The name was coined when Maximilian conveniently »forgot« to include a room for his wife in the plan. However he remembered to build his lover a house of her own in the park, which is now home to a herbarium, a collection of herbs and traditional medicinal plants in the **Museo de la Herbolaria**.

Casa Maximiliano

The pre-Columbian site Teopanzolco is located in the north-eastern outskirts of town close to the railway station. The structures there are mostly from the late post-classical period (1250–1521). The ruins were only rediscovered in 1910 when Zapata and his rebel troops placed their cannons on a hill to shell the city: the exploding shells unearthed ancient walls.
The site contains one of the few Tlahuica ruins left to us. The struc-tures here are from the Tlahuica capital and in the typical Aztec style. The Twin Temple Pyramid consists of two temple pyramids built one on top of the other. A double stairway leads to the top of the pyramid where remnants of two temples still exist, one dedicated to Huitzilopochtli, the other to Tláloc. Animal heads cut from stone and embedded in the walls, that were once finished with stucco, can still be recognized. Smaller pyramids were associated with the gods Ehécatl (god of the wind) and Tezcatlipoca (Smoking Mirror, the counterpart of Quetzalcoatl).

The Twin Temple Pyramid of Teopanzolco

Time permitting, visitors to Cuernavaca may like to do some more sightseeing. The **Museo Taller Siqueiros** (Calle Venus 7) is sited in the building which was once home to the artist David Álfaro Si-queiros, who spent the last nine years of his life here together with Angélica Arenal. The exhibits consist of unfinished murals, photo-graphs and other mementos.
Displays in the **Museo Fotográfico** de Cuernavaca show photographs and maps of the city. The photography museum is housed in a build-ing called Castellito in Calle Güemes 1, about 1km/0.6mi north of the city square.
The **Jungla Mágica** is a park for children and is completely focused on jungle motifs. At Bajada de Chapultepec 27 visitors can see many different species of bird, swim with dolphins, take out a boat or have a picnic.

Other sights

Around Cuernavaca

Tepoztlán

Tepoztlán is located about 26km/16mi east of Cuernavaca. Mexican weekend tourists like to visit this picturesque town, which is surrounded by bizarre cliff-like mountain walls. Tepoztlán's greatest architectural attraction is the former monastery of the Dominican order.

The fortress-like religious building **Ex-Convento Dominico de la Natividad** is supposed to have been designed by the Spaniard Francisco Becerra (1559–1588). In the corners of the atrium are interesting procession chapels (capillas posas) with gables and ribbed Gothic domes. On the right, in front of an open chapel, stands a 16th-century stone cross. The beautiful portal of the convent church Nuestra Señora de la Asunción in the Plateresque style shows Dominican elements and indigenous motifs. Sun, moon, planets, floral designs and whimsical figures exist side-by-side with the Virgin Mary and the Dominican cross. Remnants of frescoes still exist in the chapel and the procession chapels. The church has one nave. Passing through the church, visitors come to a rustic cloister; from the first level balcony at its north-west corner there is a good view of the beautiful surrounding mountains. A small archaeological museum in the back of the monastery complex shows regional pre-Hispanic finds.

Tepotzlán's main attraction: the former Dominican monastery

500 m/1,640 ft above the village on a steep rockface towers the ruin site Tepozteco. The Tlahuica built a 20m/66ft-high **three-level temple pyramid** here to pay tribute to the harvest and pulque god Tepoztécatl. A walk to the pyramid on a steep path takes about one hour; the climber is rewarded with a breathtaking view. Columns inside the pyramid display figures and abstract drawings. The walls and stone floor reveal calendar signs and symbols for pulque, water, war and blood. Other ancient Indian ruins exist nearby.

Tepozteco

Cuautla is located 42 km/26 mi south-east of Cuernavaca. The much-frequented **thermal springs** of the village were a magnet for visitors as early as the 17th century. Due to the subtropical climate, the vegetation is lush. Well-positioned at the intersection of interurban roads, Cuautla is a good strategic point from which to plan sightseeing tours, especially to the numerous monasteries (► Morelos). The springs here were known in pre-Columbian times as were those of Las Estacas in Tlaltizapán and El Roll in Tlaquiltenango. After the conquest, Cuautla became a fashionable spa and resort for wealthy Spaniards. In 1812, in the course of the Mexican War of Independence, José María Morelos led his troop of freedom-fighters in battle against the royalist Spanish troops. Emiliano Zapata – the leader of the great farmer uprising in the Mexican Revolution (1910–1920) – was born 6 km/3.7 mi south of Cuautla in **Anenecuilco**.

Cuautla

The town offers little in the way of colonial arts. The best known churches here, the churches of San Diego and San Santiago, were built in the 17th century. Mementos from the time of the War of Independence are displayed in the Casa de Morelos. The most important healing waters in and around Cuautla are mostly hot sulphur springs, to be found in Agua Hedionda (stinking water) at the eastern periphery of the town as well as in Agua Linda, Casasano and El Almeal.

The crater lake Tequesquitengo is situated 50 km/31 mi south of the city amid subtropical vegetation. The small town of the same name lies on its eastern bank. All kinds of aquatic sports, including water-skiing, are on offer here. There are also hotels and restaurants.

Crater Lake Tequesquitengo

The Zoofari (55 km/34 mi east of Cuernavaca) is the right destination for anybody who likes to observe wild animals. Free range is given here to zebras and giraffes, while emus and monkeys curiously watch the visitors.

Zoofari

The archaeological site Xochicalco (38 km/24 mi south-west of Cuernavaca) was declared a UNESCO World Heritage Site in 1999. It towers 130 m/427 ft high over a wide plain atop an artificially levelled mountain with terraces which are also man-made. The place conveys the image of a fortress. The history of Xochicalco – the name means »in the house of flowers« – is one of the big riddles in Mesoamerican

★
Xochicalco
🕐
open:
daily 9am–6pm

Xochicalco *Plan*

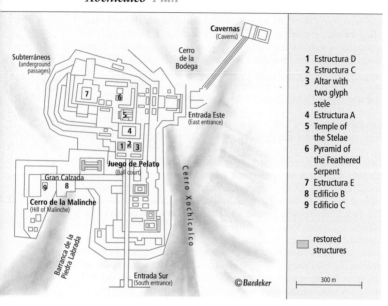

Cavernas (Caverns)

Cerro de la Bodega

Subterráneos (underground passages)

7

6

5

4

1 2 3

Entrada Este (East entrance)

Cerro Xochicalco

Juego de Pelota (Ball court)

Gran Calzada

9 8

Cerro de la Malinche (Hill of Malinche)

Barranca de la Piedra Labrada

Entrada Sur (South entrance)

©Baedeker

1 Estructura D
2 Estructura C
3 Altar with two glyph stele
4 Estructura A
5 Temple of the Stelae
6 Pyramid of the Feathered Serpent
7 Estructura E
8 Edificio B
9 Edificio C

▢ restored structures

300 m

archaeology. The site was probably already occupied by around AD 500. After the fall of Teotihuacán, the site developed into an important trading centre in the 7th and 8th centuries. Situated **at the interface between northern and southern high cultures**, the influences of Teotihuacán, the Maya, Zapotec, Mixtec and Toltec are evident. Later, Xochicalco became an important academic centre. The city lost its significance after AD 900 and, soon after, Xochicalco fell to other tribes and was then abandoned for economic reasons.

This fallen religious and military metropolis covered an area of more than 12 sq km/4.6 sq mi, while the defined ceremonial centre spanned 1,200 m/3,940 ft from north to south and about 700m/2,300 ft from east to west. The view from the top of the ceremonial site over the panorama of mountains, plains and lakes is very beautiful. To categorize the site's architecture and artistic motifs, they appear to span the cultures of Teotihuacán and Tula, as may be deduced from the **renditions of the god Quetzalcóatl** in particular. For the first time, the god is depicted in human form and not exclusively in the guise of a plumed serpent.

The most significant structure is the Quetzalcóatl Pyramid or Pyramid of the Feathered Serpent (**Pirámide de las Serpientes Emplumadas**), occasionally also called the Monumento Descubierto (uncovered monument). Some speculate that the pyramid was built to commemorate a significant assembly of priest-astronomers. The pyramid has two levels, only the lower of which still exists in its entirety. The

Relief of feathered serpent

structure was built in the Talud-Tablero style (a flat slab [tablero] over a sloped riser [talud]). In contrast to the architectural style in Teotihuacán, the sloped walls are a major focus here. A flat relief on the remaining sloped wall shows eight feathered serpents coiled around hieroglyphs and seated persons. The relief once shone in the colours white, red, black, blue and yellow, but then it was completely overpainted with red, the colour of death and rebirth, an act that may have been symbolic of the impending downfall. Reliefs on the sides of the steep wall show seated persons, stylized snakes and calendar glyphs. Patterns of stylized shells in a frieze over the forward projecting ledge are associated with the god Quetzalcóatl.

The site also features several underground **passages**, one of which ends in a raised room. A very narrow shaft in its ceiling extends to the outside surface, which presumably served as an observatory because the light falls through it exactly at the summer solstice on 21 June when it illuminates the underground room. Among other discoveries at the site are **ball courts**, an approximately 18m/59ft-long street, as well as the remnants of about 20 round altars, a palace and several wells.

The **Eco-Museum**, opened in 1996, lies a little outside the archaeological zone. It is supplied with solar energy and rainwater. In six rooms, the museum displays artefacts found in Xochicalco since 1993. One of the pieces is a large ceramic sculpture of a jaguar.

There are seven mountain lakes only 25 km/155 mi north-west of Cuernavaca in the Zempoala Lagoons National Park (Parque Nacional Lagunas de Zempoala). Some of the lakes are a real Eldorado for anglers. The forests around the lakes provide hikers with great trails and perfect locations to stop and rest.

Zempoala Lagoons National Park

Durango

K / L 14

Federal state: Durango (Dgo.)	**Altitude:** 1,890 m/6,200 ft
Population: 500,000	**Distance:** 940km/584mi north-west of Mexico City

Located in the eastern foothills of the Sierra Madre Occidental, Durango is the main city in the picturesque and fertile Guadiana valley. The climate is pleasant and dry here. The atmosphere is palpably old-Spanish. Durango is also an important regional centre of trade and industry.

History Pater Diego de la Cadena established the settlement San Juan de Analco in 1556. While Francisco de Ibarra and Alonso Pacheco gave the place the name Durango in 1563, long into the 18th century it was mostly known as Villa de Guadiana. Being an outpost of the Spaniards who were eager to find precious metals, the place was beleaguered by Indians, especially the Tepehuano. The region became more peaceful in the 17th century when Durango became the seat of a Catholic bishop and experienced considerable cultural development. However, it was to be a long wait for any economic development worth mentioning. The economic drought has abated to some degree only in the last decades.

What to See in and around Durango

Town Square (Zócalo) The tranquil city offers few cultural highlights for the tourist. Between 1695 and 1777, a cathedral was built in the main town square. The building reflects the development of the Mexican Baroque style of that time. Also notable are the Baroque Jesuit church Sagrario and the Casa del Conde de Suchil, residence of the Count of Suchil and at one time seat of the inquisition tribunals.

Cerro del Mercado The Cerro del Mercado is located north of Durango. This 200m/656ft-high mountain consists almost entirely of iron ore. Even though this was known as early as the time of the conquistadores, mining started only in 1828. Mineral collectors like to visit the Cerro del Mercado to search for pieces of apatite.

Museums **The Museum of Anthropology and History El Aguacate** (Museo de Antropología e Historia El Aguacate, located in Calle Victoria 100 Sur), owes its name to the large avocado tree in the garden. It exhibits archaeological and ethnographic finds as well as colonial and folk art.

The **Mining Museum (Colección de Minería)** is housed in the Casa del Cuerno and shows gold, silver and other precious metals. It also displays a large mammoth tooth.

▶ VISITING DURANGO

INFORMATION

Tourist information:
Calle Florida 1106
Tel. (618) 811 21 39
www.turismodurango.com

GETTING AROUND

A bus ride from Mexico City
to Durango takes about
15 hours.

WHERE TO EAT

▶ Moderate
La Casa de la Monja
Calle Negrete 308

Tel. (618) 811 71 62
Good meals on the covered patio
of a former private home.

WHERE TO STAY

▶ Mid-range to budget
Florida Plaza
Avenida 20 Noviembre y
Independencia
Tel. (618) 812 15 11
www.hotelfloridaplaza.com
This beautiful hotel (81 rooms) in the
historic centre of Durango is sur-
rounded by gardens and wells.

Thermal Springs

It is convenient to stay in Durango while making use of one of several iron and sulphur-containing thermal waters and spas in places
like Navacoyan and El Saltito.

Reservoirs

Several reservoirs close to Durango offer many opportunities for
aquatic sport enthusiasts and anglers. Notable in this context are for
example Garabitos, La Tinaja, Guadalupe Victoria and Peña del
Águila.

Western movie production sites

Movie fans will probably like to check out one of the many film locations for Westerns. The locations are to be found on the MEX 45
north starting at marker Km 12, and in the village Chupadores. Another city for movie settings is Villa del Oeste, with a saloon, church
and churchyard.

✳ Journey to Mazatlán

The MEX 40 from Durango via El Salto to ▶ Mazatlán (320 km/
200 mi) passes through impressive scenery. Parts of the road through
the wild mountain region can be a challenge because of the many
twists and turns. Be sure to obtain information on the condition of
the road before departure.

Bermejillo

Bermejillo (population 30,000) is located 45 km/28 mi north of
Gómez Palacio on the MEX 49. Townspeople find fossilized fish and
snails around town. They do some finishing work on their finds and
sell the product.

✳ Puente Ojuela

Take the MEX 30 from Bermejillo toward Mapimí. After 20km/
12.4mi, turn onto a narrow road to the mine Puente Ojuela and its

bizarre surrounding landscape. Prospecting for silver, lead and manganese still continues to some minor extent. A free-swinging wooden filigree bridge spanning a gorge is an unusual eye-catcher.

Mapimi

There are only 3 km/2 mi between Bermejillo and the old mining town Mapimi in the Sierra del Rosario. Peculiar rock formations are found in the surrounding area as well as the so-called Red Caves – the red colour is due to iron oxides.

Zone of Silence

The MEX 49 runs north and, 145 km/90 mi from Bermejillo, leads via Ceballos to the villages of San José del Centro and Mohóvano. Between these villages stretches the region called the Zone of Silence (Zona del Silencio). In this area, massive iron oxide deposits produce strong electromagnetic fields, which render all radio, TV or other electronic communications impossible.

Another remarkable characteristic in this very dry region is the absorption of solar rays, which is about 35% higher than expected for the location. Unusual plant and animal mutations have also been discovered in the region.

The settings for some Westerns have made the area around Durango very well known.

✶ El Tajín

O 21

Federal state: Veracruz (Ver.)   **Altitude:** 298m/977ft
Distance: 12 km/19 mi west of Papantla

El Tajín is one of Mexico's most important pre-Columbian excavation sites. The ruins of the Totonac city lie in lush tropical hills in a region with a warm, humid climate.

The large archaeological site occupies an area of about 11,000 sq km/ 4,250 sq mi, nearly half of which has been explored in recent years. At the height of its power, the ancient city and its surroundings were home to about 50,000 people. El Tajín has been a UNESCO World Heritage Site since 1992.

At the time of the Spanish conquest, El Tajín (lightning bolt) was occupied by the Totonac, and until now the site has therefore been associated with this tribe. The real beginnings of El Tajín however were strongly influenced by Teotihuacán. A unique culture only developed around 600; between 700 and 900, the ancient city's civilization was at its height. The first important structures were built in the 4th and 5th centuries, among them the Pyramid of the Niches. El Tajín's next building phase took place between the 6th and 8th centuries and in El Tajín Chico (the region north of the El Tajín central plaza) between the 9th and 12th centuries.

History

Toltec influences become evident in structures built in the 12th century. Around the year 1200, El Tajín disappeared from the map as a city and ceremonial site. Signs of destruction and fire point to a **conquest by the Toltec**. In the 15th century, the rulers of the Aztec empire started to extract tribute from the Totonac who lived in this part of Veracruz. In the first phase of their Mesoamerican conquest (1519–1521), the Spaniards ignored El Tajín; in 1785 Diego Ruiz became the first Spaniard to visit and report on the place. It wasn't un-

▶ VISITING EL TAJÍN

INFORMATION
www.mexconnect.com/mex_/ veracruz/tajin.html

GETTING AROUND
The best route by air is via Poza Rica. From there, it is an approximately 15km/9mi drive to El Tajín. If travelling by car, take the MEX 85 towards Teotihuacán and then the MEX 130

and 132 (Vanilla Route) via Tulancingo and Poza Rica, a total distance of about 300 km/483 mi.

El Tajín is about 240 km/149 mi from Veracruz on the MEX 180 via Nautla and Papantla. A bus ride from Veracruz to Papantla takes about 4 hours, and local bus services go on from there to El Tajín.

til 1934 that systematic excavations began. Renewed archaeological efforts since 1984 have unearthed 36 new structures. Today, visitors can see 48 structures in good condition.

Tour of the El Tajín Ruins

Site

Opening times: daily 8am–5pm

El Tajín proper and El Tajín Chico occupy several units and regions: the group of buildings around the Plaza Arroyo (Grupo Plaza del Arroyo); the centre (Zona Central) with the Pyramid of the Niches; the Complex of the Columns (Complejo de las Columnas); La Gran Greca; and La Gran Xicalcoiunqhui.

El Tajín was built in a style unique to the region (also found in Yohualichán 60km/37mi away). The style is characterized by receding ledges and window-like niches or recessed panels in the pyramid walls. The structures were painted red, black or blue and sometimes had exterior murals.

Voladores (bird-men)

Next to the visitor centre, several Indians perform the exciting Totonac ritual »Dance of the Voladores« (►Baedeker Special p.302). This is a mixture of flight, dance acrobatics and bungee jumping. The exhibition takes place around 4pm. Visitors are expected to tip the artists.

El Tajín Plan

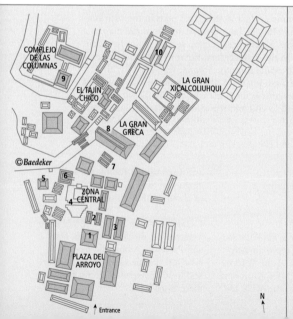

1 Edificio 16
2 Juego de Pelota 17 / 27
3 Juego de Pelota 13 / 14
4 Juego de Pelota Sur
5 Edificio 12
6 Pirámide de los Nichos
7 Juego de Pelota Central
8 Edificio I
9 Edificio de las Columnas
10 Juego de Pelota Norte

COMPLEJO DE LAS COLUMNAS
EL TAJÍN CHICO
LA GRAN XICALCOLIUHQUI
LA GRAN GRECA
©Baedeker
ZONA CENTRAL
PLAZA DEL ARROYO
N
↑ Entrance

Unique: the Pyramid of the Niches

With a total of **17 ball courts** (T, double-T and I-shaped) El Tajín is the archaeological site with the second highest number of courts in Mesoamerica, after Cantona. The game started on the Gulf Coast and spread over a large part of Mesoamerica. Although there were regional variations in rules and player's regalia, the ritual character remained constant: a contest between good and evil, day and night, and life and death, representing the duality existing between Quetzalcóatl and Tezcatlipoca, and Venus and the moon – as depicted on the walls of the two ball courts below and those of the southern ball court (►Baedeker Special p.259).

Centre of Ball Games

The buildings of the Arroya Group in the Plaza del Arroyo (Square of the Brook) near the entrance have only recently been excavated. The most beautiful building is structure 16, which consists of three structures built one on top of the other. Two ball courts (17/27 and 13/14) have been excavated behind structure 16.

Plaza del Arroyo

The southern ball court (Juego de Pelota Sur) is 60m/197ft long and 10m/33ft wide. At both ends, the side walls show extremely interesting flat reliefs between fascias with stylized snakes. Below this ar-

Southern ball court

rangement are scenes showing the initiation of a young warrior who is standing in front of gods or priests. Another scene shows the consecration of a warrior who lies on a bench, most likely to the god of the ball game (Tlachtli). The god is symbolized as a sunbird gliding in the air above the warrior. Another scene shows the preparation of pulque (agave wine with low alcohol content) as an important element of the ball game in El Tajín. Unique features on the Gulf Coast and especially in El Tajín are the so-called **yokes** (yugos), **hatchets** (hachas) and **palms** (palmas). Yugos are stone sculptures, richly adorned and up to 30 kg/66 lbs in weight, hachas are thin stone axe heads often in open work and mostly decorated with human faces, and palmas are elaborately worked, feathered triangles which were put on the sides of the yoke as a protective layer. Presumably, all these stone sculptures represent the regalia of the ball players. The sculptures are amongst the most artistic works of the pre-Columbian period.

Pyramid of the Niches The monuments II, III and IV are located in the central zone next to the Pyramid of the Niches (Pirámide de los Nichos), of which structure II and the associated monument V are notable. The magnificent Pyramid of the Niches is 25 m/82 ft high and has a square base with sides 35/115ft long. The pyramid was arguably built from the 4th to the 7th centuries and dedicated to the god of rain and wind. It has seven vertical sections including the level of the temple itself. This pyramid, too, was erected on top of an older one. 365 shallow square niches are arranged in continuous rows around the pyramid, **each niche standing for one day of the year**. A stone frame surrounds each niche. Originally, it was thought that the niches were a place to put statues, but today they are considered mere decoration.

The outer pyramid was once coated with coloured stucco and the niches painted in bright colours. The architects may have tried to create a mystical light-dark effect. A balustrade with a stone meander mosaic runs along both sides of the 10m/33ft-wide outer pyramid stairs. The stairway, which was added later, could presumably only be used like a ladder. In the centre are five equidistant platforms, each with three somewhat smaller niches.

A path leads to a historically younger building complex north of the pyramid and to a courtyard called Plaza El Tajín Chico. The architecture with roof ridges and rooms with column-framed entrances and cantilever roof are reminiscent of Maya architecture.

Hall of the Columns The Hall of the Columns (Edificio de las Columnas), also known as the Governor's Palace (Palacio del Gobierno), is the highest point of the site. It was built on top of a man-made, 45 m/148 ft-high mound. Hieroglyphs at this site tell of the ruler called »13 Rabbits« who probably lived in the 10th century. The niches of this structure are decorated with meander motifs. The design of the ledges seems to contradict the laws of gravity. It is intriguing that the massive stairways were mere decoration and could not actually be used; instead, it was necessary to use ladders to reach the inside of the uppermost rooms. On the other hand, the architects of the Hall of the Columns possessed amazing skills for their time because they covered roofs with cement slabs, a technique that was otherwise unknown in Mesoamerica. Several drum columns (cylindrical columns made from several stones), 1.20 m/3.9 ft in diameter at the base, used to be part of a gallery in the front part of the building. The columns are covered with flat reliefs, which show hieroglyphs and scenes with warriors, priests and human sacrifices. Panels with cross-shaped reliefs have been found on the eastern panel of the uppermost building. The view from the top of the building of the entire site is stunning.

Other structures

Close to the Hall of Columns is Structure I, with paintings of gods who have taken on the appearance of animals. Below the stairway lies the central ball court with six panels showing the gods Tláloc, Quetzalcóatl and Macuilxochitl. North of the ball court is La Gran Greca: unique in Mesoamerica because of its size, this platform served as a base for several buildings. Further north still, the giant spiral-shaped

Relief at the southern ball court

This rite is primarily performed by the Totonac tribe but also by the Huastecs and Otomí. Similar flying dances are also performed by the Chorti in Honduras and Quiché in Guatemala.

DANCE OF THE BIRD MEN

Papantla has become famed for the flying pole act performed by its voladores or bird men. It takes place during major celebrations such as the eight-day Corpus Christi festival. The dance is also performed by five men in traditional costume in El Tajín at the entrance to the archaeological site there.

This ceremony was originally part of a cult drama concerning a myth of growing maize and has come down in the form of hieroglyphics from pre-Spanish times.

After some preparatory ceremonials, the five men climb to a platform on a mast some 30m/98ft above the ground. The leader starts to play a flute and offer prayers for the **fertility of the land** in all directions. Then the other four men (toticones), each hanging upside down from a cable attached to the top of the mast, start to twirl around the mast in ever-increasing circles until their cables have unwound and they have reached the ground. Each man undergoes 13 revolutions, so that a total of 52 are made by the four men together. This corresponds to the 52-year cycle of the ancient pre-Columbian calendar.

Nowadays, the deeper significance of the dance has been forgotten, even though the modern voladores keep strictly to the descriptions found in old Spanish chronicles, in which the performance was seen as a kind of **sport or exercise for the body**. Only one small feature has been added: the men now ask for a small monetary reward at the end of the Dance of the bird men.

Taking pictures is allowed, but special permission (for a fee) must be obtained for taking videos.

wall called La Gran Xicalcoiunqhui can be seen; it is associated with the god Quetzalcóatl.

In a new museum at the entrance to the ruins, a display shows a miniature model of the site, as well as finds from the excavations including the otherwise rare drum columns.   Museum

Around El Tajín

The city of Papantla (population 120,000) lies 15km/9mi south-east of the El Tajín archaeological site. This pretty place in the hills, surrounded by dense tropical forest, is considered to be the centre of the largest expanse of vanilla plants in America. Papantla has become famous for the flying bird-men, the **voladores**, who epitomize the Totonac traditions. There is a statue of a volador playing the flute behind the church in the Parque Téllez.   Papantla

The industrial city of Poza Rica (population 180,000) is located only 19km/12mi north-west of El Tajín. Travellers going north from Poza Rica towards Tihuatlán take a road branching off after about 15km/9mi and arrive after 22km/14mi at the village of Teayo. The well-restored pyramid **Castillo de Teayo** stands on the main village square. The top platform of the almost 13m/43ft-tall, three-platform building still shows the remnants of a rectangular temple. Sculptures from the pyramid, mostly of Aztec origin, are now displayed inside a small museum. Similar sculptures are displayed in the districts of Zapotitlán and La Cruz. Initially, it was assumed that the Aztec built the pyramid in the 15th century at a staging post in the Totonac area. Today, people believe that Toltec from Tula built this pyramid as many as 400 years earlier.   Poza Rica
By means of a planned tunnel project it is hoped to expose a Huastec building core. The area around the pyramid was settled only around 1870. The villagers used a portion of the ancient Indian stones to build their own houses.

The airport Tuxpan is located about 55km/34mi north of Poza Rica and 10km/6mi inland from it. The city of Tuxpan (population 135,000) is known for the first-rate fishing in rivers and the ocean. Popular angling contests take place here in the summer months, mainly at the end of June or the beginning of July. An archaeological museum west of the Parque Reforma displays Totonac and Huastec finds.   Tuxpan
In 1956, Fidel Castro met with his fellow campaigners in Tuxpan to make plans for a Cuban revolution. This is the main topic of the documents in the museum of Cuban-Mexican friendship (Museo Histórico de la Amistad México-Cuba). Next to the museum stands a reproduction of the ship »Granma«, which brought Fidel Castro and 82 of his comrades to Cuba.

✳ Guadalajara

O 15

Federal state: Jalisco (Jal.)
Population: 5 million

Altitude: 1,552 m/5,092 ft
Distance: 573 km/356 mi north-west of Mexico City

Guadalajara is second in size only to Mexico City. Many foreigners regard it as the most Mexican of Mexican cities because much of what foreigners see as typical Mexican folklore had its origins here. Among such traditions, which for some express the essence of Mexico, are Mariachi music, tequila, the sombrero, charreadas (Mexican rodeos) and the popular folk dance Jarabe Tapatío.

Guadalajara is situated on a gentle hill in the fertile highland valley of Atemajac. The climate here is subtropical and temperate. For many years, Guadalajara, capital of the federal state of Jalisco, has been isolated from Mexico City. The city has therefore maintained its character as a place with a European flavour which is steeped in tradition. The people here call themselves **Tapatíos**. Thanks to their affluence and love of the arts, they have been able to create an endearing city with broad avenues, well-kept parks and light, clean buildings. However, recent strong efforts to modernize, along with rapid population growth, have diminished the traditional small-town character of Guadalajara. An excursion to the suburbs Tlaquepaque and Tonalá, both well-known for their arts and crafts, and a side trip to Mexico's largest lake, the Lago de Chapala, are well worthwhile.

! **Baedeker TIP**

Riding the Tequila Express

Every Saturday and Sunday at 11am, the Tequila Express leaves the Guadalajara station, La Querencia, for a train ride through the central highlands. Mariachi musicians and high-proof tequila ensure a party atmosphere on board. The destination is Amatitan (about 1.5 hours) where travellers can enjoy demonstrations of typical dances, visit a tequila distillery or eat Mexican food. The train arrives back in Guadalajara by 8:30pm. To enquire or buy tickets call Tel. (01) 38 89 90 99 or 31 22 79 20.

History The Spanish conquistadores initially established settlements in the region, but these were abandoned between 1530 and 1542. Finally, in 1542, Pérez de la Torre established Guadalajara, naming it after a Spanish city of the same name. The city became the capital of the province Nueva Galicia in 1560. Guadalajara escaped the devastation of war in the 19th and 20th centuries because of its distance from Mexico City and its isolation. Important historical events in Guadalajara were the declaration to abolish slavery by the independence war hero Miguel Hidalgo in 1810, Hidalgo's and Allende's defeat by the Spaniards in 1811, and the French occupation from 1863 to

Guadalajara *Plan*

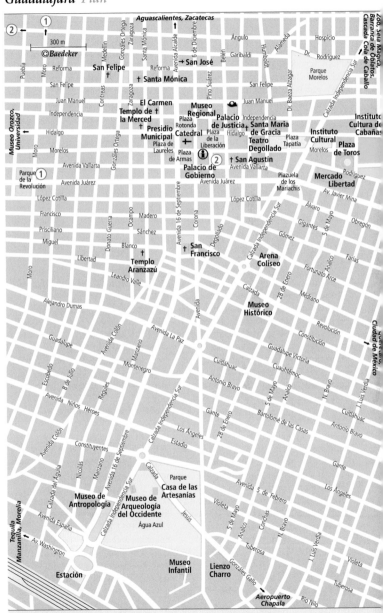

Where to stay
① Fiesta Americana Guadalajara ② Francés

Where to eat
① Copenhagen 77 ② La Destilería

▶ VISITING GUADALAJARA

INFORMATION

Tourist information
Plaza Tapatía (Morelos 102)
Tel. (333) 668 16 00
www.guadalajara.gob.mx
www.allaboutguadalajara.com

GETTING AROUND

It takes about one hour to fly from Mexico City to Guadalajara; a bus ride takes about 9.5 hours. When travelling by car, take the MEX 55 via Toluca and then the 15D via Maravatío (about 545km/339mi) or, alternatively, take the MEX 57 and the MEX 90 via Querétaro and Irapuato (572km/355mi).

EVENTS

The Basilica of Zapopan contains one of the most venerated statues of the Virgin Mary in all of Mexico. Between 13 June and 4 October, the faithful carry the statue from place to place through the Guadalajara parish communities to spread good fortune. The last stop is the Cathedral of Guadalajara. On 12 October, the statue is returned to Zapopan.

SHOPPING

Mercado Libertad
City market: street vendors and small restaurants offer gourmet food.

Tlaquepaque and Tonala
The main attractions are the arts and crafts stores with their huge selection of ceramics, glass items and souvenirs made from wood and moulded cellulose pulp.

WHERE TO EAT

▶ **Expensive to moderate**
① *Copenhagen 77*
Calle Marcos Castillanos 136

Tel. (33) 38 25 28 03
Fans of jazz music have been gathering here since 1952. Wall tiles by the well-known designer Jorge Wilmot decorate the restaurant. A culinary speciality is the Valencia paella.

▶ **Moderate**
② *La Destilería*
Avenida México 2916/Corner of Nelson, Tel. (33) 36 40 31 10
This restaurant has an attached tequila museum. Along with the typically Mexican cuisine there are more than 80 different kinds of tequila to enjoy.

WHERE TO STAY

▶ **Luxury**
① *Fiesta Americana Guadalajara*
Calle Aurelio Aceves 225
Glorieta Minerva Colonia Vallarta Poniente
Tel. (33) 38 18 14 00
www.fiestaamericana.com
This large hotel (390 rooms) features a striking glass façade and four glass elevators to the eleventh floor.

▶ **Mid-range to budget**
② *Francés*
Calle Maestranza 35
Tel. (33) 36 13 11 90
Fax (33) 36 58 28 31
www.hotelfrances.com
This is the oldest hotel in Guadalajaras (1610) and was declared a historic monument after its renovation in 1981 (72 rooms). Stone columns and continental arches enclose a marble well in the three-storey hall. The hotel is in a central location near the Governor's Palace (Palacio de Gobierno). Mariachi musicians entertain in the lobby every Friday evening.

View of the cathedral from the Plaza de la Liberación

1866. It was not until the end of the 19th century that a railway line finally connected Guadalajara and Mexico City. A tremendous explosion in the sewer lines shook the city on April 22, 1992. More than 200 people died.

What to See in Guadalajara

The Guadalajara Cathedral with its two towers is the undisputed city symbol. The cathedral was built between 1558 and 1616 and was then subject to many reconstructions. The structure is Baroque in nature with a strange mixture of different styles added to it. Some of the paintings in the chapel and side chapel (sagrario) are said to be by Cristóbal de Villalpando, Miguel Cabrera and Murillo. Over the vestry portal hangs a painting ascribed to Murillo (*The Assumption*). The cathedral stands amid plazas on all four sides; the Plaza de los Laureles in front of the main portal features a large fountain.

★
The Cathedral

True to the name, bay (or laurel) trees grow on the Plaza de los Laureles. The city hall (Presidencia Municipal), built in the 1950s, is located on the northern side of the plaza. Above its staircase, a mural by Gabriel Flores shows the inception of the city.

Plaza de los Laureles

In the most beautiful of the four plazas, the Plaza de Armas, stands the Governor's Palace (**Palacio de Gobierno**), a grand building in the Baroque style. Its columns show a zig-zag pattern, and there are also large covings (concave moldings) and ultra-Baroque wall columns known as estipites. Construction was completed in 1774. The staircase and one of the conference halls are decorated with murals by

Plaza de Armas

the famous Jalisco-born fresco painter **José Clemente Orozco** depicting Hidalgo during the War of Independence and heroes from the three major Mexican wars. Concerts take place here on Thursday and Sunday evenings. In the main, the musicians perform typical Jalisco music.

Twelve bronze sculptures of famous Jalisco personalities are placed around the **Plaza de la Rotonda** north of the cathedral. Six of these illustrious personalities are buried close to a column rotunda in the centre of the plaza, the Rotonda de los Hombres Illustres. The Guadalajara regional museum (Museo Regional de Guadalajara) is housed in the former Jesuit seminary (San José Liceo 60), a

Pater Hidalgo in Orozco's fresco

✷ ✷
Museo Regional ►

two-storey, late Baroque building on the east side of the plaza. This museum covers a wide range of topics: it informs the visitor about the archaeology of the western federal states and the west coast and enlightens people about the ethnology of the Huichol and Cora Indians and the life of the charro (farm hand); it displays religious items as well as collections concerning history and palaeontology; and collections of paintings show colonial art of the 17th to 19th century, European paintings from the 18th and 19th century as well as modern Mexican paintings and frescoes.

Plaza de la
Liberación
✷
Teatro
Degollado ►

Finally, there is the very large Plaza de la Liberación on the eastern side of the cathedral. In this plaza, opposite the cathedral, there is an impressive theatre building, the Teatro Degollado. This neo-classical theatre opened at the end of the 19th century. **Frescoes** in the theatre dome show impressive scenes from Dante's *Divine Comedy* by Gerardo Suárez. At the north side of the plaza stands the Palacio Legislativo (Legislative Palace) with its massive stone columns.

Palacio de
Justicia

The court building, the Palacio de Justicia, is located on the other side of the street (Hidalgo). Originally, the building served as the city's first convent. A wonderful mural by Guillermo Chávez in the stairwell of this building shows Benito Juárez, among other figures. Very close by, at the intersection of the streets Hidalgo and Carranza, stands the **Templo de Santa María de Gracia** (Temple of the Holy Mary of Grace). This temple served as the city's first cathedral from 1549 to 1618.

The Plaza Tapatía is located directly behind the theatre. It is a modern shopping mall, extending about half a kilometre (0.3 mi) east toward the Instituto Cultura de Cabañas.

Plaza Tapatia

It is a walk of four blocks east of the theatre through the new Plaza Tapatía pedestrian zone to the former Hospicio Cabañas. Manuel Tolsá built this orphanage in the neo-classical style in the 19th century. Over its lifetime, the building has been a home for the mentally disabled and has housed soldiers or prisoners. The story goes that in 1811 Miguel Hidalgo signed a proclamation against slavery here. The building is now an institute for cultural activities with a museum, a theatre and a school. On permanent display here are more than 100 works by Orozco, and there are also temporary exhibitions, dance and theatre shows, as well as concerts.

Instituto
Cultura
de Cabañas

José Clemente Orozco's arguably most beautiful frescoes line the walls of a former chapel in the building, which contains 23 patios. Orozco resided here in 1938/39 and artistically occupied himself with the four elements, the arts and sciences, the Spanish conquest and the Four Horsemen of the Apocalypse. His crowning achievement is the work in the dome of the building, »Man of Fire« (Hombre del Fuego). Orozco's works are displayed in different rooms around the patios. Since 1997, the entire building of the Hospicio Cabañas, including all Orozco frescoes, has been a UNESCO Cultural World Heritage Site.

Orozco Frescoes

◄(Fig. p.79)

The Plaza de los Mariachis between Calle Mina and Calzada Independencia Sur is a widely known landmark in Mexico. The Mariachi musicians play late into the night in the alleyway lined with restaurants and street cafés (►Baedeker Special p.311).

Plaza de
los Mariachis

Aside from the cathedral and the Templo de Santa María de Gracia, there are 13 more churches in the centre of Guadalajara. Only a few of them can be mentioned here:
The church Santa Mónica, found near the intersection Santa Mónica and San Felipe, was built in the second half of the 17th century. Its Baroque porch façade shows rich and finely-worked ornamentation (grapes, ears of maize, angels, double eagles and emblems of the religious order). On a corner high above the traffic, a very early St Christopher statue overlooks the streets.
The Baroque **Templo de la Merced**, built in 1650, is located near the cathedral (at the corner of Hidalgo/Loza). Inside, there is a wealth of gold embellishments, beautiful paintings and crystal chandeliers.
The sanctuary of **Our Lady of Carmen** (Nuestra Señora del Carmen) on the small square at the corner of Calle Juárez and 8 de Julio is also a very pretty church with a lot of gold and numerous wall paintings.
The style of the Templo de Aranzazú (at the corner of Calle 16 de Septiembre/Blanco), built in the middle of the 18th century, is rather

Other churches

◄Santa Mónica

◄Templo de
Aranzazú

austere. The three beautiful ultra-Baroque altars and the impressive paintings on the walls and ceiling are particularly notable.

Opposite this building stands the **Templo de San Francisco** with its splendid Baroque façade. The interior is however of lesser interest.

Agua Azul Park

Go south-west on Calzada Independencia to enter the beautiful Agua Azul Park (Parque Agua Azul). Here, the entire family is entertained. There are for example orchid and butterfly collections, a bird park, and children will love the pool and the playground. The simplest way to get to the park from the city centre is to take the buses 60 or 62, which go south on the Calzada Independencia.

Museo de Arqueología

The Museum of West Mexican Archaeology (Museo de Arqueología del Occidente del México), is situated opposite the modern park entrance. The museum shows an interesting collection of pre-Columbian artefacts from the western federal states. On display are mostly pottery, weapons, figures and artistic burial objects.

The **Casa de las Artesanías** at the northern end of the park offers very beautiful arts and crafts from the Jalisco region. Enter the building from the Avenida González Gallo. There is another special museum for children in the south-eastern part of the park.

Universidad de Guadalajara

Shade is often welcome and it is provided in the Park of the Revolution (Parque Revolución) west of the city centre where the Avenidas Juárez and Federalismo meet. The main building of the university is located three blocks west (Juárez 975) from this park. The so-called Parainfo, the auditorium of the university, is adorned with impressive frescoes by **José Clemente Orozco**. One of the works is a painting on the ceiling representing the oppressed masses pleading for education.

Guadalajara Zoo

Guadalajara Zoo, the Selva Mágica amusement park and a planetarium are located at the intersection of Calzada Independencía Norte and Avenida Flores Magón, north of the city centre and above the canyon Barranca de Oblatos.

Zapopan

Zapopan is situated about 8 km/5 mi north-west of the city centre. Now a suburb of Guadalajara, Zapopan used to be an Indian village. The suburb's 17th-century **Baroque Franciscan Church** is widely known. It is dedicated to the Virgin of Zapopan, the patron saint of Guadalajara. In summer (June to October), her statue is carried from church to church in Guadalajara and remains in each of them for a time. On 12 October, the statue is returned to Zapopan in a spectacular procession, accompanied by dancers, charros and Mariachis.

A museum (**Museo Huichol**) is associated with the church. In it, Huichol Indians from the mountains of Jalisco and Nayarit display and sell arts and crafts.

MUSIC OF THE MARIACHIS

Many see them as the most typically Mexican phenomenon of all. Proud mariachis gazing from under wide-brimmed hats, dressed in black suits trimmed with silver and holding forth with traditional Mexican folk songs on the themes of love, death and honour.

In many a good Mexican restaurant, there is no avoiding the honour of being serenaded by a mariachi troupe, for many the epitome of Mexican music. The small ensembles (and occasionally quite large ones) usually consist of violinists (or a bass player), guitarists, trumpeters and a singer.

Love, death and honour

Originally the mariachis were wandering musicians from the state of Jalisco, and Guadalajara in particular. Nowadays they are found almost all over the central highlands. In their traditional dress, the ranchero cowboys impart wisdoms that are very often **tragic in nature but occasionally happy**. These dramas of love, death and alcohol sometimes reach such unforeseen depths that sensitive listeners are compelled to reach for a handkerchief. It is assumed that the

music derives from Spanish forebears, although it also has been enhanced by French and central European elements. The mariachis may have gained their name from a corruption of the French word »mariage« or marriage, since French soldiers wrongly assumed that they played mainly at wedding ceremonies. Another theory is that mariachi comes from the Cocula word for a tree, referring to the stage where the songs are played.

Meeting places for mariachis

For anyone wishing to see them for the first time in a traditional setting, the meeting place for the mariachis in Mexico City is the Plaza de la Garibaldi and in Guadalajara it is close to the Mercado Libertad. An international mariachi festival is held here every year in September.

Tlaquepaque ✳

The suburb of San Pedro Tlaquepaque 7km/4.5mi south-east of the city centre attracts many tourists. Its shops sell ceramics, glass, animals made from papier-mâché and other arts and crafts. The region has always been a pottery centre. Some of the most beautiful pieces are on display in the regional ceramics museum of Jalisco, the **Museo Regional de la Cerámica** y los Artes Populares de Jalisco. Watch workers making glass items in a factory opposite the museum.

Tonalá

Another 7km/4.5mi distant is Tonalá. The village is also known for its ceramic art, but the town caters less to tourists than Tlaquepaque. The different shapes and patterns used in Guadalajara can be seen in the **ceramics museum** (Constitución 110). Only a few years ago, the town opened a museum of archaeology and folk art (Tonalán, Calle Ramón Corona 73). Among other items, this museum displays modern ceramics, pre-Columbian finds from Jalisco and masks. Tonalá was the capital of the state of Tonalán in ancient times.

A well-earned break by an agave field: donkeys are still used in agricultural work.

Around Guadalajara

Mexico's largest natural lake, the Laguna de Chapala, is located about 55km/34mi south-east of Guadalajara. Most of the 82km/51mi-long and on average 28km/17mi-wide lake lies in the state of Jalisco. Only its south-eastern portion is in Michoacán. The names of the three islands in the middle of the lake are Chapala (Alacranes), Mezcala (Presidio) and Maltarana.

✳ Laguna de Chapala

The lake is at times badly polluted. While this hampers the joy of swimming, there are still many opportunities for aquatic sports on and around it. The mountains surrounding the lake are mostly without vegetation. Edible fish from the lake are carp, mojarra (a food fish related to perch), brown bullhead, and whiting (pescado blanco). The beautiful landscape and the comfortable climate have attracted many people from the USA and Canada who have settled along the north-west lake shore.

Chapala (population 60,000), one of the most important locations around the lake, and its associated village Chula Vista have the largest colony of foreign nationals. Early on, between 1904 and 1907, Chapala developed into a resort when the then Mexican President Porfirio Díaz chose the town as his holiday domicile. On the shore near the Avenida Madero there is a pretty park and several vending kiosks selling ornate woven items. Arts and crafts are also on sale in the Mercado de Artesanías. The large Parque La Cristiana is an inviting place to swim and have a picnic. **Ajijic** is a fishing village with an artist colony, a small archaeology museum and several shops. Handwoven fabrics and embroidery are among the offerings. Ajijic is also known for its thermal springs, which are however overrun with tourists from the USA.

Chapala

San Juan Cosalá, 10km/6mi west of Ajijic on the way to Jocotepec, is a thermal spa resort amid beautiful surroundings. The town has its own natural geyser and several pools.

Jocotepec is located about 20km/12mi west of Chapala. The town is widely known for its white sarapes (ponchos). Jocotepec, too, is a beautiful fishing town with a small artist colony, but tourism plays a lesser role here than in Chapala and Ajijic. The village celebrates its Fiesta de los Dulces Nombres (All Saints' Day celebrations) on 14/15 January.

Tequila is located just 50km/31mi north-west of Guadalajara. The town, with its pretty San Francisco church, has been the centre of tequila and mescal production since the 18th century (►Baedeker Special p.314). These high-proof alcoholic beverages are made from agave. Local people call the blue agave used for tequila »maguey«. Guided tours with tequila tasting are arranged in the local distilleries. Large agave plantations supply the raw material for the alcoholic drink.

✳ Tequila

Testing tequila for aroma, colour and taste

THE BURNING JUICE OF THE AGAVE

»Like a field of upturned swords« was Paul Theroux's description in his book »Patagonia Express« for the fields of blue maguey agaves that grow in the arid highlands of Jalisco state and some neighbouring areas (such as Nayarit, Guanajato and Tamaulipas). Hundreds of years ago, it was discovered how to make tequila from agave juice. It is possible to visit distilleries for the tasty spirit in Guadalajara and Tequila itself.

Before the coming of the Europeans, the Indians used the agave plant for food, as a raw material for clothing and paper, and because of its fierce thorns for instruments of torture as well. The Indians of the Tequila volcano are also said to have made a kind of alcoholic drink that was drunk during religious rituals and during sacrificial ceremonies. Distilleries for the manufacture of tequila only appeared after the arrival of Spanish soldiers, though. The first was founded in 1795 by decree of King Charles IV of Spain – it is still in existence today. La Rojena, the distillery for Jose Cuervo, known for its logo with the black crow, is now the biggest in the country. Around 70 million litres are distilled in Jalisco every year. The best known tequila manufacturers are Sauza and Cuervo.

How is tequila made?

Although there are more than 400 types of agave, tequila is only made from the blue maguey agave. Even today they are hand-planted and manually harvested. Due to the blue-tinted leaves, which really are remi-

niscent of upturned swords, they are often thought to be a kind of cactus but in botanical terms they are more closely related to lilies. After **about 12 years** the agave can be harvested. At this time the core (piña) is about the size of a beach ball and weighs about 50kg/110lbs. Once harvested, the spiky leaves are hacked off and the core reduced in size for roasting. This gives the drink its characteristic taste and aroma. The core is roasted for about three days until it is soft. Then it is shredded and squeezed for its juice. The juice gained in this way is called aguamiel or honey water. It is gold-coloured and has a syrupy consistency. It is then pumped into vats mixed with sugared water and yeast and is allowed to ferment for 30 to 32 hours before being distilled twice. As it is, only the agave spirits from the north of the aforementioned region are now called tequila rather than this type of spirit in general. Only the manufacturers from that specific location are permitted to give their brands the special designation.

How to drink tequila

There are four types of tequila. It is matter of taste as to which is the best and which you prefer to drink. Mexicans tend to drink it **with salt and lemon**, or carefully mixed, but sometimes it is simply enjoyed on its own. Usually some lemon is dripped onto the back of the hand between the thumb and forefinger and a pinch of salt sprinkled over it. Next the drinker licks the salt and drinks the tequila **in a single draught** before biting into the lemon. More than one glass will make the burning effect very obvious.

Types of tequila

There are considerable differences between light and dark tequila. **Tequila blanco** (silver tequila) is bottled directly after distillation. It is clear and has a fresh albeit sharp taste. Gold tequila can either be freshly distilled like the silver with colourings and flavour enhancers (usually caramel) added or alternatively a blend of white tequila with older tequilas that have been allowed to age in wooden barrels. **Tequila reposado** will have been aged in barrels for around 8 months. It also has colourings and flavourings added and a somewhat milder taste. An **añejo** tequila is aged for one or two years in oak barrels. It also contains flavourings and colour. It is very popular for its golden-brown colour, its rich bouquet and milder taste. As it becomes older, it becomes ever smoother and can be drunk like a good brandy or old rum.

Trips to the tequila distilleries

Day trips to the tequila-making regions north-west of Guadalajara including a visit to a distillery start daily from San Francisco Park in Guadalajara or from the town of Tequila. Apart from the aforementioned **Cuervo** distillery, other large installations include the **Sauza Tequila plant**. There it is also possible to view the well-known frescoes depicting former production methods and the joy of drinking tequila. It is also worth paying a visit to **Herradura**, an old hacienda in Amatítlan (8km/13mi from Tequila).

✶✶ **Guanajuato**

Federal state: Guanajuato (Gto.)	**Altitude:** 2,050 m/6,726 ft
Population: 142,000	**Distance:** 356 km/221 mi north-west of Mexico City

Guanajuato, the capital of the federal state of the same name, extends along a small valley and seems to climb up the bare mountains.

Houses painted in bright colours, narrow streets and alleyways, small cosy plazas and colonial-style buildings give Guanajuato a charm all its own. The picturesque city and its rich cultural life make it one of the most attractive travel destinations in Mexico. Guanajuato and its silver mines are a **UNESCO Cultural Heritage Site**.

History In pre-Columbian times, the Tarasca lived in the region. They called the place where the city now stands Cuanax-huato (Hills of Frogs). The Spaniards under the command of Nuño Beltrán de Guzmán took the region and settled there between 1526 and 1529. In the mid-16th century, the first silver mines were established; these were the basis of the city's riches. In 1557, the locality was named Santa Fé y Real de Minas de Quanaxhuato, but it wasn't until 1741 that it was designated a city. Ignacio de Allende was able to temporarily occupy the city after the Declaration of Independence in 1810, but the royalists under General Felix M. Calleja reclaimed the city in short order. In the course of the Reform War (1857–1860), Guanajuato became the capital of the Republic for a month at the beginning of 1858. During the dictatorship of Porfirio Díaz (1876–1911) foreign capital poured into the mining businesses, and the city experienced a boom. Public buildings rose up, such as the Teatro Juárez, the Mercado Hidalgo and the Palacio Legislativo (Legislative Palace). Thanks to its university and the Cervantes Festival, Guanajuato is today a centre of science and culture.

What to See in Guanajuato

✶✶
Teatro Juárez The tour of the city starts at the pretty little city square (Jardín de la Unión) with the Teatro Juárez on the south side. This is an opera house in the neo-classical style with Doric columns. It opened in 1903. Inside, it has a Moorish character, especially the lobby and bar which have wood carvings as well as glass and metal artefacts.

✶
Templo de San Diego Next to the opera house stands the graceful San Diego church with its beautiful ultra-Baroque façade. At the end of the 17th century, the church was destroyed and then rebuilt in an opulent Baroque style.

The museum promoting the image of Quijote (Museo Iconográfico del Quijote) at Calle Manuel Doblado 1 is a **must-see for every Cervantes enthusiast**. This special museum next to the Templo de San Francisco collects almost everything associated with Don Quijote de la Mancha. The exhibits range from huge murals to a tiny picture on an egg shell. Among the collected items are also stamps from all over the world, statues and tapestries (open Tue–Sat 10am to 6pm and Sun 10am–3pm).

Museo Iconográfico del Quijote

Located further along on the Avenida Juárez is the Plaza de la Paz, the Square of Peace, with the Baroque Basilica Nuestra Señora de Guanajuato (Basilica of Our Lady of Guanajuato). The basilica started out as a parish church in the 17th century, and was reconstructed several times afterwards. Inside, a much venerated, jewel-studded statue of the Mother of God of Guanajuato stands on a small silver platform. It is thought to have been sculpted in the 7th century. A present from King Philip II of Spain, it made its journey to Guanajuato in 1557.

Basilica of Our Lady of Guanajuato

Also situated on the Plaza de la Paz is the Casa Rul y Valenciana, a neo-classical building and private residence of the rich mine-owner Count de Rul. It was built in the 18th century by Francisco Eduardo Tresguerras.

Casa Rul y Valenciana

Panoramic view of Guanajuato

▶ VISITING GUANAJUATO

INFORMATION

Tourist information
Plaza de la Paz 14 (to the right of the basilica)
Tel. (473) 732 15 74. More information at Calle 5 de Mayo, corner of Juárez. www.guanajuato.com

GETTING AROUND
By car, the best route for the 370km/230mi between Mexico City and Guanajuato is on the MEX 57 and the MEX 45. The same ride by bus takes about 5.5 hours.

EVENTS
The annual International Cervantes Festival (Festival Internacional Cervantino) takes place in October. The festivities of international repute last for several weeks and include music, theatre and dance.

SHOPPING
Vendors in the Mercado Hidalgo sell mostly arts and crafts (pottery and ceramics). The state-run store in the Casa de Artesanías at the Union Garden (Jardín de la Union) is also well worth a visit.

WHERE TO EAT
▶ Moderate
② *La Casona del Cielo*
Calle Pastita 76
Tel. (473) 731 20 00
The restaurant is on the second floor of a house opposite the studio of the well-known ceramics artist Gorky González. It is decorated with his works and also shows paintings by Chávez Morado. The unusual Mexican food is moderately priced.

▶ Inexpensive
① *El Retiro*
Calle Sopena 12
Tel. (473) 732 06 22
This is a traditional and very popular restaurant. It is located opposite the Teatro Juárez.

WHERE TO STAY
▶ Luxury
① *Parador San Javier*
Plaza Aldama 92
Tel. (014) 732 06 26
Fax (014) 732 31 14
This restored hacienda with 113 rooms was converted into a hotel in 1971. The city centre is only 15 minutes away. Older rooms have open fire places, and the newer ones feature satellite TV.

▶ Inexpensive
② *Hostal Cantarranas*
Calle Cantarranas 50 (close to the Teatro Principal)
Tel. (473) 732 52 41
Fax (473) 732 17 08
This small, friendly bed&breakfast has a terrific roof garden and a fantastic view over the city.

※ **Plazuelas** There are many picturesque plazuelas (small plazas) on both sides of the Avenida Juárez. A small alley, the Callejón del Beso (Alley of the Kiss), branches off from the small square on the left (Plazuela de los Ángeles); it owes its name to being such a steep, narrow (68cm/27in) passage that lovers can kiss each other from opposite windows across

※ **Callejón del Beso ▶**

the lane. The market hall of the Mercado Hidalgo (established in 1910) is situated a little further down the street on the left side. On the opposite side, a street leads to the convent church Templo de Belén (Church of Bethlehem). The construction of this building, which features an ultra-Baroque façade, began in 1773.

The Alhóndiga de Granaditas, located north of the church, is a former storage building for corn. Completed in 1799, the building later served alternate purposes as the need arose, a prison at one time, a stronghold at another. The mine worker Juan José de los Reyes Martínez, nicknamed El Pípila, once blasted its door open, making him the folk hero of Guanajuato. Today, the building houses the Museo del Alhóndiga Granaditas which exhibits archaeological and ethnological finds and historic mementos from the region. The museum also documents the history of silver mining. José Chávez Morado painted the **murals** in the stairwell between approximately 1955 and 1966; the themes of the paintings, which also show folkloristic traditions, are the historic events during the revolution and the struggle for independence involving the Alhóndiga de Granaditas. Visitors can still see the hooks for the iron prison cells in which the heads of the freedom fighters Hidalgo, Allende, Jiménez and Aldama – executed in Chihuahua by the Spaniards in 1811 – were displayed from 1811 until Mexican Independence in 1821.

✱ **Alhóndiga de Granaditas**

A Chavez Morado mural

Gustave Eiffel designed the iron-and-steel construction of the Mercado Hidalgo (market hall) on the site of the former bullring, the Plaza de Toros de Gavira. The design was created in France and actually meant for a French railway station, but was then executed as the Mercado Hidalgo between 1905 and 1910. Porfirio Díaz, the Mexican president at the time, dedicated the market during the celebration of 100 years of Mexican independence.

Hidalgo Market

The birthplace of the famous fresco painter Diego Rivera is located in Calle de los Pósitos at the corner of Calle Mollas (►Baedeker Specials pp. 79, 405). Today, the building houses a museum showing the life and works of Diego Rivera. Rivera and his twin brother were born here in 1886, but the twin died at the age of two. When Diego Rivera was six, he and his family moved to Mexico City. For many years, the Marxist Rivera was not exactly well liked in the catholic Guanajuato; however, the city has now honoured him with a small exhibition. The exhibits on the ground floor consist mostly of furni-

Diego Rivera Museum

ture. First and second floor rooms display almost 70 paintings and sketches by the artist (open: Tue–Sat 10am–6:30pm, Sun 10am–2:30pm).

Plaza San Roque

South-west of Rivera's birthplace is the Plaza San Roque with a Baroque church of the same name. This square has just the right character to serve as the setting for the performance of the *Entremeses Cervantinos (Cervantine Interludes)* a one-act play written by the Spanish poet Miguel de Cervantes Saavedra (1547–1616), author of *Don Quijote*. The performances are staged annually by the university on fitting occasions, most notably during the Cervantes Festival in or around October.

Cervantes Festival ▶

Museo del Pueblo de Guanajuato

The city museum (Museo del Pueblo de Guanajuato) is housed in the former residence of the Marqués de Rayas at the end of Calle de los Pósitos. The museum displays temporary exhibitions, such as the works of the painter José Chávez Morado and collections of folk art (open: Tue–Sat 10am–6:30pm).

University

The main university building is located north of the museum. It was reconstructed in 1955. An impressive outside staircase leads to the white stone building, in a colonial style with a Moorish touch, harmonious with the rest of the city. The **Mineralogy Museum** on the university campus is one of the best of its kind worldwide. Some of its more than 20,000 items are extraordinarily rare and of a type that have so far only been found around Guanajuato.

La Compañía

The church La Compañía, a massive structure east of the university, was commissioned by Jesuits in 1747. The façade is executed in the

Guanajuato *Plan*

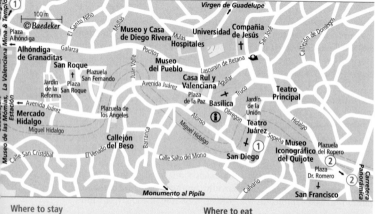

Where to stay
① Parador San Javier ② Hostal Cantarranas

Where to eat
① El Retiro ② La Casona del Cielo

ultra-Baroque style; the mighty dome in the neo-classical style. Inside the church, two paintings by the great Mexican painter Miguel Cabrera are noteworthy. The route back to the main square leads across the Plazuela del Barratillo with its beautiful fountain, a gift from Emperor Maximilian to the city.

A drive along Avenida Miguel Hidalgo is highly recommended. The avenue runs in part underground over a former river bed and emerges at the Carretera Panorámica; there are great views from here. South-west of this street stands the monument of Pípila (**Ionumento al Pípila**).

Avenida
Miguel Hidalgo

The Carretera Panorámica (panoramic road) leads in a northerly direction to the Church of Cata (also known as the Iglesia del Señor de Villaseca) in Calle Mineral de Cata. The church was built in the first quarter of the 18th century and features a remarkable ultra-Baroque façade. Other churches are those of San Francisco, Guadalupe and Pardo; the latter has a relocated façade taken from the church San Juan Rayas.

Iglesia de Cata

Travelling in the direction of Guadalajara, the Calzada de Tepetapa leads past the railway station to the cemetery (Penteón Municipal). This is the location of the somewhat macabre Mummy Museum (Museo de las Momias). In a crypt, visitors can view glass cabinets containing more than 100 mummified corpses of men, women and children who died over the past 120 years. The excellent state of preservation of the corpses is attributed to the mineral salts in the graveyard soil.

✸
Museo
de las Momias
⏲
Opening times:
daily 9am–6pm

Around Guanajuato

After 16km/10mi on the road to Silao, a road to the right leads, after another 14km/9mi, to the Cerro del Cubilete (2,700m/8,858ft). A 23m/75ft-high statue of Christ (**El Cristo Rey**) on its peak can be seen from a distance. The statue was set on the mountain top in the 1920s and has become a popular destination for an outing or a pilgrimage (particularly on Good Friday). A big part of the attraction is the magnificent view over the Bajío (lowlands) and the mountains of the Tarasca region.

Cerro del
Cubilete

Approximately 5km/3mi outside Guanajuato on the street to Dolores Hidalgo is the site of the church La Valenciana or San Cayetano. Antonio Obregón y Alcocer, Count of Valenciano and owner of the famous silver mine, commissioned the church building. Consecrated in 1788, it represents the **height of the Mexican ultra-Baroque**. The façade is executed in this style, while the side windows show arches in the neo-Mudéjar style (a combination of Moorish and Gothic architectural elements). Enter the church from the garden through a

✸
Iglesia
La Valenciana

side door, which is adorned with an ornately decorated stucco shell and a statue of St Joseph. Inside, three beautiful ultra-Baroque retables are in part gilded and in part painted in many colours. The fine inlay work with ivory and exotic woods on the pulpit are particularly notable. The entrance door, which features a carved stone Lambrequin (a stone treatment over the door in the form of a decorative hanging) on top of the Mudéjar-arch to the vestry is as eye-catching and masterfully executed as the façade. The execution of the arches is particularly stylish by virtue of the finely decorated fascias of Tezontle stone (a reddish brown stone known as blood stone).

The Valenciana Mine

Be sure to pay a visit to the La Valenciana silver mine, close to the church. First discovered in 1766 by the miner Antonio Obregón y Alcocer, who then became the mine owner and Earl of Valenciana, the silver mine very rapidly became the most profitable mine in the world. At times, as many as 3,300 miners worked in the up to 500m/ 1,640ft-deep drifts. Some of the old buildings have now decayed or tumbled down, but the pyramid-like walls still stand. The miners used to twine ropes around these walls to operate the skips. Visitors can view part of the mine.

Presa de la Olla

A beautiful park with two reservoirs, the Presa de la Olla and the Presa de San Renovato, is situated in the mountains east of the city. Here, visitors can enjoy a picnic or hire a rowing boat.

★ Guaymas · Hermosillo

G/E 8

Federal state: Sonora (Son.)
Population: 150,000

Altitude: 8m/26ft
Distance: about 1,800 km/1,120 mi north-west of Mexico City

Holidaymakers travelling to or from the USA traverse the agrarian Mexican federal state of Sonora. The main traffic artery on the Pacific coast, the MEX 15, begins at the border town Nogales, an approximately 1.5-hour drive from Tucson (Arizona). Travellers arriving from the south often cross the border into Baja California at Guaymas.

Tip

It must be emphasized that it is not always without risk to use these streets after nightfall. When planning such a tour, please first enquire with the Ministry of Foreign Affairs (State Department).

The Gulf of California Region

The port of Guaymas (population 150,000) is located in **a quiet bay** on the Sea of Cortés, as the people here call the Gulf of California. The city lies amid **spectacular mountains**. A tongue of land separates the harbour district from the bays of Bacochibampo and San Carlos

▶ VISITING GUAYMAS · HERMOSILLO

INFORMATION

Turismo Hermosillo
Comfort/Paseo Canal
Edificio Sonora Norte
Tel. (658) 217 00 60

GETTING AROUND

The MEX 15 runs from Guaymas about 1,000km/621mi along the coast and then turns inland toward Tepic. Travellers can continue their trip from there to Guadalajara or Mexico City.

WHERE TO EAT

▶ Expensive to moderate

Xochimilco
Calle Obregón 51
Hermosillo
Tel. (662) 250 40 89, 250 40 52
www.restaurantxochimilco.com
The restaurant is located in the southern part of the city. Sit on the large, shady patio and enjoy the very good regional food.

▶ Inexpensive

Los Delfines
Blvd. Sánchez Taboada
Guaymas
Tel. (622) 224 05 95
This is a large family restaurant near

to the end of the harbour. The fresh fish dishes are very reasonably priced.

WHERE TO STAY

▶ Luxury to mid-range

Fiesta Americana Hermosillo
Blvd. Kino 369
Tel. (662) 259 60 00
Fax (662) 259 60 60
www.fiestamericana.com
This is the largest hotel (220 rooms) in the city. It is popular with business travellers.

Baedeker-recomendation

Sunset at the Playa de Cortés

The Playa de Cortés hotel (Bahía de Bacochibampo 66, San Carlos, Tel. 622 / 14 99 26) is furnished in the style of a traditional Spanish hacienda. It is located in the Bahía Bacochibampo about 15km/9mi from Guaymas in the direction of San Carlos. The sunset behind the bizarre twin peaks of Mount Tetakawi (tetas de cabra = goat teats) is a unique experience. In pre-Hispanic times, the Yaqui Indians travelled to this sacred mountain to renew their spiritual strength.

---

where tourists prefer to stay. The Spaniards first explored the bay in 1535 and named it Guaima after a Seri Indian tribe. Around 1700, Pater Francisco Eusebio Kino established the mission station San José de Guaymas around today's harbour region. The village Guaymas de Zaragoza however was not established until 1769. Being an important port for precious metals from the hinterland, Guaymas was for a long period the target of adventurers, pirates and foreign invaders. Guaymas was occupied several times in the second half of the 19th century: by US troops in the war between the USA and Mexico (1847/48); by a French expedition wanting to establish a private colony in Sonora; and by French troops during the War of Intervention. The town features rather few notable buildings with the exceptions of the Church of San Fernando, the Banco de Sonora building and the town hall (Palacio Municipal).

Aquatic sports Tourists love Guaymas for its water sports and use the city as a base for offshore fishing. Some of the town's popular beaches are Mira-mar, San Francisco, San Carlos Lalo and Catch 22. The islands of San Nicolás, Santa Catalina and San Pedro offer very good conditions for scuba diving and watching birds or sea lions.

Ferry to Baja California The ferry to Santa Rosalía leaves from Guaymas. Santa Rosalia is located close to the centre of Baja California peninsula (► practicalities, traffic). Airlines offer direct flights to Guaymas from La Paz, Tijuana, Guadalajara and Tucson (Arizona).

San Carlos The village of San Carlos (population 5,000) is located 20km/12mi north-west of Guaymas. It has evolved into an attractive tourist centre for sport anglers and divers.

San José de Guaymas The village of San José de Guaymas is situated about 10km/6mi north of Guaymas. Jesuits established a pilgrim's church here in the 18th century.

✴ **Rock paintings** To reach La Pintada take the MEX 15 toward Hermosillo. After about 80km/50mi, turn right and travel another 6km/4mi along a country lane. From there, it is a 20-minute climb to see the interesting rock paintings on the walls of a canyon. The paintings show riders, boats, dance and hunting scenes as well as what are presumably Seri Indian animal emblems and blazonry. The predominant colours are **black, ochre and red**.

In the Cueva La Pintada

The modern city of **Ciudad Obregón** (population 380,000) is located about 130km/81mi south of Guaymas. Until 1924, the city was named Cajeme after a Yaqui chief. Nowadays, Ciudad Obregón is an important processing centre for regional agricultural products. The construction of the Álvaro-Obregón reservoir has enabled farmers to grow grain, cotton, alfalfa, rice and other crops.

Navojoa (population 145,000) is a further 68km/42mi south-east. **Navojoa**
This rapidly growing modern city and centre of agriculture (cotton,
fruit and vegetables) has become productive thanks to artificial irrigation.

The former mining city Álamos (about 53km/33mi east and inland **Álamos**
of Navojoa) has been put under a land preservation order. About
10,000 people now live here. The town experienced rapid growth
after the first veins of gold and silver were discovered, and 100 years
later had more than 30,000 inhabitants. Its fortunes sank however
with falling silver prices. Maya warriors trying to take back the city
and the ravages of the revolution hastened its decline until, finally, it
became a ghost town. When a group of artists from the USA settled
in Álamos after the Second World War, restoration of some of the
buildings began.
The parish church, the house of Mexican folk art and the ceramics
centre 3km/2mi outside the town are worth seeing. In recent years,
many retirees from the United States have made Álamos their home,
preferring a North American version of colonial style.

Hermosillo and the Surrounding Region

The two rivers Río Sonora and Río Zanjón meet in Hermosillo, **North-south**
about 140km/87mi north-east of Guaymas. Land bearing fruit, vege- **corridor**
tables and other crops surround the city; farmers also supply the region with meat, particularly turkey and beef. As elsewhere, **processing plants** (maquiladoras, see p.39) have recently established themselves here. Most colonial buildings have disappeared in recent years,
making room for the modernization of the rapidly growing city.
Tourists like the comfortable winter climate in the coastal region opposite the island of Tiburón. However, most travellers only pass
through, on their way north or south.

The first Spaniards who came to the region in 1531 encountered In- **History**
dians who fought for their lands. In 1742, Agustín de Vildósola established a stronghold by the name of El Real Presidio de la Santísima Trinidad de Pític here. The city has been known as Hermosillo
since 1828 in honour of the freedom fighter General José María
Gonzáles Hermosillo and has been capital of the federal state of So-
noro since 1879.

Architectural sights are a rarity here. The neo-classical 19th-century **Places of interest**
cathedral, the Governor's Palace (Palacio del Gobierno), the Madero
Park and the vantage point on top of Mount (Cerro de la) Campana
are particularly noteworthy. A statue at the northern exit to the MEX
15 shows the Jesuit missionary Eusebio Francisco Kino on horseback. His extensive travels through western Mexico led to the first
accurate maps of Baja California and the Gulf of California.

Regional museum

The modern university hosts the Museo Regional de la Universidad de Sonora (regional museum of Sonora) on its campus. On display are archaeological finds and ethnologic collections showing Indian cultures, in particular the cultures of the **Seri, Pima, Ópata and Yaqui**. The human Yécora mummy is of interest. It was found in a cave near Yécora and is thought to be at least 10,000 years old.

Centro Ecológico de Sonora

The feeder road Periférico Sur and the MEX 15 lead to the Centro Ecológico de Sonora (Sonora ecology centre) 5km/3mi from the city centre. Fauna and flora of the Sonora desert and other parts of north-west Mexico can be viewed in the zoo and botanical garden.

Bahía Kino

A drive of about 115km/71mi west from Hermosillo through irrigated land brings you to the beautiful bay of Bahía Kino. The fishing village Viejo Kino is worth a visit and the tourist spot Nuevo Kino provides many opportunities to enjoy aquatic sports. Both places are named after the famous Jesuit and explorer **Padre Eusebio Francisco Kino** (1644–1711). By the end of the 17th century, Kino had established more than 25 missions in Sonora. This Jesuit priest from South Tyrol was able to prove, amongst other facts, that Lower California is not an island but a peninsula. In Nuevo Kino, pay a visit to

The colours of paradise – the El Garrafón National Park in the south of Isla Mujeres

the new regional museum (Museo Regional in Calle Puerto Peñasco) and see the arts and crafts of the Seri Indians. Vendors in both parts of town offer carvings by this tribe.

Punta Chueca

The small village Punta Chueca is situated a mere 15km/9mi north of Kino. The beach is especially beautiful. The village is an important meeting place for the Seri Indians.

Isla Tiburón

Isla Tiburón (Shark Island) is more than 50km/31mi long and up to 30km/19mi wide, making it the largest Mexican island. It lies only a few miles off the shore of Sonora in the Gulf of California. The first Spaniard to discover the island was Fernando de Alarcón in 1540 and for a long period it was a settlement area of the Seri Indians. It has been an uninhabited nature preserve since 1976, when the Indian population was relocated. Travellers need a permit to visit the island and see the rich fauna and flora.

✳ Isla Mujeres

Federal state: Quintana Roo (Q. R.)
Distance: 10km/6mi north-east of Cancún

Population: 40,000

Isla Mujeres (Women's Island), about 8km/5mi long and up to 2km/ 1.2mi wide, lies off the shore of the Yucatán peninsula in the Caribbean Sea across the water from Cancún. It boasts large coconut palm groves and beautiful white sandy beaches, crystal clear lagoons and coral reefs teeming with fish.

History

Little is known about the pre-Spanish history of Isla Mujeres. A number of buildings here were created by the Maya in the 8th and 9th centuries. Most of the temples discovered on the island were probably dedicated to Ix-chel, the goddess of the moon and fertility. Spaniards under the command of **Francisco Hernández de Córdoba** were the first Europeans to discover the island in 1517, i.e. two years before Cortés landed in Mesoamerica, but it was Cortés who gave the island its name: he and his men had noticed that a surprising proportion of the clay figures in the Maya ruins were female. Like most of the Caribbean islands, Isla Mujeres later harboured its share of pirates and smugglers.

It took a while before tourists discovered the sleepy and slightly dilapidated island. In the meantime, the island has become a rather **popular beach destination**, and not just for backpackers. Still, in comparison to Cancún, Playa del Carmen or Cozumel, the island is fairly quiet and most accommodation for tourists is still on the simple side. Isla Mujeres has been declared a free-port to stimulate trade.

⏵ VISITING ISLA MUJERES

INFORMATION

Tourist information

Avenida Rueda Medina (west of the passenger ferry pier) or at www.isla-mujeres-mexico.com

GETTING AROUND

Ferries from Puerto Juárez or from Punta Sam (▶Traffic) bring passengers to Isla Mujeres. Both ports can be reached by bus from Mérida or Chetumal. There is also the option of taking a hydrofoil from Cancún to the island.

WHERE TO EAT

▶ Moderate to inexpensive

① *Bucanero*
Calle Hidalgo 11
Tel. (987) 877 02 10
www.bucaneros.com
This spacious bistro offers fish dishes and Yucatán speciality foods.

② *Pizza Rolandi*
Calle Hidalgo

(between Madero and Abasolo)
The Pizza Rolandi serves very good Italian meals, pizza from a wood oven as well as fish and seafood.

WHERE TO STAY

▶ Luxury

① *La Casa de los Sueños*
Carretera a Garrafón
Tel. (998) 877 06 51
Fax (998) 877 07 08
www.casadelossuenosresort.com
This bed&breakfast (10 rooms, non-smokers only) at the south end of the island used to be a private residence. All rooms have patios and an ocean view.

▶ Mid-range to budget

② *Casa Maya Zazil-Ha*
Calle Zazil-Há 129 (Playa Norte)
Tel. (998) 877 00 45
www.kasamaya.com.mx
This small hotel still conveys the atmosphere of the old, pre-tourism Isla Mujeres.

Tourist Attractions on Isla Mujeres

Beaches and coral reefs
The main attractions are beside and in the sea – all within easy reach on foot, by bike or by motorbike.
Visit Playa Cocoteros (Los Cocos) on the western side of the island for a terrific swim. At the northern tip of the island, across the bridge to the barren islet (islote) Yunque, snorkellers can explore the coral reefs. More beauty awaits at the beaches and reefs of the eastern, Caribbean coast: Playa Pancholo, for example. However, strong currents can make swimming risky here.

✱ El Garrafón
The delightful El Garrafón bay (carafe) in the southern part of the island can be reached by car or by boat. Numerous tropical coral reef fish can be observed in this marine reserve. The new Pueblo Caribe hotel with a view of a modern sculpture garden is situated at the tip of the island overlooking the bay.

Isla Mujeres *Map*

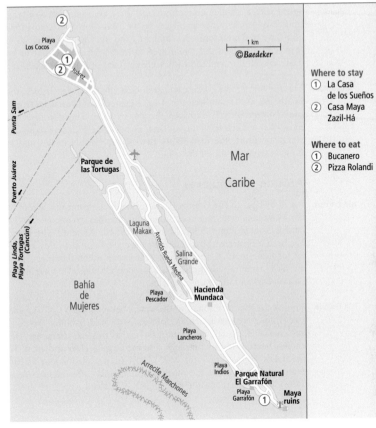

Playa
Los Cocos

① La Casa
de los Sueños
② Casa Maya
Zazil-Há

Punta Sam

Puerto Juárez

Playa Linda,
Playa Tortugas
(Cancún)

**Parque de
las Tortugas**

Mar

Caribe

Laguna
Makax

Avenida Rueda Medina

Salina
Grande

Bahía
de
Mujeres

Playa
Pescador

**Hacienda
Mundaca**

Playa
Lancheros

Arrecife Manchones

Playa
Indios

Playa
Garrafón

**Parque Natural
El Garrafón**

**Maya
ruins**

1 km
©*Baedeker*

Where to stay
① La Casa
de los Sueños
② Casa Maya
Zazil-Há

Where to eat
① Bucanero
② Pizza Rolandi

The Los Manchones reef stretches as a barrier between El Garrafón **Los Manchones**
bay and the ocean. Divers love to explore the waters here. Experienced scuba divers can take part in excursions by boat to dive to the Caves of the Sleeping Sharks about 30m/100ft below. A local fisherman discovered the caves at the end of the 1960s. Movies have made the caves famous worldwide.

Animal lovers will wish to stop off on their way to El Garrafón bay **Turtle** at the turtle park (Parque de las Tortugas) and the marine biology **park** station near the centre of the island. See the station's fish and amphibians, and watch exhibitions featuring dolphins and other marine animals. At Dolphin Discovery at the centre of the island you can even meet and swim with the dolphins. Isla Mujeres is one of their four sites in Mexico.

Hacienda Mundaca Located above the Playa Lancheros, the Hacienda Mundaca is pervaded with a unique atmosphere, and there are remnants of a large house and garden once belonging to the 19th-century Basque pirate and slave trader Antonio de Mundaca. The story goes that he fell in love with an island girl and vowed to lead a decent life, but to no avail: she left him and soon afterwards he died of a broken heart.

Maya ruin The most interesting Maya archaeological site is located behind the lighthouse at the southern tip of Isla Mujeres. Unfortunately, Hurricane Gilbert severely damaged the site in 1988. The structure was most likely dedicated to the goddess Ix-chel and also served as an observatory. Enjoy the marvellous view of the Caribbean Sea and ▶ Cancún from the top of the ruin.

Around Isla Mujeres

Isla Contoy A trip by boat to Isla Contoy (Pelican Island: conto means pelican in the Maya language) makes an interesting one-day excursion. The island is located about 20km/12mi north of Isla Mujeres. The island has been a protected bird sanctuary since 1961 and provides a habitat for more than 70 bird species. Visitors can watch flamingos, frigate birds (man-o-war birds), ducks, spoonbills (ibises), cormorants (sea ravens) and many other species.

Isla Holbox Among the marine animals in the waters between Cabo Catoche and Isla Holbox are marlin, shark, sailfish, barracuda, grouper (jewfish) and mackerel. So far, the island has kept its original character. The endless beaches teem with shells, and the water is clear and calm. To reach Isla Holbox, take the MEX 180D from Valladolid to Puerto Juárez and turn off at the junction to Chiquilá (after about 90km/56mi). From there, boats ferry visitors to the island.

✴✴ Jalapa (Xalapa)

P 22

Federal state: Veracruz (Ver.)	**Altitude:** 1,420m/4,659ft
Population: 650,000	**Distance::** 315km/196mi east of Mexico City

Jalapa is the capital of the federal state of Veracruz. The city, which has a well-known university, has been built atop several hills at the foot of Mount Macuiltepec (Cerro de Macuiltepec), and is surrounded by a garden landscape.

Of all the mountain peaks around Jalapa, the Cofre de Perote (Nauhcampatépetl) stands out. To the south lies the 5,700m/18,700ft-high Pico de Orizaba (Citlaltépetl), Mexico's highest mountain. The geography of the region accounts for the city's rich precipitation and the consequently **lush vegetation**. Occasionally, a damp fog shrouds the city.

In 1519, Cortés passed through Jalapa on his way to Mexico City. At that time, the Indian city Jalapa was flourishing under Aztec rule. After the Spanish conquest of the Aztec empire, Jalapa gained a reputation for its important annual fair, where Spanish goods brought by returning Spanish silver ships were sold. The distance between Jalapa and Veracruz is a mere 120km/75mi, and it is only 300km/186mi from Jalapa to Mexico City. This made the city an important station for stage coaches.

History

What to See in Jalapa

Spanish architecture and city design has left narrow alleys and roads lined with brightly coloured houses and lush gardens, contrasting with the broad avenues of the modern parts of the city. There are few important colonial buildings. The huge cathedral, built at the end of the 18th century and situated diagonally opposite Juárez Park is of note, and the light-coloured Governor's Palace (Palacio del Gobierno) on the other side of the park contains interesting frescoes. Hidalgo Park (Parque Hidalgo, in the Paseo de los Berros) is also very beautiful. The new stadium (Estadio Jalapeño) and Jalapa University are located only a few blocks to the east; the university offers summer courses for foreign students. At the end of 1999, the Pinacoteca Diego Rivera gallery opened next to Juárez Park. The gallery contains three dozen of Rivera's works on loan from the owner, the federal state of Veracruz.

Sights in Jalapa

The anthropology museum (Museo de Antropología de la Universidad Veracruzana) is located in the north-west part of the city on the exit road towards Mexico City. It is one of the two most attractive and important such museums in Mexico, the other being the anthropology museum in Mexico City. A large orientation hall with wall charts, models and visual aids connects the three inner courtyards and six exhibition halls. Most of the 3,000 items on display are from the pre-Hispanic Gulf Coast cultures of the Olmec, Huastec, Remojada and Totonac. **Olmec colossal heads**, carved from basalt, are on display outside in the park. They were brought to the

★★
Anthropology museum

Terracotta figure of a Tláloc priest from El Zapotal (approx. 700 BC)

▶ VISITING JALAPA

INFORMATION
Tourist information
Parque Juárez
(under the arcades of the city hall /
Palacio Municipal)
Tel. (228) 842 12 00
www.xalapa.gob.mx

GETTING AROUND
Those driving the 315 km/196 mi
from Mexico City to Jalapa should
take the MEX 140; from Veracruz take
the MEX 180 and the MEX 140
(120km/75mi).
Bus services to Jalapa are available
from Mexico City and Veracruz.

WHERE TO STAY
▶ Luxury
Posada Coatepec
Calle Hidalgo 9
(corner of Aldama),
Coatepec (10 minutes from Jalapa)
Tel. (228) 816 05 44
www.posadacoatepec.com.mx
A tastefully decorated lodge, this was
the residence of the Fernández family
in the 19th century. The hotel offers
24 suites, all grouped around the
patio. The Posada is located in the
coffee-growing region of Veracruz
and serves as an excellent base for
excursions, e.g. to the archaeological
sites of Zempoala or Quiahuitzlán, to
the Pico de Orizaba or to the Cofre de
Perote.

▶ Mid-range
Mesón de Alferes
Calle Sebastián Camacho 2
Tel. (228) 818 63 51
The 20 rooms in this former private
residence (built in 1808) are named
after historic streets in Jalapa. The
dining room was once the chapel. The
hotel entrance is on Calle Zaragoza.

WHERE TO EAT
▶ Moderate to inexpensive
La Casona del Beaterio
Calle Zaragoza 20
Tel. (228) 818 21 19
Enjoy the colonial ambience on the
patio or in your room. The restaurant
offers traditional regional food and
there is sometimes live music in the
evening.

museum from their original location in San Lorenzo. Colossal head
No. 8 is special: in contrast to the other heads, the stone lips are
shown slightly open and there are no ritualistic mutilations. Other
impressive Olmec stone sculptures are also on display, such as altars,
stelae and life-sized clay figures (AD 600–900), which were found in
El Azpotal, west of Alvarado, as late as 1986. The museum also owns
the **largest collection of stone artefacts connected with the ritualistic ball game** (yokes, hatchets and palm fronds), and displays the
»laughing faces«, terracotta sculptures from the Remojada culture
around the central Gulf. Among newly acquired items are parts of a
polychrome wall painting from Las Higueras (AD 600–900); Las Higueras was probably a satellite city of El Tajín. Ethnological collections relating to regional Indian tribes complete the picture.

A flower seller arranges poinsettias in front of a house in Coatepec.

The interesting Galeria de Estado is located in a renovated colonial building almost 1km/0.6mi east of the city centre on Xalapeños Ilustres. This art gallery of the federal state of Veracruz exhibits mostly contemporary paintings.

Galeria de Estado

Paseo de los Lagos Park stretches around a lake east of Juárez Park. In the northern part of the park in the Casa de Artesanías, visitors can see and buy regional arts and crafts. The ecology park (Parque Ecológico Macuiltépetl), at the highest point in Jalapa north of the city, was established on a long dormant, now forested volcano. Some of the trails loop all the way up to the peak of the volcano, from which there is a wonderful view. The botanical gardens (Jardín Botánico Clavijero) in the south-west of Jalapa are also very beautiful.

Parks

Around Jalapa

12km/7.5mi from Jalapa in the direction of Veracruz, a companion of Cortés established the large hacienda El Lencero. The driveway is lined with large trees. Parts of the hacienda structures and gardens have been restored in recent years, and the hacienda is now furnished as the original building was when it was first finished, thus exemplifying the almost **450-year history of the hacienda** in Mexico. La Antigua (district of ►Veracruz) is located on the same route about 75km/47mi away from Jalapa.

El Lencero

Jardín Lecuona The beautiful botanical garden Jardín Lecuona is situated about 7km/4mi north-west of Jalapa on the MEX 140 to Puebla in the garden city of Banderilla. Among the many plants are about 200 orchid species alone.

Perote 53km/33mi further along this road lies the city of Perote (population 40,000) at the foot of the coffer-shaped Cofre de Perote (4,282m/14,048ft). The massive Fort San Carlos de Perote (18th century) was once positioned at the periphery of Perote to defend the city against bandits and rebels. The fort later served as a prison.

Teziutlán The friendly colonial town of Teziutlán is a 110km/68mi drive north via Perote and Altotonga. After another 15km/9mi west the road passes the springs of Chignautla.

Zacapoaxtla 46km/29mi west of Teziutlán, a road branches off shortly after leaving Zaragoza behind. After going north for 17km/10.5mi, this road leads to the town of Zacapoaxtla (population 31,000), nestling in beautiful, often misty mountains. This is an appealing place, thanks to its pristine and diverse landscape as well as the lively traditions of several Indian tribes. The traditional **celebrations of the Náhua, Otomí and Totonac** are among the most colourful and interesting events in Mexico. The Guadalupe de Libres church and the San Pedro parish church are situated in the town.

Cuetzalán The 95km/59mi ride north from Zacapoaxtla to Cuetzalán (1,200m/3940ft) is magnificent. Situated amid the mountains of the Sierra Norte in the federal state of Puebla, Cuetzalán is very picturesque. Various Indian tribes live in and around town, and particularly on holidays and market days the Indians visit the town wearing their most beautiful costumes, their presence adding to the surrounding beauty. At some of the annual celebrations, select regional **folklore groups** (Quetzales, Negritos, Santiagos and Voladores) perform their characteristic dances. Cuetzalán offers the chance to do some sightseeing. There is the town hall with its European-style architecture, the parish church with the unusual Torre de los Jarritos (the bell tower in the cemetery is decorated with 80 clay vessels) and, a little way outside the village, Guadalupe church in front of which are elaborately decorated grave sites. The most important source of income in and around Cuetzalán is the cultivation and processing of coffee.

> ! **Baedeker TIP**
>
> **Coffee town**
>
> The delightful town of Coatepec is located about 15km/9mi south of Jalapa in the midst of coffee plantations and orchid gardens. A delicious aroma floats out of the cosy coffee houses which border the plaza, where there are also stands selling coffee liqueur. A tastefully furnished posada with a restaurant is an inviting place to dine and stay the night.

For those interested in archaeology, a visit to the excavation site Yohualichán is highly recommended. An all-terrain vehicle is required
for the 50-minute ride to the site. This **ancient religious centre** was
built on four different terraces, and it is the only other structure so
far discovered in the same style as ►El Tajín. Among the important
sights are niche pyramids, one of them with seven platforms, and the
90m/98yd-long ball court, which is one of the largest in Mesoamerica.

★
Yohualichán

Los Cabos

L / M 9

Federal state: Baja California Sur

Distance: about 200km/124mi south of
La Paz

**The holiday region Los Cabos consists of the former fishing village
Cabo San Lucas and the town of San José del Cabo at the barren
southern tip of Lower California. Spectacular rock formations, beaches in a variety of natural settings and excellent infrastructure attract travellers, especially from the United States. Offshore anglers
enjoy the rich fishing grounds.**

*The Arco is Baja California's main landmark:
here, the Gulf of California meets the Pacific.*

Tourist Attractions

Cabo San Lucas

The beach resort at the southern end of the 1,700km/1,056mi-long Transpeninsular Highway is now crowded with hotel and apartment buildings all the way along the coast and into Cabo San Lucas. Further inland, between the Avenues Niños Héroes and 20 de Noviembre, visitors also find a quiet town square and an anthropology museum. **All kinds of aquatic sports** are on offer, such as offshore fishing, water skiing, diving and snorkelling, paragliding and bungee jumping.

El Arco ►

The Arco del Carbo San Lucas cliff, the symbol of the resort city, can be reached by boat. The ocean has hollowed out the rock and shaped it into an archway. At this famous arch, the currents of the Gulf of California and the Pacific collide. Visitors can observe the sea lions here; most also stop at one of the small beaches, frequently Playa Amor with its sandy stretches bordering both oceans.

Beaches

Beaches and bays are found on both sides of the cape (Solmar, Del Amor, Médano, Cementerio, Barco Varada, De las Viudas, Santa María, Punta Chileno, Canta Mar, Punta Palmilla and Costa Azul). The beaches feature a variety of types of sand and rock, some with cliffs, some bordering a calm ocean and others with strong surf. The water teems with fish. Among the multitude of interesting diving spots is the unique and amazing **underwater sand cascade**, which

The place to weigh anchor: the yacht harbour in Cabo San Lucas

⏵ VISITING LOS CABOS

INFORMATION
www.allaboutcabo.com

GETTING AROUND
Take the Transpeninsular Highway, the MEX 1, either by car or bus to Los Cabos from Tijuana via Ensenada, Mulegé, Loreto, La Paz, Cabo San Lucas and San José del Cabo. The ferry from Puerto Vallarta is currently not in service.
Many Mexican and foreign airlines offer flights to Los Cabos.

WHERE TO EAT

▶ Expensive
Damiana
Blvd. Mijares 8
San José del Cabo
Tel. (114) 142 04 99
This high-class restaurant used to be an 18th-century hacienda. Nowadays, guests enjoy sitting on the patio or in the dining room. The cuisine is international, and in the evenings Mariachis entertain the guests.

▶ Moderate
Da Giorgio II
Transpeninsular Km 5.5
Misiones Del Cabo

Cabo San Lucas
Tel. (624) 145 81 60
This is an ideal place to enjoy the sunset and the view of the Arco del Cabo San Lucas, the famous cliff arch high over the ocean. Simple Italian cuisine.

WHERE TO STAY

▶ Luxury
Melia San Lucas
Playa El Médano
Tel. (624) 143 44 44
www.melia-san-lucas.com
This very popular hotel (150 rooms) in Cabo San Lucas has the best view of the famous Arco above Médano Beach.

▶ Mid-range to budget
Tropicana Inn
Blvd. Mijares 30
Tel. (624) 142 15 80
www.tropicanacabo.com
The wall tiles around the swimming pool show reproduced scenes and images from Diego Rivera murals. The small, pleasant hotel (40 rooms) is located away from the beach in San José del Cabo.

divers can reach from the beach, as well as an area on the ocean floor covered with manganese nodules.

There are many beaches and interesting coastal landscapes to be enjoyed while travelling the 70km/44mi north along Highway 19 towards Todos Santos. For a few years now, the coastline around Todos Santos has been considered a surfers' paradise. Surrounded by fruit trees and palms, the city has also become a magnet for artists. The **Hotel California** made famous by the Eagles song is also here. The road continues on from Todos Santos to San Pedro and La Paz (80km/50mi).

Todos Santos

San José del Cabo The history of the well-kept, small town of San José del Cabo (35km/22mi north-east of Cabo San Lucas) stretches back to the 18th century. In 1535, Cortés visited the bay here. Today the town is an important agricultural centre and also the focal point of the significant holiday area stretching to Buenavista. Annually on 19 March, the citizens here celebrate the day of San José. The coastline in this area has many beaches with great fishing and surfing and where the waves are sometimes wild. Visitors will find good restaurants and cafés along the main street, Boulevard Mijares, and a small museum has opened in the Casa de la Cultura. It is calm and quiet here compared with Cabo San Lucas.

A Side Trip to La Paz

La Paz La Paz (population 190,000) beside the Sea of Cortés (Gulf of California) is the capital of the federal state of Baja California Sur situated on the bay of the same name. On the MEX 1, the distance to Cabo San Lucas via San José del Cabo is 215km/134mi and via Todos Santos on the MEX 9 it is 150km/93mi. The rapid development notwithstanding, the port city has managed to maintain a little of its tranquil atmosphere. The port still counts as the most Mexican settlement of the Baja. The ferry ship docks here, which many travellers use to enter or leave Baja California. Indian tribes, such as the Pericúe, Cochimí and Guaicura lived in the southern part of Lower California before the Spanish conquest. Initially, the Indians greeted the Spaniards peacefully. Later however, they did their best to prevent them from settling on Indian lands. By the end of the 16th century, the region around La Paz had become a hide-out for pirates who targeted Spanish ships coming from the Philippines. In 1720, Jesuits established a mission here, but by 1745 disease and lack of water had forced them to give it up. A permanent settlement could not be established until 1800; 30 years later, La Paz became the capital of the Southern Territory. The city was occupied by US troops from 1847 to 1848 during the war between Mexico and the USA. In 1853, the American adventurer William Walker conquered the port with the intent of establishing himself as leader of an independent state, but failed. For a long time, La Paz was a centre for pearl fishing, a trade which soon became obsolete. The main sources of income now are tourism, fishing, retailing and the processing industries.

La Paz is a relatively new city, and there are consequently only a handful of places of interest for tourists. These are the parish church (19th century), the Governor's Palace (Palacio del Gobierno), the house of folk art, the anthropology and history museum, the clam market and the boardwalk (Malecón). Perhaps most importantly, La Paz is an excellent place to board a ship and head out for an **offshore fishing excursion**, to go diving or find a place on one of the many beautiful beaches in the area. The free-port adds economic life to the city.

Among the notable and well-known beaches near and not quite so near the city are Playa Sur in the south, Centenario in the west, Costa Baja in the north and north-east as well as Eréndira, Pichilingüe, El Tecolote, and Puerto Balandra. Beaches close to Las Cruces are El Saltito, El Palo, Los Muertos and El Rosarito.   **Beaches**

A boat trip to offshore islands such as Espíritu Santo, La Partida and Islotes is highly recommended. These islands are ideal for watching sea lions and various species of bird, and conditions for fishing and diving are also good. Take a trip via Los Planes to Punta Arenas, La Ventana and Ensenada de los Muertos and have a dip at one of the beautiful, solitary beaches.   **Trips**

Mazatlán

L 12

Federal state: Sinaloa (Sin.)
Population: 410,000

Altitude: sea level
Distance:: about 1,040km/646mi north-west of Mexico City

Mazatlán is home to the largest Mexican import-export harbour and fishing port on the Pacific and has one of the largest shrimp fleets in the world. Geographically, the port city of Mazatlán is located near the Tropic of Cancer in a natural bay. The long beaches have made the city a booming ocean resort.

View of Mazatlán

⏵ VISITING MAZATLÁN

INFORMATION

Tourist information
Edificio Banrural
Avenida Camarón Sábalo
(opposite the hotel Quijote)
Tel. (669) 916 51 60

GETTING AROUND

A flight from Mexico City takes about 1.5 hours, and there are connections to Mazatlán from several other Mexican and US airports. Travelling by car or bus from Mexico City to Mazatlán takes about 17 hours; by train the trip takes 6 hours more.

WHERE TO EAT

▶ Moderate
Bahía Mariscos
Calle Mariano Escobedo 203
(corner of Olas Altas)
Tel. (669) 981 26 45
A historic city mansion from the turn of the 19th century has been converted into this pretty restaurant. The house speciality is seafood.

WHERE TO STAY

▶ Luxury
Hacienda Las Moras
Carretera a la Noria Km 9
Tel. (669) 914 13 46
www.lasmoras.com
This former tequila ranch is located at the foot of the Sierra Madre an approximately 30-minute ride outside Mazatlán. The hotel has six suites and particularly attracts horse riders.

Indians lived in Mazatlán long before the Spanish conquest. The Spaniards under Hernando de Bazán came in 1576, but the city was not established until 1806. Before that, the region around Mazatlán had been a target for pirates and a hide-out for buccaneers. In the middle of the 19th century, German settlers enlarged the harbour and thus laid the cornerstone for a more prosperous Mazatlán. At this time, the larger harbour was meant to facilitate the export of agricultural products and the import of farm equipment.

Tourist Attractions

Sights in Mazatlán
There are no particularly striking buildings in Mazatlán. The Canobbia Arcades are reminiscent of the old times and the historic Teatro Angela Peralta is also pretty. The theatre was named after the grand dame of the opera who died in a cholera epidemic in 1863. Visit the 154m/505ft-high lighthouse El Faro, which is considered the highest

active lighthouse in the world. The **cliff-divers** near to the vantage point El Mirador are also magnets for tourists: every morning and afternoon, they jump from a cliff into the narrow bay Glorieta Sanchez Toboada. You may also like to visit the Cerro del Vigia, with an observatory from which the pirates scanned their territory. Another look-out point is the Cerro del Neveria, so named after the underground drifts in which ice kept the fish catch cool. The aquarium in 111 Avenida de los Deportes is one of the largest of its kind in Mexico. A botanical garden and a zoo are part of the aquarium complex. The museum Seashell City (Rudolfo Loaiza 407) exhibits seashells from all the world's oceans. The magnificent Fisherman's Monument (Monumento al Pescador) represents Mazatlán's fishing tradition. There is also a small archaeology museum.

✶
◄ Aquarium

The conditions for every conceivable aquatic sport are excellent, in particular fishing on the high seas for sailfish, marlin, shark, swordfish and tarpon. Among the most popular beaches north of the city are Olas Altas, Norte Camarón, Las Gaviotas, Sábalo, Los Cerritos and El Delfín.

Aquatic sports

A favourite trip is to the offshore islands where many birds have their nesting places. Boats pick up travellers from the hotels of the Zona Dorada and carry them to Isla Pájaros and Isla Venados. Board a ferry to Isla de la Piedra at the ferry harbour.

Trips

Taking the MEX 15 south to Villa Unión and then on toward Durango leads via Concordia with its pretty 18th-century parish church to the picturesque old mining town of **Copala**. The narrow alleys, colourful house façades and wrought-iron balconies are all reminiscent of the Mexico of times gone by.

Around
Mazatlán

Ferries sail daily to ► La Paz, the capital of Baja California Sur (► practicalities).

Ferry to
Baja California

✶ Mérida

O 29

Federal state: Yucatán (Yuc.)
Population: 820,000

Altitude: 8m/26ft
Distance: 1,550km/963mi east of Mexico City, 320km/199mi west of Cancún

The export of sisal to Europe once brought prosperity to Mérida. The capital of the federal state of Yucatán is located at the northern end of a porous limestone plateau, which is especially suitable for the cultivation of agave. Agave leaves are the source of a coarse fibre called henequen or sisal.

Sisal   Before the invention of synthetic fibres, income from sisal export made Mérida **very prosperous**, and the city developed a marked orientation toward Europe thanks to these trade relations. It was in this era that Mérida earned the name **Ciudad Blanca** (white city) because the citizens were in the habit not only of wearing white but also of keeping their streets clean. Colourful flowers abound in the warm, humid climate, which also determines the steady and tranquil rhythm of life in this beautiful city.

History   The conquistador Francisco de Montejo the Younger (El Mozo) established the city on 6 January 1542. The Maya fought fiercely but the Spaniard took most of Yucatán in the four years that followed. The city of Mérida was built where the Maya city Tihó once stood. Stones were taken from the Maya temples and used as building material. A pivotal role was played by **Diego de Landa**, the second bishop of Mérida, who was determined to completely destroy the ancient Indian culture with all possible means. In his ignorance, he had a large number of irreplaceable hieroglyphic Maya scripts burnt. The bishop was also the author of the famous book *Relación de las Cosas de Yucatán*, in which he documents the conquest of Yucatán and its civilization from the Spanish viewpoint.

Due to the geographical location, Mérida and Yucatán hardly played any role in the Mexican War of Independence against Spain. On the contrary, there were several attempts to separate Yucatán from Mexico. A bloody civil war, the Caste War of Yucatán – a Maya insurgency against Mexican domination – raged in Yucatán throughout the second half of the 19th century. Peace was only to return in the first years of the 20th century.

> ## !   *Baedeker* TIP
>
> **Songs of Mérida**
>
> The art of the troubadours, the »trova«, is a typical aspect of the culture of Mérida. Every Thursday, singers and musicians show off their abilities at the Serenata de Santa Lucía in the park of the same name. The Museum of Yucatecan Music (Museo de la Canción Yucatéca, Calle 57, No. 464; open daily 9am–5pm) illustrates the history of the trova with portraits of composers and singers, musical notation and examples of the music

What to See in Mérida

City centre   The historic city centre and the Paseo Montejo still exhibit the former colonial grandeur and the wealth of the sisal barons. The streets are defined by numbers, not names. All north-south streets have even numbers; all east-west streets are odd-numbered.

Plaza Mayor   The main city square and centre of Mérida is the Plaza de la Independencia. Spanish rulers designed it as an ostentatious place for parades. Bay trees provide ample shade in the plaza, and some of the city's most beautiful and important buildings are at its periphery.

At the eastern side of the plaza, on the site of the former Maya temple, now stands the San Idelfonso Cathedral. Pedro de Aulestia and Miguel de Auguero designed the cathedral and had it built between 1561 and 1598, in part using the former Maya temple as a stone quarry. The church with its double tower is considered the tallest Christian religious building of the Yucatán peninsula.

Cathedral

Above a door inside the cathedral visitors can see the picture of the Maya ruler Titul Xiú of Mani (in Maya: gone is [the age of greatness]) visiting his conqueror Francisco de Montejo in Tihó, today's Mérida. In the chapel of the Christ of the Blisters (**Capilla del Cristo de las Ampollas**) stands an Indian wood carving from the 16th century. According to legend, the carving was made from a tree that the Indians claim to have seen burning for many nights but which afterwards showed no sign of the fire. Originally, the sculpture was placed in the Church of Ichmul; when a fire destroyed this church it also blackened and blistered the sculpture. It has stood in the cathedral since 1645 and every year in early October becomes the object of religious veneration.

Next to the cathedral, separated only by a single street, stands the former palace of the archbishop (the Most Reverend), once the residence of the fanatical missionary Diego de Landa. Today, the building houses the contemporary art museum in Yucatán, the MACAY

★ MACAY

A short break to read the paper on the Plaza Mayor

▶ VISITING MÉRIDA

INFORMATION

Tourist information
in the Teatro Peón Contreras
corner of Calle 60 and Calle 57a
Tel. (999) 923 08 83
Other information offices are located
on the north-west side of the town
square, at the airport and at the
CAME bus terminal.

GETTING AROUND

A flight from Mexico City to Mérida
takes only about 1.5 hours. Of course,
there are many other flights from
Mexican and US airports to Mérida.
There are connections from Cancún
by bus or plane.

WHERE TO EAT

▶ Expensive
① *Alberto's Continental Patio*
Calle 64 No. 482
Tel. (999) 928 53 67
www.albertoscontinental.com
This restaurant has been converted
from an 18th-century mansion with
tile floors. The dining rooms are
arranged around a shady patio. Guests
have a choice of Lebanese, Italian or
local food. A reservation is necessary.

▶ Moderate
② *Los Almendros*
Calle 50a No. 493
(between Calle 57 and 59)
Tel. (999) 928 54 59
The best-known restaurant in Mérida
serves typical regional food. Live
music entertains the guests between
2pm and 5pm.

WHERE TO STAY

▶ Luxury
② *Fiesta Americana Mérida*
Paseo de Montejo 451
corner Ave. Colón Colonia Centro
Tel. (999) 942 11 11
Fax (999) 942 11 12
www.fiestamericana.com
The hotel (350 rooms) was built in
the style of palatial mansions as seen
in the houses in the Paseo de
Montejo. The rooms have every
modern amenity, such as internet
access.

▶ Mid-range
① *Casa del Balam*
Calle 60 and 57
Tel. (999) 924 81 30
Fax (999) 924 50 11
The hotel rooms are arranged around
a patio with flowers and a well. Guests
can play tennis and golf in a nearby
sports club.

Baedeker-recomendation

Hammocks made to measure
Mérida is widely known for its hammocks.
Have one designed to your own specifica-
tions at El Aguacate (Calle 58 No. 614/Calle
73) or La Poblana (Calle 65, between Calle
58 and 60).

Mérida *Plan*

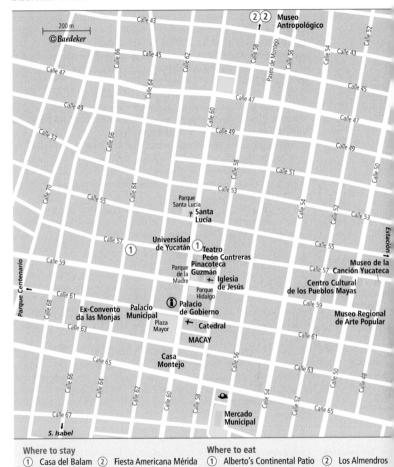

Where to stay
① Casa del Balam ② Fiesta Americana Mérida

Where to eat
① Alberto's Continental Patio ② Los Almendros

(Museo de Arte Contemporáneo Ateneo de Yucatán). On display here are mainly the works of well-known painters and sculptors from Yucatán.

In the north-east corner of the plaza stands the Governor's Palace (Palacio de Gobierno), which was built in 1892. The walls of its ballroom are decorated with interesting **murals** by Fernando Castro Pacheco. The artist from Campeche created these murals between 1971 and 1974. Visitors have a nice view from the balcony onto the Plaza de la Independencia and the cathedral.

Governor's Palace

The Municipal Palace

The municipal palace (Palacio Municipal) is located opposite the cathedral. It is an 18th-century building with colonnades and a clock tower. Yucatán independence was proclaimed here in 1821. Today, the building is often the backdrop for dance demonstrations, in particular for regional folk dance exhibitions. One of the dances, the Jarana, is accompanied by guitar players; the dancers wear white embroidered costumes.

✳ Casa Montejo

The southern side of the main city square is dominated by the Casa Montejo, which some consider **one of the most beautiful buildings from the times of Spanish colonial rule**. Built in 1549, it was the residence of the conquistador and his family. The mansion was built to span an entire side of the city square with its ornate Plateresque façade. The large, beautiful rooms are arranged around two inner courtyards and furnished with imported European antiques.

Convento de las Monjas

A stately convent, a relic of the late 16th-century Convento de las Monjas, is located one block west of the Municipal Palace. The convent building features a look-out tower from the year 1633.

Church of Jesus

The Church of Jesus (Iglesia de Jesús) was also known as the Temple of the Third Order (Iglesia de la Tercera Orden). It is sited at the Hidalgo Park, one block away from the main city square, and is a popular venue for weddings amongst the inhabitants of Mérida. A Plateresque altar painting made of carved and gilded wood is positioned to the left of the high altar.

Juan Gamboa Guzmán Gallery

The Juan Gamboa Guzmán art gallery, located next to the church, is an inviting place to browse 19th and 20th century paintings. The gallery entrance is on Calle 59. On display are mostly portraits and religiously motivated paintings as well as works by Gamboa Guzmán. The **Gottdeiner Museum** is located next to the art gallery. Visitors can view impressive bronze sculptures of Yucatán Indians by Enrique Gottdeiner, Yucatán's most famous sculptor.

The University

Originally, the University of Yucatán was built in 1618 as a Jesuit boys' school at the corner of Calles 57 and 60. Guests may take **summer courses**, for example in Spanish and archaeology.

Churches

The **Church of Ermita de Santa Isabel** (Calles 66 and 77) is remarkable mostly for its garden with Maya statues. Once, travellers from and to Campeche met at the hermitage to pray for a safe journey or give thanks for a safe return.

Originally, the Spaniards had the church **Santa Lucía** on the corner of Calles 60 and 55 built exclusively for their black or mulatto slaves.

The frescoes in the Palacio de Gobierno depict scenes from the history and culture of the Maya. →

The Monument of the Nation depicts scenes from the history of Mexico.

Enjoy the weekly evening concerts (mostly on Thursdays) in Santa Lucía Park.

At the height of prosperity in Mérida, at the beginning of the 20th century, the city's citizens built the ostentatious boulevard called **Paseo Montejo**, modelled on Paris boulevards.

Paseo Montejo is lined with expensive houses and many monuments, the most eye-catching of which is clearly the National Monument. The Colombian sculptor Rómulo Rozo created the **Monumento a la Patria** (Monument of the Nation) between 1946 and 1957. True to Maya style, the monument represents the significant events in Mexican history and their main protagonists.

Museum of Anthropology and History

⊙ Opening times: Tue–Sat 8am–8pm, Sun 8am–2pm

The former government building (Palacio del General Cantón) at the corner of Paseo Montejo and Calle 43 now houses the Museum of Anthropology and History (Museo de Antropologia e Historia). Displays in the impressive 19th-century building show **collections from Maya high culture** along with items from the other major pre-Columbian cultures in Mesoamerica.

Exceptional pieces are the retrieved sacrificial offerings from the Chichén Itzá sacred well (cenote or sinkhole). Frederick Catherwood made drawings of the Maya archaeological sites, and the museum exhibits include reproductions of these drawings (▶ Baedeker Special p.471), as well as photographs of these sites made by Teobert Maler around the turn of the century. Some of the Maya habits and practices are explained in an interesting way, for example how they flattened their foreheads or filed their teeth to comply with the beauty standards of their time.

Regional museum of Folk Art

The regional folk art museum (Museo Regional de Arte Popular, La Mejorada) at Calle 59 No. 441 displays textiles, traditional costumes, ceramics, jewellery, toys and musical instruments.

Centre of Pueblo Maya Culture

The centre of Pueblo Maya culture (Centro Cultural de los Pueblos Mayas) is located directly behind the folk art museum and shows how the Maya carved ceremonial masks or tied their excellent hammock knots.

The market takes place south of the main city square. The goods on offer are mostly **products made of sisal fibres**, such as panama hats (jipijapas), bags, carpets and sandals. Other products are the so-called huipiles, i.e. white embroidered cotton blouses, and Guayabera shirts (white 4-pocket shirts). The colourful **hammocks**, a most pleasant way to take the weight off your feet, are also very popular. Those interested in buying one should take note of differences in quality.

★
City market

Around Mérida

Mérida is a convenient place from which to venture out to the archaeological sites in Yucatán, such as Dzibilchaltún, Izamal (see below), ►Uxmal, Kabah (►the Puuc Route), ►Chichén Itzá and other places.

The excavation site Dzibilchaltún is located only 17km/10.5mi north of Mérida near the road to Progreso. The ruins are part of an ancient pre-Columbian city with the largest area (80 sq km/31 sq mi) of any ruined city in Yucatán. It is also the Maya city to have been continuously populated for the longest time. The ancient Dzibilchaltún was probably established as early as 1500 BC; the Maya still lived there when the Spaniards landed on the peninsula. Dzibilchaltún was likely a **pilgrimage destination** as well as a **significant political metropolis**; 40,000 people are thought to have lived in this city at the height of its culture.

Dzibilchaltún
🕐
Opening times:
daily 8am–5pm

The archaeological site includes various ceremonial centres, which were once connected by causeways (sacbeob). Today, only a few structures in the large excavation area are sufficiently restored to be worth a visit.

The Temple of the Seven Dolls (Templo de las Siete Muñecas) was built in the 7th century. It is a curious building. In contrast to other known Maya buildings, the architectural style is simple. The temple has a square base and there is one window on each side of the entrance. So far, no windows have been found in a Maya temple anywhere else. The roof ridge consists of a pyramid stump and thus also deviates from the traditional Maya style. At excavation, archaeologists found seven partially distorted clay effigies or "dolls", which gave the temple its name. The temple and several other smaller buildings rest on a 250 x 90m (820 x 295ft) platform with an exterior stairway on each of the four sides.

★
◄ Temple of the Seven Dolls

The **Xlacah cenote** (a sinkhole) in the centre of the city was of great importance. It is almost 30m/98ft wide and estimated to be 45m/148ft deep. Research divers have recovered about 30,000 archaeological finds from the sinkhole, such as clay vessels and ceramic figures, jewellery and some skeletal remains. Today, the cenote is used to bathe in. The small museum at the entrance of the archaeological site displays stelae, sculptures and ceramics. Many of the artefacts have

★
◄ Pueblo Maya museum

been recovered from the well (cenote). The large Pueblo Maya museum (Museo del Pueblo Maya) mostly consists of the recreation of an »**authentic**« **Maya village**. Inside and around the huts, visitors see Indians cook their meals and attend to their gardens and handicrafts. The Ecopark with its rich flora and fauna is also remarkable.

Progreso

On the same route, about 35km/22mi north of Mérida, lies Yucatán's main port Progreso. The harbour boasts a 2km/1.2mi-long pier. While the town is not particularly pretty, it does have a wide, white, sandy beach. In a limited way, construction is under way to prepare Progreso for tourism.

Scorpion Reef

Scorpion Reef (Arrecifes Alacranes) is located about 130km/81mi north of Progreso in the Gulf of Mexico. It is made up of several **islands, sandbanks and reefs**, which are grouped in a semi-circle around a lagoon. The rich marine life and many sunken shipwrecks have made the reef a first-rate destination for ambitious divers. It can only be reached by charter boat from Progreso.

Beach resorts

The people of Mérida go to their traditional beaches around Chicxulub east and west of Progreso. Between September and June, bungalow hotels are available for rent here at very favourable prices, as are furnished private homes. Of course, there is no comparison between this Yucatán coast and the one on the Caribbean side.

Izamal

On your way to Chichén Itzá, stop off in the market town of Izamal (26km/16mi north on the MEX 180 from Mérida to Chichén Itzá). The town demonstrates in classical form the historic **collision between Indian and Spanish culture**. Izamal was a place of pilgrimage in pre-Columbian times. In 12 sacred sites, the Indians honoured the sun god Kinich-kakmó, the creator deity Itzamná and other gods. It might have been Izamal's high status as a spiritual centre that inspired the Spaniards to act extremely destructively: immediately after they took Izamal (around 1540), they destroyed most of the pyramids and used the stones to build their churches.

✳

The monastery of San Antonio de Padua ▶

The houses in Izamal are mostly painted bright yellow, and so the city is also known as the Yellow City. A wide flight of steps leads from the main city square to the monastery of San Antonio de Padua. Juan de Mérida had this monastery built between 1553 and 1561 for the Franciscans. The vast atrium and the surrounding arcade with 75 arches are considered second only to St Peter's Square in Rome. Every year on 5 August, the people of Izamal celebrate the day of the Virgin of Izamal.

The main pyramids were inscribed with the names Itza-matul, Kabul and Kinich-kakmó. Today, it is mostly the latter pyramid of the sun god which still shows some of the impressive greatness of its past. The proportions of this pyramid make it one of the largest in Mexico. The particularly high risers of the uppermost stairway are remarkable. Visitors can enjoy an excellent **panoramic view** over the city from the top of the pyramid.

About 35km/22mi south of Mérida in the direction of Uxmal, visitors can learn about life on the 19th-century sisal-producing Hacienda Yaxcopoil. The large former plantation, now a museum, is in quite good condition.

Hacienda Yaxcopoil

The town of Sisal is 52km/32mi west of Mérida: travel there via Hunucmá. In the times of the sisal boom, Sisal was the most important port city of Yucatán. Empress Charlotte Amalie once came to Sisal for an overnight stay, before boarding a ship bound for Europe in 1865 to solicit help for her emperor husband. The house where she spent the night is open to visitors.

Sisal

The beautiful town of Celestún lies 92km/57mi west of Mérida on a large green lagoon. Its citizens live from fishing, coconut cultivation and obtaining salt by evaporating water from salt brine. The lagoon itself is part of an amazing nature preserve with countless seabirds, such as pelicans, flamingos, herons, cormorants and ducks.

Celestún

Hackney-coaches wait at the entrance to the San Antonio monastery in Izamal.

★ Mexico City (Ciudad de México)

Distrito Federal (D.F.)
Population (including suburbs): 25
to 30 million (2005 estimate)

Altitude: 2,240m/7,350ft

The Mexican capital is situated in the Valley of Anáhuac, often also referred to as the Mexican Highland Valley. Surrounded by towering mountains, Mexico City's location at the feet of the snow-capped, more than 5,000m/16,400ft-high volcanoes Popocatépetl and Iztaccíhuatl is singularly beautiful. Due to the elevation, the climate is temperate all year round.

A large number of monuments and artefacts tell of the city's more than 650-year history. The pre-Columbian period is however mostly represented by individual pieces of art or reconstructions in museums because the Spanish conquistadores destroyed the ancient Aztec metropolis **Tenochtitlán** to build their own city on the ruins. Extensive excavations have only recently unearthed the ruins of the main temple of Tenochtitlán. In contrast, churches and palaces from colonial times, mostly in the Baroque style, are everywhere. In addition, modern Mexican architecture, especially that of the 1950s and 1960s, has given rise to interesting buildings.

From north to south, Mexico City spans more than 40 km/24 mi, and on average 25km/15mi from west to east. A federal district, the Distrito Federal, has been created for the city; its most senior administrator, the Regente, was until 1997 appointed by the Mexican president. In the north however, this district has become too confining and the newer industrial suburbs have already grown into the adjacent federal state of Esta de México.

The population is growing very rapidly. Many Mexicans from agricultural areas with less than favourable living conditions move to the city. According to current estimates, 25 to 30 million people live in Mexico City, making it the most densely populated city in the world. Overcrowding and increasing industrialization of the capital cause severe economic and social problems. Jobs are scarce, but nevertheless every day hundreds of people come here to seek their fortune. Most of the newcomers or »paracaidistas« (sky divers) land in the slums in the east of the city and live there under the poorest of conditions in shacks made from cardboard, corrugated iron sheeting and plastic foil. Add to this the high birth rate in this particular part of Mexico City. In 1910, the estimated number of people living in and around Mexico City was about 800,000. This number had increased to more than 1 million by 1930, 3 million by 1950 and up to

Population growth

← *Aztec dancers in front of the Catedral Metropolitana on Mexico City's Zócalo*

Highlights Mexico City

Historic Centre
The centre of Mexico City reveals a long history, especially in the area around the main city square with the cathedral, the Aztec ruins, the main Aztec temple (Templo Mayor) and the National Palace with frescoes by Diego Rivera.

► page 370

Alameda Park
The park is a green oasis west of the main city square with the look-out tower Torre Latinoamericana, the Museum of Fine Arts (Palacio de Bellas Artes) and several small museums.

► page 383

Bosque de Chapultepec
Chapultepec Park is a large, forested area at the end of Paseo de la Reforma. It is a popular recreational area for weekend outings with several special attractions. Without doubt, the highlight is the impressive anthropology museum with the most comprehensive collection of original artefacts from pre-Hispanic Mesoamerican cultures in Mexico.

► page 390

San Ángel
This pretty city district has a colonial ambience. Visit the Saturday bazaar (Bazar del Sábado) in the picturesque Plaza San Jacinto.

Coyoacán
A peaceful neighbourhood in the centre of the metropolis with the museums of Frida Kahlo, Diego Rivera and Leon Trotsky.

► page 409

Xochimilco
This labyrinth of lakes and canals is a popular tourist destination. Rent a colourfully painted boat and listen to the Mariachi music. Don't miss the Museo Dolores Patiño in this part of town!

► page 412

5 million by 1960. 10 years later, the number was 7.5 million; in 1980 it reached a total of 12 million, and by the end of the 20th century the population of Mexico City was more than 22 million strong. Today, an estimated 25 to 30 million Mexicans live in the capital (2005 estimate).

Environmental problems Traffic congestion has been somewhat alleviated through the expansion of public transport and the construction of both the Metro and city highways without intersections (Anillo Periférico highway). However, conditions are still chaotic during peak hours: there are an estimated 4 million cars in Mexico City. To make matters worse, heavy industry has settled around the single mouth of the Valley of Anáhuac, the only direction from which fresh air could stream into the city. Now, in part unfiltered industrial **emissions** blow into the city and add to the air pollution. Mexico City's citizens have to deal with more than 11 tons of pollutant particles per day. Meanwhile, the Mexican government are trying to reverse this trend: Mexico spends 1% of its GNP on environmental protection and the NAFTA agreement also contains provisions to curb the pollution of air and water.

Mexico City is built on shaky foundations. Every year, the city sinks by about 20 cm/7.9 in into swampy soil and many buildings therefore no longer stand on level ground. When the Spaniards came to Tenochtitlán they found a city enclosed by lakes with many canals running through it. They immediately started draining the area and today there are dust fields where the lakes once were. Since **the wells no longer provide enough drinking water**, about one third of the water for the high-altitude metropolitan area must be pumped in at a high energy cost. At the same time, many city districts are on a level that is significantly lower than the sewer system. The waste water must therefore be pumped out of the city. Failing pumps would leave a large portion of Mexico City flooded with waste water.

These disastrous environmental problems notwithstanding, Mexico City fascinates visitors. There are beautiful boulevards such as Paseo de la Reforma, art treasures in the many museums, parks with old trees and cosy corners steeped in colonial atmosphere. Mexico City is also an ideal starting point for tours into the country.

A shortage of water, along with air pollution and huge population growth, is one of the most urgent problems. Mexico City is the only city in the world with millions of inhabitants but no river.

▶ VISITING MEXICO CITY

INFORMATION

Tourist information
at the airport, Hall A
Tel. (55) 57 86 90 02, or in the Zona
Rosa, Amberes 54 (corner of Londres)
Tel. (55) 525 93 80

Get more information from mobile
information kiosks in the main city
square (Zócalo), at the anthropology
museum and other main tourist spots
as well as in the four large bus
terminals.

Ciudad de México Plan

Where to stay
① Gran Hotel ③ Casa de los Amigos ⑤ Del Principado
② Hotel de Cortés ④ Casa Vieja ⑥ Maria Cristina

GETTING AROUND

Flights to and from Cancún, Mérida and Acapulco

CITY WALKING TOURS

Tour 1 (about 3km/2mi)
Most tourist features in Mexico City are located west of the great traffic axis Paseo de la Reforma. Close to Alameda Park, where people enjoy the shade of the trees and policemen on horseback wear sombreros, the first attractions can already be seen: the Mayer Art Museum, the Church of Santa Veracruz and pretty colonial houses. The most striking sight here

Where to eat
1. Café de Tacuba
2. La Opera Bar
3. Casa de los Azulejos
4. Los Girasoles
5. Vegetariano Madero
6. San Angel Inn

The patio in the Casa de los Azulejos forms the magnificent backdrop for the popular Sanborn restaurant which has been here for four decades.

is the Fine Arts Museum (Palacio de Bellas Artes), built from white Carrara marble (from Italy) in a grandiose Art Nouveau style. The 170m/558ft-tall look-out tower, the Torre Latinamericano (built in the 1950s), is only a few steps away on the opposite side of Avenida Lazaro Cárdenas. A ride to the top of the tower is expensive but the view is worth it, especially shortly before sunset. A stone's throw away is the Casa de Azulejos, a colonial mansion which was once the seat of the Count of Orizaba. The building is completely covered with tiles. It is possible to view the interior of the mansion, or have a snack in the restaurant on the first floor. To reach the Plaza de la Constitución walk down Avenida Cinco de Majo; on the way, check out the main post office in pure Art Deco style. Alternatively, take the parallel F.I. Madero or Tacuba with the Museo Nacional de Arte e Industrias Populares (folk art and craft museum) to reach the gigantic main city square (Zócalo). This plaza measures 240m/790ft on each side and is one of the largest city squares in the world. The buildings around the traffic-engulfed plaza are

in the lavish Art Nouveau or neo-colonial style. The cathedral (Catedral Metropolitana) on one side of the plaza leans slightly toward the Templo Mayor, the main temple of the destroyed Aztec city Tenochtitlán and the impressive museum at the excavation site. The National Palace with famous murals by Diego Rivera is situated on the eastern side of the plaza.

Tour 2 (about 8km/5mi, the suburb of Coyoacán excluded)

Start in the main city square. The first leg of the tour is a Metro ride to the Hidalgo bus stop on Paseo de la Reforma. Emperor Maximilian planned this boulevard, which was opened in 1877 after 10 years of construction work. Continue by small bus or cab to the Chapultepec Park (alternatively, take the Metro from the main city square to Pino Suárez and then continue to Chapultepec Park on bus route 1). In the northern part of this huge park stand the impressive National Museum of Anthropology and another museum with a collection of works by the painter Rufino Tamayo. In the district south of Paseo de la Reforma two lakes sparkle in the sun and a castle towers over the city on Chapulin Hill (Chapultepec, or Grasshopper Hill: chapulin = grasshopper, tepec = hill). The Mexican Emperor Maximilian of Habsburg and his wife Charlotte once resided in the castle. You may wish to spend the evening in the nearby district of Condensa, the part of town where young, intellectual urbanites want to be seen.

As an alternative, take a 6km/3.7mi trip south or south-west by taxi or bus to the colonial suburb of San Ángel with its mansions and narrow alleys. The suburb is protected as a national monument. A visit to the Saturday Bazaar (Bazar de Sábado, an arts and crafts market in a former hacienda) in this part of the city is a special treat. This extended tour 2 also takes in the district of Coyoacán where visitors can see the famous Blue House of the painter Frida Kahlo and visit the Leon Trotsky Museum (Museo Casa de Trotzkij). The museum used to be the residence of the Russian revolutionary and is the place where he was shot to death. The Plaza Hidalgo in the centre of Coyoacán with the neighbouring Centennial Garden (Jardín del Centenario), the city hall and the San Bautista church is also charming. The weekends are particularly lively here when the street life includes ice cream and balloon vendors. Bus route 3 runs from the Metro station in Coyoacán back to the city.

EVENTS AND CELEBRATIONS

Festival del Centro Histórico
The Festival del Centro Histórico takes place over almost three weeks in March. Enjoy a broad spectrum of music ranging from classical to rock, dances, children's programmes, street theatre, guided tours for those who are interested in architecture and much more.

Aparición de la Virgen de Guadalupe
The Apparition of Our Lady of Guadalupe is celebrated on 12 December. This is the most important religious holiday in Mexico. Thousands of pilgrims come to Mexico City on this day to honour the Virgin (Our Lady) of Guadalupe. A large midnight Mass is held on the evening before the celebration. The Aztec dance performances in front of the basilica on 11 and 12 December are also very impressive.

SHOPPING

Markets
Mexico City has a variety of interesting and attractive markets. Tourists especially like the Saturday Bazaar (Sábado in San Ángel), and the Lagunilla flea market east of the intersection Paseo de la Reforma/Lázaro Cárdenas. The market La Merced with its many sections is located south-east of the city centre, and the Sonora market is in Calle Fray Servando Teresa de Mier. Both these markets offer beautiful ceramics and all kinds of esoteric implements.

Baedeker-recomendation

Arts, crafts and souvenirs
In the artisans' centre (Centro de Artesanías de la Ciudadela) in Calle Balderas, all kinds of handiwork from every part of Mexico is on sale. There is something here for everyone: clothing, ceramics, baskets, items made from papier-mâché, jewellery and much more (open daily 8am–7pm, Metro: line 3, Balderas).

Museum shops

All Mexican public museums offer very good reproductions of their displayed items. In their usually well-organized shops, they also stock silver or gold-plated jewellery in the style of pre-Columbian art. These artistic mementos make nice travel souvenirs or gifts.

WHERE TO EAT

► Expensive

⑥ *Antiguo San Ángel Inn*
Diego Rivera 50 (San Ángel)
Tel. (55) 56 16 22 22, 56 16 14 02
www.sanangelinn.com
This beautiful old hacienda has well-kept gardens, colonial furniture and first-rate Mexican cuisine.

► Moderate

① *Café de Tacuba*
Tacuba 28 (Centro)
Tel. (55) 55 18 49 50
In 1912, this traditional café opened in a monastery. See the 18th-century painting in the dining room, which shows how to make mole poblano, a sauce with chili peppers and chocolate. The Oaxaca cuisine is very good.

② *La Opera Bar*
Cinco de Mayo 10 (Centro)
Tel. (55) 55 12 89 59
Although this old house is a cantina, you can also get Spanish and Mexican food here. The ceiling still shows bullet holes: the story goes that they were put there by Pancho Villa when he rode into the house on horseback. Be sure to make a reservation.

④ *Los Girasoles*
Xocoténcatl 1
Tel. (55) 55 10 32 81
This is one of the most pleasant city-centre restaurants with Mediterra-nean-style furnishings in a casual setting and excellent, creative cuisine.

③ *Sanborn's Casa de Azulejos*
Madero 4 (Centro)
Tel. (55) 518 66 76
The famous 16th-century House of Tiles (one of the 60 Sanborn chain restaurants in Mexico City) stretches over two floors. The restaurant itself is such a special experience that the food takes second place.

► Inexpensive

⑤ *Vegetariano Madero*
Madero 56 (Centro)
Friendly, spacious vegetarian restaurant, although the entrance and the stairway would suggest otherwise. The lunch menu is very good and the breakfast menu imaginative.

WHERE TO STAY

► Luxury

④ *Casa Vieja*
Eugenio Sué 45
Tel. (55) 52 82 00 67
Fax (55) 52 81 37 80
www.casavieja.com
This small, luxurious restaurant is beautifully decorated with mosaics and paintings. The exquisitely furnished suites feature all amenities, such as a Jacuzzi, kitchenette and stereo system as well as fax and internet connection. A well-stocked library and a collection of music and videos also reflect the superior standard of this hotel. Naturally, the restaurant and bar are also first-rate.

► Luxury to mid-range

① *Gran Hotel de la Ciudad de México*
16 de Septiembre 82 (Centro)
Tel. (55) 10 83 77 00
granhotelmexico_ventas@
yahoo.com.mx

The foyer of this 19th-century hotel (124 rooms) is executed in the Belle Époque style with an extraordinary filigree glass dome ceiling by Tiffany. Another style element is the 19th-century wrought-iron elevator. The location near the main city square (Zócalo) and the main Aztec temple (Templo Mayor) make this hotel an ideal base for sight-seeing tours.

② **Hotel de Cortés**
Avenida Hidalgo 85
(Centro Histórico)
Tel. (55) 55 18 21 81
Fax (55) 55 12 18 63
www.hoteldecortes.com.mx
This Best Western hotel, a very beautiful colonial building, was built in 1780. Its 29 rooms are arranged around the cool and quiet patio with a restaurant and a small café. Here, visitors feel far removed from the loud bustle of the city, but the Franz Mayer Museum is only a block away and the Museum of Fine Arts is also close by.

► **Mid-range**
⑥ **María Cristina**
Río Lerma 31 (Zona Reforma)
Tel. (55) 55 66 96 88
Fax (55) 55 66 91 94
This hotel (149 rooms) was built in 1937 in the Spanish colonial style and renovated in 1995. It is located within one block of Paseo de la Reforma and close to the Zona Rosa. The beautiful rooms offer various amenities and the hotel also has a restaurant and a bar.

⑤ **Del Principado**
Londres 42
Tel. (55) 55 33 29 44
www.hoteldeprincipado.com.mx
Spacious rooms, laundry services and parking spaces make this hotel (50 rooms) a comfortable place to stay.

Imposing: the glass dome of the Hotel de la Ciudad

► **Budget**
③ **Casa de los Amigos**
Ignacio Mariscal 132
Tel. (55) 57 05 05 21
www.avantel.net/~friends.
Currently, this lodge is managed by Quakers. It is said that José Clemente Orozco spent his last years here. Long-term visitors to Mexico City in particular appreciate the clean, plain, yet comfortable rooms. The lodge offers single and double rooms as well as dormitories for four or more people. Alcohol and smoking are prohibited inside the building. There is a two-night minimum stay provision.

History

1325	Foundation of Tenochtitlán (now Mexico City) by the Aztec.
1521	The conquistadores under Hernán Cortés subjugate the Aztec and Tenochtitlán falls to Spain. 300 years of colonial rule follow.
1535	Capital of the viceroy of New Spain, i.e. of all Spanish provinces on the American continent north of Costa Rica.
1821	Mexican War of Independence: revolutionists reclaim Mexico City under their leader Agustín de Itúrbide.
1847	Mexican-American War: US forces take the city and occupy it for five months.
1863 to 1867	Emperor Maximilian I and the French army reign in Mexico City. In 1866 Benito Juárez and his US ally chase the French out of Mexico City and the entire country. Juárez then takes over the government.
1920s	Urban renewal in Mexico City: creation of new housing and clean-up of slums.
1968	Mexico City hosts the summer Olympic Games.
1985	Devastating earthquake: horrendous damage, 9,500 people perish and 30,000 become homeless.
1997	For the first time in Mexico City, the city mayor is elected by direct vote.

Tenochtitlán and Tlatelolco

The Aztec or México shaped most of the pre-Columbian history of the metropolitan area. Their language was Náhuatl. In 1345, the Aztec established their city of Tenochtitlán, the »Place of the Prickly Pear«, on a swampy island in the Texcoco Lake (see p.376). At the time of the Spanish conquest, Tenochtitlán covered the eastern part of today's Mexico City. As Tenochtitlán grew rapidly, other city states emerged independently in the region. These settlers were Chichimec tribes like the Tenayuca, Texcoco, Chalco, Tlatelolco, Coyoacán, Tlacopán (today's Tacuba), Atzcapotzalco, Xochimilco and Culhuacán. Three large causeways and an aqueduct connected the island metropolis with the mainland across the lake. The Aztec built many interlaced canals and bridges through the island. Among other structures, they erected the magnificent main pyramid with two temples, one dedicated to the war and sun god Huitzilopochtli and the other to the rain god Tláloc. A snake wall enclosed the ceremonial centre with temples for other important gods, such as Tezcatlipoca, Xochiquetzal, Quetzalcóatl and Chicomecóatl. The ruins of these grand buildings are buried underneath today's main city square in Mexico City, or close to it. In recent years, some of the ruins have been excavated. Outside the ceremonial centre, palaces, houses, market places and small temple groups have been found. The older city of Tlatelolco was first a rival and then an ally of Tenochtitlán. The city had a main pyramid, which showed similarities to the one in Tenayuca. The temples of Tlatelolco were dedicated to the gods Tláloc and Quetzalcóatl. The city's largest source of power was its role as an Aztec trading centre. After the conquest, the Spaniards built their new city on top of the ancient structures. The old, pre-Cortés city of Tlatelolco is now buried beneath La Lagunilla market, the church Santiago, the Foreign Ministry and modern apartment blocks. Both Tenochtitlán and Tlatelolco were surrounded by lakes and wetlands and soon also by fertile agricultural plots with drainage canals on at least three sides (chinampas). Remnants of this agricultural method are visible in the floating gardens of Xochimilco. The lake regions around Chalco (south) as well as the wetlands around Xaltocán and Tzompanco (now Zumpango in the north) were probably used in this way too.

Hernán Cortés with his small group of Spanish soldiers and their many Tlaxcaltec allies first set foot in the Aztec metropolis on 8 November 1519. The city at that time spread over 12–15 sq km (4.6–5.8 sq mi), and with a population of 200,000 to 300,000 it was probably the world's third largest city after London and Beijing. The Spanish conquistadores placed the Aztec ruler Montezuma II (also Moctezuma II or Motecuhzoma Xocoyotzín) under arrest in his own palace. After Montezuma's violent death, the México under their new ruler Cuitláhuac drove Cortés and his men out of Tenochtitlán. The night of 30 June 1520, when Cortés and his men fled the Aztec city, has become known as **La Noche Triste** (the sad night). During the course of this night, more than half of Cortés's men lost their lives and half of their heavy loot was taken. Cortés then replenished his troops and also manned and equipped 13 two-mast sailing ships (brigantines) so that he would be able to control the shores. This accomplished, Cortés once again marched against Tenochtitlán in 1521. The city fell to Cortés when its last ruler Cuauhtémoc surrendered after his capture on 13 August 1521. The Spaniards levelled Tenochtitlán and filled in its system of canals.

The Spanish conquest

The Spaniards hated the temples of the Aztec »tin gods«. In 1522, they therefore hurried to build a city of their own on the ruins of Tenochtitlán with building materials recovered from the ruins. They called the city Méjico. 33 years later, Franciscan friars established in Santiago Tlatelolco the famous College of Santa Cruz as a school for the children of the Aztec nobility. In the same year, the Spanish crown declared New Spain a viceroyship, in which the city of Méjico was to play a prominent role. In 1537, the population in the new capital of New Spain had grown to around 100,000 Indians and 2,000 Spaniards. The city became the seat of an archbishop in 1546, and the first university on the American continent opened its doors here in 1551. During the Indian insurgency of 1692, several public

Capital of the province New Spain

buildings were burned down, the viceroy's palace among them. Originally, the palace had also been Cortés's residence. The Mexican freedom fighters initially struggled to rid their capital of the royalist troops. This changed when Agustín de Iturbide joined the movement and they successfully ousted the royalists in 1821.

Residence and capital

Iturbide then became emperor for a short time. After he fled the city, liberals and conservatives struggled with each other as did the centralists and federalists. US troops occupied Mexico City during the Mexican-American War (1846–1848), In 1863, French troops conquered the capital and from 1864 to 1867 the Austrian Archduke Maximilian became emperor over both city and country. His residence was the castle Chapultepec. The exiled president Benito Juárez fought the French occupiers and won. After his victory and after Emperor Maximilian was shot in Querétaro, he returned to the capital. Brisk construction activities took place during the dictatorship of Porfirio Díaz (1876–1911); the architecture in this era followed French patterns. In the years that followed, the capital city became the scene of repeated conquests and bloody skirmishes between the revolutionary leaders Francisco Madero, Victoriano Huerta, Álvaro Obregón, Francisco (Pancho) Villa and Emiliano Zapata. Progress in the capital had to wait until after the revolution. In 1930, Mexico City's population passed the one-million mark.

Recent developments

Mexicans finally started to modernize and industrialize their capital in the 1940s. To this day, a steady, unrelenting stream of the rural poor contributes to the population explosion in Mexico City. 20 years ago, 50% of Mexico's industrial activity took place in the metropolis. This proportion has now shrunk to 30%, mostly due to the development of the processing and finishing industries in the northern border states. In the same time period, banking business has declined from 70% to 60% and trade activities have dropped from 50% to 40%.

Mexico City hosted the summer Olympic Games in October 1968. Shortly before the games started, 250 people were killed during a demonstration on the Plaza of the Three Cultures. On 19 September 1985, an earthquake ravaged the capital. According to official reports, almost 10,000 people perished and more than 100,000 people became homeless. The material damage was enormous and changed the city forever.

Mayor of the metropolis

In July 1997, the PRI (Mexican International Revolutionary Party) lost its absolute majority in the federal congressional election. The party had appointed the mayor of Mexico City for more than 60 years running. Conditions had changed, and **Cuauhtémoc Cárdenas**, son of the former Mexican president Lázaro Cárdenas, now became the first freely elected mayor of the metropolis. **Marcelo Ebrard** has been mayor of Mexico City since 2006.

Orientation

Administratively, Mexico City is subdivided into 16 precincts with names such as Álvaro Obregón, Benito Juárez, Cuauhtémoc, Coyoacán, Atzcapotzalco, Xochimilco and so on. The precincts in turn are divided into more than 240 colonias (subdivisions) with street names that often relate to, for example, well-known rivers, philosophers or European cities. It is quite possible for several streets in different districts to have the same name: more than 100 streets are named after Emiliano Zapata alone. An address must therefore always include the respective colonia.

Government

In general, Spanish colonial city plans follow a chequerboard pattern, and this applies to a certain extent to Mexico City. The **explosive development of the metropolis** however has confused this system to such a degree that it is bound to puzzle the visitor. In general, avenidas (avenues) run in an east-west direction and calles (streets) in a north-south direction. However, there are also boulevards, calzadas (former causeways), callejones (alleys), prolongaciones (extensions), ejes viales (freeways, motorways) and expressways. Only the very large and important avenues run their whole length under one name, such as Avenida de los Insurgentes (north-south) and Paseo de la Reforma (running north-west to west). Other important streets running north-south are the Calzada Vallejo, Avenida Lázaro Cárdenas (formerly San Juan de Letrán), Calzada Niño Perdido and Avenida

City plan

Huge demand: Mexico City has around 90,000 taxis.

Ciudad de México Metro

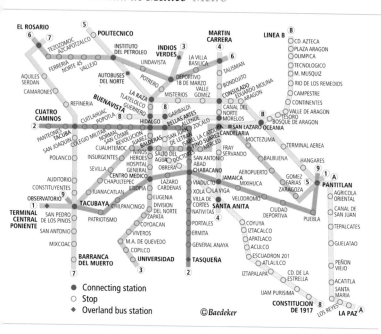

EL ROSARIO
POLITECNICO
MARTIN CARRERA
LINEA B

TEZOZOMOC AZCAPOTZALCO
INSTITUTO DEL PETROLEO
INDIOS VERDES
LA VILLA BASILICA
CD. AZTECA
PLAZA ARAGON
OLIMPICA
TECNOLOGICO
M. MUSQUIZ
RIO DE LOS REMEDIOS
CAMPESTRE
CONTINENTES
VALLE DE ARAGON
TESORO
BOSQUE DE ARAGON

FERRERIA NORTE 45
VALLEJO
LINDAVISTA
TALISMAN

AQUILES SERDAN
AUTOBUSES DEL NORTE
POTRERO
DEPORTIVO 18 DE MARZO
BONDOJITO

CAMARONES
LA RAZA
TLATELOLCO
MISTERIOS
VALLE GOMEZ
CONSULADO
EDUARDO MOLINA
ARAGON

REFINERIA
BUENAVISTA
GUERRERO
GARIBALDI
CANAL DEL NORTE
MORELOS

CUATRO CAMINOS
CUITLAHUAC
POPOTLA
HIDALGO
BELLAS ARTES
ALLENDE
ZOCALO

PANTEONES
TACUBA
COLEGIO MILITAR
NORMAL
SAN COSME
REVOLUCION
JUAREZ
BALDERAS
SAN JUAN DE LETRAN
ISABEL LA CATOLICA
PINO SUAREZ
CANDELARIA
SAN LAZARO OCEANIA
MOCTEZUMA

SAN JOAQUIN
CUAUHTEMOC
NIÑOS HEROES
SALTO DEL AGUA
MERCED
FRAY SERVANDO
TERMINAL AEREA

POLANCO
INSURGENTES
HOSPITAL GENERAL
DOCTORES
SAN ANTONIO ABAD
BALBUENA
HANGARES

SEVILLA
OBRERA
CHABACANO
AEROPUERTO

AUDITORIO
CENTRO MEDICO
CHAPULTEPEC
LAZARO CARDENAS
VIADUCTO
JAMAICA
MIXIHUCA
GOMEZ FARIAS
PANTITLAN

CONSTITUYENTES
JUANACATLAN
ETIOPIA
XOLA
LA VIGA
VELODROMO
ZARAGOZA
AGRICOLA ORIENTAL

OBSERVATORIO
TACUBAYA
CHILPANCINGO
EUGENIA
VILLA DE CORTES
SANTA ANITA
CIUDAD DEPORTIVA
PUEBLA
CANAL DE SAN JUAN

TERMINAL CENTRAL PONIENTE
SAN PEDRO DE LOS PINOS
PATRIOTISMO
DIVISION DEL NORTE
ZAPATA
NATIVITAS

SAN ANTONIO
COYOACAN
PORTALES
COYUYA
IZTACALCO
TEPALCATES

MIXCOAC
VIVEROS
ERMITA
APATLACO
GUELATAO

M.A. DE QUEVEDO
GENERAL ANAYA
ACULCO

BARRANCA DEL MUERTO
COPILCO
UNIVERSIDAD
TASQUEÑA
ESCUADRON 201
ATLALILCO
PEÑON VIEJO

IZTAPALAPA
CD. DE LA ESTRELLA
ACATITLA

UAM PURISIMA
SANTA MARIA

CONSTITUCION DE 1917
LOS REYES
LA PAZ

● Connecting station
○ Stop
◆ Overland bus station

©Baedeker

Universidad. An alternative east-west axis consists of Avenidas Chapultepec, Dr. Río de la Loza and Fray Servando Teresa de Mier. The beltways or bypasses are in part also expressways. Some important beltways (circuito interior) are Calzada Melchor Ocampo, Avenida Río Consulado, Bulevar Puerto Aéreo and the Viaducto Miguel Alemán. Avenida Río Churubusco complements the southern beltway and, like the viaducto, feeds traffic to the outer beltway Anillo Periférico.

Traffic Travellers who are unfamiliar with the muddle of the streets and the chaotic traffic conditions should **avoid driving in Mexico City**. Taking the **Metro** is the best and also the most economical way to get around town. So far, the Metro offers 12 routes, which include most of the important attractions. 4.6 million passengers daily use a Metro network of about 200 km/124 mi. The symbols and signposts are easy to understand and make orientation simple; most stations also have information desks. Heavy luggage is not permitted. If possible, avoid riding the Metro during peak traffic hours (before 10am and after 4pm) when the crowds are overwhelming and pick-pockets have easy pickings. During these times, a portion of a main station platform may be reserved for women and children and the train may also have compartments for women and children only. At night, women should not use the Metro unaccompanied because harassment is quite common.

Only travellers who speak Spanish and have a good sense of direction should hazard using one of the **approximately 60 bus lines**. Many tourists like to ride the 76 line from the main city square (Zócalo) via Paseo de la Reforma to the Chapultepec Park (Bosque de Chapultepec). But beware: with different motivation, pick-pockets like to ride on this bus, too.

About 90,000 taxis of different kinds offer their services in Mexico City. Peseros are usually VW buses, which double as cheap shared taxis. These cruising cabs service defined routes, for example Paseo de la Reforma, Avenida Insurgentes and stops along these streets. The driver indicates with his fingers how many passengers he can still pick up. Slowly but surely, somewhat larger midi-buses with 22 seats are replacing the peseros. You can also hail one of the yellow taxis or the slightly newer green taxis libres (free), which will go anywhere in the city. In recent years, the number of assaults in taxis and by fake taxi drivers has increased. Therefore it may be wise to avoid these taxis and use hotel taxi services or one of the red radio taxis (taxis de sitio). The latter park in a depot and will pick up passengers upon request. Large hotels also offer so-called turismos: these are usually limousines without meters and cost the passenger dearly. Under all circumstances, passengers should negotiate the price before boarding the taxi. For a reliable radio taxi, call 52 71 91 46 or 52 71 90 58. The drivers of yellow taxis at the airport charge a fixed standard rate.

Sightseeing

To begin a sightseeing tour, providing that you can spend several days in Mexico City, first seek out the attractions in the near vicinity of the Zócalo, such as the cathedral, the ambry, the National Palace and the new Main Temple museum (Museo del Templo Mayor) at the excavation site. Spend another day visiting places of interest around Alameda Park and the adjacent Avenida Juárez: the Fine Arts Museum (Palacio de Bellas Artes), Latin American Tower (Torre Latinoamericana), the House of Tiles (Casa de los Azulejos) and the San Francisco church (Iglesia de San Francisco). The Garden of Chapultepec (Bosque de Chapultepec) offers some peace and quiet after the noise of the city. Sights in the park are the botanical garden, the zoo

! **Baedeker TIP**

Tren Turístico

An ideal way to view the historic centre of the largest city in the world is a tour on the old-fashioned Tren Turístico. The ride in the replica of a trolleybus from the 1920s begins in front of Alameda Park (Juárez 66 and Revillagigedo, tel. 512 10 12) every hour from 10am to 5pm. The trip takes in various sights of the city, including the Zócalo, the Museum of the Former College of San Ildefonso, the Plaza de Santo, the Mining Palace, the National Museum and the Franz Mayer Museum as well as the Iturbide Palace (Spanish tour guide).

and the Castle of Chapultepec (Castillo de Chapultepec) with the Mexican National Museum of History. The highlight is a visit to the National Anthropology Museum: plan to spend an entire day there. Don't forget to visit the Museum of Modern Art (Museo de Arte Moderno). A lively evening can be spent in the Plaza de Garibaldi listening to Mariachi bands. Further excursions venture out to places a short distance from the city centre: stroll through the district of Coyoacán with the Frida Kahlo Museum and the Leon Trotsky Museum and explore University City (Ciudad Universitaria). Another trip may include an outing by boat to the Floating Gardens of Xochimilco and a visit to the Basilica of Guadalupe (see city map and itineraries [tours 1 and 2] pp.358/359).

Historic Centre

A starting point The historic centre (Centro Histórico) makes a good starting point from which to explore Mexico City. Today's historic centre is the area between the streets Abraham González and Paseo de la Reforma in the west, Calle Anfora in the east, the Bartolomé de Las Casas in the north and the José María Izazaga in the south. Since 1987, the historic centre has been a **UNESCO World Heritage Site** featuring countless historic sites and a wealth of treasures in art and architecture dating from the Aztec era to colonial times. Mexico City's most captivating museums are sited in this part of the city. At the same time, visitors feel part of the excitement of a large modern metropo-

The starting point for a sightseeing tour of the city is usually the Zócalo with the cathedral.

lis. Sunday is the best time to visit the historic core of the city because the atmosphere is relaxed, there are fewer people, the traffic is
less hectic and the museums don't charge entry fees. Metro Station:
Zócalo (line 2).

The main city square, the Zócalo (Plaza de la Constitución), is the **Zócalo**
centre of Mexico City and also the midpoint of the historic centre.
The first Mexican constitution was proclaimed here in 1813. The city
square measures 240 x 240m (787 x 787ft) and is one of the largest
plazas in the world. Immediately after the Spanish conquest of Tenochtitlán, the Spaniards began to rebuild the main square in such a
way that the northern part of the new plaza covered the south section of the destroyed Aztec temple (Teocalli). At the beginning of
colonial rule, the plaza served mostly as a bullfight arena and as a
market. Today, the plaza appears somewhat empty, although every
morning a very large national flag is raised in its centre. The plaza is
also a place for celebrations, parades and various tent exhibitions.
The view of the plaza is best from the roof garden of the Majestic
hotel.

The National Palace (Palacio Nacional) with its more than 200m/   ✱
656ft façade takes up almost the entire eastern side of the main city   **National Palace**
square. The palace was built in 1523 from tezontle (blood stone), a
brownish-red volcanic stone. Cortés had the building foundation put
on top of the levelled new palace of Montezuma II. The National
Palace is one of the oldest and most impressive buildings in Mexico
City. Currently, it serves as the office of the president and contains
many administrative offices; in colonial times, it was the domicile of
the Spanish viceroy and later it became the office of the presidents of
the republic. The palace was rebuilt and enlarged several times
throughout its history and then, during the insurgency of 1692, it
was partially destroyed. President Calles added the third floor during
his term in office in the 1920s.
The **Freedom Bell** (Campana de Dolores) occupies its place above
the central portal and underneath the Mexican coat of arms. The
priest Miguel Hidalgo rang this bell on 16 September 1810 in Dolores when he called the independence movement to action. Every
year on 15 September, one hour before midnight, the Mexican president repeats Hidalgo's Grito de Dolores (cry of Dolores) from the
balcony of the National Palace while the freedom bell rings.
The inside of the palace consists of 14 courtyards and a large number   ✱ ✱
of halls. Only some of the courtyards are open for visits. The main   ◀ Frescoes of
courtyard is surrounded by arcades and a stairway leads from there   Diego Rivera
to the first floor. The walls of both the courtyard and the stairway
bear one of the most famous murals by Diego Rivera (▶ Baedeker
Special pp.79, 405). The title of the mural is *México a Través de Los
Siglos* (Mexico through the centuries). Between 1926 and 1945, Rivera depicted Mexican historic scenes on a surface area of 450 sq m/

4,844 sq ft **from the ancient Indian eras to the time after the revolution**. The sweeping scope of this mural and the inclusion of the main historic players demonstrate Rivera's social and political awareness. This is apparent especially at the base of the stairway in the picture »La Lucha de Clases« (class strategy).

A painting in the first floor gallery entitled *La Gran Tenochtitlán* is another famous Rivera mural.

Benito Juárez Museum

Visitors can now walk through the rooms off the northern inner courtyard that were once the living quarters of Benito Juárez. Furniture and personal items in the room where Juárez died in 1872 commemorate the great president. Visitors can also see some of the halls and the chamber of deputies in which the reform constitution was adopted in 1857. The constitution of 1917 and the reform constitution are on display.

The National Palace also houses the main national archive with interesting historic documents and the Biblioteca Miguel Lerdo de Tejada, one of Mexico's largest and most important libraries.

★
Catedral Metropolitana de la Asunción de María

The cathedral on the north side of the main square is one of the oldest and largest sacral buildings in the western hemisphere. Together with the National Palace, it dominates the main square. Buried underneath the cathedral is the south-western part of the former Aztec temple area with the Wall of the Skulls and the Temple of Xipe Tótec, among other structures.

Construction of the original cathedral began in 1525. However, this original church has been partially demolished and partially reconstructed. The current cathedral dates back to 1563. It took 250 years to build the massive building from basalt and grey sandstone and it therefore represents many styles; nevertheless, the cathedral captivates onlookers because of its **outstanding harmony**. The massive covings and spiral columns give the façade an overall Baroque appearance, despite the two neo-classical open work towers and other architectural elements. The bell towers were added in 1793. In 1813, the dome was completed and three statues were added to the clock tower, representing faith, hope and compassion. The statues are ascribed to Manuel Tolsá. The way the bells are hung in the tower is uncommon, as is their varying sizes. One of the bells, named Guadalupe, weighs a hefty 5,600kg/12,346lbs.

The interior of the cathedral is divided in a main nave and two side naves. There are also 14 side altars. Again, the cathedral exhibits all the artistic styles and fashions that were prevalent in colonial times. The most outstanding feature is the elaborately carved ultra-Baroque

★
Altar of the Kings ►

Altar of the Kings (Altar de los Reyes, 1718–1739) behind the high altar. 14 chapels line the two side naves. The chapel west of the main altar contains the mortal remains of the Mexican emperor Agustin de Iturbide. Visitors now find a statue of the Señor del Cacao, which used to stand in front of the church, in the third chapel left of the

View of the cathedral and the remains of the walls of the once powerful Tenochtitlán

main entrance. The Indians once placed sacrifices in the form of co-coa beans in front of the statue, and the proceeds were used for the construction of the church. The other chapels and side altars are dec-orated with valuable paintings, most of them in the Baroque style. The carved cedar wood choir stalls (1696) are also notable. The Altar of Mercy (Altar del Perdón) opposite the main entrance is the south-ern boundary to the choir. Its ultra-Baroque retable features the painting *Virgin Mary* (1568) by Simon Pereyns. The paintings by Cristóbal de Villalpando (around 1665) in the vestry, with its ribbed Gothic dome, are well worth seeing. Most archbishops of Mexico City were buried in the crypt left of the main entrance, among them Juan de Zumárraga, the great teacher of the Indians and the main pastor of the metropolis. A museum of religious art is part of the ca-thedral. It shows precious religious artefacts.

The sacrament tabernacle is situated east of the cathedral. This parish church (consecrated in 1768) is one of the best examples of Mexican ultra-Baroque architecture. Estípites are the dominant characteristic feature of the façade; the seamless transition from the high central façade to the low support sides is also remarkable. Inside the chapel, the main altar attracts the most attention: it was created in 1829 by the Indian artist Pedro Patiño Ixtolinque, an apprentice of Manuel Tolsás, to whom the altar in the chapel of the Virgin Dolorosa is at-tributed. In the 18th century, fire and earthquakes destroyed part of the inner chapel. Like so many other old buildings in Mexico City, the structure leans to one side.

✳
◀ Sagrario
Metropolitano

Tradesmen offer their services at the eastern chapel wall, their tools spread out in front of them.

★ ★
Main Temple
⏲
Opening times:
Tue–Sun 9am–5pm

Behind the cathedral, at the corner of the streets Argentina and Guatemala, **ruins of the Tenochtitlán temple region** were excavated years ago and then left alone. In 1978, Metro construction workers found a cut stone. The stone turned out to be a round disk with a diameter of about 3.25m/10.7ft and a weight of 8,500kg/18,700lbs, the relief on the disk an artistic rendition of the decapitated and dismembered goddess Coyolxauhqui. This find triggered new excavations. Up to this point, archaeologists had anticipated that the remnants of the major pyramid (**Grand Teocalli**) would be underneath Mexico City's main square, but now they knew to look for the ancient religious and political centre of the Aztec Empire around the place where the disk had come to light. The temple pyramid had once been the sacred ceremonial centre of the Aztec city. On its top platform towered two temples, the temple of the rain god Tláloc (facing north) and (facing south) the temple of the supreme deity Huitzlopochtli, god of sun, wind and warriors; Aztec priests addressed these, the two most important gods, at these sacred temples. A Chac-mool figure with its colouring still intact was discovered in front of the Temple of Tláloc. The size and material of the temple walls suggest that these structures were built before the Aztec established their rule, in 1428, over the Valley of Anáhuac. Spaces between structures from different construction periods contained the skulls of sacrificed humans and many other sacrificial items. It is interesting that only a fraction of the more than 7,000 finds are actually of Aztec origin, most of them originating from the regions of other Indian tribes. They were most likely the tribute paid to the Aztec by subjugated tribes to be used as sacrificial offerings to the gods when a newly built pyramid was dedicated.

A circular path through the excavation site also skirts the zone of the feathered warriors where excavations have exposed the remnants of the eagle warriors' accommodation with many polychrome reliefs.

★ ★
**Main Temple
Museum**
⏲
Opening times:
Tue–Sun 9am–5pm

A new museum was built at the excavation site (at the entrance Seminario 8) when the National Museum of Anthropology could no longer accommodate the wealth of new finds. Its large windows allow a view onto the excavation site, and it features 8 exhibition halls, an auditorium and a library on four floors around an inner courtyard. Commentaries on the more than 3,000 exhibits are provided in the form of excerpts from Aztec codices in Spanish. Audio guides in English are also available. At the museum entrance, visitors see a **tzompantli** (skull rack) from the northern part of the excavation site. A **model** in the inner courtyard provides an overview of the temple area of Tenochtitlán before the Spanish conquest.

The museum is divided into a north and a south wing, just as the temple pyramid has a north and south temple. The items in the south wing relate to Huitzilopochtli, the god of sun, wind and warriors. The first exhibition hall maps out the migration of the Aztec until their arrival in the Valley of Anáhuac. War and the type and sig-

TEMPLE AREA OF TENOCHTITLÁN

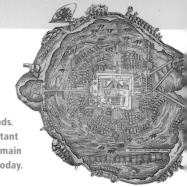

✳✳ Until the Spaniards conquered the city in 1521, the Aztec capital Tenochtitlán stood where modern Mexico City now stands. Divided into four quarters, the most important was the temple area. The remnants of the main temple, the Templo Mayor, can be visited today.

🕐 Open Tue–Sun 9am–5pm

Plan of Tenochtitlán from the letters of Cortés to Karl V (1524

① Double Temple
The Templo Mayor was consecrated to Huitzilo-pochtli and Tláloc. As the main goddess, she symbolized war and death as well as life and water.

② Temple of the Eagle Warriors
Two life-sized clay statues of elite Aztec soldiers were found here.

③ Temple of Tetzcatlipoca
Consecrated to Tetzcatlipoca, the all-powerful Aztec god

④ Ball court
As well as numerous temples, a ball court was found on the site. The other structures served as accommodation for the priests.

⑤ Temple of Ehécatl
One guise of Quetzacóatl was the wind god Ehécatl, whose temples were usually round so as not to disturb the flow of air.

⑥ Wall of skulls
made of the skulls and limbs of human sacrifices

A model of Tenochtitlán on the Plaza Templo Mayor

Templo Mayor *Plan*

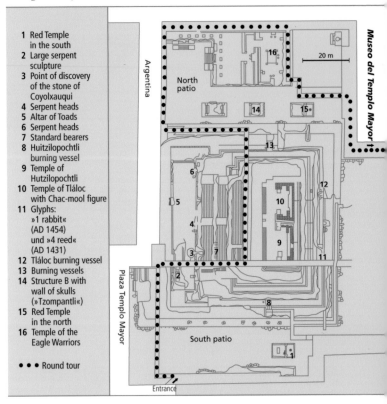

1 Red Temple in the south
2 Large serpent sculpture
3 Point of discovery of the stone of Coyolxauqui
4 Serpent heads
5 Altar of Toads
6 Serpent heads
7 Standard bearers
8 Huitzilopochtli burning vessel
9 Temple of Hutzilopochtli
10 Temple of Tláloc with Chac-mool figure
11 Glyphs: »1 rabbit« (AD 1454) und »4 reed« (AD 1431)
12 Tláloc burning vessel
13 Burning vessels
14 Structure B with wall of skulls (»Tzompantli«)
15 Red Temple in the north
16 Temple of the Eagle Warriors

● ● ● Round tour

Argentina

North patio

20 m

Museo del Templo Mayor

Plaza Templo Mayor

South patio

Entrance

nificance of sacrificial offerings are the topics of exhibitions in the second hall. Exhibits in the third hall elucidate the systems of trade and collecting tribute (tax) in the Aztec Empire. Finally, the fourth hall shows some of the most significant monoliths from the excavation site. Two life-sized stone statues of eagle warriors with stylized wings (also from the excavation site) flank the foot of the staircase. A depiction of the god of light and fire Xiuhtecutli is remarkable.

A particularly impressive exhibit is a stone used to perform human sacrifices. It shows a relief of the **moon goddess Coyolxauhqui** as a naked female figure. Her head, arms and legs have been separated from her body. According to myth, her brother, the warrior god Huitzilopochtli killed and dismembered her and her cortege of 400 on the snake hill Coatepec near Tula. He did this because Coyolxauhqui was determined to kill her mother, the earth goddess Coatlicue, and because she opposed human sacrifice – Huitzilopochtli gained

✳
◄ Stone for human sacrifice

been attributed to Lorenzo Rodriguez who was also the architect of the Sagrario Metropolitano. The bell tower in the shape of a papal tiara is notable.

The Supreme Court (Suprema Corte de Justicia) building (1929) occupies the south-east corner of the main city square. Inside, there are several murals by Orozco, among them *Justicia* and a rendition of a goddess of justice. She sleeps while bandits rob the people of their rights.

The Supreme Court

The Museo de la Ciudad de México (Mexico City Museum) in Pino Suarez 30 is housed only a few blocks away in the colonial palace of Count de Santiago de Calimaya. The exhibits include historic documents, photographs, furniture and other items concerning Mexico City from prehistoric times to the present. Two models are notable, one of the Teocalli (Aztec ceremonial centre) and the other of today's Mexico City. A stone in the shape of a snake head from the main Aztec temple forms one corner of the building.

★ **Mexico City Museum**

A short side trip of a few blocks on the road east toward El Salvador leads to the modern market buildings (La Merced). This used to be the largest trading place in the city. However, the market has been relocated to Itzpalapa which has made it less popular. While in the former market region, visit the 17th century convent (Convento de la Merced) at the corner of the streets Uruguay and Jesús María. The convent was remodelled in 1834 and features different styles, among which the Mudéjar (Moorish) style dominates.

Market

★ ◄ Convent at the market

Opposite the city museum is the site of the 17th-century Baroque Church of Jesus of Nazareth (Hospital y Iglesia Jesús Nazareno). Orozco painted the frescoes in the church dome in 1944. It was at this site that Hernán Cortés supposedly met the Aztec ruler Montezuma II for the first time, on 8 November 1519. Cortés died in 1547 in Seville (Spain); his remains are buried here. The church runs the associated Hospital La Purísima Concepción (Hospital of the Immaculate Conception). Cortés established this hospital in 1524 as the first of its kind in the Americas and, until recently, it was administered by his descendants. Consider visiting an excavated Aztec round pyramid south of the church near the Metro station Pino Suárez.

Church of Jesus of Nazareth

The former San Jerónimo Convent is situated in the plaza of the same name (No. 47), west of the Metro station in Calle San Jerónimo. The famous poet and painter Juana Inés de la Cruz (1651–1695) spent time here. Her mortal remains were recently discovered in the convent church. The convent museum (Claustro de Sor Juana Museum) was established in her memory. The Mexican Nobel prize laureate Octavio Paz wrote her biography and her poirtrait graces the front of the Mexican 1000 peso banknote.

San Jerónimo Convent

Charro Museum Go one block south on the street Isabel la Católica to reach Avenida José María de Izazaga. There, near the Metro station Isabel la Católica, stands the small Church of Our Lady of Monserrat (Iglesia de Nuestra Señora de Monserrat). The former convent now houses the Charro Museum (Museo de la Charrería). The museum is devoted entirely to horses and sports on horseback, and includes traditional charro garb and the saddle used by the revolutionist Pancho Villa.

Monte de Piedad (pawn shop) Back in the main city square, on the west side of the cathedral there is an often remodelled building from colonial times. This building houses the giant national pawn shop, the Monte de Piedad (House of Pity). It is currently the largest pawn brokerage in Latin America. The pawn business was established by Pedro Romero de Terreros in 1775 and moved to its current location in 1850.

Plaza de Santo Domingo The Plaza de Santo Domingo is located two blocks north of the cathedral and west of Avenida República de Brasil. This plaza from colonial times has retained much of its original traditional Spanish at-

Plaza de Santo Domingo

mosphere. Public scribes (evangelistas) sit under the arcades at the west side and offer their services to often illiterate potential clients. On the edge of the plaza at Calle Cuba 95, a plaque indicates that Malinche (Doña Marina), Hernán Cortés's Indian lover, advisor and interpreter, once lived here. She inhabited the house, however, in the year 1527 with the man she later married (Juan de Jaramillo).

On the north side of the plaza stands the beautiful Baroque church **Santo Domingo**. This is all that remains of a massive Dominican monastery complex. The current building is made of tezontle (blood stone) and dates back to the first half of the 18th century. Notable are the elegant tower with outside tiles, the harmonious façade, the two ultra-Baroque retables and the neo-classical main altar by Manuel Tolsá.

Museum of Mexican Medicine The Museum of Mexican Medicine (Museo de la Medicina Mexicana) is located on the east side of the plaza at the corner of the streets Brazil and Venezuela. It is housed in an 18th-century palace During colonial times, the building served as the jail of the inquisition (Santa Inquisición), the highest religious tribunal of the Catholic Church. Indians were not subject to the rules of this court. The inquisition was put in force in 1571 and lasted until 1815. An item of particular

Opening times: daily 9am–6pm

interest in the museum's history is the model of a baño de temazcal. This is the type of sweating hut or sauna which the Indians used for spiritual purification..

Following Calle Ildefonso to Calle Loreto leads to Plaza Loreto with the Church of Our Lady of Loreto (Iglesia de Nuestra Señora de Loreto). This is one of the most interesting neo-classical churches (1809–1816) in the country. Particularly notable are the elegant dome, the large windows between the buttresses and in the vestry, a reproduction of the Holy House of Loreto with beautiful paintings from colonial times. That the building shows no signs of damage, even though it stands on soft ground, speaks for its solid construction. The eastern part of the church, built from heavy stone, has sunk down significantly more than the western part which is composed of the lighter volcanic tezontle (blood stone).

Church of Our Lady of Loreto

Only a short distance away (Donceles 99), the Museum of Caricature shows a collection of works by known Mexican caricaturists.

Museum of Caricature

The Jesuit Prep School Ildefonso (built 1749) is sited two blocks west of the Plaza de Loreto in Calle Ildefonso 33–45. Today, the building houses the Escuela Nacional Preparatoria (ENP prep school) Gabino Barreda, the best known of the state grammar schools, and an office of Mexico's National Autonomous University (UNAM). The frescoes in the patio and the stairway are of great importance. The represented artists are Fermín Revueltas, Ramón Alva de la Canal, Fernando Leal, Jean Charlot, David Álfaro Siqueiros and José Clemente Orozco. In 1921, the minister of education, José Vasconcelos, invited these artists to decorate the building. This heralded the birth of the internationally known School of Mexican Muralism (▶Baedeker Special p.79).

Escuela Nacional Preparatoria

◀ Frescoes

Most significant are the murals created by José Clemente Orozco between 1922 and 1927, in which spiritual-religious themes merge with the revolutionary history of the country. The auditorium (called El Generalito) contains the choir stalls of the former Augustinian church (later turned national library). Having been rescued from a fire in the Augustinian church, the choir stalls bear some of the most artistic wood carvings of their type, which show scenes from the Christian Bible (the New Testament).

◀ Baroque choir stalls

In the same building complex, which was renovated in 1992 (enter from Justo Sierra 16), there are frescoes by the three great muralists Orozco, Rivera and Siqueiros. Today, important pre-Columbian exhibitions are shown in the building.

Museum of the Former College of San Ildefonso

Vasconcelos also proposed the creation of the frescoes which can now be seen in the building of the Ministry of Education (SEP, Secretaría de Educación Pública). The ministry is housed in the former

Ministry of Education (SEP)

17th-century convent La Encarnación. To reach it, go north-west on Calle Republica Argentina; it is situated between the streets Venezuela and L. G. Obregón.

Frescoes ► The building of the Ministry of Education contains excellent murals by Amado de la Cueva, Juan O'Gorman, Carlos Mérida and others, but most are by Diego Rivera. Rivera's frescoes depict predominantly the everyday life of the Mexican Indians. He created these frescoes between 1923 and 1928 and expressed in them his customary socio-critical spirit. Equally famous are the works by José Clemente Orozco in the stairway and the first floor above the main patio.

National Museum of Art The monumental National Museum is located a few blocks west of the Zócalo (Calle Tacuba 8, Metro station: Bellas Artes, line 2). The building used to house the Ministry of Transport and Public Works. Today, visitors can marvel here at a cross-section of Mexican art. Exhibits in the 22 halls of the National Museum of Art (Museo Nacional de Arte) include interesting Maya sculptures, religious art of the colonial period, landscape paintings from the 19th century and con-

El Caballito temporary art. In front of the palace stands a famous bronze statue by Manuel Tolsá showing Charles IV of Spain on horseback, dubbed »El Caballito« (the little horse) by the people. Tolsá's model was a similar statue by the French sculptor Girardon. El Caballito's original location was the Zócalo. However, after the Mexican War of Independence the statue was taken on an odyssey through several plazas in the city until it found its present place.

Mining Palace The Mining Palace (Palacio de Minería) is located opposite the museum at Calle Tacuba 5. The palace was built around 1800 by Manuel Tolsá in the French neo-classical style. Until 1954, the building housed the College for Mining Engineers. The palace contains a sizable collection of meteorites.

Correo Mayor (main post office) The main post office is situated next to the Mining Palace. The architect who designed this post office also designed the Museum of Fine Arts (Palacio de Bellas Artes). The top levels of the buildings house a postal museum. Philatelists will appreciate the wide range available at the counter for special issue stamps.

House of Tiles A special sight for visitors is the House of Tiles (Casa de los Azulejos) one block south between Avenida Cinco Mayo and Madero. The house was built in 1598, and 150 years later the Count of Valle de Orizaba had the house decorated with blue and white tiles from Puebla. From 1881 it served as a men's club until it was later converted into a drug store and soda fountain. **José Clemente Orozco** created the frescoes in the stairway in 1925. In 1914, **Emiliano Zapata and Pancho Villa** met here for breakfast after they had gained political power in Mexico City; a photo of the important historic meeting is displayed in the café.

At 181m/588ft the Torre Latinoamericana is the second tallest building in Mexico City, topped only by the 230m/755ft, 55-storey Torre Mayor, the tallest building in Latin America.

Since the completion of the Hotel de México, the 44-floor, 181.33m/ 594.9ft Latin American Tower is now only the second tallest building in Mexico City. The tower is situated at the corner of Avenida Madero and Lázaro Cárdenas south of the Metro station Bellas Artes. The look-out terrace on the 42nd floor provides an excellent view on the few clear days.

Latin American Tower

🕐
Opening times: daily 9am–10pm

The next building on the right is the Iturbide Palace (Palacio de Iturbide). Today, the Banco Nacional de México owns this nicely restored Baroque palace designed by Francisco Guerrero y Torres in 1780. Until 1823 it served as the residence of Agustín de Iturbide, the first emperor of Mexico. Now and then, the Banco Nacional (BANAMEX) hosts exhibitions in the inner courtyard of the building.

✷
Iturbide Palace

Study the colourful costumes of Indians from all regions in Mexico in the Serfin Museum (Museo Serfin), located one block east at Avenida Madero 33.

Serfin Museum

Alameda Central and Surroundings

The entrance to the beautiful Alameda Park (Parque Alameda Central) is less than 1km/0.6mi east of the main city square. This well-kept park offers shade and delights with its old trees, fountains and sculptures. It was established as early as 1592 and used to be a mar-

Alameda Central Park

ket (Tianguis) in pre-Columbian times. Nowadays, Sundays are particularly lively in the park when street vendors are numerous and musicians entertain the visitors. The Metro stations Bellas Artes and Hidalgo (lines 2 and 3) are located in the north-west part of the park.

Museum of Fine Arts

🕐 Opening times: Tue–Sun 10am–4pm

The massive marble building east of Alameda Park in Avenida Lázaro Cárdenas is the Museum of Fine Arts (Palacio de Bellas Artes). The building (1900–1904) was commissioned by the government under the dictator Porfirio Díaz and, for the most part, designed by the Italian architect Adami Boari. The palace clearly shows **Art Nouveau and Art Deco style elements**. Much of the building material consists of Carrara (Italian) marble. Due to its weight, the massive building has sunk more than 4m/13ft into the swampy ground over its lifetime; the sinking continued even after removing part of the dome covering in an attempt to reduce its weight. During construction work in front of the palace in the 1990s, about 2,000 pre-Hispanic artefacts and 200 graves from colonial times came to light. The headquarters of the National Institute of Fine Arts (Instituto Nacional de

Green oasis in the middle of the metropolis: the Alameda Park

Bellas Artes) since 1946, the palace now serves mostly as an opera house and concert hall.

Visitors can marvel at some of the most beautiful Mexican murals on the second and third floors of the building. Two of the murals are the works of **Rufino Tamayos** from the early 1950s titled *México de Hoy* (Mexico now) and *Nacimiento de la Nacionalidad* (birth of a nation). **Diego Rivera** contributed the *El Hombre, Contralor del Universo* (man, controller of the universe), which had originally been commissioned for the Rockefeller Centre in New York. The Rockefeller family had the work destroyed because it very clearly showed Rivera's anti-capitalistic ideology. Rivera however created the picture once again in 1934 in the Museum of Fine Arts – now showing his ideology with even more drama: see on the left the personification of capitalism, accompanied by death and war, while on the right, socialism unifies prosperity and peace. The northern part of the third floor shows the three parts of the work *Nueva Democracia* (new democracy) by **David Álfaro Siquieros** and the four part work *Carnival de la Vida Mexicana* (carnival of Mexican life, 1936) by Rivera. However, the most eye-catching and impressive mural is the one entitled *La Katharsis* (catharsis) created by **José Clemente Orozcos** in the mid-1930s.

◄ Frescoes

The large hall, the **Fine Arts Theatre** (Theatro de Bellas Artes), seats an audience of 3,500. The stage features a stained glass curtain weighing 22 tons. Dr. Atl (Gerardo Murillo) designed this curtain and Tiffany of New York executed it. Clever lighting effects enhance the rendition of the Valley of Mexico with the towering volcanoes Popocatépetl and Iztaccíhuatl in the background. The famous Ballet Folklórico gives three performances weekly here.

◄ Stained glass curtain

Don't miss the Franz Mayer Museum (Museo Franz Mayer) next to the San Juan de Dios church (Avenida Hidalgo 45 on the Plaza de Santa Veracruz). The German immigrant Franz Mayer created this **peaceful, quiet oasis** around an enchanting colonial patio on the premises of a beautifully restored 16th-century hospital.

F. Mayer Museum

Franz Mayer emigrated to Mexico in 1882. His collections include Chinese and Arabian art works from the 16th to 19th centuries as well as Mexican arts and crafts, such as tapestry, wood carvings, works in glass and paintings. Take some time out to relax here or have a snack and coffee in the cafeteria next door (open daily Tue to Sun 10am–5:45pm).

Atmospheric patio of the Franz Mayer Museum

Museum of Engraving

The Museum of Engraving (Museo de la Estampa) is also located in the Plaza de Santa Veracruz. The displays include works by important 19th and 20th-century artists. Interested visitors can also learn how engravings are made and what tools the artists use.

Museum of Mexican Arts and Crafts

In the Museum of Mexican Arts and Crafts, (Museo de Artes e Industrias Populares) at Juárez 44 opposite the Benito Juárez monument, visitors can see and also buy contemporary arts and crafts.

✳
Diego Rivera Mural Museum

🕐
Opening times:
Tue–Sun
10am–6pm

The famous painting **Dream of a Sunday Afternoon in Alameda Park** by Diego Rivera (1947/48) was first exhibited in the hall of the Hotel del Prado (Juárez 70). When the hotel was destroyed in the earthquake of September 1985, the famous painting was recovered and can now be seen in a new building in the Plaza de Solidaridad. This plaza, which was constructed to take the place of buildings ravaged by earthquakes, is next to Alameda Park. The mural shows historic Mexican personalities like Cortés, Juárez, Santa Anna, Emperor Maximilian, Porfirio Díaz, Francisco Madero and General Victoriano Huerta. Between these personalities, there is a skeleton in a beautiful evening gown and next to it Rivera as a small boy and his wife Frida Kahlo.

A **scandal** erupted when the painting was first shown, because Rivera had included the inscription »Dios no existe« (God does not exist). For years, the mural remained covered until Rivera finally removed the controversial inscription by painting over it in 1958. It wasn't until the end of 1997 that a reproduction of the mural was displayed in place of the destroyed Prado hotel.

Vice-Regal Gallery of San Diego

The Vice-Regal Gallery of San Diego (Pinacoteca Virreinal de San Diego) is situated around the corner from the Rivera Mural Museum. Here, visitors can view colonial art. The style and ambience of this former convent have made it a venue for occasional evening concerts featuring classical music.

Around the Plaza de la República

Plaza de la República

The Plaza de la República is located about 600m/0.4mi west of Alameda Park. Once, a huge monument to the revolution stood here. The Metro station Revolución (line 2) is nearby.

Monument to the Revolution

Construction of today's Monument to the Revolution (Monumento de la Revolución) started at the beginning of the 20th century. Then, it was still intended as a meeting place for members of the Mexican parliament; however, the concept and construction plan changed after the Mexican revolution. The remains of the revolutionary leaders Francisco Madero, Venustiano Carranza, Pancho Villa, Lázaro Cárdenas and Plutarco Elías Calles (not public) are now entombed in the columns of the 67m/220ft-high domed monument. The museum exhibitions (**Museo de la Revolución**) on the ground floor inform about the revolution and how it started.

Spectators watch **Jai alai**, a popular sport in Mexico, in the large Art Deco stadium Frontón México on the northern side of the Plaza de la República.

Frontón México

The former palace of the Count of Buenavisto is located at the corner of Calle Puente Alvarado (No. 50). It is a neo-classical building which was designed by Manuel Tolsá at the beginning of the 19th century. In 1865, Emperor Maximilian of Mexico gave the palace as a gift to Marshall François Bazaine, at that time the supreme commander of the French troops. Today, the building houses the San Carlos Museum (Museo San Carlos). Its new name is a reference to King Carlos III of Spain who commissioned the first collection of paintings. The museum displays a good collection of works by both Mexican and European artists, once exhibited at the Academia San Carlos. Among the paintings are works by Titian, Tintoretto, Goya and El Greco.

✱
San Carlos Museum

🕒
Opening times:
daily 10am–6pm
except on Tuesdays

The tall Art Deco building at the western side of Paseo de la Reforma and opposite Avenida Juárez houses the administrative centre of the National Lottery (Lotería Nacional). Picking the weekly winning numbers in the lottery is almost a national obsession.

National Lottery

View of the Paseo de la Reforma

Paseo de la Reforma · Zona Rosa

Paseo de la Reforma Paseo de la Reforma is the main traffic artery through Mexico City. Going east to west, it runs a total of 15km/9mi from Tlatelolco to the affluent district of Las Lomas at the western city limits. The actual boulevard however starts only at the corner of Avenida Benito Juárez and ends at Chapultepec Park. The boulevard is 60m/200ft wide and has six to eight lanes with a grass strip in the centre. It is lined by bronze statues of famous Mexicans, mostly heroes of the Wars of Independence and Intervention. The intersections are executed as large traffic islands (glorietas) with monuments and several trees. Modern high-rises with offices, hotels, restaurants, cinemas, shops and so on have almost completely replaced the patrician residences of colonial glory. The city owes this beautiful boulevard to Emperor Maximilian who wanted a direct connection between his residence in the Chapultepec Palace and his official domicile at the Zócalo. The boulevard is now named after the reforms implemented by Maximilian's opponent Benito Juárez in 1861. Metro stations: Hidalgo (lines 2 and 3), Chapultepec (line 1). There are also several bus stops along the boulevard.

Glorieta Cristóbal Colón The first large traffic island (glorieta) after Avenida Juárez crosses the boulevard is the Glorieta de Cristóbal Colón (Columbus statue). The French artist Cordier created the statue of Christopher Columbus and it was placed in the traffic island in 1877. A group of scholarly friars are shown as if gathering around the monument base; they are given credit for good works during colonial times and the integration of the Indians. Their names are Juan Pérez de Marchena, Diego de Deza, Pedro de Gante and Bartolomé de Las Casas.

Cuauhtémoc Monument The next traffic island south-west on Paseo de la Reforma features a statue of the last Aztec ruler Cuauhtémoc, donated to the city by Porfirio Díaz. Here, the 26km/16mi-long north-south axis, Avenida de los Insurgentes, intersects with Paseo de la Reforma.

Jardín del Arte The Jardín del Arte is located two blocks north-east of these monuments. The quiet garden provides some shade. On Sundays, it is a popular platform and stage for all kinds of street artists in the city.

Centro Bursátil Arguably the most interesting of the many modern buildings is the Centro Bursátil with its mirrored glass fronts (No. 255). This beautiful building houses the stock exchange.

Zona Rosa The Zona Rosa (pink zone, colonia Juárez) stretches south parallel to Paseo de la Reforma as far as the Avenida Chapultepec. This quarter of the city is the preferred domicile of many hotels, restaurants, night clubs, art galleries and elegant shops. Calle Londres 6 is the address of the Cabinet of Absurdities (Aunque Usted no le crea) and the Wax

On Sunday, thousands of Mexicans visit the Chapultepec Park. Great bunches of balloons are on sale, as well as pink candy floss, trays of sweets and filled tortillas.

Museum (**Museo de Cera**). The main attraction of the Wax Museum is a chamber displaying images of sacrificial victims of the Aztec. On this same street, go bargain hunting in the markets for clothing or arts and crafts.

The Independence Monument (Columna de la Independencia or Monumento de la Independencia) in the centre of the next but one traffic island (glorieta) after the Cuauhtémoc Monument can be seen from afar. The main part of the monument consists of a winged victory goddess on a high column, known as **El Ángel** (the angel). This monument, too, was commissioned by the dictator Díaz to commemorate the first 100 years of Mexican independence in 1910. At the base of the column stand statues of Mexican heroes, among them the leaders of the independence movement Miguel Hidalgo, Guerrero and Morelos.

Independence Monument

The crypt with the skulls of the freedom fighters Hidalgo, Adama, Allende and Jiménez has occasionally been open for viewing since March 1998. The monument sits on a thick cement foundation to prevent it from sinking further into the swampy ground. The surrounding ground however sinks by about 20cm/8in per year. Relative to the ground, therefore, the monument is getting taller and new steps to access it must be added in due time.

Bosque de Chapultepec

Popular destination for outings

Chapultepec Park (Grasshopper Hill Park) is an important recreational park for the city dwellers. With about 4 sq km/1.5 sq mi it is also **the largest park in Mexico City**. Chapultepec was once a Toltec castle, where the last Toltec ruler Huémac is said to have hanged himself in 1177 after fleeing from Tula. In 1299, the México (Aztec) ended a long period of migration by settling around the hill. Neighbouring tribes however chased them away only 20 years later. The poet-king Netzahualcóyotl (also known as the philosopher king) reputedly first created this park in the first half of the 15th century. As the power of the temple city of Tenochtitlán grew, the hill became the summer residence of the Aztec rulers. Via an aqueduct, springs from the hill provided water for the city; ruins of the aqueduct still stand in Avenida Chapultepec in the block between Calle Praga and Calle Warsovia. Portraits of the México rulers were sculpted into the eastern slope of the hill; fragments of these sculptures still exist. The park is full of old trees. The most impressive are the giant cedars and Montezuma cypresses (Ahuehuete in Nahuatl). Lakes, sport facilities, a beautiful botanical garden, a zoo, several museums and Chapultepec Castle attract many visitors. Mexico City residents in particular like to come here to hike, ride on horseback, have a picnic or enjoy the many events, such as concerts, plays, children's programs and other entertainment. Metro station: Chapultepec (line 1) Bus: several bus stops along Paseo de la Reforma (part of the boulevard traverses the park).

Chapultepec Castle

Monument to the Child Heroes

The monument to six young cadets, the Monument to the Child Heroes (Monumento a los Niños Héroes), stands at the main entrance to the park near Chapultepec Metro station. Three columns each flank a central statue in a semi-circle. Fountains in front of the semi-circle add style to the impressive monument. The statues with torches on top of each column represent six military cadets; the central sculpture shows a mother cradling a dying child cadet. The monument commemorates the heroic last stand of the cadets when US troops laid siege to Chapultepec Castle in 1847.

On a hill behind the monument towers Chapultepec Castle (Castillo de Chapultepec)). Visitors can reach the castle on foot or by bus or elevator. On the site of the Aztec grounds and constructions and later a Spanish hermitage, the viceroy, the Count of Gálvez, built himself a summer residence on the hill at the end of the 18th century. In 1841, the castle was converted to a military academy, which in 1847 became the last stronghold against the invading US troops. Emperor Maximilian and his wife Charlotte had the building remodelled in 1864/65 and used it as their residence. In 1884, the dictator Porfirio Díaz also chose to make the castle his summer residence.

Chapultepec Castle

In 1944, Chapultepec Castle became the site of the National Museum of History (Museo Nacional de Historia) with 193 exhibition halls. The museum shows a collection of pre-Columbian artefacts and reproductions of codices. There are also many exhibits elucidating the history of Mexico after the Spanish conquest. Among the exhibits are portraits of important figures in Mexican history as well as frescoes by Orozco (La Reforma y la Caida del Imperio, room 7), by Siqueiros (Del Porfirismo a la Revolución, room 13) and by O'Gorman (Retablo de la Independencia, room 7). The state coaches used by Emperor Maximilian, Benito Juárez and others are also notable. Emperor Maximilian and his wife lived in a part of the castle in the neo-classical style. They brought furniture from Europe with them to furnish their residence. There is a stunning view from the terrace.

★
◄ National Museum of History

On the way down from the castle visitors pass by the white, round building of the Historic Gallery, which displays portrayals of Mexican history from the War of Independence (1810–1821) to the time after the revolution. Enter the gallery on the uppermost floor and then follow the spiral path (caracol = snail) down to a round hall at the bottom. The exhibits in this hall deal exclusively with the foundation of Mexico in 1917.

Caracol Museum

North of the Monument to the Child Heroes amid a sculpture garden stand two round buildings which house the significant Museum of Modern Art (Museo de Arte Moderno). Alongside a retrospective of the art before and during colonial times, the exhibits consist of paintings and sculptures by 20th century Mexican artists like Dr. Atl, Rivera, Siqueiros, Orozco, Kahlo, Tamayo and O'Gorman. There are also temporary exhibitions of works by both Mexican and foreign artists. Among other notable works are the portrait of Lupe Marin (1938) by Rivera, Frida Kahlo's portrait of the two sides of her personality (Las Dos Fridas, 1939) and Zuniga's sculpture of an Indian woman.

★
Museum of Modern Art
🕐
Opening times:
Tue–Sun 10am–6pm

The beginnings of the zoo in Chapultepec Park (Parque Zoológico de Chapultepec) date back about 500 years. The zoo may have already been established under the ruler Nezahualcóyotl before the Spaniards arrived; it may quite possibly be the first zoo in the world.

Chapultepec Park, Zoo

Museo Nacional de Antropología Plan

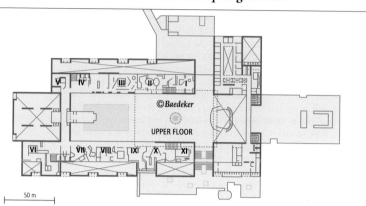

UPPER FLOOR
- I Introduction to ethnology
- II Sala Cora-Huichol
- II Sala Purépecha (Tarascans)
- IV Sala Otomi-Pame (Toluca Valley, Querétaro)
- V Sala de Puebla (Otomí, Tepehua, Totonac, Nahua)
- VI Sala de Oaxaca (Zapotec, Mixtec)
- VII Sala Totonaca y Huasteca
- VIII Sala Maya (highland)
- IX Sala Maya (lowland)
- X Sala del Norte (Seri, Tarahumara)
- XI »Indigenism« (measures to promote advancement of the Indians)

GROUND FLOOR
- I Sala del Resumen (overview)
- II Temporary exhibitions
- III Auditorium
- IV Most recent excavations
- V Introduction to anthropology
- VI Overview of Mesoamerican cultures
- VII Sala de Prehistoria (prehistory)
- VIII Sala del Periodo Preclásico (pre-classical or formative period)
- IX Sala de Teotihuacán
- X Sala de Tula (Toltec classical period)

- XI Sala Méxica (Aztec post-classical period)
- XII Sala de Oaxaca (Zapotec-Mixtec culture)
- XIII Sala de las Culturas del Golfo de México (cultures of the Gulf Coast)
- XIV Sala Maya
- XV Sala de las Culturas del Norte (northern cultures)
- XVI Sala de las Culturas de Occidente (western cultures)
- XVII Salón de Venta (museum shop)
- XVIII Statue of Chalchiuhtlicue (known as »Tláloc«)

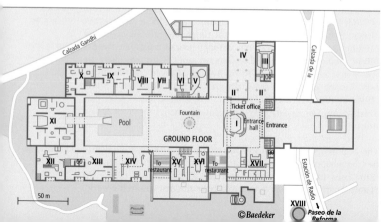

The zoo was the first outside China to raise a giant panda, a quite remarkable accomplishment. There are about 2,000 animal species here. Children are sure to like the animals, as well as the pony rides, train rides and rowing boats. Also worth seeing are the botanical garden (Jardín Botánico) and the National Auditorium (Auditorio Nacional) in the newer part of the park. The auditorium is a giant hall for cultural, sports and other events. It accommodates 15,000 people.

◄ National Auditorium

The National Museum of Anthropology (Museo Nacional de Antropología) in the northern part of the Chapultepec Park is one of the most remarkable museums in the world. The giant monolith at the entrance was generally accepted to be the rain god Tláloc. According to newer theories however, the statue probably represents Chalchiuhtlicue, the sister of Tláloc and goddess of the waters of the earth. The monolith weighs 167 tons. Found near San Miguel Coatlinchán in the area of Texcoco, transporting the unfinished colossus was very difficult. The museum was built in the 1960s and was designed by the architect Pedro Ramírez Vázquez. The building conveys harmony and impresses with its generous proportions. The presentation of the museum's extraordinary exhibits is also remarkable. Of particular note is the construction of architect José Chávez Morado's inner courtyard: an enormous stone shield on an 11m/36ft column provides shade for part of the area, and a screen of water falls from this shield and seeps into the ground as a symbol of the life-giving force of water.

★ ★
National Museum of Anthropology
⏱
Opening times:
Tue–Sat 9am–7pm,
Sun 10am–6pm

In both design and content, the museum is separated into two clearly defined areas: on the ground floor, visitors find an introduction to anthropology and finds from past Indian cultures, while the upper level exhibits tell about the lifestyles of the existing Indian cultures in Mexico. In the museum lobby, visitors find a good collection of books, museum guides and catalogues in several languages, as well as reproductions of pre-Columbian art. Video shows in the centre of the introductory exhibition room (Sala de Resumen) elucidate the content of the collections. On the right, a mural by Rufino Tamayo catches the eye. It shows the plumed serpent and the jaguar as incarnations of ancient

Wall paintings in the Sala Oaxaca (Zapotec-Mixtec culture)

Stone of the Fifth Sun Plan

1 Sun god Tonatiuh, ruler of the cosmic era of the »fifth sun«
2 Symbols of the previous four worlds, in between the points of the compass (clockwise): jaguar, water, fiery rain, wind
3 Circle with the 20 days of the Aztec month (clockwise): flower, rain, flint, movement, vulture, eagle, jaguar, cane, herb, monkey, hairless dog, water rabbit, deer, skull, snake, lizard, house wind, crocodile
4 Decorative ring wit the following symbo emphasizing the va of the sun:
  a eagle feathers
  b sunbeams
  c precious stones
  d drops of blood
5 Turquoise snakes w the sun god Tonati and the fire god Xluhtecutli looking of their throats

Indian gods. Here, visitors pay admission and buy tickets for guided tours.

The **round tour through the museum**, (anti-clockwise) also starts at the ticket counter. First stops on this circuit are the exhibition halls with alternating collections of artefacts from pre-Columbian cultures. Visitors who are pressed for time should at least see the Méxica and Maya exhibitions. However, please keep in mind that each exhibition hall features at least one highlight.

Exhibition hall: Pre-classical period ►
In the pre-classical or formative period (1400–300 BC), the Indians made the transition from a nomadic to a semi-sedentary society. The exhibits show the development of ceramics and other technical skills during this transition. Special exhibits in this hall are the figurines of Tlatilco, among them the so-called acrobat vase in the shape of a grotesquely distorted human form (mujer bonita) and the model of the pyramid of Cuicuico.

Teotihuacán exhibit ►
Exhibits in the next large exhibition hall elucidate the development of Teotihuacán, the first city in the Highland Valley of Mexico. The use of new materials such as shells, precious stones and stones show the advancement of the culture. Especially remarkable objects are the sculptures of various gods, among them Xipe Tótec (from Tlamimiloplan), Chalchiuhtlicue and Huehuetéotl. A section from the Quetzalcoátl Temple of Teotihuacán has been restored to show its original colouring. The fresco *Paradise of Tláloc* is also a reconstruction. It shows the souls of warriors and drowned people.

Tula exhibit ►
The most significant example of the Toltec culture in Tula is a gigantic Atlantean column. Further exemplary finds from the classical Toltec period (900–1200 AD) are stelae, Chac-mool sculptures and the

head of a warrior adorned with mother-of-pearl. The exhibits describe the Aztec culture from the immigration of the Chichimec to the fall of Tenochtitlán. Visitors find the museum's most precious exhibit here in this hall: the Stone of the Fifth Sun. It is sometimes mistakenly referred to as a calendar stone or sun stone. The stone has a diameter of 3.57m/11.7ft and weighs about 24 tons. It was created in 1479 shortly before the Spanish conquest. Depicted on the stone's surface is the Aztec belief regarding the five creations of the universe. Some believe that many humans were sacrificed on this stone to secure the favour of the sun god.

◄ Méxica exhibit

The centre of the stone shows the sun god Tonatiuh, the ruler of the cosmic age of the fifth sun. His tongue has the shape of a ritual knife and his claws hold human hearts. This is an indication that the sun god, or the sun, accepted sacrificed humans as nourishment. Glyphs for the four past cosmic eras are seen around the sun god: jaguar, water, rain and wind. This arrangement pointed to the date, on which the fifth – the current – universe would fall. It could be said that this prediction did indeed come true, albeit through the actions of the Spanish intruders. Two tur-

★ ★
◄ Piedra del Sol
(Stone of the
Fifth Sun)

quoise snakes can be seen at the outer bottom ring. From the mouths of these snakes emerge the rain god Tonatiuh and Xluhtecutli, the god of fire.

Further interesting items are the stone of Tizoc, codices, maps and sculptures of Coatlicue and Xochipillis, the god of love, dance and poetry. Montezuma's headdress made from the yellow feathers of the quetzal is unfortunately only a reproduction. The original is on show in the Vienna Museum of Ethnology.

DON'T MISS

- Stone of the Fifth Sun: it is impossible to overlook this very significant exhibit with its rendition of Aztec mythology.
- Olmec Heads: colossal basalt heads from San Lorenzo.
- Teotihuacán death mask: studded with turquoise and jade slivers.

Monte Alban was the central city of the Zapotec-Mixtec culture (500 BC to AD 1520). The majority of ceramic and gold artefacts originates from that region. Visitors can also see a recreation of the Monte Alban grave No. 7. Centrepieces in the collection are the green stone mask representing the bat god and the Yanhuitlán breast shield made from gold and turquoises.

◄ Oaxaca
exhibition

The list of artefacts representing the Indian cultures of the Gulf Coast includes Olmec colossal sculptures outside the museum building, Huastec stelae and painted ceramics as well as stone sculptures of hachas (small axes), yugos (yokes) and palmas (palm fronds). The latter stone sculptures are from El Tajín and probably relate to the regalia of players during ceremonial ball games.

◄ Exhibition of
Gulf of Mexico cul-
tures

During the night at Christmas in 1985, thieves robbed the museum. About one third of their loot consisted of pieces from the Maya exhibition – more proof, if it were needed, of how attractive this depart-

◄ Maya exhibition

ment is. The better part of the burial objects from Palenque, among them a jade mosaic mask and various artefacts made of gold, mother-of-pearl, turquoises and coral from the sacred well (cenote) of Chichén Itzá, were recovered in 1989. A reproduction of the famous sarcophagus lid of Palenque (Pakal's tomb) and, in the open-air exhibit, the reconstruction of the Temple of Murals in Bonampak with the famous frescoes are well worth seeing.

Northern and western cultures ► Burial objects, articles of daily use, ceramics and various finds from Casas Grandes and La Quemada give evidence of the northern Indian cultures. The exhibit also contains clay figures from Jalisco, Nayarit and Colima, representing the western cultures before the Spanish invasion. Finds from Tarasca complete the picture.

National Museum of Ethnology ► On the first floor, which is also subdivided into halls like those on the ground floor, exhibits concerning bygone cultures are replaced with those showing the lifestyles of the descendants of the respective tribes. The ethologic collections include the traditional costume, tools and houses of the Indian tribes in Mexico today. The concluding exhibits document existing programmes to support the Indian population and also show examples of their arts and crafts.

The museum also houses the National Anthropology Library, established in 1831 by Lucas Almán and sponsored by Emperor Maximilian. The library now owns more than 300,000 volumes.

Rufino Tamayo Museum
🕐
Opening times: daily 10am–6pm

East of the National Museum of Anthropology, at the corner of Paseo de la Reforma and Calzada Ghandhi, stands the Rufino Tamayo Museum.. Rufina Tamayo (1900–1991) is one of the most famous Mexican painters. The unusual concrete-and-glass multi-storey building was designed by Abraham Zabludovsky and Teodore González. Aside from the works of Tamayo, the museum also displays Tamayo's collection of works by contemporary artists (graphic arts, paintings, sculptures, tapestry etc).

Chapultepec second section Discover a few interesting places and events for children in the second section of Chapultepec Park, west of López Boulevard (Metro station: Constituyentes). There is for example **La Feria – Chapultepec Mágico**, which is a mixture of park and fair. Note also the **Papalote Children's Museum**. This is a large interactive museum (not only) for children with almost 300 attractions in five different categories. Visitors can either continue gathering information in the neighbouring Technology Museum and the Museum of Natural History, or relax at one of the lakes.

Polanco

Polanco is a pretty residential area north of Chapultepec Park (close to the National Museum of Anthropology). It features a number of interesting museums, an abundance of art galleries and restaurants, several embassies, and expensive hotels and stores.

An impressive red marble building next to the Presidente Chapultepec hotel in Calle Campos Elíseos (Metro station: Auditorio) houses the new Cultural Centre of Contemporary Art (Centro Cultural de Arte Contemporáneo). This cultural centre, run by the television group Televisa, shows contemporary and especially vanguard art. Be sure to enquire about opening times before your visit.

Cultural Centre of Contemporary Art

North of the National Museum of Anthropology stands a museum dedicated to works by David Álfaro Siqueiros (Museo Sala de Arte Público David Álfaro Siqueiros, Tres Picos 29). The family of the famous muralist and member of the communist party has turned their former residence into a showcase for Siqueiro paintings, drawings, photographs, awards and documents.

David Álfaro Siqueiros Museum Hall of Public Art

Tlatelolco · Guadalupe

The city district of Tlatelolco, in which the almost 1 million sq m/0.4 sq mi residential area Conjunto Urbano Nonoalco-Tlatelolco is situated, is west of Tepito within reach of the city centre by taxi via Paseo de la Reforma in a northerly direction. The earthquake of 1985 severely damaged this part of Mexico City. One block of flats collapsed and buried hundreds of victims in the rubble. Many buildings in the area are currently empty because they are structurally unsafe. Metro station: Tlatelolco (line 3)

Tlatelolco

The Plaza de las Tres Culturas stands for the merging of three cultures: that of the Atzecs, the Spanish and modern Mexico.

Plaza de las Tres Culturas

The focal point and main attraction of the quarter is the Plaza de las Tres Culturas (Plaza of the Three Cultures, also known as Plaza Santiago de Tlatelolco). The plaza is intended to be a reminder of the pre-Columbian and Spanish heritage and its influence on the Mexican identity. One indication of this is the co-existence of different buildings, such as the Aztec pyramids of Tlatelolco, the 16th-century Baroque church Santiago de Tlatelolco and the modern building housing the Mexican State Department. The plaza is situated at approximately the same place that the main square of the pre-Columbian city **Tlatelolco** once was. Tlatelolco was Tenochtitlán's rival city until 1473 when the México took charge of the city and its ruler Moquihuix plunged to his death from the main pyramid. However, Tlatelolco remained the most important city for trade in the region. According to reports from the conquistadores, 60,000 buyers and sellers met every day to do business in the famous market. The Aztec mustered their last stand of resistance during the Spanish siege of Tenochtitlán in 1521. A commemorate plaque reads: »Cuauhtémoc heroically defended Tlatelolco but in August 1521, it fell into the hands of Hernán Cortés. There was no triumph and no defeat; rather the painful birth of **today's Mexico, a nation of Mestizos**«.

The plaza is also the symbol for modern day troubles: in 1968, the police used deadly force against demonstrators at the plaza. According to unofficial counts, 250 people died. After the earthquake of 1985, homeless people crowded the plaza, where tents provided makeshift shelter.

A path surrounds the ancient ruins with a main pyramid, remnants of several pyramid structures, platforms, stairs, walls, altars and a wall of skulls. One of the minor pyramids displays a well-preserved and beautiful relief of Aztec calendar glyphs. The Spanish invaders quickly recognized the significance of the plaza. First they built a monastery there and then, in 1609, the Baroque church Santiago de Tlatelolco. Part of the church was an old monastery, which housed the famous Colegio Imperial de Santa Cruz. In this school, Franciscan friars taught the talented sons of the Aztec nobility. One of their most significant teachers was Bernardino de Sahagún, the annalist of New Spain.

Basílica of Guadalupe

Those determined to understand the cult of Mexico's patron saint must make the trip to the Basílica de Guadalupe. Two churches are named after Guadalupe: one is the old Basilica of Our Lady of Guadalupe (Basílica de Nuestra Señora de Guadalupe), built in 1709 to replace a 16th-century shrine and subsequently remodelled several times; the other is the new basilica in a gigantic building which contains the cape with the effigy of the Holy Virgin.

The cult has its roots in a **legend**. On 9 December 1531, the baptized Aztec Juan Diego had a vision of the holy Virgin as a dark-skinned

View of the old Basílica de Guadalupe →

Indian woman. In the vision, the Virgin told him to go to the bishop and have him build a chapel for her in a certain place. Bishop Juan de Zumárraga did not believe the report and demanded evidence. Sure enough, the Virgin appeared to the Indian a second time on 12 December and made roses bloom on a hill in the midst of the dry season. Juan Diego picked the roses and brought them to the bishop wrapped in his cape. When he opened the cape with the roses it showed the image of the Virgin in a corona of light. Many catholics believe that this is the miraculous image of the Virgin of Guadalupe which now hangs in the new basilica. In 1531, the bishop had a shrine built on the hill Tepeyac, exactly at the location where an Aztec temple used to stand; the church and the image in it quickly became the destination for many pilgrims. Especially in view of the brutal colonial regime, Indians had been reluctant to become catholic. Now, converting them became much easier. Over centuries, the Virgin of Guadalupe was revered as the patron of the Indians and Mestizos. Later, the Mexican independence movement also laid claim to her. In 1810, the priest and freedom fighter Miguel Hidalgo went to fight under her banner.

In the Basilica of the Virgin of Guadalupe, there is an image of Mexico's patron saint which many believe can perform miracles.

Throughout the year, **tens of thousands of pilgrims** visit the basilica. On 12 December however, the anniversary of the second apparition of the Virgin Mary, the church and the plaza in front of it are crowded with countless worshippers. Dancers and pantomime artists in colourful garb perform, giving the celebration the character of a large folk festival (p.130). The faith in Our Lady of Guadalupe has taken hold in all parts of Mexican society and the faithful from other parts of Latin America come here as pilgrims. This type of popular faith is called the Guadalupe cult; clearly, many of its elements do not fit catholic doctrine and are often reminiscent of pre-Christian myths.

Basilica of Our Lady of Guadalupe

The main destination of the pilgrims is the modern Basilica of Our Lady of Guadalupe (Basílica de Nuestra Señora de Guadalupe) at the foot of the hill named Tepeyac. The new basilica was built because the old one was sinking further and further into the swampy ground, thus jeopardizing the safety of the worshippers. Some of the faithful approach the basilica on their knees to keep a vow or express their veneration. This modern church (consecrated in 1976) was built of concrete and marble. The designer was Pedro Ramírez Vázquez who also designed the National Museum of Anthropology. The church is spacious inside and can accommodate up to 20,000 people. Aside from the image of the Virgin of Guadalupe, the church does not contain any other paintings or statues. Visitors may wonder about the **conveyor belt** behind the main altar, which automatically transports the faithful past the image of the Virgin. A museum in the back of the old basilica (Museo de la Basílica de Guadalupe) displays a collection of retables and a variety of religious items.

The **Capilla del Pocito** (well chapel) from the late 18th century stands next to the old basilica. The architect of the building was Francisco de Guerrero y Torres. The domes are revetted with glazed tiles. Inside the chapel, water springs from a rock and visitors – believing in its healing attributes – collect it in containers.

Chapel on the hill

About 100m/106yd up the hill is the place where Juan Diego saw the apparition of the Virgin and where the Capilla de Cerrito (chapel on the hill) was built in the 18th century. Steps lead from the chapel to the Garden of Tepeyac and from there another path downhill ends in the main plaza. The Capilla de Indios (chapel of the Indians) is located at the plaza, close to the residence of Juan Diego, where he lived until his death in 1548.

Along the Insurgentes Sur

The fastest way to go south is on Avenida Insurgentes. After passing the traffic island dedicated to the Mexican insurgents (Glorieta de Insurgentes) at the Metro station Insurgentes, the avenida leads to the Ciudad Universitaria (University City).

Lama Park Visitors find Parque de la Lama about 3 km/ 2 mi after the intersection of the Insurgentes Sur and Paseo de la Reforma. This is the location of the Hotel de México, Mexico City's highest building.

Ciudad de México *Overview*

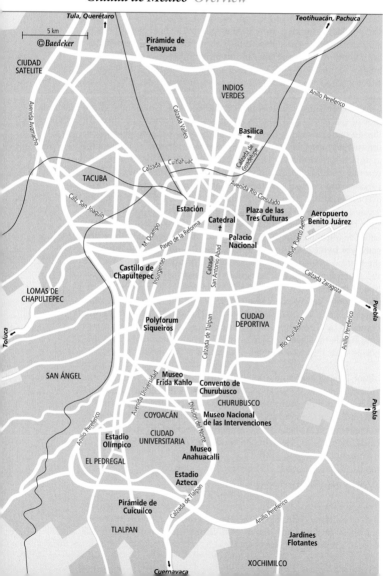

The modern Polyforum Siqueiros is situated in the hotel park in Calle Filadelfia. It is a dodecagonal, mushroom-shaped building. David Álfaro Siqueiros himself designed the building and the interior with its large egg-shaped room (1965–1969) featuring the giant mural *The March of Humanity*. The mural covers 2,400 sq m/25,933 sq ft. Regular video and audio shows in the hall explain what the mural represents.

✱ Polyforum Siqueiros

🕐 Opening times: daily 9am–6pm

The City of Sports (Ciudad de los Deportes) is situated another 3km/2mi south. Its soccer stadium seats 65,000. Another component, the Plaza Mexico, accommodates almost 60,000 and is the world's largest bullfight arena.

City of Sports

Shortly before San Ángel visitors pass the Teatro de los Insurgentes. The design of the mosaic covering its façade goes back to Diego Rivera and shows episodes and personalities from the theatre history of Mexico. The upper part features the insurgents from the War of Independence: on the left, Hidalgo, Morelos and Benito Juárez and on the right, Emiliano Zapata.

Teatro de los Insurgentes

San Ángel

Once a small village amid fields, San Ángel is now one of the prettiest suburbs of Mexico City and a popular destination for outings,

Tourist attraction: the Saturday market (Bazar Sábado) in San Ángel

with old colonial-style houses as well as modern buildings along the cobbled streets. The suburb, located 8.5km/5.3mi south of Chapultepec Park, features many historic sites, cafés, fine stores and restaurants. Avenida Insurgentes Sur runs in a north-south direction through the eastern part of San Ángel.

Saturday Bazaar

The Saturday Bazaar (Bazar Sábado) takes place in the picturesque Plaza San Jacinto. Here, Indians offer interesting crafts, such as wood carvings, ceramics and jewellery as well as woven or embroidered fabrics. Artists also display their works here. The turbulent and colourful market tends to spill over into the neighbouring streets all the way to the Plaza del Carmen. The garden of the Church of San Jacinto is the ideal place for a well-earned rest.

Casa del Risco Museum

The buildings No. 5 and 15 at the north side of the plaza house the Casa del Risco Museum (Museo Casa del Risco, also known as Cliff House). This is an 18th-century palace with valuable antiques and an interesting two-storey fountain made from tiles and porcelain. The displayed paintings are by 14th to 18th-century Mexican and European artists. The plaza also has historic significance: 16 Irish deserters from the US Army who had fought on the side of the Mexicans were caught and hanged here in 1847.

Diego Rivera and Frida Kahlo Studio-House Museum
⏱ Opening times: Tue–Sun 10am–6pm

In 1929, Juan O'Gorman built this vanguard utilitarian residence at the corner of today's streets Altavista and Rivera (Palmas). In two separate houses, Diego Rivera and Frida Kahlo lived here from 1934 until their divorce in 1940. Rivera remained in this residence until his death in 1957.

Today, the building houses a studio-museum. Visitors get a glimpse of Diego Rivera's life through personal documents, clothing, furniture, paintings, drawings and photographs.

Carrillo Gil Art Museum

The Carrillo Gil Art Museum at Avenida Revolución 1608 shows an unusually interesting collection of Mexican art. Works of the »three greats« (Rivera, Siqueiros and Orozco, ►Baedeker Special p.79) are on display here among others. The contemporary works in this museum consist mostly of graphic art.

El Carmen Museum

The Museo Colonial del Carmen (El Carmen Museum) is housed in a former Carmelite convent (Avenida Revolución 4), built by Fray Andrés de San Miguel in 1617. It was dedicated to the martyr San Ángel who gave the city its name. Richly decorated with glazed tiles, the building contains the Virgin of Carmen (made of Talavera tiles), a statue of Christ (made of sugar cane paste), a painting by Cristóbal de Villalpando and valuable religious items. There is a beautiful tile-covered well in the patio, and several mummies in the crypt, which also contains the graves of the nobility and nuns. See the beautifully panelled ceiling and fine colonial furniture in the vestry.

FRIDA AND DIEGO

**The marriage between perhaps
Mexico's two most famous artists was once described as being »like a
relationship between an elephant and a dove«. Frida Kahlo and Diego Rivera
were certainly an unusual couple to look upon. Rivera was an imposing giant
of a man whereas Frida was dainty and beautiful, often dressed in traditional
Indian garb and hardly reaching to her husband's shoulder.**

Diego Rivera (1886–1957) first met
Frida Kahlo when she was 21 years
old, while working on his first mural
for the Escuela Nacional Preparatoria
in Mexico City (see page 79) as she
paid a visit to the work. He was
already notorious at the time as an
inveterate womanizer.

Frida Kahlo (1907–1954) had suffered
from polio at the age of six and as a
result her right leg remained perma-
nently thinner then the left. This
turned out, though, to be just the
start of her tribulations. In 1925 she
suffered a serious **bus accident** from
which she was rescued more dead
than alive. She suffered innumerable
broken bones, a serious injury to the
spine and her lower body was smas-
hed. She was to suffer from the
consequences of the accident for the
rest of her life. However, her artistic
career began while she was recovering
in hospital. While she was forbidden
to move for months on end, a special
frame was set up alongside her bed.
This enabled her to start writing a
diary and to paint. Pain and suffering,
both physical and emotional, became
a central theme of her work.

1939: Frida Kahlo and Diego Rivera at the Hospital Inglés in Mexico City

Love-hate relationship

Kahlo and Rivera both associated with left leaning artists. They met again later in 1928 and married the following year. It was always an extraordinarily passionate love-hate relationship. Both were said to have had **several affairs**. Kahlo's beauty and unconventional manner were the talk of the town. During this period, Diego worked like a man possessed. He designed frescoes for dozens of the country's official buildings. His work also took him abroad to the U.S.A. where he was accompanied by Frida. In 1934, though, after four years in the States, Frida demanded that they return home. She was homesick, hurt by her husband's endless affairs and a painful miscarriage was the final straw. On their return the couple moved into a new home in San Ángel. It was in response to their invitation that the Russian revolutionary Leon Trotsky and his wife Natalia fled into exile in Mexico, moving into the house where Frida had been born, the Blue House in the suburb of Coyoacán. It was not long before Kahlo and Trotsky started an affair. After a series of fights, Frida and Diego **divorced** in 1939. However the following year **they married again**. Now she moved into the Blue House while he remained in San Ángel. There were still numerous affairs but the relationship between them persisted. Despite their rifts, Kahlo remained Rivera's most trusted critic and Diego was her most devoted fan. Kahlo had only one exhibition in Mexico in her whole life, which took place as late as 1953. A year later she died in the Blue House. Diego survived her for another four years.

Works in Mexico City

By contrast with Rivera's monumental murals with their clear social and political messages, Frida's paintings

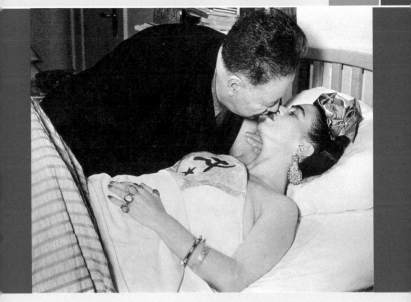

are small and puzzlingly intricate. Mostly, she herself is the centrepoint, gazing incorruptibly and challengingly at the viewer. It is obvious that her paintings contain **autobiographical references**, her childlessness, her declared love for Diego, her tormented body (enshrouded in a plaster corset or in the midst of an operation), her love of Mexico and its culture or her association with death are all present in her work.

In Mexico City more of Rivera's works can be seen than those of his wife, partly because he was more prolific and more in the public eye, but perhaps also because much of her work is to be found in private collections or in museums abroad.

In the **Centro Histórico** murals by Rivera can be seen in the Museo de Ildefonso (formerly the Escuela Nacional Preparatoria), in the Palacio Nacional and in the Secretría de Educación Pública (SEP). The Museo Mural Diego Rivera has the famous »Dream of a Sunday Afternoon in Alameda Park« and the Palacio de Bellas Artes has various other Rivera murals from the 1930s. They are both close to Alameda itself.

In **Coyoacán** you can visit Anahuacalli, the museum that Rivera himself designed for his collection of pre-Hispanic art and the Museo Frida Kahlo, situated in the famous Blue House where she was born and where Leon Trotsky briefly lived with his wife Natalia.

The house where the two artists lived together in the suburb of **San Ángel** is now the Museo Casa Estudio Diego Rivera y Frida Kahlo. The Museo de Arte Moderno in the Bosque de **Chapultepac** has works from both artists as does the Museo Dolores Olmedo Patiño **near Xochimilos**. The latter has more than 100 of Rivera's works and a room of paintings by Kahlo.

Álvaro Obregón Monument

The Álvaro-Obregón Monument commemorates the revolutionary hero and president who was murdered here in 1928. Located east of Avenida Insurgentes, it was created by Ignacio Asúnsolo. A rather macabre exhibit is found inside the granite monument: in a glass container, the right hand and underarm of the revolutionist, who lost this limb in battle during the revolution, is preserved in alcohol.

University City · Cuicuilco

Largest university in Latin America

Mexico City boasts Latin America's largest university. With more than 80 buildings on roughly 3 sq km/1.2 sq mi, University City extends east of Insurgentes Sur (2km/1.2mi south of San Andrés and 12km/7.5mi south-west of the Zócalo). Construction of the university began under President Miguel Alemáns and most of the buildings were added between 1950 and 1955. José García Villagrán, Mario Pani and Enrique del Moral were responsible for the main design and about 150 architects participated in the project.

University rector's office with Siqueiro frescos.

The most significant buildings are often decorated with ancient Indian symbols. The rectorate, with its harmoniously structured horizontal and vertical building elements (frescoes by Siqueiros), is one of these. Another is the central library which features a ten-storey, windowless book tower, whose façades Juan O'Gorman has covered with **the word's largest natural stone mosaic** (4 x 1200 sq m/12,900 sq ft). A distinctive attribute of the science auditiorium is a glass mosaic by José Chávez Morado and a special attraction in the Medical School is a mural by Francisco Eppens Huelguera. The sports facilities include large swimming pools, soccer pitches and baseball, tennis and Frontón (jai alai) courts. The modern concert hall (Sala de Netzahualcóyotl) south of the university's main building complex can seat 2,500 people.

Olympic Stadium

The Olympic Stadium (Estadio Olímpico) on the west side of Avenida Insurgentes was built for more than 80,000 spectators, and Diego Rivera decorated it with a colourful stone relief. Here, as in many other university buildings, the architects have integrated the art of pre-Columbian builders into the new designs. The university's botanical garden is situated not far from the Olympic Stadium.

About 3.5km/2.2mi south of the Olympic Stadium and immediately following the underpass Anillo Periférico, a street on the left leads to the archaeological site Cuicuilco (Plaza of Song and Dance) with its small museum.

Cuicuilco was probably established in the pre-Columbian formative period by agrarian people and was at the height of its civilization between 600 and 300 BC when it played a dominant role in the region. At this time the city state numbered 20,000 people. The rise of the rival city Teotihuacán however quickly diminished Cuicuilco's standing, and at the time of the cataclysmic eruption of the volcano Xitle, around 50 BC, people had already left the city.

Lava flow has engulfed the once 27m/89ft-high **Round Pyramid** with a diameter of 112m/367ft, and its ruin now stands only 18m/59ft tall. A part of the pyramid was damaged during the difficult excavation and the restoration is not considered very authentic. In all probability, the pyramid started out as an artificial mound, on top of which a new construction was built several times, each time over the existing pyramid. The architecture of the simple, fortress-like structure marks the beginning of pre-Columbian monumental architecture. The pyramid consists of five round sections of decreasing circumference ending in a platform with the remnants of an altar.

Further discoveries have also been made: next to the major pyramid, another pyramid which is probably even older; remnants of a horseshoe-shaped altar covered with gravel; and a chamber made of stone slabs on the right hand side of the main entrance to the major pyramid. Residual red paintings are still visible on the slabs. The excavations also turned up a large number of figurines, jewellery and items of daily use made from stone or clay.

Coyoacán

In Náhuatl, the language of the Aztec, Coyoacán means »place of coyotes«. Hernán Cortés resided here after he had destroyed Tenochtitlán. The famous Aztec stadium is sited on the periphery of Coyoacán.

The **three major attractions** of the district are the museums Frida Kahlo, Diego Rivera and Leon Trotsky, but many visitors and local people simply enjoy life in the streets and plazas. Weekend festivities clearly show that there mainly two focal points for social events: the Plaza Hidalgo in the eastern part of Coyoacán and the Centennial Garden (Jardín de Centenario) in the west. Metro: Coyoacán, Viveros, Quevedo (line 3) or General Anaya, (line 2).

Calle Francisco Sosa is lined with beautiful houses from the 17th and 18th centuries. The street leads to the main plaza, the Plaza Hidalgo, with the convent church San Bautista. In 1538, Dominicans had this church built in the typical architectural style of the 16th century. The side portal to the atrium, which shows rich decorations in the

Indian style, is notable, and the high-Baroque Capilla de Santisima inside the church on the left is well worth seeing.

Plaza Hidalgo and Centennial Garden
On the north side of the plaza stands the former city hall, also known as Casa de Cortés. Cuauhtémoc, then ruler of the Aztec, may have once been tortured here to extract the whereabouts of a treasure from him. At that time, the building (like all of Coyoacán) was the property of the Cortés family.

National Museum of Folk Culture
The building at Hidalgo 289 is located half a block east of the plaza, and houses the National Museum of Folk Culture (Museo Nacional de Culturas Populares). The museum offers more than just exhibits, it also puts visitors in touch with the current living traditions of the Mexican ethnic groups. An example of the engaging approaches taken to folk culture is an introduction to a Mexican version of wrestling, the »lucha libre«.

Plaza de la Conchita
It is believed that Cortés once built a house for his Indian lover and interpreter Malinche at the Plaza de la Conchita, formerly Plaza de la Concepción. The red house, named Casa Colorada, is situated at the corner of Avenida Higuera two blocks east of the Plaza Hidalgo. Some also claim that Cortés murdered his Spanish wife Catalina Juárez de Marcaida in this house.

★ ★
Frida Kahlo Museum
It is well worth visiting the Frida Kahlo Museum at the corner of Calle Allende and Londres. The well-known, rather small Blue House with green shutters is the birthplace of the painter (1907–1954), and she lived here with her husband Diego Rivera periodically from 1929 until her death.

The rooms have been kept as they were during the lifetime of the artist who spent much of her life in a wheelchair. Leon Trotsky was a guest here when he lived in Mexico (after 1937). Aside from personal items and works by both artists, the studio-museum shows mostly paintings and sculptures by 18th and 19th-century Mexican artists. Pre-Columbian artefacts from Frida Kahlo's private collection are also on display. While the exhibited works of Kahlo are less significant, they quite well express the pain in her life. The painting *El Marxismo Dará la Salud a los Enfermos* (Marxism gives health to the sick)

Figures in the patio of the Frida Kahlo Museum

shows the artist tossing her crutches aside. An unfinished portrait of Josef Stalin, a picture of her wheelchair and, famously, Rivera's hat lend the memorial a personal note (opening times: Tue–Sun 10am–6pm).

Exiled in Mexico, Leon Trotsky lived in a house turned fortress at the corner of the streets Viena and Morelos, now the Leon Trotsky Museum (Museo León Trotsky). Ramón Mercader, an agent working for Stalin, struck the Russian revolutionist Trotsky with an ice pick and killed him on 20 August 1940.
Trotsky's office has been kept as it was on the day of his murder. Even his broken glasses still sit on a desk. The plain bedroom shows the bullet holes from an earlier attack by Stalinists, in which the muralist David Álfaro Siqueiros participated; a plaque at the front door commemorates Robert Sheldon Hart, Trotsky's bodyguard, who was shot dead in the attack. Visitors can see the **graves of Trotsky and his wife** in the garden.

✳
Leon Trotsky Museum
🕐
Opening times: daily 10am–5pm

A former Franciscan monastery now houses the National Museum of the Interventions (Museo Nacional de las Intervenciones) in Calle 20 de Agosto, only a few minutes from the Metro station General Anaya (line 2). The museum opened in 1981 and its exhibits deal with the wars Mexico fought against foreign invaders. These are the War of Independence (1810–1821) and the following Spanish Intervention, the Mexican-American War (1846–1848), the French Interventions (1838 and 1861–1867) and, finally, the time of the revolution when US troops intervened in Mexico. The exhibits include photographs, weapons, paintings, flags and other historic documents. The documentation is interesting, albeit a little subjective.
In 1847, Mexicans fought the battle of Churubusco where the museum now stands. The Mexicans under General Anaya were outnumbered and lost this crucial battle against US troops under General Winfield Scott.

✳
National Museum of the Interventions
🕐
Opening times: Tue–Sun 9am–6pm

Follow Avenida División del Norte further south for a somewhat longer but very worthwhile side trip (about 3.5km/2.2mi south of the centre of Coyoacán). After 3km/2mi, turn right onto Calle del Museo to reach the Diego Rivera Museum. Rivera himself designed the House of Anáhuac (Anahuacalli) to exhibit his excellent collection of pre-Columbian artefacts.
The building is made of dark volcanic stone, shaped like a pyramid and reminiscent of a Maya tomb. The museum exhibits roughly 2,000 objects, mostly ceramics of the western cultures and Aztec stone sculptures. There is also a reconstruction of Rivera's studio. Among Rivera's works, *El Hombre en el Cruce de los Caminos* (man at the crossroads) is particularly interesting: it is a study for *El Hombre, Contralor del Universo* (man, controller of the universe), which is on display in the Palacio de Bellas Artes (Museum of Fine Arts).

✳ ✳
Anahuacalli (Diego Rivera Museum)
🕐
Opening times: Tue–Sun 10am–6pm

Aztec Stadium (Estadio Azteca)
The Aztec Stadium has become famous worldwide through the summer Olympic Games in 1968 and the Soccer World Cup in 1970 and 1986. From Avenida Division del Norte visitors can reach the stadium via Calzada Tlalpan. Completed in 1966, the stadium which was first known as »Estadio Guillerma Cañedam« but has since been renamed accommodates about 115,000 spectators.

Xochimilco and Surroundings

A labyrinth of lakes and canals
Xochimilco (in Náhuatl: place of the flower fields) is a popular destination for outings and excursions by boat. The small village is located well south of Mexico City, outside the beltway Anillo Periférico (about 20km/12.4mi south-east of the main city square). Some of the villagers are Nahua Indians. Probably, Toltec who had fled from Tula first settled in Xochimilco around the end of the 12th century. In the 13th century, a nomadic tribe related to the Aztec settled here; this tribe belonged to the Náhuatl language group. These settlers later became famous for their Chinampa system and were therefore named the Chinampanec. The Chinampa system refers to an agricultural method in which small, floating patches of mud and aquatic plants were held together with wickerwork and used for planting.

With time, these floating garden patches took root on the bottom of the lake. The abundance of water and the addition of fertile mud allowed up to seven harvests per year. The same system was also used elsewhere in the lake region, and the rich harvests secured the food supply for Tenochtitlán. Around 1430, the Aztec subjugated the settlers in Xochimilco. Heavy fighting took place here in 1521 during the Spanish conquest. Finally, the city was burned down. Visit the Dolores Olmedo Patiño Museum, one of the most beautiful museums in Mexico, a little more than 2km/1.2mi west of Xochimilco. Metro station: Tasqueña (line 2), and from there by tram or bus, or make use of a shared taxi service.

★★
Floating Gardens
The region around Xochimilco is still an important growing area for vegetables and flowers. Only a small portion of the lagoon is left today. Scarce water supply caused severe setbacks for the region in the 1980s. However, financial help from the UN has helped to open up more waterways: about 100km/62mi of these canals are now accessible. This means that the Floating Gardens of Xochimilco are a popular recreational region, where barques painted in bright colours navigate the network of canals, vendors offer food and beverages from boats and Mariachi musicians entertain the public. Xochimilco is a UNESCO **Word Heritage Site**. Standard boat rides start at the pier close to the Xochimilco village centre.

Xochimilco Ecological Park
The Xochimilco Ecological Park (Parque Ecológico de Xochimilco) has been created 4km/2.5mi north of the village. The nature preserve (2 sq km/0.8 sq mi) features a botanical garden, a sight-seeing train

Visitors can drift through a 150km/90mi maze of branching canals on colourfully decorated and painted boats.

and environmentally friendly canoes and pedal boats for discovery tours through the park. The beltway Anillo Periférico cuts through the park. A large market takes place north of the beltway, where people buy flowers and plants as well as arts and crafts.

At the Xochimilco village square, the parish church San Bernardino is well worth seeing. The church was built around 1590 and is one of the oldest religious structures in Mexico. The Indian Plateresque

San Bernardino

façade of the main porch and a rare 16th-century Renaissance retable are of particular note. The crucifix shows a Christ figure made of corn stalks using Indian techniques. The Saturday market is also worth a visit, and the same is true for the archaeology museum at the intersection of Avenida Tenochtitlán and Calle La Planta: see the 10,000-year old mammoth bones, regional pre-Hispanic finds and other exhibits.

✳
Dolores Olmedo Patiño Museum

🕐
Opening times:
Tue–Sun
10am–6pm

The Dolores Olmedo Patiño Museum is located at Avenida México 5843. The museum is housed in the private residence (La Noria Xochimilco) of one of Diego Rivera's some-time companions. It is situated in a landscape garden in which peacocks live. The exhibits include a large number of Rivera paintings, and works by his two wives (Angelina Beloff and Frida Kahlo) alternate with photographs by Dolores Olmedo. Dolores Olmedo died here in 2003.

On display is also a collection of arts and crafts as well as pre-Columbian artefacts.

Around Mexico City

Two important roads go north from Mexico City. The MEX 57D runs past the quiet colonial city of Tepotzotlán, and after the turning to ▶ Tula with its Toltec ruins, heads north-east toward Querétaro. The MEX 130D runs north-east from the capital to the former mining city ▶Pachuca. The MEX 132D branches off east towards the old convent in Acolman and the huge archaeological site of ▶Teotihuacán.

✳
Tenayuca

🕐
Opening times:
Tue–Sun
10am–4:45pm

Just outside the borders of the Distrito Federal and 12km/7.5mi north of central Mexico City, near Tlalnepantla, stands the magnificent **Serpent Pyramid of Tenayuca**. The first pyramid was created between the 13th and 16th centuries, and a new pyramid was built like a mantle around the existing one six times. As a product of the overlap of Toltec high culture and the rising Chichimec Empire, this pyramid is a classic example of the architecture of Aztec temple pyramids. The Serpent Pyramid was presumably dedicated to the sun god and was newly constructed every 52 years as prescribed by the rhythm of the Aztec calendar. The last times this was carried out were in 1351, 1403, 1455 and 1507, largely under Aztec influence.

Most of the currently visible structures originated with the last three rounds of re-building. The structure is in principle similar to the Templo Mayor of Tenochtitlán, which was destroyed almost completely, its remnants being discovered only a few years ago. A low wall with interlocking serpents surrounds the Serpent Pyramid on three sides. Today, this serpent wall (coatepantli) features 138 from an assumed 800 original snake sculptures. A crypt to the right of the pyramid is decorated with skulls and skeletal bones and probably symbolizes the setting sun.

The beautiful Augustinian settlement of San Agustín de Acolman is located in the highlands north-east of Mexico City (about 40km/ 25mi on the MEX 132D). It represents a 16th-century fortress-monastery building typical of New Spain. The monastery's cornerstone was laid as early as 1539; 40 years later, the monastery residents numbered 24 friars, 19 of which pursued their studies and five of which worked as missionaries to convert Indians. The construction of today's church started only around the middle of the 16th century: it features a wide Gothic interior and an early-Plateresque façade.

✱ **Acolman**

A small museum with displays from the early missionary period is located inside the monastery. The church has integrated an open chapel, typical for Mexico, to accommodate the newly baptized Indians. Floods destroyed the associated procession chapels, one of which has however been reconstructed. Outside the current atrium stands a beautiful **stone sculpture in the shape of a cross**. The centre

Mary Magdalene on the crucifixion fresco in the cloister of Acolman

of this cross shows the face of the suffering Christ. His arms and legs carry symbols of the path of his passion as well as flower ornaments.

Tepotzotlán

The pretty town of Tepotzotlán is situated only 35km/21mi north of Mexico City. It is especially well-known for a most interesting religious museum and its well-restored church, which is considered a **jewel of Mexican Baroque art**. The Jesuit school San Martín was established in 1582 in Tepotzotlán, which was then an Otomí settlement. The school was built by local craftsmen with the assistance of privileged, friendly Indians. In this Jesuit school, the Spaniards learnt the Indian languages Náhuatl and Otomí and the sons of the Indian nobility were taught the new religion.

In the 17th and 18th centuries the monastery was enlarged to a considerable extent. In 1767, the Jesuits were banned from New Spain. Church and school changed hands at that time. After Mexico had won its independence, the Jesuits returned to Tepotzotlán, albeit with less influence. They remained in Tepotzotlán until the secularization of Mexican monasteries in 1859. Nowadays, the monastery and church are administered by the National Institute of Anthropology and History (Instituto Nacional de Antropología e Historia).

! **Baedeker** TIP

Pastorelas

The Pastorelas (pastoral plays) are performed every year from 16 to 23 December in various towns, but especially impressively in the church patio in Tepotzotlán (about 50km/30mi north of Mexico City). Launched by the Spaniards in the 16th century to demonstrate to the Indians ideas of good and evil, the moralistic pastoral plays first took place in the church; later they were performed on the plaza. They portray dramatic, mysterious and comical aspects around the birth of Christ

---

★ ★

Church of San Francisco Javier ►

The façade of the convent church is one of the most excellent examples of the **ultra-Baroque style** in Mexico, next to similar church façades in La Valenciana near ►Guanajuato and in Santa Prisca in ►Taxco. The Church of San Francisco Javier was for the most part built between 1628 and 1762. Several artists worked on the church between 1760 and 1762, which in superbly harmonious design features estípites (upward flaring pedestals), niches with platforms and sculptures, and medaillons with reliefs.

Visitors see the statue of San Francisco Xavier above the window, and in the side niches the statues of St Ignacio de Loyola, St Francisco de Borja, St Luis Gonzaga and St Estanislao de Kotska, i.e. the most important personalities in the Jesuit order. The steeple consists of two sections and is also decorated with estípites. The small, backward recessed steeple on the left belongs to the Casa de Loreto.

Enter the church through the monastery. The wide nave contains seven beautiful altars in the typical ultra-Baroque style. They are mostly carved from wood and gilded. The main altar consists of three parts and its design resembles that of the outside façade. The statue of San Francisco Xavier forms the centre of the altar, which also features particularly expressive sculptures of the immaculate conception in the upper centre and of John the Baptist in the left niche. Adjacent to the nave is an octagonal room called the camarín, a highpoint of the Mexican high Baroque. Design and execution of the retables as well as the ceiling reveal the handiwork of Indian artists. Especially notable are the figures of the archangel and the black, oxidized designs made of silver. The early ribbed cross dome of the camarín still shows Mudéjar (Moorish) influence. Light streams in from alabaster windows and enhances the overall grandiose impression.

Today, the former Jesuit school houses the National Museum of the Viceroyship (Museo Nacional del Virreinato). Access the house chapel (Capilla Doméstica) via the cloister of the wells (Claustro de los Aljibes) and see in its vestibule (Portería) paintings by Miguel Cabrera. The building of the chapel dates back to the middle of the 17th century but it was later remodelled. The decorations in its dome show the crests of the six most important orders in New Spain, and the altar with sculptures, mirrors and paintings of Jesuit saints is particularly interesting. The exhibits in the numerous halls and corridors of the museum are from alternating art collections from the past viceroyship of New Spain. They are mostly religious art treasures from the 16th to 19th centuries. Some of the rooms are regularly used for concerts and theatre performances.

◄ National Museum of the Viceroyship

The MEX 190D east runs via fairly dry highlands to ►Puebla. Four scattered volcanoes are visible in the highlands, the well-known ► Popocatépetl (5,452m/17,887ft), the Iztaccíhuatl (5,286m/17,343ft), the peak of the ►Orizaba – at 5,747m/18,855ft Mexico's highest mountain – and La Malinche (4,461m/14,636ft). There is also the possibility of taking a trip to Tlaxcala and the murals of Cacaxtla (both ►Tlaxcala).

East of Mexico City

The MEX 95 and 95D from Mexico City south soon lead from an often sticky valley to the pleasant, aromatic shade of pine forests. Next on the route is ►Cuernavaca, the capital of the federal state of Morelos. An alternative route is the MEX 115D south-east to the Dominican monastery of Tepoztlán. To travel all the way to the silver city ►Taxco, continue south (about 170km/106mi south-west of Mexico City).

South of Mexico City

The MEX 15D runs west of Mexico City to ►Toluca, which boasts an interesting museum, several excavation sites and villages with an extensive arts and crafts industry. Consider a trip to Valle de Bravo if you would rather take a break from sight-seeing. En route to Taxco (see above), there are some interesting villages, such as the resort Ixtapan de la Sal (►Baedeker Tip p.576).

West of Mexico City

★ Mitla

S 22

Federal state: Oaxaca (Oax.)
Distance: 46 km/29 mi south-east of Oaxaca

Altitude: 1480m /4810ft

Although the ancient ruins of Mitla may not seem all that impressive in comparison to other archaeological sites, the elaborate stone ornaments here are unparalleled in Mesoamerican art history. Located south-east of Oaxaca, the site at the periphery of the small Zapotec town also called Mitla is one of the best known archaeological travel destinations in Mexico.

Archaeological finds in caves provide evidence that settlements existed in the mountains around today's Mitla as early as 6000 BC. Different tribes left their mark on Mitla (place of the dead) and the history is therefore often hard to fathom and still a matter of debate.

The well-known **abstract geometrical patterns** on Mitla's ancient buildings are reminiscent of Mixtec art. Recent research however points to the Zapotec as the builders of these sites and Mitla was their ceremonial centres. Their shaman (high priest) Uija-tao (Náhuatl: he who sees everything) probably resided here.

Ceramics unearthed in Mitla from the 14th century are however almost exclusively of Mixtec origin. This is consistent with a short Mixtec rule before the Zapotec regained power. Eventually, the Aztec conquered Mitla.

Mitla has certainly kept at least one of its secrets: in his 1679 report, the friar Francisco de Burgoas wrote about an as yet undiscovered tomb of Zapotec kings.

A Visit to the Archaeological Site

The archaeological zone comprises five important building groups and many houses and graves. The stone mosaics seem the most beautiful in the late afternoon when more intense **light and shadow effects** enhance the impressions and most visitors have left (opened daily 8am–6pm).

Typical stone mosaic in the Patio de las Grecas

The Columns Group (Grupo de las Columnas) is the most significant building complex. It is located in the eastern part of the site. The palace-like structure consists of two quadrangular courtyards, which meet at one corner. Three rooms surround each inner courtyard. A stairway on the north side of the first courtyard leads to the Hall of Columns (Salón de las Columnas), so called by the Spaniards because of the six large, round monolithic columns of volcanic stone. These columns once supported a roof.

A narrow, low passage leads to an inner courtyard known as Patio de las Grecas. This was supposedly the residence of the high priest (shaman) Uija-táo who was also the highest judicial authority in the region. The walls of the courtyard and the rooms are decorated with the typical Mitla **stone mosaics**. To create the mosaics, the builders covered the wall with plaster and then set precisely cut stones into it in very elaborate and always geometric patterns; there are **14 variations** of these.

★ **Columns Group**

MITLA

GETTING AROUND

From Oaxaca, drive east on the MEX 190 via El Tule for 38km/24mi, then turn left and drive another 4km/2.5mi to Mitla. A bus ride from Oaxaca to Mitla takes about 1 hour.

WHERE TO STAY

► **Budget**

Hotel Mitla
Independencia 12
Simple rooms with showers opposite the old hacienda with the La Sorpresa restaurant.

Bands with cross and woven patterns alternate with tiered meander lines, zig-zag friezes and other Greek ornamentation, the interplay of light and shadow enhancing the effect of this geometry. Some believe that the different repeating patterns symbolize the serpent god of the sky (Quetzalcóatl) or the duality of heaven and earth. An estimated 100,000 or more mosaic stones were used to decorate this building. The massive, expertly cut stone cubes, which serve as lintels and posts, are also typical of Mitla architecture. These blocks are up to 8m/26ft long and can weigh as much as 23 tons. The transport and placing of these stones is an amazing feat, all the more amazing in light of the fact that these people chose not to use the wheel and had neither pack nor draught animals.

★ **Patio de la Grecas**

Compared with the Hall of Columns, the adjacent inner Patio of the Tombs (also called the Patio de las Cruces) shows a less elaborate execution. The two cross-shaped tombs were found emptied. The so-called Pillar of Death (Columna de la Muerte) supports the ceiling in one of the northern chambers. Put your arms around the pillar: The amount of space between your hands indicates how long you have to live.

Patio de las Cruces

Mitla Plan

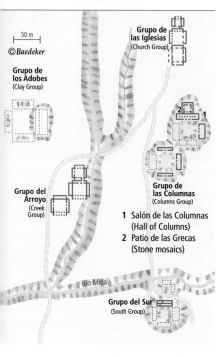

50 m

©Baedeker

Grupo de
los Adobes
(Clay Group)

Grupo de
las Iglesias
(Church Group)

Grupo del
Arroyo
(Creek
Group)

Grupo de
las Columnas
(Columns Group)

1 Salón de las Columnas
   (Hall of Columns)
2 Patio de las Grecas
   (Stone mosaics)

Río Mitla

Grupo del Sur
(South Group)

The **Church Group** (Grupo de las Iglesias) north of the Columns Group is so called because of the church of San Pablo, built by the Spanish conquerors in the midst of the ancient stonework. The layout of the Church Group is similar to that of the Columns Group, but the dimensions of the Church Group are smaller. A patio and part of the surrounding building were however destroyed when the church was built. The northern courtyard is still relatively intact and shows the characteristic mosaics on the walls and inside the chambers, as does a small inner courtyard.

These structures also feature the remains of friezes and murals which once decorated most lintels in the site. The friezes were mostly executed in the style of the Mixtec pictorial/ iconographic scripts, the most famous of which are the Codex Vindobonensis (Mexicanus I) and the Codex Becker I (Manuscript of the Chieftain).

Other building groups
Other building groups are located on the other side of the Río Mitla. There is the South Group (Grupo del Sur), the western Creek Group (Grupo del Arroyo) and the Clay Group (Grupo de Adobes). These structures have not as yet been completely excavated and restored.

Arts and crafts
All kinds of arts and crafts are for sale in the car park and also in the village where small shops line the main street. They offer a variety of embroidered, crocheted and woven items.

✳ Frissell Museum
The Frissell Museum (Museo Frissell de Arte Zapoteca) in the town of Mitla (population 11,000) displays the largest collection of pre-Hispanic ceramics from the Oaxaca Valley.

Around Mitla

Hacienda Xaaga
An interesting cruciform tomb has been found on the former sugar hacienda Doleres near Xaaga, which is also decorated with meander motifs and still shows parts of the original painting. The town of Xaaga is also known for treadle-loom weaving.

The Grupo de las Iglesias was built on top of Indian structures.

The so-called petrified waterfalls are located 25km/15.5mi south-east of Mitla in Hierve el Agua (travel via San Lorenzo). In two places, carbonate-containing, mineral-rich water tumbles over a cliff into a natural basin. Changes in pressure and temperature, the action of micro-organisms and particularly the release of carbonic acid have created a limy mineral-containing crust that sparkles in many colours. Bubbles rise up as the water percolates over and through the limy crust as if it was boiling (hence the name Hierve el Agua – where the water boils). Over thousands of years, this process has created a veritable petrified waterfall.

Hierve el Agua
(see fig. p. 9)

⚹ Monte Albán

Federal state: Oaxaca (Oax.)
Distance:: 10 km/6 mi south-west of Oaxaca

Altitude: 2,000m/6,500ft

Once the centre of Zapotec religion and power, Monte Albán – one of the most magnificent pyramid sites in Mexico – is raised up on a 400m/1,300ft-high artificial platform and towers over the subtropical Valley of Oaxaca.

The Monte Albán settlement stretches over 40 sq km/15 sq mi of land, including several mountains. In the course of 2,500 years, tribes other than the Zapotec have also used the site for their ceremonies. Built in 500 BC, Monte Albán was at its height between AD 500 and 600 when about 25,000 people lived in and around the city.

History There were settlements in the Valley of Oaxaca as early as 6000 BC. The beginning of the civilization which occurred around 1500 BC is called Tierras Largas. San José Mogote was the dominant civilization in the Oaxaca Valley until its fall around 1100 BC. Monte Albán (white hill) came probably into existence around 600 BC. The first calendar glyphs, particular the day glyphs in the 260-day calendar (Tzolkin), appear to have been carved in stone earlier than this. It is still not known whether the first settlers and builders of Monte Albán were Zapotec.

In any case, the **Monte Albán I** period (500–200 BC) also shows Olmec artistic influence. Between 500 and 400 BC, the people in the region created a settlement with urban character, and tombs with ceramics and carved stone blocks with flat reliefs showing human figures and the glyphs of the Tzolkin 260-day calendar remain from this time. The **Monte Albán II** period (200 BC–AD 200) reveals elements of the pre-Classical Maya culture in the south. The quality of the ceramics improved, the calendars became more comprehensive, and people built larger Cyclopean buildings.

 MONTE ALBÁN

GETTING AROUND

Travel the 10km/6mi between Oaxaca and Monte Albán by car or bus (30 minutes).

The height of the civilization coincides with the appearance of the Zapotec in Monte Albán. This cultural zenith is divided into the following periods: **Monte Albán III a** (until about AD 600) and **Monte Albán III b** (until about AD 800). These periods are characterized by the building activities; most of the important structures were built at that time. The architecture followed the talud-tablero style with sloped and very steep walls between platforms). The tombs of the time were executed with great artistry and contained beautiful frescoes and clay burial vessels in various shapes. The expanding high culture of Teotihuacán made its presence known and style elements from the central highlands appeared in Monte Albán in the first of these periods. At their close there were already Mixtec cultural influences. At the time, as many as 25,000 people lived in Monte Albán.

The fall began in the next period, **Monte Albán IV** (800–1200). Building activities ceased and decay befell the grandiose site, while the ancient cities of Lambityeco, Yagul, Mitla and Zaachila were either established or enlarged. Monte Albán probably declined to become a burial place for the Zapotec and later primarily for the Mixtec. The artistic execution of the ceramics became simpler and the tombs less lavish. The Mixtec dominated the last phase before the Spanish conquest, **Monte Albán V** (1200–1521). They built many tombs and re-used existing ones. The Aztec, who in 1486 established a base for their warriors where Oaxaca is situated today, had as little influence on the development of Monte Albán as the Spanish conquerors after their arrival in 1521.

Serious research was not done in Monte Albán until the 19th and 20th centuries. ► Oaxaca and Monte Albán became UNESCO World Heritage Sites in 1987.

A Visit to the Ruin Site

From the entrance to the site, adjacent to which is a small museum, a path winds its way uphill to the north platform and the Gran Plaza (200 x 300m/656 x 984ft), flanked on its eastern side by a ball court, a palace and a small temple platform, and on its northern side by three large temple complexes. At the southern end towers the pyramid on the Plataforma Sur (south platform). Various other buildings

Site design

Opening times:
daily 8am–6pm

At almost 2,000 years old, the temple city of Monte Albán is the oldest religious centre of the Zapotec in Mexico. It has been a UNESCO World Heritage Site since 1987.

Monte Albán Plan

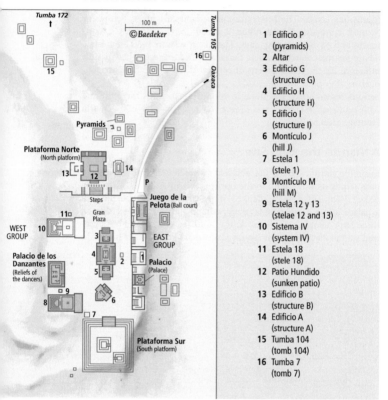

Tumba 172

100 m
©Baedeker

Tumba 105
Oaxaca

15

16

Pyramids

Plataforma Norte
(North platform)

13   12   14

Steps   P

Juego de la Pelota (Ball court)

Gran Plaza

11

WEST GROUP   10

3

EAST GROUP

Palacio de los Danzantes
(Reliefs of the dancers)

4   2   **Palacio** (Palace)

5   L

9

8   6

7

Plataforma Sur
(South platform)

1 Edificio P (pyramids)
2 Altar
3 Edificio G (structure G)
4 Edificio H (structure H)
5 Edificio I (structure I)
6 Montículo J (hill J)
7 Estela 1 (stele 1)
8 Montículo M (hill M)
9 Estela 12 y 13 (stelae 12 and 13)
10 Sistema IV (system IV)
11 Estela 18 (stele 18)
12 Patio Hundido (sunken patio)
13 Edificio B (structure B)
14 Edificio A (structure A)
15 Tumba 104 (tomb 104)
16 Tumba 7 (tomb 7)

in between do nothing to diminish the feeling of being in a vast space. Almost all structures are from the Monte Albán III period.

Gran Plaza   The Gran Plaza is the centre of the archaeological site. Because the plateau for the plaza was created by clearing away ground in some places and adding it in others – when rock was too hard to move it became part of a building, as with the north platform, the south platform and the building groups G, H and I – the structure is not perfectly symmetrical: the outside steps of the north and south platforms are for example not exactly opposite one another.

To hide this flaw the Zapotec added in period III two additional small buildings, one each in front of the buildings M and IV, which are separated by patios. As was common practice in pre-Columbian architecture, almost all buildings were eventually covered by a similar new one, some up to six times over. The walls received a coating of coloured stucco.

The first structure at the eastern side of the plaza (on the left when viewed from the car park) is the ball court (Juego de Pelota) in the shape of a Roman I. There are no stone rings on facing sides to serve as goals; these have been found in no ball courts in Oaxaca.

Ball court

The pyramid (Structure P) is the most important of the adjacent buildings. It features an inside stairway; priests could descend from the tip of the pyramid and reach the building group with structures G, H and I through tunnels – unnoticed by spectators outside.

Pyramid

The next structure in this group is called El Palacio (the palace). It too has a wide stairway. On the top platform, only remnants of walls are still standing; the now destroyed rooms probably served as residences for the priests. A cruciform tomb from the Monte Albán IV period has been found under the ground of the inner courtyard. There is a sunken altar between the palace and the middle row; the famous bat god mask made of jade was found here.

Palace

The fourth solitary building is named Montículo J (hill J). Unusual by shape and particularly by orientation, this interesting structure does not seem to fit into the site design. The building is aligned in a 45° angle relative to the other structures. The layout resembles the **tip of an arrow** with the stairway as the obtuse end. A vaulted tunnel traverses the front part of the building and leads upward. In Mesoamerican architecture, tunnels of this type served as part of observatories, but strangely, the heavens are not visible from this tunnel. Stone slabs with human figures and hieroglyphs are visible on the wall of the broad side: they appear to show the successful conquests of cities. For the most part, Montículo J seems to have been built quite some time before the Common Era, i.e. at the beginning of the Monte Albán II period.

✱
Montículo J

The Plataforma del Sur (south platform) at the southern end of the plaza is a huge structure. So far, only a small portion has been excavated. A 40m/131ft-wide stairway leads onto a platform from which there is a magnificent view of the entire site. The view is especially good at sunset.
Stele 1 stands at the north-west corner. It is one of the best preserved and most artistic stelae in Monte Albán. On the left, a jaguar sits on a hill wearing the headdress of the rain god Cocijo with a decorated lance in his hand. Other glyphs are visible in the top part and on the right side. Other stelae from this platform are located in the National Museum of Anthropology in Mexico City.

South platform

✱
◄ View

✱
◄ Stele 1

Montículo M (hill M) is located in the south-west corner of the plaza. The structure consists of two buildings that are separated by a patio with a small altar. As is the usual arrangement at this site, central stairs lead over 2 platforms with slanted rising walls between them to

Montículo M

the top platform. The four columns of the façade are all that remains of the temple on this platform. The front building on the north side was added during the Monte Albán III period to correct the symmetry. On the north side of the main building stand reproductions of stelae 12 and 13. The originals are also in the National Museum of Anthropology in Mexico City. The stelae are covered with number glyphs and relate to the adjacent building L (Palacio de los Danzantes).

✳
**Building L
(Palacio de los
Danzantes)**

Building L (Palacio de los Danzantes) is without doubt the most interesting structure on the site. Its altar dates to the 6th/5th century BC (Monte Albán period I). The first structure was covered by newer buildings several times; the final structure is a high two-platform building from the periods III a and III b.

✳ ✳
**Danzantes
(dancers) ▶**

The most important elements are the stone slabs, which once decorated a terrace wall. Reliefs on the slabs show figures, the so-called Danzantes (dancers). Today, the reliefs are subdivided into several groups and are known as »Galería de Prisoneros«. The facial expressions and glyphs show a clear similarity to Olmec art (La Venta Culture) on the Gulf of Mexico.

Calendar systems

Evidently, the inhabitants of Monte Albán used **a writing system as well as numerical and calendar systems** at the very beginnings of their time here. Previously, the distorted figures on the stone slabs were interpreted as being intoxicated dancers or possibly tortured slaves. The glyphs over the heads of the figures indicate to today's researchers that the figures represent important captives under the influence of drugs. Several of the stone slabs have been recently brought to museums; polyester reproductions have replaced the originals.

System IV

System IV, a pyramid complex, lies further south. It very closely resembles Montículo M. On the north side of the building complex stands the weather-beaten stele 18, which probably dates back to the period Monte Albán II.

North platform

A wide stairway leads up to the massive, 12m/39ft-high Plataforma del Norte (north platform). It is almost as large as the Gran Plaza. One cult room decorated with figures and glyphs and containing a tomb flanks each side of the stairway. Stele 9, showing reliefs on all four sides and considered the most important find of its kind, was found opposite the western cult room. This stele, too, is now displayed in the National Museum of Anthropology in Mexico City. Remnants of columns still stand in double rows; they have a diameter of 2m/6.6ft and once supported the roof of an enormous hall. Stairs lead down to the sunken patio (**Patio Hundido**) with an altar at its centre. This once finely sculpted rectangular altar served as the base for the stele 10 (now also in Mexico City).

The Palacio de los Danzantes contains bas-relief figures which due to their unusual posture have been interpreted as either dancers or captives.

Following a path north-west brings visitors to tomb 104 (Tumba 104), the **most beautiful of the tombs discovered in Monte Albán**. It was created around AD 500. A niche above the elaborate façade around the entrance contains a clay urn in the shape of a seated person who wears the headdress of the rain god Cocijo. All three sides of the burial chamber are decorated with coloured frescoes.

On the right side stands the statue of Titao Cazobi, the Zapotec god of maize with a large headdress showing the plumed serpent. There is a picture in the centre of the back wall above a niche depicting the head of an unknown red deity with a bow-shaped headdress, the hieroglyph »5 Turquoise« and the opening to heaven. The statue at the left wall has the face of a very old man. He carries a copal pouch in his hand and his waist, neck and head are richly adorned. The statue probably represents the god Xipe Tótec, the god of rebirth and protector of jewellers and the oppressed for the Zapotec, Mixtec and Aztec. The remains of an adult male were discovered in the burial chamber with a large urn – showing the same dignitary who is also depicted on the back wall. There are also four smaller urns.

Tomb 172   Tomb 172 lies below the hill with tomb 104 and contains the skeleton and the burial objects the way they were found.

Tomb 7   North-east of the Gran Plaza but slightly outside the actual ceremonial site (on the right when using the access road), lies the famous Tumba 7 (tomb 7). When it was discovered in 1932 the tomb, created by the Zapotec in the Monte Albán III period, became an archaeological sensation because it contained the largest treasure found in Mesoamerica to date. The antechamber contained Zapotec vessels and burial urns. Later, probably around the middle of the 14th century, the Mixtec buried the remains of their nobles here: among the

★ ★
Burial objects ►   Mixtec burial objects are **about 500 elaborate and finely crafted works of art**, created using gold, silver, jade, turquoise, rock crystal and alabaster. The burial objects are now kept in the Oaxaca Regional Museum (monastery Santo Domingo).

Tomb 105   Tomb 105, located on the Plumaje Hill, features a gate and interesting murals.

★ Montebello Lakes (Lagunas de Montebello)

S 27

Federal state: Chiapas (Chis.)
Distance: 52km/32mi east of Comitán

Altitude: from 1500m/4,921ft down

The Lagunas de Montebello (Montebello Lakes) comprise 60 small and medium-sized lakes. Sparkling in a variety of beautiful colours, the lakes cover the area from the entrance to the National Park (6,700ha/16,566ac) as far as Guatemala in the east and into La Selva Lacandona.

The lakes stretch through a terraced landscape, covered in large part by pine forests and still almost untouched. Aside from the lakes, there are also quite a number of sinkholes, grottoes and waterfalls. This is indeed a beautiful region for a holiday or an outing.

Lagunas de Colores   The road from the entrance to the National Park leads directly to the Lagunas de Colores (lakes of colours). True to their name, the lakes shimmer in **all shades from emerald-green to night-blue**. The shades of blue and green depend on the sun's rays, the depth of the water and its properties as well as the type of lake bed. The names of the lakes and their surroundings are as beautiful as the lakes themselves: Esmeralda, Bosque Azul (forest blue) and Agua Tinta (coloured water). It is possible to pitch a tent in Bosque Azul.
The **Arco de San Rafael** (Arc of San Rafael), a natural limestone bridge, is close to a small village. The Río Comitán flows under the bridge into a cave where it seemingly disappears. Another path leads

The Montebello Lakes glisten in a great variety of shades – from crystal turquoise to moss green.

from the park entrance in the direction of Tziscao. After about 3km/2mi, a path branches off to the **Laguna de Montebello**, one of the larger lakes.

The lake region called **Cinco Lagunas** (five lakes) is situated 3km/2mi further along the same road towards Tziscao. Four of the five lakes are in plain view right away. The last and the most beautiful lake, La Cañada, comes into view after taking a right turn and travelling another 1.5km/1mi.

A few miles further on Lago Tziscao, one of the largest lakes, comes into view. This lake forms border to Guatemala. Take the new road east along the Guatemalan border on to San Javier via Matzán and Benemérito. In San Javier, turn off and drive the 16km/10mi to Frontera de Corazal (from there a river boat sails to Yaxchilán, ►Bonampak • Yaxchilán).

Lago Tziscao

Around the Montebello Lakes

After 32km/20mi on the road which branches off the MEX 190 towards the Montebello Lakes, a left turn leads 2km/1.2mi along an unpaved road to Chinkultic. This **archaeological site** in the rocky cliffs at the edge of a forested mountain (elevation 1,600m/5,249ft) consists of ruins from the Maya classical period. The site is surrounded by a **charming lake and meadow landscape**. Remarkably,

Chinkultic

▶ VISITING MONTEBELLO LAKES

GETTING AROUND

The best route by bus or shared taxi to the Montebello Lakes is from Comitán de Domínguez.

By car, take the MEX 190 (Pan-American Highway) and drive 103km/64m from San Cristóbal de Las Casas to Comitán de Domínguez. Another 16km/10mi on, take a left turn close to La Trinitaria and drive another 40km/25mi to the Lagunas de Montebello National Park.
Only the first part of the road through the National Park is asphalted; country roads in various conditions lead to the individual lakes. Discovering this vast unmapped area without assistance is not an easy feat: it may be wise to hire a guide.

WHERE TO STAY

▶ Mid-range

Parador Museo Santa María
Carretera La Trinitaris –
Lagos Montebello Km 22
Tel./Fax (963) 632 51 16
www.paradorsantamaria.com.mx
The Parador Santa María is a converted hacienda (6 rooms). The hacienda was originally built in 1830. Each of the six rooms is furnished with antiques from a different period; some have open fireplaces. The food is excellent.

there is a sinkhole (cenote) here, far away as it is from the karst formations of Yucatán. In recent years, vegetation has reclaimed some of the already cleared structures. Archaeologists expect to find more Maya structures hidden under more than 200 hills of various sizes in the vast area. Today, little of the six main building groups is visible.
Among the finds so far are a **ball court** (juego de pelota) and several stelae with reliefs showing figures and glyphs. The north-western Structure A with the excavated Temple 1 (El Mirador) can hardly be overlooked. The temple stands atop an approximately 40m/131ft-high pyramid and rests on a terrace which is the base for four platforms. The forest has once again overgrown the wide outside stairway to the top of the pyramid.

Agua Azul The picturesque turquoise-blue cenote Agua Azul lies about 50m/164ft below the temple. Its presence raised the expectation of finding human sacrifices and sacrificial offerings, and the water was pumped from the cenote into the nearby Lake Chanujabab so that further excavations could be made. Indeed, this brought several ceramics to light. Aside from stelae and smoking vessels, a very valuable stone disk was unearthed. The so-called Chinkultic Disk has a diameter of 55cm/21.7in, weighs 78kg/172lbs and bears the date 590. It is a marker stone for the ceremonial ball game and shows a ball player with an elaborate headdress and cult regalia. The stone is on display in the National Museum of Anthropology in Mexico City.

Monterrey

J 18

Federal state: Nuevo León (N.L.)
Population: 3,300,000

Altitude: 538m/1,765ft
Distance:: 934km/580mi north of
Mexico City

The peculiarly jagged peaks of Cerro de las Silla (Saddle Mountain, 1,740m/5,711ft) and Cerro de la Mitra (Mitre Mountain, 2,380m/7,811ft) dominate the city of Monterrey in the Valley of Santa Catarina.

Monterrey is the capital of the federal state of Nuevo León and Mexico's **third largest city after Mexico City and Guadalajara**. As an important industrial centre, Monterrey is second only to Mexico City. FEMSA (Coca Cola Latin-America) for example is based here, and runs a large brewery which produces brands such as Sol and Dos Equis, among others. The city has undeniably developed into a modern metropolis, yet narrow alleys, flat roofs and picturesque patios will suddenly bring alive the old-Spanish atmosphere in some areas. The climate is hot and dry in summer, the winters cold and damp. Monterrey is a purely Spanish city with no recognizable Indian influence.

The area around Monterrey does not have an ancient Indian history. **History**
Nomads who passed through the region left few traces of their presence. In 1584, the first Spanish settlers under Luis Carvajal y de la Cueva arrived here and established the outpost Ojos de Santa Lucía. It wasn't until eleven years later that twelve Spanish families under the leadership of Diego de Montemayor made their home here, naming their village Villa de Nuestra Señora de Monterrey after the reigning viceroy, the Count of Monterrey. In 1775, the isolated settlement numbered only 258 inhabitants who often had to defend their homes against nomadic Indians. Troops occupied the village during the war between Mexico and the USA and French troops took the city in 1864. The city's

Palacio de Gobierno

fortunes changed only in 1882 when **the railroad between Laredo and Monterrey was built**. The city's economy has been growing ever since.

▶ VISITING MONTERREY

INFORMATION

Tourist information
Calle Hidalgo 477
Tel. (81) 83 45 08 70 or at
www.go2monterrey.com

GETTING AROUND

Flying from Mexico City to Monterrey takes 1.5 to 2 hours. The same trip takes about 16 hours by train or 12 hours by bus.

WHERE TO EAT

▶ Expensive

① *Luisiana*
Calle Hidalgo Ote. 530
Tel. (81) 83 43 15 61
This is most likely the swankiest restaurant in Monterrey with piano music in the evening. Specialities of the house are steaks and fish.

▶ Moderate

② *La Casa del Maíz*
Calle Abasolo Ote 870b (Dr Cross, Barrio Antiguo)
A trendy place with a creative menu. The memelas la maica are a special treat: thick, generously filled tortillas with a zesty spinach-and-cheese sauce. Spend a pleasant evening in the hip Akbal Lounge on the top floor (closed Sunday evenings and Mondays).

WHERE TO STAY

▶ Mid-range

① *Colonial*
Calle Hidalgo Ote. 530
Tel. (81) 83 80 68 00
The oldest hotel in Monterrey (100 rooms) is situated right in the centre of town. Check out the interesting antique lift. Nightly noise from a neighbourhood club especially affects guests who stay in rooms with windows onto the street.

② *Fundador*
Calle Montemayor 802
(Matamoros)
Tel. (81) 342 01 21
www.travelbymexico.com.mx
A good choice in Barrio Antiguo: colonial ambience, comfortable rooms and a recommended in-house restaurant.

Economy The favourable location in terms of transport connections have led to the rise of Monterrey as a centre for heavy industry. Consumer goods manufacturing in the area is based on the production of glass, cement, textiles and synthetic materials. An important factor is also the production of food and beer. Monterrey can take pride in its Instituto Tecnológico, which ranks as one of the best and largest Technical Universities in Latin America.

What to See in Monterrey

Gran Plaza The Gran Plaza was established in 1984 and is located between the Governor's Palace and the modern new city hall in the south. Modern and historic buildings surround its green spaces, trees and fountains. The plaza is almost 1km/0.6mi long and about 100m/328ft wide. The monuments of Miguel Hidalgo, José María Morelos, Benito Juárez and Mariano Escobedo are located along the Esplanada de los Héroes (Esplanade of the Heroes) close to the government building. The water of the spectacular 60 x 30m/197 x 98ft Neptune Fountain **Fuente de la Vida** cascades over three levels between the bronze sculptures of Luis Sanginio. Between 1603 and 1851, the **cathedral** with its single spire was built on the west side of the plaza. On the opposite side, a laser beam points up at night from the remarkable, 76m/249ft-high **monument by Luis Barragán** known as the Lighthouse of Commerce. The equestrian statue of General Zaragoza and the monument to the city's founder Diego de Montemayor stand in the centre of the southern part of the Gran Plaza. Rufino Tamayos's sculpture **Homenaje al Sol** (homage to the sun) has found its place next to the new city hall (Palacio Municipal).

The Plaza de Cinco Mayo with the statue of Benito Juárez in the centre forms the northern part of the Gran Plaza. This is the site of the Governor's Palace, which was built from sandstone. It is worth taking a look at the colonial patio and the representation rooms with a small exhibition of historic items, among them the guns used to shoot Emperor Maximilian and his generals in 1867. The rooms are decorated with frescoes. Diagonally opposite, the tower of the federal building offers a nice view.

Governor's Palace

The Museum of Contemporary Art (Museo de Arte Contemporáneo, MARCO) at the corner of Zuazo and Ocampo in the Gran Plaza, opened in 1991. Ricardo Legorreta designed the architecturally magnificent building. The interior design of the 14 exhibition halls around the atrium with a pond is very interesting. As well as from temporary exhibits, the museum also possesses a good collection of modern paintings. The focus is on Latin American and particularly on Mexican artists.

★
Museum of Contemporary Art

North of the museum towers the cathedral with its Baroque façade and a bell tower from 1851.

Cathedral

The Museum of Mexican History (Museo de la Mexicana) is situated a few streets further along in the direction of the Governor's Palace. Here too, much care has been taken over the architecture and interior design. The exhibits are related to the ancient Mesoamerican cultures, and there are also documents concerning the revolution as well as a collection of traditional costumes.

Museum of Mexican History

On the other side of the Gran Plaza opposite the cathedral, the small Plaza Hidalgo offers shade. Old colonial houses surround the statue of Hidalgo. The old city hall houses the **Metropolitan Museum of Monterrey** (Museo Metropolitano de Monterrey).

Plaza Hidalgo

Iglesia (Church) La Purísima ✴ West of the Plaza Hidalgo at the intersection of Avenida Padre Mier and Calle Serafín Peña stands the church La Purísima by Enrique de la Mora y Palomar, one of the best examples of modern sacral architecture in Mexico.

Cerro del Obispado At the western end of Avenida Padre Mier, the 18th-century Bishopric Palace towers over the Cerro del Obispado (Bishopric Mountain) or Chepe Vera. Later, the palace served alternately as a fortress and a hospital. In 1913, the infamous bandit and revolutionary hero **Pancho Villa** barricaded himself inside it. Today, the palace houses the Nuevo León Regional Museum (**Museo Regional de Nuevo León**). Significant sights include the chapel with its beautiful ultra-Baroque façade, the printing press used by Pater Servando Teresa de Mier during the Mexican War of Independence (1810–1821) to produce pamphlets against the Spanish rulers, and the two rifles reputedly used to shoot Emperor Maximilian and his generals in Querétaro.

Monterrey Plan

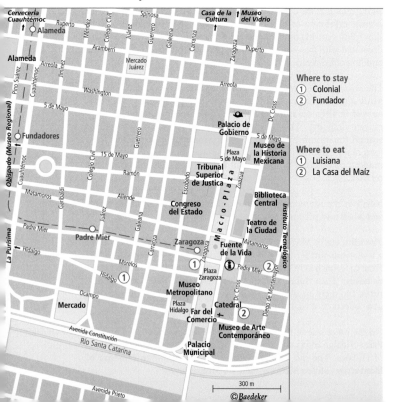

Where to stay
① Colonial
② Fundador

Where to eat
① Luisiana
② La Casa del Maíz

300 m

©Baedeker

The modern Institute of Technology (Instituto Tecnológico) in Calle Eugenio Garza Sada 2501 Sur, known as »El Tec«, has a **library** well-stocked with books about 16th-century Mexican history, books in Indian languages and a comprehensive collection of different editions of *Don Quijote*. Jorge González Camarena painted the mural in the library.

Institute of Technology

Mexican families like to visit the Child Heroes Park (Parque Niños Héroes), which is located about 3km/2mi north of the brewery Cervercería Cuauhtémoc. Aside from well-kept flower beds, there is also a small lake and a small art gallery.

Child Heroes Park

Other sights are the Espíritu Santo church, an asymmetrical building designed by Armando Rauize with a wall mosaic, the **House of Culture** (Casa de la Cultura in Calle Colón 400 Ote), the **Museo del Vidrio**, a museum about glass (Calle Zaragoza and Magallanes) and an old-timer museum in the suburb Del Valle (Calle Río Suchiata and Vasconcelos).

Other sights

Around Monterrey

Leaving the city heading south on Avenida Mesa Chipinque toward Club de Golf, the suburb of San Pedro Garza García is found 8km/5mi south of the centre. There, the Centro Cultural Alfa displays pre-Hispanic finds, works by Mexican painters, folk art, shells and minerals. There is also a planetarium providing insights into the world of astronomy. The planetarium has been built in the shape of an inverted cylinder.

Centro Cultural Alfa

After San Pedro Garza García the road leads to a forested mountain ridge (18km/11mi south of Monterrey), the Mesa Chipinque. There are beautiful views from the mountain over Monterrey and its surroundings.

Mesa Chipinque

Villa de Saniago is another 36km/22mi south on the MEX 85 towards Ciudad Victoria. From there, branch off to the impressive Cascadas Cola de Caballo (Horse Tail Falls). The water cascades down 30m/98ft, although sometimes the falls dry up.

Cascadas Cola de Caballo

Branching off to the left after about 18km/11mi on the MEX 40 to Saltillo brings you to the (Cañón de la Huasteca). The canyon is surrounded by bizarre rocks and its walls descend almost vertically to a depth of about 300m/984ft.

Huasteca Canyon

After 6 km/3.7mi on the same arterial road, turn off to the right and drive another 24km/15mi to the Garcia Caves (Grutas de Garcia). Here, **one of the largest and most beautiful cave systems in Mexico** awaits. The entrance to the caves is accessible only by cable car.

✴
Grutas de García

Morelia

P 17

Federal state: Michoacán (Mich.)
Population: 710,000

Altitude: 1,950m/6,400ft
Distance: approx. 300km/180mi west of Mexico City

Morelia is the beautiful capital of the federal state of Michoacán on the right bank of the Río Grande de Morelia. The city is situated in a wide, fertile valley between Mexico City and Guadalajara, the two largest Mexican cities. To this day, Morelia has retained the character of a genteel Spanish colonial city. The city centre has been a UNESCO World Heritage Centre since 1991.

History   In the middle of the 15th century, a group of Matlatzinca Indians (Purépecha), fleeing Aztec rule, settled in Morelia, then dominated by the Tarasca. Immediately following the Spanish conquest, the first Spaniard under Cristóbal de Olid came to the area and subjugated the Tarasca. The Franciscan cleric Juan de San Miguel established a mission convent in the region in 1537, an event which received first mention in the Spanish chronicle of the city. Commissioned by the first viceroy of New Spain, Antonio de Mendoza founded a township here with the name of Valladolid in 1541. Only six years later, Valladolid received the rank of a city. Competing with the Indian Pátzcuaro where the Bishop Vasco de Quiroga had his diocese, the Spanish Valladolid also became the seat of a Bishop in 1570 and then capital of Michoacán in 1582. In the 17th and 18th centuries, Morelia developed into a trade centre for regional agricultural products. From time to time, the city served the freedom fighter Miguel Hidalgo y Costilla as his temporary operational base during the Mexican War of Independence (1810–1821). In 1828, after Mexico won independence, the city was renamed Morelio to honour the local fighter for independence, priest **José María Morelos y Pavón** (1765–1815). Founded on Spanish cultural heritage, Morelio became an important intellectual centre over time, thanks mostly to its university.

> ! **Baedeker TIP**
>
> **Help us St Anthony!**
>
> Every Morelia local knows the restaurant San Miguelito and likes to show strangers its special atmosphere. A special favourite is the corner where San Antonio is standing on his head. Statues of the saint are closely packed, all of them with their feet pointing at the ceiling. Here, the single women of Morelia ask – either just for fun or rather more seriously – for a man who can stand on his own two feet. There is, however, a ritual to complete: take 13 coins from a plate of small change, light a candle, say a prayer and write a personal dictum in the "book of miracles, wishes and thanks". All of this must be done in full view of the other guests. Some women making the plea to the saint have already had success – though only those who entered their email address.

Morelia was named after the priest and freedom-fighting hero José Maria Morelos.

What to See in Morelia

On three sides, the beautiful main city square (Zócalo) is lined with arcades. The impressive cathedral occupies the entire east side. Construction of the cathedral using the light red-brown trachyte started in 1640. Even though construction took a long time, the unity of style did not suffer. A pure Baroque style predominates.

★ **Cathedral**

Strikingly, the dome is clad with glazed wall tiles, and the inner wings of the double door portal are covered with leather. Interesting interior features include the neo-classical retables, the silver baptismal font, a crucifix by Manuel Tolsá, and the impressive organ (built in Germany in 1903). Note also several paintings in the choir and the vestry which are attributed to the most significant painters of the first half of the 18th century. An Indian Christ figure (made from corn stalks) is kept in the vestry. The Spanish King Philipp II donated a gold crown for it.

● VISITING MORELIA

INFORMATION

Tourist information
Palacio Clavijero
Calle Nigromante 79
Tel. (443) 312 80 81

GETTING AROUND

Flying from Mexico City to Morelia takes about 45 minutes. The same trip lasts 10 hours by train and about 6.5 hours by bus.
The distance by car is 309km/192mi taking the MEX 15 via Toluca.

SHOPPING

Exhibits in the House of Artists (Casa de las Artesanías in the Plaza Valladolid/Avenida Humboldt) give visitors a good idea about the many arts and crafts in the region. There are beautiful woven textiles, wickerwork, lacquered items, ceramics and items made of wood or copper.

WHERE TO EAT

► Moderate

Las Trojes
Calle Juan Sebastián Bach 51
Tel. (443) 314 73 44
»Troje« is the term for the traditional house built by the Purépecha Indians. The restaurant consists of seven such nested wooden houses. It serves cuisine from the region.

WHERE TO STAY

► Luxury

Virrey de Mendoza
Avenida Madero Pte. 310
Tel. (443) 312 06 33
Fax (443) 312 67 19
www.hotelvirrey.com
The colonial house was built for a Spanish nobleman in 1565 and still displays some of its original lustre. The 55 rooms are furnished elegantly with antiques and Persian rugs.

Michoacán Regional Museum A Baroque building (mid-1700s) at the corner of the streets Allende and Abasolo houses the Michoacán Regional Museum (Museo Regional de Michoacán). The exhibits are from pre-Columbian times and the colonial era. Unti 1886, the museum building was the property of Francisca Román, one of the court ladies of Queen Charlotte. Therefore, we can assume that Emperor Maximilian of Habsburg stayed here in 1864 when he visited Morelia.

Governor's Palace Opposite the cathedral on the other side of Avenida Madero Oriente a Baroque building with an interesting patio serves as the Governor's Palace (Palacio de Gobierno). It features very large murals by the local artist Alfredo Zalce showing historic scenes relating to Mexican independence, the reform movement and the revolution.

Colegio de San Nicolás North on Calle Galeana and across Avenida Madero Poniente is the Colegio de San Nicolás (San Nicolas College). First founded 1540 in Pátzcuaro, the school later operated in a building built in the year 1580. After a similar school in Santa Cruz de Tlatelolco (1537), it is the second oldest college of its kind in the Americas. The freedom fighter and priest Miguel Hidalgo once taught here, and José María Morelos is the school's most famous student so far. Today, the Colegio de San Nicolás is part of the University of Morelia. The large patio with beautiful Baroque arcades is of particular note.

Opposite the San Nicolas College stands the massive Clavijero Palace (Palacio de Clavijero), named after the Jesuit professor Francisco Javier de Clavijero. The former Jesuit church (built between 1660 and 1681), the Iglesia de la Compañía, is part of the building complex. Today, the church serves as the **Public Library** (Biblioteca Pública). Next to the Clavijero Palace, the vendors in the sweets market (Mercado de Dulces) offer arts and crafts as well as sweets.

Palacio de Clavijero

✷

◄ Mercado de Dulces

Cross Calle Santiago Tapia to find the Santa Rosa de Lima church in a pretty little plaza. Construction of the church building started as early as the end of the 16th century. Its double-portal shows the influence of the Renaissance style, although for the façade as well as the gilded and painted retables the Baroque style in its Churrigueresque form (ultra-Baroque) dominates. The oldest conservatoire in the Americas is associated with this church.

Santa Rosa de Lima

Diagonally opposite, in the so-called House of the Empress (**La Casa de la Emperatriz**) in Calle Guillermo Prieto 176, is where Doña Ana Huarte, wife of the Emperor Agustín de Iturbide, spent her youth. Since 1986, the palace has housed the National Museum (Museo del Estado). Among the many exhibits are pre-Columbian pieces, traditional Indian costumes, a valuable collection of precious stones and minerals and a complete pharmacy from the 19th century. There are also mementos and documents relating to the history of Michoacán.

✷

Museo del Estado

The Museum of Colonial Art (Museo del Arte Colonial) is located a small distance further east along Calle Santiago Tapia; turn onto Avenida Benito Juárez (No. 240) at the intersection.

Museum of Colonial Art

The House of Culture (Casa de la Cultura) is found in the former monastery Convento del Carmen further north at the corner of Calle Humboldt and Fray Juan de San Miguel. Aside from archaeological artefacts, the exhibits include beautiful masks and Christ figures from all over Mexico.

Casa de la Cultura

The Church of San Francisco, located behind the Plaza Valladolid, was built in 1540: it is the oldest sacral building in the city. The façade is in the Renaissance style with Plateresque elements, and the small bell tower is covered with glazed tiles (azulejos). The convent used to be part of the church. Today, it houses the House of Artisans (Casa de las Artesanías). A variety of first-rate regional folk art, such as lacquered and copper items, wood carvings, ceramics and embroideries is on sale.

Church of San Francisco

✷

◄ House of Artisans

Morelos Museums	Two buildings in Morelia's old town are dedicated to the memory of the hero and fighter for independence José María Morelos. One is **the birthplace of Morelos** at the corner of Corregidora and García Obeso, a house containing letters and mementos. The second is the **Morelos Museum** in Morelos's later residence (Avenida Morelos 323). His weapons, uniform, frock and various documents are on display here.
Aqueduct	The aqueduct in the eastern part of the city was built between 1785 and 1789 and has become a Morelia landmark. The conduit carries water over a distance of 1,600m/5,250ft and is supported by 253 arches.
Other attractions	The churches San Agustín, Guadalupe, Santa Catalina and the Museum of Contemporary Art (Museo de Arte Contemporáneo) in the beautiful Cuauhtémoc Park are all worth a visit, as is Mexico's largest and most advanced planetarium.

Around Morelia

✳ Augustinian Monastery Cuitzeo	The northbound MEX 43 crosses the almost dry Cuitzeo Lake and after 35km/22mi leads to the township of Cuitzeo (population 17,000). This former fishing village is a favourite for the itinerary because of its Augustinian monastery built in 1551. The associated church features a beautifully ornamented façade mostly in the Spanish Plateresque style. The emblem of the Augustinian order (a flaming heart pierced by an arrow) can be seen above the portal, and each flanking column displays the sculpture of the Habsburg double eagle. The fortress-like design of the church and monastery, with its once much larger and enclosed atrium, is evident.
Pátzcuaro	Situated 58km/36mi along the road from Morelia to Uruapan is the city of Pátzcuaro. This city is a good base for outings to the interesting locations around ►Pátzcuaro Lake, in particular the archaeological site Tzintzuntzan.
✳ San José Purúa	Going toward Zitácuaro, there is a turnoff to the right after passing through the village Tuxpan (19km/12mi). A ride of about 8km/5mi on this road leads to the town of San José Purúa (population 35,000), whose picturesque thermal bath lies amid tropical vegetation at the rim of a deep gorge.
Los Alzati	Returning from San José Purúa on the MEX 15, a country lane on the left leads to the archaeological site of Los Alzati (Camají), 4km/2.5mi away. Recent investigations ascribe the ruined city to the Puréchepas (1200–1520). The site consists of a huge, multi-level pyramid. However, the pyramid complex has been excavated only to a small degree.

The next township after a ride of 2km/1.2mi on the MEX 15 is San Felipe de Alzati. From there, a road to the left leads after 24km/15mi via Ocampo to the former mining town of Angangueo, where it is possible to book a tour to the Mariposa Sanctuary (Santuario de la Mariposa Monarco). This is one of the pine forests in the volcanic highlands (elevation 3,000m/9,850ft) where monarch butterflies spend the winter, and the only one of these regions to be open to the public. Millions of monarch butterflies per year fly from Canada and the northern USA to these rare places in Mexico in the autumn. They will return north in April, lay their eggs and die. In recent years, deforestation, too many tourists and the often cold winters have considerably reduced the number of butterflies.

Angangueo

✹ ✹
◄ Monarch butterfly

The distance from San Felipe de Alzati to Zitácuaro is 9km/6mi, and from there it is another 97km/60mi to ► Toluca. ► Mexico City is now a mere 70km/43mi away.

Other destinations

Every year in late summer, millions of Monarch butterflies undertake the journey from southern Canada via the USA to Mexico, where they find optimal conditions until spring.

✳ ✳ Oaxaca

R 22

Federal state: Oaxaca (Oax.)	**Altitude:** 1,545m/5,069 ft
Population: 480,000	**Distance:** 440 km/264 mi south-east of Mexico City

In contrast to other Mexican colonial cities, Oaxaca has largely retained the character of a tranquil residential city. The mixture of Indian and Spanish elements is particularly attractive.

The historic centre of Oaxaca has been a **UNESCO World Heritage Site** since 1988. The charming city is located almost exactly in the centre of the federal state of Oaxaca. It lies in a valley with subtropical vegetation and is surrounded by the tall mountains of the Southern Sierra Madre.

History   Though Indian groups inhabited the Valley of Oaxaca as early as 6000 BC, an independent culture did not exist until San José Mogote (San-José phase, 1450–1050 BC). The transition to the Monte Albán I period took place between the 8th and 7th centuries BC. The development of the pre-Zapotec developed in the following periods into the Zapotec and Mixtec cultures, which spread through the regions around today's Oaxaca at a time when Oaxaca was still to be established. In 1486, invading Aztec under their ruler Ahuítzotl chose this location for the **Huaxyaca military fort** (Náhuatl: at the acacia grove). Spaniards under Francisco de Orozco invaded the area in 1521, subjugated the Indians and founded a small settlement, which was known as Antequera from 1529. As early as 1532, Emperor Karl V declared the settlement a royal city and gave it the name Oaxaca, which derives from the original name of the Aztec fort. Porfirio Díaz was born here in 1830. He was a Mestizo and partially of Mixtec descent. The national hero and later Mexican president Benito Juárez, a Zapotec, lived here as a governor of the federal state of Oaxaca from 1847 to 1852.

What to See in Oaxaca

Main city square (Zócalo)   ✳   The main city square (Plaza de Armas or Plaza Central) is the centre of the lively city of Oaxaca. The square features a pretty music pavilion, magnificent old trees and pretty arcade cafés. Not far away another pedestrian zone, the Alameda, is a good place to meet people. The unique and very lively annual Radish Festival (Fiesta de Rábanos) on 23 December takes place here.

The **Governor's Palace** (Palacio de Gobierno) on the south side of the plaza is built in the colonial style. A **mural** by Arturo García Bustos in the stairway shows the history of Oaxaca: the central part depicts Benito Juárez and his wife Margarita among others; on the right there is an image of old Mitla; and on the left several women are depicted, such as the nun and poet Juana Inés de la Cruz.

Construction of the **cathedral** on the north-west side started in the middle of the 16th century and lasted for roughly 200 years. The compact architecture with the two low towers is striking: it is meant to prevent damage during earthquakes. The mechanism of the unique tower clock, a gift from the king of Spain, is made entirely of wood. The Baroque façade exhibits finely worked statues and flat reliefs on the columns. In the church interior, executed in the neo-classical style, take a look at the eight engraved glass pictures and the chapels.

> **! Baedeker TIP**
>
> **The art of photography and more**
>
> The Centro Fotográfico Álvarez Bravo is situated at Calle Murguia 302. It has already created a stir with temporary exhibitions of high quality photographic artists such as Cartier-Bresson, Man Ray, Nacho Lopez or Walter Reuter, but also shows works by younger photographers and offers workshops. In addition, there is a specialized library here, containing thousands of volumes. For over a decade now, the Galeria Quetzcalli just a few steps away from the side entrance of the Santo Domingo church has been presenting regular works by contemporary artists and sculptors from Oaxaca, whose reputation has meanwhile extended as far as New York.

Like most **markets** in Oaxaca, the **Mercado Benito Juárez** in the main city square is a lively scene. Taking place in the old building in Calle Colón between the streets 20 de Noviembre and Miguel Cabrera, the activities are particularly interesting on Saturdays when Indians from the surrounding areas join in. The items on sale include textiles, pottery, leather articles, knives and machetes. The Artisan's Market (**Mercado de Artesanías**) in Calle J. P. García, near the I. Zaragoza, specializes in textiles. Vendors at the **Mercado del 20 de Noviembre**, framed by the streets Las Casas, Cabrera, Mina and 20 de Noviembre (south of the church San Juan de Dios), offer mostly food. Another lively market (mostly food) is the **Mercado de Abastos**, which is held on the other side of the train tracks south of the second-class bus station. Here too, on Saturdays, Indians from the region make it even busier than usual.

The pedestrianized Calle Alcalá runs from the city centre directly to the church of Santo Domingo. A beautiful colonial building in Calle Alcalá 202 houses the **Oaxaca Museum of Contemporary Art** (Museo de Arte Contemporáneo de Oaxaca, MACO). On display are works by painters from the federal state of Oaxaca, the famous Rufino Tamayo included.

Calle Alcalá

The church of Santo Domingo, built by the order of the Dominicans, is located five blocks north of the Zócalo. Construction started in 1575 and lasted more than 200 years. The total cost was more than 12 million gold pesos. The **Baroque façade** and the gilded frame of the portal are particularly impressive.

★ ★
Church of Santo Domingo

▶ VISITING OAXACA

INFORMATION

Tourist information

SEDETUR in the Palacio Municipal
Independencia 607
Tel. (951) 16 01 23 or
www.oaxaca.gob.mx/sedetur

GETTING AROUND

Flying from Mexico City to Oaxaca
takes about 50 minutes. The same trip
by train lasts about 15 hours and by
bus about 10 hours. The best route by
car is via the MEX 190.

EVENTS

Every year on 23 December since
1879, the Noche de Rábanos (night of
the radishes) takes place in the Plaza
de la Constitución. The showing of
the elaborately sculptured radishes
begins in the afternoon, as does the
hotly contested competition. Spectacular dance celebrations known as
Guelaguetzas are fun events on the
last two Mondays in July. Dance
groups from all over the state of
Oaxaca come and show their gorgeous, colourful costumes and perform their stirring traditional dances.

SHOPPING

Near and far, artists in Oaxaca are
known for the quality of their arts and
crafts, which are sold by Indians in
the streets. Women from the region
offer their textiles, ceramics, woven
items and jewellery in the cooperative
Mujeres Artesanas de las Regiones de
Oaxaca (women artisans of the
Oaxaca region) at Calle Cinco de
Mayo 204.

WHERE TO EAT

▶ Expensive

① *El Asador Vasco*
Portal de Flores 11
(on the west side of the Zócalo)
Tel. (951) 514 47 55
El Asador Vasco has the best and most
requested tables in town. This excellent restaurant offers Basque specialities and a view of the main city
square.

▶ Moderate

② *El Naranjo*
Calle Trujano 203
Tel. (951) 514 18 78
www.elnaranjo.com.mx
Only half a block away from the
Zócalo, the proprietor of El Naranjo
cooks the most delicious regional
meals in the covered patio.

WHERE TO STAY

▶ Luxury

① *Camino Real Oaxaca*
Calle 5 de Mayo 300
Tel. (951) 501 61 00
Fax (951) 516 07 32
www.caminoreal.com
The hotel is a converted, 400-year old
monastery and also has a colourful
history as a city hall, prison, cinema
and school. Some frescoes can still be
recognized on the first and second
floors. The 91 rooms are decorated
with Mexican textiles and ceramics.

▶ Luxury to mid-range

② *Victoria*
Lomas del Fortín 1
Tel. (951) 515 26 33
Fax (951) 515 24 11
www.hotelvictoriaoax.com.mx
Located on a hill about 10 minutes
away from the city, this hotel (150
rooms) is surrounded by well-kept
gardens. There is a beautiful view over
Oaxaca.

The church interior shows many gilded ornaments and coloured sculptures in high relief on the walls and ceiling, which contrast splendidly with the white background, creating the impression more of a palace than a church. The peasant style of the coloured sculptures gives the nave, the choir arch and the chapels an unmistakable Mexican note.

On the ceiling over the main entrance is a sculpture of a grapevine from whose golden branches and leaves grow 34 portraits making up the **family tree of St Domingo de Guzmán**, the founder of the Dominican order who died in 1221. Almost all the skilfully executed portraits wear a crown and the Virgin Mary sits on the top of the vine.

The largest and most beautiful of the twelve chapels is the **Rosary Chapel** (Capilla de la Virgen del Rosario), with its own choir, a vestry and even its own towers. The richly decorated altar with a figure of the Virgin Mary is considered a jewel of Mexican Rococo. Most of the original altars and decorations were destroyed in the 1860s when the church was temporarily used as a stable. The church was restored according to old records. (Open daily 7am–1pm and 2pm–8pm providing there is no Mass).

Stucco Dominican family tree in the Santo Domingo church

The adjacent former monastery of Santo Domingo now houses the Oaxaca Museum of the Cultures (Museo de las Culturas de Oaxaca). The exhibits on two floors include **archaeological and ethnologic collections relating to the Indian cultures** as well as Catholic and secular **colonial exhibits**. The ethnology collection includes traditional costumes, masks, jewellery and items for ceremonial and daily use of different Indian tribes in the region. Displays next door consist of finds from surrounding Zapotec and Mixtec sites. Photographs, charts and maps complete the exhibition.

The highlight of the archaeological department is the Mixtec treasure made from gold, jade, turquoises and other semi-precious stones. It

✳ **Oaxaca Museum**

✳ ✳ ◄ **Mixtec treasure**

Oaxaca *Plan*

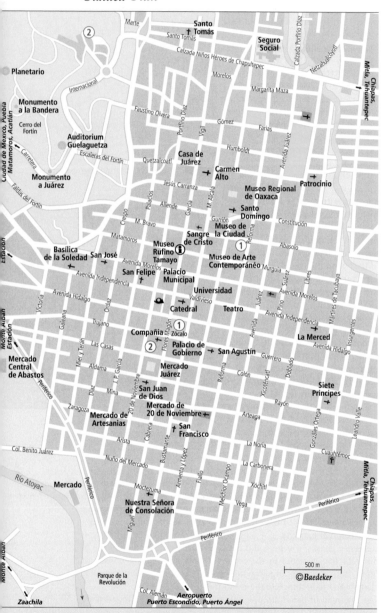

Where to stay
① Camino Real Oaxaca ② Victoria

Where to eat
① El Asador Vasco ② El Naranjo

was found in 1932 in tomb no. 7 in Monte Albán. Brilliant ancient artists formed these colourful materials into very beautiful arm bands, necklaces, adornments for the ears, breast shields and masks (open: Tue–Sun 10am–6pm).

The Rufino Tamayo Pre-Hispanic Museum (Museo Prehispánico Rufino Tamayo) is housed in a palace in Avenida Morelos (No. 503) four blocks away from the main city square. The famous Mexican painter Tamayo donated this museum to the people of Oaxaca. Exhibits in five rooms show **archaeological artefacts** left by the most important ancient cultures (open: Mon, Wed–Sat 10am–2pm and 4pm–7pm, Sun 10am–3pm).

Rufino Tamayo Pre-Hispanic Museum

Benito Juárez was born in 1806 in Guelatao near Oaxaca in 1806. Between 1818 and 1828 he served as a domestic servant in the house in García Vigil 609, now a museum featuring a variety of mementos of the man who later became Mexican president.

Museum Casa Benito Juárez

The patron saint of Oaxaca is Our Lady of Solitude. Her church (Basílica de Nuestra Señora de la Soledad) is located five blocks west of the main city square. Built between 1682 and 1690, it features a limestone cobbled atrium surrounded by a raised colonnade. The statue of the Virgin of Solitude (Virgen de la Soledad) wears a robe of black velvet embroidered with gold and precious stones and is adorned with an especially large pearl on its forehead.

✷ **Basilica of Our Lady of Solitude**

About 100m/328ft above the town on top of the hill Cerro de Fortín de Zaragoza stands an open-air theatre (also called the Guelaguetza amphitheatre) as well as a national monument in honour of Benito Juárez and the Mexican national flag. This hilltop ist he setting for the largest and most colourful annual event in the country, known as Guelaguetza or Lunes del Cerro (feast of Mondays on the hill). The festival takes place on the two Mondays following 16 July. The dances, performed by Indians from the federal state of Oaxaca, show a mixture of pre-Hispanic and Christian elements.

Cerro de Fortín de Zaragoza

✷ ◄ Guelaguetza

A communal public service association (Museos Comunitarios del Estado de Oaxaca, Dept. 12, Tinoco y Palacios 311, Tel. 516 57 86) offers **trips to a number of local museums** in the Valley of Oaxaca. These tours provide first-rate insights into the arts and crafts of the region and the agricultural methods, traditional forms of medicine and more. Tours also include participation in local festivities.

Museos Comunitarios

Around Oaxaca

The small village of Santa María del Tule is located about 10km/6mi east of Oaxaca on the MEX 190. The famous Tree of Tule (Árbol de Tule) stands in front of a charming little chapel. The **magnificent cy-**

✷ **Árbol de Tule (Tree of Tule)**

press is estimated to be 2000 years old. The tree is 40m/131ft high and has a circumference of 42m/137ft.

Tlacochahuaya
✳
Indian
paintings
(see fig. p.85) ▶

A branching road to the right after another 10km/6mi leads immediately to Tlacochahuaya with the 16th-century San Jerónimo church containing unique and colourful paintings. Here, Indians have expressed their artistic and religious ideas by painting the walls with suns, stars, angels, birds and flowers.

Teotitlán del Valle

Another 3km/2mi further on, a road branches off and leads after 5km/3mi to Teotitlán del Valle. This village with a pre-Hispanic history was built around a 17th-century church. It is known worldwide for its production of **ponchos** (serapes). Visitors can watch how the cochenilla dye (see Cuilapan p.450) is obtained from cochineal (scarlet red) bugs in La Grana Tejido.

Dainzú
🕐
Opening times:
daily 8am–6pm

Shortly after La Grana Tejido, a road branches off to the archaeological site Dainzú. The excavations have shown that Dainzú is a very old city which was inhabited from about 600 BC to AD 400, i.e. during the Monte Albán I to V periods. The city lies in beautiful surround-

The mighty Tree of Tule

ings and had its time of prosperity probably in the formative period (500–300 BC). Only a few of the buildings of this large Zapotec centre have been researched so far.

One of the most important buildings has a pyramid-shaped base and appears similar in architecture to the north platform in Monte Albán. Archaeologists have found a gallery of highly interesting flat processed stones on the south side of the lowest level. The reliefs on these flat stones show Olmec features similar to the »Danzantes« in Monte Albán. Among the images on the stones are ball players during a game and priests or deities with jaguars as patrons of the game. The main stairway of the building was added later (about 700). Rocks at the peak of the hill show figures and scenes similar to those on the gallery wall. The tomb of a ruler or priest has also been found at this site.

★
◄ Reliefs

Next to the road only a few miles from this site lies the archaeological site Lambityeco. This city was much larger than indicated by today's ruins. The time of its greatest power was between 900 and 1200, parallel to the fall and abandonment of Monte Albán by the Zapotec. The site has a small pyramid, underneath which an old house has been excavated, revealing seven tombs. Cut into the stone of the façade of tomb 5 are two heads and two names that may belong to the former owner of the house and his wife. Two impressive sculptures of the **Zapotec rain god Cocijo** were discovered in tomb 2, which was built over several prior structures. In a patio, friezes carved in stone show human figures and hieroglyphs. The patio also contains an altar and a tomb. According to current assumptions, the inhabitants left this city because it did not provide much natural protection and settled 5km/3mi away in the older cult site of Yagul (see below).

Lambityeco

About 2km/1.2mi further on, a short side road to the right leads to the old Zapotec city of Tlacolula with a parish church from the year 1647. The church is worth taking a look at. The Baroque façade is divided into three parts with round arches, columns, niches and a choir window. The interior is also predominately executed in the Baroque style, albeit with the usual local adaptations. The gate to the Christ Chapel (Capilla del Santo Cristo) and the choir and the pulpit balustrade are an excellent example of simple colonial wrought iron works. The chapel's imaginative and **masterfully executed stucco ornamentation** is similar to that in the Santo Domingo church in Oaxaca or the Rosary Chapel in ► Puebla. Depictions show Jesus Christ, the Virgin of Guadalupe and martyrs who carry their heads underneath their arms. The gold-framed mirrors (some showing the Habsburg double eagle), the silver chandeliers, the pews and the main altar made from silver are also worthy of note.

★
Parish Church of Tlacolula

The town of Tlacolula is also known for its picturesque and very lively Sunday market. From here, it is only 10km/6mi to ►Mitla.

★
◄ Sunday market

Yagul

⊙ Opening times:
daily 8am–6pm

In a landscape rich with cacti on the slope of a hill north-east of Tla-colula lies Yagul (15km/9mi west of Mitla, 34km/21mi east of Oaxa-ca). Yagul was once a **Zapotec and Mixtec religious centre**. On the top of a hill, from which there is a view of the Valley of Oaxaca, a fortress towers over temples and palaces built on three levels. While the earliest finds are from the time between 500 and 150 BC, Yagul was probably at its zenith around 1250 AD.

Most of the lower part of the archaeological zone has been excavated. This part contains the **Patio of the Triple Tomb** (Patio de la Triple Tumba) with four temples and an altar for sacrifices in the centre. On the left a sculpture of the rain god has the appearance of a seated frog. Stairs lead down from a platform in the centre of the patio to a tomb consisting of three chambers, the walls of which are elaborately adorned with stone skulls and which contained skeletons of dignita-ries as well as rich burial objects. The **ball court** (juego de pelota) is located in the second row of buildings. It is the second largest ball court of its kind in Mesoamerica after the one in Chichén Itzá. West of the ball court lies the large **Patio I**, which is framed by low terra-ces. The patio, which contains several tombs with decorated façades, is bordered at its northern end by the **Council Chamber** (Sala del Consejo), behind which is a path with mosaics in the Mitla style. The last row of buildings is called the **Palace of the Six Patios** (Pala-cio de los Seis Patios). This spacious labyrinth may have served as the residence of the ruler. In a long, narrow passage visitors can see stone mosaic patterns in the Mitla style.

The ascent to the fortress or **Structure U**, which is surrounded by a massive defensive wall, is cumbersome; but its interesting architec-ture and the marvellous view make the climb well worth the effort. Tombs were found here which may date back as far as the Monte Al-bán I period (600–200 BC).

Cuilapan

Cuilapan (12km/7.5mi south of Oaxaca) means »coyote river« in Na-huatl. It is the centre for the once important **cochinilla processing**, in which a scarlet-red dye is extracted from the cochineal bug which lives on cacti.

The church and monastery Santiago Apóstol, one of the largest buildings of its kind in Mexico, stand on a raised bank. Construction of the huge monastery began in 1555 but the structure was never completed. The Renaissance façade of the roofless basilica stands in front of two inner colonnades, parts of which have collapsed in an earthquake. On the left, a small staircase leads up to a pulpit cut from stone. The monastery was abandoned in 1663, when the Cath-olic order moved to Oaxaca. Its walls are almost 3m/10ft wide, and there are murals at the entrance describing the history of the reli-gious order. The Mexican president Vicente Guerrero was once in-carcerated here before his enemies shot him dead in 1831. There is a good view from the terrace on the second floor; the monks' cells were once to be found here. On the back wall, a highly interesting

Panorama of the ruins of Yagul

stone slab shows the pre-Columbian calendar glyph »10 Reef« and the date 1555. The church is the only building that is still in use; it is the burial place of a Zapotec princess, the daughter of the ruler Cocijo-eza who took the Christian name Juana Donaje after her baptism. The restored part of the monastery houses a museum with ethnological exhibits as well as colonial and modern art.

Ancient Indian ruins have been found near Cuilapan, among them a remarkable tomb with a pyramid built around it. This is an unusual architectural form for Mexico. An outer stairway with nine steps leads into an antechamber from which visitors pass underneath a beautiful stone lintel into the tomb.

Ancient Indian ruins

Further south on the same road, about 6km/4mi after Cuilapan, lies the village Zaachila. A market, at which mostly livestock is traded, takes place here every Thursday. The ruins of the last Zapotec capital, re-discovered only in 1962, stood here. As of yet, only the foundations of some buildings have been excavated. These are located on a low hill behind the Virgen de Juquila church.

Zaachila

The large central pyramid has been investigated only to a small extent. Tombs 1 and 2 are found in a patio within a rectangular platform. Two jaguar heads decorate the façade of tomb 1; in its antechamber there are two stucco owls with their wings spread. Inside the chamber itself stand statues of two rulers of the underworld with hearts hanging from their shoulders. They are each accompanied by a priest, called respectively »5 Flower« and »9 Flower«; both carry

★
◄ Graves

Cuilapan: the Renaissance façade unfortunately remains incomplete.

copal pouches. The back wall of the tomb shows a very old man with a headdress, tortoise-shell body armour and fire stones in his hands. Tomb 2 is much less elaborately furnished; however, this tomb contained valuable burial objects made of gold, jade and precious stones, now in the National Museum of Anthropology in Mexico City.

San José Mogote About 10km/6mi north-west of Oaxaca on the MEX 190 to Guadalupe Etla lies the archaeological site of San José Mogote. Of the several cities in the Oaxaca Valley, this was the most powerful in the period between 1100 and 900 BC. Around 500 BC, Monte Albán overpowered San José Mogote. One of the finds from the site at its zenith is a clay and stone structure with reliefs depicting the heads of a jaguar and predatory birds: these are the oldest stone sculptures found so far in Oaxaca.

Between 800 and 600 BC, ancient artists created a relief slab which served as the threshold to a structure. The relief depicts a naked, bent human form reminiscent of the later »Danzantes« of the Monte Albán I period. The displays in the small museum include reconstructions of tombs.

The small city of Huitzo is another 21km/13mi further on. Having passed through the town, a left-turn over railway tracks leads to the excavation site Huijazoo (Náhuatl: in the war fortress). This site also had a pre-Olmec history, and recently nine tombs were discovered here. The most remarkable is Tomb 5, which lies under a not yet fully explored pyramid. A snake mask forms the entrance to the tomb, which contains elaborately sculpted columns and coloured murals. In all likelihood, Zapotec created these frescoes of rulers and priests between the 8th and 10th centuries. The architecture and paintings are unique for this part of the country.

Huijazoo

! *Baedeker* TIP

Guelaguetza in Zimatlán de Álvarez

About 30km/19mi south of Oaxaca on the Carretera 131 towards Sola de Vega lies the Zapotec village Zimatlán de Álvarez. At the end of July, on the first Monday after the celebrations for the Virgin of Carmen, a Guelaguetza or Lunes de Cerro takes place here. This is a smaller version of the Guelaguetza in Oaxaca with a mixture of traditional Indian dances and Catholic rites.

The site is sometimes closed, and travellers should therefore ask for information before embarking on the trip.

Monastery Route in the Mixteca Alta

Aside from visiting the many interesting sights in and around the capital Oaxaca, a tour of the famous 16th-century Dominican monasteries in the Mixteca Mountains is also recommended. The monasteries are in easy reach on the MEX 190 not too far north-west of Oaxaca.

16th-century Dominican monasteries

For the most part, the road passes through cool highland valleys. In pre-Columbian times, this region was the core region of the Mixtec who settled here in large cities mostly between 1000 and 1521. The Spanish conquistadores, keen on a quick colonization, built a series of grand Dominican monasteries using destroyed Indian temples for their foundations.

It is a distance of 120km/75mi on the MEX 190 to the first monastery in Yanhuitlán , whose construction was completed in 1575. In the early years, this was probably the seat of the archbishop of the Mixteca. The relatively simple monastery church Santo Domingo was built on a platform to show the Mixtec how superior the new religion was. The wooden roof in the Moorish style is especially beautiful in the choir, and the resplendent main altar from the 17th century is decorated with sculptures and paintings that are ascribed to Andrés de la Concha.

Yanhuitlán
★
◄ Main altar

After another 15km/9mi north-west on the MEX 190, the MEX 125 turns south-west and leads after 12km/7.5mi to San Pedro y San Pablo Teposcolula. The ravages of time and an earthquake have all but

Teposcolula

destroyed the monastery in this small town where the Dominicans once introduced silkworm breeding; the townspeople still live from this industry. Although in ruins, the **open chapel** is one of the most excellent examples of 16th-century sacral architecture in Mexico.

Such open-air chapels, where mass baptisms were performed and sermons given, have been found exclusively in the New World. Based on Mixtec tradition, the town is host to the historic seat of the Teposcolula chieftains (La Casa de la Teposcolula), built in 1560 and serving as the centre of power for more than 200 years. The centre of the chieftains, a unique power structure in Latin America, reigned over the region of the Mixteca Alta.

The route of the Dominicans leads from Puebla to Chiapas: Teposcolula is one of the most impressive of the more than 70 monasteries and churches.

Tlaxiaco is located about 45km/28mi south-west of San Pedro y San Pablo on the MEX 125 via Santa María Asunción. The town's monastery is dedicated to the Assumption and was built in 1550. The Plateresque façade and the Gothic dome are noteworthy. The altars inside this church are in the neo-classical style.

Tlaxiaco

Returning to the MEX 190, a branching road on the right side 12km/7.5mi north-west leads, after a further 24km/15mi, to the town of San Juan Bautista Coixtlahuaca. This town was once the capital of the Mixteca Alta kingdom and an important trade centre. The church (1546) associated with the Dominican monastery has a notable Plateresque main façade with interesting sculptures and ornaments, and an ultra-Baroque altar in the interior. Sermons were once delivered to the masses from the beautiful **open chapel**, the ruins of which are close to the church. Late classical pre-Columbian buildings and many tombs have been discovered nearby.

Coixtlahuaca

✱

◄ Monastery church

Orizaba · Córdoba

Q 21/22

Federal state: Veracruz (Ver.)
Population: 320,000

Altitude: 1,250m/4,100ft
Distance: 285km/177mi east of Mexico City

The city of Orizaba at the foot of Mexico's tallest mountain, the 5,747m/18,855ft-high Pico de Orizaba, is located halfway between Puebla and Veracruz en route east from Mexico City to the Gulf of Mexico.

The Pellet hut, a base for a climb with pick axe and climbing iron in the thin air (7 hours up, 4 hours down) can be reached via the village Tlachichuca after 32km/20mi (see also the surroundings of ► Puebla, Acatzingo). Less avid climbers may prefer to visit the nearby colonial city of Córdoba and the beautiful park of Fortín de las Flores.

Orizaba (population 320,000) is an important traffic hub and also one of Mexico's most important industrial centres. Nevertheless, the city has retained its colonial character to some degree. Situated between mountains in a fertile valley with ample rain in the Eastern Sierra Madre, Orizaba has a temperate climate, and rain and the fertile land have helped the steady development of agriculture and industry. There are regional coffee and fruit plantations as well as marble quarries and power plants. The Moctezuma brewery, cement plants as well as cotton spinning and weaving works thrive in the city.

Important traffic hub

The once unimportant Indian village was conquered by the Aztec in the 15th century and became one of their staging posts. They named

► VISITING ORIZABA – CÓRDOBA

INFORMATION

Turismo in Córdoba
Palacio Nacional in the main city
square (opposite the cathedral)
Tel. (271) 712 11 40

GETTING AROUND

The MEX 150D is the best option to
go by car from Mexico City to
Orizaba and Córdoba. The trip takes
about 8 hours by train, a bus ride
takes about 4 hours.

WHERE TO EAT

► **Inexpensive**
El Cordobés
in the Zócalo (main city square)

Córdoba
Tel. (271)13 01
Good Mexican food served in
generous portions.

WHERE TO STAY

► **Mid-range**
Fiesta Cascada
Autopista Puebla-Córdoba
Km 275
Tel. (272) 724 15 96
Fax (272) 724 55 99
This hotel (50 rooms) is located on
the route from Puebla to Córdoba. It
has a pleasant garden, a restaurant
and conference rooms.

the post Ahuaializapán (pleasant water). In the 16th century the
Spaniards occupied the strategic site, and Emperor Maximilian of
Mexico and his wife Charlotte enjoyed staying here at the Hacienda
Jalapilla on the edge of the settlement. In 1973, an earthquake de-
stroyed part of the old city.

Sights
The massive, fortress-like **San Miguel** parish church is located on the
north side of the Castillo Park. Built between 1620 and 1729, this interesting church has several spires and a rectangular bell tower which
also serves as a meteorological station and observatory. One of the
spires is clad with wall tiles in the Mudéjar (Moorish) style. The remarkable vestry contains inlays, murals and paintings by the local artist Gabriel Barranco (19th century).

The **Palacio Municipal** (city hall) is a rarity. Starting out as the Belgian pavilion at the 1889 World Fair in Paris, the green and yellow
building is made entirely of steel. After the exhibition, it was taken
apart, transported to Orizaba in pieces and rebuilt to be put to use
again in 1914.

Since 1992, the former church San Felipe Neri houses the **Museum
of the State of Veracruz** (Museo del Estado de Veracruz), which displays works by European and Mexican painters.

★
Pico de
Orizaba
The Pico de Orizaba (Citlaltépetl), the highest mountain in Mexico,
rises 5,760m/18,900ft up into the sky. It is located at the border to
the federal state of Puebla, about 30km/19mi north of Orizaba. The

The highest volcanoes in Mexico are Citlaltépetl (also known as Pico de Orizaba) which at 5760m/18720ft is also Mexico's highest mountain, Popocatépetl and Iztaccíhuatl.

best way to approach the mountain is from the west side (surroundings of the city ▶Puebla).

Córdoba

Córdoba (population 200,000) is a picturesque city set amid lush vegetation in the valley of the Río Seco. Tropical fruits grow in the lowlands toward the hot coastal plains, and at medium altitudes coffee and tobacco is cultivated. The mountain slopes are often forested and mighty cedars and walnut trees grow here. Spaniards founded the city in 1618 and named it Córdoba after the Moorish residence in Andalusia. On 24 August 1821, Agustín de Iturbide (general and later Mexican emperor) and the last viceroy Juan O'Donojú (just newly sent over from Spain) signed the treaty of Córdoba, thus acknowledging Mexican independence. It was some time before Spain accepted the treaty.

Coffee, tobacco and sugar cane

The best coffee is harvested in the vicinity of Córdoba and Orizaba.

In the **Zócalo** (main city square) with its arcades stands the classical city hall (Palacio Municipal) and the Zevallos hotel, of historic interest because the treaty of Córdoba was signed here.

Another historic landmark is the **Casa Quemada** (burnt house) at the corner of Calle 7 and Avenida 5. When the War of Independence began, a small troop of Mexican freedom fighters staged their last stand against the Spaniards in this house.

The small **Córdoba City Museum** (Museo de la Ciudad de Cordoba in Calle 3 No. 303) exhibits finds mostly from the Totonac culture and also possesses a copy of the Treaty of Córdoba.

The market **Mercado Juárez** takes place between Calles 7 and 9 and Avenidas 8 and 10. A visit is especially enjoyable on Saturdays and Sundays when business is particularly active.

The **Fortín de las Flores** (Fort of Flowers) is situated only 6km/3.7mi west of the city on the MEX 150. There was a Spanish fortress here in colonial times but today the flowers blooming in abundance in the temperate climate make this a very pleasant place to spend some time. The beautiful main square consists of two equally sized parks connected by a narrow street. In the plaza stand the town hall and the public library.

At higher elevations, coffee plantations surround Fortín de las Flores, while fruits like mangoes, oranges, bananas, pineapple and papayas thrive in the lowlands. On a clear day and especially early in the morning, the **view of the snow-covered Pico de Orizaba** is excellent. It is worth browsing around Sunday's market. The annual flower festival takes place from 15 to 17 April.

Pachuca

O 20

Federal state: Hidalgo (Hgo.)
Population: 425,000

Altitude: 2,426m/7,960ft
Distance: 86km/53mi north-east of Mexico City

Pachuca, the capital of the federal state of Hidalgo, is surrounded by mountains on three sides. It is the centre of the oldest and richest mining region in Mexico. The city, with its steep sinuous alleys and beige painted houses, boasts a unique photography museum with a large historic collection. Interesting examples of colonial art can be found in villages in the surrounding area.

It is said that the Aztec founded a settlement here as early as 1490 to dig gold and silver from just under the surface of the earth. It was the conquistador Francisco Téllez who established the village Pachuca in 1528. The first boom occurred when, in 1555, Bartolomé de Medina discovered the process of amalgamation, a method to extract precious metals from ore via the formation of an alloy of mercury. New developments in the 18th century increased the yields of precious metals from the ore, thus creating another boom; most of the colonial buildings in the city were created around this time. Mines are still in operation at the edge of the city and in Real de Monte. Two acquirements go back to the mining tradition: one is »paste«, a special meat pasty, and the other is the game of soccer, both of which were introduced by miners from Cornwall in the 19th century.

What to See in Pachuca

One of the historic landmarks of the city is the fortress-like former treasury building Las Cajas from 1670, located at Calle Venustiano Carranza 106. The Quinto Real used to be deposited here, i.e. the fifth which the Spanish crown demanded from all mining proceeds.

Las Cajas

The former Franciscan convent Archivo Casasola e Hidalgo was built at the end of the 16th century. It has been remodelled and new parts have been added several times over the years. The centrepiece of the 18th century chapel, the Capilla de la Luz, is a beautiful ultra-Baroque altar. The convent complex houses the Hidalgo Cultural Centre (Centro Cultural Hidalgo), the museum of regional history (**Museo Histórico Regional**), which exhibits archaeological and ethnologic collections concerning the cultures of the Huastec, Chichimec, Toltec, Aztec and about Teotihuacán. It also displays military and religious objects.

Convent of San Francisco

In the adjacent building, the interesting and unique photography museum shows the famous **Casasola Collection**. Some of the photo-

★
Photography museum

● VISITING PACHUCA

INFORMATION

Tourist information
Reloj Monumental
in the main city square
Tel. (771) 715 14 11

GETTING AROUND

The distance between Mexico City
and Pachuca on the MEX 85 is about
86km/53mi. This trip takes about 2.5
hours by train and about 1.5 hours by
bus.

WHERE TO EAT

► **Inexpensive**
La Blanca
Calle Matamoros 201
(Col. Centro)
Tel. (771) 715 18 96

www.restaurantlablanca.com.mx
The restaurant offers folkloristic ambience and very good, simple and
inexpensive food.

WHERE TO STAY

► **Mid-range**
Hacienda San Miguel Regla
Huasca de Ocampo
Tel. (771) 792 01 02
This lodge (53 rooms) is a former
hacienda from the 18th century in the
village of Huasco about 30km/19mi
north-east of Pachuca. There is a pre-
Columbian aqueduct in the park
around the lodge.

graphs are from the late-19th and 20th centuries, and there are also
pictures from the Mexican revolution. The masterworks of star photographers such as Hugo Brehme, Tina Modotti (►Famous Persons),
Charles B. Waite, Edward Weston and Guillermo Kahlo are of particular interest.

Torre de Reloj The clock tower (Torre de Reloj) in the centre of the city is 40m/
131ft high with four sculptures in separate niches representing freedom, independence, reform and the Republic. The tower was built
on the occasion of the 100th anniversary of the Mexican independence. The clock was purchased from the same English clockmaker
who also created the legendary chimes of Big Ben in London.

Other buildings Other remarkable buildings include Las Casas Coloradas (built in
the 18th century and today the Court of Justice) and the 20th-cen-
tury theatre Teatro Efrén Rebolledo.

Around Pachuca

MEX 105 north Along the MEX 105 north, which runs through a **varied landscape**
featuring rock formations, mountains, canyons and fertile valleys,
are also many old mining towns and the interesting 16th-century sacral buildings of the Augustinian order.

A little further on from the old silver city Mineral del Monte (12km/7.5mi east of Pachuca) a road branches off toward the north-west. It leads to the picturesque old mining city Mineral del Chico (25km/15.5mi north of Pachuca), which is part of the **National Park El Chico**. Climbers will appreciate the park's interesting rock formations and walls and hikers love the trails through the pine forests. There are also beautiful rivers for all to enjoy, especially anglers.

Mineral del Chico

About 11km/7mi north of Mineral del Monte travellers get a chance to turn off to Huasca , visit its 17th-century church, its spas and take advantage of the many opportunities to see and buy arts and crafts. Many haciendas in the area are in the process of being turned into beautiful new hotels or lodges.

Huasca

An **Augustinian monastery** from the middle of the 16th century and a swimming pool next to hot springs await the traveller in the town of Atotonilco El Grande (34km/21mi north-east of Pachuca). The monastery church features a long nave with a very high ribbed dome and remnants of frescoes. The stairway of the monastery is adorned with depictions of great philosophers from antiquity.

Atotonilco El Grande

Typical church in a village near Pachuca

✳
Metztitlán

From there, the road runs downhill to Metzquititlán and the fertile valley of the Río Tulancingo. After 31km/19mi, a road branches off to the left. Metztitlán, once the capital of the independent domain of the Otomi also named Metztitlán, is another 22km/14mi further along this road. The Aztec never managed to subjugate the Otomi. Metztitlán is also the location of a **convent ruin** which is worth taking a look at. It has two large atriums, two open chapels, and one posa chapel. The view down to the valley is very beautiful from here. There is a large variety of cacti to be discovered.

Metzquititlán

10km/6mi further north on the main road lies the township of Metzquititlán. The 16th-century Augustinian church Señor de la Salud has a beautiful Indian-Plateresque portal frame in the Tequitqui style (Indian master masons sculpting European motifs using Indian craftsmanship).

Tulancingo

Tulancingo (population 112,000), the second largest city in the state of Hidalgo, is another 34km/21mi east on the MEX 130. For a short time, the city was the Toltec capital, until it was succeeded by Tula. A pyramid in Huapalcalco gives testimony to the city's time of glory.

Tenango de Doria

Tenango de Doria (40km/25mi north of Tulancingo) is an Otomi village and known for its colourful textiles with plant and animal patterns.

✳
Monastery fortress Actopan

The MEX 85 is also known as the Pan-American Highway. In a northern direction, it runs through the thickly forested and sometimes hazy Sierra Madre to the former monasteries Actopan and Ixmiquilpan.

✳ ✳
Renaissance frescoes ▶

Visitors find an interesting example of the sacral fortress building in the town of Actopan (37km/23mi north-west of Pachuca). The town's citizens are mostly Otomi. In 1548, Augustinian friars founded the **San Nicolas Monastery** (Convento San Nicolás) here, one of a series of monastery fortresses in the federal state of Hidalgo. Its beautiful Renaissance façade with Plateresque style elements is unique because the inner framing of the portal is repeated in the outer framing on a larger scale. The massive tower shows a Moorish influence. The 24m/79ft-high nave with its Gothic dome ends in an angular apse.

The former graveyard is located left of the church. It is surrounded by a defence wall. At the end of the churchyard stands the **open chapel** (Bóveda de Actopan = Dome of Actopan). The chapel consists of a large arch with bold vaulting; Indian artists have decorated the chapel with wall mosaics and colourful depictions of hell and perdition.

In a small room (Sala de Profundis), the history of the monastery is chronicled in medieval style. **Black and white Renaissance frescoes** (in various stages of preservation) decorate most of the monastery walls, an obvious contrast to the colourful art in the chapel. The frescoes are the most beautiful from this era in Mexico and mostly depict church elders and saints of the Augustinian order.

A side building of the monastery houses a museum of Otomi folk art.

Augustine as founder of a religious order

The city of **Ixmiquilpan** (75 km/ 47mi north-west of Pachuca) used to be the capital of the Otomi in pre-Columbian times. It is the site of an interesting **Augustinian monastery** (1550–1554). The monastery church is consecrated to San Miguel Arcángel and has a beautiful Renaissance Plateresque façade, Corinthian columns and an archivolt decorated with ceiling panels. Inventive frescoes created by an Indian artist and including battle scenes between Indian warriors and mythological figures from antiquity were found in both the church and the monastery in 1960. Other attractions in the city are the church El Carmen with its ultra-Baroque façade and Baroque retables as well as two bridges from colonial times. Artists at the Monday market and in the Casa de Artesanías (house of artists) offer local arts and crafts, among them miniature musical instruments, embellished mirrors and combs, embroidered blouses and handbags.

✶ Palenque

R 26

Federal state: Chiapas (Chis.)
Distance: about 210km/130mi north-east of San Cristóbal de las Casas

Altitude: 150m/492ft

A style unique in beauty and technical perfection developed between 600 and 800 in the classical Maya site Palenque.

Palenque lies at the foot of low hills lush with rainforest above the alluvial plains of the Río Usumacinta. This landscape is very different from the flat land of northern Yucatán where the Maya built their impressive cities around spacious squares. The builders of Palenque had to adapt their architecture to the more confining spaces of the hill country.

▶ VISITING PALENQUE

INFORMATION

Tourist information
in the Plaza de Artesanías
Calle Juárez at the corner of Abasolo
(1 Poniente Nte)
Tel. (916) 345 03 56 or
www.palenque.com.mx

GETTING AROUND

On the MEX 186, drive 114km/71mi
from Villahermosa to Cataja and from
there take the MEX 199 south to
Palenque (23km/14mi). The Palenque
archaeological site is another 9km/
5.6mi further on. Starting out from
San Cristóbal de Las Casas, follow the
MEX 199 for 205km/127mi via Ocosingo to Palenque. Small air taxi
services to Palenque are available
from Villahermosa, San Cristóbal de
Las Casas and Tuxtla Gutiérrez. An
alternative is a bus ride of about 2.5
hours from Villahermosa.

WHERE TO EAT

▶ Inexpensive

Restaurante Maya
Avenida Independencia
Tel. (934) 345 10 96
This restaurant in the north-west
corner of the city square is popular
with both locals and tourists.

WHERE TO STAY

▶ Luxury to moderate

Misión Palenque
Comicilio Conocido
Rancho San Martín de Porres
Tel. (916) 345 02 41
Fax (916) 345 03 00
www.hotelesmision.com.mx
Located four blocks from the main
city square and 20 minutes away from
the first class bus terminal, this hotel
offers more than 200 spacious rooms
with air conditioning. The 8km/5mi
bus ride to the archaeological site is
free.

▶ Budget

Hotel Maya Tulipanes
Touristic and Ecological Zone
of La Cañada
Cañada 6
Tel. (916) 345 02 01
Fax (916) 345 10 04
In this two-storey hotel all 48 rooms
have air conditioning. The hotel is
located one long block north of the
Maya statue in La Cañada.

The climate here is hot and humid, especially in March and April.
The months from October to February are the coolest. There are
many mosquitoes in this region, and travellers should therefore be
sure to use malaria tablets. There are relatively few mosquitoes in
the months from December to April.

History   Palenque was populated as early as the pre-classical period (300 BC
to AD 300), but its history becomes particularly relevant only in the
early classical period of the Maya (AD 300–600). As a religious and
political centre, Palenque was at its zenith between AD 600 and 800.

New research on deciphering Maya glyphs has provided us with the names of the Palenque rulers from the time Bahlum-kuk (Jaguar Quetzal, born in 397) became ruler in 431 until the death of Cimi-pacal (»6 dead«) in 799. By this time, Palenque was one of the great cities in the central Maya region, along with Yaxchilán (Chiapas), Caracol (Belize), Tikal, Piedras Negras, Quiriguá, Uaxactún (all in Guatemala) and Copán (Honduras). During this period, the Maya developed their culture to the highest degree of maturity: among the developments were the use of the cantilever roof, the advancement of the hieroglyphic script, the art of carving stelae and the calendar.

Like all other cities in the central Maya region, Palenque was abandoned in the 9th century. The last dated reference is from the year 799. Only 20 years later, Palenque had ceased to exist. Within the shortest time, the magnificent sites in the region decayed and became engulfed with jungle.

Panoramic view of the ruin site of Palenque

Re-discovery of Palenque

The first Europeans to visit the ruined city were Ordónez y Aguilar, José Antonio Calderón and Antonio Bernanconi in 1784. The Spanish captain José Antonio del Río followed two years later, delivering a report about Palenque to Charles III of Spain. In 1841, John Lloyd Stephens and Frederick Catherwood spent some time in Palenque, and their reports and drawings drew attention around the world. Many other explorers followed. The Mexican I.N.A.H. (Instituto Nacional de Arqueología e Historia) has undertaken important research and restorations. Palenque has been a UNESCO World Heritage Site since 1987.

Exploring the Archaeological Site

Tip

A museum about 1.5km/1mi away from entrance of the archaeological site gives a good overview of the area. A map and a model give an impression of the way the ancient site may have once looked.

Site map
🕐 **Opening times: daily 10am–5pm**

The archaeological zone measures about 300m/984ft east to west and 500m/1,640ft north to south. This is only a small portion of the ancient city of Palenque, which probably stretched over six to eight kilometres (3.7–5mi). An aqueduct brought water from the river Otulum through underground canals to Palenque. The **view from the top of the pyramid over grey temples with the jungle as background is marvellous**; however, in the imagination the buildings should be painted in their original bright red colour. In contrast to the flat ground in Chichén Itzá and Uxmal, Palenque lies amid hills and a visit involves exercising the leg muscles.

Temple XII and Temple XIII

One of the first sights when entering the site is the impressive Temple of the Inscriptions, but the first structures to be reached are Temple XIII and Temple XII. In 1994, the discovery of a tomb in Temple XIII made the headlines: a sarcophagus in a tomb chamber contained the remains of body of a woman painted vermilion (typical for buried Maya nobility). The age of the buried woman at her death was estimated to be 40 years. She was about 1.70m/5ft 7in tall and adorned with a jade mask, an chest shield with precious stones, ear studs and many pieces of jade. Two other skeletons of high-ranking Maya were found in a chamber. While there were no glyphs in the tomb, it is safe to assume that the woman was of high rank (**La Reina Roja**), possibly even the mother of Pacal and the female ruler of Palenque. This seems to confirm that the central plaza in Palenque was a necropolis for the ruling class.

✳
Temple of the Inscriptions

The construction of the impressive Temple of the Inscriptions (Templo de las Inscripciones) started under the ruler Pacal (603–683) in 675 and was completed in 683 under the rule of his son. This is so far the largest known structure in Palenque. The

New research on deciphering Maya glyphs has provided us with the names of the Palenque rulers from the time Bahlum-kuk (Jaguar Quetzal, born in 397) became ruler in 431 until the death of Cimipacal (»6 dead«) in 799. By this time, Palenque was one of the great cities in the central Maya region, along with Yaxchilán (Chiapas), Caracol (Belize), Tikal, Piedras Negras, Quiriguá, Uaxactún (all in Guatemala) and Copán (Honduras). During this period, the Maya developed their culture to the highest degree of maturity: among the developments were the use of the cantilever roof, the advancement of the hieroglyphic script, the art of carving stelae and the calendar.

Like all other cities in the central Maya region, Palenque was abandoned in the 9th century. The last dated reference is from the year 799. Only 20 years later, Palenque had ceased to exist. Within the shortest time, the magnificent sites in the region decayed and became engulfed with jungle.

Panoramic view of the ruin site of Palenque

PALENQUE

✱ ✱ **Palenque was one of the most significant Maya cities. For a long time, its history was a mystery. It was known that it was already inhabited before the Common Era, but did not experience its prime until the 6th century. Through the deciphering of heiroglyphic scripts part of Palenque's history has become clear: according to the scripts the dynasty began on 11.3.431, when Bahlum-Kuk (Jaguar-Quetzal) took to the throne.**

🕐 Open:
Tue–Sat 8am–4.45pm

① Templo de las Inscripciones
The tomb of the ruler was found in this, the most imposing building on the site. A ten-generation history of the dynasty could be reconstructed from the glyphs on three huge stone panels.

② Palacio
The maze-like Palace, raised on a platform, is grouped around four inner courtyards. On its walls are carefully executed reliefs, glyphs and stucco ornamentation. A tower, probably serving as a vantage point for astronomical observations, dominates the maze of columns and galleries arranged around interior yards.

③ Templo del Sol
In the interior of the Temple of the Sun visitors find the beautiful bas-relief of a sacrifice ceremony with the symbol of the sun at its centre.

④ Templo de la Cruz
The temple is named after the large stone panel on the back wall of the shrine depicting a cruciform, stylized world tree. The roof comb is well-preserved.

⑤ Templo de la Cruz Foliada
The Temple of the Foliated Cross is named after the relief of a cruciform maize plant.

⑥ Templo del Conde
The archaeologist Count Friedrich von Waldeck lived in this temple during his research work at the site.

A relief in the Palace shows the ancestors of Pacal II handing over the crown and the oblation as attributes of his power. Below, a script describes the coronation ceremony.

Palenque *Plan*

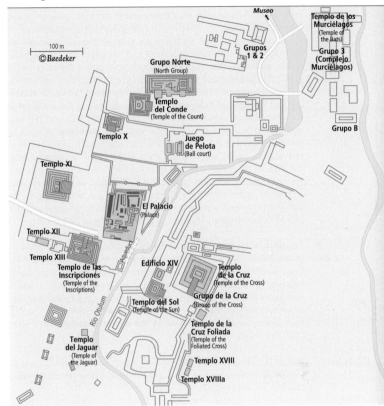

100 m
©Baedeker

Museo

Templo de los Murciélagos
(Temple of the Bats)

Grupos 1 & 2

Grupo 3 (Complejo Murciélagos)

Grupo Norte
(North Group)

Templo del Conde
(Temple of the Count)

Templo X

Juego de Pelota
(Ball court)

Grupo B

Templo XI

El Palacio
(Palace)

Templo XII

Templo XIII

Edificio XIV

Templo de la Cruz
(Temple of the Cross)

Templo de las Inscripciones
(Temple of the Inscriptions)

Grupo de la Cruz
(Group of the Cross)

Templo del Sol
(Temple of the Sun)

Río Otulum

Aqueducto

Templo de la Cruz Foliada
(Temple of the Foliated Cross)

Templo del Jaguar
(Temple of the Jaguar)

Templo XVIII

Templo XVIIIa

classical step pyramid consists of nine stacked platforms and is 20m/ 66ft high including the temple on top of it.

Six columns, adorned with stucco figures, flank the five entrances to the temple.The **620 hieroglyphs** to which the pyramid owes its name are carved into the stone right and left of the main entrance. It is thought that these glyphs are mainly **a chronicle of the ruling family in Palenque**.

✶ ✶
◀ Burial treasure and crypts

One of the sensations in pre-Columbian archaeology was a find by the Mexican archaeologist Alberto Ruz I'Huillier who is also buried on the grounds of Palenque. In 1949, he discovered a stairway in the middle chamber of the temple hidden under debris. When the entrance was cleared a wall was revealed with burial objects in front of it. When the wall was torn down the discoverers found a triangular upright plate, in front of which were **the ruins of a burial site with six skeletons**. Turning the triangular stone plate around its axis, opened the crypt underneath the temple platform. The chamber walls were adorned with nine stucco reliefs depicting gods or priests (shamans). Two stucco heads lay on the ground. The sarcophagus in the chamber was closed with a stone slab, on which a relief depicts the ruler Pacal, his knees pulled up and his upper body bent backwards, seated on the mask of the earth god. Above the ruler circles the bird of heaven, and symbolic death glyphs are placed next to Pacal. It is now known that the depictions **represent the death and rebirth of the ruler of Palenque Pacal**. The skeleton of Pacal still lay in the sarcophagus. A jade mask had slipped off his face, and his face, neck and arms were also adorned with **jade jewellery**. A piece of jade was placed in the ruler's mouth and one in each of his hands. A clay tube from the crypt to the stairs at the tomb entrance ensured the Pacal's connection with the world of the living. This 1952 discovery indicated for the first time that the Maya had, at least once, used a pyramid as the tomb of a ruler as was the practice in Egypt. The burial objects and a reconstruction of the Palenque crypt are displayed in the National Museum of Anthropology in Mexico City.

✳ Palace

The next building on the left is the Palace (Palacio). The architecture of the Palace on its huge, trapezoid artificial mound is unusual for a Maya building. The irregular structure consists mainly of a dozen buildings arranged around four inner courtyards. A tower, which dominates the structure, and connecting underground passages (subterráneos) suggest that the palace served as an observatory. The human figures on the **stone slabs in the eastern courtyard** are especially interesting.

Jaguar Temple

East of the Temple of the Inscriptions, a path leads downhill through the jungle to the ruins of the Jaguar Temple. There are many other ruins in the near vicinity.

✳ Temple of the Sun

Cross the narrow Río Otolum to reach another plaza with a group of three elevated pyramids, all of which were dedicated to Chan-Balum. The **most charming structure** is undoubtedly the Temple of the Sun (Templo del Sol), completed in 692. The temple has three entrances, which lead to two passages and one shrine in the back. The well preserved **roof comb** (cresteria), once the most common roof construction in this ancient city, is remarkable. The roof combs provided space for decorations and created the illusion of added height; they also resulted in longer supportive walls. The columns around the entrance are decorated with stucco human figures and hieroglyphs, of which only remnants are still visible.

✳ Bas-relief ▶

A masterful bas-relief decorates the back wall opposite the central entrance. In its centre, the relief shows a shield with two crossed lances representing the sun god. The altar depicted underneath the god is supported by two seated figures that possibly symbolize gods of the underworld. On either side of the altar stands a figure; some be-

Frederick Catherwood only spent a few years in Central America but we have him to thank for many accurate and detailed drawings of remains of the Maya culture, such as this, the Nunnery Complex at Chichén Itzá.

ON THE TRAIL OF THE MAYA

When American explorer John Lloyd Stephens (1805–1852) heard about the discovery of ruins in Mesoamerica, he undertook two expeditions to Central America and Mexico between 1839 and 1842 along with British artist Frederick Catherwood (1799–1854). Although initially unsuccessful, they finally discovered traces of walls in Copán, Honduras and purchased the ruins for 50 dollars. They subsequently made more discoveries including Palenque, Chichén Itzá, Kabah, Labna and Uxmal.

Stephens described his first impressions of the finds at Palenque in his book »**Incidents of Travel in Central America, Chiapas and Yucatán**«:
»At half-past nine we left the village. After a short crossing of open terrain, we entered some forest that continued unbroken until we arrived at the ruins and undoubtedly continued further for mile upon mile. We took the narrow footpath used by the Indians, including paths muddied by rain where the branches hung so low that we were forced to stoop. Even then our hats and coats rapidly become thoroughly soaked.« (...)

The palace

»After two hours we arrived at the Michol and half an hour later at the Otula that flowed majestically through its stony bed in the shadow of the forest. Then came a rocky climb that rose so steeply that the mules could hardly cope with it. At the top we found a kind of terrace, as overgrown with trees as the paths below so that it was impossible to determine its extent. After a short time we came on foot to a second terrace where our Indian guides suddenly called out »El palacio!« – »the palace!«

A bleak beauty

»Through the gaps in the trees we caught a glimpse of a large building, the front of which was beautifully decorated with strange, finely chiselled figures. Even here the trees were so dense that the branches were practically growing through the entrance. It was a unique sight that **truly impressed us** with its bleak beauty. (...)
For the first time we stood in a building built by the ancient natives of this land, a building that had stood before the Europeans even knew this continent existed.«

lieve that these two figures represent the ruler Pacal on the left and his son and successor Chan-bahlam (who ruled from 684 to 702) on the right.

Temple of the Cross The Temple of the Cross (Templo de la Cruz), built in 692 on the orders of Chan-bahlam, is similar to and in the same group as the Temple of the Sun. Some suspect it to be the burial place of Chan-bahlam.

Large relief panels were found in the temple at the back of the shrine, and the middle panel, now displayed in the National Museum of Anthropology in Mexico City, shows Chan-bahlam on the right and his father Pacal on the left with a cross-shaped object, possibly a **Ceiba, the holy tree of the Maya**. This scene gave the temple its name. The left relief panel shows Chan-bahlum after his ascent to power. Carved into the right panel is the glyph of the god L, an old god of the underworld who is connected to the house of the ruler. In the relief, he smokes a cigar.

Agua Azul: the turquoise-blue colouring gave the waterfalls near Palenque their name.

The Temple of the Foliated Cross (Templo de la Cruz Foliada) stands opposite the Temple of the Sun, which is similar in appearance. Both temples were built in the same decade. The relief in this temple once again shows the transfer of power from Pacal to Chan-bahlam. The main motif is a cross growing from the head of the sun god. A sun bird sits on top of the cross, and **the leaves of the maize plant form the arms of the cross**. The leaves are decorated with human heads. Again, on each side stands a ruler, the deceased father on the right and the son and successor on the left.

Temple of the Foliated Cross

North of the Palace stand the low buildings of the north group, consisting of several temple ruins and the remnants of a ball court. The best known and best preserved of the buildings is without doubt the **Temple of the Count** (Templo del Conde). The structure was built between 640 and 650 and is the oldest excavated building to be found in Palenque so far. Typical for the Palenque style are the two parallel passages, of which the rear one is divided into three chambers. For the first time, this building features the mansard effect, created by the sloping outer walls.

North group

To explore the surroundings of Palenque visitors can follow the path behind the Temple of the Inscriptions into the jungle. A path between the former ball court and the north group leads to a beautiful waterfall, the Baño de la Reina (queen's bath), and continues on to the Murciélagos group, which consists of late Palenque houses (770–850).

Surroundings

The small town of Palenque (population 20,000) possesses no attractions other than the archaeological site. The main traffic axis through the town is Avenida Juárez with travel agents, hotels and restaurants. However, a visit to the nearby cascades is enjoyable. Excursions into the mountains of Chiapas are very interesting as are sightseeing trips to ▶Bonampak or Yaxchilán.

Town of Palenque

Around Palenque

About 20km/12mi south-west on the road toward Ocosingo there is a turning to the right leading to the Cascades of Mizol-há. These beautiful cascades in romantic surroundings fall almost 30m/98ft into a large pond in the midst of a beautiful jungle area. It is safe to take a swim here. There is a camp site nearby, as well as cabins and a small restaurant. A path lined with ferns leads around the cascades giving visitors a chance to experience the regional fauna.

Mizol-há

After approximately 45km/28mi, a 4km/2.5mi path to the right leads to the Cascades of Agua Azul (blue water). Water rushes in several wide cascades over limestone steps into the Río Bascán, flowing on into the Río Tulijá. Between the cascades and the rivers are several

Agua Azul

natural turquoise basins, in some of which it is possible to swim. The falls, located near the road to San Cristóbal de las Casas, are very beautiful, and have therefore become a major destination for outings by bus. In the close vicinity are a camp site, simple restaurants and a runway for small planes.

✴ Pátzcuaro Lake (Lago de Pátzcuaro)

P 17

Federal state: Michoacán (Mich.)
Distance: 65km/40mi south-west of Morelia, 350km/217 mi west of Mexico City

Altitude: 2,050m/6,726 ft

Pátzcuaro Lake (19km/12mi long and about 5km/3mi wide), considered by many the most beautiful lake in Mexico, lies amid forested mountains and extinct volcanoes. The most important islands in the lake are Janítzio, Jarácuaro, Tecuén, Yunuén and Pacanda.

Picturesque Indian villages are situated along the lakeshore and in the surrounding areas, and some of the Indians still live in the style of their forefathers. Its location and surroundings make Pátzcuaro Lake one of the most attractive travel destinations in Mexico, a fact which can lead to overcrowding. In recent years, the beauty of the lake has suffered somewhat from environmental pollution.

Pátzcuaro

✴
Pretty town by the lake

The most important town in the region is Pátzcuaro (population 90,000) about 4km/2.5mi away from the lake shore. In this charming town, whose name means place of stones for temple buildings, time seems to have stood still. As in times past, the Indian element dominates the former **Tarascan metropolis**, while the most beautiful old buildings go back to around 1550 when Pátzcuaro was the seat of a Spanish bishop.

Now as then, the memory of this great guardian and teacher of the Indians, Bishop Vasco de Quiroga (1470–1565), is kept alive. Pátzcuaro received its town charter from Emperor Karl V in 1553. Its history is closely related to the histories of Tzintzuntzan and ►Morelia.

! **Baedeker TIP**

Baile de los Viejitos

On 8 December (Día de Nuestra Señora Salud = day of our lady of health) the »Baile de los Viejitos« (dance of the old men) takes place in Pátzcuaro. It is supposed to remind people of the victory of Hernán Cortés over the Tarascan people, in which the Tarascan chief came forward dressed as an old man. The dancers wear wooden masks and at first make a very frail impression; they then accelerate their movements, in the end revealing themselves as young men.

Two plazas form the town centre. The larger of the two plazas is the spacious and quiet Plaza Vasco de Quiroga (Plaza Grande). It is framed by arcade walkways and mansions which, in the meantime, have mostly been converted into hotels, restaurants and stores. A fountain featuring a statue of the bishop marks the centre of the plaza and gives it its name. On the right stands the town hall (Palacio Municipal), which is a former 18th-century palace, and on the plaza's eastern side is the **House of the Giant** (Casa del Gigante), with a beautiful portal and decorated balcony windows. It is said that the last Tarascan ruler had his residence in the Palacio de Huitzimengari on the northern side, which today houses a tourist office.

Plaza Vasco de Quiroga

Fishermen at work in the early morning. In the background Janitzio island rises out of the mist on Pátzcuaro Lake.

▶ VISITING LAKE PÁTZCUARO

INFORMATION

Tourist information
Palacio Municipal
Pátzcuaro or
www.patzcuaro.com.mx

GETTING AROUND

On the MEX 15 (via Morelia), it is a drive of about 350km/217mi from Mexico City to Lake Pátzcuaro. By train, the trip through the beautiful landscape lasts about 12 hours.

WHERE TO EAT

▶ **Moderate**
① *El Primer Piso*
Plaza Vasco de Quiroga 29
Tel. (434) 342 01 22

Guests have a nice view onto the plaza from this first floor restaurant, which is also a gallery. It serves a creative menu inspired by Tarascan and Italian cuisine.

WHERE TO STAY

▶ **Luxury to mid-range**
① *Posada Don Vasco Best Western*
Avenida Lázaro Cárdenas 450
Tel. (434) 342 02 27
Fax (434) 342 02 26
www.bestwestern.com
This hotel is situated a few minutes' walk away from the centre and on the road to the lake. The 103 new rooms have either a patio or a balcony.

House of the Eleven Patios

The House of the Eleven Patios (Casa de los Once Patios) is located on the south-east side of the Plaza Grande. This 18th-century convent now serves as the Casa de las Artesanías de Michoacán (Michoacán Artist's House) where first-rate arts and crafts are for sale. While browsing, visitors can learn about the special skills of craftsmen from different regions: copper ware from Santa Clara del Cobre, items made from straw come from Tzintzuntzan and excellent musical instruments from Paracho. There are lacquered items with gilded decorations, hand-painted ceramics and beautifully woven or embroidered textiles.

Plaza Gertrudis Bocanegra

The second important plaza in Pátzcuaro is named after Gertrudis Bocanegra, famous for her role as hero of the independence movement. Here, visitors are aware of the hustle and bustle of the neighbouring market, where vendors offer fruit, vegetables, fresh fish and medicinal herbs, as well as ponchos and shoulder wraps. The plaza is a busy place with shoe-shine stands, street vendors and small buses. The **Gertrudis Bocanegra Library** is located in the former **San Agustín** church at the northern end of the plaza. The library is decorated with murals by Juan O'Gorman and shows the history of Michoacán until the revolution in 1910. Interesting and inexpensive arts and crafts are to be found in the small artists' market, the **Mercado de Artesanías**. The theatre **Teatro Emperador Caltzonzín** is located west of the library in a former monastery, now a place for cultural

Pátzcuaro Lake Map

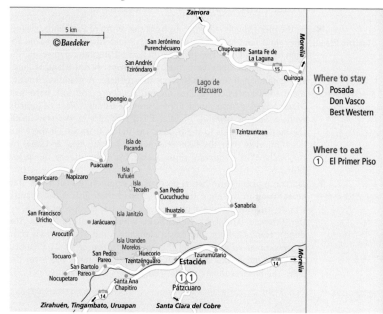

events. The frescoes in the stairway are very interesting. Among other scenes, they show the meeting of the Tarascan ruler Tangahxuan II with the Spanish conqueror Cristóbal de Olid in 1522.

Next to the former monastery is the site of the Basilica of Our Lady of Health (Nuestra Señora de la Salud, otherwise known as La Colegiata). Bishop Quiroga ordered the construction of this cathedral in 1543 but it was never finished. Inside the building stands a statue, the **Virgin of Health** (Virgen de Salud), made of sugar cane paste (pasta de Caña) in the traditional Tarascan way. **La Colegiata**

At the next corner, at the intersection of Calle Enseñanza and Alcantarillas, stands the former San Nicolás College, founded in 1540 by Bishop Quiroga.

The former sacral rooms arranged around a patio now house the **ethnologic and arts and crafts collections** of the Museum of Folk Art (Museo de Artes Populares). Aside from ceramics, masks, textiles and lacquered items, it is worth taking a look at a room in which a typical regional kitchen is set up. ★ ◄ **Museum of Folk Art**

Don't miss the wonderful view over the lake and the beautiful landscape around it from the look-out point El Estribo (4km/2.5mi west of the town centre). **El Estribo**

Other Attractions

Janítzio Island

At the pier (Muelle) 4km/2.5mi from the centre of Pátzcuaro, visitors can rent a boat to make a trip to the various islands. The island **Tecuén** is considered the prettiest in Lake Pátzcuaro. However, the most important albeit very touristy and overcrowded island is Janítzio. It takes half an hour by boat to get there. A grandiose monument to the Mexican fighter for independence and folk hero José María Morelos towers over the picturesque fishing village of Janítzio with its narrow winding alleys and red roof-tiles. A stairway inside the monument leads to the head of the statue, from which there is a beautiful view over the lake. Frescoes by Ramón Alva de Canal on the walls of the stairway show scenes from the life of the priest Morelos.

Morelos Statue ▶

Janítzio is also known for its particularly ceremonious **All Souls' Day celebration** in the night from 1 to 2 November. This is the Spanish Día de los Muertos (day of the dead, ▶ Baedeker Special p.128) or the Tarascan Animecha Kejtzitakua, which means (**gifts for the dead**). Here, Catholic and pagan elements combine to form a vivid expression of religious belief. In the early morning of 31 October, the ceremonial wild duck hunt (Kuirisi-ataku) takes place on the lake. The hunters throw 2.5m/8ft-long spears (Atlatl) at the ducks.

Day of the dead ▶

Important elements during the Day of the Dead celebrations: skeleton and decorative flowers

Around Pátzcuaro Lake

About 30 picturesque Indian villages exist on the islands and around the lake. Their inhabitants are mostly fishermen who still use boats made from hollowed trees to fish with nets for the tender whiting (pescado blanco) or different kinds of perch and trout. Nowadays, the famous butterfly nets (Uiripu) are only used to put on a show for tourists.

The ruined Tarascan city of Tzintzuntzan (place of the humming-birds) is situated on top of a hill above a village of the same name about 15km/9mi away from the village of Pátzcuaro. The view from the archaeological site over the nearby Pátzcuaro Lake is magnificent. Tzintzuntzan, with its unusual architecture, was once the most significant **Tarascan religious centre**.

✳
Tzintzuntzan

🕑
Opening times:
daily 10am–5pm

The original city of Tzintzuntzan was probably built in the 12th century. Together with Pátzcuaro and Ihuatzio the city formed the reigning triumvirate in the Tarascan Empire. The Tarascan people in Tzintzuntzan were excellent warriors, and the city dominated the region. About 40,000 inhabitants populated the city of almost 7 sq km/ 2.7 sq mi. When, in 1478, the Aztec invaded their territory after they had conquered Toluca, the Tzintzuntzan warriors defeated them, a victory due not in small part to their copper weapons. Later Aztec attempts to conquer the Tarascan Empire also failed. The Spanish conquistadores under Cristóbal de Olid entered Tzintzuntzan in 1522. Without a battle, the Tarascans agreed to submit to Spanish rule. Seven years later however, the infamous conquistador Nuño Beltrán de Guzmán killed the Tarascan ruler Tangáxoan II, leading to revolts. The Spanish crown responded by sending the priest and jurist **Vasco de Quiroga** (1470–1565), who succeeded in re-establishing peace. In 1537, Vasco de Quiroga was appointed bishop of Michoacán; the episcopal see was initially in Tzintzuntzan, and later transferred to Pátzcuaro. The bishop encouraged the development of Indian arts and crafts, a fact still evident in the regional craftsmanship.

The ancient city is interesting more because of its architectural style than the execution of the building. Only fragments are still intact. Five T-shaped flat temples (yácatas) sit on the huge platform (425 x 250m/1,394 x 820ft). The rectangular foundations of the temples ended in oval platforms. Originally, the temples had a covered round upper level. These structures were obviously tombs, while the main portions of the yácatas were used as **ceremonial places dedicated to the fire god Curicáveri**. Excavations of the round structure have yielded tombs of Tarascan rulers and their families as well as many burial objects. On the eastern side, a monumental 30m/98ft wide outer stairway leads up to a terrace. The row of yácatas (numbered I to V, counted from the right with your back turned toward the lake) once featured 12 stacked terraces each rising of 0.9m/3ft, accessible via steps. These temples were constructed by stacking flat stones,

◀ Yácatas

held together by flat facing stones called janamus. For the outer covering, the Tarascan builders used stones from the volcanic rock Xanamu, which were joined in an even pattern using a mixture of clay and pebbles.

Town of Tzintzuntzan

On the opposite side of the road to Quiroga lies today's town of Tzintzuntzan. The **Franciscan convent**, which was reconstructed in 1570, has a large atrium and old olive trees, remarkable because of their rarity in Mexico: the Spanish crown had prohibited the cultivation of olives in the American colonies. The convent church San Francisco (16th century), with its open chapel and Plateresque façade, was ravaged by a fire in 1944. Next door stands the church of the Third Order. Tzintzuntzan is famous for its painted ceramics and wood carvings, stone statues and braided items.

Quiroga

The town Quiroga is located on the northern lake shore, about 25km/15.5mi north of Pátzcuaro and 8km/5mi away from Tzintzuntzan. Take a look at the 16th-century Franciscan monastery here. Quiroga is known as an outlet for regional folk art, such as wood and leather products as well as woollen ponchos (sarapes).

Erongaricuaro

Visitors will discover the pretty Tarascan village of Erongarícuaro on the western shore of the lake, about 18km/11mi away from Pátzcuaro. There are old houses with a Spanish appearance and an attractive church. During the Second World War, the village harboured a group of **French surrealists**.

Santa Claradel Cobre

A drive of 20km/12mi south from the city of Pátzcuaro leads to Villa Escalante or Santa Clara del Cobre. This old Tarascan town has earned fame for its beautiful **artefacts made of forged copper**, a craft already well developed in pre-Hispanic times. Back in the 16th century, this was one of the crafts that Bishop Vasco de Quiroga especially helped to advance. The Museum of Crafts documents this development.

✳ Lake Zirahuén

A road west leads from Villa Escalante to the beautiful, quiet Lake Zirahuén (20km/12mi south-east of Pátzcuaro). With a length of about 4km/2.5mi, it is smaller than Pátzcuaro Lake, but much deeper.

✳✳ Santiago Apóstol de Tupátero

15km/9mi after leaving Pátzcuaro, heading toward Tiripetío and Morelia, there is a turning to Guanajo, and just 4km/2.5mi down this road is the village Tupátero. In the interior of the **simple adobe church** Santiago Apóstol there is an altar which is consecrated to St Jacob. The church features a dome, surprisingly in the Mudéjar (Moorish) style, decorated with **singularly beautiful wood paintings** showing an impressive rendition of the life of Christ and his mother Mary as conveyed by the Spanish missionaries to the Indians in the

16th century. Similar religious paintings were found in only two other churches near Cuzco in Peru. Opening times are irregular and should be confirmed with the tourist office in Pátzcuaro.

Tarascans

The Tarascan people lived mainly from fishing, hunting and the cultivation of corn (maize). There were **two main classes in Tarascan society**: the military elite and priests, and the fishermen, farmers and slaves. Their highest ranking god was the fire god Curicaveri. Subordinate gods were the earth mother Cuerauáperi, Tata Uriata (father sun) and Nata Cutzi (mother moon). While Tarascans were mainly warriors, they were also very skilled in **metal work** and used copper as well as gold and silver. The Tarascan metal work was clearly superior to similar work anywhere else in Mesoamerica. Working with copper was rare in Mexico at the time, and it has therefore been speculated that this technique was introduced by people from Peru or Colombia. The quality of Tarascan feather works, ceramics, textiles and the processing of obsidian was, however, also famous throughout Mesoamerica. The **rough stone sculptures appear archaic** and seem identical to the Toltec Chac-mool statues. The **yácatas** with temple platforms and oval structures dominate in the simple but nevertheless unique architecture.

Beautiful location: ruin site Tzintzuntzan

** Popocatépetl · Iztaccíhuatl

P 20

Federal states: México (Mex.) and
Puebla (Pue.)

**A volcanic belt forms the southern rim of the great Mexican high-
lands and traverses Mexico from the Pacific to the Atlantic. In the
early and middle Tertiary period (65 to 20 million years ago), enormous quantities of lava flowed over the country.**

The second phase of eruptions started in the Pliocene (about 2 million years ago), and has not yet ended. The giant volcanoes Popocatépetl (5,452m/17,887ft) and Iztaccíhuatl (5286m/17,343ft) were created in this phase. The two volcanoes of the Sierra Nevada are the
mountainous barrier between the highlands of Mexico and highlands
of Puebla. Popocatépetl has been active since 1994 and frequently
casts out rocks, ashes and smoke; for this reason it is currently forbidden to climb the mountain. 14 of the 16th century monasteries
on the low slopes of the volcano have been declared **UNESCO World
Heritage Sites**.

Tip Climbers don't need to have the skills of an Alpine mountaineer to
make the ascent to the two volcanoes. However, it is not advisable to
start the tour without proper equipment. The ascent should be slow
but steady; a hasty ascent can lead to circulatory problems due to the
altitude. Unskilled climbers should hire a guide. (►Practicalities, active vacations). The best time to climb the mountains is during the
months from November to April. Depending on the wind direction,
sulphur fumes may impede the ascent.

National Park The road from Amecameca to Tlamacas passes through the Popoca-
tépetl-Iztaccíhuatl National Park. The park stretches between the two
volcanoes and ends at the **Cortés Pass** (Paso de Cortés). The conquistador Hernán Cortés and his men crossed this pass on their
march from the Gulf of Mexico to Tenochtitlán on 3 November
1519.

**
Popocatépetl Drivers reach the cabin on the right hand side (Albergue, 3,998m/
13,117ft). This is the last stop by car before making the ascent of Popocatépetl, in Náhuatl **»smoking mountain«**. Until 1994, two routes
to the peak with its immense crater (about 800 x 400m/2,625 x
1312ft) were possible. Since the times of the conqueror Cortés, large
quantities of sulphur have been extracted from the crater. The sulphur was initially used to produce gunpowder.
In December 2000, 40,000 people had to be evacuated during the
heavy eruptions, the largest in 500 years. The »smoking mountain«
has had active periods ever since. In March 2005, an eruption set a

The snow-capped peak of Popocatépetl

forest near the city of San Nicolás de los Ranchos on fire. A smoke cloud often hangs over the peak.

Travellers reach the mountain Iztaccíhuatl or Ixtaccíhuatl (Náhuatl: white woman) via the road from the Cortés Pass toward La Joya. This **craterless mountain** is located about 15km/9mi from the volcano. In legends, Iztaccíhuatl is associated with a lovelorn princess who was united with her warrior lover, Popocatépetl, in death. Coming from the direction of Mexico City and providing it is a clear day, the three snow-covered peaks of the Iztaccíhuatl resemble the head, chest and knees of a prone woman. The difficult ascent and descent requires two days. Emergency accommodation is available. The radio station Torre Retransmisora (elevation 3,950/12,960ft) offers a good opportunity for an overnight stay before and after a climb.

★ ★
Iztaccíhuatl

The town Amecameca lies at the foot of the two snow-covered volcanoes Popocatépetl and Iztaccíhuatl. The location of the town in this sparse but impressive mountain region is advantageous because of its proximity to some remarkable landmarks of colonial art. Amecameca is therefore a **good vantage point for outings, trips and tours through the mountains**. The parish church in the main town square features beautiful Baroque altars, and the associated 16th-century Dominican monastery has a well preserved cloister.

Amecameca

▶ VISITING POPOCATÉPETL

INFORMATION

Tourist information
www.cenapred.unam.mx or
www.volcano.si.edu/gvp/volcano

GETTING AROUND

The distance from Mexico City via Chalco and Amecameca to the Albergue cabin near Tlamacas is about 86km/53mi. The starting point for an ascent of Popocatépetl is as follows:

go from Puebla to Chalco, and from there another 43km/27mi on poor roads via San Nicolás de los Ranchos to the Cortés Pass; there, take the road south and go 4km/2.5mi to Tlamacas. Turn north onto the road and drive 7km/4.3mi to La Joya (the starting point of the tour to Iztaccíhuatl). Popocatépetl often ejects ashes and is at times therefore closed to climbers or hikers.

Sacromonte   The peak of the Sacromonte (Holy Mountain) towers 150m/492ft over the town. On Ash Wednesday, it becomes **the destination for many pilgrims and tourists**, while down in the town people enjoy the colourful market. A way of the cross, with stations decorated with colourful tiles, leads to a small church on top of the hill with a painting of Christ which reputedly works miracles. The small church was built to honour the friar Martín de Valencia, one of the first Franciscan priests in New Spain, who until then had been living in a cave as an anchorite. Above the church, there is a chapel dedicated to the Virgin of Guadalupe, built at the former Indian ceremonial site Teteoinán. There is a **magnificent view** from the hill over the Valley of Mexico, the surrounding mountains and especially of the snow-covered peaks of Popocatépetl and Iztaccíhuatl.

✶ **Puebla**

P 20

Federal state: Puebla (Pue.)
Population: 2,000,000

Altitude: 2,162m/7,096ft
Distance: 126km/78mi south-east of Mexico City

Puebla is located in a fertile highland valley, surrounded by Popocatépetl (5,452m/17,887ft), Iztaccíhuatl (5,286m/17343ft) and La Malinche (4461m/14,636ft). History and colonial architecture gave the city its character, which has 65 churches and is well-known for the production and use of colourful tiles.

Puebla is also known for the creation of »**mole poblano**« (a gourmet sauce made with plenty of chili) which was probably first concocted in a monastery kitchen. While Puebla has developed into an important industrial centre in recent decades (Volkswagen for example produces its VW Mexico cars and trucks here), the city has still retained some of its original colonial charm. The historic centre of Puebla has been a **UNESCO World Heritage Site** since 1987.

History

As far as we know today, Puebla has no pre-Hispanic history. Monks founded the town in 1531 under the name of Ciudad de los Ángeles on behalf of Bishop Julián Garcés of Tlaxcala. Puebla had its own university as early as 1537. In the same year, the town became the seat of a bishop and has been called Puebla de los Ángeles ever since. The town soon became the centre of the surrounding agrarian region and a traffic hub between the Gulf of Mexico and the Pacific. Around the middle of the 16th century, Puebla citizens had already started to produce glazed tiles (azulejos) according to Spanish guidelines, and the tiles from Talavera de la Reina (see p.145) in particular became the template. With its predominantly European flair, Puebla was in competition with the neighbouring ancient Indian metropolis Cholula, and in the 17th century Puebla started to outperform Cholula.

In the war between the United States of America and Mexico (1846–1848) acrimonious battles took place between the troops of

Puebla Plan

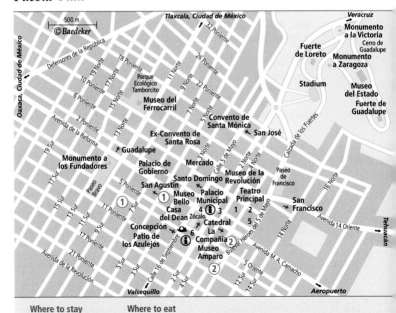

Where to stay	Where to eat		
① Camino Real Puebla	① Fonda de Santa Clara	1 Casa del Alfeñique	4 Las Galerías del Palacio
② Mesón Sacristía de la Compañía	② La Guadalupana	2 Barrio del Artista	5 Antiguo Parián
		3 Casa de los Muñecos	6 Casa de la Cultura

the generals Winfield Scott and Antonio López de Santa Ana, leading to a temporary occupation of Puebla by US troops. During the French Intervention, the Mexican troops under General Ignacio Zaragoza defeated the French on 5 May 1862: Cinco de Mayo is now a national holiday all over Mexico. The French were finally to conquer Puebla a year later. The city remained under the reign of Emperor Maximilian until General Porfirio Díaz successfully chased the emperor's troops out of town in April 1867. Puebla was also the scene of heavy fighting in the Revolutionary War (1910–1920).

In the summer of 1999, a strong earthquake shook the historic centre of Puebla. In the meantime, the damaged buildings have been restored to their original beauty, particularly the Palafoxiana Library (Biblioteca Palafoxiana), the city hall, the José Luis Bello Museum, the Carolino Structure and several church spires.

! *Baedeker* TIP

Raisin glasses

Opposite the Plazuela de los Sapos, on which a flea-market takes place on Sundays, stands the La Pasita bar where the popular raisin liquor of the same name is served; it normally comes with a raisin in the glass.

What to See in Puebla

✱ Zócalo

The beautiful main city square (Plaza de la Constitución) with its tall trees, flower beds and fountains is framed by arcades (portales). It is the busy centre of the city.

✱ Cathedral

The cathedral, the second-largest in Mexico after the one in Mexico City, stands on the south side of the plaza. The construction of the impressive building (built mostly in the Renaissance style) started as early as 1575, but was not finished until 1649. The north portal toward the main city square is decorated with the high relief depictions of the four Spanish kings from Habsburg House (Charles V, Philipp II, Philipp III and Philipp IV). The crest of the Spanish kings is placed below the arch apron. The main façade and portal already show elements of the coming Baroque style. The two spires, one built in 1678, the other completed 90 years later, are unusually high and airy. The huge dome is noteworthy, **clad with the glazed tiles (azulejos)** that are typical for Puebla. The magnificent interior of the cathedral measures 90 x 47m/295 x 154ft and is 25m/256ft high. The cathedral features three long naves and a large cross nave. Especially remarkable is the neo-classical upright altar (around 1800) by Manuel Tolsá and José Manzo, the wrought-iron choir balustrade (1679) by Mateo de la Cruz, the wood-carved choir stalls (1719–1722) by Pedro Muñoz and the two impressive organs from the same time.

Casa de la Cultura

South of the cathedral, the former palace of the archbishop now houses the Casa de la Cultura (House of Culture), as well as govern-

▶ VISITING PUEBLA

INFORMATION

Tourist information
Avenida 5 Oriente 3
(south of the cathedral)
Tel. (222) 246 12 85
www.visitpuebla.com

GETTING AROUND

Take the MEX 150 for the 126km/
71mi trip from Mexico City to
Puebla.
The same journey takes about 5 hours
by train and 2.5 hours by bus.

SHOPPING

There is a tradition stretching back
many centuries of hand-painted Talavera ceramics in Puebla. Particularly
beautiful pieces are to be found at
Uriarte (factory and shop), Calle 4
Poniente 911. On Sunday mornings,
antiques are on sale at a flea market in
the small square Plazuela de los Sapos
(Calle 5 Oriente/Calle 6 Sur).

WHERE TO EAT

▶ Expensive
② *La Guadalupana*
Calle 5 Ote. 605
(Plazuela de los Sapos)
Tel. (222) 242 48 86
This is a highly praised restaurant in a
very beautiful colonial building. Regional cuisine is served in special
vessels called Molcajetes.

▶ Moderate to inexpensive
① *Fonda de Santa Clara*
3 Poniente No. 307
(opposite the Bello Museum)
Tel. (222) 442 26 59
www.fondadesantaclara.com
This restaurant is very popular in
Puebla. It serves delicious food at
moderate prices.

WHERE TO STAY

▶ Luxury to mid-range
① *Camino Real Puebla*
7 Poniente 105
Centro Histórico
Tel. (222) 229 09 09
Fax (222) 232 92 51
The hotel (83 rooms) opened in 1996
in a former 16th-century convent. It
is located less than 3 blocks south of
the Zócalo between Calle 3 Sur and
Avenida 16 de Septiembre. The Camino Real offers two restaurants, a
bar, an art gallery and a business
centre.

▶ Mid-range to Budget
② *Mesónes Sacristía de la Compañia*
Calle 6 Sur 304
Tel./Fax (222) 242 3554
www.mesones-sacristia.com
The 15-room lodge is a 200-year old
private residence. Because the owners
are a family of antique traders, guests
can buy the antique furniture in the
rooms!

ment agencies and a tourist office. The Palafoxiana Library (Biblio-
theca Palafoxiana) on the upper floor was founded in 1646 by Bishop
Juan Palafox. It has a large **collection of bibliophilic treasures**,
among them a Nuremberg Chronicle of 1493 and a beautiful Baroque reading room.

◀ Palafoxiana
Library

Amparo Museum

✳ Also located on the south side (Calle 2 Sur), the Amparo Museum displays the pre-Columbian collection of José and Jacqueline Sáenz, one of the largest private collections of its kind. Among the highlights is the »Maya Altar of the Lords of Yaxchilán«.

Casa del Dean

The House of the Dean (Casa del Dean at Calle 16 de Septiembre 505) in the next block west of the archbishopric palace is a beautiful old residence in the Renaissance style (1580). Inside, **murals** are sure to impress. They are a painted Indian interpretation of the Petrarca poem *I trionfi* on the themes of love, death, virtue, fame, time and eternity.

Bello y Gonzalez Museum

A captain of industry and his son once built their home in Avenida 3 Poniente 302 in the Puebla style. Now a museum (Museo Bello y Gonzalez), the house contains Chinese, Japanese, English and French porcelain, Talavera ceramics and smithery.

Las Galerías del Palacio

The gallery next to the tourist bureau of the state of Puebla shows contemporary Mexican art or presents works which make Mexican everyday life their theme.

Doll's House

At the beginning of Calle 2 Norte, near the north-west corner of the city square, stands a house in the **sugar baker style**, the Doll's House (Casa de los Muñecos). The wall tiles on the façade tell the story of nefarious Puebla city elders who allegedly brought the house owner to court in an attempt to take the house from him. According to the story, they were jealous because the house was larger than their own. Inside, the Museo Universitario documents the city's cultural history.

Temple of the Holy Spirit

Two blocks east of the main city square stands the Jesuit Church of the Holy Spirit (Templo de la Compañía, consecrated in 1767). The church has an ultra-Baroque façade and a dome clad with white and blue wall tiles. Of all things, the church consecration occurred in the same year that the Jesuits were banished from Mexico. The church vestry contains a grave said to be the final resting place of a Chinese princess who pirates abducted and sold as a slave in Mexico. In the story, she regained freedom in Puebla at the end of the 17th century. She supposedly created the widely accepted fashion of the quaint **china Poblana costume**, which consists of a white blouse with frills, a long skirt and a shoulder wrap. The adjacent former Jesuit school now houses the university.

Almond Cake House

From Calle 2 Norte, Avenida 4 Oriente branches off to the right. Here, visitors find the unique Casa del Alfeñique (Almond Cake House). This guest house, probably designed by Antonio de Santa María Incháurregui at the end of the 18th century, is one of the best

Elaborate grandeur – in the style of the icing on the cake: the Casa de Alfeñique. →

examples of the **Puebla style** with its colourful wall tiles, red bricks and white stucco. The house exhibits the typical local Baroque style. Today, the **Regional Museum** is here, which displays mostly ceramics, weapons, paintings, traditional costumes and furniture.

Teatro Principal

The main theatre (Teatro Principal, built 1756 to 1769) is situated north of the museum. Considered one of the oldest theatres in Latin America, it burnt almost to the ground in 1902 but was rebuilt in the 1930s. The **artists' quarter** is not far away in Calle 8 Norte. There, it is possible to visit the studios of painters and sculptors and buy their works.

Church of San Francisco

A short side trip takes in the Church of San Francisco (Templo de San Francisco) located in Avenida 14 Oriente. The convent was built in 1551 and features a nicely tiled façade. The ultra-Baroque main portal and the carved choir stalls from the 18th century are noteworthy. The building was remodelled around 1800 in the neo-classical style. The mortal remains of San Sebastián de Aparicio are displayed in a glass cabinet; such relics still attract many people. San Sebastián de Aparicio was a Spaniard who came to Mexico in 1533 and planned many roads through the country, finally becoming a monk. The chapel exhibits paintings with scenes from his life and his statue stands in a church niche.

Santo Domingo de Guzmán in Puebla is one of the most splendid Baroque churches in Mexico.

The Church of Santo Domingo is located two blocks away from the main square in Calle de Cinco de Mayo. The church façade is executed in a deliberate Baroque style. The Rosary Chapel (Capilla del Rosario, 1690) is a crowning achievement in Mexican Baroque art: not an inch of wall space, ceiling, columns or portal is left without tiles, gold leaf, sculptures or carving. Particularly remarkable is an orchestra of cherubs fully encircled by very elaborate arabesques, from which God seems to descend.

✸
Church of Santo Domingo

Situated at Calle 3 Norte 1203, the former Convent of Santa Rosa now contains the **Museum of Arts and Crafts** (Museo de Artesanías), a library, shops and an exact reconstruction of a convent kitchen, complete and true to the original with tiles and old utensils. It is believed that in around 1680 a nun worked in this kitchen on the chili sauce known as »**mole poblano**«, eventually perfecting the very famous sauce with many spices and chocolate (► Baedeker Special p.120).

Former Convent of Santa Rosa

Further along Calle Cinco de Mayo visitors come to the former convent of Santa Monica (Avenida 18 Pte. 103), founded in 1609 and remodelled 70 years later. After the Mexican Reform of 1857, the convent had to be closed, but the nuns kept the convent going in secret until they were discovered in 1934.
The original secret chambers and their furnishings were unfortunately lost during remodelling. However, some cells with pallets, instruments for self-flagellation and an old kitchen with dining room are still on display. The former convent also houses the **Museum of Religious Art**.

✸
Former Convent of Santa Monica

A unique railway museum (Museo Nacional del Ferrocarril) has been created in the north-west end of Puebla in an old railway terminal (11 Norte, corner of 10 Poniente). Almost 200 old locomotives, wagons and other mementos from the heyday of the Mexican railway are displayed here.

Railway museum

On top of a hill in the north-east of Puebla towers the **Fortress of Loreto** (Fuerte de Loreto, built in 1816). Today the stronghold has become a museum, the **Museo de la No Intervención**, which documents the fights against the French around this hill in 1862. The view from the fortress over the city is beautiful. On the southern hillside stands the **Fort Guadalupe**.

Cerro de Guadalupe

The Cívic Centre Cinco de Mayois located between the two forts. Here, visit the planetarium, an open-air theatre and exhibition halls for arts and crafts. The **National Museum of Puebla** (Museo del Estado de Puebla) is also situated here and displays interesting archaeological finds from the Olmec, Toltec and Aztec cultures. There are also exhibits describing the regional ethnology.

Cívic Centre Cinco de Mayo

Around Puebla

Cantona ✱

Cantona lies about 115km/71mi north-east of Puebla (via Carretera 150 to Carretera 129, junction near Oriental toward Tepeyahualco). Excavations started here in 1993 to unearth **one of the most important archaeological sites in the central highlands**. Cantona was at the height of its civilization between AD 600 and 950. The fortified city covered 12 sq km/4.6 sq mi, and its location between the Gulf of Mexico and the Mexican Highland Valley gave it great significance. The site includes a series of magnificent pyramids, wide patios, palaces and platforms as well as a network of 500 cobbled roads. So far, archaeologists have identified over two dozen ball courts, more than at any other ancient site in Mesoamerica to date.

Amozoc

A ride of 16km/10mi on the MEX 150 toward Tehuacán leads to Amozoc where pottery and the silver embellishments for the costumes of the charros (equestrian farmhands) are produced.

Tepeaca ✱

Tepeaca (population 40,000) is another 20km/12mi on. Founded by Hernán Cortés as early as 1520 as his second settlement after Veracruz, this village is now known for its Friday market. The watchtower (Rollo) in the main square of this former stopover for coaches shows both Moorish and Renaissance elements. Cortés had the house with the red façade built on the opposite side of the square. This house may have served as his retreat after his defeat in Tenochtitlán in the **noche triste** (sad night) on 30 June 1520. The massive 16th-century Franciscan monastery was built like a fortress and is one of the earliest and most impressive monasteries in Mexico. Note the battlement parapet around the monastery church, the colonial Plateresque façade and the execution of the monastery atrium.

> ! *Baedeker* TIP
>
> **Candlelight concerts**
>
> The pretty town of Tecali is located about 42km/26mi south of Puebla and 10km/6mi away from Tepeaca. From time to time, candlelight concerts are given within the walls of the venerable Franciscan church or in the small wood-panelled theatre. Enquire about details at the tourist office in Puebla.

Franciscan monastery ✱ ▶

Acatzingo

Only a few miles after leaving Tepeaca on the MEX 150, take a left turn and drive the 11km/7mi to Acatzingo (population 48,000). The 16th-century Franciscan monastery is a smaller replica of the monastery in Tepeaca and contains a beautiful Indian-made baptismal font.

Pico de Orizaba ✱
(fig. p. 457) ▶

There are two routes from Acatzingo to the foothills of Mexico's highest mountain the Pico de Orizaba, otherwise known as Citlaltépetl (mountain of the star). To reach the mountain's southern slope, first take the MEX 140 north-east to El Seco and then go 25km/15.5mi on the MEX 144 to reach El Serdan. The northern slope is best reached from Tlachichuca, where it is possible to rent an all-terrain vehicle (the road is fairly difficult) or arrange to be driven the 32km/20mi to the cabin at the Piedra Grande (with overnight accommodation) at an elevation of 4,260m/14,976ft. Experienced mountain hikers can negotiate the beautiful volcano with its glacier in one day. Information about the state of the access roads and the ascent routes can be obtained from the official sources (►Practicalities, active vacations).

Moving along the MEX 150 (115km/69mi south-east of Puebla) travellers reach the resort town of Tehuacán (population 160,000) with the churches San Francisco and El Carmen as well as the Dr. Miguel Romero mineral collection. The thermal springs are well-known as is the drinking water, which has become the **epitome of all mineral waters** (Peñafiel) in Mexico. The Museo del Valle de Tehuacán (three blocks from the main square) provides explanations of finds from regional excavations, such as the preserved ears of corn (maize), which are the first ever planted in the area.

Tehuacán

✶ Puerto Escondido

T 21

Federal state: Oaxaca (Oax.)
Population: 35,000

Altitude: sea level
Distance: 400km/250mi south-east of Acapulco

Surfers were at home here long before asphalt roads to Puerto Escondido (hidden port) existed. Meanwhile, the town has lost the character of a fishing village and has taken on the atmosphere of a small resort.

Puerto Escondido lies in a protected bay on the Pacific and is surrounded by hills with lush vegetation. The **most beautiful long beaches** stretch out on both sides of the town. The surf can be high in some places. Only a few years ago, Puerto Escondido was a secret location for travellers seeking the simple life away from the tourist circuit. Those times have past, especially since the new airport opened to bring in more visitors.

Tourist Attractions

The town consists mostly of small restaurants, bars and shops lining the main street Pérez Gazga. Also called »Adoquín«, this street turns into a traffic-free zone in the late afternoon, allowing pedestrians to mill around without worry. The western end of the main street leads to the MEX 200 or coastal road. Below the city lies the narrow beach Playa Principal, which merges at its southern end with Playa Zicatela. The long beaches and the lagoons in small bays (Puerto Angelito,

▶ VISITING PUERTO ESCONDIDO

INFORMATION
Turismo
shortly before the approach road on
the MEX 200 toward the airport
(Fraccionamiento Bacoch)

Small info kiosk:
Pérez Gasga
Tel. (954) 582 01 75 or at
www.puerto-escondido.com.mx

GETTING AROUND
A flight from Oaxaca or Mexico City
to Puerto Escondido lasts 45 and 60
minutes, respectively. By bus, the trip
from Oaxaca takes 6 to 10 hours and
from Acapulco about 7.5 hours.
The distance by car is about 265km/
165mi on the winding MEX 131 via
Miahuatlán and Pochutla or about
310km/193mi on the better MEX 175
and MEX 200 which takes 5 to 6
hours. Puerto Escondido is 420km/
261mi from Acapulco on the MEX
200.

WHERE TO EAT
▶ Moderate to inexpensive
La Perla Flameante
Pérez Gasga
This second-floor restaurant serves
or, if desired, delivers very tasty sushi
and seafood.

Los Candiles
1a Poniente
(road-side)
This is a pleasant and diligently-run
restaurant with hand-woven table
cloths and various arts and crafts,
specializing in traditional food from
Oaxaca.
The seafood specials of the day are
highly recommended.

Restaurante de Doña Celia
Bahía Santa Cruz
Huatulco
Tel. (958) 587 01 28
The real name of the restaurant is
Avalos but it is known only under the
name of its owner, Doña Celia. She
cooks a wide variety of seafood dishes
and serves generous portions.

WHERE TO STAY
▶ Luxury to mid-range
Las Brisas Huatulco
Bahía de Tangolunda Lote 1
Santa Cruz de Huatulco
Tel. (958) 583 02 00
Fax (958) 583 02 40
www.brisas.com
Each of the 483 rooms has its own
patio with hammock and all have an
ocean view. Three beaches are part of
the extensive club premises.

▶ Mid-range to budget
Posada Cañón De Vata
Playa Panteón
Tel. (958) 584 31 37
The nice, simple bungalows
(22 rooms) are a little hidden above
the Panteón beaches.

Santa Fé
Calle del Morro
Col. Marinera
Tel. (954) 582 01 70
Fax (954) 582 02 60
The hotel (62 rooms) is built in the
hacienda style. It is located between
the beaches Marinera and Zicatela.
Some of the rooms have balconies and
a view onto the swimming pools,
patios or the ocean. It pays to ask
about these when making reservations.

Carrizalillo, Manzanillo and Bacocho) are the habitat of many water birds. Part of the coastline is fit for swimming despite the surf but swimming is not without risk in places with an undertow. **Surfers still like to come to Puerto Escondido** because the waves are excellent for their sport. Surfing competitions mostly take place on Playa Zicatela. Visitors can rent the necessary equipment on the beach to take advantage of the opportunities to dive, snorkel or surf.

At the beach of the town itself, the **Bahía Principal,** visitors find restaurants at the western end, fishing boats in the central part and mostly modern sun worshippers in the eastern part, also called Playa Marinero. Now and then, pelicans fly only inches above the water surface hunting for food.

The long, sandy beach of Zicatela stretches behind the rocks of the headland. This part of the beach is however only safe for hard-core surfers with the best of swimming skills, as the currents here can be very dangerous. It is however pleasant to watch the surfers for a while, enjoy the beach life or relax in one of the bars or small parks.

Surfers' paradise on the Pacific: Puerto Escondido

Still further west lies the beautiful Puerto Angelito bay with two small beaches divided up by a few cliffs. A taxi or boat brings visitors here from the centre of Puerto Escondido. It may be pretty crowded on weekends and holidays.   **Puerto Angelito**

Playa Carrizalillo lies behind the headland. In the meantime, a flight of 165 stone steps has been built to allow access to this beach, which is stoney but still suited for swimming. A boat sails to the beach from the Bahía Principal; alternatively, follow the trail with the signs to »Trailer Park Carrizalillo«.   **Playa Carrizalillo**

The beach Bacocho, with its palms, is a little further away. Enjoy the ocean west of the hotel Posada with care: the currents can be treacherous here as well. The best way to reach Bacocho is by boat from Puerto Escondido.   **Bacocho**

Fun by the water in Bahía Principal

West of Puerto Escondido

Beautiful lagoons and untouched natural beaches are visible from the MEX 200 to Acapulco. Travellers can observe many interesting animals and enjoy the variety of plants. The history of this region is not limited to that of the Mixtec and the Spanish: some of the people living in the area are the descendants of escaped slaves, displaced Chinese and shipwrecked sailors from Chile. The latter are known for the local folk music called »La Chilena«.

Manialtepec Lagoon   The veritable bird paradise Manialtepec Lagoon (Laguna de Manialtepec) is about 15km/9mi from Puerto Escondido. The 8km/5mi-long lagoon provides a habitat for ibis, various hawks (falcons), herons and ospreys. Birdwatchers are especially well rewarded early in the morning and in June or July. Special tours can be booked in Puerto Escondido.

San Pedro Tututepec   After 75km/47mi west on the MEX 200, a road branches off and leads after 10km/6mi to San Pedro Tututepec. This mountain village is home to the Chatino Indians. Some pre-Columbian sculpture are on display behind the old church.

Chacahua Lagoons   A few more miles along the MEX 200 leads to a road going to the Chacahua Lagoons National Park. within the park boundaries are three lagoons and several islands with many species of birds and amphibians. A large number of migratory birds from Alaska and Canada spend the winter months here. Mangroves border the islands where cormorants, storks, egrets and ospreys, as well as crocodiles and tortoises are seen. With a little bit of luck, visitors can discover a black orchid among the wealth of tropical plants.

Chacahua

The village Chacahua is a five-minute walk along the beach of the Chacahua Lagoon. There is a wonderful opportunity to relax here; surfers in particular love the place. At the end of the lagoon, pay a visit to a small crocodile farm.

East of Puerto Escondido

Puerto Ángel

The fishing port Puerto Ángel (population 9,000) with its beautiful beaches (Puerto Ángel and Panteón) is located about 84km/50mi east of Puerto Escondido. This is just the place for anybody in need of peace and quiet.

Zipolite

Young campers love Playa Zipolite, a white beach with a spectacular headland 10km/6mi west.

Mazunte

North of Zipolite, behind a rocky tongue of land lies another beautiful beach, an ideal location for lounging in a hammock: San Agustinillo. Behind it lies the village of Mazunte , a former place to catch tortoises. It is much more tranquil here than in Zipolite and there is also a terrific beach and a **tortoise museum** (Centro Mexicano de las Tortugas).

★
Huatulco

About 35km/22mi east of San Pedro Pochutla (about 110km/68mi from Puerto Escondido) there are **nine picturesque bays** known under the collective name the Huatulco. The beaches are especially beautiful here, and a number of first-class and mid-range hotels provide ample accommodation. There are chances to engage in various aquatic sports, from offshore fishing to canoe rides; the underwater world is still intact here. The solitude and the fine white sand on the beach are compelling reasons to stay.

The town **Santa María Huatulco** (with an international airport) lies 12km/7.5mi inland. In recent years, the Mexican Government and private investors have built a 20,000ha/49,420ac tourist centre around the town, which mushroomed into being just like Cancún.

San Agustín Bay near Huatulco

✷ Puerto Vallarta

O 13

Federal state: Jalisco (Jal.)
Population: 350,000

Altitude: sea level
Distance: 462km/287mi south of Mazatlán

Puerto Vallarte is situated in a wide bay among green hills. It is one of the best known and most popular travel destinations for those who like to spend time on the beach.

History Puerto Vallarta was established in 1851 and named in 1918 after Ignacio Luis Vallarta, the governor of the federal state at the time. Puerto Vallarta was then a sleepy fishing village. The place attracted attention only when, in the beginning of the 1960s, scenes for the Hollywood movie ***The Night of the Iguana*** (starring Richard Burton and Ava Gardner, 1964) were shot in the neighbouring village Mismaloya. Elizabeth Taylor also turned up and thus the headline-making love affair between Taylor and Burton took its course.

It was only in 1968 that a road was built between Puerto Vallarta and Tepic. This heralded Puerto Vallarta's meteoric rise.

Tourist Attractions

Puerto Vallarta looks very pretty with its cobbled alleys and white houses with red tiled roofs, but it is the extended beaches with aquatic sports opportunities and the tropical landscape which attract most of the visitors.

Aside from the boardwalk (Malecón), the impressive yacht harbour Marina Vallarta and many hotels, restaurants, bars and shops, Puerta Vallarta also has a small museum in Escuela 15 de Mayo and then there is the Guadalupe church with its curiously shaped tower reminiscent of a crown.

Puerto Vallarta lies on **Banderas Bay** (Bahía de Banderas, Bay of Flags) with more than two dozen

Puerto Vallarta Plan

©Baedeker

Where to stay
① Pasada de Roger
② Fiesta Americana
   Puerto Vallerta

Where to eat
① Chef Roger
② El Palomar
   de los Gonzáles

⏵ VISITING PUERTO VALLARTA

INFORMATION
Tourist information
in the Presidencia Municipal
(north-east corner) on the Plaza
Principal
Tel. (322) 22 20 24 or
www.allaboutpuertovallarta.com

GETTING AROUND
Plane
Flying from Mexico City to Puerto
Vallarta takes about two hours. Many
more flights to Puerto Vallarta exist
from other Mexican or US cities.

Car or bus
A bus trip from Guadalajara lasts
about five hours. By car, it is 170km/
106mi on the MEX 200 from Tepic,
and about a 320km/200mi drive from
Guadalajara on the MEX 15 and the
MEX 200.

Ferry
A ferry connection exists from Cabo
San Lucas to Puerte Vallarta.

WHERE TO EAT
▶ Expensive
① *Chef Roger*
Augustín Rodríguez 267
Tel. (322) 259 00
In the small but luxurious restaurant
of a Swiss gourmet cook guests can sit
either inside or outside on the patio.
The cuisine is a mixture of Mexican
and European cooking. Reservations
are required.

▶ Moderate
② *El Palomar de los González*
Calle Aguacate 425
Tel. (322) 227 95
This is just the right place for a
romantic evening in the mansion of
the González family. Enjoy the beautiful view over Puerto Vallarta and the
bay. The cuisine is international.
Reservations are necessary during the
peak season.

WHERE TO STAY
▶ Luxury to mid-range
② *Fiesta Americana Puerto Vallarta*
Blvd. Francisco Medina Ascencio
Km 2.5
Tel. (322) 224 20 10, Fax 224 21 08
www.fiestamericana.com
The 290 rooms of this 9-storey hotel
all have a white marble floor and a
balcony. An extraordinary feature of
this hotel is the high Palapa hall.

▶ Mid-range to inexpensive
① *Posada de Roger*
Calle Basilio Badillo 237
Tel. (322) 222 08 36
Fax (322) 223 04 82
www.hotelposadaderoger.com
All 48 rooms in this good value,
friendly hotel have air conditioning
and a TV.

beaches. The beaches stretch north and south of the Río Cuale,
which flows through the city.
The most popular beaches are located north of the river, among
them Playa de las Glorias, Las Palmas, de Oro and Chino (already in
the federal state of Nayarit). In this area, there are now large hotel
complexes almost everywhere.

Puerto Vallarta's old city with a view of the cathedral and the Bahía de Banderas.

Beaches

The beaches south of the river are Playa del Sol (or Playa de los Muertos), Las Amapas and Conchas Chinas (below the cliffs), Las Estacas, Punta Negra, Palo María and Gemelas (all with pretty bays). The most enjoyable albeit somewhat overcrowded beach is located 12km/7.5mi south of Mismaloya. This beach also features a waterfall and natural basins. In front of the bay are the rock formations of the Los Arcos underwater park.

✳
Mismaloya ▶

✳
Yelapa ▶

This nature preserve includes a group of islands, of which Yelapa is the most important. The park and islands are very popular with snorkellers and divers. Watching the humpback whales is a spectacular experience at the Jalisco and Nayarit coasts from December until March. The whales swim thousands of miles from the North Pacific to Mexico's warmer waters to mate.

Around Puerto Vallarta

The holiday centre Nuevo Vallarta in the federal state of Nayarit lies about 15km/9mi north on the MEX 200. Nuevo Vallarta features one of the largest yacht harbours in Mexico. The next destination on the same road is the town Bucerías, and then after another 15km/9mi the towns Rineón de Guayabitas and Peñita de Jaltemba (▶Tepic). South along the MEX 200 stretches the ▶Costa Alegre, namely the coastal region up to Manzanillo with wonderful beaches and a rich flora and fauna.

Puuc Route

Federal state:: Yucatán (Yuc.)   **Altitude::** 25–28m/82–92ft

In the hills of the Puuc region west of Ticul and about 80km/50mi south of Mérida, travellers find idyllic Maya villages as well as small excavation sites. While Uxmal is without doubt the most beautiful and most significant ruined city in the region, the sites Kabáh, Sayil, Xlapak and Labná show the Mayan Puuc style much more clearly.

Maya centres are dominated by a central building. Despite all the common features shared by Maya sites, there are also typical and unique features. In this regard, Codz-poop (Palace of the Masks) in Kabah and El Palacio in Sayil are worth a trip. To learn about the present day Maya culture, an overnight stay in Maní or the busy market town of Oxkutzcab is worth considering – even if levels of excitement and energy are high enough to cover the whole of this route in a single day.

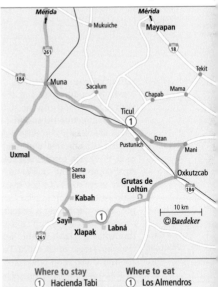

Puuc Route Map

Kabah

Continuing south-west on the MEX 261 at Uxmal past Santa Élena, the ruins of the ceremonial centre Kabah are reached after 25km/15.5mi. The ancient Maya executed the now excavated structures in their traditional Puuc style. However, there was a remarkable deviation in style, pointing to the influence of the Chenes culture (open daily 8am–5pm).

Where to stay
① Hacienda Tabi

Where to eat
① Los Almendros

In the southern part of the excavation site, east of the road, stands the Palace of the Masks (Templo de las Máscaras) or Codz-poop. The latter name means »rolled up mat« in the Maya language and is a reference to the trunk-shaped nose of the rain god Chac. This feature was used here in the design of the steps.

Recent discoveries indicate that this is in fact not the rain god Chac (as assumed before) but rather the faces of the mountain monster

▶ VISITING PUUC ROUTE

INFORMATION

Tourist information
www.mayakultur.de/puuc.htm oder
www.yucatan-guide.de/mayas

GETTING AROUND

Day trips are possible by bus from
Mérida to the Puuc sites (the bus
stops everywhere). By car, take the
MEX 261 via the village St. Elena
directly to the Maya site Kabah.

WHERE TO EAT

▶ **Inexpensive**
① *Los Almendros*
Calle Principal (in the direction of
Oxcutzcab)
Ticul

This is a popular restaurant with very
good regional cuisine and a swimming pool. Children especially enjoy
swimming and playing in the pool.

WHERE TO STAY

▶ **Mid-range**
① *Hacienda Tabi*
Contact: Fundación Cultural Yucatán
in Mérida
Calle 58 No. 249-D
Tel. (999) 923 94 53
www.fcy.org.mx
The main building of this former
sugar plantation is still awaiting
renovation. However, it is already
possible to stay here overnight and
enjoy the beautiful park and pool.

signifying the structures as holy mountains. The Temple of the
Masks is 6m/20ft high and 45m/148ft long and stands on a platform
with a horizontal row of stylized masks. The temple is unique in
Puuc architecture because the façades of the walls between the lower
floors are already completely decorated. This style of ubiquitous decoration is associated with the Chenes style. Above a decorated cornice, there is **a continuous row of masks with rolled up noses**. The
cornice above the masks is decorated with geometrical patterns.
Three more rows of Chac masks are arranged above the cornice. The
skills of the sculptors who created more than 250 masks are as impressive as the façade is puzzling.

Palace (Teocalli) Immediately north of the Temple of the Masks stands the palace
(Palacio), most often called Teocalli. The difference between the palace and Codz-poop could not be more pronounced. The palace has
two storeys (the lower one is badly damaged) and follows a strikingly
simple design, very different from the richly decorated Temple of the
Masks. On the palace, the decorations are panels of rows of columns
between two raised cornices.

Arch of Kabah Many structures in the Central and West Groups are still in bad dis-
repair. The Arch of Kabah (Arco de Kabah) however has already
been completely reconstructed. The arch is a text book example of
the cantilever roof so characteristic of Maya architecture. The con-

struction is also called a **false arch**. In this technique, stones on opposite sides are made to project slightly more with each layer of the wall. Thus, the ends of these projections (corbels) grow toward each other until they can be capped with a stone. The unadorned Kabah arch was presumably the entrance to the religious centre of the site.

A causeway or **sacbé**, that is a raised ceremonial road, probably led through this arch to Uxmal. The causeways were constructed from limestone and covered with cement. They were raised above the surrounding ground by about 0.5–2.5m/1.8–8ft and were on average 4.5m/15ft wide.

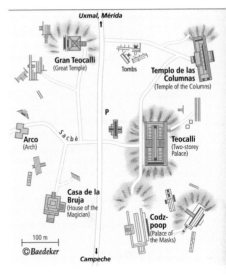

Kabah Plan

Sayil

About 5km/3mi past Kabah on the MEX 261, there is a turning onto a country road east to Sayil. No dates have been found on artefacts here and archaeologists therefore date the structures according to style. This method suggests that the two main structures were built in the 9th century (open: daily 8am–5pm).

★
Religious Maya site
🕐

The palace (Palacio) dominates the site. The partially restored building with three terraces and a base measures 80 x 40m/262 x 131ft. It is one of the architecturally most consummate Mayan creations in the **classic Puuc style**.

★
Palace

The western section of the middle floor is the most interesting part of the building. The section features two doors and four openings flanked by two stone columns each with square capitals. Between these features, embedded columns in the shape of the logs used in Maya huts create a harmonious overall impression. The upper frieze displays the giant mask of the rain god Chac in the centre and the stylized motif of the descending god between open snake mouths. A large cistern (Chultún) once existed at the north-west corner of the palace.

★
◄ Western section

Aside from the remnants of the ball court (juego de pelota) and a small temple, there is also a badly weather-beaten temple in Sayil, which is known as the Mirador. The structure was once connected to the palace via a sacbé. The Mirador rests on a platform and has a remarkable roof comb, which was probably once decorated with

Mirador

stucco ornaments, a relatively rare feature in the Puuc region because mosaics were mostly made from limestone.

An approximately 100m/330ft-long path leads from the Mirador to a roughly made stele showing a figure with an over-emphasized phallus, which looks rather misplaced here considering the usual Maya style.

Xlapak

The excavation site Xlapak is located about 6km/3.7mi east of Sayil on the road to Labná. Here too, the most important restored building is the palace (Palacio) built in the typical Puuc style. Over the first floor, a frieze under a cornice is decorated with column ornaments. Above the simple first level, the main façade shows a richly decorated frieze under a cornice. There are three doors close to the ground. Above the central door is a square upright structure with elaborate decorations involving masks. Panels on both sides show geometrical adornments. The panels transition into a wide cornice. The still preserved corners show one upright top structure each with elaborately stacked Chac masks.

Labná

✳
Religious site of the Maya

🕐
Opening times: daily 8am–5pm

Covered by dense tropical forest like the neighbouring sites Sayil and Xlapak, Labná was an important Maya centre which has not yet been analyzed fully. The few dated finds suggest that the known structures in Labná were built in the 9th century, i.e. in the Maya late classical period. **More than 60 cisterns (chultunes) have already been found at the site**, leading researchers to deduce that the ancient city of Labná was densely populated.

Palace

The building group known as the palace (Palacio) in the northern section of Labná is one of the largest temple complexes in the Puuc region. The somewhat haphazardly built, asymmetric group of buildings rests on a terrace. A large patio lies in front of the building, which is traversed by the remnants of an ancient causeway (sacbé).

The façade of the east section shows decorations in groups of three in the form of embedded columns, bands with geometrical ornaments and nose masks. At the south-east corner, above three bundled columns, there is an unusual Chac mask with a wide open snake mouth from which a human head emerges. The trunk-shaped nose is rolled up toward the forehead.

Mirador

The South Group is dominated by a pyramid with a temple, which has been restored only to a small degree. It is called the Mirador (look-out tower). An **impressive roof comb** looms above the two restored platforms and the temple as a quasi free-standing façade. As reported by J. L. Stephens (▶Baedeker Special p.471), the giant wall once showed a large, colourful seated figure in a stucco relief. The protruding stones of the roof comb façade used to be the basis for the stucco work. The only preserved part of the temple decorations is the lower part of a figure at the south-west corner of the Mirador.

The best known work of art in Labná is the beautiful **Labná Arch** (Arco de Labná), south-west of the Mirador. A straight causeway (sacbé) is said to have led from here to Kabah. Since the Maya did not know the proper arch, they made do with the so-called cantilever roof. The richly decorated corbelled arch has a clearance of 5m/ 16.4ft and is 3m/9.8ft deep. It is flanked by two small rooms with entrances on the north-west side. Protruding cornices frame the frieze with mosaics that are reminiscent of Uxmal. Above the two entrances, a high relief depicts two typical Maya houses with feather-adorned thatched roofs. Presumably, figures once stood in the Maya house entrances. The opposite side of the structure is much more prosaic: above the similarly decorated cornice runs a generously dimensioned frieze with a meander-like motif on a background of embedded columns.

✱ **Labná Arch**

The impressive Caves of Loltun (Grutas de Lol-tún) are about 20km/ 12mi along the road toward Oxcutzcab. On the outer rock face, close

✱ **Caves**

The most important buildings of Labná are the false arch and the look-out tower.

to the Nahkab entrance to the caves, stands the larger-than-life bas-relief figure of a **richly adorned Maya warrior** with a lance in his right hand. The relief is dated to 400–100 BC. The **dripstone caves** are well worth visiting, containing remnants of wall paintings, rock drawings and the stone head of Lol-tún with Olmec features. Research has shown that the caves were probably already inhabited in 2500 BC. In excavations, archaeologists have discovered ceramics which have been dated to a time after 1200 BC. The caves were probably also used to hide from the Spanish invaders. Guided tours are the only way to visit the Loltun Caves. Tour schedule: daily 9:30am and 12:30pm (Spanish) and 11am and 2pm (English).

Oxkutzcab The market city of Oxkutzcab is another 10km/6mi along the same road. A particularly interesting sight in this town is the church whose façade shows depictions of the sun and moon. An altar painting dominates the church interior. In this lively town, visitors can observe the Maya women with their colourfully embroidered huipiles (wide blouses) and carriages which are reminiscent of rickshaws.

Return to Mérida Travellers who are pressed for time can take the MEX 184 from Oxkutzcab to Ticul. Close to Muna, return to the MEX 261 toward Mérida.

Mani Those with plenty of time should consider visiting the pretty town of Main (10km/6mi north) with its cenote (sinkhole) and the chapel San Miguel Árcangel. In 1562, Mani experienced the **auto-da-fé**, in which the infamous fanatical Spanish missionary and later bishop Diego de Landa burnt more than 5,000 valuable scripts, art and the remains of Maya ancestors. As bishop, Diego de Landa initiated the construction of a monastery. Only the church with a very beautiful stone sculpture of Christ still stands.

Mayapán ruins Next on this route are the Maya villages Chapab, Mama, Tekit, Tecoh and Acancah as well as the ruins of Mayapán 8km/5mi north-west of Tekit. The Maya Chronicles give contradictory information about the history of Mayapán, but it is probable that the Itzá came to Yucatán around 1200, re-settled in the once abandoned Chichén Itzá and finally established Mayapán. For almost 200 years, Mayapán became the dominant city in Yucatán under the Cocom dynasty. Revolting Xiú who had once lived in Uxmal destroyed Mayapán around 1450 heralding the final fall of the Maya civilization. In the following period, the Maya empire dissolved into about 20 insignificant small settlements.

In its heyday Mayapán occupied about 6.5 sq km/2.5 sq mi, had about 6,500 buildings and was surrounded by a massive protective city wall. The architecture in Mayapán was a smaller, very simple **copy of the architecture in Chichén Itzá**. The structures have been unearthed and restored only to a minor degree. The Casa del Viejo is

Market in Oxkutzcab

located on the right side, followed by the wall of skulls, and the Palace of the Columns with its giant stone mask is sited on the left. The Castillo was once the dominant structure of the site; from here, there is a nice view of the surrounding beech forest.

On the east side, a path turns left to a low structure with masks of the rain god Chac. Strangely, this building is in the Puuc style, which had passed its time of significance 300 years earlier.

★ Querétaro

Federal state: Querétaro (Qro.)
Population: 780,000

Altitud: 1,836m/6,024 ft
Distance: 225km/140mi north-west of Mexico City

Nestled into a valley in the Mexican highlands in the foothills of the Cerro de las Campanas (hill of the bells), Querétaro is surrounded by mountain peaks. The city is known for its beautiful houses, churches and plazas from colonial times as well as its nicely kept fountains and parks.

▶ VISITING QUERÉTARO

INFORMATION

Tourist information
Plaza de Independencia
(north side)
Tel. (442) 238 50 00 and
at the corner of Pasteur 17 and
Andador Libertad
or at
www.turismoqueretaro.com.mx

GETTING AROUND

The best route from Mexico City is to
take the MEX 57 D (212km/132mi).
The trip takes about 5 hours by train
and about 2.5 hours by bus.

WHERE TO EAT

▶ **Expensive**

① *Fonda del Refugio*
Jardín de la Corregidora 26
Tel. (442) 212 07 55
The restaurant is located in the Jardín
de la Corregidora. Guests can enjoy
their meals (Mexican cuisine) in the
dining room or out on the terrace
with a view of the garden.

▶ **Inexpensive**

② *La Mariposa*
Calle Angela Peralta 7
Tel. (442) 212 11 66
The restaurant is located two blocks
north of the Obregón Gardens (Jardín
Obregón). It is easily recognized by
the wrought-iron butterflies (= mar-
iposa) above the entrance. Light
Mexican cuisine as well as coffee and
cakes are the house specialities.

WHERE TO STAY

▶ **Luxury to mid-range**

② *Fiesta Americana Hacienda
Galindo*
Carretera a Amealco
Km 5.5
Tel. (427) 271 82 00
Fax (427) 271 82 50
www.fiestaamericana.com
This 16th-century hacienda turned
hotel (166 rooms) started out as a gift
from Hernán Cortés to his Indian
lover and interpreter Malinche. The
rooms are tastefully decorated and
some of them have terraces and
Jacuzzis. Tennis courts and an 18-hole
golf course are available.

▶ **Mid-range to budget**

① *Mesón de Santa Rosa*
Pasteur Sur 17
Tel. (442) 224 26 23
Fax (442) 212 55 22
www.mesondesantarosa.com
This hotel building with 21 rooms is
200 years old. It is situated in the
quiet Plaza de Independencia and has
a shaded patio around which the
tastefully decorated suites are arranged.

At its core, Querétaro has retained its tranquil character, even though
some industrialization has begun in recent years. UNESCO declared
the historic monuments of the city a **World Heritage Site** in 1996.

History Long before the Europeans discovered Mexico, the Otomi Indians established this town and in the 15th century the Aztec conquered it.
The Spaniards brought the region under their control between 1531

Querétaro *Plan*

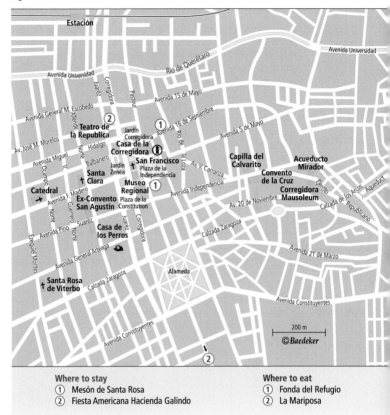

Where to stay
1. Mesón de Santa Rosa
2. Fiesta Americana Hacienda Galindo

Where to eat
1. Fonda del Refugio
2. La Mariposa

and 1570. The town served the conquistadores as a supply centre for the rich mines in Guanajuato and Zacatecas. Querétaro was granted its town charter in 1699.

As no other town, Querétaro later became the setting for historic events. The **plot against Spain** which led to the uprising headed by **Miguel Hidalgo** started here in 1810, an event that resulted in the fight for freedom and finally independence from Spain. The Treaty of Guadalupe Hidalgo was signed in Querétaro in 1848, which ended the war between the USA and Mexico. The last battle between the troops of Emperor Maximilian of Mexico and Benito Juárez took place here in 1867. The emperor from the House of Habsburg was imprisoned in Querétaro, convicted and shot to death. The current Mexican constitution was put down in black and white in Querétaro (1917).

What to See in Querétaro

Aqueduct The impressive aqueduct east of the town centre, a defining element in the townscape, still carries water. Marqués de la Villa del Villar del Aguilar ordered the construction of the system, and the aqueduct was built between 1726 and 1738. The construction is almost 1.3km/0.8mi long and has 74 arches, which are up to 29m/95ft high.

San Francisco Monastery

✳

Museum ▶

The old monastery of San Francisco was founded in the middle of the 16th century. It is located south of the main city square (Plaza Principal or Jardín Obregón). A century later, the church and the monastery were remodelled. The monastery is now the site of the Regional Museum (Museo Regional).

✳

Former San Agustín monastery

The beautiful former Augustinian monastery was built in the first half of the 18th century. It is situated at the corner of Calle Allende Sur and Pino Suáres. The main features are the three-part Baroque façade with niches and statues; there is also a beautifully worked arch and a column in the cloister. The monastery complex now houses the interesting **Art Museum of Querétaro** with a comprehensive collection of Mexican and European paintings. Exhibits on the ground floor show contemporary Mexican art.

Theatre of the Republic The **trial against Emperor Maximilian** and his two generals Mejía and Miramón took place in the Theatre of the Republic (Teatro de la República) and concluded with death sentences. The theatre (built in the 19th century) is located north of the main city square at the corner of the streets Juárez and Peralta. Historic events took place in

View over the roofs of San Francisco

Querétaro's Theatre of the Republic twice more after the conviction of Maximilian. The constitution of the federal Mexican Republic was declared here on 31 January 1917, and in 1929 the **PRI** (Institutional Revolutionary Party, Partido Revolucionario Institucional) was established here.

The quiet Plaza de la Independencia (Plaza de Armas, Independence Square) has retained its colonial character. In the centre stands the monument in honour of Marqués de la Villa del Villar del Aguilar who ordered the construction of the aqueduct.

Plaza de la Independencia

At the corner of Avenida Cinco de Mayo and the Plaza de la Independencia stands a pretty building from the year 1770 with wrought-iron balconies. This is the town hall, also called Casa de la Corregidora. Here, Josefa Ortiz de Domínguez, the wife of the mayor (corregidor), warned the conspirators working in the independence movement of 1810 about the impending disclosure of their planned coup. This led to the **early outbreak of the War of Independence**.

Governor's Palace

Avenida Venustiano Carranza leads in an easterly direction to the Convento de la Cruz (de la Cruz monastery). The original building was erected in the 16th century; however it was replaced 100 years later by a Baroque construction. **Emperor Maximilian** had his headquarters here in 1867, and after his capture he was kept in the monastery from time to time. There is also a legend associated with the founding of the monastery: in 1531, the Spaniards fought to conquer Querétaro. At the height of the battle, the heavens darkened at the place where the monastery was later built. The appearance of the apostle James on a horse and a shining cross helped the Spaniards win.

Convento de la Cruz

The open chapel (middle of the 17th century) Capilla del Calvarito now stands at the place of that the apparition of Jacob appeared. After they had conquered the city, the Spaniards are said to have celebrated their first Mass here. In the monastery garden stand 50 unique trees (acacias); this species belongs to the mimosa family and its thorn-like needles have a cruciform shape.

Capilla del Calvarito

Heading south-west on Avenida Francisco Madero, the Hostería de la Marquesa (middle of the 18th century) is seen on the left and the San José de Gracia church (late 17th century) on the right. In the small park at the corner of Madero and Allende stands the Neptune fountain (Fuente de Neptuno), a neo-classical work by the artist Francisco Eduardo Tresguerras (1797).

Avenida Francisco Madero

The adjacent Santa Clara church was once part of a powerful monastery. It has a simple façade (17th century), but its interior is a **particularly beautiful example of the ultra-Baroque style** from the 18th

★
Church of Santa Clara

century with opulently carved and gilded retables. The wooden lattice work in the choir with the statue of Christ in the centre and the draped curtains at the sides is of particular note.

Santa Rosa de Viterbo

The Santa Rosa de Viterbo church (built in 1752) stands at the intersection of Arteaga and Montes. It is one of the town's most interesting churches, and its most striking feature is the protruding buttresses with supporting volutes. The clock in the bell tower is said to have been the first repeating striking clock in the Americas. The retables in the church are richly decorated in the ultra-Baroque style and there are also valuable paintings from colonial times. As in some other churches that are part of a convent, the choir features particularly intricate lattice work. Behind it, the nuns were able to partake in Masses. The beautifully carved confessional, the high-Baroque organ and in the vestry, the life-sized statues of the twelve apostles at the Last Supper. Behind the statues, a wall-sized painting by Tresguerras shows Saint Rosa surrounded by her nuns.

Hill of the Bells

On the Hill of the Bells (Cerro de las Campanas) on the western outskirts of town (in Avenida Justo Sierra) stands the **Capilla de Maximiliano** (Chapel of Maximiliano). The Austrian Emperor Franz Joseph donated the chapel to uphold the memory of his brother Emperor Maximilian of Mexico who was shot here. The chapel was consecrated in 1901. Close to this chapel now stands the taller **colossal statue of Benito Juárez**, Maximilian's victorious opponent and later Mexican president.

Opal mining

The area around Querétaro is a centre for opal mining. Opals and other regionally mined semi-precious stones such as topaz, aquamarine and amethyst are processed in the area and sold in speciality shops.

Around Querétaro

San Juan del Río

The town of San Juan del Río (population 100,000) is located 55km/ 34mi south-east of Querétaro on the MEX 57D. The area is a centre for basket weavers and makers of wooden furniture.

Tequisquiapan

The charming resort town of Tequisquiapan (population 30,000) is situated 20km/12mi north-east of San Juan del Río on the MEX 120. The hotels and thermal spring spas (radioactive springs) as well as the opportunities to ride and fish attract predominantly visitors from Mexico City.

Bernal

The road to Bernal branches off at Ezequiel Montes, about 17km/ 10mi north of Tequisquiapan. The town lies on the slopes of a spectacular hat-shaped mountain. The area is known for the manufacture of heavy woollen ponchos (sarapes).

From San Joaquín, after about 95km/59mi on the MEX 120 through the very beautiful Sierra Gorda region, travellers reach Jalpan (elevation 770m/2,526ft). The town lies amid sugar cane and coffee plantations and has a Baroque church which is worth a visit. The church was built by Indians in the middle of the 18th century and is dedicated to St James; in the lower part of the façade, the double eagle of the emperor is combined with Aztec eagle with a snake in its beak. The legendary Franciscan priest Junipero Serra is responsible for the construction of the church. He was sent as a missionary to convert Indians in the region, and later founded several missions in California, some of which developed into large cities, such as San Diego, San Francisco and Santa Clara. Serra and his fellow friars established other missions around Jalpan whose churches are worth taking a look at because of their unique Baroque façades. The names of these mission towns are Concá (38km/24mi), Landa (22km/14mi), Tilaco (49km/30mi) and Tancoyol (60km/37mi).

Jalpan

◄ Baroque Churches

! *Baedeker* TIP

Fantastic castle in the jungle

Xilitla is about 84km/50mi away from Jalpan. Going in the direction of Ciudad Valles, 4km/2.4mi after this little town there is a small bridge, and after this a track leads off left to Las Pozas. Eccentric British millionaire Edward James purchased a 100ha/250ac area of jungle here after the Second World War and created a surreal dream-world in the midst of lush tropical vegetation, the construction of which he on principle never completed. James however died in 1984 and since then the fate of this fantastic rainforest palace, whose bizarre architecture is becoming more and more overgrown, has remained uncertain.

★ Riviera Maya

Federal state:: Quintana Roo (Q.R.)

The Riviera Maya or Cancún-Tulum Corridor is the approximately 140km/87mi-long section along the MEX 307 from Cancún to Tulum. In this area, enjoy the beaches or visit smaller archaeological sites, among them the Tulum fort from the post-classical Maya period.

From here, Cobá is in easy reach as is the picturesque nature and biosphere reserve (Reserva de la Biósfera de Sian Ka'an) in a southerly direction. Sponsored by the Mexican tourist authority and private investors, in the last years the region has been developing fast. There is accommodation in the form of luxury bungalows but also simple cabañas on the beach, as well as beaches, nature parks, aquatic sports facilities and recreational parks. The main city in the area is Playa del Carmen. Movie buffs will remember the film »Against All Odds«, which was in part shot in this charming coastal region.

Riviera Maya Map

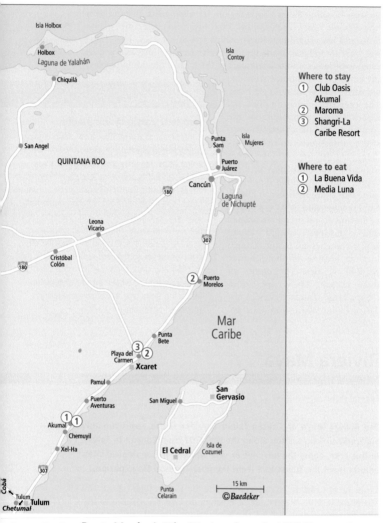

Isla Holbox

Holbox
Laguna de Yalahán

Chiquilá

Isla
Contoy

San Angel

QUINTANA ROO

Punta
Sam

Isla
Mujeres

Puerto
Juárez

Cancún

180

Laguna
de Nichupté

Leona
Vicario

307

Cristóbal
Colón

180

② Puerto
Morelos

Mar
Caribe

Punta
Bete

③ ②
Playa del
Carmen
Xcaret

Pamul

Puerto
Aventuras

San Miguel

**San
Gervasio**

① ①
Akumal

Chemuyil

Xel-Ha

El Cedral

Isla de
Cozumel

307

Cobá

Tulum
Chetumal **Tulum**

Punta
Celarain

15 km

©*Baedeker*

Where to stay
① Club Oasis
  Akumal
② Maroma
③ Shangri-La
  Caribe Resort

Where to eat
① La Buena Vida
② Media Luna

Puerto Morelos

Puerto Morelos is 37km/23mi south on the MEX 307, past Cancún airport. Ferries carry people and cars from Puerto Morelos to the island of ►Cozumel.

Playas Secreto and Paraíso

These two very beautiful beaches (15km/9mi south of Puerto Morelos) are the habitat of ocean turtles. Overnight accommodation is available.

▶ VISITING RIVIERA MAYA

INFORMATION
Detailed information about this recreational area is available at www.rivieramaya.com

GETTING AROUND
Bus services from and to Cancún

WHERE TO EAT
► Moderate
② *Media Luna*
Avenida 5 and Calle 8 (opposite the Plaza Rincón del Sol)
Tel. (984) 873 05 26
This is a favourite restaurant for vegetarians and connoisseurs of fish and seafood. It features beautiful wall hangings from Guatemala and guitar music.

► Moderate to inexpensive
① *La Buena Vida*
Bahía Media Luna
Akumal
Tel. (984) 75 90 60
The popular beach hotel with bar offers mainly fish and seafood.

WHERE TO STAY
► Luxury
① *Club Oasis Akumal*
Carretera Chetumal-Puerto Juárez
Km 251
Akumal
Tel. (984) 875 73 00
Fax (984) 875 73 16
www.oasishotels.com

This is a luxury class hotel (120 rooms) next to a beautiful beach on a half moon-shaped bay, which is protected by a barrier reef. Guest can take part in many aquatic sports and there are opportunities for outings. All rooms have either an ocean view or a view on the garden.

② *Maroma Resort and Spa*
Carretera Cancún Tulum Km 51
Punta Maroma
Tel. (988) 872 82 00
Fax (998) 872 82 20
www.maromahotel.com
The hotel (36 rooms) lies somewhat hidden on a beach at the Punta Maroma. The area around the hotel used to be a coconut plantation. The thatched bungalows have neither TV nor telephone.

► Mid-range
③ *Shangri-La Caribe Resort*
Calle 38 Norte con Zona Federal Maritima
Playa del Carmen
Tel. (984) 873 0611
Fax (984) 873 05 00
www.shangrilacaribe.net
These bungalows (70 rooms) each have a porch with hammock and fans. A diving sport centre offers equipment for rent and organizes tours. Riders can take out horses.

Puntas Maroma and Bete
Between Punta Maroma and Punta Bete (about 40km/25mi from Cancún), an underground river surfaces and soon reaches the ocean where its fresh water mixes with the salty ocean water. This creates a unique ecological system. Pleasant lodging is offered on both of the river's banks.

Xcalacoco

Those who love camping find their ideal spot in Xcalacoco, the newest recreational park of the region Tres Rios. Campers are provided with solar power, public showers, several fish restaurants and can even venture out to a small archaeological site. A large number of palms provide welcome shade.

Playa del Carmen

Finally, after another 10km/6mi, travellers reach Playa del Carmen. For many decades, Playa as it is known for short was just a simply fishing village opposite the island of ▶Cozumel, about halfway between Tulum and Cancún. Now, the fast growing village is crowded out by hotels and restaurants. The new, luxurious tourist zone Playacar is located right next to »old Playa« in the midst of a tropical park. **After Cancún, Playa del Carmen is the second largest travel destination in the federal state of Quintana Roo.** The area offers many miles of beautiful white beaches, especially in the northern part. There are opportunities to dive or go offshore fishing.

Avenida Juárez leads from the MEX 307 to a park near the ocean. A block south, the ferry from and to Cozumel docks or casts off. Avenida 5, lined with various types of hotels, restaurants and shops, runs parallel to the beach; the new modern bus terminal and a direct connection to the airport Cancún and other destinations is also here. In the evening, Avenida 5 is completely closed to cars.

It is easy to reach Cancún or Tulum from Playa del Carmen or to visit other tourist attractions along the coast or inland, such as the tropical bird sanctuary Xaman-Ha or the Sacbé Caves.

> ! **Baedeker TIP**
>
> **Pelota game**
>
> IIn Yucatán's Xcaret leisure park it is not only ecology that is writ large – Maya history is also presented in a lively way. Every afternoon, the show programme includes the demonstration of a Pelota game in appropriate historical costume on an authentic replica of a Pelota court (information at www.xcaretcancun.com).

Calica

Calica is located about three miles south of Playa. It is a large international landing stage for cruises and also the place where the car ferry to Cozumel docks or leaves.

Xcaret

A turning to the left shortly after Playa del Carmen on the MEX 307 leads to the Xcaret recreational park where visitors can see the vestiges of a ruined Maya city. This is the old port of Pole from where boats used to cast off to Cozumel. The park features several cenotes (sinkholes) as well as a lagoon and the most beautiful bays on the Riviera Maya. Aside from the ruins, there is a botanical garden with a small camp where visitors learn about the method of extracting Chicle, a replica of a Maya village, a butterfly pavilion, an aquarium

Tropical vegetation at the Yal-ku lagoon →

Relaxing in the Xcaret nature and leisure park

and a dolphinarium. It is also possible to watch the free swimming turtles, watch Indian dance demonstrations, ride or dive.

Paamul   Near the park stretches the beautiful beach Paamul, a paradise for snorkellers or divers. During the night in May and June, ocean turtles come to the beach to lay their eggs. Travellers can camp out here or stay in a hotel or guesthouse. There is also a pleasant Mexican restaurant.

Puerto Aventuras   About 30km/19mi south of Playa del Carmen stands a glamorous, village-like hotel complex of huge proportions named Puerto Aventuras with a **marina** (ferry to Cozumel), golf courses, hotels, restaurants and apartment complexes. A fishing competition takes place here every year around the end of May. Recently, a cultural and religious centre opened here. A **shipwreck museum** in the harbour is a recommended attraction.

Xpu-Ha   Xpu-Ha is a large and very beautiful bay perfect to visit and rest for a while. The nearby village offers hotels, restaurants and shops with diving gear. The Cenote Manati (sinkhole) is situated in the northern part of the bay.
Another beautiful beach in the area is **Kantenah** with palms and an amazing coral reef very close to the coast.

Akumal (meaning »place of the turtles«) is situated in a half moon-shaped bay with a 15km/9mi-long snow-white beach lined with palms. As well as a small village, there are more than two dozen hotels and many clubs. Now a tourist centre, Akumal used to be a small Maya village, only gaining popularity when CEDAM, an association dedicated to the discovery and preservation of archaeological underwater finds, moved its offices here. In the course of many expeditions, researchers have succeeded in discovering **Maya sites** and recovering old Spanish shipwrecks from the ocean floor. The **Ecology Centre Ukana I**, whose purpose is to boost awareness of the regional ecology, is located in the village. Dancing, painting and yoga delight the guests.

✱ Akumal

Tourists and locals alike love the bays of Chemuyil and Xcacel. Chemuyil is a pretty bay with white beaches and a small stretch of woods. The coastal water is shallow here and therefore ideal for children. Several restaurants offer fresh fish and seafood. It is possible to camp out or stay in a hotel.

Chemuyil and Xcacel

Covering a relatively small area, the charming Nature Park Xel-há features **a fresh-water lake, an ocean bay and Maya ruins**. By walking, swimming and snorkelling, visitors can enjoy the rich fauna and flora on land and in the ocean. Diving gear is offered for rent. At weekends however, the lagoon (10km/6mi south) is hopelessly overrun. More than other places along the bays in this region, Xel-há (meaning »birthplace of the water«) seems to have been an important Maya religious site in classical times. The extent of the waters and the locations of the archaeological artefacts support this theory. A battlement from the post-classical period as well as several underwater altars have been discovered here; one altar was found in a chapel-like grotto, which had obviously served as a sacred site. Recently, inland Maya ruins close to the MEX 307 have been excavated and partially restored. Do consider visiting the three groups Mercado, Palacio and Jaguar, their pyramids, palaces, temples and the cenote in a very romantic setting.

✱ Xel-há

The ruined Maya city of Tancah with a cenote (sinkhole) lies about 10km/6mi south on the grounds of a hacienda. The unearthed temples are similar to those found in Tulum, although they seem to be much older. In the post-classical period, Tancah was presumably some kind of satellite city of the nearby ►Tulum.

Tancah

Moving further along the Riviera Maya, the impressive Maya fortress ►Tulum appears, set off by a grandiose panorama directly on the ocean. From there, a road leads south to the biosphere reserve Sian Ka'an and via Boca Paila to the picturesque fishing village Punta Allen. Alternatively, travel north-west from Tulum to reach the ruins of ►Cobá.

Along the Riviera Maya

✳ San Cristóbal de las Casas

S 26

Federal state: Chiapas (Chis.)
Population: 140,000

Altitude: 2,200m/7,218ft
Distance: 1,085km/674mi south-east of Mexico City

Even though San Cristóbal de las Casas exhibits typical colonial flair with many churches, low houses with red tiled roofs and window grilles, the essence of the town derives from its Indian history and present. This gives San Cristóbal de las Casas its own special atmosphere.

San Cristóbal de las Casas and its surroundings certainly make the list of the most interesting travel destinations in Mexico. The town in the Jovel Valley is the oldest Spanish settlement in Chiapas, surrounded by forested mountains including Tzontehuitz (2,858 m / 9,377 ft) and Huetepec (2,717 m / 8,914 ft).

History

The Maya were the first to settle in Huezecatlán, but in the 15th century the Aztec extracted tribute from the Maya inhabitants of the settlement. The Spanish conquistadores had a hard time subjugating the Maya tribes and managed to advance only after bitter fights. In 1528, the Spanish conqueror Diego de Mazariegos founded Villa Real, but the settlement was later renamed after the patron saint San Cristóbal and the great protector of the Indians and bishop of the town, Bartolomé de las Casas. Chiapas and consequently San Cristóbal were subject to the rule of the Spanish administration in Guatemala until Mexico became an independent nation. Until 1892, San Cristóbal was the capital of Chiapas. On New Year's Day in 1994, the town was temporarily occupied by insurgent Tzotzil and Tzeltal tribes fighting in the **Zapatist liberation army**. The negotiations between the government and the rebel army took place in the cathedral (▶ Baedeker-Special pp.52–54).

> **! Baedeker TIP**
>
> **How did the Maya heal?**
> Predominantly with herbs, natural remedies and magic rituals. How did the herb gardens and pharmacies look, and how were illnesses diagnosed? Visitors can test the latter on their own bodies in the Casa de Curación: headaches, diarrhoea and similar complaints are treated here (Museo de la Medicina Maya, Av. Salomón González Blanco 10, www.laneta.apc.org/omiech/museum.htm; open Tue–Fri 10am–2pm, Sat/Sun 10am–4pm).

What to See in San Cristóbal de las Casas

Plaza 31 de Marzo

Around the Zócalo (Plaza 31 de Marzo) stands an array of beautiful colonial buildings, such as the town hall, the tourist office and the

Woollen dolls, on the left with Zapatist masks

cathedral. The construction of the **Church of Our Lady of Assumption** started as early as 1528; however, it was completed only at the end of the 17th century. The church contains several Baroque altars, paintings and sculptures, among them a picture of Magdalena by Miguel Cabrera and the centre panel of the Altar del Perdón by Juan Correa. Also note the wood carvings, in particular the beautifully decorated pulpit.

The house of the town's founder, the **Casa de Mazariegos**, stands at the corner of Avenida Insurgentes and is now the Hotel Santa Clara. In the stone sculptures at the portal, heads of the Castilian lion are visible.

The most important sacral building of the city is the Church of Santo Domingo north of the city square and up Avenida General Utrilla. It was built between 1547 and 1560 by order of Bishop Francisco de Marroquin of Guatemala. Created in the 17th century in the typical Mexican Baroque style, the church façade is by area the largest of its kind in Mexico. The church interior **is decorated with extreme opulence** and contains several sculptures and wooden gilded altars. The elaborately carved pulpit especially is richly decorated; its foot is made of a single piece of wood.

✷
Santo Domingo

The market is located near the Church of Santo Domingo where the **indigenous population** from the surrounding mountain villages con-

✷
Market

VISITING SAN CRISTÓBAL DE LAS CASAS

INFORMATION

Tourist information

at the right corner of the Palacio Municipal in the Zócalo,
Tel. (967) 678 06 60 or
Secretaría de Turismo de Chiapas
Calle Hidalgo (immediately behind the south-western corner of the Zócalo)
Tel. (967) 678 65 70

GETTING AROUND

The best route is to drive 83km/52mi from Tuxtla Gutiérrez on the MEX 190 (Pan-American Highway), which begins in Mexico City. By bus, the trip from Mexico City lasts about 18 hours, and 1.5 hours from Tuxtla Gutiérrez.

SHOPPING

The main market in the area around San Cristóbal is doubtless the Mercado Indígena which offers almost anything, including fruit and vegetables, flowers, small livestock, clothing and pottery. Bargain-hunters should visit weavers' cooperative J'Pas Jolovitelic.

WHERE TO EAT

▶ Moderate

① *El Fogón de Jovel*
Calle 16 de Septiembre 11
Tel. (967) 678 11 53

The waiters in this restaurant wear traditional Maya dress, and on the walls hang prints from Guatemala as well as regional folk art. The kitchen serves Chiapas specialities.

▶ Inexpensive

② *Normita's*
B. Juárez y Dr. José Flores
This small, very good restaurant is located two blocks south-east of the Zócalo and serves specialities from the Jalisco and Chiapas regions.

WHERE TO STAY

▶ Mid-range

① *Ciudad Real*
Plaza 31 de Marzo No. 10
Col. Centro
Tel. (967) 678 04 64
A beautiful colonial building right on the Zócalo, with friendly staff and a pleasant patio.

② *Na Bolom*
Vicente Guerrero 33
Tel. (967) 678 14 18
www.nabolom.org
The 12 rooms have a rustic feel and are decorated in the Indian style; they feature photographs of the different tribes by the former owner and photographer Duby-Blom. Guests also enjoy the museum and the well-stocked Maya library. (see p.525).

gregate. For a few years now, part of the market has been taking place in a modern market hall, detracting from the market's unique character. The participants in the San Cristóbal market are mostly members of the Tzotzil and Tzeltal, both Maya tribes. Visitors can tell the tribes from different settlements apart by their unique traditional costumes; the garb of the Chamula and the Indians from Tenejapa and Zinacantán is the most striking

A monastery was built at the same time as the church. In the 19th century the monastery served as a prison and it is now occupied by the Indian Textile Cooperative Sna Jolobil. A religious museum stands next to it.

Weavers' cooperatives

Another cooperative going by the name of **J'pas Joloviletic** (weavers) operates from a building behind the La Caridad church in Avenida Utrilla. Each of these associations represents approximately 800 Indian weavers who create very interesting, high quality textiles from wool and cotton. There are many different styles of woven textiles because every village in the Highland of Chiapas has its own traditional embroidered or woven costumes. At first glance, the patterns appear abstract but on closer inspection stylized snakes, frogs, butterflies or birds can be picked out.

The exhibits in the Museum of Archaeology, Ethnography, History and Art (Museo de Arqueología, Etnografía, Historia y Arte) mostly elucidate the history of San Cristóbal de las Casas. The museum is close to the Church of Santo Domingo.

Museum of Archaeology

A daily market takes place in front of the Dan Domingo church in San Cristóbal.

San Cristóbal de las Casas *Plan*

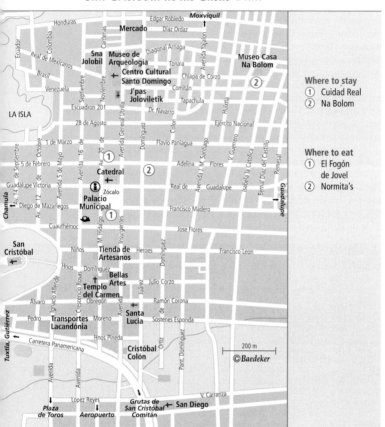

Where to stay
1 Cuidad Real
2 Na Bolom

Where to eat
1 El Fogón de Jovel
2 Normita's

©Baedeker

200 m

Church of Carmen
Fine Arts

Calle Hidalgo south leads from the Zócalo to the Church of Carmen (Templo del Carmen) located at the moorish gate over the street, once the access gate to the city.

The church was once part of a monastery (1597) and has a conspicuous tower. Opposite, stands the Casa de la Cultura with a library, gallery and auditorium; a small shop and café are also part of the set-up.

Centro Cultural
El Puente

The centre for information and culture (Centro Cultural El Puente, Real de Guadalupe 55) attracts locals, tourists and artists. The exhibits in the gallery change from time to time. Readings, theatre plays and movies entertain the visitors. The associated café serves good food.

Outside the church in San Juan Chamula

On the premises of the guest house Casa Na-Bolom (House of the Jaguar) in Avenida Vicente Guerrero 33 there is also a museum of archaeology and ethnology as well as a library, both established by the Danish archaeologist Frans Blom, who died in 1963. They are dedicated to the **Indians of Chiapas** and their cultural heritage. Particular attention is paid to the **Lacandon Maya**. Frans Blom's wife Gertrude Duby-Blom created an excellent photographic portrait of the disappearing culture. A board of directors has administered the house since her death in 1993. The house opens at 4pm.

✱
Casa Na-Bolom

After 10km/6mi on the MEX 190 toward Comitán, a road branches off to the right leading to the nearby San Cristóbal caves (Grutas de San Cristóbal). Only a small fraction of these extended dripstone caves is accessible to the public.

San Cristóbal caves

Excursion to Indian Villages

When visiting Indian villages, remember that the indigenous people do not like to have their photographs taken. Therefore, either do not take photographs, or first ask permission to do so. Very revealing attire or loud and overbearing behaviour may be met with an irritated reaction.

Respect for the indigenous people

San Juan Chamula is the ceremonial centre of the Chamula with the largest of the Tzotzil speaking Indian groups. Most of the approxi-

✱
San Juan Chamula

mately 40,000 Chamula live in scattered small villages. The site lies about 11km/7mi north-west of San Cristóbal. Here, as in many Indian villages or on hill tops, stand **three large crosses**, which symbolize the tree of life. Candles are lighted in the small church in memory of deceased family members or friends. The church is well worth a visit because it shows how Catholic rites have merged tightly with Maya myth.

The Chamula wear woollen wraps over white skirts and slacks, which are often held by an orange leather belt. On holidays, straw hats with colourful bands hanging down in the back give a festive look to the attire. Men who play an official role in the village wear black wraps. Women wear black wrap-around skirts which go half way down their calves as well as orange-red-green belts. Traditionally, women's blouses were white, but today they tend to prefer blue cotton or dark wool blouses. **Festivities** take place from 16 to 22 January to honour San Sebastian or to celebrate carnival or Easter. There are also feasts to honour Santa Cruz (3 May), San Juan Bautista (22–25 June) or Santa Rosa (30 August).

Photographs prohibited ► Visitors should note that it is considered most inappropriate to photograph people when they congregate for church services. Doing so may cause an angry reaction. Taking photographs inside the church is also strictly prohibited.

✳ Zinacantán
Zinacantán is situated about 12km/7.5mi west of San Cristóbal de Las Casas. Only a few hundred people live in this village, but it is nevertheless a religious and political centre for the roughly 14,000 Zinacantec in surrounding villages. The language of this tribe is Tzotzil. The special features of the men's attire are a grey chequered wrap over white shorts and **flat straw hats with bands in many colours**. The way these bands are arranged indicates whether or not the wearer is married. The celebrations in honour of San Sebastián (18 January), San Lorenzo (8–11 August) and the Virgen de la Navidad (8 September) are well-known events.

✳ Tenejapa
About 28km/92mi north-east of Cristóbal de Las Casas lies the Indian village of Tenejapa. Only a few hundred of the approximately 15,000 Tzeltal-speaking Indians in the area live in the village. The men's attire consists of black woollen tunics over white trousers and a straw hat. The women of Tenejapa wear embroidered blouses and dark-blue skirts with narrow bands and a red and black striped belt under a white one. Festivities take place every year in honour of San Ildefonso (23 January) and Santiago Apóstol (22–24 July).

✳ Huixtán
About 90km/56mi further on, a road branches off to the left and leads to Ocosingo and ►Palenque. The village of Huixtán is another 20km/12mi along this road. As elsewhere, only a few members of the **Tzotzil tribe** live in the village itself in the old Maya tradition; most Indians live in the surrounding hills. The village features a church,

an administrative office building and a few shops. Most men still wear the traditional wide, white cotton trousers with a broad red sash. The majority of their white shirts are embroidered on the collar and sleeves, and a black or brown woollen wrap serves as outerwear. The flat hats with the decorative red band are made in the village. The women wear long, dark-blue skirts and a red belt with yellow stripes. Their cotton blouses show blue embroidery on the collar and they embroider their white wraps with colourful animal and flower patterns. Only 10% of the approximately 12,000 Huixtec of the Tzotzil tribe live in the village of Huixtán. **Festive events** take place from 14 to 16 May (San Isidro), from 27 to 30 June (San Pedro) and on 28 and 29 September (San Miguel Arcángel).

Other Indian villages may not be quite as well known, but they are certainly just as interesting to visit, especially at fiesta time. These include San Andrés Larrainzar, San Pedro Chenal-hó and Amatenango del Valle.

Other Indian villages

Further Afield

Ocosingo is about 50km/31mi from Huixtán. Until recently, this was an isolated, small town in the territory of the Tzeltal. The town, set in very beautiful landscape, is important to Indians as a **centre for the woodcutters, chicle gatherers and hunters**. In addition to various remote and often hard to reach but unspoilt Indian villages and haciendas (El Real, Australia and others), there is also the picturesque village Altamirano.
The MEX 199 north leads to the Agua Azul Cascades, Misol-ha and ►Palenque.

Ocosingo

The excavation site Toniná, with its small museum, lies about 14km/9mi east of Ocosingo. This Maya city had its heyday in the **Maya classical period**, i.e. the 8th and 9th centuries. Inscriptions on stelae suggest that Ruler 3 of Toniná captured the ruler Kan-xul of Palenque in 711. The site covers seven terraces on a hill, and two ball courts have been found at its base. Among the excavated finds are many **stelae** with inscribed dates between 495 and 909, round calendar stones and sculptures of humans without heads. Of special interest is the discovery of an underground chamber with cantilever arch and wooden lintel, as well as a tomb with sarcophagus, large stone

 Toniná

Maya relics in Toniná

Opening times:
daily 9am–4pm

masks and stucco statues. Finds from the early 1990s include the **Palace of the Underworld** (Palacio del Inframundo). The palace with a base of 4 x 12m/13 x 39ft was built from stones that had not been used in the region prior to this building. Maya motifs, Toltec elements and the large stucco mural of the Fourth Sun suggest that Toniná continued to exist after the Maya classical period, submitting to Toltec influence. The beautiful *Frieze of the Dream Lords* was discovered in September 1997. The unique mural depicts, in red, four lords of the underworld who symbolize war, agriculture, trade and tribute. A small museum was established here in 1998.

Comitán

Comitán (population 63,000) is another 57km/35mi south-east of San Cristóbal de Las Casas on the MEX 190 (Pan-American Highway). This friendly colonial city is known for the cultivation of orchids. A small museum in the Casa Dr. Belisario Domínguez (Avenida Central Sur 29) and another one in the Casa de la Cultura (a former monastery next to the church on the corner of the plaza) show regional archaeological finds.

Montebello Lakes

After another 16km/10mi on the MEX 190, a road branching off to the left leads to the ▶Montebello Lakes (40km/25mi).

Outings by air taxi

San Cristóbal de Las Casas is a convenient hub to hire an air taxi and venture out to Maya sites in the Lacandon Jungle (Selva Lacandona). The largest sites are ▶Palenque, ▶Bonampak and Yaxchilán.

★ San Luis Potosí

M 18

Federal state: San Luis Potosí (S.L.P.)	**Altitude:** 1,877m/6,158ft
Population: 950,000	**Distance:** about 420km/261mi northwest of Mexico City

San Luis Potosí is the capital of the federal state of the same name. Stretching out on a steppe-like upland plain, the city serves as an important trade centre and traffic hub. While modernized, San Luis Potosí has still kept some of its colonial character with beautiful old buildings and parks.

History

Little is known about the pre-Hispanic history of the city. Supposedly, there once was a Cuachichil-Indian settlement called Tanjamanja in this area. Europeans came here between 1585 and 1590, first Spaniards led by Miguel Caldera and soon afterwards the Franciscan friars. At this time, significant deposits of silver and gold were discovered. This led to the establishment of the township Real de Minas de San Luis Potosí, the name Potosí (place of great riches) simply being taken from a silver city of that name in Bolivia. Philipp IV of

Spain granted the town its charter in 1658. Until 1824, San Luis Potosí was the capital of an extended region administered by Spanish officials, an area that included Texas. In the French Intervention War (1862–1866) and for a short while afterward, San Luis Potosí served temporarily as the seat of the Benito Juárez administration when it was exiled from Mexico City.

What to See in San Luis Potosí

The Plaza de Armas with the Hidalgo Gardens (Jardín Hidalgo) is the centre of the city. At the western end of the plaza stands the Governor's Palace (Palacio de Gobierno), a massive 18th-century structure in the neo-classical style. Inside, the Sala Juárez contains life-sized wax statues depicting the meeting of Benito Juárez with the princess Salm-Salm on 18 July 1867 during which the princess begged for the life of Emperor Maximilian. He was nevertheless executed on the following day in Querétaro.

Governor's Palace

The temple of San Francisco in San Luis Potosí was built in the 17th century.

▶ VISITING SAN LUIS POTOSÍ

INFORMATION

Tourist information
in the Palacio Municipal
Tel. (444) 812 27 70
The state of San Luis Potosí offers an information office at Calle Obregón 520, west of the Plaza de los Fundadores.

GETTING AROUND

The MEX 57 connects Mexico City and San Luis Potosí (417km/259mi). The trip takes about 10 hours by train and about 5.5 hours by bus.

WHERE TO EAT

▶ **Moderate**

② *La Corriente*
Carranza 700
This is a pretty restaurant, with shaded places in the inner courtyard, which serves delicious food including various steaks and enchiladas.

① *El Callejón de San Francisco*
Callejón de Lozada 1
Tel. (444) 812 45 08

Guests can sit either in the roof garden of this romantic restaurant or in the dining room with its old movie posters. The Mexican food is first-rate. Dinner reservations are required.

WHERE TO STAY

▶ **Luxury**

② *Westin San Luis*
Real de Lomas 1000
Tel. (444) 825 01 25
Fax (444) 825 02 00
www.westin.com
The former Quinta Real (123 rooms) is decorated with tasteful antiques and Mexican folk art.

▶ **Mid-range**

① *María Cristina*
Juan Sarabia 110
Centro Histórico
Tel. (444) 812 94 08
Fax (444) 812 88 23
www.mariacristina.com.mx
The 74 rooms in this large, modern hotel feature heavy wooden furniture, TV and fans.

✳ **Cathedral**
The Baroque cathedral is also located at the main plaza. It was built between 1670 and 1740 and the façade was fitted with an unusual hexagonal anteroom with statues of the twelve apostles standing in niches. The excessively ornate design of the interior is a mixture of many different styles.

✳ **El Carmen**
The 18th-century El Carmen church stands at the Plaza del Carmen east of the cathedral. This church façade is a beautiful example of **Mexican Baroque**, and the dome is covered with glazed tiles (azulejos) in different colours. The main altar inside the church is in the neo-classical style and several side altars are in the ultra-Baroque style. There is a particularly beautiful **sea shell-shaped alcove** (a niche for a statue) as well as two frescos by Francisco Eduardo Tresguerras.

San Luis Potosí Plan

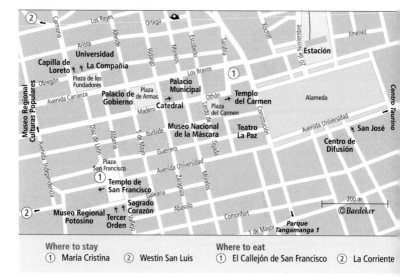

Where to stay
① María Cristina   ② Westin San Luis

Where to eat
① El Callejón de San Francisco   ② La Corriente

The Teatro La Paz next to the El Carmen church was built at the end of the 19th century using the regional reddish variety of the Cantera stone. The interior is decorated with murals by Fernando Leal.

Teatro La Paz

The Palacio Federal from the times of the Porfiriato across the street from the theatre now houses the National Mask Museum (Museo Nacional de la Máscara). The museum displays a formerly private collection of old and new **masks from all parts of Mexico**.

✳
National Mask Museum

An old Franciscan monastery in Calle Galeana south of the Zócalo now houses the Potosi Regional Museum (Museo Regional Potosino). The museum displays mostly regional archaeological finds (Huastec, Totonac and Aztec).

Potosi Regional Museum

The Capilla de Aránzazu, considered a **masterpiece of the 18th-century ultra-Baroque style in New Spain**, is on the first floor of the building.
The carved door leaves made from mesquite wood, the oversized estípites (inverted pilasters) supporting the dome, the Christ statue in the ante-hall and the paintings in the chapel and its adjoining rooms are all remarkable.

✳
◀ *Capilla Aránzazu*

The San Francisco monastery church, featuring a beautiful ultra-Baroque façade and situated next to the Guerrero Gardens, was built in the 17th century. The crystal chandelier in the shape of a ship and finely crafted saint statues are particularly noteworthy.

San Francisco monastery church

Other attractions

Other attractions in the city include the San Agustín church (at the intersection of Morelos and Abasolo) with a Baroque façade, a beautiful tower and a neo-classical interior. There is also the Jesuit church of Loreto (Avenida Obregón and Avenida D. Camona) with the adjoining shrine (sagrario). Also interesting to visit are the Federico Silva Museum of Contemporary Sculpture near the park Jardín de San Juan de Dios, the Museum of Religious Art in the former monastery, the Casa de la Virreina (house of the viceroys) and the historic train station.

The popular **Regional Museum of Folk Art** (formerly Jardín Guerrero 6) has been relocated under a new name to the former Hacienda de Tenería (about 5km/3mi from the city centre) in the Tangamanga Park (opposite the main park entrance). The items in the **regional art and sales exhibition** are very interesting to browse through and of excellent quality (ceramics, items made from wood or paper pulp, masks, musical instruments, baskets, wraps etc).

> ! **Baedeker TIP**
>
> **Technology back then**
>
> The Presa San José outside of the gates of San Luis de Potosí is an awesome sight. This giant dam was built already in 1863 as the artificial closure to a 5-kilometre long (3-mile) S-shaped canyon. Meanwhile nature is taking shape around it as the Parque Ecológico Urbano and is very popular among the Potosini. Especially on weekends and holidays crowds stream in, fill up the long tables at the eateries, pant over hundreds of steps to the top of the dam or just quietly dangle their hook and line in the water.

Around San Luis Potosí

Media Luna Lagoon

A side road about 15km/9mi east of San Luis Potosí leads to the warm and perpetually clear Media Luna Lagoon (half moon lagoon). These qualities make the lagoon particularly popular with divers who have also found quite a few archaeological artefacts.

Santa María del Río

Santa María del Río is located 50km/31mi south of San Luis Potosí. The town is known for the rebozos (wraps, baby slings, etc.) produced there. The radioactive thermal springs Gogorrón, Lourdes and Ojo Caliente are not far away.

Real de Catorce

The **impressive ghost town** Real de Catorce is about 30km/19mi north-west of Matehuala; the site is accessible via a mountainous road and a roughly 2.5km/1.6mi-long tunnel.It was reputedly named after 14 soldiers who were killed here in around 1700 by Indians. The mining town played a significant role mostly at the end of the 19th century, when 45,000 people lived there (today about 800), and there was a theatre, a mint and an electric mining railway.

San Francisco church, to which thousands make a pilgrimage every year on 4 October, is well worth taking a look at. The pilgrims leave

The ghost-town Real de Catorce

many votive boards with their thanksgivings for answered prayers for health, wealth and protection from disaster.

The **peyotl cactus** grows in the region around Real de Catorce. Considered sacred by some Indian tribes, such as the Huichol and Tarahumara, the peyotl (button cactus, mescalito) contains the psychedelic drug mescaline. After ingesting it, the Indians believe they can hear messages from their gods. Since the peyotl cactus does not grow in the current settlements of the Huichol, some of them will make large pilgrimages in winter, sometimes over distances of more than 500km/311mi, to come to the Holy Land of Wirikuta where the cactus still grows. This pilgrimage involves complicated ceremonies and ends with spearing and then harvesting the peyotl.

**Holy Land
Wirikuta**

★ ★ San Miguel de Allende

Federal state:: Guanajuato (Gto.)
Population: 135,000

Altitude: 1,910m/6,266ft
Distance: 280 km/174mi north-west of Mexico City

San Miguel de Allende is one of the most beautiful colonial towns in Mexico. Nestling against a hill and stretching from there into a valley, the town's splendid residences line the steep, cobbled alleys, and there are churches and shady plazas.

Attractive landscape	From the town the wide bend of the Río Laja is visible, and in the distance the blue mountains of Guanajuato. As one of the few towns in Mexico under preservation order, San Miguel de Allenda has almost completely retained its colonial character. Especially beautiful residences with patios and gardens are often hiding behind quite simple façades.

The charming appearance, the attractive landscape and the temperate climate, all make San Miguel Allende a favourite destination for foreigners who take up temporary or permanent residence here. Moreover, the city is an **academic centre and centre for the arts**, especially painting, sculpture, pottery, music, literature and the theatre.

 VISITING SAN MIGUEL DE ALLENDE

INFORMATION

Tourist information
Delegación de Turismo
Plaza Principal
(next to the parish church)
Tel. (415) 152 65 65

GETTING AROUND

A bus ride from Mexico City to San Miguel de Allende takes 4 hours. The MEX 57 D connects Mexico City and San Luis Potosi via Querétaro (about 280 km / 174 mi).

WHERE TO EAT

► **Expensive**
① *La Capilla*
Cuna de Allende 10
Tel. (415) 152 06 98
This is a new restaurant with unique ambience in a great location. The international cuisine is excellent. The restaurant occupies two floors in an old building next to the parish church. Guests can sit outside or in the dining room. On the first floor, a pianist entertains the guests. Reservations are necessary.

► **Moderate**
② *Mama Mía*
Umarán 8
Tel. (415) 152 20 63

Enjoy Italian and Mexican cuisine in a patio with a lush garden and Latin American music in the evening. There is also a video bar and a listening room for salsa and jazz.

WHERE TO STAY

► **Luxury**
② *Hacienda Taboada*
Carretera a Dolores Hidalgo
Km 8
Tel. (415) 152 08 50
www.hoteltaboada.com
This is an exclusive hotel (70 rooms) with thermal spa 12km/7.5 mi north of San Miguel. The hotel offers a restaurant, bar, three different temperature-adjusted swimming pools (one for children), two tennis courts, table-tennis tables, horses for hire, a playground for children and other amenities.

► **Inexpensive**
① *El Hotel Posada Carmina*
Cuna de Allende 7
Tel. (415) 152 04 58
Fax (415) 152 10 36
www.posadacarmina.com
This two-storey former colonial mansion (12 rooms) next to the parish church is more than 200 years old. The large patio offers shade.

History

The Tarasca and the Chichimec settled in the area around San Miguel de Allende in pre-Columbian times. The Franciscan priest Juan de San Miguel, who had a reputation for his beneficial work on behalf of the Indians in Michoacán, established an **Indian mission** here in 1542 and named it San Miguel de los Chichimec after his own patron saint and the indigenous Indians. Soon, Indian settlers came from Tlaxcala and settled here but still had to ward off attacks from the bellicose Chichimec. The village became a provincial town in 1555 and was renamed San Miguel el Grande. In colonial times, rich mine owners and landholders from Guanajuato and Zacatecas also came and settled here; some of their palaces and houses are still among the most beautiful buildings in town. In 1779 **Ignacio de Allende** was born here, and in 1810 he joined Juan Aldama and the priest Miguel Hidalgo in the fight for Mexican independence, finally being executed by the Spanish royalists. In appreciation for his actions, the town assumed the surname Allende (1862). In recent decades, the town has developed into an important cultural centre, but not at the cost of its traditional charm.

Life is colourful at the Zócalo.

What to See in San Miguel de Allende

Parroquia

The parish church (Parroquia) at the pretty main square (El Jardín, Plaza de Allende) has become the landmark of the city. The church was built around 1880 in a unique neo-Gothic style to replace an older, simple church. The new church is the work of the Indian architect Ceferino Gutiérrez who modelled it on a number of European cathedrals.

To the left of the parish church stands the chapel of the Señor de la Conquista with the statue of the **Cristo de la Conquista**. Indians from Pátzcuaro created this 16th-century statue from maize stalks, using an old technique in which the stalks are glued together with a paste made from orchid tubers. The form is then covered with lime (de caña). In the chapel, the remaining parts of murals by Federico Cantú are still visible. Considering the murals too radical, a priest ordered the offending parts destroyed. The universal artist Tresguerras created the neo-classical alcove behind the main altar.

The 18th-century church **San Rafael** adjoins the Parroquia at a right angle. The church interior contains simple sculpture.

Allende Museum

⏲
Opening times:
Tue–Sun
10am–4pm

On the western side of the main city square stands a corner building which is decorated in the Baroque style. This is the birthplace of Ignacio de Allende. Today, it is the Allende Museum (Museo Allende) and contains archaeological and historic exhibits as well as arts and crafts. One exhibition is about Allende and his role in the independence movement. The façade shows the inscription »Hic natus ubique notus« (born here, known everywhere).

Casa del Mayorazgo de Canal

The imposing Casa del Mayorazgo de Canal shows elements of the Baroque and neo-classical style. It occupies the north-west corner of the plaza on Calle Canal. The carved wooden doors and the elegant iron-wrought window grilles are of particular note.

On the north side of the plaza stand beautiful 18th-century colonial buildings, including the town hall (Palacio Municipal).

La Concepción monastery

The La Concepción monastery (Convento La Concepción, also called Las Monjas) is west along Calle Canal, another block after the beautifully carved gate of the Casa de Canal. The construction of this building started in the middle of the 18th century, but it was finished only near the end of the 19th century.

The **grand dodecagonal church dome** (finished in 1891) is remarkable. Inside the church there are paintings ascribed to Miguel Cabrera and Juan Rodríguez Juárez. The monastery features an impressive inner courtyard with old trees and two-storied arcades. The building now houses the **Ignacio Ramírez Cultural Centre**.

Angela Peralta theatre

Diagonally opposite, at the corner of Calle Mesones (entrance) stands the Angela Peralta theatre (Teatro Angela Peralta). The build-

San Miguel de Allende *Plan*

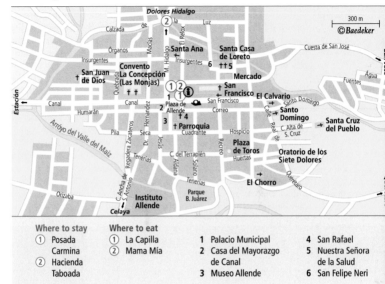

Where to stay	Where to eat		
① Posada Carmina	① La Capilla	**1** Palacio Municipal	**4** San Rafael
② Hacienda Taboada	② Mama Mía	**2** Casa del Mayorazgo de Canal	**5** Nuestra Señora de la Salud
		3 Museo Allende	**6** San Felipe Neri

ing started out as an opera house and had its heyday in 1873 when Angela Peralta, the »Mexican Nightingale«, performed here. Passing by the monastery, Calle Hernández Macías runs south; the former prison and the inquisition (Calle Cuadrante 18) are on opposite sides of this street.

In the same direction out of town, on the left hand side on Calzada Ancha de San Antonio, stands the beautiful former 18th-century mansion of Don Manuel Tomás de la Canal. The mansion now houses one of the two significant schools of the arts, the Allende Institute (Instituto Allende).

Allende Institute

The San Francisco church is situated one block north-east of the city square. Built at the end of the 18th century, the church has a beautiful ultra-Baroque façade and a high neo-classical spire, reputedly designed by Francisco Eduardo Tresguerras.

✳
San Francisco

In a northern direction, beyond Calle Mesones, stands the church El Oratorio de San Felipe Neri (founded in 1712).
The façade shows strong **Indian style elements**. This is particularly apparent in the five statues of saints in the niches.
In the right nave stands an altar with the painting of the Virgin of Guadalupe by Miguel Cabrera, to whom the 33 paintings depicting the life of St Felipe Neri are also ascribed.

✳
San Felipe Neri

Santa Casa de Loreto

Turning left, you come to the Santa Casa de Loreto. This is a replica of the Holy House of Loreto (Italy) from the 18th century and contains a statue of the Virgin Mary. An aisle on each side leads to the Camarín an octagonal room with six altars, of which five are in the Baroque style and one the neo-classical style. The retables are examples of Mexican ultra-Baroque.

★

◄ Camarín

Our Lady of Health

The 18th-century Church of Our Lady of Health (Nuestra Señora de la Salud) is located east of the church San Felipe Neri. A large sea shell forms the top part of the ultra-Baroque façade. The interior contains neo-classical altars and paintings, including some by Miguel Cabrera, Antonio Torres and Tomás Xavier de Peralta. Since 1993, the equestrian statue of Ignacio de Allende has been standing in front of the church in the renovated Plaza Allende.

Indian chapels

Indian chapels are rare now in San Miguel. Sporadically however, they can be found in neighbouring villages and on ranches. The sim-

The simple façades often conceal exceptionally beautiful rooms.

ple buildings show idiosyncratic depictions of saints, crosses and religious motifs with rather personal interpretations. These chapels allowed Indians to conduct their own Indian-Catholic services free of Spanish supervision.

There is an ecological reserve in the hills of El Charco del Ingenio on the north-eastern outskirts of the city. The 65ha/161ac reserve is used to grow succulent plants, mostly cacti. Some rare cactus species are cultivated here.

Ecological reserve

The lookout point El Mirador is by the road leaving San Miguel Allende toward Querétaro. It provides a panoramic view over San Miguel de Allende.

View

Around San Miguel de Allende

There are many thermal springs and spas close to the town, mainly in the direction of Dolores Hidalgo.

Thermal springs

Cañada de la Virgen is an archaeological site which has received only scarce attention so far. To reach it, follow the street south in the direction of Celaya, then turn right and, passing the reservoir (Presa de Allende), go 15km/9mi toward Guanajuato. Among the finds are a 18m/59ft-high pyramid, a temple, terraces and a causeway. Present dating suggests that this site was an ancient city between 800 and 1000. The finds at the site point to Toltec influence.

Cañada de la Virgen

Atotonilco (place of the hot water) is a much visited **place of pilgrimage** about 15km/9mi north of the city and 3km/2mi off the road. This monastery founded in 1740 by the priest Felipe Neri de Álfaro has a much revered statue of Christ. When Mexico declared itself independent from Spain, the priest Miguel Hidalgo and his motley crew interrupted their march here. He took the painting of the Virgin of Guadalupe out of the church and attached it to his banner, making the Madonna the patron saint of the Mexican freedom movement.

Atotonilco

The interior of the Santuario de Jesús Nazareno monastery church and the different chapels are decorated with beautiful frescoes depicting popular subjects. There are sculptures of the Virgin Mary and the apostles in the alcove behind the high altar. The rosary chapel (on the right) with frescoes depicting the battle of Lepanto leads to an alcove with a ceiling in the shape of a sea shell.

✴
◄ Santuario de Jesús Nazareno

✴
◄ Frescoes

The monastery complex is the destination of **annual pilgrimages from all over Mexico**. Two weeks before Easter Sunday, the Christ statue of the Señor de la Columna is carried in a nightly procession into the church San Juan de Dios in San Miguel de Allende. A church festival with Indian dances takes place on the third Sunday in July.

! *Baedeker* TIP

An icy treat

The Dolores Hidalgo park is not only home to the statue of the priest and revolutionary Don Miguel Hidalgo y Costilla; on the corners of the park the ice-cream sellers have their patch. Their home-made »nieve« (snow) is available in an abundance of flavours, among them such unusual varieties as cactus, tequila and seafood.

The small town of **Dolores Hidalgo** (population 41,000) is situated about 28km/17mi north-west of Atotonilco. With the independence movement in danger of being discovered, the priest **Miguel Hidalgo y Costilla** shouted his legendary **grito de Dolores** (cry of Dolores) in the early hours of 16 September 1810 in front of the parish church. His alarm cry initiated the War of Independence in Mexico. The parish church (Parroquia), built between 1712 and 1778, has a beautiful façade. The two retables show a similarly impressive design. The first of the altars is gilded and shows the historic painting of the Virgin of Guadalupe.

✳

◄ Parroquia

A museum in the Casa de Don Miguel Hidalgo shows items that commemorate the freedom fighter and hero. The city is also known for the coloured glazed tiles (azulejos) produced here.

✳

Mineral de Pozos

A few miles past San Miguel toward Querétaro, a street to the left heads in the direction of Dr. Mora. Turn left again after the overpass on the main road 57 to reach San Luis de la Paz (population 31,000) after 11km/7mi. Another 14km/9mi further on is Mineral de Pozos, which used to be a mining town with 60,000 citizens but now is largely abandoned and has the **the atmosphere of a ghost town**. Only the large number of ruined buildings and deep mining shafts still tell of its past. Visitors can see temporary exhibitions in the gallery at the main square.

Tampico

M 21

Federal state: Tamaulipas (Tamps.)
Population: 760,000

Altitude: 12 m/39 ft
Distance: 515km/320mi north-east of Mexico City

Tampico, the southernmost and largest city in Tamaulipas is completely dominated in the oil industry. Situated on the northern bank of the Río Pánuco, along with Veracruz it is the most important port on the Gulf of Mexico.

Originally an oil and cotton harbour, Tampico is today a well-equipped busy trans-shipment centre for goods destined mostly for the United States of America, Europe and South America. Oil tanks and refineries, the busy harbour, estuaries, lagoons and beaches shape life in and around Tampico.

▶ VISITING TAMPICO

INFORMATION

Tourist information
Calle 20 de Noviembre
(between Obregón and
Altamira)
Tel. (833) 212 28 68

GETTING AROUND

A flight from Mexico City to Tampico
lasts about
45 minutes; a bus ride takes about 10
hours. There is a rail connection via
San Luis Potosí.

WHERE TO EAT

▶ **Inexpensive**
Super Cream
Altamira y Olmos 201
This is a nice bistro with tasty snacks.

WHERE TO STAY

▶ **Mid-range to budget**
Hotel La Central
Rosalio Bustamante 224
Tel. (217) 03 88
This hotel has a pleasant atmosphere
and is conveniently located close to
the bus terminal.

History

The area around Tampico was probably settled very early by the Huastec, a Maya-speaking tribe. Ceramics finds in the region date their settlements back as far as 1000 BC. In the 15th century, the Aztec managed to extract tribute from the Huastec. In 1519, a river expedition brought the first Spaniards, under Alonso Alvárez de Pineda, to the region and they subjugated the Huastec in the decade that followed. The Franciscan priest Andrés de Olmos had a monastery built on the ruins of an Aztec staging post in 1532 and the future Tampico evolved around it. In 1560, the village San Luis de Tampico was granted the title »villa« (= small township).

Over the next hundred years, the port became the target of attacks by Indians from the north and by pirates from the ocean. Tampico was destroyed in 1683 and was not rebuilt until 1923, i.e. after the War of Independence. Then, successive occupations by Spanish, US and French troops followed. The discovery of **crude oil** in the beginning of the 20th century under the Porfirio Diaz presidency brought in US and British capital. For a while, the oil boom made Tampico the largest oil port in the world.

Plaza de Armas

The Plaza de Armas (city square, Zócalo) is a good place to observe the city night life. The cathedral and city hall (Palacio Municipal) are located at the plaza.

Museum of Huastec Culture

The Museum of Huastec Culture (Museo de la Cultura Huasteca) is located in the technology institute (Instituto Tecnológico) about 7km/4.3mi north of the plaza in the Ciudad Madero. It contains statues, terracotta figurines, clay vessels, jewellery, ritual stone objects and also weapons and traditional costumes.

Playa Miramar   Playa Miramar is a very popular beach about 15km/9mi outside Tampico. There are a few shady palapas (palm huts) in the area, but it is very quiet here during the week.

✶✶ Taxco

Q 19

Federal state: Guerrero (Gro.)
Population: 125,000

Altitude: 1,670m/5,479ft
Distance:: about 150km/93mi south-west of Mexico City

Taxco is situated in a beautiful, undulating landscape. The self-contained city character, the low, red-tiled colonial houses, the small alleys and plazas, have all made Taxco one of the most popular travel destinations in Mexico.

History   In pre-Columbian times, the region was inhabited by the Náhua tribe Tlahuica. The Indian city Tlachco (place of the ball game) was located about 10km/6mi from present day Taxco. Under the rulers Itzcóatl and Montezuma I, the Aztec forayed into the region and annexed it in the middle of the 15th century. The Spaniards came to the region in 1522 in search of tin and silver and established the settlement El Real de Tetzelcingo in 1529, which finally became the town of Taxco in 1581.

Large silver finds were not made until the middle of the 18th century when **José de la Borda** discovered and exploited the large San Ignacio mine. The people in the region began sinking into poverty after the Mexican Revolution (1910–1920) until in 1930 **William Spratling** (1900–1967) moved from the USA and settled here. He was successful at reviving the old arts and crafts industry by bringing silversmiths from Iguala into the region to manufacture jewellery in the tradition of the Indians. Today, people in Taxco live almost completely on tourism and the **art of silversmithing**. More than 1,500 craftsmen practise the art of making jewellery in small shops in the area. The precious metal they use is an alloy of 950–980g silver and 20–50g copper (95–98% silver, 5–2% copper).

What to See in Taxco

✶✶
San Sebastián y
Santa Prisca

The small city square (Plaza de la Borda) with the church San Sebastián y Santa Prisca is particularly picturesque. The church, a **masterpiece of ultra-Baroque architecture**, was commissioned by the silver mogul José de la Borda in the middle of the 18th century and designed by the architects Diego Durán and Juan Caballero. As the

Detail of the Santa Prisca parish church,
a splendid example of the ultra-Baroque style →

▶ VISITING TAXCO

INFORMATION

Tourist information
in the city square and at the bus terminal Flecha Roja. Information is also available at the Subsecretaría Fomento Turístico in Avenida de los Plateros at the northern edge of the city or at www.taxco.com.mx

GETTING AROUND

The best route by car from Mexico City to Taxco is (150km/93mi) on the MEX 95 or 95 D (take the junction to Amacuzac). The same trip takes about 3 hours by bus.

SHOPPING

The name Taxco is synonymous with silver. While the prices for jewellery are not really lower than elsewhere, the choice of necklaces, rings, ear-rings, arm bands, belt buckles and other silver items is stunning. There are good shops around the city square (e.g. Los Castillos at the Plazuela Bernal) and a silver market next to the Santa Prisca church. Both here and with street vendors don't be afraid to negotiate on price, and make sure that the pieces on sale carry the 925 stamp.

WHERE TO EAT

▶ Moderate

① **Cielito Lindo**
Plaza Borda 14
Tel. (762) 622 06 03
This is a particularly popular restaurant which serves Mexican and international food.

② **Sotavento Restaurant Bar Galería**
Calle Juárez 8
Tel. (762) 622 12 17
The former »La Taverna« serves Italian specialities.

WHERE TO STAY

▶ Luxury

① **Montetaxco**
Fracc. Lomas de Taxco
Tel. (762) 622 13 00
Fax (762) 622 14 28
www.montetaxco.com.mx
This hotel (156 rooms) is situated high above the city and offers a great view. It can also be reached by cable car (teleférico). All rooms have a terrace and a TV. Other amenities include a 9-hole golf course, three tennis courts, horse rental, a fitness centre with massage and steam bath, and a discotheque.

▶ Mid-range

② **Hacienda del Solar**
Paraje el Solar
Tel. (762) 622 03 23
The hotel is located south of the city on a hill and has a wonderful view over the city and the valley. The hotel (23 rooms) consists of several Mexican bungalows in different catego-ries, some with terrace, others with folksy murals. There is also a restau-rant and a bar.

story goes, de la Borda lived by the motto »Dios da a Borda, Borda da a Dios« (**God provides for Borda, Borda provides for God**). The church portal is flanked by two Corinthian columns on each side, which include a series of sculptures. There is no central window in the top part of the façade above the papal tiara but rather a large medallion depicting the baptism of Christ. The **opulent decorations** with statues, crests, leaves, shells, bands, cherubim and so on is worked in a particularly intricate way. The spires over the façade show richly decorated columns and sculpted grimacing heads. **Blue and yellow glazed tiles** (azulejos) cover the dome and complete the magnificent picture.

The church interior contains beautifully carved, painted and gilded ultra-Baroque retables with many pictures of apostles, angels and saints amid opulent motifs of flowers, fruits, birds, etc. A painting by Miguel Cabrera above the entrance to the Indian chapel (**Capilla de los Indios**) shows the martyrdom of Santa Prisca, the patron saint of the church. There are more paintings by the artist in the chapel and the vestry.

The William Spratling Museum is located at Calle Porfirio Delgado 1 and shows archaeological artefacts belonging to the western cultures as well as exhibits from Taxco's heyday as a silver mining town.

Museo Guillermo Spratling

The Antigua Casa Humboldt (Museum of Colonial Art) in Calle Juan Ruíz de Alarcón is a magnificent 18th-century building with a remarkable Moorish portal. The building owes its name to the fact that in April 1803 the German naturalist and geographer **Alexander von Humboldt** spent a night here on his several-year-long journey through the Spanish West Indian colonies. Today, the museum shows a variety of silversmith art. (Open: Tue – Sat 10 am – 5pm, Sun 9 am – 3 pm.)

Museo de Arte Virreinal (Antigua Casa Humboldt)

Visit the **Silver Museum** (Museo de la Platería) at the Plaza Borda and admire some of the extraordinary work of William Spratling or learn about the development of silversmithing in Taxco (open daily except Wednesdays, 10:30 am – 5 pm).

Silver Museum

The market (mercado) in Calle del Arco is enjoyable. Further southeast stands the Baroque church Santísima (1713), and from here the streets Real de San Nicolás and Progreso lead to the Iglesia de Ojeda church (finished in 1822).

Capilla de la Santísima

When returning from the church to the main city square via Calle de San Agustín, take a look at the Plaza de los Gallos and the Casa Figueroa (Calle Guadalupe 2), which still exhibit their **old Spanish atmosphere**. This building from the middle of the 18th century originally went by the name Casa de las Lágrimas (house of tears). The owner, the Count of Cadena, had the house built by Indians in slav-

Casa Figueroa

Taxco Plan

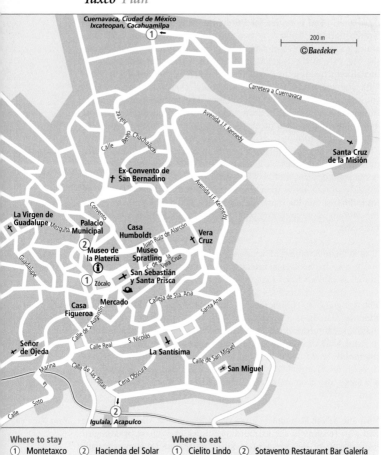

Cuernavaca, Ciudad de México
Ixcateopan, Cacahuamilpa
① ←

200 m
©Baedeker

Carretera a Cuernavaca

Avenida J.F. Kennedy

Santa Cruz
de la Misión

Calle Benito Juárez Chachalacas

Ex-Convento de
† San Bernadino

Avenida J.F. Kennedy

Convento

La Virgen de
Guadalupe
†   Palacio   Casa
Mezquita   Municipal   Humboldt   Vera
②   † Cruz
Museo de   Museo   Juan Ruiz de Alarcón
Guadalupe   la Platería   Spratling   C. de Vera Cruz
ⓘ   la
① Zócalo   San Sebastián
y Santa Prisca

Casa   Mercado   Calleja de Sta. Ana
Figueroa

Santa Ana

Calle de S. Augustín

Señor   Calle de San Miguel
† de Ojeda   Calle Real   S. Nicolás ✝
                            La Santisima
Marina   Calle de San Miguel
Calle de las Piñas   Cena Obscura   ✝ San Miguel
Calle Soto   er

②
Igulala, Acapulco

Where to stay		Where to eat	
① Montetaxco	② Hacienda del Solar	① Cielito Lindo	② Sotavento Restaurant Bar Galería

ery. Many Indians died due to the hardship of this enforced labour. In 1943, the artist Fidel Figueroa bought the house. Today, it is a museum.

Church of Our Lady of Guadalupe Looking to the west, the church of the Virgin of Guadalupe is visible, standing on a hill. The view from the 18th-century church (remodelled in 1877) over the city square and the Santa Prisca church is beautiful.

San Bernardino monastery The former San Bernardino monastery (Ex-Convento San Bernadino) is located in Calle Convento where the city hall is also to be

Alleyway in Taxco

found. Originally founded by the Franciscans in the 16th century, it burnt down in the 19th century and was rebuilt in the neo-classical style.

Small buses and taxis bring people from the city square to the ground terminal of a cable car at the north end of the city near the Hacienda del Chorillo. The cable car ascends 240m/787ft to the chain of hills called Lomas de Taxco. Visitors enjoy the **extraordinarily beautiful view** during the ascent and from the plateau.

Lomas de Taxco

Unique annual processions take place in Taxco during the **week before Easter**. They begin on Palm Sunday and reach their climax on Maundy Thursday and Good Friday when all kinds of symbolic acts are performed during the processions. There are penitents wearing ankle chains, encruzados who express their faith by carrying heavy thorn bushes on their shoulders, and flagelentes who flagellate themselves using thin lashes. They all perform these rites in the hope of forgiveness for their sins.

✳
Processions

Around Taxco

Ixcateopan (population 8,000) is located 40km/25mi west of Taxco in an enchanting mountain region. The 16th-century village church Santa María de la Asunción now houses a museum. Some believe the **remains of the last Aztec ruler Cuauhtémoc**, who Cortés had killed in Honduras in 1525, were found underneath the altar of this church.

Ixcateopan

<table>
</table>

★★
Cacahuamilpa caves

The Taxco National Park is located 31km/19mi north-west of Taxco. Here, at an elevation of 1,100m/3,610ft, are the **Cacahuamilpa dripstone caves** (Grutas de Cacahuamilpa, Cacahuamilpa = in the growing fields of cocoa), Mexico's largest and most interesting cave system. Since the caves were discovered in 1835, people have been driving drifts (now 16km/9.6mi in length) into the interior without ever coming to the end of the system. There are various types of dripstone formations in 16 caverns, which can be up to 80m/262ft wide and up to 77m/253ft high.

Tehuantepec

Federal state: Oaxaca (Oax.)	**Altitude:** 110m/361ft
Population: 90,000	**Distance:** 260 km / 162 mi south-east of Oaxaca

The town of Tehuantepec, which has also given its name to the Pacific gulf and the isthmus, is an important hub for overland traffic and rail connections. The Isthmus of Tehuantepec measures only 200km/125mi across and is Mexico's narrowest point.

Tehuantepec (Náhuatl: jaguar hill) is a hot and humid tropical town set amid lush vegetation. It lies in a dip and is surrounded by low hills and the wide bend of the Río Tehuantepec. The Zapotec and Mestizos populate the area.

History

Tehuantepec probably had a very long pre-Hispanic history because it used to be a Zapotec centre. Axayácatl, the ruler of the Aztec, and his warriors subjugated Tehuantepec in 1470. When the Spaniards arrived in 1521/22 Cocijo-pii was the ruler, the son of the Zapotec ruler Cocijo-eza and an Aztec princess. Cocijo-pii became an ally of the Spaniards against the Aztec. At the beginning of the colonial period, Tehuantepec constituted part of the land owned by Hernán Cortés. Tehuantepec's strategic significance as the **shortest overland connection between the Gulf of Mexico and the Pacific** in Mexico did not escape Cortés or later the Spanish viceroys and Mexican Government. It triggered speculations about creating convenient trade routes. Roads and the railway were built, but plans to dig a canal never came to fruition. The significance of Tehuantepec reduced sig-

! Baedeker TIP

Flying fruit

An odd custom is carried out at many festivals in Tehuantepec. First, the women put on their costumes, adorning themselves with flowers and various kinds of jewellery. Then they hand out sweets, toys and small gifts – and last but not least they climb, magnificently decked out, onto the roofs and bombard the men with fruit.

▶ VISITING TEHUANTEPEC

GETTING AROUND

The trip from Mexico City to Te-huantepec takes about 23 hours by train or 12 hours by bus via Oaxaca. The Pan-American Highway (MEX 190) is the best route to take by car.

WHERE TO EAT

▶ Inexpensive
Café Colonial
Calle Juana 66
This restaurant serves very good local food. The chicken dishes, prepared in countless ways here, are particularly tasty.

WHERE TO STAY

▶ Budget
Donaji del Istmo
Calle Juárez 10
Tel. (971) 715 00 64
This 23-room hotel is located south of the city square and has a view over the park.

---

nificantly when, in 1914, the Panama Canal opened. However, the Mexican oil boom and the construction of a pipeline from Teapa (state of Veracruz) to the port city Salina Cruz once again changed the significance of Tehuantepec for the better.

Tehuantepec has only a few significant buildings. The former Domi-nican church (1544), now the city's cathedral, has been rebuilt sev-eral times, but has however retained its old arches and the domes. The column-supported town hall is remarkable. The decidedly self-assured women of Tehuantepec enjoy a special reputation all over Mexico (Fig. p.102). At celebrations, they wear richly embroidered garb made from special fabrics.

Self-assured women

Around Tehuantepec

Juchitán de Zaragoza (population 100,000) is located 26km/16mi further along the MEX 190 east of Tehuantepec The town is an im-portant regional trade centre. Visitors enjoy the market and the pret-ty traditional costumes, which are mostly worn for celebrations.

Juchitán de Zaragoza

Only 17km/10mi south lies the port city of Salina Cruz (population 120,000). Recently, the port has significantly grown in importance as a **trans-shipment centre and site of oil refineries**. However, it is in-teresting for tourists only as a stop-over en route to the extensive beach of La Ventosa (Posada Rustrian), 7km/4mi distant.

Salina Cruz

About 15km/9mi west of Tehuantepec, a country road branches off to the right from the MEX 190 and leads to the archaeological site Guiengola (large rock). At the end of the approximately 6km/4mi-long country road, a path leads through a **picturesque landscape**

Guiengola

with rocks, forest and cacti to the top of a hill (ascent about 1 hour). Here, roughly 400m/1300ft above the valley, the **ruins of the last great fortress of the Zapotec** stand on the Guiengola mountain. Part of a large wall still standing is about 3m/10ft high and 2m/6.6ft thick; at one time, the wall extended all around the mountain. Around the large courtyard stand the ruins of a large four-step temple pyramid and the remnants of three small ceremonial buildings and the ball court. The palace of the Zapotec ruler Cocijo-eza once stood on the mountain slope. The view from the mountain cliffs over the valley of Tehuantepec is magnificent.

Coastal Tour along the Gulf of Tehuantepec

The coastal road (MEX 200) can be reached via the MEX 190, which connects Oaxaca and Tuxtla Gutiérrez. Leave this road after San Pedro Tepanatepec and turn right toward Arriaga (44km/27mi).

Tonalá   A drive of another 23km/14mi leads to Tonalá (population 50,000). This small town lies amid lush vegetation and has a small archaeological museum. A road branching south leads to the fishing port Puerto Arista (17km/10mi). Ruins and other finds at the excavation site close to the port reveal Aztec influences.

Dunes on the Pacific near Salina Cruz

The distance from Tonalá via Huixtla to Tapachula (population **Tapachula** 190,000) is 221km/137mi. Beautifully located, the city nestles in the foothills of the extinct volcano Tonaná (height: 4,093m/13,428ft). Tonaná is the economic centre of a region which revolves around the **cultivation of coffee**. Places of interest for visitors to Tapachula are the zoo and the Soconusco Archaeological Museum (Museo Arqueológico de Soconusco) with finds from Chiapas, especially from Tonalá and Izapa.

The archaeological zone of Izapa, **the largest pre-Hispanic cultural** **Izapa** **centre on the Pacific coast in Mesoamerica**, is less than 11km/7mi east of Tapachula.
The temple city is very old: its most significant period stretched from 1500 BC to AD 900. On 4 sq km/1.5 sq mi, the site features many artificial mounds, temple platforms, inner courtyards and a ball court; however, the more than 50 stone monuments (300 to 50 BC) are the most outstanding feature. Most of monuments point to Olmec influence and show the burgeoning transition to the Maya style. Among other finds are stelae with bas-reliefs, which depict a peculiar god with long lips.
The most important find is arguably **stele 5** with the carved tree of life and old gods, probably a depiction of the creation myth. Some of the stelae are on display in the Museum of Tapachula.

The port and popular ocean resort Puerto Madero lies approximately **Puerto Madero** 27km/17mi south of Tapachula.
Travellers can **cross the border to Guatemala** at Puente Talismán (18km/11mi) or close to Ciudad Hidalgo (another 20km/12mi). The railway line runs parallel to the coastal road between Salina Cruz via Tehuantepec to Guatemala.

✶ ✶ Teotihuacán

P 20

Federal state: México (Mex.)   **Altitude:** 2,28 m/7,484 ft
Distance: 50 km/31 mi north-east of
Mexico City

During the first 600 years of the common era (CE), Teotihuacán was politically and culturally the most influential power in Mesoamerica. Thanks to its symmetrical design and consistent architecture, this gigantic ruined city now counts as one of the most magnificent archaeological sites in the world. Situated at the periphery of the highland valley of Anáhuac, Teotihuacán is so far the largest excavated ancient city in Mesoamerica, and has been a UNESCO World Heritage Site since 1988.

▶ VISITING TEOTIHUACÁN

INFORMATION
www.teotihuacan.com

GETTING AROUND
By bus
To reach Teotihuacán from Mexico City take the Metro line 5 to the bus station Autobuses del Norte and continue by bus (ticket counter 8, stop 6) or take the bus line 3 to the Indios Verdes station and change there.

By car
The best way to reach the excavation site by car is to take Avenida Insurgentes Norte, which becomes the MEX 85 D. Then take the exit to the MEX 132 D which leads to the ruined city.

EVENTS
Tens of thousands of people climb up the Sun Pyramid on the spring equinox around March 21 when the sun passes in an exact vertical position over the pyramid.

WHERE TO EAT
▶ **Moderate to inexpensive**
Las Pirámides
Puerta 1
The restaurant's main attraction is its location at the main entrance of the site. There is a great view of the archaeological site from the upper floor.

WHERE TO STAY
▶ **Mid-range budget**
Club Med Villas Teotihuacán
Zona Arqueológica
Tel. (558) 36 90 20
Fax (558) 956 02 44
www.clubmedvillas.com
This hotel (40 rooms) is located near the archaeological zone in the middle of a huge garden.

History Nothing is known about the builders of Teotihuacán, their language and history. It was first assumed that the Toltec founded this city, but excavations in Tula have revealed that Teotihuacán was abandoned and destroyed around 200 years before the Toltec came to power. The name of the city itself and those of the individual structures derive either from the Náhuatl language or have more recent origins, and are therefore of no help in identifying the builders. Teotihuacán means »the place where men become gods«.

Small settlements were established here during the so-called **proto-Teotihuacán** period (600–200 BC), by the end of which a larger village had grown up in what would become the north-west part of the later city. The first obsidian workshops emerged at the same time. The hyaline (glass-like), mostly grey and green obsidian was not only essential for making tools, it was also indispensable as a commodity for trade. The actual development of the city occurred in the **Teotihuacán I** period (200 BC–0 CE), in which the north-south axis, the Avenue of the Dead, and the core buildings, the Sun and Moon Pyramids, were constructed. Influences from Oaxaca become apparent in this period, as deduced from finds in the Monte Albán II period. In the following building phase, known as **Teotihuacán II** (0–AD 350) the city reach its largest expanse (calculated at 20 sq km/7.7 sq mi), exceeding the size of Rome at that time. During this period, the

Teotihuacán Plan

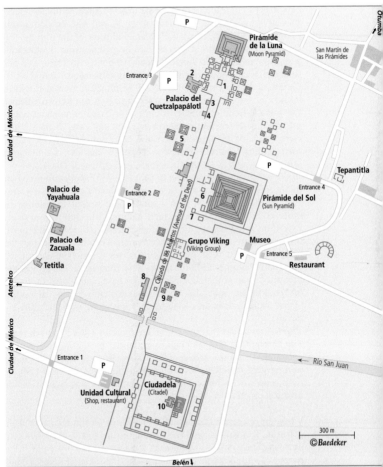

1 Plaza de la Pirámide de la Luna (Pyramid of the Moon Plaza)

2 Palacio de los Jaguares (Palace of the Jaguar)

3 Templo de la Agricultura (Temple of Agriculture)

4 Templo de los Animales Mitológicos (Temple of Mytho-logical Animals)

5 Group of Columns

6 Plaza de la Pirámide del Sol (Pyramid of the Sun Plaza)

7 Casa de los Sacerdotes (House of the Priests)

8 Edificios Superpuestos (Superimposed buildings)

9 Excavations of 1917

10 Templo de Quetzalcóatl (Temple of Quetzalcóatl)

Sun and Moon Pyramids were, for the time being, completed, and the Quetzalcóatl Temple and the Citadel complex of buildings were built. In the fine arts, the ancient people of Teotihuacán created the important thin-orange ceramics, three-legged cylindrical vessels with lids and monumental sculptures. The **Teotihuacán III** period (350–650 AD) was the most prosperous time for the city with probably 200,000 inhabitants. During this time the builders erected most new structures on top of the existing ones, predominantly the Quetzalcóatl Temple and the Pyramid of the Moon. Also created in this period were the Quetzalpapálotl Palace and most of the murals. The mutual cultural learning process among people from Teotihuacán and Monte Albán, El Tajín, Panuco, Cholula, Guerrero and the southern Maya region reached astounding dimensions, and between the 5th and 6th centuries the city of Teotihuacán exerted the most influence on the cultures of Mesoamerica. It is not known whether this was the result of military conquests or based on peaceful political, cultural or economic interchange. In any case, elements that were typical of Teotihuacán have also been found in distant places, such as Xochichalco (Morelia), Cacaxtla (Tlaxcala), Kaminaljuyú (Guatemala) and in Petén (Guatemala, particularly in Tikal).

In the last period, **Teotihuacán IV** (AD 650–750), work continued on the Avenue of the Dead and excellent murals and ceramics were created. Then, the city met with a sudden and violent end similar to other classical Mesoamerican high cultures, but 200 years earlier. Even though the reasons for the demise of the city are still unknown, the methodical destruction of the ceremonial centre suggests that the priests destroyed their temples themselves, possibly under attack from barbaric tribes from the north-west. Internal revolts against the theocracy or an economic crisis may also have contributed to the fall of Teotihuacán. Soon the city deteriorated into a regional centre, whose 30,000 inhabitants lived in the ruins along with the alien intruders.

There is no doubt that the fall of Teotihuacán caused a **shock reaction throughout Mesoamerica** as evidenced by the fact that in the following period the strongholds of power decayed and trade routes were severed, heralding an economic decline. For the later civilizations, such as the Toltec and Aztec, Teotihuacán was a ghost city of mythical origins.

After the Spanish conquest When the Spaniards first passed by the site of Teotihuacán after their defeat in Tenochtitlán in 1520 (on the noche triste), the fallen city was completely covered with earth. Almaraz was the first to excavate parts of Teotihuacán in 1864, and in the 1880s Désiré Charnay and Leopoldo Batres continued the excavations.

Reconstructions undertaken in the 20th century partially destroyed and distorted the original shapes of some main buildings. Manuel Gamio and Ignacio Marquina did valuable work with their excavations and restorations in the 1920s, as did the experts from the National Mexican Institute of Archaeology and History (Instituto Nacional de Arqueología e Historia) who started their work in 1962. The Arizona State University is helping to continue this work.

Visiting the Archaeological Site

Only a portion of the ruins have been excavated. The archaeological zone covers more than 20 sq km/7.7 sq mi, while the actual centre covers only 4.2 sq km/1.6 sq mi. When looking at the somewhat uniform appearing architecture of the site you should consider that originally all façades were covered with stucco in many colours and were in part decorated with sculptures.

Site design

Opening times: daily 7am–6:30pm

Directly after the main entrance (entrance no. 1), there is a museum in the Unidad Cultural, giving an overview of the development of Teotihuacán using a combination of exhibits, time charts and a large model. At one time, this was the site of the huge Teotihuacán market.

Unidad Cultural

Strict alignment of the buildings around the Avenue of the Dead

The 366 sculptures on the Quetzalcóatl Temple represent the feathered serpent, the rain god and the fire snake.

✴ Avenue of the Dead

The 2km/1.2mi-long and 45m/148ft-wide main street, Miccaotli, which has been erroneously named the Avenue of the Dead (Calzada de los Muertos), is behind the Unidad Cultural. The entire city was planned with this thoroughfare as the **main axis**, which looks less like a street than a series of connected open terraces between the Citadel complex in the south and the Pyramid of the Moon at the northern end. Originally, the Avenue of the Dead stretched 2km/1.2mi south from the Citadel (Ciudadela), but little of it still exists. The structures on the right and left of the avenue – three or four-stepped platforms attached to sloped walls – were presumably used for ceremonial purposes. Sometimes, new structures were built on top of existing ones as can be seen in the superimposed buildings (edificios superpuestos) behind the river on the left.

Citadel

Across the street is an impressive rectangular complex bordered by four platforms called the Citadel (La Ciudadela). Some speculate that these were cult sites and residences of the priests and ruling classes. The Citadel exemplifies very well the **talud-tablero style** prevalent in Teotihuacán, in which steeply sloped walls with framed panels predominate. Both frames and panels were once covered with a thick layer of stucco adorned with colourful frescoes.

✴ Templo de Quetzalcóatl ▶

In the centre of the Citadel stands the Temple of the Feathered Serpent (Temple of Quetzalcóatl). The pyramid was twice rebuilt, the new building being structured around the old one. The pyramid is mainly characterized by its originally **366 sculptures**, a rarity in a city with only a few stone sculptures. To which god the pyramid was dedicated is not known but there is a connection to rain and maize. One of the two alternating sculptures depicts a snake with a head and a body framed by flower petals or feathers and surrounded by sea shell and spiral motifs symbolizing water. The other type shows a stylized mask, possibly of the rain god Tláloc or the maize god, featuring large round eyes (goggle eyes) and two fangs. Some residual paint is still visible on the stucco covered stone statues.

In 1986, a **tomb with the skeletons of 18 priests** was found here. They were obviously ritually sacrificed around the year 150. This sensational find demonstrates that high-ranked nobility, not just slaves or captives, were ritually sacrificed. The victims' hands were bound behind their backs, and they had jade and other precious stones embedded in their teeth. Their bodies were surrounded by sea shells, arrowheads and small clay figures.

After passing the Casa de los Sacerdotes (house of the shamans or priests) a wide stairway leads to the Pyramid of the Sun Plaza. The plaza is 70m/230ft wide, and in its centre stands an altar. At the corners stand the ruins of temples and other structures.

Pyramid of the Sun Plaza

At the eastern side of the plaza towers the largest structure in Teotihuacán, the Pyramid of the Sun. By circumference, only the pyramid of ► Cholula is larger in the whole of Mesoamerica. The gigantic structure is oriented in a way that on the day of the **summer solstice** the sun sets exactly opposite the pyramid's front side. The base of the Pyramid of the Sun (220 x 225m/720 x 738ft) is almost as large as the base of the Cheops Pyramid in Egypt. However, the Cheops Pyramid is 70m/230ft higher than the Pyramid of the Sun (63m/207ft, with the once present temple 74m/243ft).

✳ ✳
Pyramid of the Sun

An at least 7m/23ft-thick stucco and stone layer was lost from the original pyramid covering in the course of an unsuccessful restoration in the beginning of the 20th century. Two flights of stairs lead across a three-part front building to the first step of the pyramid. From here, a **wide outside stairway** leads via several pyramid tableros to the top platform where the temple once stood. From the last pyramid platform, climbing a stairway with 248 steps, **the view over the entire archaeological site is magnificent**. By chance, a 7m/23ft-deep shaft was discovered at the foot of the stairway in 1971. This shaft leads to a 103m/338ft-long passage at the end of which is a group of four chambers in a clover leaf shaped arrangement. The chambers contained remnants of ceramic objects and discs of slate (mirrors?), which had presumably been left there after robberies. There has been plenty of speculation about this passage and the chambers, which were probably built around AD 250. Such guesses make the chambers a place for sacrifice, a tomb or a ceremonial place in honour of the rain or maize god.

Museo

The first-rate main museum of the site is located south of the Pyramid of the Sun (entrance no. 5). The museum provides a site map and information about the ancient inhabitants, and exhibits include recently unearthed finds and a collective tomb with nine male and four female sacrificial victims. The tomb was found at the Temple of the Feathered Serpent (Quetzalcóatl Temple). The glass floor with the large model of Teotihuacán in the main exhibition hall is particularly impressive. The Manuel Gameo Museum is located in front of entrance no. 5 and mostly concerns itself with the history of the excavations.

Pyramid of the Moon Plaza

The Pyramid of the Moon Plaza is located at one end of the Avenue of the Dead. The symmetry and spatial design of this plaza most impressively exemplifies the architectural planning in Teotihuacán. The **ceremonial plaza** consists of steps and pyramid-like platforms generally with four levels, which were originally topped by a temple. In the centre of the plaza stands a large square altar.

Palacio del Quetzalpapálotl

On the left side stands the Palace of the Plumed Butterfly (Palacio del Quetzalpapálotl), which probably served as a residence for the high priests. Richly decorated and with well preserved frescoes, it is arguably the most beautiful residential building of the city. A stairway adorned with a snake head leads to an ante-hall with murals, and in the connecting patio with arcades, quadrangular columns show bas-reliefs depicting the **mythological plumed butterfly and birds**. The reliefs were once painted and featured embedded obsidian pieces. Note the stylized figures on a red background and the roof spikes with year glyphs.

Palace of the Jaguars

The next structure is the Palace of the Jaguars (Palacio de los Jaguares) with remarkably early murals depicting, for example, felines with human heads and jaguars blowing into conch horns. A frieze shows the glyphs for the rain god and the year.

Temple of the Plumed Conches

A tunnel allows entry to what is arguably the oldest structure in Teotihuacán. It is called the Temple of the Plumed Conches (Templo de las Conchas Plumadas) and lies hidden underneath the Palace of the Plumed Butterflies. The largest of the still intact temple façades shows beautiful reliefs, depicting **conch shells adorned with colourful feathers** (musical instruments?), green birds (parakeets?) and flowers with four petals.

Pyramid of the Moon

At the north side of the plaza stands the impressive Pyramid of the Moon (Pirámide de la Luna). The front side consists of a five-level pyramid-like structure in the **talud-tablero style**. Using the wide outer stairway, visitors come to the actual pyramid with its four staggered levels. The base measures 140 x 150m (459 x 492ft) and the structure is 46m/151ft high. While 17m/56ft lower than the Pyramid of the Sun, the Pyramid of the Moon stands on higher ground so that the tops of both pyramids are on the same level. The stairs only reach up to the third level. The view from the top of the Pyramid of the Moon over the entire site is also very beautiful.

Outside the Ceremonial Centre

The ruins of residential structures are visible some distance away from the centre; they are best reached by car.

The Tepantitla Complex (place of the thick walls) lies about 500m/ 0.3mi east of the Pyramid of the Sun and features several very beautiful murals.

✳ **Tepantitla**

About 1.5km/1mi away from the Pyramid of the Sun on the west side of the Avenue of the Dead lies the site Tetitla (place with stones), where visitors can also see beautiful frescoes from two building phases. The Zacuala Palace (Palacio de Zacuala) and the Yayahuala Palace (Palacio de Yayahuala) are a mere 100m/328ft away from this site.

Tetitla

At the equinoxes, masses of people come to the Pyramid of the Sun which is said to emanate psychic forces at these times.

✳
Atetelco
Roughly 400m (a quarter of a mile) west of Tetitla is the archaeological site Atetelco with two patios decorated with beautiful frescoes.

Burial objects
A large platform (500 sq m/5,380 sq ft) was unearthed in April 1997 during construction work on the highway between Mexico City and Tulancingo. Underneath the platform, located about 2.5km/1.6mi north-east of the Pyramid of the Moon near the town of Metepec, an interesting tomb was found containing the remains of a noble person who died in childhood. The interesting part is that the 50 female figurines in rich costumes seem to deliver a **theatrical rendition of life in Teotihuacán**. As no script has been found in Teotihuacán so far, this rendition could be of historical value.

Tepic

N 14

Federal state:: Nayarit (Nay.)	**Altitude::** 915m/3,002ft
Population:: 390,000	

Tepic, the capital of the federal state of Nayarit, is situated at the foot of the dormant volcano Sangangüey (2,360m/7,743ft), amid verdant hills about 50km/31mi east of the Pacific coast. East of the city stretches a wide plain with tobacco and sugar cane plantations. The city is a hub for traffic by rail, bus or car, and is also a good central point from which to make trips to the coast, San Blas, Mexcaltitán or Puerto Vallarta.

History
The city of Tepic (hard stone) was founded in 1531 by Nuño Beltrán de Guzmán. In 1711, Philipp V of Spain granted Tepic its municipal charter. The modern development of Tepic and the region however started only with the establishment of a railway connection (1912).

Attractions
Tepic is a convenient base when planning trips or outings to the beaches on the Pacific coast or to the nearby Indian villages. Of particular note are the cathedral at the Plaza Principal with neo-Gothic spires as well as the church La Cruz de Zacate, so called after a cross made of lemongrass (zacate de limon) which is revered by the Indians in the area.

Museums
The Amado Nervo Museum (Calle Zacatecas 284) is dedicated to the well-known Mexican poet who was born in Tepic. Another interesting museum is the Regional Museum of Anthropology and History (Museo Regional de Antropología e Historia) at Avenida México 91. On display are regional archaeological finds, paintings from colonial times as well as exhibitions showing the lifestyle of the Cora and Huichol.

✳
Regional
Museum ▶

⏵ VISITING TEPIC

INFORMATION
Tourist information
in the Palacio Municipal at the city
square
Tel. (323) 285 02 21

GETTING AROUND

A trip from Mexico City via Guadalajara to Tepic takes about 19 hours by
train or about 14 hours by bus.

WHERE TO EAT
▶ Inexpensive
La Terraza
Insurgentes 98 Pte

Tel. (311) 13 15 73
This is a simple but popular and
inexpensive restaurant.

WHERE TO STAY
▶ Budget
Melanie
Blvd. Tepic-Xalisco 109
Tel. (311) 214 23 10
www.hotelmelanie.s5.com
The Hotel Melanie is located close to
the university and not too far from
the city centre. All 57 rooms have
telephone and TV. The staff are very
pleasant and helpful.

Around Tepic

After 70km/44mi on the MEX 15 toward Guadalajara, a road turns   **Ixtlán del Río**
off and leads through a bizarre landscape shaped by lava flows from
the volcano Ceboruco. Travellers reach the town of Ixtlán del Río
(population 40,000) shortly after these lava fields.
About 3km/2mi past this town on the left side lies one of the few archaeological sites in West Mexico which does not consist exclusively
of graveyards, the **Centro Ceremonial Rincón de Ixtlán y Los Toriles**.
The partially excavated site was probably already inhabited in the 6th
and 7th centuries. The currently uncovered structures were probably
built in the early post-classical period (900–1250) during which the
culture in the area was certainly influenced by the Toltec. Among the
most interesting structures are an L-shaped building on a low platform, a round building with tapered windows and two altar platforms. Other finds include residential buildings, platforms and altars.
There are other buildings as yet unexcavated.

Compostela (population 55,000), an old mining town with an inter-   **Compostela**
esting 16th-century parish church, is located about 40km/25mi south
of Tepic in a tobacco growing area. Some fishing villages south-west
of Compostela have turned into popular spas, among them the picturesque locations Peñita de Jaltemba and Rincón de Guayabitos.

After 34km/21mi on the MEX 15 toward Mazatlán, there is a road   **San Blas**
leading to San Blas (population 12,000), 36km/22mi away. This sea
resort has been popular since the 1970s. It is also possible to reach

the town from Tepic via Santa Cruz (51km/32mi) and another 25 km / 15.5 mi along the beaches. San Blas used to be an important commercial harbour for trade with East Asia in colonial times as evidenced by the remnants of the old Spanish fortress Fuerte San Basilio and the custom house. From the **picturesque fishing village** visitors can make pleasant boat tours through a tropical river and lagoon landscape with many different birds (La Tovara). Beautiful beaches stretch for miles, among them in a southern direction Playa El Borrego and toward the south-east Playas Las Islitas (9km/5.6mi), Matanchén (11km/7mi), Los Limones, de los Cocos and Miramar (23km/14mi).

Playa Los Corchos

To reach the popular beach resort Playa Los Corchos travel northwest of Tepic on the MEX 15 to Santiago Ixcuintla, then turn west to the ocean. The entire trip is about 100km/62mi.

Lagoon village of Mexcaltitán

A side trip from Santiago Ixcuintla of the road to Playa Los Corchos to Mexcaltitán lagoon (25km/15.5mi) is well worthwhile. The village of Mexcaltitán is a kind of **mini-Venice**, situated on a circular island in the middle of a lake with numerous fish and birds. Some historians see in the island the legendary Aztlán, the original home of the Náhua people and consequently the Aztec.

The harbour at San Blas is home to a fishing fleet. With its relaxed atmosphere it is a favoured destination for holidaymakers from all over the world, especially in winter.

Tijuana

B 1/2

Federal state: Baja California Norte (B.C.N.)
Altitude: 152m/499ft

Distance: about 2,840km/1,700mi north-west of Mexico City
Population: 1.5 million

Tijuana is located immediately on the border with the US state California and has become a magnet for the typical consumer and the tourist who enjoys a drink; it has never been able to shake off its reputation as a city of sin. Of all Mexican cities, Tijuana displays American influence the most. Office buildings, shopping malls and industrial areas dominate here.

The main industries in Tijuana are tourism and the finishing industry. The city attracts millions of visitors a year, mostly Americans from Californian metropolitan areas such as San Diego (25km/15.5mi) or Los Angeles (260km/162mi). With about 50 million visitors per year, Tijuana registers the most border crossings; the Trans-peninsular Highway (MEX 1) across Baja California starts in Tijuana. Part of the attraction is based on a large offering of **duty-free goods** as well as Mexican folk art and souvenirs, events (bullfights, horse and dog races, Jai alai, and baseball) and the night life of Tijuana. The centres of activity are the main city square, the Guerrero city park, the shopping area around Avenida Revolución and the Boulevard Agua Caliente with hotels, restaurants, various shops and sports arenas.

Tijuana has a short history. Today's large city developed from a cattle hacienda by the name of Tía Juana (Auntie Anna), founded in 1829 by José María Echandi. Tijuana's rise began with Prohibition in the USA (1920–1933) when streams of people thirsty for alcohol crossed the border to Mexico for a good time and supplies.

History

What to See in Tijuana

One of the few remarkable buildings in the city is the 20th-century cathedral, which has been consecrated to the Virgin of Guadalupe.

Cathedral

The architecturally interesting Centro Cultural Tijuana offers a first impression for tourists who start their visit to Mexico in Tijuana, with a multimedia show and a museum at the intersection Paseo de los Héroes and Independencia. A branch of the museum, the **Museo de Identidades Mexicanas**, does a good job of familiarizing visitors with Mexico and its customs and traditions.

Centro Cultural Tijuana

In a large park, the Mexitlán Museum (Museo Mexitlán, Calle 2 / Avenida Ocampo) shows **150 models of the best known pre-Colum-**

Mexitlán Museum

As the figure on the fountain demonstrates, Jai alai is especially highly thought of in Tijuana.

bian and modern monuments in Mexico. Visitors can also enjoy music and ballet performances in the park.

Around Tijuana

Playas de Rosarito

The valley of Rosarito south of Tijuana once marked the border between California and Baja California. The town (21km/13mi away from Tijuana) was founded in 1885, and as early as the 1920s it gave a glimpse of what effect modern tourism can have. Playas de Rosarito is known for a **long sandy beach** and its busy main street, the Boulevard Juárez.

In the amphitheatre near the beach in the city park Parque Municipal Abelardo L. Rodríguez, you can admire the mural *Tierra y Libertad* (land and freedom) by Juan Zuñiga Padilla.

Tecate

Driving east on the MEX 2 from Tijuana leads after 55km/34mi to the town of Tecate (population 47,000). The border town is an agricultural and industrial centre, and it has a large brewery.

★
La Rumorosa

Proceeding on the MEX 2 east, you come to La Rumorosa with its bizarre rock formations and a **beautiful view of the desert panorama**.

Salada Lagoon

The Salada Lagoon (Laguna Salada), another 30km/19mi distant, stretches south. It is a shallow lake that may dry out overnight.

● VISITING TIJUANA

INFORMATION

Tourist information
corner Revolución / Calle 1
or at
www.tijuana.com

GETTING AROUND

Mexican and US airlines offer many flights. Cross the US-Mexican border from the USA to Tijuana by bus (Greyhound terminal on the US side), by car or even on foot.

WHERE TO EAT

► **Expensive to moderate**
Cien Años
Avenida José María 1407
Zona Río
Tel. (664) 634 30 39
This pretty restaurant in the colonial style serves first-rate Mexican food in very pleasant surroundings.

WHERE TO STAY

► **Mid-range to budget**
Camino Real Tijuana
Paseo de los Héroes 10305
Tel. (664) 633 40 00
Fax (664) 633 40 01
www.caminoreal.com
The 240 rooms in this classy hotel (close to the Centro Cultural) have different modern amenities.

La Villa de Zaragoza
Avenida Madero 1120
Tel. (664) 685 18 32
www.hotellavilla.biz
The newer rooms in this popular hotel (66 rooms) feature a kitchen, air conditioning and cable TV.

Mexicali

From Tecate, it is another 140km/87mi to Mexicali (population 880,000), whose name is of course a contraction of the first syllables of Mexico and California. As recently as 1898, a village of the Cucapá Indians by the name of Laguna del Álamo existed here.

Today, Mexicali is the dynamic **capital of Baja California Norte** and a centre for the finishing industry as well as agriculture (cotton, fruit and vegetable). It is also the **border crossing** to the US sister city Calexico. In the University Museum, visitors learn more about the palaeontology, archaeology, ethnography and the history of the missions in Lower (Baja) California.

Cerro Prieto

Only about 24km/15mi south of Mexicali a road branches off from the MEX 5 to the Cerro Prieto geothermal area. This volcanic field is the second largest geothermic generator on earth, and provides a fair proportion of the electricity for the Valley of Mexicali.

San Felipe

The much frequented fishing village and ocean resort San Felipe (population 30,000) is located at the Sea of Cortés (Gulf of California), 193km/120mi south of Mexicali. San Felipe is also popular with offshore anglers.

✴ Tlaxcala

P 20

Federal state: Tlaxcala (Tlax.)
Population: 100,000

Altitude: 2,255m/7,398ft
Distance: 120km/75mi east of Mexico City, 30km/19mi north of Puebla

Tlaxcala is the capital of Mexico's smallest federal state. The inhabitants of the city, located in the foothills of the Eastern Sierra Madre, have always been known for their friendly attitude toward strangers. Being on bad footing with the Aztec city Tenochtitlán, the Tlaxcala residents and their allies were quick to forge an alliance with Cortés when he arrived in 1519. After its retreat from Tenochtitlán, the Cortés alliance was able to regroup here with the help of the Tlaxcala natives.

The town of Tlaxcala was founded in 1525 by Franciscan friars. Even though it was meant to be a place for the Indian people in the area, it was nevertheless built in the ostentatious style of the Spanish Renaissance. Once heavily populated, and at one time one of the largest urban areas in Mexico, Tlaxcala lost most of its inhabitants during a plague epidemic (1544–1546). It never recovered from this disaster, and its role in history remained small from then on. Many people from Mexico City come to Tlaxcala to escape the metropolitan noise and bustle, and the archaeological site of Cacaxtla Pyramid is easy to reach for an outing as are the many small colonial cities in the area.

 VISITING TLAXCALA

INFORMATION

Tourist information
corner Avenida Juárez / Lardisábal
Tel. (246) 466 21 22
www.tlaxcala.gob.mx

GETTING AROUND

Taking the MEX 150 and the MEX 119 is the best way to reach Tlaxcala from Mexico City (113km/70mi) by car. The trip by bus lasts about 2 hours.

WHERE TO EAT

► **Moderate**
Los Portales
Plaza de la Constitución 8

Tel. (246) 462 54 19
This is a simple restaurant in a central location offering Mexican cuisine.

WHERE TO STAY

► **Luxury to mid-range**
Posada San Francisco
Plaza de la Constitución 17
Tel. (246) 462 60 22
Fax (246) 462 68 18
www.posadasanfrancisco.com
The remodelled 19th-century grey-reddish villa (68 rooms) in a central location at the southern end of the city plaza offers its guests a swimming pool and a tennis court.

But the beauty of Tlaxcala itself is reason enough for a visit. There are buildings in all **shades of yellow and red**, well groomed trees line the main streets and there are fountains all over town.

What to See in Tlaxcala

The large, shady town square (Zócalo) is one of the most beautiful plazas in Mexico. The town hall (built 1550), whose second-floor window arches are designed in the Indian-Moorish style, takes up much of the northern edge of the square, while the rest is occupied by the Governor's Palace (Palacio de Gobierno) next door. Tlaxcala-born Desiderio Hernández Xochitiotzi's modern frescoes in the hall-ways of the palace depict the history of the town. The Parroquia de San José church, its red brick façade decorated with colourful wall tiles, stands at the north-west side of the square.

Zócalo

Founded in 1526, the church and monastery of San Francisco (Ex-Convento San Francisco) stand close to the plaza in a north-eastern direction. The former monastery is one of the earliest of its kind in Mexico. The main monastery complex was built between 1537 and 1540. The cathedral **Church of the Assumption** (Iglesia de la Asun-ción) is also notable for its cedar wood ceiling decorated with stars, which is Moorish in character. The baptismal font in the chapel of the Third Order was probably used to baptize the four rulers of the city. Next to the chapel stands the **Tlaxcala Regional Museum** (Mu-seo Regional de Tlaxcala), which documents the history of the region from pre-Hispanic times to the Mexican revolution.

✳
Former San Francisco monas-tery

In the Museum of Folk Art and Tradition (Museo de Artes y Tradi-ciones Populares) in Calle Emilio Sánchez 1, local people provide in-sights into their lives and artistic accomplishments, such as weaving, carving or making carpets. They also elucidate on pulque produc-tion. Beautiful pottery and textiles are on display next door in the Casa de Artesanías (house of artists).

Museum of Folk Art and Tradition

Above the city and north-east of the city square stands one of the most beautiful sacral buildings in Mexico, the Sanctuary of Our Lady of Ocotlán (Santuario de la Virgen de Ocotlán). The Indian **Francis-co Miguel** created this church in the middle of the 18th century. The white stucco ornaments in the central part of the ultra-Baroque façade and the towers are set off in an appealing contrast by the arched outer elements, which are covered with hexagonal wall tiles. This combination and the exceedingly vivid conch arches give the Baroque building an **exquisitely graceful** appearance.
It took the artist 25 years to complete the church interior. The high altar, the two side altars and the **octagonal alcove with the statue of the Virgin Mary** are especially remarkable. In this case, the latter is a small chapel behind the high altar with colourful stucco decorations

✳ ✳
Sanctuary of Our Lady of Ocotlán

showing Indian style elements. An apparition of the Virgin Mary is said to have appeared here in 1541 and now, every year, a **procession** takes place in her honour. The celebrations attract many pilgrims, participants and onlookers.

Santa Ana Chiautempan

The town of Santa Ana Chiautempan has grown together with the eastern part of Tlaxcala and is of about equal size. The town is particularly known for its woven and embroidered textiles. Visitors can admire and buy arts and crafts at the Sunday market or in various shops.

San Esteban Tizatlán

San Esteban Tizatlán is located about 5km/3mi north-east of Santa Ana Chiautempan on the road to Apizaco. Here stand the ruins of the Palace of Xicoténcatl and two altars with interesting **pre-Columbian wall paintings**. These frescoes are executed in the style of Mixtec pictorial script and display for example the mythological figure of Xochiquétzal, the god and protector of Tlaxcala. Next to the site stands a 16th-century church with an open chapel and frescoes showing angels who are playing medieval instruments.

Cacaxtla · Xochitécatl

✳ Cacaxtla
⏲ Opening times: daily 9am–5pm

The excavation site Cacaxtla is located not quite 20km/12mi southwest of Tlaxcala near San Miguel del Milagro. In 1975, the site received a lot of attention when grave robbers dug a tunnel and discovered pre-Hispanic murals in the process. They reported the find to the authorities. Cacaxtla probably had its heyday between AD 700 and 900 and the impressive frescoes were most likely created in the 8th century.

The frescoes show style elements of the Maya and the late period of Teotihuacán, i.e. cultures that are characterized by slight modifications to the talud-tablero style and by the framing scenes and glyphs in the wall paintings. It is striking that in Cacaxtla **Venus symbols** predominate. These symbols closely relate to Mesoamerican war rituals and sacrifice. A roof now covers most of the site, which has been named Los Cerritos. When entering the site, first Hill B (Montículo B) is seen, with a three-tiered pyramid base. The round tour of the site then leads over the Gran Basamento (large base), an enormous stepped complex with many structures of various ages, such as palaces, column passages, platforms, courtyards and altars. The paintings around the stairs of the Red Temple are protected by a glass plate.

✳ Mural ►

The tour leads via the North Plaza to **Structure B** and the depiction of a battle. The two murals show the brutal **battle between the victorious jaguar warriors against the bird people, who are about to be defeated**. In the centre of the battlefield stand two monumental figures observing the scene, wearing the garb of the highland Indians but walking in platform sandals like the Maya. The most interesting building in the archaeological site is the adjacent Structure A or

The wall paintings in Structure B show the victorious jaguar warriors in a battle against the bird people.

Structure of the Paintings (Edificio de las Pinturas). The interior of the structure contains five wall paintings, most of them probably symbolic depictions of the gods **Quetzalcóatl and Tláloc**. The fresco in the northern column passage shows a life-sized person with the appearance of a jaguar with a broad ceremonial wand from which water drips onto a snake in a jaguar skin. A painted glyph (9 reptile eye) is conspicuous, painted in the style of Teotihuacán with bar and dot numbers. The wall painting at the door jamb again shows a person disguised as a jaguar with Tláloc vessel and a snake in his hand. The headdress and the cross-band motifs on the belts are typical of the Maya style. The beautiful figure in the painting at the southern entrance depicts a winged being standing on a snake. The oversized ceremonial staff ends in a stylized snake head. The glyphs for the number 13 as well as the hand and footprints are Teotihuacán elements. The figure on the southern door jamb seems to show a figure who appears to be connected to the ocean, holding a large conch and wearing an octopus in its headdress. This is reminiscent of the conch god of the Gulf Coast Maya.

✱ ✱
◁ Wall paintings

Xochitécatl
🕐
Opening times:
same as for
Cacaxtla; ticket valid
for both sites

On top of a hill, about 1.5km/1mi east of Cacaxtla, lies the excavation site Xochitécatl Xochitécatl (Náhuatl: xochitl = flower and técatl = place). The site consists of two plazas with a round pyramid (Edificio de la Espiral, spiral structure), which was dedicated to the wind god, the Building of the Serpent (Edificio de la Serpiente) from the formative period (1000–700 BC) and the Pyramid of the Flowers (Pirámide de las Flores). The latter pyramid is the fourth largest in Mesoamerica. In front of the Pyramid of the Flowers stands the Platform of Volcanoes (Basamento de los Volcanes) and two tall columns with a diameter of 1.70m/5.5ft.

Other Travel Destinations around Tlaxcala

**Huamantla
de Juárez**

Apizaco is a further 20km/12mi on the MEX 119, and from there the MEX 136 leads south-east to Huamantla de Juáre (27km/17mi), where you can pay a visit to the 16th-century Franciscan monastery, the Baroque church and the Bullfight Museum (Museo Taurino). The August celebrations in this town with colourful **festivals** are known near and far. On 15 August (Assumption Day) the city organizes a bull run like the one in the Spanish city of Pamplona. On the same day, flower mosaics are laid out in the streets (Xochipetate) for the Virgin of Charity (Virgen de Caridad). The celebrations also involve markets for livestock as well as arts and crafts.

✳
**Volcano
La Malinche**

Returning from Huamantla to Apizaco on the MEX 136, a new road after 13km/8mi turns off to Centro Vacacional Malintzín, 14km/8.7mi away. The town (elevation 3,000m/9,843ft) is convenient as a base to climb the now inactive volcano Malinche (4,461m/14,636ft). The volcano is named after Cortés' Indian interpreter and lover. The ascent takes about 2.5 hours, the descent 2 hours. An alternative ascent from San Miguel Canoa (north-east of Puebla) is considerably longer and should only be made by experienced mountain climbers.

Toluca

P 19

Federal state: México (Mex.)
Population: 1,200,000

Altitude: 2,680m/8,793ft
Distance: 67km/42mi west of
Mexico City

The colonial centre of Toluca captivates with pretty plazas and beautiful arcades. The city offers visitors many museums and galleries.

Toluca is the capital of the federal state of Mexico. Built at an elevation of 2,650m/8,694ft at the south-western edge of the Anáhuac Plateau, about 70km/43mi from Mexico City, Toluca is the **highest city**

▶ VISITING TOLUCA

INFORMATION

Tourist information
in the Edificio de Servicios
Administrativos
Urawa 100 (at the corner of Paseo
Tollocan)
Tel. (722) 212 60 48

GETTING AROUND

The best route by car from Mexico
City to Toluca is on the MEX 15
(67km/42mi). The same trip takes
about 1 hour by bus and about 2
hours by train.

WHERE TO EAT

▶ **Inexpensive**
Hostería de las Ramblas
Portal 20 de Noviembre 107
Good value, tasty Mexican cuisine.

WHERE TO STAY

▶ **Mid-range**
Del Rey Inn Hotel
Carretera México-Toluca Km 63.5
Tel. (722) 212 21 22
Fax (722) 212 25 67
www.delrey.com.mx
This hotel (257 rooms) with a large
garden is located in the industrial part
of the city (between Chrysler and
Pfizer).

Baedeker-recomendation

Trees of Life
Arts and crafts galore are on sale in Mexico,
but nothing is quite so characteristic of the
country as the Tree of Life (árbol de la vida).
The most beautiful and the best known
variety are found in Metepec. The finely
crafted clay figures with fruit and bird
ornaments are reminiscent of Adam and
Eve in paradise and the impending fall of
mankind.

in Mexico. It is also the seat of the Autonomous University in Mexico
and of many companies in trade and industry, among them breweries and large mills.

Indians had settled in the area around Toluca by the 13th century.   **History**
Over and over again, the Matlazinca in the region fell under the rule
of one or the other tribe from the Valley of Anáhuac. Remaining allies of the Aztec until the beginning of the 15th century, they finally
had to concede to them and many fled into the surrounding region
which is today's Michoacán. The Spaniards received limited help
from them in their conquest of Tenochtitlán, and their settlements as

part of the Marquesado del Valle de Oaxaca therefore became the personal property of **Hernán Cortés**. The Franciscans built the first monastery here in 1529, and in 1667 Toluca de San José was granted its municipal charter. In 1830, Toluca became **the capital of the federal state of Mexico**, which borders the Distrito Federal on three sides. The city assumed the surname "de Lerdo" at the end of the 19th century after the statesman Sebastián Lerdo de Tejada.

What to See in Toluca

City square, Plaza de los Mártires

Around the beautiful city square (Plaza de los Mártires) is the cathedral, a neo-classical 19th-century building, and the Governor's Palace (Palacio de Gobierno) on the northern side. There is a long shopping street with 120 arcades (**Portales**) one block to the right of the city square. Not far away is the Baroque El Carmen church, whose associated convent now houses the **Museum of Fine Arts** (Museo de las Bellas Artes). The museum displays paintings from the 17th, 18th, and 20th centuries. At the opposite side of the Plaza de los Mártires stands the 19th-century **cathedral** and the mustard-yellow church, the Iglesia de la Cruz. The plaza is lined with arcades containing shops, restaurants and cafés.

Malinalco: House of the Eagle

Immediately to the north-east lies the Plaza Garibay with one of the most beautiful botanical gardens in Mexico, the Jardín Botánico Cosmo Vitral. Originally, the Art Nouveau building with the majestic lead windows by the Mexican artist Leopoldo Flores was designed to be a market, and the native people used it as such throughout most of the 20th century.

Botanical garden

A huge market, the Mercado Juárez, takes place near the road to Mexico City. It is one of the most lively markets in Mexico with pots, baskets, dresses, fruit and vegetables on offer. Friday is the best day to visit.

Mercado Juárez

The interesting cultural centre, the Centro Cultural Mexiquense (10km/6mi from the city centre in a park-like portion of the former Hacienda de la Pila), consists of several museums and a library. Visitors have the choice of either learning more about the history of the state in the **Regional Museum**, visiting a small **Museum of Art** or marvelling at the exhibits in the **Museum of Folk Arts and Crafts**, which include sometimes strange All Saints' Day statues and amazing Trees of Life. The **Charro Museum** (Museo de la Charrería), exhibiting cowboy (charro) gear and attire, saddles, lassos and other items, is also part of the cultural centre.

Centro Cultural Mexiquense

Around Toluca

About 8km/5m south-east of Toluca lies the town of Metepec with the Franciscan monastery San Juan Bautista (16th/17th century) and the pretty del Calvario church with its large atrium. The town is known for the green earthenware and colourful clay figures manufactured here, mostly in the shape of Trees of Life or suns.

Metepec

Returning from Metepec to the MEX 55, drive on toward Ixtapán de la Sal. After a few miles, a road near Mexicaltzingo branches off to the left. Driving another 16km/10mi on this road leads to Santiago de Tianguistenco. The market, which has existed since pre-Hispanic times, is especially interesting. Every Tuesday, about 3,000 vendors offer their wares here. The 18th-century parish church Santa María del Buen Suceso is part of the pretty town.

Santiago de Tianguistenco

★

◄ Market

The town Tenango del Valle is a roughly 25km/15.5mi drive south on the MEX 55. Close to this town lies the large archaeological site Teotenango. This ancient city was at its zenith between the 10th and 12th century. The typical feature of this site are the **pyramid platforms** with three or four stepped terraces. Once, temples stood on the top platforms. The first structures seen when entering the site belong to Complex A in the Plaza of the Jaguar, beyond which is Complex E with a ball court and a sweat bath. The remnants of several residences which had to be taken down to make room for the con-

Teotenango

struction of the ball court are still visible. Within the North Group, Complex D covers the most ground. Aside from platforms, residences and patios, Complex D features a 120m/393ft-long and 40m/131ft-wide structure called Platform of the Serpent (Basamento de la Serpiente). The Plaza of the Serpents in front of the platform extends in a western direction to the Street of the Frogs (Calle de la Rana) and in a northern direction to the Square of the Peach (Plaza del Durazno). The museum displays remarkable archaeological finds belonging to the federal state of México, mostly from Teotenango, Malinalco and Calixtlahuaca.

Tenancingo

Tenacingo (population 40,000) is about 50km/31mi away from Toluca on the MEX 55. The town is known for its 18th-century Carmelite monastery (Convento del Santo Desierto de Tenancingo) and for the wooden furniture and the rebozos (a Mexican shawl used to carry infants) produced here. There is also a beautiful waterfall.

✳ Malinalco

⏲ Opening times: Tue–Sun 9am–5.30pm

The archaeological site Malinalco is located in a landscape with verdant forests and craggy rock formations. To go there, take the MEX 55 and about 20km/12mi east of Tenancingo look for the branching road to Malinalco. Malinalco is located on top of the Cerro de los Ídolos (Hill of the Idols) which towers over the town by 220m/722ft. This Aztec-built ceremonial centre is unique in that it is one of the few pre-Columbian sites which have been carved into the rocks. The Matlatzinca ruled the area until in 1476 the Aztec under Axayácatl conquered it, but construction of the main ceremonial structures probably did not start until 25 years later and had not been completed when the Spaniards, under Andrés de Tapia, conquered Malinalco in 1521.

When climbing up to the site, visitors see on the left side of the steps a small temple, which was dedicated to the rain god Tláloc. A stairway flanked by jaguars leads to the main temple (**Templo Principal**). In the centre of this temple sits the damaged statue of a standard bearer. This temple was completely carved out of the rock. Initially, it was covered with a thin layer of coloured stucco. As **the House of the Eagle** (Cuauhcalli), symbolizing the sun, it served the initiation of men into the religious warrior orders named Eagles and Jaguars. The entrance to the round shrine is framed by a flat relief, designed to make the opening look like the open mouth of a snake. A serpent and a war drum throne were placed next to the shrine. The temple chamber, which has a diameter of 6m/20ft, contains sculptures of three sacred animals carved from the circular rock wall. Several structures remained unfinished at the time of the Spanish conquest, among them are the chambers left of the entrance and a low pyramid in front of the main temple. Behind the unfinished pyramid stand the ruins of two larger temples. **Structure III** consists of an ante-hall with frescoes and a round chamber with a hollowed-out altar. The structure was probably a **Tzinacalli** (Temple of the Bat). It may have possibly be used as a temple in which the corps of warriors who had fallen in battle against the enemies of the Aztec were burnt, thus elevating them to the rank of a god. According to Aztec belief, a warrior death was richly rewarded and the warriors' spirits would turn into stars.

The adjacent large structure to the north, **Structure IV**, which had in part been cut out of the rock, is believed to have contained a sun temple. A remarkable **wooden drum** (Tlapanhuéhuetl) with intricately carved depictions and glyphs of the eagle and jaguar has been found here. They are intrepreted as being connected with killed or sacrificed warriors who, after passing the underworld, became messengers of the sun god. The drum is on display in the museum of Tenango.

In the town of Malinalco, take a look at San Salvador church which is associated with the Augustinian monastery. The church has a prosaic 16th-century Renaissance portal and early frescoes on the right behind the entrance on the back wall. A dance festival takes place in the monastery atrium from 6–8 January at Epiphany (adoration of the three magi).

Malinalco

The town of Malinalco is perhaps not as well known as the ruin site, but is nevertheless very pretty.

Chalma

Chalma is located only 12km/7.5mi to the east. It is **one of the most significant places of pilgrimage** in Mexico. In pre-Columbian times, people worshipped Otzoctéotl, the god of the grottoes, and visited his statue in Chalma. After the Spaniards destroyed the statue and replaced it with a large crucifix from the Augustinian friars in 1533, the worshippers changed over to the new symbol. Since then, people have been making pilgrimages to the church (built in 1683), in which the Christ of Chalma (El Santo Señor de Chalma) is revered. Thousands make pilgrimages to this church on high religious holidays, but especially on the first Friday of Lent, on Ascension Day and also on the Day of San Agustín (August 28). In the festivities, Catholic and ancient Indian rites mix. The seven **Zempoala Lagoons** are found 40km/25mi north-east of Chalma in a beautiful landscape reminiscent of the Alps.

! **Baedeker TIP**

Wellness the Mexican Way

Fancy being spoiled for a couple of days? If so, the health resort in Ixtapán de la Sal is just the place for you. Located in the spacious grounds of a 14ha/35 ac subtropical park with old trees and a small stream, about 200 rooms are at guests' disposal, as well as tennis courts, a golf course and horses. There are four swimming pools of various temperatures, whose mineral rich water is good for muscles and circulation problems. Guests can choose between the sauna and the steam bath, take part in water areobics, or receive massages and treatments with herbs, paraffin or fango packs.

After almost 35km/22mi on the MEX 55 in a southerly direction, you come to the resort **Ixtapán de la Sal** (population 40,000) set in very pretty surroundings. There are radioactive springs in the area, and the resort town is also popular because it offers many opportunities to take part in sports. The Ixtapán Vacation Centre Aquatic Park in particular attracts many visitors. The spas offer thermal bath basins at various temperatures, and there are also waterfalls, small lakes and water slides.

Nevado de Toluca

You may also like to make an excursion to the often snow-covered dormant **volcano**, also known as Xinantécatl (4,575m/15,010ft). The volcano is located south-east of Toluca, and can be reached via the roads 103, 134 and 3 (50km/31mi from Toluca), leading up to the 4,200m/13,780ft-high Laguna del Sol (Sun Lagoon) and the Laguna de la Luna (Moon Lagoon). From the top of the volcano and the crater rim there is a magnificent view over the beautiful valley of Toluca, the mountains of Guerrero, the forests of Michoacán, the peaks of the Sierra Nevada, Popocatépetl and Iztaccíhuatl.

Valle de Bravo

A 70km/44mi drive west from Toluca leads to the pretty **vacation spot** Valle de Bravo (population 35,000). The town lies near a reservoir (Presa de Valle de Bravo or Presa Miguel Alemán) amid lush vegetation and mountains. Special attractions around the town are the rock formation La Peña and the Salto de Ferrería waterfall.

Stone altar at the crater lake of the volcano Nevado de Toluca

Leaving Valle de Bravo on the MEX 55 north, a country lane branches off to the left after about 8km/5mi, and the archaeological site Calixtlahua lies about 2.5km/1.6mi along this lane. The early history of this religious site is unknown. It was presumably a Matlatzinca settlement, until the Aztec conquered the city, occupying Calixtlahuaca for the first time in 1474 and exerting great influence on later building activities. The Aztec are said to have sacrificed 11,000 Matlatzinca at this site after a revolt.

The Temple of Quetzalcóatl (Structure 3) is the most important building at this site. It stands on a large terrace and over time several structures were built over the original one. The **four-step round pyramid** has a wide outside stairway and an altar. The temple was dedicated to the wind god Ehécatl, a god which originated with the Huastec but was then also accepted by the Aztec and later incarnated by Quetzalcóatl. On a higher, secluded plain stretches a building complex consisting of the Temple of Tláloc (Structure 4) and a pyramid platform (Structure 7) with a wide stairway. On the small platform stands the T-shaped Altar of the Skulls. Spikes and skulls project from the top plate of the altar. A third, still higher plain, displays two partially overgrown platforms (Structures 5 and 6) and two carved stone slabs.

When leaving the site in the direction of the intersection of two paths, the fourth building group of Calixtlahua is seen a little further to the left. This group was named after the Aztec school of higher education Calmecac (Structure 17). At this site, several rooms and platforms are grouped around a large inner courtyard.

★ Tula

0 19

Federal state: Hidalgo (Hgo.)
Distance: 75km/45mi north of Mexico City

Altitude: 2,030m/6,660ft

Tula (Tollán), once the capital of the Toltec, can be visited in half a day from Mexico City. Although not quite as spectacular as the Teotihuacán site, Tula particularly impresses with the famous, slightly ominous looking 4.5m/15ft-high warrior statues carved from black basalt.

The Toltec people not only dominated the development of the early post-classical period in central Mexico, but also influenced Maya culture in Yucatán 1,200km/750mi away. How this interaction was managed is not yet clear. According to legend, Tollán was considered a kind of **paradise**, full of golden palaces, and richly endowed with turquoises, jade and Quetzal feathers. Quite conceivably, the Aztec or Chichimec plundered Tollán. The ruins of Tollán stand on a hill, separated from today's town of Tula de Allende by a river. The small but modern town has a refinery and cement plants but no tourist attractions.

History It has been confirmed that the ruler Ce Ácatl-Topiltzin (born in 947) established the new Toltec capital in 968. The name Tollán means »Place of Reeds«. About 20 years later, the priest king Ce Ácatl-Topiltzin – or Quetzalcoátl as he now called himself – ostensibly started a brawl with his mythical rival Tezcatlipoca, the bellicose god of the night, and was forced to leave Tollán. As legend has it, he roamed via

Tula *Plan*

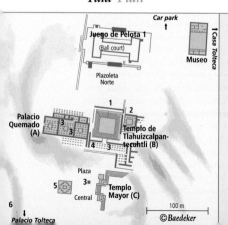

Car park

Juego de Pelota 1
(Ball court)

↑ Casa Tolteca

Museo

Plazoleta Norte

Palacio Quemado (A)

Templo de Tlahuizcalpan-tecuhtli (B)

Plaza

Templo Mayor (C)

Central

Palacio Tolteca

100 m

©*Baedeker*

A »Burnt Palace«
  (Edificio 3)
B Temple of the Morning Star
  (Edificio B)
C Main Temple
  (Edificio C)
1 Coatepantli
  (Serpent Wall)
2 Edificio 1
3 Chac-mool
4 Gran Vestíbulo
  (Great Vestibule)
5 Adoratorio (Altar)
6 Juego de Pelota
  (Ball court)

VISITING TULA

GETTING AROUND

Travelling from Mexico City on the MEX 57 D toward Querétaro, there is a branching road to Tepejí del Río after 58km/36mi (26km/16mi after the toll station Caseta). From Tepejí del Río it is only a 22km/14mi drive to Tula de Allende and another 3km/2mi to the archaeological site. The bus ride from Mexico City (Terminal del Norte) to Tula lasts about 1.5 hours.

WHERE TO STAY

► **Budget**

Hotel Casa Blanca
Pasaje Hidalgo 11
(cul-de-sac, starts at the Calle Hidalgo)
Tel. (773) 732 11 86
casablanca@yahoo.com.mx
This is a relatively new hotel with small but comfortable rooms. Parking is available.

WHERE TO EAT

► **Moderate to inexpensive**

Casa Blanca
Hidalgo 114
Enjoy the delicious buffet with simple Mexican food and various salads.

Cholula and Veracruz to Yucatán and brought the Toltec culture to the Maya. The victory of the warring faction in Tollán brought about a militaristic empire with the **Eagle and Jaguar orders of the warrior elite** emerging as the ruling class. The fall of Tollán began in 1125 with a conflict between the Chichimec and the Nonoalca. In the following period, there was a great fire in the city and other Chichimec groups settled in Tollán. The end finally came in 1175 under the two rulers Topiltzín and Huémac, who both fled south. Most inhabitants of Tollán left and settled in various places in the Valley of Anáhuac or moved on to the coastal regions on the Gulf of Mexico, Chiapas, Guatemala or Nicaragua. Afterwards, the Aztec ruled Tollán, and considering themselves the heirs of the Toltec they emulated elements of Toltec culture and in particular their religion.

Visiting Tollán (Tula)

Site layout

Opening times:
Tue–Sun 10am–5pm

The archaeological site of Tula lies on a hill with a view over the land. Once, the ancient city stretched over 13 sq km/5 sq mi almost to today's city. Upon entering the site, visitors see the small Northern Plaza (Plazuela Norte) next to the **ball court no. 1** (Juego de Pelota No. 1), which measures 67 x 12.5m/220 x 41ft.

Serpent Wall (Coatepantli)

At the south side of the small plaza runs the 2.20m/7.2ft-high and 40m/131ft-long Serpent Wall (Coatepantli), which abuts one side of the Temple of the Morning Star. Between two friezes with geometrical designs, a relief shows a snake devouring human skeletons.

✳
Temple of the Morning Star (Pyramid B)

Passing Structure 1, which was over-built several times and probably served as a residence for priests, visitors see the main courtyard of the site in front of them. Here stands the Temple of the Morning Star (Templo de Tlahuizcalpantecuhtli), also called the Pyramid of Quetzalcóatl or simply Structure B. An outer stairway leads up the five-tiered, 10m/33ft-high step pyramid. Once, a temple crowned the top of the structure.

✳
Atlantean statues ▶

The columns and **colossal statues**, also called telamons or Atlantean statues, discovered here have been placed on the platform of the temple pyramid. The left statue and the upper part of the right statue are reproductions; the originals are on display in the National Museum of Anthropology in Mexico City. These magnificent, 4.60m/15ft-high colossal statues which once supported the roof of the temple symbolize the god **Quetzalcóatl as the morning star**. They hold a spear sling (atlatl) in their right hands and a bundle of arrows, an incense pouch and a small sword in their left. Their breast shield has the form of a butterfly and the rear belt buckle is interpreted as the setting sun. The rectangular columns show reliefs with the symbols of the earth (crocodile head), and there are also depictions of warriors and weapons.

The incomplete column shows the face of Quetzalcóatl. The round columns are decorated with intricate feather patterns because they were originally in the shape of snakes with the snake head as the base. When Tollán was destroyed, the temple was abraded and the colossal statues and the broken columns thrown a long distance down over a ramp. Fragments of friezes with impressive reliefs are still visible on the rising walls of the structure, built in a modified talud-tablero style. The most common motifs in the reliefs are eagles and jaguars, some holding or devouring human hearts.

Great Vestibule

All columns in the Great Vestibule (Gran Vestíbulo) have been rebuilt. Remnants of a painted relief in the north-west corner are still recognizable. One relief shows a procession of warriors and priests. To the right of a stairway reclines a headless Chac-mool statue.

Burnt Palace

To the left of the Temple of the Morning Star lies Structure 3, the Burnt Palace (Palacio Quemado). The building once featured rooms of various sizes, colonnades and courtyards. Two Chac-mool sculptures lie in the central courtyard, and in its north-west corner there is a border with painted reliefs showing a procession of richly dressed and decorated noblemen.

Central courtyard

South of the palace, in the middle of the central courtyard (Plaza Central), stands a small altar (Adoratorio) on a square platform. **Structure C** is located on the east side of the courtyard. This is the Main Temple (Templo Mayor). A Chac-mool statue guards the stairway to its upper platform, and on a stone slab to the right of the stairs appears the Venus glyph, one of the symbols of Quetzalcóatl.

To the west of the Main Temple lies the **largest ancient ball court in Central Mexico** (Juego de Pelota No. 2). The more than 100m/328ft-long ball court is lined with Chac-mool sculptures on both sides.

Very impressive: the Atlantean statues of Tula once supported the roof of the Temple of the Morning Star.

Museum · The Jorge R. Acosta Museum at the entrance to the archaeological site displays stone sculptures of all shapes and sizes, obsidian objects and jewellery.

Around Tula

El Corral · About 1.5km/0.9mi north of the ruined city stands a strange monument called El Corral. The centre is round, and two rectangular structures are added, one on the east side and one on the west side. Once, an interesting altar stood here, which now resides in a museum.

El Cielito · The ruins of an Aztec palace have been found on the small hill (little heaven) about 6km/3.7mi south-east of Tula. The palace stands on top of an older Toltec site. The palace was still inhabited in the early years of the Viceroyship of New Spain. Historians have discovered that it was used as the **residence of Pedro Montezuma**, the son of the Aztec ruler Montezuma II, appointed Chieftain of Tula by the Spaniards. Pedro Montezuma was a student of the first Franciscan school for the Indian elite.

Cerro de la Malinche · The Cerro de la Malinche (Malinche Mountain) is situated west of Tula de Allende on the other side of the Río Tula. Here, people found carved in a polished rock the calendar glyph "1 Pipe 8 Flint" (980), which could point to the reign of Ce Ácatl Topiltzín. However, it is likely that the glyphs were carved into the rock later by the Aztec.

Tula de Allende · The city Tula de Allende (population 70,000) is 3km/1.8mi away. Franciscan friars established the city in 1529 and between 1550 and 1553 built the massive **San José church fortress**. The church façade was executed in the pure Renaissance style. The choir and the side naves in particular show remarkable ribbed domes.

✶ Tulum

O 31

Federal state: Quintana Roo (Q. R.)   **Altitude:** 14m/46ft
Distance: 320km/200mi south-east of
Mérida, 132km/82mi south of Cancún

Tulum is the only known large Maya fortress on the ocean. Visible for miles around, the fortress is protected by a wall on the inland side and, built on 12m/39ft cliffs, towers over the white sandy beaches of the Caribbean Sea.

In comparison with other Maya sites, Tulum is architecturally of limited importance. Still, **the unique and extraordinary location** as

▶ VISITING TULUM

GETTING AROUND

A bus ride to Tulum takes about 2 hours from Cancún and about 4 hours from Chetumal. By car, drive 131km/81mi on the MEX 307 from Cancún or 250km/155mi from Chetumal on the MEX 307. From Mérida take the MEX 180, exit on the road close to Nuevo Xcan and continue through Cobá (total distance 320km/200mi).

WHERE TO EAT

▶ Moderate

Paris de Noche
Corner Avenida Tulum / Beta Sur
This restaurant serves international cuisine, mainly Mexican, French and Italian.

Que Fresco
in the hotel Zamas, Boca-Paila-Street, about 3km/2mi from the great intersection
This restaurant serves very good Italian and Mexican food, including wood-oven pizza, delicious fresh pasta and traditional foods of the Maya.

WHERE TO STAY

▶ Mid-range

**Maya Tulum –
Wellness Retreat and Spa**
PO Box 1496
Conyers, GA 30012
Tel. (770) 483 02 38
Fax (770) 785 92 60
www.mayatulum.com
Comfortable lodgings (32 rooms) with simple but pretty cabañas. A place to meditate. Among the extras are Yoga lessons, vegetarian food, and interesting offers of outings into the surrounding areas.

Caphé-Ha
30km/19mi south of Tulum, 5km/3mi after the bridge in Boca Paila on the road to Sian Ka'an. Pleasant surroundings (1 villa, 2 bungalows) for fishermen and anglers.
No electricity, no fans, and solar energy for cooking. The minimum length of stay in the peak season is 3 days.

well as the wall paintings discovered here make it one of the archaeological sites on the Yucatán peninsula well worth seeing.

Little is known about the history of Tulum. The city's original name may have been Zama (dawn). Today, the style of the site is classified as **late Maya post-classical** (after AD 1200), i.e. in the period when the Maya and Toltec cultures mixed. The buildings, which today are considered most important, were probably erected as late as 1450. A stele with the inscribed date of 564 has been found in Tulum, but chances are that this calendar stone came from another site, most likely the neighbouring Tancah. Members of a Spanish expedition under Juan de Grijalva sailed along the Yucatán coast and happened to come upon Tulum in 1518; they were the first Europeans to set foot here. The city still seems to have been inhabited when the Span-

History

iards conquered the north-east of Yucatán in 1544. Toward the end of the 19th century while the Yucatán Caste War raged, the Maya once more barricaded themselves in Tulum. The American John Lloyd Stephens and the British illustrator Frederick Catherwood together explored Tulum in 1842 and delivered the first illustrated description of the archaeological site (►Baedeker Special p.471).

Exploring Tulum

Site layout

Tulum is a relatively small archaeological site. Landside, the city was protected by a battlement, an arrangement also seen in other Toltec-influenced Maya sites of the post-classical period, for example the sites of Mayapán and Ichpaatún. The walled-in area measures 280m/918ft from north to south and 165m/541ft from east to west. The stone battlement was originally 3m/10ft to 5m/16ft high and on average 7m/23ft thick. The five exits were enforced with stone slabs. The site plan suggests that the Tulum was not only a ceremonial site. A balustrade secured the wall-walk on top of the battlement. In two corners inside the battlement, a small temple presumably served as a look-out tower.

🕐 Opening times: daily 8am–7pm

★ Temple of the Frescoes

From an archaeologist's point of view, the most important structure in Tulum is the Temple of the Frescoes (Templo de los Frescos, Structure 16). The temple stands approximately in the centre of the wall-enclosed city area and consequently halfway across the east-west axis. For the most part, the temple was probably built in 1450. As was the custom with Maya sacral structures, the original temple was over-built several times with a new structure on top of the old one, as prescribed by the calendar.

The temple contains only one chamber on the ground level with an entrance on the west side. Four columns partition the entrance. Above the columns, a double lintel is divided into three parts, each with one niche. A stucco statue of the **descending god** is installed in the centre niche. Stucco reliefs depicting seated figures with elaborate headdresses decorate the niches on either side. Large bas-relief masks form the cornices; they were originally painted and probably depict Itzamná, the ancient **sky god of the Yucatán Maya**. The top level of the temple has a niche above a door, which contains remnants of a stucco relief. Originally, it probably depicted the de-

! *Baedeker* TIP

Beware false guides!

If you visit Tulum under your own steam you should only pay for your ticket to the archaeological site at the entrance. Time and time again, tricksters pass themselves off as tour guides. They wear »official looking« name tags and will drastically overcharge for their »special tour offers« or »package prices«, sometimes up to ten times the regular price.

A unique location on the Caribbean Sea: Tulum →

Tulum Plan

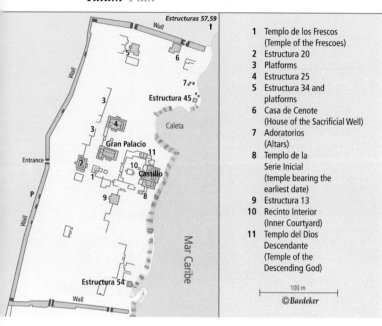

1 Templo de los Frescos
   (Temple of the Frescoes)
2 Estructura 20
3 Platforms
4 Estructura 25
5 Estructura 34 and
   platforms
6 Casa de Cenote
   (House of the Sacrificial Well)
7 Adoratorios
   (Altars)
8 Templo de la
   Serie Inicial
   (temple bearing the
   earliest date)
9 Estructura 13
10 Recinto Interior
   (Inner Courtyard)
11 Templo del Dios
   Descendante
   (Temple of the
   Descending God)

100 m

©Baedeker

scending god. The interior wall is decorated with interesting paintings that are reminiscent of codices. As far as the content is concerned, these paintings seem Mayan but in terms of style they appear Mixtec. They mainly show the Mayan gods. Two embodiments of the sky god Itzamná face each other in the centre top part, and the rain god Chac stands on their right. The central part of the frescoes shows the moon god and the fertility goddess Ixchel, the wife of Itzamná, as well as two unknown figures. The lower part of the fresco again depicts the goddess Ixchel in a maritime scene with stylized fish. The 1.30m/4.3ft-high stele no. 2 stands on an altar in front of the temple. According to the post-classical Maya calendar and the inscription, the stele was created in AD 1261.

Castle The most conspicuous and largest structure in Tulum is the Castle (El Castillo or Structure 1), situated in the eastern part of the site **high up on a cliff, overlooking the ocean**. It has been shown that the Castle was created in three construction phases. A wide stairway leads to a terrace with the temple. A stone in front of the temple was probably used as an altar for human sacrifices. The temple has two chambers and two serpent columns partition the entrance. A niche above the central door opening contains the stone statue of the descending god.

Templo del Dios Descendente North of the Castle and adjacent to it stands the Temple of the Descending God (Templo del Dios Descendente, Structure 5). It was built over an existing temple. A particularly striking feature is the width of the walls, which taper off toward their base, a design that was meant to add to the stability of the building. The temple has only one chamber.

Temple of the Descending God

The niche above the entrance contains a stucco statue of the descending god. This god (of the setting sun) appears frequently in the Tulum designs. The god has winged arms and shoulders as well as a bird tail. Different interpretations of the figure include the downward flying bee, the setting evening star, the setting sun or the lightning bolt. Only traces of colour are left from the paint on the main façade and the interior east wall.

Other structures are also remarkable, including Structure 25 with a polychrome descending god, Structure 35 which was built over a small cenote (sinkhole) and Structure 45 with a round platform and a breathtaking view of the Caribbean Sea and the Castle. The site also has a visitor centre, an interesting museum and a restaurant.

Other structures

Around Tulum

Driving south for 26km/16mi on 307 leads on to Chunyaxché. An archaeological site of 2.5 sq km/1 sq mi lies very close to the street. Among the finds are pyramids, temples and palaces from the late classical and the post-classical periods. The highest structure is a 19m/62ft-high pyramid. The site is almost unexplored and vegetation covers most of the ruins. Finds include two early tombs with valuable burial objects, among them intricately made jade objects, which are dated between AD 200 and 600. A path leads to the Chunyaxché lagoon, a place which invites a dip.

Chunyaxché

A great number of pre-Hispanic Maya ruins have been found along the coast north of Tulum and the same is true for the southern part of Quintana Roo. A few examples of the archaeological sites are Las Milpas, San Miguel de Ruz, Chamax, Chacmool (Santa Rosa) and Tupak.

Other Maya sites

In 1986, an area of more than 485,000ha/1,200,000ac was set aside as the Sian Ka'an Biosphere Reserve (Reservación de la Biosfera Sian Ka'an). These areas of land are almost untouched and largely uninhabited by people. A region of lagoons, tropical forest, mangrove swamps, palm groves, marshlands and coral reefs, it stretches to Tulum in the north, to Felipe Carrillo Puerto in the west, to Punta Herrero in the south and to a coral reef in the east.

✷ Sian Ka'an nature reserve

The nature reserve is designed not only to protect fauna and flora, but also to create an atmosphere of cooperation with the people in the area. The common goal is to establish a balanced use of the land.

Aside from countless species of fish, crustaceans, and conches, the reserve also provides a habitat for crocodiles, turtles, manatees, tapirs, monkeys, deer, jaguars, ocelots, mountain lions and many species of bird ranging from parakeets to pelicans and flamingos.

Tuxtla Gutiérrez

S 25

Federal state: Chiapas (Chis.)
Population: 450,000

Altitude: 530m/1,739ft
Distance: 1,000km/621mi south-east of Mexico City

Many travellers know Tuxtla Gutiérrez – the capital of the federal state of Chiapas – only as a stopover on the way to San Cristóbal de las Casas. Situated on the Pan-American Highway in a fertile subtropical valley, Tuxtla Gutiérrez has developed into a modern city thanks to its central location and the discovery of crude oil in Chiapas.

Members of the Maya tribe Zoque used to live in the region around today's Tuxtla. They called their settlement Coyactocmo, which later turned into Tuxtlán. Both in Zoque and Náhuatl, the name means

Parque de la Marimba in Tuxtla Gutiérrez

"Place of the Rabbits". In the 16th century, other settlers soon followed the first Spanish monks; the settlers had to fight off many attacks from the Zoque Indians.

In the beginning of the 19th century, Tuxtla was still an obscure place. In 1848, the city added the surname Gutiérrez and in 1892, the town replaced San Cristóbal de Las Casas as the capital of Chiapas. Today, the city is an important administrative and cultural centre as well as a trans-shipment centre.

What to See in Tuxtla Gutiérrez

The city has few old buildings. The cathedral, which has been remodelled several times, and the red and white Governor's Palace (Palacio de Gobierno) are of particular note.

The Francisco Madero park 1.5km/1mi north-east of the city centre is a cultural area with a museum and theatre. This is also the location of the Chiapas Regional Museum (Museo Regional de Chiapas), which displays **Olmec and Maya archaeological finds** as well as regional ethnological objects.

Parque Madero Complex

★

◄ Chiapas Regional Museum

The modern Emilio Rabas theatre and the botanical garden are also part of the park centre. Further popular attractions include a swimming pool and a children's park with models and exhibitions on historic topics, a small railway, mini golf and pony rides.

The small museum of Indian cultures, the Casa de Artesanías (House of the Artists) at Blvd. Dr. Belisario Domínguez 2035 also sells folk arts and crafts from Chiapas.

Casa de Artesanías

Marimba music groups play in the evenings in the popular garden Jardín de las Marimbas, Avenida Central y 8 Pte.

Jardín de las Marimbas

The small forest El Zapotal, situated in the south-east part of the city, is the location of the Miguel Álvarez del Toro Zoo which covers an area of 100ha/247ac and is one of the most interesting zoos in Mexico. Only animals from the Chiapas region live in the zoo, such as jaguars, eagles, parakeets, peacocks, mountain lions, ocelots, coatimundis (a racoon-like animal very common in Mesoamerica), monkeys and nutrias (coypus).

★

Miguel Álvarez del Toro Zoo

Around Tuxtla Gutiérrez

The town of Chiapa de Corzo (population 60,000) is situated along the Pan-American Highway roughly 15km/9mi east of Tuxtla Gutiérrez. A single-tiered restored pyramid is already visible from the intersection. A tomb was found inside this pyramid. Excavations have shown that the area of Chiapa de Corzo harbours one of the oldest pre-Columbian sites in Mesoamerica, similar to the Izapa site. As in-

Chiapa de Corzo

► VISITING TUXTLA GUTIÉRREZ

INFORMATION

Tourist information
North-west corner of the Plaza Cívica
Tel. (961) 612 55 11

GETTING AROUND

Flights are available from Mexico City (about 1hr 20min) and other Mexican airports.
A bus ride from Mexico City to Tuxtla Gutiérrez takes 16 hours, the ride from Oaxaca takes about 7 hours.

EVENTS

Festivities in honour of various saints is absolutely normal in Mexico. In a rather practical manner, Chiapa de Corzo has combined various commemorations to one large city event and people celebrate the Fiesta Grande from 9–23 January. The festival includes everything: processions, fireworks, music, dance, and the parachicos – young men dressed as proud Spaniards.

WHERE TO EAT

► Budget

La Selva
Blvd. Dr. Belisario Domínguez 1360
Tel. (961) 615 07 18
The restaurant opposite the Hotel Camino Real (see below) has plenty of atmosphere. In the afternoon, guests are entertained with Marimba music. On Sundays, the restaurant offers a large buffet.

WHERE TO STAY

► Mid-range

Camino Real Tuxtla Gutiérrez
Blvd. Dr. Belisario Domínguez 1195
Tel. (961) 617 77 77
Fax (961) 617 77 99
www.caminoreal.com
The 210 rooms in this luxurious hotel are grouped around a large swimming pool amid exotic vegetation. All rooms have a splendid view of the mountains.

dicated by ceramic finds in the area, Indians lived in the region between 1400 BC and AD 950. At this site, archaeologists have discovered the so far oldest date inscription ever found in the archaeology of the Americas: the stele 2, now on display in the Regional Museum of Tuxtla Gutiérrez, shows an inscribed date corresponding to 8 December 36 BC. The culture responsible for building this ceremonial site remains unknown.

The conquistador Diego de Mazariegos founded today's city in 1528 around a giant Ceiba tree, sacred to the Indians, called La Pochota. The 16th-century Santo Domingo church, which has been remodelled several times, is well worth taking a look at. In 1552, the priest Rodrigo de León began building an octagonal fountain in the city square, which was completed 10 years later. The somewhat curious fountain, **La Pila**, was built in the Moorish style and has the shape of the Spanish crown. Also located in the Zócalo is a small museum (Museo de Laca) whose exhibitions compare in a clear fashion local and Chinese lacquered works.

About 22km/14mi north of Tuxtla Gutiérrez, the vantage point Los Chiapas (Mirador) affords visitors a splendid view over an area **featuring the magnificent Cañon del Sumidero (Sumidero Canyon)**. It is more than **1,000m/3,281ft** from the rim of the canyon to the winding Río Grijalva (Río Grande de Chiapa) on the canyon floor.

Sumidero Canyon

In 1528, when the Spaniards invaded the area, the Chipanec living in Chiapa reportedly jumped into the canyon to their deaths rather than submit to the invaders. The Chicoasén dam was completed in 1981. It turned the canyon into a narrower, 35km/22mi-long water reservoir. Starting a tour by boat in Chiapa de Corzo or Embarcadero Cahuare, it is possible to make dramatic excursions through the canyon. In many places, almost 1,200m/3,937ft-high rock walls rise up almost vertically. A sweater and a sun hat are recommended for the approximately 2.5-hour boat tour. A rich variety of birds is to be seen, including cormorants, kingfishers, herons, and you sometimes even spot a crocodile. On the tour, guides will point out some unique rock formations such as a moss-covered cliff known as the Christmas tree (Árbol de Navidad).

Around Tuxtla Gutiérrez are several large reservoirs, some of which offer opportunities to take part in aquatic sports. The nearest reservoir (about 35km/22mi north) is the Presa Chicoasén with one of the largest hydroelectric power plants in Latin America.

Reservoirs

The Río Grijalva winds through the Cañon del Sumidero.

Uruapan

P 16 / 17

Federal state: Michoacán (Mich.)
Population: 350,000

Altitude: 1610m/5233ft
Distance:: 430km/267mi west of Mexico City

A mild climate, lush vegetation and beautiful parks are the main assets of the very pleasant, scarcely visited Uruapan. The city lies on the banks of the Río Cupatitzio amid forests and fruit orchards.

The city's Tarascan name means "where the flowers bloom". The Franciscan priest Juan de San Miguel founded the city in 1532 and gave it the name San Francisco de Uruapan. The city was built in a checkerboard pattern and divided into nine districts (barrios) which have retained their self-contained character to this day.

✱ **Guatápara hospital chapel**

The Plaza Principal (Jardín Morelos, Morelos Garden) is the centre of the city. In the early colonial days, the square was designed to be a large market. Juan de San Miguel established the Guatápara hospital chapel here. The hospital with its beautiful patio now houses the **Museum of Folk Art** (Museo de Artes Populares) displaying the lacquer crafts typical of the region.

▶ VISITING URUAPAN

INFORMATION

Tourist information
Casa del Turista
Emilio Carranza 44
(west of the main city square)
Tel. (452) 524 30 91 or

Juan Ayala 16
Tel. (452) 524 71 99
or at www.uruapan.gob.mx

GETTING AROUND

By car from Mexico City, take the MEX 15 via Toluca, Morelia and Pátzcuaro.
The trip takes about 13 hours by train and about 7.5 hours by bus.

WHERE TO EAT

▶ **Moderate**
La Pérgola
Portal Carillo 4
This is a popular restaurant on the south side of the city square. It serves international and local cuisine.

WHERE TO STAY

▶ **Mid-range**
Mansión del Cupatitzio
Parque Nacional
Tel. (452) 523 21 00
Fax (452) 524 67 72
www.mansiondelcupatitzio.com
The 57 comfortable rooms are grouped around a patio. This hotel is located next to the National Park and 5 minutes from the city centre.

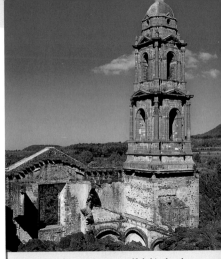

The daily **market** is well worth a visit. Aside from lacquered items, vendors also offer beautiful hand-woven fabrics and traditional clothing. Sample local food in the market behind the hospital chapel, the Mercado de Antojitos (market of snacks).

The principal park of all the beautiful parks here is the **Eduardo Ruiz National Park** at the Río Cupatitzio Canyon. The entrance to this tropical park is only 600m/0.4mi away from the city centre, and it then stretches about 1km/0.6mi along the river bank. Pleasant walkways lead through lush vegetation around waterfalls, rock forma-

In 1943, lava from Paricutín engulfed this church.

tions and springs. The park has a playground for the children. There is also a turkey farm.

Around Uruapan

One of the most beautiful waterfalls in Mexico, the Tzaráracua Falls (Cascada La Tzaráracua), is situated about 12km/7.5mi south on the MEX 37. The water cascades down almost 40m/131ft. The falls are situated in the beautiful forest around the Cupatitzio Lagoon. About 2km/1.2mi upstream there is a smaller version of the waterfall, logically bearing the name Tzaráracuita.

✶
Tzaráracua Falls

Only 18km/11mi north of Uruapan on the MEX 37 a road branches off to the left and after 21km/13mi leads to the Purépecha village of Angahuan (population 35,000). The Santiago parish church (1562) boasts a particularly impressive Moorish-Plateresque portal, which benefited from the art of Indian masons. The portal is opulently decorated and shows similarity with the portal of the Guatápara chapel in Uruapan.

Angahuan

From Angahuan, a 50-minute ride on a mule or on horseback (5km/3mi on foot) leads to the **lava field** of the volcano Paricutín (2,575m/8,448ft) which attracted worldwide attention when it erupted on 20 February 1943. The volcano's lava flows buried several villages. The eruptions continued for almost three years, and more than 5,000 people were forced to leave their homes. The upper portion of the church San Juan Parangaricútiro protrudes desolately above the lava field. It is a good idea to hire a local guide for an ascent to the top of the volcano.

✶ ✶
Paricutín

Paracho   Returning to the MEX 37 from Angahuan, Paracho de Verduzco (population 40,000) is another 20km/12mi distant. The town is known for its wood crafts, such as the making of guitars, violins, toys and furniture. The most festive time in town is at the beginning of August during the Feria Nacional de Guitarra. The festivities last a week with music, dance, markets and cockfights.

✶✶ Uxmal

O 29

Federal state: Yucatán (Yuc.)   **Altitude:** 12m/39ft
Distance: 80km/50mi south of Mérida

Uxmal was once an important city in the Puuc Mountains, after which the typical architectural style of the region is named. The city was at the height of its influence in the late classical period (AD 600–900). Excavation sites, such as Sayil, Kabah, Xlapak and Labná surround the archaeological site of Uxmal (▶Puuc Route).

The famous Maya site Uxmal spreads out over a densely forested plain. The archaeological site is located 80km/50mi south of Mérida in the north-western part of the Yucatán peninsula. By area, Uxmal certainly does not rank among the other larger excavation sites in

Uxmal *Plan*

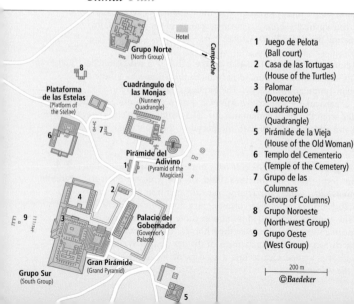

1   Juego de Pelota
    (Ball court)
2   Casa de las Tortugas
    (House of the Turtles)
3   Palomar
    (Dovecote)
4   Cuadrángulo
    (Quadrangle)
5   Pirámide de la Vieja
    (House of the Old Woman)
6   Templo del Cementerio
    (Temple of the Cemetery)
7   Grupo de las
    Columnas
    (Group of Columns)
8   Grupo Noroeste
    (North-west Group)
9   Grupo Oeste
    (West Group)

200 m
© Baedeker

Mexico. However, Uxmal is mostly built in the classic Maya Puuc style and by virtue of its consistent, self-contained architecture it is without doubt **one of the most beautiful pre-Columbian sites in Mexico**. Since 1996, Uxmal has been a UNESCO World Heritage Site.

Uxmal (= built three times) was probably established by a tribe who came to the region from Petén (Guatemala) in the 6th century, i.e. during the Maya classical period. Earlier settlements cannot however be ruled out. The 9th and 10th centuries witnessed the most glorious architectural achievements in Uxmal. The first Spaniard to report on Uxmal was Fray Alonso Ponce who visited Uxmal in 1586. Frans Blom undertook the first systematic excavations here in 1929.

History

Exploring Uxmal

In contrast to Chichén Itzá, the architecture of Uxmal displays almost no Méxica or Toltec influence, and so the structures remained **in the classical Maya Puuc style** (AD 700–1000), named after a chain of hills, Puuc, in the north-west of Yucatán. Characteristic of this style are thin, square or grid-like limestone sheathing over smooth walls, a technique which replaced stucco decoration in the Maya

Puuc Style

🕐
Opening times:
daily 8am–5pm

▶ VISITING UXMAL

GETTING AROUND
On the MEX 261, it is an 80km/50mi drive from Mérida to Uxmal; from Campeche, it is a 172km/107mi drive on the MEX 261.
Alternatively, there are bus services from both Mérida (Via Ruinas, about 1.5 hours) and Campeche.

WHERE TO STAY
▶ Luxury to mid-range
Hacienda Uxmal
Carretera Mérida–
Campeche Km 78
Tel. (997) 976 20 11
Fax (997) 976 20 12
www.mayaland.com/hotels.html
The 73-room colonial hotel of the Barbachano family (built in 1955) is located near the archaeological sites. All rooms are air conditioned, with fans and TV.

▶ Budget
The Flycatcher Inn
Santa Elena
www.mexonline.com/flycatcher-inn.htm
This is an attractive guesthouse with beautiful rooms and a generous breakfast buffet. The atmosphere is relaxed and there are hammocks on the patio.

WHERE TO EAT
▶ Moderate to budget
Hacienda Ochil
on the MEX 261
(between Uxmal and Mérida)
The partially restored Hacienda serves simple meals, but there are many more highlights. A small museum provides insights into sisal processing. Products from the craftsman's workshop are on sale.

classical period. This kind of embellishment, used almost exclusively for the top part of a building, is complemented by panels showing **masks of the rain god Chac** with long bent noses and snakes with stiff bodies, as well as round stone columns in the entrances and embedded columns in long rows.

The excavated part of the Maya city covers an area of 700 x 800m/ 2,296 x 2,625ft. As in the case of other pre-Columbian sites, only a fraction of the original ancient city has been unearthed so far. Unlike other pre-Columbian cities in Yucatán, Uxmal was not designed around one or more cenotes (natural sinkholes) because there are no such sinkholes in the area. People had to make do with aguadas and chultunes, i.e. sealed earth troughs or artificial cisterns in which rainwater was collected. The lack of ground water made the rain god Chac dominant among the gods, and the temple decorations certainly bear this out. Visitors enter the site through the Unidad-Uxmal building, which houses a museum and auditorium, a restaurant and a shop.

Site layout

The 35m/114ft-high Pyramid of the Magician (Pirámide de Adivino) opposite the entrance is the highest structure in Uxmal. The pyramid rests on an oval platform. According to legend, a dwarf built this pyramid in one night with the help of his mother who was a witch. In fact, the pyramid was built during the course of more than three hundred years and consists of five pyramids with the original one in the centre and the others built successively around it; the different layers can be clearly distinguished from one another.
The slightly sloping sides were restored in the fifth building phase. Unfortunately, the older structures were entirely over-built except the entrance to Temple IV (Chenes Temple), which has the appearance of a gaping mouth of a stylized mask. In contrast to the usual Uxmal structures in the Puuc style, this temple is built in a **pure Chenes style**. The façade of the cube-shaped building is completely covered with **Chac masks and lattice work**. Both Temple IV and Temple V, the latter from the period around AD 1000 and also called the House of the Magician, can be accessed either directly via the stairs on the eastern side or alternatively via two smaller side stairways along the Chenes Temple on the western side, a rectangular building (late 9th century) apparently a smaller replica of the Governor's Palace. A small part of the temple façade is decorated with lattice work, and the temple consists of three chambers. The ascent is only advisable for people with a head for heights or experienced climbers because the **stairway is steep and the step width small**, but the view of the site and the surroundings from the top of the pyramid is well worth the climb.

★
Pyramid of the Magician (Pirámide de Adivino)

★
◄ View

← *The ascent of the pyramid is only recommended for those with a head for heights.*

✳
Nunnery Quadrangle

Next to the Pyramid of the Magician and north-west of it stands the beautiful building called the Nunnery Quadrangle (Cuadrángulo de las Monjas). The Spaniards gave the structure this nickname because of its **many cells**. Four long buildings are arranged around the trapezoidal inner courtyard. They rest on terraces of various heights and were built at different times.

Visitors enter the inner courtyard through the cantilever arch entrance to the **South Building**, the second largest structure of this complex. The arch has a common axis with the ball court in front of the quadrangle. Eight rooms each are arranged along both sides of the centre aisle, of which half face the outside and half the inner courtyard. The frieze above the doors contains raised sculpted images of Maya huts. On the opposite side rises the 100m/328ft-long **North Building**, the oldest and most significant building of the Nunnery Quadrangle. It rests on an almost 7m/23ft-high platform. The 30m/98ft-wide stairway is flanked by two small temples. The temple on the western side, the only building in Uxmal supported by columns, is called the Venus Temple because archaeologists relate a motif in the frieze to the planet Venus. The north building consists of

Explanations outside the Nunnery Quadrangle

26 chambers and eleven entrances to the inner courtyard. Four mask towers rise over the cornice, each one with four stacked Chac masks. Located next to the Chac masks are small depictions of thatched houses and reliefs showing monkeys and serpents. The third oldest structure is the **East Building**, with five entrances. The cornice consists of a serpent ornament with the heads protruding beyond the north side. The frieze is relatively basic in style and consists mainly of lattice work. Trapezia around owl heads continue the design. The youngest tract is the **West Building** with seven entrances; some consider its frieze the most artistic in Puuc architecture. A throne with canopy is located above the main entrance. Once a creature – half man, half turtle – sat on the throne. The **beautiful panel** shows alternating sculptures of Maya huts, rows of masks, geometrical patterns and serpents coiled in a meandering pattern. The latter, added later, represents one of the few Toltec style elements in Uxmal. Three stacked masks of the rain god Chac protrude from each of the vertical corners of the building.

The ball court is located south of the Nunnery Quadrangle. The date 649 is inscribed in the two stone rings discovered here.

Ball court

Further south stands the House of the Turtles (Casa de las Tortugas), one of the best proportioned buildings in Uxmal. Three entrances lead from the east side through the unadorned lower floor to the interior of the house. The frieze over the central cornice consists of a row of closely spaced columns. The building owes its name to the turtles in the frieze on the top cornice.

House of the Turtles

The next building on the southern side is arguably the **architecturally most accomplished building of the pre-Columbian Americas**. It is called the Governor's Palace (Palacio del Gobernador). The building sits on a giant platform and a terrace and consists of a main building and two side wings that are connected via two vaulted passages. Later, these passages were walled off.

✷ ✷
Governor's Palace

The façade on the lower level is smooth. Eleven entrances in the front of the structure and one on each side lead to 24 chambers, which all feature the typical cantilever ceiling. The 3m/9.8ft-high frieze above the central cornice shows in its top part an almost uninterrupted row of 103 Chac masks with many geometrical patterns in the background. Above this frieze, a row of s-shaped geometric patterns form a serpent, whose body once reached around the entire building. The restored figure over the central entrance with a Quetzal feather headdress could be a depiction of the Uxmal ruler. According to estimates, about 20,000 cut stones with a weight of 20–80kg/44–176lbs each were used for the giant mosaic frieze. An altar stands in front of the palace, and a double-headed jaguar forms its centre. This figure could have been a symbol of the ruler and may have served as a throne; it is cut from a single block of stone.

The roof comb with its window-like openings gave the Dovecote its name.

Grand Pyramid South-west of the Governor's Palace stands the Grand Pyramid, which has been partially restored. The once nine-tiered 30m/98ft building had a flat top surface which carried no temple; instead a palace-like smaller building stood on each of the four sides. The top level shows decorations in the Puuc style, among them masks, parakeets, lattice work, flowers and meander patterns.

Palomar West of the Grand Pyramid stands the Palomar (Dovecote or Dovecot, House of Pigeons). The structure resembles the Nunnery Quadrangle with its inner courtyard. The unique design of the serrated roof comb inspired the name of the structure. On top of a row of columns rise nine triangular structures with window-like openings, creating the appearance of a dovecote. This building is presumably 200 years older than the Nunnery Quadrangle and the Palace of the Governor, meaning it was probably built between AD 700 and 800. The buildings of the South Group and the Quadrangle (north) have a ground plan resembling that of the Palomar (Dovecote).

Other structures One of the oldest structures in Uxmal is the **House of the Old Woman** (Pirámide de la Vieja) in the south-eastern part of the site. According to legend, the mother of the dwarf who ruled Uxmal resided here. Photographers can take a good shot of the Governor's Palace from the top of this pyramid. From the Pyramid of the Old Woman a 400m/0.25mi walk along a path leads to the ruins named the **Temple of the Phallus**. Visitors find a series of stone sculptures in the form of a phallus in this temple, which may have served as water spouts.

The **Cemetery Group** stands east of the Nunnery Quadrangle. The West Temple of this group has been lovingly restored. The complex was named after the four small round platforms, which probably served as altars. This is indicated by the depictions of skulls with eyes and the cross-bones as well as the hieroglyphs on the altar.

Close to the Temple of the Cemetery stands the **Platform of the Stelae**. Only a few stelae are left and they are in poor condition.

Every evening, a spectacular light and sound show takes place in the Nunnery Quadrangle. Accompanied by drums and flutes, flood lights illuminate the most striking features of the site. A speaker tells the history of Uxmal. The spectacle, in four languages, starts at 7pm from November to March, otherwise at 8pm, and lasts almost 45 minutes.

Light and sound show

About 15km/9mi north-west of Uxmal, visitors can also admire other ceremonial sites in the Puuc style, in particular the Maya centres Kabah, Labná and Sayil. The tour goes through singularly beautiful hill country in Yucatán, passing small Maya villages and excavation sites along the ►Puuc-Route.

Around Uxmal

Veracruz

P 22

Federal state: Veracruz (Ver.)
Population: 800,000

Altitude: 3m/10ft
Distance: 450km/280mi east of Mexico City

Mexico's most important port city was built on a sandy beach only a few feet above sea level and is located in the hot and humid climate zone. For centuries, the city has played an important role as a customs station and a focal point for the coastal areas along the Gulf of Mexico and the tropical hinterland. This also provided for an interesting history.

Today, Veracruz is a lively city, popular with Mexican tourists. The city has a likeable mixture of **colonial buildings and modern architecture**. Veracruz is internationally known for its unparalleled Marimba sound and its open, happy flair. The catchy tune **La Bamba** was created here and is now performed all over the world.

▶ VISITING VERACRUZ

INFORMATION
Tourist information
in the Palacio Municipal at the city square
Tel. (229) 939 88 17 or at
www.veracruz.gob.mx or
www.veracruzinfo.com

GETTING AROUND
The flight from Mexico City to Veracruz lasts about 45 minutes. The same trip takes 10 hours by train and about 6 hours by bus. By car, take the MEX 150 (424km/263mi) or the MEX 190 via Puebla and Córdoba.

EVENTS
Veracruz stands for carnival, the craziest carnival between Río de Janeiro and New Orleans. The festivities last nine full days. Every year, many Caribbean countries reserve the last two weeks in July to celebrate life, their country and their peoples in the colourful Festival del Caribe.

WHERE TO STAY
▶ Luxury
① *Fiesta Americana Veracruz*
Blvd. Manuel A. Camacho s/n
Fraccionamiento Costa de Oro
Tel. (229) 989 89 89
Fax (229) 989 89 04
www.fiestamericana.com
The hotel (233 rooms) at the Costa de Oro (opposite the Congress Centre) provides all modern amenities and is therefore ideal for business people. All rooms have a patio and a marble bath. The hotel features a diving centre as well as a fitness studio with massage.

② *Imperial*
Calle Miguel Lerdo 153
Tel. (229) 932 12 04
The colonial hotel building (81 rooms) is located in the historic centre close to the cathedral. It has an antique lift and large rooms with air conditioning and TV.

▶ Mid-range
③ *Hotel Mar y Tierra*
Paseo del Malecón/ corner of Figueroa
Tel. (229) 931 38 66
www.hotelmarytierra.com
This hotel (176 rooms, 22 suites) is located on the ocean and only about 10 minutes away from the main city square. In addition the good service and value for money speak for this hotel.

WHERE TO EAT
▶ Moderate
② *Mariscos Villa Rica Mocambo*
Calz. Mocambo 527
Tel. (229) 922 21 13
This palm-thatched beach hotel is located near the Mocambo Hotel and is popular with local people who like the good regional cuisine.

▶ Inexpensive
③ *El Cochinito de Oro*
Calle Zaragoza 190 (corner Serdán)
This restaurant prides itself on its preparation of fish and seafood.

Baedeker-recomendation

① *Gran Café del Portal*
Every Mexican president since Benito Juárez has at least once been a guest of the Gran Café del Portal opposite the cathedral. While people-watching, visitors enjoy not only the excellent coffee but also the Marimba and Mariachi bands and the lively atmosphere. If you'd like your coffee refilled, simply tap your teaspoon on the glass.

Veracruz *Plan*

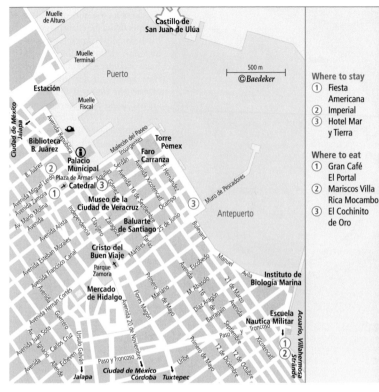

Muelle
de Altura

Castillo de
San Juan de Ulúa

Muelle
Terminal

Puerto

500 m
©Baedeker

Estación

Muelle
Fiscal

Ciudad de México
Jalapa

Avenida República

Biblioteca
B. Juárez

Malecón del Paseo
Insurgentes

Torre
Pemex

Faro
Carranza

Palacio
Municipal

Aquiles Serdán

Avenida 16 de Septiembre

J. Hernández

B. Juárez

Plaza de Armas

Avenida Miguel Lerdo

Catedral

Muro de Pescadores

Ocampo

Antepuerto

Avenida Zamora

Museo de la
Ciudad de Veracruz

Av. Mario Molina

Independencia

Clavijero

Zaragoza

Baluarte
de Santiago

25 de Junio

Bulevard

Avenida

Avenida Arista

Cristo del
Buen Viaje

Mártires Fallán

Avenida Esteban Morales

Parque
Zamora

Avenida Francisco Canal

Primero de Mayo

Flores Magón

Avenida 20 de Noviembre

Mariano

de Mayo

Manuel

Avenida Escobedo

Ávila

Instituto de
Biología Marina

Mercado
de Hidalgo

Avenida Hernán Cortés

Guerrero

M. Abasolo

Díaz Aragón

21 de Marzo

Avenida

Septiembre

Barragán

y

Avenida Juan Soto

Av.

Iago de Carlos Cruz

Ursulo Galván

Escuela
Nautica Militar

Troncoso

Paso de Mayo

Xicotencatl

Acuario, Villahermosa
Strande

Avenida Juárez

Alende

Paso y Troncoso

Primero de Mayo

12 de Diciembre

12 de Octubre

Uribe

Jalapa

Ciudad de México
Córdoba Tuxtepec

Where to stay
① Fiesta
   Americana
② Imperial
③ Hotel Mar
   y Tierra

Where to eat
① Gran Café
   El Portal
② Mariscos Villa
   Rica Mocambo
③ El Cochinito
   de Oro

In the time before the birth of Christ the region around Veracruz was inhabited by Indians, probably first by the Olmec and later the Totonac. Their capital was Zempoala, about 40km/25mi away from today's Veracruz. **Hernán Cortés and his men landed on the coast near La Antigua** on Good Friday (22 April) in 1519. Shortly thereafter, he welcomed a delegation sent by the Aztec ruler Montezuma whose native religion tricked him into believing that Cortés was the returning god Quetzalcóatl. According to Aztec belief, the legendary Quetzalcóatl had been chased from the Toltec capital of Tula 530 years earlier. Quetzalcóatl had disappeared over the ocean, promising to return. Before the Spaniards settled near the Totonac city Quiahuiztlán, Hernán Cortés symbolically founded the city Villa Rica de la Veracruz (rich city of the true cross). In the years to come, the Spaniards changed quarters several times until in 1599, they settled in La Nueva Veracruz in the location of today's Veracruz. Even though the city did not immediately grow much, the harbour played a crucial role for shipping traffic to and from Cádiz and Seville

History

Pescado a la Veracruzana is savoured with a spicy tomato sauce.

(Spain). It was here that in 1821, i.e. close to the end of the War of Independence, General Agustín de Iturbide (the later emperor of Mexico) defeated the troops of Juan O'Donojú, the last viceroy of New Spain. Finally, after 10 years of war, the defeated O'Donojú accepted Mexican independence in the Treaty of Córdoba. Veracruz was subjected to constant attacks right into the 20th century.

What to See in Veracruz

Veracruz is one of the oldest cities in Mexico but it has only a few significant buildings in the colonial style. The city hall from the early 17th century, with an interesting façade and a romantic patio, is well worth seeing. There is also the parish church (La Parroquia, consecrated in 1734), now know as the Cathedral of Our Lady of the Assumption (Nuestra Señora de la Asunción). Both city hall and church are located on the Plaza de Armas, also known as the Plaza de la Constitución. This beautiful plaza is framed by palm trees, tropical plants, flowers and arcades. It is the centre of the city where people meet in the evening, have a bite to eat and listen to the sounds of Marimba music or the Jarocho players.

Museums The **City Museum** (Museo de la Ciudad, Calle Zaragoza 397) displays archaeological finds and artefacts from the regional Indian cultures (Olmec, Totonac and Huastec). The museum also shows paintings, arts and crafts, as well as documentary photographs from the history of Veracruz. The revolutionary General Venustiano Carranza conducted his political activities from the **Faro Carranza lighthouse** in 1914/15. The **Museo de la Revolución**, which has been established in the lighthouse in Avenida Insurgentes to commemorate this time, shows furniture and documents from the life of the revolutionary and hero.

Baluarte de Santiago The Baluarte de Santiago between Avenida 16 de Septiembre and Calle Gómez Farías is the only remaining building belonging to the city's wall from the 18th century. It now houses the small historic museum with the famous **"Jewels of the Fisherman"**, 35 pre-Columbian pieces of jewellery found by a fisherman in 1976. Some still wonder whether the jewels are part of the treasure of Montezuma.

A visit to the harbour to observe the business there and a stroll along the Malecón (waterfront) are recommended. There is a parade every morning in front of the Faro Carranza lighthouse. One-hour harbour tours start at the Malecón de Paseo.

Harbour

In the harbour you can also catch a boat to the large island fortress Castillo de San Juan de Ulúa. The Spaniards started building the stronghold in 1528. In the 19th century, it became an infamous prison, in which ocean water would sometimes flood the cells. The fortress is now a **Veracruz landmark**. Today, a road connects the island with the city of Veracruz.

★
Island fortress Castillo de San Juan de Ulúa

The spectacular Veracruz Aquarium (Acuario de Veracruz) is located in the middle of a modern shopping centre in the Plaza Acuario Veracruzano (Blvd. M. Avila Camacho). It was designed by a Japanese architect. The aquarium affords people a look at sharks, barracudas, turtles and a formidable number of other tropical sea creatures daily 10am–7pm

★
Veracruz Aquarium

🕐

The beaches closest to Veracruz are Playa de Hornos and Playa Villa del Mar. The beach of Mocambo lies about 8km/5mi south of the city. After this beach comes the fishing village Boca del Río, and still further from the city lies the village of Mandinga with its beaches. Some of the beaches close to the city are very dirty.

Beaches

Around Veracruz

Driving north on the coastal highway, a road branches off after 25km/15.5mi toward the town of La Antigua. The fishing village had its historic moment when Hernán Cortés landed there in 1519 and made it his temporary headquarters. Cortés burnt his ships in the Bay of Antigua to make withdrawal from his planned conquest impossible. Five years later, the Spaniards established their main administrative centre here. Remnants of the fort still exist.
The pride of the village is the **Hernán Cortés residence**, which seems almost to hide under the aerial roots of centuries-old trees. River rocks served as the floor, and the walls were built from volcanic stone, corals and bricks brought in the ships as ballast. The walls were painted blue and red with a dye extracted from plants and lice. A small, white chapel is said to have been the first church built by Spaniards on Mexican soil.

La Antigua

Leaving José Cardel behind and following the coastal road another 10km/6mi, a road branches off left to Zempoala or Cempoala (20

★
Zempoala

🕐
Opening times:
daily 9am–4.30pm

water) 3km/2mi away. This was the **last capital of the Totonac**, from the 13th century until the Spanish conquest. In the second half of the 15th century, the Aztec defeated the Totonac and made them subject to tribute payments. 23 days after he landed in Mexico, on 15 May 1919, Cortés met the Totonac ruler Chicomacatl. There was no love lost between the Totonac and the Aztec and so it was easy for Cortés to win the Totonac as allies.

The ruins of Zempoala cover a total of 5 sq km/2 sq mi and consist of 10 groups of buildings. However, only a few buildings have been restored and are ready for visitors. The excavated structures were built in the 300 years preceding the Spanish conquest. Some of the buildings clearly show Aztec style elements, and some point to the fact that Zempoala was arguably already inhabited in the first millennium AD. The **Templo Mayor** (Main Temple, or Temple of the Thirteen Steps) is located on the northern side of the Quadrangle. The pyramid is 11m/36ft high and the height of each of the 13 steps measures 85cm/33.5in. The pyramid sits on a platform measuring 67 x 40m/220 x 131ft, and remnants of a temple on the top of the pyramid are still recognizable. On the east side of the Quadrangle stands

Today, centuries-old aerial roots are entwined around the Casa de Cortés.

the **Temple of the Chimneys** (Templo de las Chimeneas). A wide stairway leads to the top of the six-level structure. The remnants of the columns which gave the pyramid its name are on the top platform.

The **Great Pyramid** in the western part of the site was built later. The pyramid is made of stacked platforms, whereby each successive platform is smaller than the preceding one. The interesting **Temple of the Little Faces** (Templo de las Caritas), whose construction is similar to that of the Great Pyramid, lies east of the Quadrangle. The niches in the walls once contained a total of 360 small stuccoed heads which gave the temple its name. A small museum at the entrance to the archaeological site displays local finds.

20km/14mi north of Zempoala on the MEX 180 lies the archaeological site Quiahuitzlán (Place of the Rain), first an Olmec site, then a Totonac and Toltec site, and finally conquered by the Aztec. At the site there are three not particularly well-preserved pyramids and a ball court. The three cemeteries with 78 stone tombs in the shape of small temples are of particular interest.

Quiahuitzlán

The huge ruined city of El Pital, which was discovered in the beginning 1990s, lies 15km/9mi inland of Nautla (about 150km/90mi north of Zempoala). The site was probably inhabited from AD 100 to 600 and played a role as a cultural and economic corridor between the highlands and the northern coastal areas on the Gulf of Mexico. There are probably more than 100 pyramids hidden amongst thick forest. El Pital is the most significant archaeological discovery in this region since the discovery of El Tajín in 1785.

El Pital

Zempoala Plan

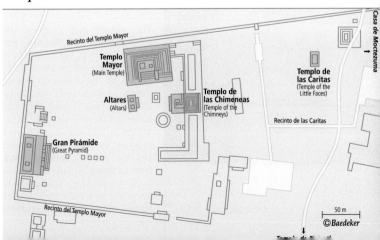

Recinto del Templo Mayor

Templo Mayor (Main Temple)

Altares (Altars)

Templo de las Chimeneas (Temple of the Chimneys)

Gran Pirámide (Great Pyramid)

Recinto del Templo Mayor

Templo de las Caritas (Temple of the Little Faces)

Recinto de las Caritas

Casa de Moctezuma

50 m

©Baedeker

★ Villahermosa

R 26

Federal state: Tabasco (Tab.)
Population: 600,000

Altitude: 11m/36mi
Distance: 840km/522mi east of Mexico City

Until a few years ago, Villahermosa was a sleepy town in tropical surroundings on the Río Grijalva. There are no indications of an ancient Indian history. In 1598, the Spaniards established a village in the area under the name of Villa Felipe II. Later, the name was changed to Villahermosa (beautiful village). Over time, this village has developed into the largest city in the federal state of Tabasco, due in no small part to the rich crude oil reserves discovered in Tabasco and Chiapas. New traffic connections have also boosted the city's growth.

Villahermosa has developed into a pretty city with wide boulevards, pleasant parks and many cultural institutions. There are only a few

historic buildings but the city offers two of the most interesting museums in Mexico. One is the archaeological open-air La Venta Park-Museum, and the other is the Regional Museum of Anthropology (Museo Regional de Antropología). A short trip to the ruins of Comalcalco is also recommended.

What to See in Villahermosa

The archaeological open-air museum **La Venta Park-Museum** (Parque-Museo de la Venta) is located on the south-western shore of the Laguna de las Ilusiones. Monumental artefacts from the **Olmec culture**, whose heyday occurred between 1200 and 400 BC, are on display in this tropical park, such as altars, stelae, animal sculptures and the famous **colossal heads from La Venta**. To save the original from weathering, several stone sculptures have been replaced with reproductions made of synthetic

Olmec head from La Venta

materials. The artefacts were often found in inaccessible swamps in the federal states of Tabasco and Veracruz. The zoo keeps animals of the jungle in several enclosures, such as alligators, deer, jaguars, coatimundis (animal from the racoon family), monkeys and many others. It also boasts a large aviary.

Some archaeologists consider the Olmec to be the ancestors of all cultures in Mesoamerica. Without doubt, this mysterious people created the oldest known culture in Mexico. Moreover, their influence reached large parts of Mesoamerica. According to current theories, the Olmec, along with the proto-Zapotec, were the first to develop a hieroglyphic script and were very adept at handling numbers. They are therefore considered the predecessors of the Maya. The oldest known dating (31 BC) found so far is on the Olmec Stele C in the Tres Zapotes archaeological site. The Olmec not only created impres-

Olmec

Parque-Museo La Venta *Plan*

- ▲ Introduction
- ▪ Bust of C. P. Cámaras
- 1 Pacing figure monument
- 2 Stone block seat
- 3 The Grandmother
- 4 Stele 3
- 5 Mosaic
- 6 Group of basalt columns and tomb
- 7 Basalt columns
- 8 Colossal head
- 9 Colossal head
- 10 Incomplete head
- 11 Altar 6
- 12 Altar 5
- 13 Figure with mantle
- 14 Feline head
- 15 Altar 7
- 16 Anthropomorphic jaguar
- 17 Cactus
- 18 Sculpture with cone
- 19 Anthropomorphic animal
- 20 Contortionist
- 21 Various basalt fragments
- 22 Human type head
- 23 Altar 4
- 24 Mosaic
- 25 Stele 2
- 26 Colossal head
- 27 Figure with standard
- 28 Split head
- 29 Silhouette
- 30 Altar 3
- 31 Altar 2
- 32 Model
- 33 Stele 1
- A Ticket office
- B Information
- C Lockers
- D Telephone
- E Monkeys
- F Aquatic birds
- G Martens
- H Racoons
- J Otter
- K Nocturnal animals
- L Toucans
- M Bird enclosure
- N Snake house
- O Monkeys
- P Reptiles
- Q Game animals
- R Pheasants
- S Big cats
- T Big cats
- U Turtles
- V Crocodiles
- W Toilets
- X Various rooms
- Y Café

© Baedeker

► VISITING VILLAHERMOSA

INFORMATION

Tourist information

Tabasco 2000 (see p.611)
Av. de los Ríos 113 (behind the city hall)
Tel. (993) 316 36 33
Information kiosks also in the first class bus terminal and at the airport

GETTING AROUND

A flight from Mexico City to Villahermosa lasts about 1hr 15min. This trip takes about 15 hours by bus.

WHERE TO EAT

► Expensive

Los Tulipanes

Calle Carlos Pellicer 511
Tel. (993) 312 92 09
The fish restaurant between the Teatro Esperanza Iris and the Carlos Pellicer Museum in the CICOM Complex offers a nice view of the Río Grijalva.

► Moderate

El Mirador

Madero 105
This is a good seafood restaurant with a beautiful view over the ocean.

WHERE TO STAY

► Luxury

Cencali

Juárez y Paseo Tabasco
Tel. (993) 315 19 99
Fax (993) 315 66 00
www.cencali.com.mx
The two-storey hotel (120 rooms) has a tropical garden and is located opposite La Venta Park. A mural in the lobby depicts life in the Aztec Empire.

sive, large sculptures, they were also masters of finer clay design and intricate work with jade. The most significant finds from the Olmec culture have so far come from La Venta, San Lorenzo Tenochtitlán, Tres Zapotes and Cerro de las Mesas.

It is still a mystery how the Olmec were able to move the up to 50-ton **3.40m/11ft-high colossal heads**, which are made of basalt. The basalt came from a quarry about 120km/42mi away from La Venta. The features of some of the colossal heads appear to have negroid qualities, and in others human and jaguar features seem to mix, an observation that has prompted some to proffer extremely bold theories. Some people have proposed that the heads are depictions of Nubian noblemen who had been sent west by Ramses III of Egypt in search of the underworld. Others are of the opinion that the heads are images of kings from prehistoric megalithic cultures in the south of England and northern France.

★
Regional
Museum of
Anthropology

The Cultural Complex CICOM (Centro de Investigaciones de las Culturas Maya y Olmeca) on the west bank of the Río Grijalva is also the site of the Regional Museum of Anthropology (Museo Regional de Antropología Carlos Pellicer Cámara). The museum was named after the poet, art collector and museum founder **Carlos Pellicer** (1897–1977). The round tour starts on the second floor with an outline of the pre-Columbian cultures. Important points are underlined using stone masks and ceramics from Teotihuacán, ceramic heads and urns made by the Zapotec and Totonac as well as Aztec stone sculptures. On the first floor, the exhibits concern the Olmec and Maya: there are extraordinary clay figurines made by the Maya in Jaina and Olmec jade from La Venta. On the raised ground floor, select pieces from the two cultures are presented. The monumental artefacts of the Olmec and Maya are displayed on the ground floor.

Further west stands the Tabasco 2000 complex, which includes a planetarium, a convention centre, department stores and the city hall. Built after the oil boom started, the complex conspicuously displays the new wealth of the city.

Tabasco 2000

The La Choca Park is a short 600m/0.4mi walk from the Tabasco 2000 area. This is the location for trade fairs, exhibitions and the annual arts and crafts festival at the end of April.

La Choca Park

The modern building of the Angel Aldrete Chávez Museum of Natural History of Tabasco (**Museo de Historia Natural Angel Aldrete Chávez**) is located in Avenida Adolfo Ruíz Cortínes next to the park entrance next to the Laguna de las Ilusiones. The museum shows protected plants and animals as well as objects related to geology, evolution and the solar system. The Museum of Popular Culture (**Iuseo de Cultura Popular**) at Calle Ignacio Zaragoza 810 shows regional traditional costumes, folk art and a reproduction of a typical Indian Chontal house. The memorabilia of the famous poet and archaeologist Carlos Pellicer are on display in the Carlos Pellicer Museum (**Casa Museo Carlos Pellicer**) at Calle Saénz 203, where he was born. The exhibits in the neo-Baroque **Museo de Historia de Tabasco** (Casa de los Azulejos, Juárez 402) include the national coat of arms, 18th-century paintings and an oil painting of the revolutionary and hero Emiliano Zapata by Alfredo Zalce.

Other museums

Around Villahermosa

The Yumká Ecology Park covers 100ha/247ac about 15km/9mi outside of Villahermosa close to the airport. The park includes a savannah region, virgin forest and a lagoon where Asian, African and domestic wild animals are given a habitat. Such animals include monkeys, toucans, parakeets, manatees, alligators, jaguars and deer. Visitors can experience the park on foot, by local railway or by boat (dependent on the water level).

✱
*Yumká
Ecology Park*

Take the MEX 180 via Nacajuca (52km/32mi) or the MEX 180 and 187 via Cárdenas (82km/51mi) from Villahermosa to reach the town

✱
Comalcalco

🕐 Opening times:
daily 10am–4pm

Comalcalco. The archaeological site of the same name, the western-most of the significant Maya sites, is located only 5km/3mi north-east of the town. The finds at the site are from the **late Maya classical period** (AD 600–900). The ancient city was probably at the height of its culture in the 8th century. The temple design, the execution of the stucco decorations and the ornamentation in the tomb discovered here are reminiscent of the art in Palenque. In the absence of stone and with the ocean nearby, the Maya used flat fired bricks and mortar made from pulverized conches, a type of construction unusual for the period. At the western side of the **North Plaza** (Plaza Norte) stands Temple One. The pyramid has several levels, and there are still remnants of a temple on the top level.

Temple II is located on a hill at the north side of the plaza, and more structures are being excavated. At the south end of the site, bordering the **Plaza de la Gran Acrópolis** on three sides, is the building complex called the Great Acropolis on whose platform stand two small temples and a palace. The Tomb of the Nine Lords of the Night (Tumba de los Nueve Señores de la Noche) was found next to the Acropolis. Nine stucco reliefs, three on each side of the walls of the tomb, probably represent the nine rulers of the underworld. The figures were once painted red, and only partially show classical Maya features. In 1993, excavations unearthed the clay pipes of an ancient sewer system which is unique for the region and the period.

! **Baedeker** TIP

Steamboat on the Grijalva

A popular excursion is the two-hour trip on the river Grijalva aboard the »Capitán Buelo II.« Get to know the delicious cuisine of Tabasco in the boat's restaurant, while music plays and the tropical landscape floats by. The trip starts at Malecón Carlos A. Madrazo Becerra.

Yucatán

N?P 28?32

Federal states: Yucatán (Yuc.), Campeche (Cam.), Quintana Roo (Q.R.) and the northern parts of Guatemala and Belize

The Yucatán peninsula borders on the Gulf of Mexico in the west and north and on the Caribbean Sea in the east. The coastal areas in the west and north consist mostly of sand banks, lagoons and mangrove swamps, while coral reefs and islands like Cozumel or Isla Mujeres characterize the east coast.

Geologically, Yucatán is a large, flat, limestone plate, slightly ascending in a southerly direction. As a karst region, most of Yucatán is covered by savannahs and jungle. Precipitation increases from north to south. The rain quickly seeps through the thin soil and the limestone creating underground rivers and lakes. The moving water also creates underground caves, and when the ground over these caves gives way, round sinkholes with the features of a well appear. These sinkholes or cenotes are of various sizes. Before the Spanish conquest, the Maya built their cities around these cenotes, which to this day retain their importance as a water supply.

What to see

Beach tourists unwind best in the luxury beach resort ►Cancún, on the ►Riviera Maya, on the island of ►Cozumel or on ►Isla Mujeres. The Palancar Reef with its gorgeous coral gardens, caves and steep rock faces off the south-west coast of Cozumel attracts divers from all over the world. Many significant Maya archaeological sites in Yucatán are within easy reach for a day's outing from the holiday centres. Among these sites are ►Chichén Itzá, ►Uxmal and the ruins

The main beach of Isla Mujeres is the modestly sized Playa Norte.

⏵ VISITING YUCATÁN

INFORMATION
www.mayayucatan.com.mx or
www.yucatan.gob.mx

GETTING AROUND
A flight from Europe to Cancún takes
about 10 hours.

WHERE TO EAT
► Moderate
② *Yaxche*
Calle 8 (between Av. 10 and Av. 5)
Tel. (984) 873 25 02
Playa del Carmen
The Maya restaurant serves typical
specialities, such as tamales with
pumpkin seeds or fish with various
salsas.

① *La Palapa*
Calle Quetzal 13
(behind the Hotel Imperial Laguna)
Cancún
This restaurant, which is thatched
with palm straw, has a Belgian
proprietor.

WHERE TO STAY
► Luxury
② *Casa de los Sueños*
Ila Mujeres
Carr. Garrafón, Fracc. Mar Turquesa
Tel. (998) 877 06 51
Fax (998) 877 07 08
www.casadelossuenosresort.com
Designer hotel with wonderful spa
and wellness centre.

► Mid-range
① *Hotel Deseo*
Quinta Avenida / Calle 12
Playa del Carmen
Tel. (984) 879 36 20
Fax (984) 879 36 21
www.hoteldeseo.com
Basically equipped hotel in the pe-
destrian zone.

---

along the ►Puuc-Route. The walled-in fortress of ►Tulum high up
on the cliffs above the ocean is very impressive as is the romantic ►
Cobá hidden in dense, verdant jungle.
As in ►Mérida, Izamal, Valladolid (around ►Chichén Itzá), Motul
and Tikul, the colonial arts have left their mark almost everywhere
in Yucatán. The Franciscan churches and monasteries from the 16th
and 17th centuries in particular bear witness to the colonial style. In
part, these sacral buildings still lie in a pristine landscape. They are
well worth visiting, if only to savour their atmosphere.
Nature lovers are also well provided for in places such as the Calakmul biosphere reserve, the Si'an Ka'an biosphere reserve (south of
Tulum), around Celestún with its flamingos and on the banks of the
Río Lagartos.

Maya Route The Maya Route (Ruta Maya) was mapped out in the 1980s and includes the archaeological sites and colonial cities of Mexico, Guatemala, Belize, Honduras and El Salvador. The programme has involved the modernization of transportation, the restoration of the ar-

Yucatán Map

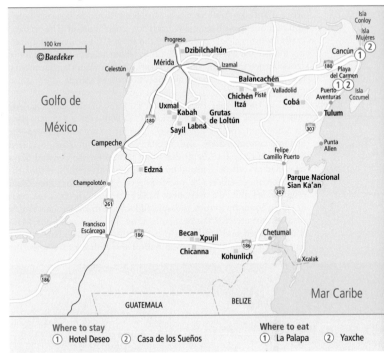

Where to stay
① Hotel Deseo ② Casa de los Sueños

Where to eat
① La Palapa ② Yaxche

chaeological sites and the creation of new overnight accommodation. The region covers the territory from the Isthmus of Tehuantepec in the east across the entire Yucatán peninsula into Honduras and El Salvador.

Within a short time, the Riviera Maya, i.e. **the coastal region between Cancún and Tulum** with the main city Playa del Carmen, has developed into one of the most popular destinations for beach vacations in Mexico. Many international – mostly European – investors financed new hotel complexes here. The area now also has a number of marinas and recreational parks. In the meantime, the area south of Tulum is also being developed for tourism.

Riviera Maya

Jaguars and ocelots still live in the dense jungle of Yucatán, as well as deer, wild pigs, pheasants, wild ducks, wild turkeys, monkeys, iguanas, snakes and countless tropical birds. Palm trees used to be abundant but a tree disease has considerably reduced their number. Attempts are now underway to replenish the trees on the beaches by planting disease-resistant South-East Asian varieties.

Fauna and flora

Economy **Culture and beach tourism** is the backbone of the economy in wide areas of Yucatán. Sisal haciendas have been turned into luxury hotels and harbours have been made ready for cruise tourism. The arts and crafts industry clearly profits from the stream of tourists. The finishing industry in Mexico's advantageous labour market (maquiladoras, cross-border industry) and agriculture remain important economic factors, and some breweries also operate around Mérida.

History With its ruins from bygone Maya cultures of the classical (AD 300–900) and post-classical periods (AD 900–1450), Yucatán plays an important role in archaeology. The first contacts between the Spanish conquistadores and Yucatán's native population occurred between 1512 and 1519. At this point in history, the classical Maya cities had already been abandoned, with a few exceptions. It took the Spanish conquistadores 20 years of fierce fighting before they could establish Spanish rule over about half of Yucatán. Through the years of ruling Spanish viceroys, the isolated location made Yucatán a fairly insignificant area for the Spaniards. Over and over again, the Maya tribes rebelled and tried to win back their lands. The battles were particularly bitter in the second half of the 19th century when the

Typical Maya hut

Maya managed to temporarily establish their independence from the Mexican central government (Caste War of Yucatán); not until the beginning of the 20th century could the Mexican government establish full sovereignty over the Yucatán peninsula, when many defeated Indians retreated into the wilderness of Quintana Roo. Aside from a number of Spaniards mostly in and around Mérida, the population of the federal state of Yucatán consists predominantly of Maya Indians and Mestizos. Some Indians only speak their Maya language.

Hardly any other region in Mexico has as many archaeological sites as Yucatán. The post-classical Maya culture (AD 900–1450), stemming from the indigenous and immigrant Maya tribes as well as some Toltec tribes from the Mexican highlands, created magnificent architecture. However, the later ceramics and stone artefacts no longer equalled the quality of objects from the early and late classical periods (AD 300–900) that originated predominantly in South Campeche, Chiapas, Guatemala, Belize and Honduras.

Maya

The so-called Long Count, the historic **calendar**, which counts each day from the beginning of the Maya calendar, was only used in an abbreviated form in the late Maya classical period. Day zero of the Maya calendar coincides with 13 August 3114 BC. The Maya calendar is considered the most complete and most accurate of its time. The Maya were the first to use the zero in their numerical system, and through this it was possible for them to handle immense periods of time. The oldest Maya date so far identified with a high degree of certainty is the inscription AD 292 on Stele 29 in Tikal, Guatemala.

As far as we know, the Maya had the only **hieroglyphic script** which was both logographically as well as phonetically fully developed. So far, around 800 Maya glyphs have been identified. Each glyph can stand for a syllable or for a word. Today, 80–90% of the 400 frequently used glyphs can be read and pronounced. It was a breakthrough discovery that helped researchers decipher the Maya glyphs: when Heinrich Berlin, a German living in Mexico, found emblem glyphs he discovered that certain signs always appear in particular sites, and from this the glyphs of the eight classical Maya cities Palenque, Yaxchilán (Mexico), Tikal, Piedras Negras, Quiriguá, Seibal, Naranjo (Guatemala) and Copán (Honduras) could be deciphered. This led Berlin to the conclusion that the glyphs on stelae and monuments told the story of the cities. Tatjana Proskouriakoff then determined that the dates in specific groups of stelae were the dates of birth and marriage of rulers and the period of their reign. At the same time, it became possible to associate certain glyphs with the names of rulers and their family members. Since then, many famous researchers have helped to further decipher the Maya glyphs.

The **Maya Codices** are the »books« of the Maya civilization. They have a leporello fold and are made of plaster-coated, bark-derived paper. The codices that were not lost or deliberately destroyed by Spanish zealots mostly survived in the form of »gifts« to Charles V or

The Palace of Sayil with its multi-level terraced construction is one of the most accomplished architectural creations in the classical Puuc style of the Maya.

otherwise found their way to Europe. Today, they are to be found in Dresden, Madrid and Paris. The Grolier Codex was introduced in 1971 and at first not accepted. Today it is kept in Mexico City.

★ Zacatecas

Federal state: Zacatecas (Zac.)
Population: 250,000

Altitude: 2,496m/8,189ft
Distance: 130km/81mi north of Aguascalientes, about 600km/373mi from Mexico City

Situated in a highland area sporadically interspersed with mountains, Zacatecas, the capital of the state of the same name, was for centuries an important silver mining centre. The charming colonial city lies in a narrow canyon surrounded by the hills La Bufa, Mala Noche and El Padre. Today, with its pretty, aged buildings and cobbled alleys, Zacatecas is one of the most beautiful colonial cities in Mexico.

In pre-Hispanic times, various Indian tribes lived in the region **History** around Zacatecas (land where zacate grass grows), but little is known about them. Their history may have at times been influenced by the Chalchihuites and by the Chicomóztoc from La Quemada. In search of silver, a few conquistadores under Juan de Tolosa established a small village here in 1546. Philip II granted the place its municipal charter forty years later. In 1914, bitter battles took place here during the revolution between the troops of the dictator Victoriano Huerta and **Francisco Pancho Villa**, battles which Pancho Villa won. Since 1993, the historic centre of the city has been a UNESCO World Heritage Site.

What to See in Zacatecas

The magnificent cathedral on the Plaza Hidalgo is **one of the most** ✶✶ **perfect examples of the Mexican ultra-Baroque** (Churriguerism). **Cathedral** The constructions first started on the site of an existing church in 1612, but the cathedral was modelled in its current form mostly between 1730 and 1760. The façade is opulently decorated with the great variety of shapes typical for the Spanish-Mexican Baroque. The façade depicts Christ and the twelve apostles, four church elders around the choir window and, in the top part, God surrounded by eight angels making music. The artistic treatment mixes **Romanesque elements with motifs from the Indian world view**. The dome was remodelled in 1836. The scant interior, mostly in the neo-classical style, is disappointing. Once, the interior design was unusually rich (with items made from gold and silver, European paintings etc), but these items disappeared during the Reform War and in the upheaval of the revolution.

The Governor's Palace (Palacio de Gobierno) is located on the east **Governor's** side of the Plaza Hidalgo. This 18th-century palace with pretty **Palace** wrought-iron balconies displays a mural by Antonio Rodríguez (1970) in the top part of its main stairwell. The mural illustrates the history of the federal state of Zacatecas.

The commanding, white Palacio de la Mala Noche (Bad Night Palace) on the west side of the plaza is today the seat of several government agencies. The palace was originally built for the Basque owner of the Mala Noche mine close to the city. It contains a mural by the artist Ismael Martinez Guardado. Its pretty interior is worth a look and open to the public. **Bad Night Palace**

▶ VISITING ZACATECAS

INFORMATION

Tourist information
Avenida Hidalgo 403, 1st floor
Tel. (492) 924 40 47

GETTING AROUND

The flight from Mexico City to
Zacatecas lasts about 1 hour.
The same route by bus takes about 7
hours.
By car, take the MEX 75 D and the
MEX 45 via León, Querétaro and
Aguascalientes (613km/381mi).

EVENTS

An international week of culture takes
place here during Easter Week. On the
anniversary of the day Zacatecas was
founded, i.e. the Friday before 8
September, a two-week fair begins.
The festivities include bull and cockfights, athletics competitions and
concerts.

WHERE TO EAT

▶ Moderate

Cenaduría Los Dorados
Plazuela de García 1314
Tel. (492) 257 22
The restaurant is decorated with

memorabilia from the War of Independence. It is a little hidden away at
a small square next to the former San
Francisco monastery. The Mexican
cuisine is simple but good.

WHERE TO STAY

▶ Luxury

Quinta Real
Avenida Ignacio Rayón 434
Colonia Centro
Tel. (492) 922 91 04
Fax (492) 922 84 40
This unique hotel with 49 rooms
was built around a bullfight arena.
All rooms face the paved Plaza de
Toros.

▶ Mid-range

Mesón de Jobito
Jardín Juárez 143
Tel. (492) 924 17 22
Fax (492) 924 35 00
www.mesondejobito.com
These lodgings (31 rooms) from the
19th century are located a few blocks
away from the cathedral on a small
square. The rooms are furnished in a
tasteful, modern style. All rooms have
cable TV.

González Ortega Market	South of the cathedral, there is a cast-iron building which used to be a market hall (1880). You can reach the top level of this building via Avenida Hidalgo; in the 1980s, this top level was remodelled into a shopping gallery with restaurants.
Calderón Theatre	The elegant Calderón Theatre (Teatro Calderón) is situated on the opposite side of Avenida Hidalgo. It was built in the last years of the 19th century and is still used for cultural events.
✶ **Santo Domingo Temple**	Callejón de Veyna begins at the city hall and leads to the 18th-century Santo Domingo church, a somewhat soberly designed Baroque structure. The church interior features eight finely-carved ultra-Bar-

oque retables and a neo-classical main altar. The 18th-century paintings in the vestry are notable.

The adjacent former Jesuit school now houses the Pedro Coronel Museum (Museo Pedro Coronel). Pedro Coronel was a Zacatecas artist (1923–1985) who left not only his own works to his home town but also a **very remarkable art collection** which includes pre-Columbian, European, African and Asian art. Among the treasures are also works by Goya, Picasso, Chagall, Kandinsky and Miró.

★ ★
Pedro Coronel Museum
🕐
Opening times:
Fri–Wed 10am–5pm

The Casa de la Moneda, in 19th-century Mexico the country's second largest mint, is located about 150m/165yd south of the small square Plazuela de Santo Domingo. Today, the Zacateno Museum (Museo Zacateno) occupies the building. Most of the museum exhibits relate to the culture of the Huichol Indians.

Zacateno Museum

About 100m/110yd south, stands San Agustín church, once the most magnificent sacral building of Zacatecas. Now, the building has in large part decayed, though the **Plateresque side portal** remains captivating. The portal design, showing the proselytism of St Augustine, is one of the most beautiful in Mexico. The church was built by Augustinian friars in the 17th century. During Mexico's anti-cleric phase in the 19th century, the church was used as a casino. In 1882, American Presbyterians found the church "too Catholic": when they replaced the façade they put in a white wall.

★
Church of San Agustín

North-west of the city centre (Calle Antonio Doval) visitors can explore the El Edén mine using the mine's railway line. The visit provides an insight into the harsh, often inhumane working conditions in the silver mines. Indians, among them many children, were forced into slave labour, and historic records show that every day labourers died in accidents or from disease, sometimes as many as 5 in a single day. The El Edén mine was worked from 1586 into the 1950s.

Mina El Edén

The La Bufa mountain (Cerro de la Bufa, 2,700m/8,858ft) is a landmark of the city located 4km/2.5mi from the city centre. On its peak stands the chapel **Capilla de los Remedios**. The view from here is beautiful. You can reach the top of the mountain by aerial tramway (teleférico): the aerial tramway station Cerro del Grillo is a few minutes walk to the left of the El Edén mine.
The museum documenting the taking of Zacatecas (**Museo de la Toma de Zacatecas**) has been erected on top of the La Bufa mountain. There, pictures and documents in connection with the battle (1914) in which the División del Norte under Pancho Villa and Felipe Ángeles defeated the troops of President Victoriano Huerta are on display. This victory gave the revolutionaries control over Zacatecas, their first step on the way to Mexico City. Next to the museum stands the 18th-century **Capilla de la Virgen del Patrocinio**, a chapel

La Bufa mountain

named after the patron saint of mine workers. Some people believe that the painting of the Virgin Mary above the altar can heal the sick, and many faithful people make pilgrimages to see the image all through the year, but especially around 8 September when the painting is carried to the cathedral. Three impressive **equestrian statues** stand to the east of the chapel and the museum. The statues show the heroes of the battle of Zacatecas (Villa, Ángeles and Pánfilo Natera). The path behind the equestrian statues leads up to the rocky peak of La Bufa mountain. The view from here over the city and the surrounding land is marvellous. The metal cross is illuminated at night. A path to the right of the statues leads to the **Mausoleo de los Hombres Ilustres de Zacatecas** (Mausoleum of the Illustrious Men of Zacatecas) where the heroes of the city have been buried from 1841 until the present day. A path next to the aerial tramway leads back to the city; it starts close to the statues.

Rafael Coronel Museum
⊙ Opening times: Thu–Tue 10am–4.30pm

The Rafael Coronel Museum (Museo Rafael Coronel) displays the private collection of the Coronel family. The museum occupies part of the ruined early Baroque San Francisco monastery in the northern part of Zacatecas (bus line 5 or 8). Rafael Coronel was the brother of the above-mentioned Pedro Coronel and the son in law of Diego Rivera. The museum displays about 4,000 mostly **pre-Hispanic masks** from all regions of Mexico, worn by performers of traditional dances or rites. Among the exhibits is also a puppet collection as well as drawings and sketches by Rivera.

Francisco Goitia Museum
⊙

It's worthwhile visiting the Francisco Goitia Museum (Museo Francisco Goitia), a neo-classical building in the former Casa del Pueblo (Calle Enrique Estrada 102) close to the ruins of the old aqueduct. It exhibits works by Francisco Goitia (1884?1960), an expressionist from Fresnillo and annalist of the revolution in Mexico (open Tue to Sun 10am–4.30pm).

Around Zacatecas

Museum and Church of Guadalupe

The town of Guadalupe lies about 7km/4.3mi east on the MEX 45. In 1707, the Franciscans established the Convent Of Our Lady of Guadalupe here, which has made the town famous. The convent library is not open to the public, but visitors can enjoy a collection of valuable paintings from Mexico's colonial times.

The convent church (consecrated in 1721) has an **interesting Baroque façade**. Two pairs of columns are placed on each side of the entrance gate. The columns flank niches with statues. The columns and niches are decorated with figures, spirals and basketwork in three sections. A high relief above the door shows the Virgin of Guadalupe and the apostle Luke who is painting her. The top part of the façade is executed in the style of the local masters, which is reminiscent of the design used for the cathedral of Zacatecas.

The neo-classical chapel inside the church, the Capilla de la Purísima (or Capilla de Nápoles, 19th century) **is richly gilded**, decorated and furnished with valuable paintings. The chapel is the most precious of its kind in Mexico. The **unique mesquite wood floor** features inlays in imaginative combinations of compass rose, signs of the zodiac and biblical scripture.

◄ Capilla de la Purísima

On the right of the convent stands the **Museo Regional de Zacatecas** (Regional Museum of Zacatecas). It displays an interesting collection of automobiles, hackney coaches and other vehicles.

The **feria** (annual festival) of the city takes place from 3 to 13 December around the Day of the Virgin of Guadalupe (December 12).

The pre-Columbian ruined city La Quemada or Chicomóztoc (seven caves) is located about 53km/33mi south of Zacatecas on the MEX 54. The archaeological site covers a large hill. The ancient city was settled around 300 and flourished especially between AD 700 and 1100. La Quemada, together with Chalchihuites and other cities in Zacatecas and Durango, is part of the region that forms the **northern border of the Mesoamerican cultures**. Very early on, the city began to thrive on regional trade. However, strong signs of smoke amongst other things suggest that La Quemada met a violent end. An Indian

La Quemada
⏱
Opening times:
daily 10am–4.30pm

On the Cerro de la Bufa three statues commemorate the heroes of the battle of Zacatecas.

legend refers to the destruction of a city in the region after it had attempted to monopolize the Peyotl trade. The buildings of La Quemada **were mostly constructed using stone slabs and adobe bricks** and they were spread over a mountain ridge. An entrance on the east side leads into a 40 x 31m/131 x 102ft portico (Hall of the Columns), which presumably served as a ceremonial hall. Although ball courts are extremely rare in this region, there is one located higher up on the hill. In the same area stands the impressive 11m/36ft-high Votive Pyramid and there is also a steep stairway to the top part of the site.

A path from the main hill leads in a western direction to a ledge with remnants of buildings called La Ciudadela. A wall, probably a battlement, stretches along the northern slope.

Casco de la Hacienda Bernández The Don Ignacio de Bernárdez mansion is just 2.5km/1.6mi along the MEX 45 in the direction of Fresnillo. Here, visitors can watch silversmiths at work and buy their products.

Fresnillo The old silver mining city Fresnillo (population 80,000) is situated about 60km/37mi north-west of Zacatecas. Visitors enjoy the thermal springs and spas in the vicinity, but the main reason for a stop is to see one of Mexico's most visited sacred sites, the Santuario de Plateros (Sanctuary of Plateros), situated about 5km/3mi away from the centre of the village Plateros. In the 18th-century church, worshippers revere El Santo Niño de Atocha, a curious embodiment of the child Jesus with staff, basket and feather hat. In the rooms to the left of the entrance visitors can marvel at the miracles he has performed which are recounted on small retables.

✱ Zihuatanejo · Ixtapa

R 17

Federal state: Guerrero (Gro.)	**Altitude:** Sea level
Population: 60,000	**Distance:** 240km/149mi north-west of Acapulco

Heading south from Manzanillo on the coastal road, travellers soon reach the former fishing port Zihuatanejo about 240km/149mi before Acapulco. The village is situated in a protected bay, surrounded by beautiful beaches, forested hills and cliffs. Along with the beach resort Ixtapa – a paradise planned on the drawing board only in 1975 – Zihuatanejo is one of the most restorative travel destinations on the Mexican Pacific coast.

Fishermen prepare their catch on Playa Municipal in Zihuatanejo. →

▶ VISITING ZIHUATANEJO / IXTAPA

INFORMATION

Turismo
in Zihuatanejo:
Calle Juan N. Alvarez
Tel. (755) 554 23 55
in Ixtapa:
Information booth close to Sefotur
(opposite the Hotel Presidente)
Blvd. Ixtapa or
www.zihua-ixtapa.com or www.ixta-pa-zihuatanejo.com

GETTING AROUND

There are daily flights to Zihuatanejo
from Mexico City and other Mexican
or US airports (the airport is located
14km/8.7mi south-east of Zihuatanejo). A bus trip to Zihuatanejo takes 9
hours from Mexico City and 4 hours
from Acapulco. Driving from Mexico
City on the well-maintained wide
Autopista del Sol (MEX 95) and the
MEX 200, you will reach Zihuatanejo
in about 7.5 hours. From Acapulco it
is a 240km/149mi drive on the MEX
200. It is not advisable to take the
route via Toluca and Ciudad Altamirano because the roads are bad and
there is a high risk of hold-ups.

WHERE TO EAT

▶ Expensive

② *Villa de la Selva*
Paseo de la Roca
(after the Hotel Westin Brisas Ixtapa)
Tel. (755) 553 03 62
The romantic terraced restaurant sits
on a cliff over the ocean. The
international cuisine is excellent.
Closed at midday, reservations required.

▶ Inexpensive

① *La Sirena Gorda*
Paseo del Pescador 90
Tel. (755) 554 26 87
This restaurant is decorated with a
huge mural showing a fat mermaid
(sirena gorda). It is located near the
landing stage, has a relaxed atmosphere and serves good food.

WHERE TO STAY

▶ Luxury

② *La Casa Que Canta*
Camino Escén. Playa La Ropa
Col. La Madera, Zihuatanejo
Tel. (755) 555 70 30
Fax (755) 554 79 00
www.lacasaquecanta.com
"The singing house" (26 rooms) is
built into a cliff over Playa La Ropa.
The setting is unusually tasteful and
inventive. Almost all rooms are in fact
suites and have a patio with ham-
mock.

▶ Mid-range

① *Puerto Mio*
Paseo del Morro
Playa del Almacén 5
Tel. (755) 436 24
This romantic little hotel (25 rooms)
is built into a cliff at the marina where
guests also find the diving centre.

Zihuatanejo

The former fishing village offers hardly any tourist attractions, even though it gained some importance as a commercial port during colonial times. As early as 30 October 1527, Cortés ordered ship crews to set sail on a voyage from Zihuatanejo to the Philippines. The name Zihuatanejo derives from Cihuatlán (in Náhuatl: place of the woman, probably relating to the goddess of creation, Cihuatéotl). In pre-Hispanic times, Zihuatanejo is said to have been the winter resort for the last ruler of the Purépecha (Tarascans), complete with protective wall against sharks. Remnants of this wall are still preserved on the beach Las Galas. The local **Museum of Archaeology** at the northern end of the Paseo del Pescador is worth a visit. The museum exhibitions revolve around the culture on the Guerreros coast. As early as 1960, tourism discovered the **Bay of Zihuatanejo** with its wide beaches of white or golden sand and its fairly calm waters.

There has followed a gradual modernization of the port town, especially since Ixtapa and its new development was founded only 10km/6mi away.

The beach closest to the harbour is **Playa Municipal**, where the fishermen still bring in their catch. The **Playa Madera**, with its hotels and restaurants, stretches further east. The next beach is **Playa de La Ropa**, a beach surrounded by cliffs and lined with palm trees, where luxurious accommodation is available and there are many opportunities to take part in sports in, on and out of the water. **Playa de La Gata** at the end of the bay is also surrounded by a reef; there are pretty Palapa restaurants near the beach. **Playa Majahua** in the direction of Ixtapa is also worth a visit. However, here bathers will already notice the stronger surf, which is characteristic of the entire Bay of Ixtapa.

500-year old fishing village

Ixtapa

Ixtapa is located about 10km/6mi to the north-east. Known especially

Zihuatanejo Plan

300 m
© Baedeker

Morelos · Morelos
Juárez
Mercado
Circo de
Mercado
Turístico
Alvarez
Museo Arqueológico
Playa Madera
Playa Municipal

Bahía de Zihuatanejo

Punta Godornia

Playa la Ropa

Playa Las Gatas

Where to stay
① Puerto Mío
② La Casa Que Canta

Where to eat
① La Sirena Gorda
② Villa de la Selva

for the **luxury hotel complexes** which line its long, wonderful beach, the resort is characterized by golf courses, tennis courts, terrific shops and fancy restaurants. Having had your fill of life on the beach, you may turn to hotel hopping to see the other hotels along Playa Palmar, evaluate the bars and compare pools. With few tourist attractions in Ixtapa, the obvious places to visit are the lagoon or the Marina Ixtapa, where between canals, boats and luxury yachts, fancy bars and high-class boutiques beckon.

During the development of Ixtapa into a beach resort, special attention was given to protecting as much of the natural environment as possible.

Playa del Palmar borders directly on the Ixtapa hotel zone. However, beware of the strong undertow when venturing out for a swim. The beach on the west side shortly ahead of the lagoon attracts surfers. The locals call the beach **Playa Escolleras** (breakwater, jetty). There are three more beaches past the harbour, further west: Playa San Juan, Playa Casa Blanca and Playa Cuates. The name **Playa Quieta** (quiet beach) is misleading because there are many motor boats in this area (about 5km/3mi north of Ixtapa). It is possible to take a boat from here to **Isla Ixtapa**, a few miles distant. This is a small island with four beaches and a special diving area. Passenger boats to the island also run from Zihuatanejo: the exact schedules for boat tours are available on site. Beyond Playa Quieta lies the quieter **Playa Linda**, a good place for a swim.

Beaches

INDEX

PHOTO CREDITS

LIST OF MAPS AND & ILLUSTRATIONS

PUBLISHER'S INFORMATION

Illustrations etc: 310 illustrations, 63 maps and diagrams, one large city plan

Text: Anita and Karl Anton von Bleyleben, Rita Henss, Beate Szerelmy, with contributions by Dr. Hedwig Nosbers, Rainer Eisenschmid and Helmut Linde

Editing: Baedeker editorial team (Beate Szerelmy, Robert Taylor)

Translation: all-lingua/ Robert Taylor

Cartography: Christoph Gallus, Hohberg; Franz Huber, Munich; MAIRDUMONT/Falk Verlag, Ostfildern (city plan)

3D illustrations: jangled nerves, Stuttgart

Design: independent Medien-Design, Munich; Kathrin Schemel

Editor-in-chief: Rainer Eisenschmid, Baedeker Ostfildern

1st edition 2008

Copyright: Karl Baedeker Verlag, Ostfildern
Publication rights: MAIRDUMONT GmbH & Co; Ostfildern

DEAR READER,

We would like to thank you for choosing this Baedeker travel guide. It will be a reliable companion on your travels and will not disappoint you.
This book describes the major sights, of course, but it also recommends the most attractive beaches, as well as hotels in the luxury and budget categories, and includes tips about where to eat or go shopping and much more, helping to make your trip an enjoyable experience. Our authors ensure the quality of this information by making regular journeys to Mexico and putting all their know-how into this book.

Nevertheless, experience shows us that it is impossible to rule out errors and changes made after the book goes to press, for which Baedeker accepts no liability. Please send us your criticisms, corrections and suggestions for improvement: we appreciate your contribution. Contact us by post or e-mail, or phone us:

▶ **Verlag Karl Baedeker GmbH**
Editorial department
Postfach 3162
73751 Ostfildern
Germany
Tel. 49-711-4502-262, fax -343
www.baedeker.com
E-Mail: baedeker@mairdumont.com

Baedeker Travel Guides in English at a glance:

▶ Andalusia

▶ Dubai · Emirates

▶ Egypt

▶ Ireland

▶ London

▶ Mexico

▶ New York

▶ Portugal

▶ Rome

▶ Thailand

▶ Tuscany

▶ Venice